797,885 Books
are available to read at

Forgotten Books

www.ForgottenBooks.com

Forgotten Books' App
Available for mobile, tablet & eReader

ISBN 978-1-330-14070-3
PIBN 10035710

This book is a reproduction of an important historical work. Forgotten Books uses state-of-the-art technology to digitally reconstruct the work, preserving the original format whilst repairing imperfections present in the aged copy. In rare cases, an imperfection in the original, such as a blemish or missing page, may be replicated in our edition. We do, however, repair the vast majority of imperfections successfully; any imperfections that remain are intentionally left to preserve the state of such historical works.

Forgotten Books is a registered trademark of FB &c Ltd.
Copyright © 2015 FB &c Ltd.
FB &c Ltd, Dalton House, 60 Windsor Avenue, London, SW19 2RR.
Company number 08720141. Registered in England and Wales.

For support please visit www.forgottenbooks.com

1 MONTH OF FREE READING

at

www.ForgottenBooks.com

By purchasing this book you are eligible for one month membership to ForgottenBooks.com, giving you unlimited access to our entire collection of over 700,000 titles via our web site and mobile apps.

To claim your free month visit:

www.forgottenbooks.com/free35710

* Offer is valid for 45 days from date of purchase. Terms and conditions apply.

English
Français
Deutsche
Italiano
Español
Português

www.forgottenbooks.com

Mythology Photography **Fiction**
Fishing Christianity **Art** Cooking
Essays Buddhism Freemasonry
Medicine **Biology** Music **Ancient Egypt** Evolution Carpentry Physics
Dance Geology **Mathematics** Fitness
Shakespeare **Folklore** Yoga Marketing
Confidence Immortality Biographies
Poetry **Psychology** Witchcraft
Electronics Chemistry History **Law**
Accounting **Philosophy** Anthropology
Alchemy Drama Quantum Mechanics
Atheism Sexual Health **Ancient History**
Entrepreneurship Languages Sport
Paleontology Needlework Islam
Metaphysics Investment Archaeology
Parenting Statistics Criminology
Motivational

THE CONTEMPORARY SCIENCE SERIES.

EDITED BY HAVELOCK ELLIS.

THE JEWS:

A STUDY OF RACE AND ENVIRONMENT.

Of the same Publishers, and Uniform with this Volume.

THE CRIMINAL. New and Enlarged 3rd Edition. By HAVELOCK ELLIS. 6/-.

HYPNOTISM. New and Enlarged 6th Edition. By ALBERT MOLL. 6/-

MODERN ORGANIC CHEMISTRY. By C. A. KEANE, D.Sc. 6/-

And 47 others.

THE JEWS:

A STUDY OF RACE AND ENVIRONMENT.

BY

MAURICE FISHBERG,

FELLOW OF THE NEW YORK ACADEMY OF SCIENCES; MEMBER OF
THE AMERICAN ETHNOLOGICAL SOCIETY, THE AMERICAN
ASSOCIATION FOR THE ADVANCEMENT OF SCIENCE,
THE AMERICAN ANTHROPOLOGICAL
ASSOCIATION, ETC.

THE WALTER SCOTT PUBLISHING CO., LTD.
PATERNOSTER SQUARE, LONDON, E.C.
CHARLES SCRIBNER'S SONS
597 FIFTH AVENUE, NEW YORK

PREFACE.

THIS volume is an attempt to present the results of anthropological, demographic, pathological, and sociological investigations of the Jews. Considering that one-fifth of all the Jews in the world live at present in English-speaking countries, and that the migrations of Eastern European Jews tend toward the United States and England with its colonies, I believe I need not apologize for claiming attention to this subject. The facts presented are not available in any book, and it may safely be declared that the whole world is interested in the subject of the Jews as a race, and the getting into closer touch with the ethnic relations of the Jews. Moreover, the perennial problem, whether it is possible to assimilate the vast number of Southern and Eastern immigrants to the United States and British colonies has been applied more to the Jews than to any other white people. It has even been questioned whether there is ever a probability of incorporating the Jews into the body politic of Anglo-Saxon communities.

That anthropology only is competent to answer this question is agreed. Yet there is no book in English treating of the race traits of the Jews. The literature on the subject in English consists mostly of investigations by special parliamentary commissions, containing opinions of statesmen, social workers, educators, etc. It appears that the prevailing opinion is that the Jews, alleged to have maintained themselves in absolute racial purity for three or four thousand years, may prove hard to assimilate. On the one hand we have those Jews who take great pride in the purity of their breed, and, on the other, the people among whom they live who see a peculiar peril in the prospect of indefinitely harbouring an alien race which is not likely to mix with the general population. This apprehension is confirmed by the Jewish nationalists, who look for repatriation in Palestine, or some other territory, thus corroborating the opinion that they are aliens in Europe, encamped for the time being, and waiting for an opportunity to retreat to their natural home in Asia. Indeed, the problem has of late been given official recognition in Anglo-Saxon countries. When bills were introduced in Parliaments aiming at the exclusion of Asiatic immigration, it was questioned whether Jews might not be considered Asiatics under the law; and in the United States a bill was recently introduced in Congress specifically declaring that the law prohibiting immigration and naturalization of Asiatics does not refer to Jews, Armenians, and Syrians.

This inquiry into the race traits of the Jews could not be carried out by a study of these people in any one country, because we find at the outset that they present significant differences depending greatly on their birth-place, social and political conditions, and, in general, the environment in which they find themselves. Their anthropological characteristics could best be studied in New York City, where exist a million Jews from Europe, Asia, and Africa; and we have taken advantage of the material thus offered by obtaining anthropometric measurements of about three thousand Jews in this city. The conclusions as to the anthropological types of the Jews are based on these measurements, as well as on a collation of the scattered literature on the subject. The demography of the Jews could best be studied from official government publications in those countries where the censuses classify the population by religious confession. The changes in the physical, social, and economic conditions of the Jews under emancipation could best be studied in Western Europe and America, and this study involved a careful search into the literature on the Jews to bring out certain points which might have practical social bearings, especially on the problem of assimilation.

While speaking of the changes which the contemporary Jews

have been undergoing within the last fifty years, we have avoided taking the position of partisan or advocate, and have treated the subject objectively. Books aiming at sympathetic apologies, defending, often excusing, Israel's existence among the nations, are on the same plane as those containing venomous diatribes full of scurrilous invectives against the Semites. It should also be understood that while pointing at the process of assimilation of the Jews, we by no means advocate their absorption by the surrounding people of different faiths. We do not find it important for the welfare of the remnants of Israel, or of those around them, that Jewry should commit race suicide. What is aimed at, however, is to point out what appears to be the tendencies, the *Zeitgeist,* of the Jews at the threshold of the Twentieth Century. Showing that while discarding the greater part of their separative ritualism the modern Jews commit suicide as Jews, because they cease to be peculiar, it is difficult to avoid describing in detail the metamorphosis this change works on the children of Israel. The large number of mixed marriages, which keeps on growing, could only take place among Jews who have discarded the separative tenets of their religion. People obeying the dietary laws religiously could not come in close and intimate contact with those whose table they could not share. The fact that the differences between Jews and Christians are not everywhere racial, due to anatomical or physiological peculiarities, but are solely the result of the social and political environment, explains our optimism as regards the ultimate obliteration of all distinctions between Jews and Christians in Europe and America. This optimism is confirmed by conditions in Italy, Scandinavia, and Australia, where anti-Semitism is practically unknown. When intermarriage between Jews and Christians will reach the same proportions in other countries, and the facts presented in Chapter IX. clearly show that the time is not distant, anti-Semitism will everywhere meet with the same fate as in Italy, Scandinavia and Australia. Both Jews and Christians have been contributing to this end, the former by discarding their separative ritualism, and thus displaying willingness to bridge the gulf which separated them from others, and the latter by legalizing civil marriage. Whether this means that ceasing to be peculiar may prove deadly to Judaism can only be conjectured. All I could do was to present the facts.

I am indebted to Dr. Joseph Jacobs for reading the greater part of the manuscript and proofs and making some helpful suggestions. Drs. S. Weissenberg and A. D. Elkind of Russia have generously loaned me some photographs of types of Jews which could not readily be obtained in New York. Dr. Joseph Fraenkel, physician to the Montefiore Home in New York, deserves my gratitude for reading the proofs of the chapter on nervous diseases. I am also indebted to Mr. M. Mandelkern for the patience and interest he manifested when I sent to him persons to be photographed for this work.

MAURICE FISHBERG.

NEW YORK, U.S.A.,
    1911.

CONTENTS.

CHAPTER I.

NUMBER AND DISTRIBUTION OF THE JEWS IN THE WORLD—ACCLIMATIZATION - - - - PAGE

Number of Jews in ancient times—During mediæval ages—Ubiquity during the nineteenth century—Distribution of the Jews in Europe—Number and distribution in North and South America—In Asia, Africa, and Australasia—Total number of Jews—Recent changes in distribution—Jews in English-speaking countries—Jews as town-dwellers—Causes of preference for city life—Acclimatization—Causes of the superior power of acclimatization of the Jews.

CHAPTER II.

PHYSICAL CHARACTERS - - - - - 21

The alleged purity of the Jewish race—Stability and persistence of racial traits—Race and environment—Stature of the Jews—Height of the ancient Hebrews—Height of modern Jewish conscripts—Growth of the body Height of Jewesses—Influence of the environment on the stature of the Jews—Influence of occupation—Social selection—Selection by immigration—Ethnic Factors.

CHAPTER III.

PHYSICAL CHARACTERS (*Continued*) - - - 47

The head-form—Skulls of ancient Hebrews—Of mediæval Jews—Of modern Jews—The three types of head-form among Jews—Uniformity of cranial type of Eastern European Jews—Origin of the types of skulls of the Jews—Size of the head—Weight of the brain—Brain weight and intellectual capacity.

x   CONTENTS.

CHAPTER IV.

PAGE

PHYSICAL CHARACTERS (*Concluded*) - - - 60

Complexion—Types of pigmentation of the ancient Hebrews—The ideal Jewish type—Types of pigmentation among modern Jews—Complexion of Jewish children in various parts of the world—Erythrism—The blonde Jews—Origin of the blonde elements among the Jews—Artificial selection—The nose—Fallacy of considering the aquiline and hook noses as typically Jewish—Forms of the nose among modern Jews—The Jewish chest—Vital capacity—Fitness for military service.

CHAPTER V.

TYPES OF JEWS - - - - - - 90

The "indelibility" of the Jewish type—The type of the ancient Hebrews—The characteristics of the Jewish face—The artist's conception of the Jewish face—The novelist's conception of the Jewish face—The anthropologist's conception of the Jewish type—The alleged prepotency of the Jewish physiognomy—The two Jewish types—The *Sephardi* type of Jew—The *Ashkenazi* types of Jews—The Slavonic type—The Teutonic type—The Turanian type—The Mongoloid and the Negroid types of Jews—Other types.

CHAPTER VI.

TYPES OF JEWS IN VARIOUS COUNTRIES   121

Jewish types in Palestine—The Samaritans—Jews of Bokhara—The Persian Jews—Jews in the Caucasus—The Daghestan Mountain Jews—The white and black Jews in India—Chinese Jews—The various types of Jews in North Africa—Berber Jews—Jewish cave-dwellers in Tripolis—Falashas in Abyssinia—Other Negro Jews—In Jamaica and Surinam—The Karaites—Crypto-Jews—The Dönmeh in Salonica—The Chuetas—The Annussim—The distinction between Jews by race and Jews by religion.

CHAPTER VII.

ORIGIN OF THE VARIOUS TYPES OF JEWS   162

Dress and deportment as contributory causes of the distinctive type of Jews—The attitude of the body—The psychic type of the Jew—The Ghetto face—The Jewish

CONTENTS. xi

eye—The ubiquitous Ten Lost Tribes of Israel—Jewish type met with among many peoples and races in various parts of the world—Isolation and selection as factors in the production of the Jewish type.

CHAPTER VIII.

PROSELYTISM AND INTERMARRIAGE AMONG JEWS · 179

The Jewish race—Mixtures during the period of consolidation of the Hebrews—Intermarriages of the patriarchs and kings of Israel with other races—Intermarriages during the Babylonian captivity—Ezra's admonition about the purity of race—Intermarriage during the Greco-Roman period of Jewish history—Extent of Jewish proselytism—Graetz's and Reinach's estimates of the extent of intermarriage and proselytism of the Jews during that period—Intermarriages prohibited by Church edicts—Intermarriages in Gaul and Spain—In Slavonic countries—The Chozars—Origin of the Eastern European Jews.

CHAPTER IX.

INTERMARRIAGES BETWEEN JEWS AND CHRISTIANS IN MODERN TIMES - - - - - 195

The legal status of intermarriages between Jews and Christians—What is a "mixed" marriage?—Number of mixed marriages in Scandinavia, Germany, France, Italy, England, Australia, and the United States—The opposition of the Church and the Synagogue to intermarriages between Jews and Christians—Intermarriages between followers of various Christian denominations—The Ghetto is the best preventive of intermarriage—Fertility of mixed marriages—Distinguished persons of half-Jewish origin—The loss sustained by Judaism through intermarriages—Frequency of divorce among mixed couples—Decrease of Jewish population as a result of intermarriage—Intermarriage and missionary work among Jews—Ethnic effects of mixed marriages—Jewish Theological attitude toward inter-marriage.

CHAPTER X.

DEMOGRAPHIC CHARACTERISTICS - - - - 225

The alleged superior fecundity of the Jews—Birth-rates of the Jews in various countries—Differences between Eastern and Western Jews—The decline in the fecundity of the Jews—The marriage fecundity of the Jews—Causes of the low birth-rates of the Jews—Sex at birth—The enormous excess of male births only apparent—Proportion of still-births—Illegitimacy among the Jews.

CHAPTER XI.

DEMOGRAPHIC CHARACTERISTICS (*Continued*)   245

Marriage rates among the Jews in various countries—Differences between Eastern and Western Jews—Age at marriage—Proportion of celibates—Causes of low marriage-rates of the Jews—Consanguineous marriages—Dissolution of marriage.

CHAPTER XII.

DEMOGRAPHIC CHARACTERISTICS (*Concluded*)   255

Mortality of the Jews in various countries—Tenacity of life of the Jews—Jewish infant mortality—Expectation of life Causes of the low death-rates of the Jews—Effects of the demographic phenomena on the Jews—Excess of births over deaths—Differences between Eastern and Western Jews—The recent decline in the natural increase of the Jews.

CHAPTER XIII.

PATHOLOGICAL CHARACTERISTICS   270

Race and disease—Effects of social conditions on the incidence of pathological processes—Alcoholism—Contagious diseases among Jews—The Black Death—Typhoid fever, cholera, endemic diseases among Jews—Causes of differences in frequency of certain diseases among Jews and others—Tuberculosis—Causes of infrequency of tuberculosis among Jews.

CHAPTER XIV.

PATHOLOGICAL CHARACTERISTICS (*Continued*) -   296

General diseases—The diatheses—Diabetes as a "Jewish disease"—Diseases of the respiratory, circulatory, and digestive organs—Goitre—Cancer—*Foetor Judaicus*—Skin diseases among Jews—Syphilis, leprosy, eye diseases among Jews—Blindness, colour-blindness, and myopia.

CHAPTER XV

PATHOLOGICAL CHARACTERISTICS (*Concluded*) -   324

Nervous and mental diseases among Jews—Hysteria and neurasthenia—Paralysis agaitans—Intermittent claudication—Causes of the nervousness of the Jews—Frequency of idiocy and imbecility among Jews—Deaf-mutism—Insanity among the ancient Hebrews—Insanity among the modern Jews—Forms of insanity among Jews—*Psychosis Judaica*—Causes of the excessive incidence of insanity among Jews—Suicide among Jews—Recent increase in the tendency to self-destruction.

CHAPTER XVI

SOCIAL AND ECONOMIC CONDITIONS OF THE JEWS IN VARIOUS COUNTRIES - - - - 356

Factors influencing social and economic conditions—Distribution of the population by ages—Differences between Eastern and Western Jews—Poverty—Absence of the pauper element—The economic conditions depend mostly on their political status—Poverty of the Jews in Russia, Poland, and Roumania—Prosperity of the Western Jews—Differences in the economic conditions of the native and immigrant Jews in the United States—Capacity for regeneration of the Jewish immigrant.

CHAPTER XVII.

EDUCATION OF THE JEWS IN VARIOUS COUNTRIES - 370

Facilities for education an important factor—Illiteracy among Jewish immigrants—Illiteracy in Russia—Superiority in countries in which the schools are open to them—Higher education—Jews in high schools and universities—Disabilities in Russia—Preference for the study of medicine and law—Jewish students of philosophy and applied sciences—Languages spoken by Jews—There is no Jewish vernacular—Chaldaic displaced Hebrew at an early age—Greek, Arabic, and the Romance languages used by Jews during the Middle Ages—Effects of isolation—Characteristics of Jewish jargons—*Spagnuoli*—*Yiddish*—Its centre of diffusion—English displacing Yiddish—Language as a test of social contact—The alleged inability of Jews to pronounce European languages.

CHAPTER XVIII.

OCCUPATIONS - - - - - 393

Effects of political disabilities on the occupations pursued by the Jews—Influence of the Jewish religion on the choice of occupation—Preference for the garment industry—Jews in various trades—Commercial pursuits—Changes observed in the occupations of American Jews—Jews as agriculturists.

CHAPTER XIX.

CRIMINALITY 407

Differences between Jews and Christians as to the number of arrests and convictions—Effects of occupation on criminalty—Criminality of the Jews in Germany, Hungary, Holland, and Russia—Differences in the nature of the crimes committed by Jews and Christians—Infrequency of crimes of violence committed by Jews—Recent changes among the Jews in England and the United States.

CHAPTER XX.

POLITICAL CONDITIONS OF MODERN JEWS 419

Proportion of emancipated Jews—Effects of the union of Church and State on the political conditions of the Jews at various periods of their history—Political status in ancient Greece and Rome—Effects of the spread of Christianity—Effects of the separative ritualism of Judaism—Aims of mediæval legislation against the Jews—Political conditions of the Jews in Roumania—Conditions in Russia—Summary of restrictions imposed on the Jews of Russia—Causes of Russian persecutions—Political status of the Jews in Western Europe—First admission to citizenship in France—Emancipation in England—In Holland, Austria, Germany, Italy, Switzerland, etc.—Analogy between conditions of the modern Jews in Russia and Roumania and those in mediæval ages—General effects of the recent political disabilities—Migrations of modern Jews—The United States the point of destination of the vast majority of Jewish immigrants.

CHAPTER XXI.

SOCIAL DISABILITIES AND THEIR EFFECTS 438

The entry of the emancipated Jew into modern society—Discrimination in the armies and navies in Europe—Social ostracism in the United States—Discrimination in German academic circles—Number of Jewish professors in German universities—Baptism the usual pre-requisite for academic appointments—Fear of the "Semite" by "Aryan" jingoes—Baptismal waters the specific means of clearing the "Semite" of his objectionable racial traits—Singular position of the emancipated Jews—Causes of baptism—Baptism and apostasy in ancient and medieval times—Prominent modern Jewish converts to Christianity—Number of

CONTENTS. XV

PAGE

baptisms during the nineteenth century in Russia, Austria, and Hungary—Social conditions of the Jews baptized in Vienna and Berlin—The "Freethinkers" from the Jewish fold—Marriage and advancement the two main causes of baptisms—Effects of baptism on the social conditions of the Jews who remain true to their faith — Excessive proportion of Jewish *parvenus* — Eastern European Jews replacing those lost through baptism in Western countries.

CHAPTER XXII.

ASSIMILATION *versus* ZIONISM - - - - 466

Tendencies among the modern Jews—George Brandes' view on his relation to Judaism—Causes of the revival of the Jewish Nationalists' movement—The Zionist's programme—Zionism and assimilation — The Zionist's assumption of a distinct Jewish nationality—Attempts to avert disintegration of Judaism—Are the Jews a nation?—The Jews were a nation before their emancipation in Europe—Judaism and the laws of Christian states kept them apart from their neighbours—Assimilation of the Western Jews—Causes of denationalization of modern Jews—Religion and nationality—Language and nationality—There is no national Jewish vernacular —Adoption of culture and civilization of the countries in which they live—The failure of the Nationalists in their efforts to revive the Jewish national spirit—What is Jewish art?—Is there a Jewish literature?—Absence of a specific Jewish spirit in painting, sculpture, music, and architecture—There is no Jewish folk-lore, folktales, folk-medicine, etc.—Professor Lazarus on Jewish nationalism—Why Palestine is inadequate to shelter all the Jews—Christendom would not cherish renationalization of the Jews in the Holy Land—The fertility of Palestine—The difficulties in the way of developing Palestine industrially and commercially— Repatriation offers no solution of the Jewish problem— Zionism has not attracted the cultured Jews—Objections to an autonomous territory—The two tendencies among the modern Jews.

CHAPTER XXIII.

RECAPITULATION AND CONCLUSIONS - 504

Race pride of the Jews—The Semite and the Aryan—Influence of the environment on racial characters—The difference between the social and the anthropological type of the Jew—Anthropologically the Jews are not a race—There is no Jewish type; there are Jewish types—Mixed marriages and their significance—Failure of hostile legislation against the Jews—Decline in the fertility of the Jews—Demography as an index of the social, religious, and political status of the Jews—Decadence of the Western Jews—Alleged racial immunities—Isolation often spared them during epidemics—Mortality rates of the Jews depend more on their economic condition than on "inherent tenacity of life"—Psychic trauma as causes of nervousness of the Jews—Isolation and its significance—Mediæval legislation always aimed at isolation of the Jew—Judaism the most separative of religions—Effects of the Sabbath and the dietary laws—Judaism the best ally of the Church in keeping the Jews isolated from the Christians—Economic and social effects of isolation Alleged superiority of the Jew as a trader—Characteristics of the Jewish artisan—The "inherent thirst for knowledge" of the Jew—Causes of the peculiar criminality of the Jews—Assimilation of the Jews—Large number of baptisms prove capacity of assimilation—Disabilities in Eastern Europe the greatest barrier in the way of assimilation of the Jews.

BIBLIOGRAPHY - - - - - - - 557

INDEX OF AUTHORS - - - - - - 567

INDEX OF SUBJECTS - - - - - - 572

LIST OF ILLUSTRATIONS.

FIG.		PAGE
1.	Algerian Jewess	5
2.	Tunisian Jew	9
3.	Daghestan Mountain Jews	12
4.	Bokhara Jews	15
5-6.	Caucasian Jewess	18
7.	Young Jewess in Sfax, Tunis	22
8-11.	Types of Eastern European Jews	30
12.	Curve of stature of Jews and non-Jews in Eastern Europe	43
13-16.	Types of Jews in Austrian Galicia	45
17.	Group of Jews in Bokhara	61
18.	Face of Old Jew. (From a painting by Rembrandt)	62
19.	Jewish Faces. (From a painting by Kaufmann)	63
20.	Jewess in Tangier, Morocco. (From a painting by Portaels)	67
21-22.	Lithuanian Jews	69
23.	Algerian Jewess	71
24.	Algerian Jew	73
25.	Jewish Rabbi, Constantine	75
26-27.	Galician Jews	78
28-29.	Polish Jew, White Russian Type	80
30-31.	Polish Jew, Great Russian Type	82
32.	Diagram of Jewish Nose	85
33.	Ancient Races portrayed on the Egyptian Monuments	91
34.	Jewish Doctor (Rembrandt)	93
35.	Jewish Face. (Drawing by Lilien)	95
36-40.	Artists' conception of Jewish Face. (From paintings by Hirszenberg, Pasternack, Sichel, Gottlieb, Lilien)	96-97
41.	Composite portraiture of Jewish Type. (Galton)	100-101
42.	Jewess, Jerusalem; Sephardi Type	103
43-46.	Sephardi Types of Jews	105
47.	Jewish Rabbi, Oran	109

xviii LIST OF ILLUSTRATIONS.

FIG.		PAGE
48-51.	Ashkenazi Types of Jews	112
52-55.	Jewesses, Ashkenazi Type	113
56.	Polish Jew	115
57.	Galician Jew	115
58-59.	Russian Jewess, Mongoloid Type	115
60-61.	Polish Jew, Slavonic-Mongoloid Type	116
62-63.	Galician Jew, Ruthenian Type	116
64-65.	Polish Jew, Mongoloid Type	117
66-67.	Galician Jews, Negroid Types	117
68-69.	South Russian Jew, Slavonic Type	119
70-71.	Jew, Native of Warsaw, Polish Type	119
72-73.	Teutonic Types of Jews	122
74.	Polish Jew in Jerusalem	123
75.	Samaritan	125
76.	Group of Samaritans	126
77.	Syrian Jewess	127
78-79.	Yemenite Jews	128
80.	Bokhara Jewess	129
81.	Syrian Jewess	129
82.	Group of Persian Jewish Immigrants in New York	129
83-84.	Jews in Georgia, Caucasus	130
85-86.	Jews in Kutais, Caucasus	130
87-88.	Daghestan Mountain Jews	132
89-90.	Circassian Jews, Caucasus	133
91-92.	Black Jews of India	134
93.	White Jew in Cochin, India	135
94.	Black Jew, Cochin, Malabar, India	135
95.	Jew, Samarkand	135
96.	Jewess, Turkestan	135
97-98.	Chinese Jews	137
99.	Family of Chinese Jews	137
100.	Tunisian Jew	138
101.	Fat Jewess in Tunis	139
102.	Tunisian Jewess	140
103.	Fat Jewess in Sfax, Tunisia	141
104.	Jewess in Constantine	142
105.	Jewess in Biskra, Algeria	143

LIST OF ILLUSTRATIONS.

FIG.		PAGE
106.	Sahara Jewesses	144
107-109.	Falashas	147-8
110-111.	Karaite	151
112.	The Ghetto Bend	164
113-114.	Jew, Native of Tetuan, Morocco	167
115-116.	Muscovite Jew, Great Russian Type	168
117-118.	Imer, Caucasus, with Jewish Facial Expression	169
119.	Tartar, from Tiflis, with Jewish Physiognomy	169
120.	Circassian, Caucasus, with Jewish Physiognomy	169
121-122.	Bakaïri Indian, with Jewish Cast of Countenance	172
123.	Japanese Girls with Jewish Expression	173
124.	Hova of Tananarivo, with Jewish Cast of Countenance	175
125.	Yoro Combo, with Jewish Expression	177
126.	Young Woman of Arles, with Jewish Physiognomy	180
127-128.	The Jewish Lads' Brigade, London	185
129.	Jewess in Asia Minor	187
130.	Jew of Jerusalem, Mongoloid Type	190
131.	Hungarian Jewess	190
132.	Jew of Bukowina	193
133.	Jewess, Oran, Algiers	193
134-135.	American Jew and Jewess	198
136.	Russian Jewish Rabbi	201
137.	Caucasian Jew	201
138.	Group of Daghestan Mountain Jews	204
139.	Group of Yemenite Jews	208
140.	South Arabian Jew	212
141.	Samaritan Grand Rabbi	212
142.	The Three Types of Head-form among Jews	510

THE JEWS:

A STUDY OF RACE AND ENVIRONMENT.

CHAPTER I.

NUMBER AND DISTRIBUTION OF THE JEWS IN THE WORLD.

Number of Jews in ancient times—During mediæval ages—Ubiquity during the nineteenth century—Distribution of the Jews in Europe—Number and distribution in North and South America—In Asia, Africa, and Australasia—Total number of Jews—Recent changes in distribution—Jews in English-speaking countries—Jews as town-dwellers—Causes of preference for city life—Acclimatization of the Jews—Causes of superior power of acclimatization of the Jews.

THE facts of history, beginning with remote antiquity, show that there were never as many Jews, nor were they ever as ubiquitous, as they are at the present. Biblical tradition has it that Jacob migrated to Egypt with a retinue of seventy souls. After remaining there 430 years, his progeny returned to Palestine, and a census taken at Mount Sinai showed that there were 611,730 adult males capable of bearing arms. Haushoffer and Nossig calculate by a plausible method that the total population amounted to 3,154,000 souls.[1] Leaving the question of the possibility of taking a proper census, as well as the method employed, out of consideration, it must be borne in mind that it is questionable whether such a large number of men, women, and children could be supported with absolulely necessary food and shelter in a

[1] Haushoffer, *Handbuch der Statistik*, p. 95; A. Nossig, *Juedische Statistik*, pp. 430-432, Berlin, 1903. These Biblical figures are certainly fanciful. It is problematical where 3,000,000 people could find room and subsistence in the land of Goshen, even if many lived in the district of Rameses. The exodus must have been a movement of a much smaller body of men (*Jewish Encyclopædia*, vol. v., p. 294; see also Flinders Petrie, *Researches in Sinai*, pp. 194-222, London, 1906).

desert. In any case, it appears that during the following period of their history they increased at a fair rate. The census of King David gave a net result of 1,300,000 males over twenty years of age, which would imply a total population around 5,000,000. This would also imply that Palestine was quite densely populated, to the extent of about the density of population of Belgium of to-day. That it is possible for such a population to live on such a small area which has few high roads, navigable rivers, etc., is shown by the congested state of India and some parts of China. But even this apparently high estimate of the Jewish population in antiquity shows only five millions. Since then there have never been as many Jews before the nineteenth century.

There is only scanty information available about the number of Jews during their dispersion at the beginning of the present era. Syria, according to Josephus, was, next to Palestine and Babylonia, most densely inhabited by the Chosen People. In Damascus there are said to have been massacred, at the time of the great insurrection, 10,000 Jews, or even 18,000 according to another version. Philo gives the number of Jewish inhabitants in Egypt as 1,000,000, one-eighth of the total population. But this is only an estimate.[1] "If the sum confiscated by the propretor Flaccus in 62 represented actually the tax of a dedrachma per head for a single year," says Reinach, "the inference may be safely drawn that in Asia Minor the Jewish population numbered 45,000 persons." Josephus evidently exaggerates when he says that during the siege of Jerusalem 1,100,000 people were segregated in that city.[2] He also says that in Nero's time 2,565,000, or even 3,000,000 Hebrews offered Passover sacrifice in Jerusalem, while the Talmud states that as many as 12,000,000 congregated at one time in the holy city, which, according to the most extravagant estimate, measured thirty-three stadia, or about six square kilometres. Tacitus[3] states that shortly before its destruction, Jerusalem harboured 600,000 Jews. Beloch[4] estimates that among the 7,000,000 inhabitants of Syria in Nero's time there were a million Jews. Ruppin's estimate that in 500 B.C. the total number

[1] *In Flaccum*, § 6.   [2] *Jewish Wars*, vi., 9, 3.   [3] *Historiæ*, v., 13.
[4] *Die Bevolkerung der griechisch-römischen Welt*, p. 248.

of Jews did not much exceed 100,000 appears to be correct, while his estimate of 4,500,000 at the beginning of the Christian era is seemingly excessive.[1]

In the absence of any definite data about the number of Jews during the Middle Ages, we must resort to estimates which are often fallacious. The best estimates, based on various historical data, and especially on records of the travels of Benjamin of Tudela, are those made by Joseph Jacobs in his article "Statistics" in the *Jewish Encyclopædia*. According to this author the number of Jews during the twelfth century was about 750,000, and during the sixteenth century about 1,000,000. They had not increased during these dark days, owing to the severe persecutions to which they were subjected. Jacobs estimates that during the five centuries from 1000 to 1500 A.D., 380,000 Jews were killed during massacres. All historical evidence goes to show that even as late as the middle of the eighteenth century the total number of Jews in the world hardly exceeded one million, less than one-half of whom lived in Europe. That there were no more can easily be believed when it is considered that they were mostly city-dwellers, and there were very few cities in Europe in which the Jewish population exceeded 10,000. After the beginning of the nineteenth century the increase of the number of Jews in Europe was enormous. In addition to this increase they have also scattered all over the habitable globe, so that to-day they are met with in almost every country.

In round numbers there are twelve millions of Jews in the world at present. Of these only about 500,000 live in Asia, and only about 250,000 in their original homes, Palestine, Asia Minor, and Mesopotamia. Three-fourths of the total number of the Jews of to-day, or about nine millions, live in Europe, and 7,500,000 live in three countries, Russia, Austria-Hungary, and Roumania. The rest are scattered all over the continent, north, south and west.

Russia has the largest number of Jews. At the census of 1897, which was the first complete enumeration of the population in that country, the returns showed 5,110,548 Jews, of whom 3,578,229 lived in the so-called "Pale of

---

[1] *Die Juden der Gegenwart*, pp. 30-32.

Settlement," consisting of fifteen provinces in the west of European Russia, where the Jews are permitted to live; 1,321,100 in Poland, and 202,000 in the rest of European Russia. It can be safely assumed that their number has not increased since 1897, because of the heavy emigration which has taken place during recent years. As will be shown later, the annual excess of births over deaths among the Jews in Russia is about 75,000. During the period 1897-1909 there emigrated nearly 615,000 Russian Jews to the United States alone. In addition there was a heavy emigration to South America, Canada, South Africa, England, and many Western European countries. On the whole the excess of births over deaths among the Jews in Russia has probably been wiped out by emigration during the last ten years. Before this large exodus, the Jewish population in Russia multiplied very rapidly owing to the high birth-rate combined with a low mortality rate. From the scanty evidence available, it appears that during the second half of the sixteenth century there were about twelve thousand Jews in Lithuania, according to Bershadsky.[1] In 1897 there were in that region nearly 1,500,000 Jews. At the first division of Poland in 1772-95, a census showed that there were in that country 308,519 male Jews.[2] Considering the number of Jewesses about the same, it appears that there were at that time over 600,000 Jews in Poland. It is from these Jews that most of the Russian Jews of to-day are descended. But, after all, they constitute only 4.03 per cent. of the total population of European Russia. Inasmuch as they are segregated in the so-called "Pale of Settlement," they are more densely settled in Western and Southern Russia. In this "Pale" they constitnte 10.8 per cent., and in Poland even 14.01 per cent. of the total population. The "problem" of the Jews in Russia is thus seen to be entirely artificial, mainly due to their segregation in one part of the empire, and in that region, in cities, as will soon be shown.

[1] *Litowskie evrei*, St. Petersburg, 1883, p. 331, quoted from *La situation économique des Israélites de Russie*, vol. i. p. 17; Paris, 1906.
[2] T. Czacki (*Rozprawa o Zyach*, p. 216; Wilno, 1807) believes that this figure is rather low, and estimates 450,000 male Jews and as many Jewesses, a total of 900,000, at the end of the eighteenth century.

Austria comes after Russia with 1,224,896 Jews, according to the census of 1900. Two-thirds live in Galicia, the

Fig. 1.—JEWESS OF ALGIERS.

part of Poland taken by Austria during the division of that unfortunate country. Thus both countries which have the largest number of Jews have them as a heritage from

Poland. Hungary also has a large number of the children of Israel. At the census of 1900, 851,378 Jews were enumerated. In Roumania, where the Jewish question is most acute, it has repeatedly been asserted that there were about 400,000 Jews, but the census of 1899 showed that this statement was very much exaggerated. Only 266,652 Jews were returned by the census officials, constituting 4.5 per cent. of the total population. It can safely be stated that they have not increased in number since that census owing to the enormous emigration since 1900.

There are Jews in every country in South-Eastern Europe. In some, where censuses have been taken during 1900, the exact number is known. In Bulgaria, 33,663 were enumerated; in Greece, 8,350; in Bosnia and the Herzegovina, 8,200 (census of 1895); in Servia, 5,700; and in European Turkey the Alliance Israélite Universelle estimates their number at 189,000.

There are fewer of the followers of Judaism in Western Europe. In Germany the census of 1905 showed 607,862 Jews, 409,501 of whom lived in the kingdom of Prussia— *i.e.*, they are also in a great measure a heritage from ancient Poland. Bavaria is the next province with a large number of Jews, 55,341; while the other provinces have a much smaller number. They constitute only 1.04 per cent. of the total population of Germany, and even in Prussia, where the greater number of Jews in Germany live, they make up only 1.14 per cent. of the total population.

The census of Great Britain takes no cognizance of the religious denomination of the inhabitants, and it is therefore impossible to give the exact number of Jews in that country. According to a recent estimate made by Rosenbaum, there are about 240,000 Jews in the United Kingdom. Of these 225,700 live in England and Wales, 27,250 in Scotland, and 6,100 in Ireland.[1] The majority of these Jews are recent immigrants from Eastern Europe and their descendants, who have come to England within the last thirty years.

Just as in England, there are no denominational

---

[1] S. Rosenbaum, "A contribution to the Study of the Vital and other Statistics of the Jews in the United Kingdom," *Journal Royal Statist. Society*, vol. lxviii. pp. 526-562.

NUMBER AND DISTRIBUTION.

statistics for the population of France and Belgium, and we must rely on estimates of the number of Jews in those countries. The most recent estimate made for France shows that there are over 100,000 Jews in that country, 55,000 of whom live in the city of Paris;[1] in Belgium the number is estimated at about 15,000. Most of the Jews in these two last mentioned countries also consist of recent refugees from Russia and Roumania, who have immigrated within the last twenty-five years. At the census of 1901 there were enumerated 35,617 Jews in Italy, and inasmuch as there is no material immigration from Eastern Europe, and intermarriages with Christians are very frequent, their number has, in all probability, not increased in recent years. In Switzerland the census of 1900 showed 12,264 Jews, but there is probably now about double that number, owing to the large number of Jews from Russia who fled thither during the last ten years.

There are comparatively few Jews in Scandinavia. Only 3,476 were enumerated at the census of 1901 in Denmark, 3,912 in Sweden, and 642 in Norway (census of 1900). Among the native Jews there has hardly been any increase since these censuses, because of mixed marriages which are there very prevalent. But here again their number has probably augmented by immigration from Russia, which has been quite heavy within recent years.

After their final expulsion in 1492 there were no Jews in Spain, at least officially. According to some writers there are at present between three and four thousand of them in that country, although they are not yet permitted to have their own places of worship. But since Gibraltar passed under English rule, many Spanish Jews have returned, and about 2,000 are to be found there. It is also stated that there are about 1,200 Jews in Portugal.

The official censuses of the governments of the various countries in North and South America take no religous statistics. It is therefore impossible to state the exact number of Jews in America. It can, however, be stated that the United States has the majority of the Jews on the western continent. Indeed, there are more Jews in the United States than in any other single country in the world,

[1] *Jewish Chronicle*, Dec. 6, 1907.

excepting Russia. In 1818 Mordecai M. Noah estimated their number at about 3,000; in 1840 the *American Almanac* put down their number at about 15,000. Since then many Jews have come. First the flood started from Germany, and in 1848 it was stated that 50,000 Jews were domiciled under the Stars and Stripes. Very few Eastern European Jews came to the United States before 1880, although many of the immigrants before that period were practically Polish Jews, coming as they did from the part of Poland which Germany has sliced off for itself. In fact the majority of the "German" Jews in the United States are descended from Polish parents. In 1881, after the anti-Jewish disorders in Russia, the flood of immigrants from Eastern Europe assumed quite large proportions, so that the number of Jews in the United States, which was estimated in 1880 at 230,000, has since then increased to about nine times that number. Between 1880 and 1910 over 1,100,000 Jews came from Russia alone. In addition there also came large numbers from Austria-Hungary, Roumania, etc. Their number augmented within the mentioned period by natural increase, and in 1910 the *American Jewish Year Book* estimates their number at 1,777,185, more then one-half of whom are living in the State of New York; Pennsylvania is stated to have 150,000 Jewish residents; Illinois, 110,000; Massachusetts, 90,000; Ohio, 85,000; New Jersey, 70,000; and Missouri, 52,000. The states having the smallest number of Jewish residents are Idaho, Nevada, South Dakota and Wyoming, each of them being credited with 300 Jews by the above-mentioned authority. There are very few Jews in the extracontinental colonies of the United States. None are credited to Alaska, while the Philippines, Hawaii, and Porto Rico are given 100 Jews each. All these figures are quite below the real number of Jews in the various States of the Union. It is fairly established that New York City alone has about one million Jews.

In Canada and British Columbia the number of Jews has been estimated at 60,000; in Jamaica, 2,400; Mexico, 8,972; Brazil, 3,000; Argentine, 40,000; Cuba, 4,000; Curaçoa and Surinam, 2,158; Peru, 500, Venezuela, 450. Altogether the estimate of 2,110,000 for North and South

NUMBER AND DISTRIBUTION. 9

America is rather conservative. Most of them have come from Europe within the last one hundred years, and

Fig. 2.—Jew in Tunis.

probably seventy-five per cent. within the last thirty years.

The number of Jews in Asia is not exactly known,

because no censuses are taken by the various Governments on that Continent. One exception is Russia, where a complete enumeration was made during 1897, showing that there were 105,257 Jews in Asiatic Russia. In India, also, the census of 1901 shows that there were 18,226 inhabitants of Jewish faith. The Alliance Israélite Universelle estimates the number of Jews in Syria and Palestine at 100,000; Asia Minor, 77,500; Mesopotamia, 60,000; Persia, 49,000; Arabia, 35,000. Ruppin gives the total number of Jews in Asia as 472,000.

In Africa, there are besides the 7,000 Falashas in Abyssinia, about 150,000 in Morocco, 65,000 in Algeria, 62,500 in Tunis, 50,000 in South Africa, 38,635 in Egypt (census of 1907), and about 19,000 in Tripolis. An estimate of 380,000 Jews in Africa is as near the actual number as is possible under the circumstances.

In Australia the census of 1901 showed that there were 17,106 Jews.

Recapitulating, we find the following distribution of the Jews on the five continents:—

Europe	9,000,000 or 74.87 per cent.
America	2,110,000 or 17.66 ,,
Asia	500,000 or 4.16 ,,
Africa	380,000 or 3.17 ,,
Australasia	17,000 or 0.14 ,,

Thus seventy-five per cent. of all Jews live in Europe, and over seventeen per cent. in America. While the number of Jews in America was practically insignificant only seventy-five years ago, the recent changes in distribution of the children of Israel have brought it about that at the present one out of every six Jews in the world lives in either North or South America. In Asia and Africa, their original home, there are found only eight per cent. of all contemporary Jews; and very few have found their way to Australasia. It is interesting in this connection that while only about fifty years ago, hardly 50,000 Jews lived in English-speaking countries, the recent change in their distribution has wrought a radical change in the languages spoken by the followers of Judaism. Up till recently the bulk of the Jews in Europe, as well as their descendants on other continents, spoke either German or more often a corrupted dialect of German, known popularly as *Yiddish*.

NUMBER AND DISTRIBUTION.

To-day nearly one-fifth of all the Jews in the world live in English-speaking countries. While the older generation as yet largely uses Yiddish among themselves, their children consider the English language as their mother-tongue. If the migration of Jews from Eastern Europe keeps on for some time to come, there is no doubt that English will soon become the mother-tongue of the majority of Jews.

The distribution of the Jews is interesting for study when they are considered according to the percentage they constitute of the entire population of a country. In Russia, where nearly one-half of all the Jews live, they constitute only four per cent. of the total population of the empire. But here they are limited by law as to the choice of residence. They are permitted to live undisturbed, except during "pogroms," which are of rather frequent occurrence, so far as the Russian police can leave citizens undisturbed, in fifteen provinces at the western and southern limits of the empire, and also in Poland. This is known as the "Pale of Settlement," and extends south of the Baltic provinces and west of the Don Army Territory. The result is that while constituting only 4 per cent. of the total population of the empire, they live here in a congested state, and make up 10.8 per cent. of the inhabitants of this Pale, and even 14 per cent. of the population of Poland. In addition to the segregation in the Pale, they are further limited by law as to choice of residence by excluding them from all rural settlements. They are only permitted to live in cities and incorporated towns. They thus constitute over 18 per cent. of the province of Warsaw; 15 per cent. of the population of Lomza, Pietrokoff, and Siedlec, etc. In these provinces there are many cities and towns where the Jews constitute the majority of the population. There are in Russia 932 incorporated towns in which 13.4 per cent. of the entire population resides, while 50.5 per cent. of all the Jews live in these places. Another way of showing the congestion of Jews in cities of Russia is by recalling that while they constitute only 4 per cent. of the total population, they form 15.6 per cent. of the total urban population. In four cities of the Pale—Berditchef, Pinsk, Slonim, and Slutzk—they constitute over 70 per cent. of the population; in twenty-four cities they make up between 40 and 70 per cent. of the population; and in fifteen cities between 30 and 40 per cent.[1]

While this congestion in cities can be attributed to the special anti-Jewish legislation in Russia, still it must be

Fig. 3.—DAGHESTAN MOUNTAIN JEWS.
[*Photo, Kurdoff.*]

mentioned that it is not entirely due to this cause. The Jews in other countries, where they are not interfered with

[1] For details, see B. Goldberg, "Die Juden unter der städtischen Bevölkerung Russlands," *Zeitschrift für Demographie und Statistik der Juden*, 1905, No. 10.

in this respect, are also pre-eminently town-dwellers. In Austria-Hungary they constitute 4.5 per cent. of the entire population. But in the provinces of Galicia and Bukowina they make up 11 and 13 per cent. of the population respectively. Several cities in these parts of Austria have a majority of their population of Jewish faith. Nine cities have over 50 per cent. of Jews; twelve, between 33 and 50 per cent.; and eleven cities, between 25 and 33 per cent.[1] Similarly in Germany, where, according to the census of 1905, the Jews constituted 1.04 per cent. of the total population, two-thirds of their number lived in Prussia. Here also they live mostly in cities. In Berlin 4.88 per cent. of the inhabitants are of Jewish faith. Over 50 per cent. of all the Christians of Prussia and only one-seventh of the Jews live in rural communities. In the city of Berlin alone 22.92 per cent. of all the Jews in the German Empire were found during the enumeration of 1905. With its suburbs Berlin harboured 139,320 Jews, or 34 per cent. of all who lived in the Kingdom of Prussia. Conditions are the same in the West and South of Europe. About 60 per cent. of all the Jews of France live in Paris, and the majority of the rest live in the other cities of that country. According to the census of 1899, 86.4 per cent. of all the Italian Jews live in the sixty-nine capitals of the provinces of that country. In England, Rosenbaum estimates that 144,000 of the 240,000 Jews who live in Great Britain and Ireland live in London.[2] The same is reported from many other parts of the world—Egypt, Palestine, Persia, North Africa, etc.

The best illustration is, perhaps, furnished by the Jews in the United States. According to the figures on the distribution of the Jews in this country given by the *Jewish Encyclopædia*, it appears that here also they prefer to live in large towns. Of the 1,558,710 Jews in the United States in 1905, 672,000—*i.e.*, 43 per cent. of all—lived in New York City, where they constituted nearly 20 per cent. of the total population. The same authority estimates the number of Jews in Chicago at 80,000; Philadelphia, 75,000; St. Louis, 40,000; etc. From the figures given there, I calculate that in the nineteen cities in the United

---

[1] J. Thon, *Die Juden in Oesterreich*, pp. 17-19, Berlin, 1907.
[2] Rosenbaum, *loc. cit.*

States with more than 200,000 inhabitants at the census of 1900, in which 15.61 per cent. of the population of this country lived at that time, there lived 1,081,100 Jews, or 69.35 per cent. of all the followers of Judaism in the United States.[1] These figures give a correct statement of conditions, even considering that they are only based on estimates. Indeed, taking another country—Australia—where the Jewish population consists mostly of immigrants, we find exactly the same condition of affairs. In Australasia the census gives details as to the religious confession of the inhabitants, so that the data are as authentic as can be expected. It was found in 1901 that 79.7 per cent. of all the Jews in New South Wales lived in the city of Sydney; 60 per cent. of all the Jews in South Australia lived in Adelaide; 57.5 per cent. of the Jews in Queensland lived in Brisbane, etc.

The causes of this peculiar distribution of the Jews are not far to seek. Throughout the centuries of their dispersion legislation has always been directed to segregate them in cities, and even in certain parts of cities. While in Western Europe these laws have already been abolished, more than one-half of all the Jews in the world are not yet free to choose their abode in the country of their allegiance. In Russia and Roumania they must not, even if they choose, live in villages; in Morocco, Persia, Bokhara, etc., they are even to-day compelled to live in special parts of the cities known as *Mellahs*, or Jewish quarters. During the Middle Ages the Jews in every country laboured under these disabilities. Everywhere they were compelled to live in *Judengassen*, *Ghettoes*, or *Jewries* in English-speaking countries. The process of urbanization of the rural population, which is at the present going on in all civilized countries, is well known. The reverse has not been known to occur to any considerable extent. In other words, city dwellers do not move

---

[1] Since 1905 the number of Jews in the United States has increased by immigration and natural increase, so that at present there are about 1,000,000 of them in New York City. But the proportion of city dwellers has not undergone any change. The effort of philanthropists to disperse them all over the States, especially the activities of the Industrial Removal Office, is successful in removing Jews from New York City and transplanting them into western and southern cities, where they are again town-dwellers. Considering their occupations, the reason for this is evident.

in large numbers to the country for permanent residence. The Jews who for centuries have not been permitted to acquire land, to work the soil, or even to live in the open

Fig. 4.—BOKHARA JEWS.

country, have acquired all the characteristics of the city dweller, have been urbanized *par excellence*, and cannot be expected to change all at once after they have been relieved from these disabilities.

Quite the contrary has been observed in Western Europe. The Jews during recent years leave small towns and move into large cities. Ruppin points out that the reason for this phenomenon is to be found in their occupations. Formerly they lived in small towns which were the centres of commerce for the rural population. This is even to-day the case with the Jews in countries which are backward in their economic development, as, for instance, in Russia, Galicia, Roumania, etc. Here the Jewish small trader finds a good field to act as the merchant and middleman for the peasants. But in countries where the industrial development has reached a high plane and the facilities for transportation have been more or less perfected, it is the great city where all the commercial and industrial activities are concentrated, and the small town has been losing its significance in this respect. The Jews, owing to their peculiar occupations, have thus only followed the stream of commerce and industry. It can be stated that the higher the industrial and commercial development of a country the larger the number of Jews in large cities. The distribution of the Jews in towns and cities goes hand-in-hand with the distribution of the commercial and industrial population in the country of their residence. Germany offers an excellent illustration in this respect. It was found in 1900 that 42.72 per cent. of all the Jews lived in cities with over 200,000 population, while only 15.9 per cent. of the Christian population lived in this class of cities. This striking difference is explained when it is borne in mind that the part of the general population which is engaged in mercantile pursuits was represented in this class of cities to the extent of 35.5 per cent. according to the census of occupations taken in Germany in 1895. The differences between Jews and Christians engaged in similar occupations are not so great when viewed from this standpoint. Occupation has a great influence in determining the place of residence.[1] The rural population is essentially agricultural, and there are very few agriculturists of Jewish faith. This will be brought out in a later chapter when speaking of the occupations of the Jews.

Acclimatization.—The distribution of the Jews is inter-

[1] A. Ruppin, *Die Juden der Gegenwart*, pp. 42-43.

esting from the standpoint of acclimatization which has recently received so much attention. That most urgent problem which confronts modern statesmen, anthropologists, and sociologists is whether the *Homo Europæus* may emigrate to climates other than those he is accustomed to in Europe, especially the tropics, live a healthful life, and perpetuate his kind and ethnic type. Many claim that the European is not fit for this change, and that those who survive the difference in the physical environment, even if the new climate differs but little from that of the mother country, have to undergo a kind of transformation which effects their entire organism.[1] Virchow has shown that not only is the individual affected by a prolonged sojourn away from his native country, but his posterity is as well affected. Some authors have maintained that the Jews appear to be an exception in this respect. They live, thrive, perpetuate their kind, and preserve their identity under all varieties of climatic conditions. They are said to be a cosmopolitan race.[2] Andree thus expresses himself on this peculiarity:—"The Jew is able to acclimatize himself with equal facility in hot and in cold latitudes and to exist without the assistance of the native races. He lasts from generation to generation in Surinam (Dutch Guiana) or in Malabar (India), tropical climates where Europeans, in course of time, die out, unless they are constantly re-enforced by new immigration from the mother country."[3] A. R. Wallace speaks in a similar vein when he says that the Jews are "a good example of acclimatization because they have been established for many centuries in climates very different from that of their native land; (?) they keep themselves almost wholly free from intermixture with the people around them

They have, for instance, attained a population of near two millions [over five millions in 1897] in such severe climates as Poland and Russia." According to Mr. Brace (*Races of the Old World*, p. 185), "their increase in Sweden is said to be greater than that of the Christian population [at present the reverse is true]; in the towns of Algeria they are the only race able to maintain its numbers [many

---

[1] See Ch. E. Woodruff, *Expansion of Races*; New York, 1909.
[2] Boudin, *Mémoires de la Société d Anthropologie*, vol. i, p. 117.
[3] R. Andree, *Zur Volkskunde der Juden*, pp. 70-71, Leipsic, 1881.

other Europeans have succeeded in this since the improvement in sanitary conditions which the French have brought about]; and in Cochin China and Aden they succeed in rearing and forming permanent communities."[1] Of course all these statements are based on antiquated views of the problem of acclimatization and ancient data about the Jews. Conditions have changed at present, as will be seen later on in this work.

This peculiarity of the Jews has been considered a racial trait. Felkin even states that it is probably due to a certain amount of Semitic blood that the Southern

Fig. 5. Fig. 6.
CAUCASIAN JEWESS.

Europeans possess in a higher degree the power of adapting themselves to a subtropical climate[2]; and discussing the overwhelming superiority in adaptability of the Maltese over the Spaniard, Virchow says that it is derived from the mixture of Semitic blood.[3] This ethnic trait of the Jews is said to have been slowly acquired by their constant migrations, even their temporary stay in Egypt. Their slow progression (*petit acclimatement*) is stated by

[1] Article "Acclimatization," *Encyclopædia Britannica*, Vol. I.
[2] *Scottish Geographical Journal*, vol. ii. p. 653.
[3] R. Virchow, "Ueber Akklimatisation," *Verhandlungen der Versammlung der Naturforscher und Aerzte in Strassburg*, 1885.

Bertillon to have had its influence on their power of acclimatization.[1] This is confirmed by Schellong, who points out that the centre of Jewish dispersion in Europe was in the countries around the Mediterranean, whence they have slowly penetrated northward (which was not the case with all the Russian Jews, as will be shown later) into colder climates, for which less aptitude for acclimatization is necessary.[2]

All these theories about the superior powers of acclimatization of the Jews are disproved by the changes which have taken place during recent years in the life of those followers of Judaism who have been emancipated. They no more keep themselves free from intermixture, and, as will be shown later on, have hardly ever refrained from intermarriage to the extent with which they are credited. Physically they do not retain their identity in every country, but we distinguish types of Jews in various places which differ from each other quite as much as, and often more than, from the people around them. So that if they do prosper in tropical as well as in cold climates, it is probably more due to the racial elements which they have acquired in the countries of their present sojourn than to the "Semitic" blood which is alleged to flow in their veins.

But it must also be borne in mind that they are hardly comparable with the average colonist who engages in agriculture and allied pursuits, which necessitate severe exertion and exposure to the hot rays of the sun in tropical climates, or to the frigid cold of northern climes. The Jew mostly confines his activities to small trading, and during the greater part of the day is protected from the vicissitudes of the weather in his shop. In addition to this, his proverbial sobriety, the purity of his domestic life and freedom from vicious habits generally, contribute largely to his facility of adaptation to a new climate. The Jews cannot be compared with the average colonist who in a strange country, without the usual restraints of home life, is prone to do things which he would not dare to do at home. Wallace points out that the English, who cannot

---

[1] Article "Acclimatement," *Dictionnaire des Sciences Anthropologiques*, Paris, 1884.
[2] "Akklimatization," in Weyl's *Handbuch der Hygiene*, vol. i. p. 334.

give up animal food and the use of spiritous liquors, are less able to sustain the heat of the tropics than the more sober Spaniards and Portuguese. The Boers in South Africa are another example of a people who keep sober and prosper in a tropical land.

The wide distribution of the Jews in the world, under various climatic conditions, is not due to any special racial peculiarity; their power of acclimatization is the result of the peculiarity of their occupations and habits of life. Any other race or people adopting the habits of the Jews could just as well live under similar climatic conditions.

CHAPTER II.

PHYSICAL CHARACTERS.

The alleged purity of the Jewish race—Persistence of racial traits Race and environment—Stature—Height of ancient Hebrews Height of modern Jewish conscripts—Growth of the body—Height of Jewesses—Influence of the environment on the stature of Jews—Influence of occupation—Social selection—Selection by immigration Ethnic factors.

IT has been accepted by anthropologists that there are no pure races among civilized peoples and nations. Migrations, wars, and conquests, with their concomitant intermingling, assimilation, and absorption of different races have been in operation for ages. One exception, however, has been pointed at by many who studied the problem of races. The Jews, constituting as they do only a small fraction of civilized humanity, were alleged to have succeeded in maintaining their race in a state of purity for the last four thousand years. Moreover, during the last eighteen centuries of dispersion among all the nations of the habitable globe, among nearly all the races of mankind, they are alleged to have refrained from intermarriage outside of their pale, and thus maintained the purity of the breed of Israel to an extent unknown among any other ethnic group of people. The result, it was asserted, is a most astonishing and noteworthy phenomenon: the Jews of to-day present a uniform physical type wherever they may be encountered. One met with in Scandinavia hardly differs physically from one who lives, and whose ancestry have lived for several centuries, on one of the oases of the Sahara; nor do these differ materially from Jews who have been domiciled from times immemorial in the Caucasus, or on the Malabar coast, or from the recent immigrants to England, the United States, and Australasia. Furthermore, it has been repeatedly asserted by archæologists that the race portraits portrayed on the ancient Egyptian, Assyrian, and Babylonian monuments which have recently come to light, show faces of Jews

Fig. 7.—Young Jewess in Sfax, Tunis.

which bear a striking resemblance to the faces met with to-day in Warsaw, Frankfort, Whitechapel in London, and in the east side of New York City. Notwithstanding all the vicissitudes which he was subject to for four thousand years, it is said that the type of the ancient Hebrew survives to-day in the modern Jew, whether you meet him peddling his wares on the high road, working in a sweat-shop in New York, or speculating in the bourse of Paris.

For these reasons anthropologists in Europe have given the Jews an unusual amount of attention. Measurements have been taken of Jews in various parts of the world in order to ascertain whether the alleged uniformity of physical type can be substantiated by scientific tests. Demographers have studied the birth-rates, morbidity and mortality of the children of Israel and found that there are important differences between them and the people around them. Sociologists have given due attention to social and economic phenomena as they appeared among the Chosen People. Many have, as a result of their studies, come to the conclusion that the differences elicited were to be attributed solely to endogenic causes, that the Jews differ in racial derivation from all other Europeans, and that all their peculiarities, virtues, and vices are the result of heredity.

It is therefore important to inquire at the outset what are the traits which differentiate the Jews from other races, and also whether these race traits are persistent—*i.e.*, transmitted by heredity from generation to generation, irrespective of the environment. The material for the purpose of such an inquiry is, to a certain extent, available in anthropological literature. There are measurements and photographs of race types of Jews in many parts of Europe, and some parts of Asia and Africa. All these can be utilized in a study of the racial characteristics of the Jews, and can materially aid us in our attempt to determine whether their physical type in various parts of the world is really homogeneous from the standpoint of physical anthropology.

If the physical type of the Jews of to-day be found homogeneous, it may safely be assumed that they have preserved themselves free from any considerable infusion of foreign blood. Because, in contrast with the remarkable changes which have taken place in the cultural characters of mankind within historical times, research has shown that physically the various races of man have remained practically the same. Judging from the remains of well-preserved skeletons which have been recently unearthed, it appears that prehistoric man did not materially differ from the people of to-day. The morphologic traits which differentiate man from the anthropoids have not changed since the neolithic period—*i.e.*, for about eight to ten thousand years.[1] In fact, a glance at the reproductions of race types depicted on Assyrian, Babylonian, and Egyptian monuments reveals that at the time these portraits were produced the Nubian was black with a long head, a flat nose and thick lips, a prognathous jaw, etc.; the blonde-haired individual is represented as orthognathous with medium-sized lips, a straight nose, etc., corresponding to the fair complexioned population of to-day. The physical type of the Egyptian, as painted by artists of three thousand years ago, bears a striking resemblance to the modern Fellah. There is consequently justification for the assumption that the different races, varieties, or types of mankind which are met with at present have persisted for several thousand years, and that changes in the physical and social environment to which they have been subjected during long centuries have been powerless to alter them. This is also confirmed by observations made on skeletons of pre-historic man which have been reclaimed in various parts of the globe. The shape and form of the human skull, the proportion of the limbs, etc., are about the same as seen among modern peoples. These morphological traits have persistently been transmitted from generation to generation.

According to J. Kollmann, the most constantly reappearing racial traits are the following:—The colour of the skin, hair, and eyes; the form of the skull and face; the relative length of the limbs; and within certain limits the height, or stature. These traits are constant in a race and depend only on heredity, and are not known to be influenced by external conditions. These are to be distinguished from the secondary or fluctuating racial traits which depend greatly on the social and physical environ-

[1] See J. Kollmann, "Die Rassenanatomie der Hand und die Persisterz der Rassenmerkmale, *Archiv fur Anthropologie*, 1902, pp. 91-141.

ment. The latter are, according to Kollmann, the amount of fat on the body, the development of the muscular system, the strength of the skeleton, and, to a certain extent, also stature. All these are known to increase in well-nourished individuals.

The persistence of the racial traits just mentioned is seen to-day among the inhabitants of Australia and America. The white race has been transplanted from Europe into countries with different climates and conditions of life. In the course of three hundred years' sojourn in America no new race has appeared. The descendants of the original English, Spanish, and French settlers are of the same physical type as the parent stock, the inhabitants of England, Spain, and France of to-day. Although some maintain that they have changed both physically and mentally, still there is no case on record showing the transformation of a white man into anything like a redskin.[1] There is no new American or Australian race differing physically from the European. This tends to confirm the belief that the *milieu* does not change races, as far as the anthropological type is concerned. Crossing of human races is also not known to produce new types of mankind. Professor Boas' investigations have shown that crossing of whites with North American Indians and negroes has not produced any new type nor middle types, but generally the half-breeds showed a reversion to one of the parent types.[2]

This theory of the stability and persistence of racial characters has never been accepted in its entirety by all anthropologists. Many have insisted that the geographical and social environment has a great influence in modifying physical traits, and that the process of adaptation to a new environment involves a change in the organism with

---

[1] The statements often made by anthropologists that Europeans in America, as a result of the geographical environment, begin to resemble the Indian physical type appear to be pure fiction. Professor Franz Boas, the foremost authority on American anthropology, failed to find even a trace of evidence on which this opinion can be based. (*Science*, vol. xxix., p. 844.) W. Z. Ripley considers such observations amusing and the product of an over-excited and vivid imagination. (*Journ. Royal Anthropol. Inst.*, vol. xxxviii., p. 221.)

[2] F. Boas, "Zur Anthropologie der nordamerikanischen Indianer," *Zeitschrift für Ethnologie*, vol. xxvii. p. 401.

concomitant changes in the somatic traits. It is immaterial for our present purposes whether these changes are due to the creation of new types, or are merely the result of a process of natural selection which eliminates individuals whose head-form, complexion, etc., are not fitted to the new *milieu;* while those possessing traits best fitted to their new home survive and transmit their advantageous characters to their offspring. The followers of the environmental theory have often mentioned the Jews as a good example of a race which has maintained itself in absolute purity of blood, yet showing physical differences in different countries. The blonde Jews in Northern Europe, the brunettes in the South, the black Jews of the Malabar Coast, the Negro Jews in Abyssinia, and the Mongolian Jews in China, were thus supposed to be not a product of race fusion, but solely the result of the climate, altitude, nourishment, etc. The fallacy of this contention will appear later on in this work. Meanwhile, it must be mentioned that different races are found in many places living side by side under the same physical and social environment for centuries, and, as far as we know, showing no tendency toward changing their physical type. Indeed, investigations have shown that long-headed men usually beget long-headed children; blondes only rarely have dark-complexioned children, etc. Heredity seems at work in all directions.

The first, and thus far the only, proof of the theory that the environment is capable of modifying the physical type of human races has been brought forward by Professor Franz Boas, whose researches have recently been published. Measurements taken of about 30,000 immigrants and their descendants in New York revealed that the change in the environment from Europe to America has a profound and far-reaching influence on racial traits, such as stature, headform, and to some extent also on complexion. The Eastern European Jews with their brachycephalic heads become long-headed, while the Sicilians, who are pronounced dolichocephals, become more short-headed, so that they approach a uniform type in America. It was also evident that the influence of the American environment, as expressed by the divergence of the descendants from their European type, manifests itself with increasing intensity according to the time elapsed between the arrival of the mother and the birth of the child. The increase in stature and weight, as well as the acceleration of growth of the descendants of immigrants, may be attributed to a certain extent to economic improvement. But the change in the headform cannot thus be accounted for, as far as our present knowledge goes.[1]

Of course these observations are comparatively limited in number and extent of territory they cover. Similar investigations must be undertaken in other parts of the world before drawing definite conclusions. It is also necessary to inquire whether these changes are progressive and permanent through several generations and not temporary divergences, the result of intermixture of the various local types of Jews, Italians, Scotch, Bohemians, etc., who at home mostly married with persons in their own towns or villages, but in New York, while marrying with their own people, yet often from different cities. Such intermingling may lead to changes in certain directions, but whether it will lead toward a permanent, uniform, "American" type remains to be seen.

With these preliminary remarks on the significance of ethnic traits we can proceed to examine in detail the more important physical traits of the modern Jews, beginning with stature, a trait which is less stable than others, still of sufficient importance in our study, showing, as it does, the influence of both heredity and environment.

Stature.—No definite information is found in Biblical and Talmudic records and traditions as to the stature of the ancient Hebrews. Judging from the descriptions found in the Bible about the autochthonous races of Palestine at the time of their invasion, the Hebrews were short. The *Raphaim*, who were settled both east and west of the Jordan, are stated to have been of immense stature; also the *Emims*, "a people great, and many and tall," as the *Anakim*, who were also accounted as giants.[2] The *Amorites*, the sons of Anak, were, in the estimation of the Bible, giants, "and we were in our own sight as grasshoppers, and so we were in their sight."[3] Whether

---

[1] See Franz Boas, *Changes in Bodily Form of Descendants of Immigrants*, Washington, 1910.
[2] *Deuter.*, ii. 10, 11.   [3] *Numbers*, xiii 33.

these and others who were taller than the Hebrews constituted a distinct non-Israelitish race or nationality, or were a selected warrior class of tall individuals, is uncertain. For our purpose it is sufficient to indicate that Biblical evidence tends to show that the Jews were not as tall, and apparently could not line up an army of such tall warriors, as the indigenous population, but this did not interfere with their success in the struggle for the supremacy over Palestine.

Taking, with Topinard and Deniker, the median height of the contemporaneous population of Europe to be about 165 cm., the Jews of to-day are short of stature. General observation in the extensive settlements of the Jews in Eastern Europe reveals an immense number of stunted individuals among them. But there is no need to rely on superficial observation to reach this conclusion. There are records in anthropological literature of a large number of measurements taken of Jews in various countries. As is the rule with other races, the largest number of Jews were measured in the conscript offices of the European armies, particularly in Russia, Austria, and Poland. The following are the averages of stature of Jewish conscripts in various countries, based upon records of over 10,000 individuals reported by Snigireff, Zakrzewski, Scheiber, Pantiukhof, Himmel, Ranke, Tolwinski and others[1]:

Poland	161.3 cm.	Bavaria	162.0 cm.
Lithuania	161.2 ,,	Hungary -	- 163.3 ,,
Little Russia -	164.2 ,,	Baden	- 164.3 ,,
Odessa	166.9 ,,	Bukowina	- 165.4 ,,

The average stature of Jewish conscripts is shown by these figures to be quite variable. In Poland and Lithuania it is slightly above 161 cm.; in Bavaria, 162 cm.; in Hungary, Little Russia, and Bukowina, between

[1] Snigireff, "Materiali dlia medizinskoi statistike i geografii Rossii," *Voenno-Medizinski Zhurnal*, 1878-1879; Zakrzewski, "Wzrost w Krolewstwie Polskiem," *Zbior wiadom. do antrop. kraj*, 1891, vol. xv. pp. 1-38; Himmel, "Körpermessungen in der Bukowina," *Mitt. anthropol. Ges. Wien*, vol. xviii. pp. 83-84; Scheiber, "Untersuchnug. über den mitteleren Wuchs der Menschen in Ungarn," *Archiv f. Anthropologie*, vol. xiii. pp. 133-267; J. Ranke, "Zur Statistik der Körpergrösse, etc." *Beitr. z. Anthrop. Bayerns*, vol. iv. pp. 1-35; I. I. Pantiukhof, *Observ. anthropol. au Caucase*, Tiflis, 1893.

163 and 167 cm. These variations are of significance, and, as will appear hereafter, may be attributed to either ethnic or economic and social causes. They go far to show that the stature of the Jews is not a homogeneous trait, but that it is subject to wide limits of variation. It must be mentioned, however, that recruiting statistics are not a reliable guide. There are many sources of error, which are often sufficient to deprive them of any considerable value after a thorough analysis. Thus, most of the conscripts are persons between nineteen and twenty-one years of age, i. e., before they have attained their maximum growth. With Jews this is of importance, as will soon be shown. In addition it must be borne in mind that the largest number of measurements were recorded by Snigireff, having been obtained in Russia and Poland during 1875-77. At that time the Jews were very much averse to serve in the army, and they often presented themselves before the actual age of twenty; many have appeared at the age of nineteen, eighteen and even fifteen, hoping to be rejected because of imperfect physical development and shortness of stature. That such individuals were thus measured in large numbers at that time (1875-77) is well known to every one who knows conditions in that country. How far this may influence the average height in the records can be seen when growth is taken into consideration.

From measurements taken by Weissenberg in South Russia, Majer and Kopernicki in Galicia, Sack in Moscow and Yashchinski in Poland,[1] all of which give quite uniform results, it appears that Jewish children in Eastern Europe grow very rapidly up to the age of six, whereas observations among other European children indicate that development usually slackens at four years of age. From six to eleven, growth is slower among the Jews than among others; from eleven to sixteen the body again increases rapidly, then growth becomes somewhat slower, but it continues nevertheless, up to the age of thirty. At this age the maximum height is attained. At forty the body begins to decline and grow shorter.

[1] S. Weissenberg, "Die südrussischen Juden," *Archiv für Anthropologie*, vol. xxiii. pp. 347-423; 531-579; J. Majer, Roczny przyrost ciala, etc. *Zbior Wiad. do antropol. kraj.* vol. iv. pp. 3-32.

Weissenberg's diagrams show graphically the process of growth in Eastern European Jews based on observations

Fig. 8. Fig. 9.

Fig. 10. Fig. 11.

Figs. 8-11.—Types of Eastern European Jews.

of his own and others, and confirm the conclusion that at twenty the Jew has not yet attained his full height.

There are, however, on record measurements of adult Jews which may be of great assistance to determine the actual height of Jews in various countries.

Here again wide limits of variation are seen. The shortest Jews are found in Lithuania and Poland, averaging about 161 cm. in height; in South and Little Russia they are taller, from 163 to 166 cm.; while in England and the United States they even reach 168 and 171 cm. on the average. Altogether it is seen that the limits of variation are almost as wide as for all European races; at any rate there is no uniformity to be observed.

One peculiarity worthy of note is the large number of short persons among the Jews. This has been observed by the recruiting officials of Russia, Poland, Austria, etc. It is true that it may partly be ascribed to their aversion to military service and the means they often resorted to to escape it in Eastern Europe, as has been just stated; but measurements taken on the general population, including only persons over twenty years of age, also show an excessive number of short individuals. Taking Topinard's classification of stature, it is found that, among 3,209 Jews measured in Eastern Europe and America, 29.67 per cent. were of short stature, less than 160 cm. in height; 31.35 per cent. were below the average stature, 160 to 165 cm.; only 24.3 per cent. were above the average, 165 to 170 cm. in height; and of tall persons, measuring 170 cm. and more, only 14.68 per cent. were found. The number of stunted persons is significant. When compared with other European races, it is found that only the Magyars, Lapps, and Sardinians can show such a large proportion of short persons. The Russian recruiting officials have recognized this as a trait of the Jews, and admit them into the army even when they are a few centimetres shorter than the minimum prescribed for the non-Jewish recruits.

Jewesses are similarly short of stature. The absolute difference in height of men and women is about the same in all races. From Deniker's study of 35 series of measurements of women it is seen that in 20 cases out of 35—*i.e.*, almost two-thirds—the difference in height between the two sexes in any given population hardly varies more than from seven to thirteen centimetres; 14 times out of 35 it only varied from 11 to 12 centimetres; so that the figure 12 centimetres may be accepted as the average.[1] Measurements of Jewesses show the same results: they were found to be about eleven centimetres shorter than the Jews. The 435 Jewesses measured in New York by the present writer had an average height of 153.5 cm., as against 164.5 cm. of the average height of the Jews, thus showing the ratio of stature of men and women as being 1 to 0.931 or as 16 to 14.88, which is exactly the ratio of adult men and women in England.[2] The same has been observed among Jewesses in Poland, South Russia, Lithuania, etc. It is also significant that the number of tall individuals is very small among the Jewesses, just as has been found among the Jews. Only 23 per cent. measured over 157 cm. among 435 immigrant Jewesses in New York city. In their native homes they are even shorter: only from 9 to 13 per cent. are found of that height in Poland, White Russia, Lithuania, etc.[3]

Influence of Environment on the Stature of the Jews.— The shortness of stature of the Jews has been taken by some as a racial trait, and as one of the proofs of the uniformity of their physical type since biblical times. Even then, it is pointed out, they were shorter than the Aryan Amorites, and to-day they are shorter than the Aryans in Europe. On the other hand, others, particularly Jacobs, are of the opinion that it is not necessarily of ethnic origin, but is solely the product of the social and economic environment under which they find themselves. In countries in which the Jews are generally poor, of sedentary habits, employed at indoor occupations, deprived of the invigorating and growth-accelerating influence of outdoor life and only rarely or never engaged in agricultural pursuits, they are shorter of stature than in places where they are on a higher economic level. This is best shown by the rich Jews of the West End of London, who are as tall as the average Englishman, reaching

[1] J. Deniker, *The Races of Man*, p. 33; London, 1899.
[2] There the stature of men is 170 cm., and of women 160 cm.; the ratio then as is 16 to 14.88. See *Report of the Anthropometric Committee of the British Association*, 1883; H. Ellis, *Man and Woman*, p. 39.
[3] For detailed statistics on the subject see Fishberg, *Materials for the Physical Anthropology of the Jews*, pp. 195-199.

171.4 cm. in height, while their poorer co-religionists in the East End only average 164.1 cm. in height. The influence of the *milieu* is worthy of consideration while this particular subject is considered.

The Jews are mostly town-dwellers, and this may account for some of the shortness of their stature. "The general rule in Europe," says Ripley, "seems to be that the urban type is physically degenerate."[1] Beddoe considers it as proved that the stature of men in large towns of Britain is lowered considerably below the standard of the nation, and that such degradation is progressive and hereditary.[2] The same has been observed to be the case in Bavaria,[3] by Anutchin in Russia, and by many others. Ripley points out that the unfavourable influence of city life is often obscured by the great social selection which is at work in the determination of the physical type of the population of great cities. While the course of town life is downward, oftentime the city attracts a class which is markedly superior, in the same way as the immigrants of the United States have been distinguished in this respect. Not having a large number of agriculturists in their midst, the Jews of course cannot enjoy this advantage of renewing their physical conditions by intermarrying with country people.

The wretched social, economic, and sanitary conditions under which they labour in Eastern Europe will also account for the deficiency which they display in bodily height. As a matter of fact, in Galicia and Lithuania, where they find themselves under the worst circumstances materially, they are shorter than in any other country. Zakrzewski, in his work *Ludnosc Miasta Warszawy*,[4] shows graphically on maps of the city of Warsaw that the shortness of stature goes hand-in-hand with economic misery.

The indoor occupations in which they are mostly engaged have also a great influence in reducing their

---

[1] Wm. Z. Ripley, *The Races of Europe*, p. 95; New York, 1899.
[2] J. Beddoe, "On the Stature and Bulk of Man in the British Isles," *Mem. Anthrop. Soc.*, III.; London, 1867.
[3] J. Ranke, *Der Mensch*, vol. ii., p. 131; Leipsic, 1886.
[4] *Materiali Antropol.-archeol. Academ., umiej.*, Cracaw, vol. i., part i.; 1895. See also Ripley, *Races of Europe*, p. 381.

average height. The author has investigated this problem among the Jews in New York City, and the results showed in a striking manner that those engaged at indoor occupations were shorter than those who worked outdoors. Among 1,528 individuals thus investigated 720 (47.12 per cent.) were engaged in indoor occupations, including the various branches of tailoring, shoemaking, weaving, baking, etc.; 344 (22.51 per cent.) were outdoor workers, including carpenters, house painters, masons, ironworkers, etc.; 398 (26.65 per cent.) were engaged in mercantile pursuits and clerks; 130 were pedlars, and 66 were of the class generally termed professional, including the liberal professions, and also students. The tallest were the professional men, who average 169.6 cm. in height, and it is significant that thirty-five per cent. of these were 170 cm. and taller. The clerks and merchants come close, with 169.2 and 168.7 cm. in height on the average respectively, while the pedlars are much shorter, only 164.3 cm. on the average. Jews engaged in outdoor occupations were also taller, 166.4 cm., than the average for the Jews, which was 164.5 cm., and nearly twenty-three per cent. of them were above 170 cm. in height, as against only nineteen among the Jews generally. Masons and iron workers were the tallest in this class, while the carpenters were the shortest.

Among the Jews engaged in indoor occupations there was found an appalling proportion of stunted individuals. Thirty-one per cent. were shorter than 160 cm. in height, and only twelve per cent. were tall, 170 cm. and higher. It is also significant that only one of the entire number was 178 cm. in height, and even he was not a tailor in his early life, but only adopted this occupation after arriving in the United States at the age of twenty-one. The average stature of this class was 162 cm., 2.5 cm. shorter than the average for the Jews in New York City. Deplorably deficient in this respect were the shoemakers and tailors, the former average only 160.3 cm., and the latter 161.3 cm. The percentage of short persons was 32.79 among the tailors and as high as 38 among the shoemakers.

These figures tend to show that the deficiency of the Jews' stature, as compared with other races in Eastern

Europe, may, at least partly, be ascribed to the wretched social and economic conditions under which they find themselves in the Eastern Europe Ghettoes. Dr. Weissenberg[1] also observed the same process in South Russia, and Zakrzewski in Poland confirms it for Warsaw. It is remarkable that in contrast with this is the fact that the first generation of native Jews in New York, who are only rarely employed at indoor occupations, but lead a more active outdoor life, which is conducive to normal growth and development, are also taller, as will be seen hereafter.

Social Selection among the Jews.—Much weight cannot, however, be placed on these figures as showing the effects of the *milieu* on stature. A further analysis shows that besides social and economic conditions there is also a process of selection going on which is more potent in its effects. This process of artificial selection is well summarized by Ripley: "The physically well developed men seek certain trades or occupations in which their vigour and strength may stand them in good stead; on the other hand, those who are by nature weakly, and coincidently often deficient in stature, are compelled to make shift with some pursuit for which they are fitted. Thus workers in iron, potters, porters, firemen, policemen, are taller as a class than the average, because they are of necessity recruited from the more robust portion of the population. In marked contrast to them, tailors, shoemakers, and weavers, in an occupation which entails slight demands upon physical powers, and which is open to all, however weakly they may be, are appreciably shorter than the average." Besides this process of selection it must be added that the habits of life which are peculiar to certain occupations also have a perceptible influence on stature. The conditions in the tailoring shops of Eastern Europe, or in the "sweat-shops" in England or America, act very adversely on the physique of young tailors who have not reached their full growth. They work in cramped positions for long hours daily, amid unsanitary surroundings which by no means contribute to full growth and development of the human body.

May not the peculiar occupations of the Jews be the

[1] "Die südrussischen Juden," *Archiv für Anthropologie*, vol. xxiii.; 1895.

effect rather than the cause of their poor physique? May we not consider that so few Jews engage in occupations requiring strong and violent muscular exertion merely because they find themselves unequal to the task? Tailoring, shoemaking, weaving, etc., do not require strong muscles; any one with a spark of life may successfully pursue any of these vocations, and for this reason Jews are mostly working at these trades. The shortness of stature of the Jews working at these occupations may thus be explained as due principally to selection, the shorter persons as well as those with weakly and flabby muscles are more likely to engage in them.

The author has also observed a process of selection in connection with emigration of Jews. The Jewish immigrants to the United States were found to be taller, on the average, than those in Europe. Thus, the average stature of the Jews in Poland has been determined by Elkind and Snigireff to be 161 cm., while immigrants from that country are taller by one inch, reaching 163.4 cm. in height. In Lithuania and White Russia the average height of the Jews is around 162 cm., according to Snigireff, Talko-Hryncewicz, and Yakowenko, while immigrants from that region of Russia are 164.2 cm. The Jews in South Russia and Little Russia are known to be taller than those in Poland and Lithuania. Snigireff and Wissenberg found them to average 164 cm. in height, and immigrants from that region measured in New York were found to be taller, 165.6 cm.; and the Jewish immigrants from Hungary are also taller by one inch than those who remained at home. The only exception was found with the Jews from Galicia, who measured, both in the United States and in their native home, 162.3 cm. in height.[1] Among immigrants there are to be found a larger pro-

---

[1] These observations have been confirmed by the investigation of Professor Boas recently published. He found the following average stature for Jewish immigrants in New York:—Roumanian, 164.8 cm.; Galician, 163.6 cm.; Little Russian, 165.6 cm.; White Russian, 163.8 cm.; Polish, 163.5 cm.; Lithuanian, 164.0 cm. They are thus all taller on the average than the Jews in their native countries. (F. Boas, *Changes in Bodily Form of Descendants of Immigrants;* Washington, 1910.) There are no published data about Jewish immigrants in England, but Jacobs' investigations show that the native Jews are much taller than their alien co-religionists.

portion of persons of superior stature, as can be seen from the following figures embracing measurements of 1,681 Jews in Poland, Russia, and Galicia, compared with 1,528 Jews who emigrated to New York city:—

	Eastern Europe.	New York.
Persons of short stature	35.46%	23.30%
Persons below the average	32.48	30.10
Persons above the average	21.41	27.40
Tall persons	10.65	19.11

Individuals of short stature, less than 160 cm. in height, were found in Eastern Europe to the extent of 35.46 per cent., while among the immigrant population in New York City only 23.3 per cent. are of this class. On the other hand, tall persons were more numerous in New York, 19.11 per cent., as against only 10.65 per cent. in Eastern Europe. The process of selection by immigration is thus seen to work by leaving many of the short individuals at home and attracting to the new country many of the taller ones. The result of this selection is manifesting itself in the physical development of the children of the immigrants, who are much taller than their parents. The author has found that the average stature of 1,404 immigrants in New York City was 164.2 cm., while their children, the first generation of descendants of Eastern European Jewish immigrants, measured 167.9 cm. in height, an increase of 3.7 cm. in height in one generation. This increase in stature is yet better displayed in the accompanying table, showing the proportion of persons in each class of stature:—

	Foreign Jews.	Native Jews.
Persons of short stature	24.57%	8.77%
Persons below medium height	30.63	24.19
Persons above medium height	26.99	33.07
Tall persons	17.81	33.87

These figures show that while among the Jews born in Eastern Europe 24.57 per cent. were of short stature, there were only 8.87 per cent. of native Jews thus deficient in body-height. On the other hand, tall men, 170 cm. in height and over, are found among the native Jews, 33.87

per cent. as against only 17.81 per cent. among their immigrant parents.

A process of double selection can thus be seen at work. The immigrants are, on the average, taller than the people of whom they spring, as has already been noted. That stature is transmitted by heredity is not questioned. When to this are added other factors which are favourable to the growth and development of the body, we have good reasons for the superior stature of the native American Jews. Here during the period of most active growth, the Jewish child attends a modern public school, instead of the semi-oriental *Cheder* in Eastern Europe. During adolescence the Jew here engages mostly in outdoor occupations, instead of the dangerous "sweat-shop" which is the workshop of a large proportion of the immigrant Jews. In addition, the native Jewish youth in New York City indulges quite freely in open-air recreations, games, bicycle riding, etc., all of which is conducive to healthy growth and development of the body. This gives him an immense advantage over his immigrant co-religionist. Possessing the qualifications required for doing outdoor work successfully, he no longer engages in tailoring, weaving, shoemaking, etc., but mainly engages in occupations into which his superior muscular development has fitted him. Had he remained physically as weakly as his Eastern European co-religionists, he would surely have been compelled to seek occupations in which muscles are not the determining factor of success.

Ethnic Factors of Stature.—We have thus arrived at the conclusion that the social and economic environment in which the Jews find themselves has some influence on their stature. It is true that it usually works indirectly, by compelling persons of poor physique to seek occupations in which muscles are not essential; but still it can be stated that it has a perceptible influence. This, however, does not clear up the most important part of the problem. We are still in the dark as to the reason why the Jews in Poland are shorter than those in Roumania, although the economic and social conditions of both groups are not materially different; any difference that may be discerned is rather in favour of the Jews in Poland. Similarly, the Jews in South Russia and Bukowina are taller than those in Bavaria or Turin, Italy, although the latter are unquestionably more prosperous socially and economically; or the Jews in North Africa, in Algeria, Tunis, Morocco, and the Spagnuoli in Palestine, who are very poor, and live, even taking their oriental surrounding into consideration, in disgracefully overcrowded and unsanitary surroundings; but they are taller than the native Jews of Germany, France, and Italy.

A careful study of the height of the Jews, as compared with the height of the non-Jewish populations among which they live, shows certain relations which are important in this connection. In general it is found that in countries where the indigenous population is of tall stature, the Jews also are of superior height; and, reversely, wherever the non-Jewish population is short of stature, the Jews also are deficient in this respect. This noteworthy phenomenon is plainly seen when a comparison of the average stature of the Jews and non-Jews in various countries is considered. To begin with Russian and Austrian Poland, where a fairly large number of measurements have been taken of the population. Here the shortest Jews are found averaging 161 to 162 cm. in height. It is questionable whether the non-Jewish Poles were ever taller, as has been repeatedly asserted by many patriotic publicists of Poland, who bewail the manifestation of physical decadence of their compatriots, manifesting itself chiefly in their inferior height, averaging from 161 to 164 cm., according to the district. Some have attempted to attribute this deficiency to the presence of a large number of Jews in that country whose shortness of stature drags down the average. Of course measurements of recruits taken *en bloc* without any attempt to separate Jews from Christians can be used to prove the proposition that a large number of Jews would undoubtedly reduce the average perceptibly. But, as a matter of fact, even in cases when the Jews and Christians were considered separately, it was not found that the Poles were much superior of stature. Thus, Snigireff's statistics, taken from a large number of measurements of Jews and Christians in Poland, show that the average for the Poles is 162.5 cm., and for the Jews 161.3 cm. Similarly, Zakrzewski's series, after selecting only certain classes of

Poles, show an average stature for Jews, 162.3 cm., and for Poles, 165.5 cm. Elkind and Tolwinski found 161 cm. for Jews and 164 cm. for Poles. In Galicia the Jews are of the same average stature as the Poles in that country. Both have an average of 162.3 cm. in height, according to Majer and Kopernicki. All this shows that the Jews in Poland approach the average of the Christian population of the country. South and Little Russia is mainly inhabited by Slavs, who are taller than the Poles. The Little Russians are from 164 to 167 cm. in height, according to Ivanowski.[1] It is a striking fact that the Jews who live among these people are much taller than the Polish Jews. Weissenberg found an average of 164.8 cm. in height; immigrants from that region of Russia to the United States were 165.7 cm. in height; and even the recruits reported by Snigireff, who are only twenty years of age and often less, and have not yet attained their maximum height, were 164.2 cm. in height, and Jewish recruits in Odessa even reach 166.9 cm. in height, according to Pantiukhof, being taller than the Christian recruits from that city, who averaged only 166.1 cm.

In the north-western provinces of European Russia, in Lithuania and White Russia, where the non-Jewish population is short of stature, measuring about 163 to 165 cm. in height, being midway between the short Poles and the tall Little Russians, the Jews also approach the same height; 161.2 according to Snigireff's recruiting statistics, and 164.2 cm. in immigrants to the United States. Going further south-east, in Roumania and Bukowina, where the Slavonic population is characterized by tall stature, we find the Jews also tall, 165.4 cm. in height, according to Himmel, and the indigenous Ruthenians averaged 167.3 cm. Jewish immigrants from Roumania were 166 cm. in height, taller than the Christian Roumanians, who, according to Pittard's measurements,[2] were 165 cm. in height. The average stature of 77,579

---

[1] A. A. Ivanowski, "On the Anthropological Composition of the Races in Russia," *Memoirs Society of Friends*, etc., vol. cv. ; Moscow, 1907 (in Russian).

[2] E. Pittard, "Anthropologie de la Roumanie," *L'Anthropologie*, vol. xix., pp. 33-58 ; 1903.

Hungarian soldiers was 164.6 cm., according to Deniker, and the Jewish soldiers in Hungary measured 163.3 cm. on the average, according to Scheiber; Jewish immigrants to the United States averaged 165.7 cm. Besides these, there are evidences that in Italy the Jews in Turin measured by Lombroso gave an average stature of 163.3 cm., and the Catholic population of the city was 165.1 cm.[1]; and in England, as has already been mentioned, the native Jews are, according to Jacobs, almost as tall as the average Englishman, 171.4 cm. in height.[2]

Outside of Europe there are very few measurements of Jews recorded. In North Africa the Jews of Morocco, Algeria, and Tunis averaged 166.9 cm. in height,[3] which corresponds to the superior stature of the native tribes of Kabyls, Arabs, Berbers, etc., in that region. In Transcaucasia, Pantiukhof found the Jews short of stature, only 161.2 cm. on the average; but their non-Jewish neighbours, the Armenians, are not much taller, measuring about 163 cm.[4] The mountain Jews of Daghestan are taller, 164.4 cm. according to Pantiukhof, and even 166.3 cm. on the average according to Swiderski and Kurdoff, corresponding to the superior stature of their neighbours, the Lesghians.[5]

All these facts point to the conclusion that there is no uniformity of stature among the Jews in various countries; in some they are taller, in others they are shorter. These differences are not satisfactorily explained by the differences in the social and economic conditions under which the Jews find themselves. One thing is certain, the stature of the Jews varies with the stature of the non-Jewish population among which they live. They are tall where the indigenous population is tall, and *vice versa*.

[1] C. Lombroso, *L'antisemitismo e le scienze Moderne* (Appendix). Torino, 1897.
[2] J. Jacobs, "On the Racial Characteristics of the Modern Jews," *Journal Anthropol. Institute*, vol. xv., pp. 23-62; (with Spielman), "On the Comparative Anthropometry of English Jews," *Ibid.*, vol. xix., pp. 76-88.
[3] M. Fishberg, "North African Jews," *Boas Anniversary Volume*, pp. 55-63; New York, 1906.
[4] Pantiukhof, *loc. cit.*
[5] K. Kurdoff "Gorskie evrei dagestana," *Russian Anthropol. Journ.*, Nos. 3, 4, pp. 57-87; 1905.

An objection may justly be raised to this conclusion by showing that averages are not always exact representations of actual conditions. This is particularly true when we deal with small numbers of observations of such a variable factor as stature. A few abnormally tall or short individuals, who in fact are only chance variations, will influence the resulting average perceptibly, and may lead to erroneous conclusions.

An attempt has been made to obviate this source of error by studying the stature of the Jews by the method of seriation and co-ordination. First it is determined how many individuals were found measuring say 150 cm., then how many 151 cm., 152 cm., and so on. The figures thus obtained are used for the construction of a curve on a scale. It is expected that if more than one ethnic element is represented in the group of Jews measured, the curve will show more than one apex each corresponding to the racial element which has been infused. On diagram (Fig. 12) such a curve is shown. It is drawn from measurements of 3,209 Jews in Eastern Europe. It will be noted that the maximum frequency, corresponding to the largest number, measured about 162 cm. in height, which is about the average stature of the Jews in Eastern Europe. It will be seen that the curve toward the left, where stature below the average is represented, descends progressively downward, until the stature of 150 cm. is reached, when the number becomes almost insignificant. Similarly to the right, where heights above the medium is represented, the curve runs more or less smoothly down. Altogether it gives an impression that the Jews represent a homogeneous race, because it has been accepted by some anthropologists that measurements of a mixed people will not show a smooth curve when figures of stature are used for the construction of a diagram, but will display two or more apices, each corresponding to a racial element which entered into the composition of the people. On the other hand, when a curve shows a single apex—one maximum of frequency, around which are clustered all other observations, the lesser values to the left, and the larger to the right—it may be accepted as good proof of the purity of the race.

But in the case of the Jews under consideration this

curve does not by any means establish absolute evidence of freedom from foreign blood. A collection of measurements of 6,708 Christians in Eastern Europe, including Little Russians, Letts, Lithuanians, White Russians, Poles, and Ruthenians, has been tabulated by the author, the percentage of frequency calculated for each group of stature, and the results plotted as a curve on the same diagram.[1] A glance at this curve reveals the following salient points:—Notwithstanding the fact that it represents peoples, each of which has no special claim to exceptional racial purity; notwithstanding that no matter how pure

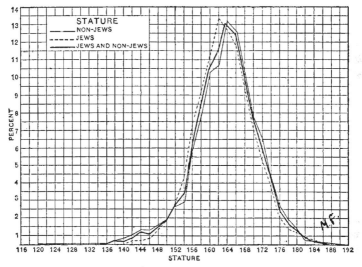

Fig. 12.—Stature of Jews and Non-Jews in Eastern Europe.

each of these races may claim to be, still a mixture of all of them cannot be considered as representing a pure type,—the resulting curve of stature is as smooth as could be expected of the purest of races. The course of the curve is almost identical with that representing the Jews, with the exception that it is moved about two centimetres to the right, showing that the Christian population of those countries is on the average about two centimetres taller

[1] The figures from which these curves are constructed are given in detail by M. Fishberg, "Materials for the Physical Anthropology of the Eastern European Jews," *Mem. American Anthropol. Assn.*, vol. i., pp. 27-30.

than the Jews. The apex points at the height of 164 cm., while that of the Jews points at the height of 162 cm. The deficiency of two centimetres in height may be due to poverty and privations under which the Jews in Eastern Europe are labouring, the indoor occupation in which they are generally employed, and the absence of agricultural labourers among them, as has already been previously stated.

The third curve on the diagram shows a combination of both Jews and Christians which are represented in the other two curves. This curve again shows no double apex, no significant elevations or indentations in its course, thus again proving that the smooth course of the curve representing the stature of the Jews cannot be considered a proof of their racial purity. It is evident that no amount of foreign blood coming from the races of Eastern Europe among whom these Jews have lived would have shown itself in a study of their stature. The reason is plain:— The difference in the height of the Jews and Christians in that region of Europe is very slight, only two to four centimetres. Intermixture could, under the circumstances, not give a double apex, or two maxima of frequency. This could only occur in case of more substantial differences, say of eight to ten centimetres; supposing, for instance, intermixture had taken place between these Jews and the Scotch, who average over 170 cm. in height, the curve might have shown a double apex.

From all the figures of measurements of the height of Jews in various countries brought together in this chapter it is evident that stature is not homogeneous among the Jews in every country. It is very variable, and the limits or variation are almost as large as is observed among European races generally. It is also evident that the shortness of their stature can only to a slight extent be attributed to the influence of the environment in which they find themselves, or to the occupations in which they mostly engage. Indeed, it appears more probable that they prefer indoor occupations, which require but little muscular exertion, as a result of their poor physique, which, being an aquired character, is not transmitted by heredity. Soon after leaving the Eastern European Ghettoes they display a remarkable capacity physically to engage in all

kinds of occupations, even the most difficult, and very few
of them engage in tailoring, weaving, etc. But what is of

Fig. 13.   Fig. 14.

Fig. 15.   Fig. 16.

TYPES OF JEWS IN AUSTRIAN GALICIA.

most importance is the fact elicited that the stature of the
Jews varies with the stature of the non-Jewish population

among whom they live. In countries where the indigenous population is tall the Jews also are tall, and the reverse. That this character cannot altogether be attributed to the influence of the environment, such as climate, altitude, etc., is shown by the fact that we meet with tall and short races in the same place, each retaining their characteristic height as long as no intermarriage occurs, as is the case in London or New York.

It must, however, be emphasized that stature alone is not sufficient to determine whether we deal here with several races of Jews each having its peculiar height. The other important criterions of race, particularly complexion and head form, must be considered before this question can be discussed.

CHAPTER III.

PHYSICAL CHARACTERS (*continued*).

THE HEAD-FORM—Skulls of ancient Hebrews—Of mediæval Jews—Of modern Jews—Uniformity of cranial type of Eastern European Jews—The three types of skulls among Jews—Origin of the types of skull of the Jews—Size of the head—Weight of the brain—Brain weight and intellectual capacity.

The Head-form.—Archæological and anthropological research in Palestine has not unearthed any skulls of ancient Hebrews. Because the Hebrews were not in the habit of embalming and preserving their dead, no skeletons have been preserved, and even when ancient cemeteries are opened up, little, if anything, is found in a condition suitable for anthropological investigation. We are not, therefore, in a position to speak of the head-form of the ancient Hebrews with any degree of certainty. We do not know whether they were of the dolichocephalic type, like some non-Hebrew Semites of to-day, the Bedouin Arabs, the Berbers, and Kabyls of North Africa, etc., or whether they were of the brachycephalic type, as are other Semitic races of to-day in Syria, Asia Minor, and the Caucasus.

The oldest Jewish skulls examined are those reported by C. Lombroso.[1] They were found in the Catacomb of St. Calixtus in Rome, and are of great scientific interest, because at the period (Second century) to which they belong there could not have been any considerable racial intermixture of the Jews with European peoples, and the type they represent may be considered the type of the ancient Hebrews. Of the five skulls thus examined three were distinctly dolichocephalic, their cranial indices being 75.1, 76.1, and 78; one was mesocephalic, with a cranial index of 80, and one brachycephalic, with an index of 83.4. The average cranial index was 78.5, or a cephalic index of 80.5 for the living. It thus appears that three

[1] C. Lombroso, *L'antisemitismo e le scienze moderne* (Appendix). Torino, 1894.

out of five skulls correspond to the type of the modern Jews who live among Semitic tribes, like those in North Africa; and also to the type of the Samaritans, as well as the Jews in Yemen, South-western Arabia, who for the last fifteen hundred years have hardly intermarried outside of their faith, at least only with Semitic races. It must be emphasized that no plausible conclusions can be drawn from measurements of only five skulls; but the fact that of five skulls, two are of the brachycephalic type and three of the dolichocephalic type, points strongly against the opinion that the ancient Hebrews were a purely dolichocephalic race.

We have no knowledge of any Jewish skulls recorded in anthropological literature unearthed from ancient cemeteries, excepting those just mentioned, and also twelve skeletons found in a Jewish burial-place in Bâle, Switzerland, which were interred during the thirteenth and fourteenth centuries. These are of a type entirely differing from the above mentioned. They are distinctly brachycephalic, having a cranial index of 84.66 on the average, or a cephalic index on the living of 86.66.[1] Only two of these skulls are dolichocephalic, all the rest are of the round type, the exact opposite of the type encountered among the modern Semitic tribes, who are said to have preserved themselves in greatest purity.

Skulls of modern Jews are, also, not found in abundance in ethnonological museums, because of the anxiety of Jews to be buried according to Jewish rites. In almost every city where a Jewish cemetery exists there is established a burial society which takes special care to bury the dead, and as a result, very few skeletons have found their way into anthropological laboratories for investigation. In all, about one hundred skulls are described by various European investigators. Of these, thirty were described by Ikoff as deriving from Karaites, and cannot, perhaps, be considered Jewish in the strict sense of the word. They are distinctly brachycephalic.[2] Eleven skulls dating from

---

[1] J. Kollmann, "Schädel und Skeletreste aus einem Judenfriedhof des 13 und 14 Jahrhundert zu Basel," *Verhandlungen der naturforschenden Gesellschaft*, vol. vii, pp. 648-656; Bale, 1885.
[2] K. N. Ikoff, "Neue Beitrage zur Anthropologie der Juden," *Archiv für Anthropologie*, vol. xv., pp. 369-389; 1884.

mediæval times, and unearthed in a cemetery in Paris, are brachycephalic, with a cephalic index of 82.2. Only two of these skulls are dolichocephalic, while seven have indices above 80 (Quatrefages et Hamy). Of the other skulls investigated, it appears that most of those derived from *Sephardim*, or Spanish and Portuguese Jews, are dolichocephalic; particularly is this the case with those from North Africa and Turkey, and examined by Pruner Bey, Quatrefages, Ikoff, Davis, etc. The few skulls of Polish and German Jews are either meso- or brachycephalic.[1] But, of course, the material is rather scanty for any definite generalization, and we must rely on measurements taken on living Jews of to-day for information on the subject.

The most noteworthy characteristic of the skulls of modern Jews is their great variability, according to the country from which they are derived. It may, in fact, be stated that there is no single type of head which is found among the Jews in all countries in which they live. Indeed nearly all varieties of skulls are met with among the Jews of to-day. In Caucasia they are extremely brachycephalic, with a cephalic index of 85.2, according to measurements taken by Pantiukhof, and 98 per cent. had round heads; among the Daghestan mountain Jews the average index is even 86.35, and no dolichocephalic have been found among them by Kurdoff. The races among which these Jews live are also brachycephalic, particularly the Aisors, Armenians, Lesghians, etc.[2]

Taking the other extreme of head-form, dolichocephaly, we find that the Jews living in Yemen, Arabia, Morocco, Algeria, and Tunis are of this type. Of 77 adults measured by the present author,[3] 70 per cent. had indices less than 80, and the average cephalic index was 78.24.

---

[1] For a table giving detailed information of these skulls, see M. Fishberg, article "Craniometry," *Jewish Encyclopædia*, vol. iv.; also S. Weissenberg, "Das jüdische Rassenproblem," *Zeitschrift für Demographie und Statistik der Juden*, No. 5; 1905.

[2] I. I. Pantiukhof, "Observations anthropologiques au Causase," *Section Caucasiéne de la Soc. Impériale de Géographie*, Tiflis, 1893; K. Kurdoff, "Gorskie evrei dagestana," *Russian Anthropological Journal*, Nos 3-4, pp. 57-87; 1905.

[3] M. Fishberg, "North African Jews," *Boas Anniversary Volume*, pp. 55-63; New York, 1906.

Similarly the Samaritans in Nâblus are dolichocephalic.[1] According to Huxley's measurements of 14 male and 5 female skulls, the average cranial index for the males was 76.5 and for the females, 78. Of 35 male Samaritans only 31.5 per cent. were brachycephalic, and the whole series gave an average cephalic index of 78.1. Those in South-western Arabia are even more dolichocephalic, showing an average index of 74.3 according to measurements by Weissenberg, while the autochthonous Jews in Palestine are mesocephalic.[2] We thus have both extremely brachycephalic and dolichocephalic Jews, and it is noteworthy that each group lives among races having a head-form similar to its own.

Between these two extremes of head-form there are the Eastern European and Central European Jews, whose headform ranges between 80 and 83. These include the Jews in European Russia, Austria, Germany, Italy, etc. Their cephalic index is as follows in various countries:—[3] Lithuania, 81.05; Poland 81.91; Roumania, 81.82; Little Russia, 82.5; Italy, 82.14; Galicia 83.33; Baden, Germany, 83.5. On the whole they are of quite a uniform type, as can be seen from the following figures, in which the percentage of each class having a certain type of head-form is indicated according to Deniker's classification of headform.

	Daghestan, Caucasus.	Jews in Europe.	North Africa.	Yemen, Arabia.
Hyperdolichocephalic (-76)		2.89%	25.97%	71.80%
Dolichocephalic (76-77)		7.36	24.67	14.10
Subdolichocephalic (78-79)	4.70%	15.51	19.48	7.69
Mesocephalic (80-81)	6.10	25.78	13.00	2.56
Subbrachycephalic (82-83)	17.37	24.01	9.09	3.85
Brachycephalic (84-85)	23.94	15.97	6.49	
Hyperbrachycephalic (86+)	47.89	8.47	1.30	
Number of observations	213	2,641	77	78

---

[1] H. M. Huxley, Article "Samaritans," *Jewish Encyclopædia*, vol. xi. pp. 674-676.

[2] S. Weissenberg, "Die jemenitische Juden," *Zeitschr. f. Ethnologie*, 1909, pp. 309-327; "Die autochtone Bevölkerung Palestinas," *Zeitschr. Demogr. Statistik d. Juden*, 1909, pp. 129-139.

[3] For details see M. Fishberg, "Materials for the Physical Anthropology of the Eastern European Jews," *Memoirs American Anthropolog. Society*, vol. i., part I., pp. 13-15, 57-92.

It will be observed that fifty per cent. of all the European Jews had a head-form ranging between the index of 80 and 83, and 80 per cent. between the indices of 78 and 85. In contrast with these can be taken the Caucasian Jews, who are of a totally different type, having 72 per cent. of individuals with indices above 84; the North African Jews are altogether at the opposite pole, having less than eight per cent. of this type of head-form, while they have fifty per cent. of persons with long heads, *i.e.*, with cephalic index less than 77, and the Yemenite Jews show 86 per cent. of such long-headed individuals.

But though Jews from Caucasia, when compared with those from Europe, Arabia, and Africa, belong to totally different races, it appears at first sight that when the Jews of Europe are considered alone they display a remarkable uniformity of type, which would indicate purity of race. In other words, it points to a striking freedom from admixture with non-Jewish blood. Considering that the Eastern European Jews constitute about eighty per cent. of all the Jews in the world, it should go very far to prove that the bulk of the modern Jews has succeeded in maintaining a uniformity of race hardly met with among any other civilized race.

A little analysis disillusions one from this presumption. The measurements of the European Jews brought forward above are of persons native of parts of Russia known as Lithuania, White Russia, Little Russia, and Poland; also of Austrian Galicia, Hungary, and Roumania. A careful study of the head-form of the non-Jewish races of these countries reveals the following remarkable facts: Their head-form is more uniform than that of the population of any other part of Europe. "The perfect monotony and uniformity of environment of the Russian people," says Ripley, "is most clearly expressed anthropologically in their head-form . . . a moment's consideration of our map shows at once a great similarity of head-form prevailing all over Europe, from the Carpathian mountains east and north. The cephalic index oscillates but two or three points above a centre of 82. . . . Our widest variation in Russia is about five units."[1]

For the last ten centuries Jews have lived among these

[1] Wm. Z. Ripley, *The Races of Europe*, pp. 341-342; New York, 1899.

races, and it is consequently safe to assume that if any non-Jewish blood has been infused into their veins during this period, it must have come from the races and peoples inhabiting just this region of Europe. A close examination of the map ingeniously prepared by Ripley shows graphically that the head-form of these peoples is about the same as that of the Eastern European Jews. Even slight differences occurring here and there are also to be observed among the Jews from these countries. Wherever there is an increase in the width of the head of the indigenous non-Jewish races, as, for instance, in Galicia, the same is to be noted among the Jews from these countries. The difference may be ever so small, it may be even of one or two units; it is nevertheless perceptible to the calipers when measurements are taken on Jews. This is shown in the following figures taken from the author's measurements, compared with the results of Ivanowski's compilation of the anthropology of the races in Russia;[1] the Jews of Galicia have been compared with the Poles measured by Majer and Kopernicki, and for Roumania Pittard's work has been utilized.[2]

Country.	Average Cephalic Index of—	
	Jews.	Non-Jews.
Lithuania	81.05	81.88
Roumania	81.82	82.91
Hungary	82.45	81.40
Poland	81.91	82.13
Little Russia	82.45	82.31
Galicia	83.33	84.40

From the above figures it is seen that the average cephalic index of the Jews in the countries mentioned approaches that of the non-Jewish races among which they live. In Lithunia, where the Lithunians are somewhat dolichocephalic, the Jews also are of the same type, while in Little Russia and Galicia, where the Little Russians, Ruthenians, and Poles are characterized by rounder heads, the Jews are about the same. A case in

[1] A. A. Ivanowski, "Ob antropologitcheskom sostave naselenia Rossii," *Trudi antropologicheskavo otdiela, Soc. of Friends, etc.*, vol. xxii. Moscow, 1904.
[2] E. Pittard, "Anthropologie de la Roumanie," *L'Anthropologie*, vol. xiv. No. 1, pp. 33-58; 1903.

point is that of the Polish Jews. The part of Poland which was taken by Russia appears to be inhabited by Poles who are more dolichocephalic than those of Galicia, the part of Poland which is now under Austrian souzerainity. The Russian Poles have an average cephalic index of 82.13, while those of Galicia, 84.4. The Jews of these two parts of ancient Poland also show the same differences; their average cephalic index is in Russian Poland, 81.91, and in Austrian Poland (Galicia), 83.33. On the whole, the slight differences which are to be observed between the Jews and non-Jews in these countries may be ascribed to the usual, and practically unavoidable errors of observation and calculation. The uniformity of cranial type of the Jews in Eastern Europe is observed only to the same extent as that of the non-Jewish populations in that region. Neither can claim racial purity on this score.

Writers on the anthropology of the Jews have devoted considerable space to the discussion of the problem presented by the cranial type of the modern Jews. As is well known, the non-Jewish races which speak Semitic languages are long-headed. Thus the Arabs, Berbers, Kabyls, etc., iu North Africa, the Abyssinians, and especially the Bedouin Arabs, who are said to have kept themselves quite free from intermixture, are decidedly long-headed, as are most of the skulls unearthed in Palestine and Egypt. It was therefore decided that the head-form of the original Semites, and among them the ancient Hebrews, was also of the same type. Up to recent years measurements of Eastern European Jews were only available, and the type of the modern Jews was said to be mesocephalic, or brachycephalic. It was thus stated that the Jews of to-day have diverted from the original cranial type of their ancestors, and various interpretations have been offered in explanation of this phenomenon. Some, who agree that the head-form is a constant trait, only transmitted by heredity, and not influenced by external conditions such as climate, social and economic conditions, have seen in this proof of intermixture with non-Jews. Luschan is of the opinion that the brachycephaly of the modern Jews is due to the intermarriages of the ancient Hebrews with the Hittites of Biblical times. These latter are said to have been brachycephalic, and in addition to the head-form, it is argued that the Jews have also inherited from them their peculiar physiognomy, and epecially the hook nose.[1] Joseph Jacobs argues that the brachycephaly of the modern Jews is due to the widening influence which superior intelligence and culture exerts on the head, and points out that nearly all available evidence goes to show that Europe was inhabited formerly by long-headed peoples,[2] but to-day they have been replaced by round-headed. Various circumstances are against this theory. In the first place, if advance of culture would invariably be accompanied by a widening of the head, some races should have been doomed to eternal barbarism. The English, for instance, have remained dolichocephalic. Indeed, it is well known that the shape of the head has absolutely nothing to do with the state of culture of a race. Moreover, the fact that in some countries in Europe we find to-day brachycephalic races, while the skeletons of the ancient inhabitants which have been unearthed show that they were dolichocephalic, is satisfactorily explained by evidence showing that the former races have been replaced by the invasions of round-headed races. It is about the same as the darkening of the hair and eyes of the modern populations of Europe. Both are due to the same cause.

Another theory about the origin of the round-headedness of the modern European Jews is that the original type of the Jews was brachycephalic. But this needs confirmation.[3] So far there is no evidence showing that they

---

[1] F. V. Luschan, "Die anthropologische Stellung der Juden," *Correspondenz-blatt der deutschen Ges. f. Anthropol.*, etc., vol. xxiii., pp. 94-102; 1892.

[2] Joseph Jacobs, "Are Jews Jews?" *Popular Science Monthly*, vol. lv., 1899, pp. 502-510. This author states that "Brachycephalism implies intellectual development." If this was the fact all the Scandinavians, most of the Englishmen, Americans, etc., would be much below the intellectual status of the mountain tribes of Caucasia, who are probably the most brachycephalic people in the world.

[3] It must be mentioned in this connection that the ancient Semites were not confined geographically to Arabia or Palestine. The Semitic dialects were also common among the inhabitants of Asia Minor and Caucasia, as the Arameans, Assyrians, Chaldæans, etc. The descendants of these peoples, the modern Syrians, and the inhabitants of Caucasia, are to-day perhaps the most brachycephalic races in the world. But if the ancient Hebrews were of this type, then the only Jews who preserved the type are

were either brachycephalic or dolichocephalic. It is only by analogy with all the other races who speak Semitic dialects, and who have more or less long heads, that the dolichocephaly of the ancient Hebrews is assumed. It appears, however, from Weissenberg's measurements of the autochthonous races in Palestine that the Jews in El-buke'a, Safed and Shefa'amr, whom he considers direct descendants of the ancient Hebrews, are dolichocephalic, as are the Samaritans and also the non-Jewish populations of that region.[1]

But no matter what type of head we assume the ancient Hebrews to have had, we must bear one fact in mind: the modern Jews are not everywhere of the same type; in countries where the indigenous population is long-headed, as in Africa, Arabia, etc., the Jews are of the same type. Now, even agreeing that these are the Jews who have maintained the cranial type of the ancient Hebrews, then it is evident that all the rest of the Jews, all those living in Europe constituting eighty per cent. of all the Jews in the world, have diverted from the original type. On the other hand, assuming that the original type of the Hebrews was brachycephalic, then the only ones who preserved that type are the few thousand now living in Caucasia, and the small percentage of brachycephalic Jews in Europe, while all the others have diverted from the type. In the present state of our knowledge of the causes of the type of the head, such diversity of cranial type can only be ascribed to heredity. Environment, physical, economic, or social, is, as far as we know to-day, impotent to change the head-form of the Caucasian Jews into the brachycephalic type, that of the African Jews into the dolichocephalic type, or that of the European Jews into the brachycephalic or mesocephalic type. If the ancient Hebrews were a pure race, then we can explain the diversity of type in the modern Jews only by racial intermixture. And even assuming them to have been a mixed race originally, it must be acknowledged

---

the mountain tribes of Jews in Daghestan. All the European, and especially the North African and Arabian Jews, have widely diverted from the original type of head.

[1] See S. Weissenberg, "Die autochtone Bevölkerung Palestinas," *Zeitschr. Demogr. Statist. d. Juden*, pp. 129-139, 1909; "Peki in und seine Juden," *Globus*, vol. xcvi.; 1909.

that the modern Jews are the product of further mixtures during their migrations after their dispersion, for the following reason:—It cannot be conceived that all the brachycephalic Jews emigrated to Caucasia, the dolichocephalic to Africa, etc. It is more in agreement with our present state of knowledge to explain the diversity of the cranial type of the Jews of to-day by fusion with their non-Jewish neighbours.

Size of the Head.—We are accustomed to hear of the great cerebral capacity of the Jew. His friends are always speaking with emphasis of his remarkable brain, while his enemies often speak of the danger the Jew, with his greater cerebral power, may be to his non-Jewish neighbour in Eastern Europe, who has not been endowed with as much brain tissue in his cranial cavity.[1] It is, however, a remarkable fact that measurements of the size of the Jews' head and brain have shown that there is no basis for this belief. Of course it must be remembered in this connection that the size of the brain, and especially of the cranium, has not by far the significance as regards culture and intelligence which some have ascribed to it.

The simplest way to determine the size of the head is the determination of its horizontal circumference, although it is not at all the most satisfactory method. Measurements taken of Jewish heads show that the average horizontal circumference is about 55.5 cm., or twenty-two inches. This is about the same as is found among the Slavonic races, amidst whom the vast majority of the contemporaneous Jews live. The differences which were found in various classes of Jews in different countries are only slight, ranging between 54 and 56.5 cm. on the average. This is exactly the range of variation encountered among the Slavonic races. In some groups of Jews it was even found that the circumference was slightly smaller than

---

[1] "If they had been forced by persecution to become mainly blacksmiths, one would not have been surprised to find their biceps larger than those of other folk; and similarly, as they have been forced to live by the exercise of their brains, one should not be surprised to find the cubic capacity of their skulls larger than that of their neighbours. When it is remembered that they are, owing to their persecutions, the shortest of all European folk, their relative superiority in brain comes out even more striking." J. Jacobs. "Are Jews Jews?" *Popular Science Monthly*, vol. lv., 1899, pp. 502-511.

PHYSICAL CHARACTERS.

that of the Christians among whom they lived. This is to be expected, considering that the Jews are usually shorter of stature than the Christians. When the ratio of size of the head to the height of the body is considered, it is found that there is a slight difference in favour of the Jews. The average circumference of the Slavonic population in Russia is around 33.4 per cent. of their stature, while that of the Jews is around 35 per cent.[1]

One of the methods of determining the volume of the brain case, and approximately the weight of the brain, is the determination of the cranial capacity. Very few direct measurements of this kind have been taken, because only few Jewish skulls have found their way into anthropological museums, where they could be studied carefully. But from the few studies of this character that have been made, it appears that the Jews are somewhat at a disadvantage. Lombroso's studies of the Jews in Turin, Italy, which were made in an indirect fashion, showed that the Jews have a smaller cranial capacity than the Catholics of that city.[2] Weinberg collected measurements of seventeen Jewish skulls in various museums of Europe, which were made properly, and are not approximations. The average cranial capacity was 1421 c.cm., which is about thirty to forty c.cm. below the average cranial capacity of the population of Europe. Of course the small number of skulls thus measured is not sufficient to draw positive conclusions.

As to the weight of the brain, there are also very few observations on record. The author knows only of twenty-three Jewish brains reported by Giltchenko,[3] four by Weisbach,[4] and three by Weinberg.[5] The average weight of these brains, as calculated by Weinberg, was 1320.4 gm. Since the average weight of the brain of the European is 1350 gms., the brain of Jews is rather lighter by 30

---

[1] R. Weinberg, "Das Hirngewicht der Juden," *Zeitschrift fur Demographie und Statistik der Juden*, No. 3; 1905.

[2] C. Lombroso, *L'antisemitismo e le scienze moderne* (Appendix); Torino, 1897.

[3] N. W. Giltshenko, "Vies golovnavo mosga . . . u raslitchnikh plemen naseliaiushtchikh Rosiu," *Trudi anthropologitcheskavo otdiela*, vol. xix., pp. 151-153.

[4] *Archiv für Anthropologie*, vol. i., p. 192; 1860.

[5] *Russian Anthropological Journal*, part iv. pp. 1-34; 1902.

gms., or nearly one ounce. Considering that the Jews are shorter of stature than the average Europeans, it would be expected that their brain should also be smaller But, as Weinberg points out, the average for Germans was found to be 8.22 gm. of brain tissue for each centimetre of stature, while for the Jews it is only 8.05 gms. This shows the Jewish brain lighter not only absolutely, but also relatively. This, if confirmed by further investigation, because thirty brains are by far too few to give reasonably certain results, tends to confirm the opinion of many physiologists that the gross weight of the brain is not invariably the determining factor in the intellectual capacities of a people. But we have no data based on observations of Jewish brains as to the cerebral cortex, or the grey substance which form the convolutions, and it has been held that the more numerous, complicated, and sinuous these convolutions are, the higher the psychic force they can evolve. Weinberg has thus studied only three brains of Jews, and found some peculiarities which he considers characteristically racial. The most curious peculiarity he describes in detail is the union of the fissure of Rolando or the central sulcus, with the fissure of Sylvius, at their lower ends.[1] This can hardly be called a racial peculiarity, because while as a rule the fissure of Rolando pursues an isolated course across the convex surface of the brain of all races, still it is occasionally observed to communicate with the præcentral or intraparietal sulci, no matter what race the individual may belong to. It is to be considered an anatomical curiosity on account of the rarity of the occurrence of this variation; there are many experienced anatomists who have never encountered it. But the cases in which this variation has been found includes many races, and the fact that it has been observed in only one Jewish brain goes far to demonstrate that it is only an accidental variation, and can by no means be considered a racial characteristic of the Jewish brain.

Anatomy is consequently, at the present state of our knowledge, unable to account for the prevalence of nervous

[1] P. Weinberg, "K-ucheniu o forme mozga cheloveka," *Russian Anthropological Journal*, 1902, No. 4, pp. 1-34; *idem*, "Ueber einige ungewohnliche Befunde an Judenhirnen," *Biologisches Centralblatt*, vol. xxiii., pp. 154-162; 1903.

and mental diseases among Jews. As will be seen in a later chapter, there are many more plausible reasons in the social and economic conditions of the Jews to account for the excessive proportion of neurotics and psychopathics among them.

CHAPTER IV.

PHYSICAL CHARACTERS (*concluded*).

Complexion—Type of pigmentation of the ancient Hebrews—The ideal Jewish type—Complexion of Jewish children in various parts of the world—Types of pigmentation of the modern Jews—Erythrism—The blonde Jews—Origin of blonde elements among the modern Jews—Artificial selection—The nose—Fallacy of considering the hook nose as typically Jewish—Forms of the nose among the modern Jews—The chest—Vital capacity—Fitness for military service.

Complexion.—Judging from Biblical data, it appears that the colour of the hair of the ancient Hebrews was black; "raven black" seems to have been the ideal of beauty, as can be seen from *Canticles*, IV. 1, and V. 11. Black hair is designated as a sign of youth in contrast with the white hair of old age. Josephus narrates that Herod dyed his grey hair black in order to appear younger. Black hair was considered beautiful, black being the general colour, while light or blonde hair was exceptional.[1] Esau and also King David are credited by the Bible with having had a red or "ruddy" complexion. Besides these, it must be mentioned that early paintings of Christ represented Him as having blonde hair, and Mary Madgalene has always been painted as blonde haired, while Judas Iscariot is traditionally known as a red-haired individual, although there is no word mentioned in the New Testament as to their complexion. "The earliest description we possess of Christ, that of John of Damascus," says Grant Allen, "states that his complexion was ' of the colour of wheat'; while in the apocryphal letter of Lentulus to the Roman Senate we read in the same spirit that his hair was ' wine coloured.' The Greek description by Epiphanius Monachus says that Christ was six feet high; his hair long and golden

[1] I. Benzinger, *Jewish Encyclopædia*, vol. vi., p. 157.

PHYSICAL CHARACTERS. 61

coloured; and in countenance he was ruddy like his father David."[1]

In one of the stories of the *Arabian Nights* entitled "The weaver who became a leech," the quack is asked how he recognized a certain patient as being a Jew, and he answered: "Thou must know that we people of Persia are skilled in physiognomy; and I saw the woman to be rosy-cheeked, blue eyed and tall statured. These qualities belong to no woman of Rome . . . and I knew she was a Jewess." Jacobs mentions that Jehuda Halevy, a Hebrew poet of the twelfth century, speaks of the golden hair of his

Fig. 17.—BOKHARA JEWS.

beloved, and mentions a Spanish Jew, Roven Salomo, in the fourteenth century, who had light brown hair, and Rembrandt's painting of a Rabbi in the National Gallery, with a red beard. Many other paintings or portraits of Jews during the middle ages show them to have had light brown, blonde, or red hair, and particularly beards.

The colour of the eyes is not indicated in either the Bible or Talmud, although this organ is mentioned more than

[1] Grant Allen, *The Origin of the Idea of God*, chap. xviii. He believes that all these descriptions are obviously influenced by the identification of the bread and wine of the eucharist with the personal Jesus.

eight hundred times in the Bible, and is described in detail as regards other characteristics, such as anatomy, expression, etc. It may be mentioned in this connection, however, that according to some Hebrew scholars, there is no equivalent in the Hebrew language for the word blue in either the Bible or Talmud.

Fig. 18.—OLD JEW.

[*From a Painting by Rembrandt.*]

The predominant type of complexion of the Jews of to-day is also dark; black and brown hair and eyes are in the majority. But still a large proportion have blonde hair and blue eyes. In the most extensive investigation of the subject made by Prof. Virchow,[1] of over 75,000 Jewish school children in Germany, it was elicited that only 66 per

[1] R. Virchow, "Gesamtbericht . . . ueber die Farbe der Haut, der Haare und der Augen der Schulkinder in Deutschland," *Archiv für Anthropologie*, vol. xvi. pp. 275-475; 1886.

cent. had dark hair, and 52 per cent. had dark eyes. Fair-haired children were found to the extent of 32 per cent., and fair-eyed even more, 46 per cent. Up till recently it was stated by ethnologists that the Jews in Germany had a large number of blondes in their midst, but that in other countries they are mostly brunettes. Virchow's investigations have

Fig. 19.—JEWISH FACIAL EXPRESSION.
[*From a Painting by Kaufmann.*]

confirmed it for Germany; and when the colour of the hair and eyes of Jews in other countries was investigated it was found that blonde Jews are to be met with almost everywhere. Thus, the 60,000 Jewish school children examined in Austria,[1] and reported by Schimmer, revealed that 27 per cent. had blonde hair and 54 per cent. had blue eyes. In

[1] G. A. Schimmer, "Erhebungen über die Farbe der Augen, der Haare, und der Haut bei den Schulkindern Oesterreichs." *Mitt. der anthropol. Gesel.*, Wien, 1884, Erganzungsband.

Hungary 24 per cent. of Jewish children had fair hair and 42 per cent. fair eyes, and even in Bulgaria 22 and 61 per cent. respectively were found.[1] The author has examined 600 children in the schools of the Alliance Israélite in Algiers, Constantine, and Tunis, and among them also six per cent. were found who had fair hair and 22 per cent. with fair eyes.[2]

These fair-haired Jews created a problem for anthropologists. It is a question whence these "Indo-Germanic" Jews, as Virchow called them, have found their way into the midst of a dark complexioned race like the Jews, and whether they are signs of racial intermixture between Jews and northern Europeans. Some have argued that inasmuch as these observations were made on children, they are of doubtful value, because the hair and eyes of at least twenty-five per cent. of fair children darken with the advance of adolescence. But investigations of adult Jews did not alter the case at all. As can be seen from the following figures, there are fair haired Jews in almost every country :[3]

Country.	Percentage of Fair Hair	Eyes.
England	25.5	41.2
Galicia	20.03	52.12
Little Russia	17.74	53 68
Roumania	14.67	51.33
Lithuania	14 09	37.81
South Russia	13.00	33.00
Baden, Germany	12.80	51.20
United States	11.29	44.35
Hungary	17.86	50.71
Poland	7.16	43.89
Caucasia	2.00	15.69
Daghestan, Caucasia	0.05	4.38

[1] J. Korósi, "Couleur de la peu, des cheveux, et des yeux à Budapest," *Annal. de démographie*, I, pp. 136-137. S. Wateff, "Anthropologische Beobachtungen der Farbe der Augen, der Haare und der Haut, etc., in Bulgarien," *Correspondenzblatt der Deutschen Gesel. für Anthropologie*, vol. xxxiii. Nos. 7, 8; 1904.

[2] M. Fishberg, "North African Jews," *Boas Anniversary Volume*, pp. 55-63; New York, 1906.

[3] These figures were obtained from the following sources:—England: J. Jacobs, "On the Comparative Anthropometry of English Jews," *Journal Anthrop. Institute*, vol. xix pp. 76-86; Baden: O. Ammon, *Zur Anthropol. der Badener*, Jena, 1899; Caucasia: J. Pantiukhof, *Observ. anthropol. au*

PHYSICAL CHARACTERS.

In fact, even the Spanish and Portuguese Jews, the *Sephardim*, who have been considered to be of a much darker complexion than the Eastern European Jews, the *Ashkenazim*, also have a fair number of blondes among them, as can be seen from the following figures :—[1]

Country.	Percentage of Fair Hair.	Eyes.
Bosnia	18.50	30.90
England	11.90	33.20
North Africa	5.19	16.88
Italy	4.80	30.00
Various	2.60	32.00
Turkey	10.00	18.70

From these figures it is evident that Jews in every country investigated had a certain proportion of fair-haired and eyed individuals, and that the percentage of these fair Jews fluctuates within wide limits. The smallest percentage of fair hair and eyes is found among the Caucasian and Arabian Jews. Pantiukhof found among the Caucasian Jews only two per cent. with fair hair and 15.69 per cent. of fair eyes. Among Georgian Jews Weissenberg found 3.33 per cent. fair hair and 12.33 per cent. fair eyes, while Kurdoff counted among the Daghestan mountain Jews less than one per cent. fair hair and only 5.63 per cent. fair eyes. Among 78 Jews from Yemen, Arabia, Weissenberg did not find one who had either fair hair or eyes.[2] On the other hand, among the English Jews, one in four was found with fair hair, while fair eyes were found among 41 per cent. Among the Austrian Jews the percentage exceeds fifty. The Sephardim, who had been reputed to

Caucase, Tiflis, 1893; Daghestan : K. Kurdoff, "Gorskye evrei dagestana," *Russ. Anthrop. Journal*, Nos. 3-4, pp. 57-87, 1905. The rest are from M. Fishberg, "Materials for the Physic. Anthrop. Eastern European Jews," *Memoirs Amer. Anthrop. Assn.*, vol. i.; 1905.

[1] These observations were reported by Glueck, "Beitr. zur physisch. Anthrop. der Spaniolen," *Wiss. Mitt. aus Bosnien und der Hercegovina*, vol. iv. pp. 587-592; Jacobs, loc. cit.; J. Beddoe, "On the Physical Characteristics of the Jews," *Trans. Ethnol. Soc.*, vol. i. pp. 222-237, London, 1861; C. Lombroso, *L'antisemitismo e le scienze moderne*, Torino, 1894; M. Fishberg, "North African Jews," *Boas Anniversary Volume*, pp. 55-63, New York, 1906.

[2] Pantiukhof, *Observ. Anthrop. au Caucase*, Tiflis (in Russian), 1893; Kurdoff. *loc. cit.*,; Weissenberg, *Archiv f. Anthropologie*, vol. viii., pp. 237-245, 1909; idem, *Zeitschr. f. Ethnologie*, pp. 309-327; 1909.

have preserved the Jewish type more perfectly, are also not lacking in a blonde element. Of the Spagnuoli in Bosnia, 18.5 per cent. have fair hair and 31 per cent. fair eyes (Glueck), and those in England 11 per cent. Even the Spanish Jews in Turkey, as well as the indigenous Jews of Algeria, Morocco, and Tunisia have blondes.[1]

Types of Pigmentation.—Typical representatives of a race show a constant interrelation between the colour of the hair and eyes: In the blonde northern races, their fair hair is usually accompanied by blue eyes, while among the dark southern races the dark hair is usually accompanied by dark eyes. The former are considered pure blonde types, and the latter pure brunette types. Individuals who do not exhibit such interrelation—*i.e.*, who have dark hair with fair eyes, or fair hair with dark eyes—are considered "mixed types." It is interesting that only about one-half of the contemporaneous Jews have preserved the pure brunette type; the rest are either of the blonde or mixed types. Among 4,235 Jews observed by the present writer in New York the following proportion of types were found:—

	Jews.	Jewesses.
Brunette type	52.62%	56.94%
Blonde type	10.42	10.27
Mixed types	36.96	32.79

The brunette type, which is considered characteristic of the Jews from time immemorial, is thus reduced to only 52 per cent. among the European representatives of the race, while among the Jewesses it is not much larger, 57 per cent. The pure blonde type was found to the extent of ten per cent., while over thirty per cent. were of the mixed type. Observations made on Jews in various countries have brought out similar results. Of the 75,377 Jewish school children in Germany reported by Virchow only 46.83 per cent. were of the brunette type, 11.17 per cent. of the blonde, and 42 of the mixed type. In Austria, Schimmer found between 32 and 47 per cent. of the brunette type among Jewish school children and 8 to 14 per cent. of the blonde type, according to the district. Wateff's investi-

[1] For England, see Jacobs, *loc. cit.*; North Africa, Fishberg, *loc. cit.*; for Turkey, Weissenberg, *Mitt. Anthropl. Ges. Wien*, vol. xxxix., pp. 225-239; Bosnia, L. Glueck, *loc. cit.*

gations in Bulgaria, where the general population is brunette, the Jews have only 49.57 per cent. of the pure brunette type, 8.71 per cent. blondes, and 41.72 per cent. of mixed types. In North Africa, where there is known

Fig. 20.—Jewess, Tangier, Morocco.

[*From a Painting by Portaels.*]

to be a strong blonde element among the Berbers and Kabyls, the Jews were also found by the present writer to have 4.62 per cent. of pure blondes and 76.40 per cent. of brunettes. The only country where all the Jews examined were brunettes is Yemen, Arabia, where Weissenberg did not find a single Jew with either blonde hair or fair eyes. Perhaps the reason is that the Bedouins in that region also have no blondes, and intermarriage could not affect the Jews in this direction. Altogether, it appears that the proportion of Jews of the pure blonde type oscillates between five to sixteen per cent., according to the country of birth. Between twenty-five and fifty per cent. are of the mixed types, and if this is one of the signs of racial intermixture, as some are inclined to believe, this is important.

Erythrism, or Red Hair.—Red hair appears not to be of recent origin among the Jews. It was known among the ancient Hebrews, for Esau was said to have been "red all over, like a hairy garment."[1] The Biblical reference to King David as "ruddy" is explained by some as meaning that he had red hair. Besides Judas Iscariot, who is, without any special reason, considered to have been red-haired, it must also be mentioned that in ancient Egyptian monuments the Canaanites are pictured as having red hair and red beards. The Edomites, if we may rely on the etymology of the word "edom," were also red-haired.

Among the modern Jews, about four per cent. of men and women are rufous, and nearly ten per cent. of men have red beards; in fact, the beard of Jews is quite frequently red, and very often it has at least a rufous tinge of a frizzly character. I find that red beards are more frequently encountered among Galician Jews than among those of other countries. As is usual, the red-haired individuals have nearly always a freckled skin, and the beards are frizzly. Many anthropologists, like Topinard, Deniker, Kopernicki, etc., believe that red hair is a special racial characteristic of the Jews. At the present state of our knowledge as to the origin of red hair in man we are unable to assign any reason for its prevalence among the Jews. Indeed, some believe that red hair is a special shade of blonde, while others class it with dark hair. One thing is certain, red hair is often encountered when intermixture between dark and blonde races has taken place to a large degree. Whether the

[1] Genesis, xxv., 25.

PHYSICAL CHARACTERS.

erythrism of the Jews is due to this cause is difficult to say.

Origin of the Blonde Jews.—One of the most important problems in the anthropology of the Jews has been the origin of the Jews with fair hair and eyes, and it has been discussed by every one who wrote on the subject. Generally speaking, two theories have been advanced. One, represented by Broca,[1] Lagneau,[2] and others, is to the effect that the blonde Jews have their origin in intermixture with North European races. Others claim,

Fig. 21.   Fig. 22.
Figs. 21, 22.—LITHUANIAN JEWS.

however, that blondeness is no proof of intermixture with Teutonic races of Europe. As has already been mentioned, there were blonde Jews in Biblical times, and the modern blonde Jews are considered as descendants of the blondes of the time of the Bible.[3] Prof. von Luschan, in fact, sees in the modern blonde Jews the descendants of the Amorites, who are said to have been blondes,

[1] *Bull. Soc. d'Anthrop.*, vol. ii., p. 416.
[2] G. Lagneau, "Sur la race juive et sa pathologie," *Bull Soc. d'Anthropalogie;* 1891.
[3] Pruner-Bey says: "Il est incontestable pour moi, qu'il y en a de très blonds juifs qui ne sont pas des métis."—*Ibid.*

and with whom the Hebrews intermarried to a great extent.¹

The suggestion made by some that the blondeness of the modern Jews is a product of climatic conditions can be eliminated as worthless. In the first place, there are blonde Jews in every part of the world, in Southern and Eastern, as well as in Northern countries, even in India and North Africa. Then it must also be borne in mind that in countries where the general population is distinctly blonde, like Germany, it is not the Northern provinces where the highest percentage of blonde Jews are met with. Indeed, the geographical distribution of the Jewish blondes proves quite the contrary. On the whole, it can be stated that most of the blonde Jews are found in countries where the general population has a considerable proportion of blondes This is exemplified by the large number of blonde Jews in England, twenty-five per cent., and in Germany, where over thirty per cent. of Jewish children had blonde hair. On the other hand, in Italy, where the Christian population is distinctly brunette, less than five per cent. of Jews are blonde, while in Algeria, Bokhara, the Caucasus, etc., the percentage is even less. But that things are not so simple can be seen when the question is studied more carefully. It must be recalled that the home of the blondes in Europe is the North, and as we proceed East and South, the proportion of fair people decreases, and brunetteness becomes predominant. It is a striking fact that with the Jews of Germany and Austria this appears not to be the case. It was elicited by Virchow and Schimmer during their investigations of the colour of the hair and eyes of the school children of Germany and Austria, that among Jewish children there were more brunettes in the Northern provinces than in the Southern. Among the Germans the largest proportion of blondes are found in the provinces of Prussia, Pomerania, Schleswig-Holstein, Hanover, Westphalia, etc., while further east, in Posen, Bohemia, Moravia, Upper and Lower Austria, and finally, Galicia and Bukowina, the number of blondes decreases. With the Jews it is the reverse. It is in Southern and Eastern parts of Germany

---

[1] F. v. Luschan, "Die Anthropologische Stellung der Juden," *Corr.-Blatt deutsch. Ges. Anthrop.*, vol. xxiii. pp. 97-102.

and Austria where most of the Jewish blondes are met with, while the highest proportion of brunettes is en-

Fig. 23.—ALGERIAN JEWESS (*Roman Nose*).

countered in the Northern provinces. These facts do away with the statement that only the Jews in Northern countries are blonde, in contrast with the Jews in Southern countries, who are of dark complexion, and that the origin of this blondeness is to be looked for in the Northern climate; a kind of transformism, as Darwin would call it. All the facts point to heredity as the basic cause, and, consequently, intermixture with blonde races. Whether this intermixture took place solely in Biblical times with the Amorites, and was transmitted by heredity to the modern Jews, as was suggested by Luschau, is doubtful. It appears to the present writer that if this was the sole cause, *i.e.*, if intermarriage with the indigenous blonde races of Palestine in ancient times were the only source of the modern Jewish blondes, the proportion of fair Jews would be about the same in every country. As a matter of fact, however, we find in some countries, like Caucasus, Africa, Arabia, Italy, etc., only from less than one to six per cent. of Jews have blonde hair; while in others, like Germany, Galicia, England, etc., the proportion exceeds thirty per cent. This points to a suggestion that in regions in which the non-Jewish population is distinctly brunette, the Jews by intermarriage have acquired again dark traits, as is the case in Caucasia, North Africa, etc., while in European countries in which the number of blondes among the Christian population is larger, they acquired by intermarriage a larger proportion of blondes. There is no way of escaping such a conclusion, when all the facts are considered. Everything points in this direction.

It is curious that the so-called "Aryan," or North European type, *i.e.*, the combination of blonde hair, blue eyes, tall stature, and long head in the same individual, appears not to be common among the European Jews. As is well known, many anthropologists speak of the ideal "European" type. The Germans have been so exalted with this type of mankind, that they have named it the "Indo-Germanic" type, in spite of the fact that less than one-half of the population of their country is tall, blonde, and dolichocephalic, and in some of the southern provinces hardly fifteen per cent. of the population is of this type. Some anthropologists have spoken of the blonde Jews as the "Indo-Germanic" or "Aryan" elements in Judaism. Majer and Kopernicki, investigating the somatic traits of the Galician population, have found that brunette Jews are usually brachycephalic, while the blonde Jews are predomi-

Fig. 24.—ALGERIAN JEW (*Aquiline Nose.*)

nantly dolichocephalic, which they, and many others who quoted their writings, consider as good proof that there is an "Indo-Germanic" element among the modern Jews.[1] But this conclusion was based on rather few observations. Among Jewish immigrants in New York City I have found that the head-form of the tall Jews is almost exactly the same as among Jews of shorter stature. I also found that the average cephalic index of 86 blonde Jews was 81.35, almost identical with that of the dark-complexioned Jews, which was 81.97. In fact, the dark-haired individuals had even a somewhat larger percentage of dolichocephalic persons. Similarly, Jews with fair eyes had the same head-form as those with dark eyes, while the percentage of brachycephalic Jews was larger among the blondes than among the brunettes.[2]

It has also been alleged that tall Jews are usually blonde, and short Jews of dark complexion. Pantiukhof found this among the Jews of Odessa, South Russia; and among the Jews in Caucasia, also, those with fair eyes are tall of stature, while those with dark eyes are shorter.[3] But these observations have not been confirmed by other investigators. Among the immigrants of New York examined by the present author, it was found that the proportion of tall Jews is about the same among the blonde and brunette Jews.[4] The same has been reported by Otto Ammon about the Jews in Baden, Germany; and Elkind finds that the dark-complexioned Jews in Poland are even taller than the blondes.[5]

It is thus seen that the ideal "Aryan" combination of tall stature, blondeness, and dolichocephaly is not observed among the European Jews. Indeed, all the facts seem to

---

[1] J. Majer and J. Kopernicki, "Charakterystyka fizyczna ludności galicyjskiej," *Zbior Wiadom. do antropol. Kraj.*, Cracow, vol. i., p. 132. 1877.
[2] For details, see M. Fishberg, "Materials for the Physical Anthropology of the Eastern European Jews," *Annals New York Academy of Sciences*, vol. xvi., pp. 280-284.
[3] I. I. Pantiukhof, "Semitic Types," *Proc. Russian Anthropological Society*, St. Petersburg, 1889, pp. 26-30. *Idem, Observations anthropologiques au Caucase* (in Russian), pp. 37-38; Tiflis, 1893.
[4] M. Fishberg, "Materials for the Physical Anthropology of the Eastern-European Jews," *Memoirs of the American Anthropological Society*, vol. i., part I. pp. 130-134.
[5] Otto Ammon, *Zur Anthropologie der Badener*, pp. 663-664, Jena, 1899; D. N. Elkind, "Evrei," *Memoirs of the Society of Friends of Natural Science, Anthropology, and Ethnography*, vol. civ. pp. 82-83, 1902.

point to a quite contrary condition. It appears that the tall Jews are more liable to be brunettes than blondes, and

Fig. 25 —JEWISH RABBI IN CONSTANTINE (*Aquiline Nose*).

also that they are more often long-headed. This tends to exclude Northern European influence as a cause of Jewish blondeness, especially for those who believe that the combination of traits in question is invariably found among persons who are of "Aryan" origin, which, however, is not the fact, as can be seen from a study of European anthropology. At any rate, it must be remembered that this does not at all exclude Slavonic infusion. It has been observed that among the various Slavonic peoples tall stature is often combined with dark complexion, and short stature with blonde complexion in the same individual This is the case, according to Weisbach's researches, with the Serbo-Croats.[1] Among the Poles and White Russians it was also found that the brunettes are taller than the blondes. Vorobyeff, who studied this question, concludes that many Slavonic peoples are characterized by traits which are the exact opposite of the conventional "Aryan" type: The larger the percentage of brunettes, having dark eyes and hair, the larger the proportion of tall and long-headed individuals.[2] The blondes in Eastern Europe, on the other hand, are often of medium stature, and brachy cephalic. Deniker describes this class of blondes as the "*race orientale*," and states that they are mostly found in White Russia, and among the Great Russians of the Northern provinces of Russia.[3] All this evidence shows that the Slavonic type does not at all agree with the so-called "North European" or "Aryan" type, in which fair complexion is combined with tall stature and dolichocephaly, but the reverse seems to be the case. Tall stature is often combined with round heads and dark complexion. It thus appears that the blonde Jews may be the result of intermixture with the Slavonic races. All available data about the interrelation of stature, complexion, and head-form point to a similarity between the Jews of Eastern Europe and the Gentile races among which they have lived for centuries.

Discussing the origin of the blonde Jews, Ripley

---

[1] A. Weisbach, "Die Serbo-kroaten der adriatischen Küstenländer," *Zeitschrift für Ethnologie*; Supplement, 1884.

[2] *Russian Anthropological Journal*, No. 2, p. 106; 1902. No. 1, pp. 43-82; 1900.

[3] J. Deniker, "Les six races composant la population actuelle de l'Europe," *Journal of the Anthropological Institute*, vol. xxxiv. pp. 181-206; 1904.

suggested that they may be a product of social or artificial selection.[1] Auerbach has developed this theory, and says that sexual selection has greatly influenced the Jews in every country in which they have been dispersed. The racial characters of the population among which they lived has become their ideal. In countries where the non-Jewish population is blonde, the ideal type of the Jews may have become persons with blonde hair, and unconsciously preference might have been given in marriage to blonde individuals. He speaks of a physical but not a cultural assimilation of the Jews. In this manner the blonde elements of the Jews has been multiplied by giving more chance to persons of fair complexion to leave a progeny.[2] I do not believe that this theory is in agreement with facts of Jewish Ghetto life. The ideal type of the Ghetto Jew is the Jewish type. As I will show when speaking of the types of Jews, they prefer in marriage persons with Jewish physiognomies. It is true that to-day, among the Western European and American Jews, blondeness is idealized, as can be seen from the comparatively large number of Jewesses who bleach their hair. But this is a recent phenomenon, going hand-in-hand with other peculiarities which have made their appearance in Jewish life since they were released from the Ghetto, and are no more isolated from the general population. Nowadays the ideals of the people among which they dwell are their ideals. In former times the ideals of their non-Jewish neighbours were not only not their ideals, but more often were very distasteful to them. One who looked like a "Goy" (Gentile) stood no more, but rather less, chance to be preferred in marriage. As the Jews of to-day are the product of the Ghetto Jews, one is at a loss to find in artificial selection a tenable explanation of the origin of the blonde Jews.

The conclusion thus reached is that while some of the modern blonde Jews may be the direct descendants of the blonde Jews of antiquity, or of the intermarriage of ancient Hebrews with the Amorites, still this will not account for all the fair-complexioned Jews of to-day. If all were the descendants of the ancient blonde element, we should

[1] Wm. Z. Ripley, *The Races of Europe*, pp. 396-400.
[2] Elias Auerbach, "Die jüdische Rassenfrage," *Archiv für Rassen und Gesellschafts-Biologie*, vol. iv., p.p 332-261; Berlin, 1907.

expect that the proportion of blondes would be about the same among the Jews in all countries. Considering, however, that in some regions, like Germany, Austria, etc., the proportion is about thirty per cent., while in others it is much less—as, for instance, in North Africa about six per cent., in Italy five per cent., in Caucasia less than one per cent., and in Yemen, Arabia, no fair Jews are met with at all—it must be concluded that the blondes have their origin in the countries in which they are found to-day. When, in addition to this, it is mentioned that the fair-complexioned Jews have other physical

Fig. 26.   Fig. 27.

Figs. 26, 27.—GALICIAN JEWS (*Retroussé Nose*).

traits of their non-Jewish neighbours in the country in which they live, the conclusion that it has been acquired by intermarriage with non-Jews is inevitable.

The Nose.—How far popular fancy is unreliable as a guide when an attempt is made to determine the type of a race or people is best shown by consideration of the Jewish nose, which most people regard as characteristic. In addition to the cartoonists, who always exploit this part of the Jewish anatomy, and never draw a Jewish face without a nasal appendage which looks like the beak of a parrot, most of the writers of fiction, in describing their

Jewish characters, only rarely omit to mention the large protruding, hooked nose of the Jew. Even anthropologists have been led astray by this popular notion. Topinard, in his classification of the forms of noses in the human being, speaks of a separate variety, the "Semitic," or "Jewish" nose. He enumerates several varieties of convex noses, generally known as aquiline: The simple aquiline, the arched, some of which have the appearance of the beak of the parrot or of the eagle ("*bec de pèrroquet*," "*bec d'aigle*") according to the direction taken by the extreme point of the nose. From all this one would be led to believe that a Jew without a "Jewish" nose must be extremely rare. It may consequently be surprising to some that observations among the Jews show that there is no valid reason for considering the arched or hooked nose as peculiarly Jewish. The reverse is rather true. If the most prevalent type of an organ is to be considered as typical of a race or people, then the Jewish nose is the straight, or Greek variety.

The present author has investigated the subject among the Jews in New York City and also in various countries of East and West of Europe, in North Africa, and among Jewish immigrants from various countries of Asia. The results of these investigations do not bear out the popular opinion that the hook nose is to be considered the "Jewish" nose, because only a small minority of Jews have the privilege of possessing this kind of nose. Among 2,836 adult male Jews in New York City the percentage of noses was as follows:—

Straight, or Greek	57·26 per cent.
Retroussé, or snub	22·07 ,,
Aquiline, or hooked	14·25
Flat and broad	6·42 ,,

Among 1,284 Jewesses the percentage of straight noses was even larger, and of aquiline and hooked noses even smaller than among the men:—

Straight, or Greek	59·42 per cent.
Retroussé, or snub	13·86 ,,
Aquiline, or hooked	12·70
Flat and broad	14·02 ,,

This shows that the predominant type of the Jewish nose is the straight. Fifty-seven per cent. of the Jews, and fifty-nine per cent. of the Jewesses, have this variety of nose. This type is known as the Greek nose, because the ancient Greek sculptors have usually produced in their statues faces with straight noses. It must be mentioned, however, that faces with noses after the form of the Greek monuments are very rare among all races. This is true especially of that part where the root of the nose joins the forehead, which is represented in the productions of the masters as almost straight, with practically no indentation at all. The straight noses observed among the modern

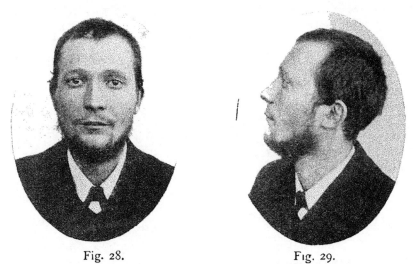

Fig. 28.   Fig. 29.

Figs. 28, 29.—POLISH JEW (WHITE RUSSIAN TYPE), (*Retroussé Nose.*)

[*Photo lent by Elkind.*]

population of Europe and America have a more or less deep depression at the root, while the dorsum is straight, without any considerable elevation or depressions in its course.[1] Nearly three-fifths of the Jews have this form of nose, which cannot be called the classic Greek nose for

[1] It appears that even in ancient Greece this perfectly straight nose was also not the rule. The figures which represent the gods who stand for evil have many other kinds of noses, as, for instance, Pan, Satyrs, etc. Socrates, also, is represented as having had a snub nose. Only the good gods were pictured with beautiful and straight noses. See O. Hovorka, *Die äussere Nase*, pp. 80-83; Vienna, 1893.

reasons just mentioned. Indeed, many of these noses are slightly convex, and could be classed with the form known as the Roman nose, a type very prevalent among Europeans of to-day.

The *retroussé*, or concave, or snub, popularly known as the saucy nose, has been found more often among Jews than popular fancy would lead one to expect. Twenty-two per cent. of the Jews, and thirteen per cent. of the Jewesses, have this form of nose. The chief characteristics of this type are that it is usually short and comparatively broad. When looked at in profile, the dorsum appears short and but little elevated, while the nostrils are often directed upward on both sides. The root is generally broad, low, and the bridge concave. This concavity may be of various degrees, some having but a slight curve hardly to be distinguished from the straight nose, while others have a deep concave curve, which makes them very ugly and animal-like. Popularly this type of nose, if not of the pathological variety due to disease, is considered rather beautiful by some, and the name, "saucy" or "cute" nose, is then given to it. It is very frequently seen among the Slavonians, especially in the Ukraine among the Little Russians, in Galicia among the Ruthenians, among the Bohemians, etc. It is a fact worthy of note that these noses are also most often encountered among Jews coming from these places.

The flat and broad noses are usually short, broad at the base, with both nostrils rather large. The bridge is flat and low, not much protruding from the face. Many of this variety of noses can be called "Negroid," for their similarity to the nose of Negroes. The latter form of nose is often seen among Jews who possess other negroid traits, such as prognathism, large bulky lips, frizzly hair, etc. When this type of nose is seen among the Jews in North Africa, Egypt, Yemen, etc., it can be assumed that its origin is about the same as the origin of negroid traits among their non-Jewish neighbours in those countries, namely, intermixture with Negroes, which is very prevalent among the Arabs, Kabyls, Berbers, etc. But it is also seen, though not very often, among Jews who have had no opportunity to come in contact with Negroes for centuries, such as the Jews of Eastern Europe, and more often yet among the Jews in Italy, and the South of France. The suggestion has been made that this may be considered a case of atavism, striking back to the ancient Hebrews, who intermarried with the tribe of Cushites, said to have been Nubians. Of course this rather far-fetched theory is just as difficult to prove as it is to disprove.

The proportion of aquiline, hooked, convex, or so-called "Jewish" or "Semitic" noses is thus rather small among the Jews of to-day. The author, as has been stated, found

Fig. 30.　　　　　　　　Fig. 31.
Figs. 30, 31.—POLISH JEW (GREAT RUSSIAN TYPE).

[*Photo lent by Elkind.*]

them to be only fourteen per cent. among the Jews, and twelve per cent. among the Jewesses. Observers in Russia, Austria, Hungary, etc., have also found a rather low proportion of this form of nose among Jews in those countries. Some report only two per cent., others ten per cent., while Majer and Kopernicki have found it among 30 per cent. of Galician Jews. This contradicts flatly the prevailing popular opinion that every Jew is the possessor of a hook nose. Moreover, this kind of nose is not infrequent among non-Jewish peoples in various parts of the world. Among the Slavic races amidst whom the bulk of the modern Jews live there was found quite a considerable proportion with aquiline and hook noses. Among the Little Russians, Talko-Hryncewicz has found that over ten per cent. of men and women have aquiline and hook noses; among the Poles and Ruthenians of Galicia, Majer and Kopernicki report over 6 per cent., and among the Germans in Bavaria thirty-one per cent. of aquiline and hook noses have been found.[1] It is noteworthy that Bavarian Jews also have a higher proportion of hook noses than their co-religionists in other countries. In fact the best specimens of the beak-formed nose, the delight of the cartoonist, which is prominent, with fleshy wings, and a dorsum forming a very convex arch, the lower end of which makes a twist backward, are mostly found among the Bavarian Jews, and extremely rare among Jews in other countries. This form of nose is also very frequently met with among the various non-Jewish Caucasian tribes, and also in Asia Minor. Among the indigenous races in this region, such as the Armenians, Georgians, Ossets, Lesghians, Aissors, and also the Syrians, aquiline noses are the rule. Among the people living in Mediterranean countries of Europe, as the Greeks, Italians, French, Spanish and Portuguese, the aquiline nose is also more frequently encountered than among the Jews in Eastern Europe. The North American Indians also have very often "Jewish" noses.

Considering, on the one hand, that only one Jew in six has an aquiline or hook nose, and on the other, that so many races in various parts of the world have just as many and often more persons with this kind of nose, there is hardly any justification for speaking of a "Jewish" or "Semitic" nose. Indeed, as has been pointed out by Luschau, the modern non-Jewish races who speak Semitic dialects, especially such as are supposed to have maintained themselves in a pure state, as the Bedouin Arabs, do not have this characteristic at all. The predominant type of nose among them is the short, straight, and very often the "snub" or concave variety. Luschan holds that the aquiline nose is by no means characteristic of Semites, and contends that the small proportion of arched noses that are found among the

[1] J. Ranke, *Der Mensch*, vol. ii., p. 50; Leipsic, 1894.

modern Jews is due to ancient intermixture with the Hittite race which reigned in Asia Minor in pre-Biblical times. One of their chief physical characteristics is said to have been the aquiline and hook nose. The same author shows that other races which have a considerable portion of Hittite blood in their veins, as the Armenians, also have aquiline noses [1] Indeed, Luschau believes the aquiline and hook nose should rather be called the "Armenoid," and not the "Jewish" or "Semitic" nose.

There are various explanations why popular fancy, artists, cartoonists, actors, and even ethnologists have always considered the arched nose peculiarly Jewish. Beddoe believes that it is due to a characteristic tucking up of the wings which is mostly seen among Jews. He believes that the common type of nose is not sufficiently described when it is called aquiline, though that term is etymologically very appropriate. Beddoe thinks that there is usually more hollowness at the root, more depression at the point, and more tucking up of the wings, than in high-nosed persons of "Aryan" race.[2] Jacobs concludes that the nose contributes much toward producing the Jewish expression, but it is not so much the shape of its profile as the accentuation and flexibility of the nostrils. He alleges that from Galton's composite photographs of Jewish faces it appears that when the nose is covered the Jewish expression disappears entirely, and that it is the so-called "nostrility" which makes these composites "Jewish," which is not in agreement with the present author's observations. "A curious experiment illustrates this importance of the nostril toward making the Jewish expression," says Dr. Jacobs. "Artists tell us that the very best way to make a caricature of the Jewish nose is to write a figure 6 with a long tail (Fig. 1); now remove the turn of the twist as in Fig. 2, and much of the Jewishness disappears; and it vanishes entirely when we draw the continuation horizontally, as in Fig. 3. We may conclude then, as

---

[1] F. v. Luschan, "Die anthropologische Stellung der Juden," *Correspondenzblatt der deutschen Gesellschaft für Anthropologie, etc.*, vol. xxiii., pp. 94-102; 1891.
[2] John Beddoe, "On the Physical Characters of the Jews," *Transact. of the Ethnological Society*, vol. i., p. 222; 1861.

regards the Jewish nose, that it is more the Jewish nostril than the nose itself which goes to form the characteristic Jewish expression."[1] Ripley agrees with Jacobs on this point, and concludes that next to the dark hair and eyes and a swarthy skin, the nostrils are the most distinctive feature among Jews.[2] But if this were the chief criterion of the Jewish cast of countenance, then very few

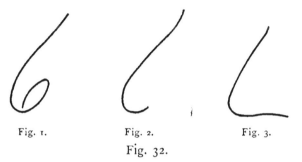

Fig. 1.   Fig. 2.   Fig. 3.
Fig. 32.

Jews would look like Jews, because the nostrility is mostly found among Jews and Christians who have arched noses, and this sort of nose is met with in less than fifteen per cent. of the Jews. Among Jews who have straight or concave noses the "nostrility" is hardly ever seen. Among the inhabitants of Asia Minor and the Caucasus, as has already been mentioned, this nostrility is also frequent.

The Girth of the Chest.—In addition to the "Jewish face," "Jewish nose," etc., there has also been described a "Jewish chest" by various authors. The chief characteristics ascribed to this chest are narrowness and flatness, and a special deficiency in vital capacity. As is well known to those who have seen many Jews of Eastern Europe, there are not many among them who can boast of a fully developed, capacious chest; most of them have emaciated, flat, and narrow chests. One of the chief criterions as to chest capacity is its circumference, which in a healthy, well-developed individual should measure more than one-half his stature. Indeed, in most Europeans the average circumference of the chest is from about fifty-five to fifty-eight per cent. of the average stature, while

[1] Joseph Jacobs, "On the Racial Characteristics of Modern Jews," *Journal of the Anthropological Institute*, vol. xv., pp. 23-62; 1886.
[2] Wm. Z. Ripley, *The Races of Europe*, p. 395.

among those who have indulged in athletic training it may reach sixty per cent., and even more. This is one of the most important measurements taken by conscript officers in continental armies when attempting to determine the fitness of recruits to do military duty. Such measurements taken in Eastern Europe have shown that the Slavonic races have a girth which exceeds half of their body-height by from two to eight per cent. Among Jewish conscripts of Russia, Poland, and Austria, it was found that they are notoriously deficient in this respect. Among 4,470 Jewish recruits in Poland, Snigireff[1] found that their girth is on the average only 49.68 per cent. of their stature. Among 2,122 Lithuanian Jewish recruits he found the girth measured only 49.55 per cent. of stature, and among Galician Jews the same condition was elicited by Majer and Kopernicki.[2] Military medical journals have on the strength of these facts repeatedly discussed the subject whether the Jews, owing to their defective "vital capacity," and their lesser "index of vitality," are at all fit for military service. It appears that the consensus of opinion, as well as practical experience with Jewish soldiers, was to the effect that this defect, if it may at all be termed a defect, by no means interferes with their efficiency to bear arms. In fact the Russian and Austrian armies have decided to disregard the girth of the chest as a primary test for recruits, and admit Jews, even when they are deficient in this respect, provided they are healthy in all other respects. The girth of the chest has thus been given an official recognition as a racial trait of the Jews.

But this official stamp is by no means convincing that the narrow chest is a racial trait, transmitted by heredity, and cannot be eradicated by proper sanitary and hygienic measures. A careful study has shown that it mainly depends on the social and economic conditions under which the Jews find themselves, and in part also on the tardy development of their physique. The precocity of

[1] "Materials for Medical Statistics and Geography of Russia," *Voyeno-Medizinski Zhurnal* (in Russian); 1878-79. See also E. Goldstein, "Des circonférences du thorax et de leur rapport à la taille," *Revue d'anthropologie*, Series II., vol. viii., pp. 639-675; B. Blechman, *Ein Beitrag zur Anthropologie der Juden*, Dorpat, 1882.
[2] "Charakterystyka fizyczna ludnosci galicyjskiej," *Zbior Wiadom. do antropol. kraj.*, vol. i., pp. 1-181; vol. ix., pp. 1-92; Cracow, 1877, 1885.

Jewish children is well known. This prococity manifests itself, however, only in their mental and intellectual development. The success they achieve in public schools and undergraduate colleges bears witness to this. But this success is usually achieved at a high price; it is gained at the expense of their physical development, which is very slow in the Jewish youth, as can be seen among the Jewish pupils of public and high schools of the United States. In Russia and Austria conditions are much worse in this respect. At a very early age the Jewish child is sent to the so-called *cheder* (Jewish religious school), which is almost invariably in a deplorable sanitary condition, and in which he remains from morning till late in the evening engaged in the study of Hebrew, the Bible, and the Talmud. Games and outdoor exercises are foreign to the Jewish child in Eastern Europe. During adolescence conditions do not change materially. Indoor and domestic occupations, sedentary habits and the lack of physical culture are notoriously frequent among them. All this does not contribute much to the healthy development of the muscular system, and their chests remain flat and contracted. It must be borne in mind that the girth does not depend entirely on the size of the skeleton of the chest, but also in a great measure on the condition of the muscles. Well-developed muscles enlarge the girth by their bulk, as well as by their ability to hold the ribs at a very obtuse angle in relation to the spinal column, while weak and flabby muscles do not elevate the ribs to any perceptible extent, but permit them to hang down at an acute angle in relation to the spinal column, producing what is known among medical men as the so-called "paralytic chest," which is of small capacity, narrow and flat. Individuals with strong, well-developed muscles have consequently capacious chests. The absence of agriculturists among Jews is also an important factor. The rural population is known to have a larger girth than the urban population, and the factory worker is at a disadvantage when compared with the outdoor worker in this respect. It has also been observed that the intellectual classes are often deficient in chest capacity unless they engage in outdoor sports and games, as is generally the case with the American college boys. Otto Ammon, speaking of the deficient girth of the Jews in Baden, attributes this condition to the fact that a very large proportion among them is engaged assiduously in study in a sitting posture, and also because they are very frequently engaged in mercantile pursuits. He ascribes this defect of the physical organization of the Jews to their faulty muscular development.[1]

The tardy development which has been mentioned already is also an important factor. It has been elicited that measurement of adults over twenty-five years of age shows that Jews have a girth which exceeds half their stature. Recruits, who are usually between nineteen and twenty-two years of age, on the other hand, have a deficient girth. Measurements taken by the author on 983 immigrant Jews in New York showed that their girth was 52.2 per cent. of the height of their body. While this may be due partly to the fact that immigrants are a selected class physically, yet the fact that they are all over twenty years of age is also important. All the measurements of adult Jews over twenty years of age taken in Russia also show that their girth is between 52 and 54 per cent. of their height. But even measurements of native American Jews in the east side of New York City have not shown that they improve materially in one generation of favourable sanitary and hygienic surrounding during their youth. This confirms Ripley's opinion that, even if granted that the narrow chest of the Jews is an acquired characteristic, the effect of long-continued subjection to unfavourable sanitary and social environment, it has none the less become a hereditary trait.

Some curious statements have been made about the ethnic relations of the Jewish chest. Pantiukhof observed that in Odessa, South Russia, the chest of the taller Jews is more capacious than that of Jews of inferior stature. He considers this another proof of the greater vitality of the "Aryan" element among the Jews, particularly because the taller Jews were also of fairer complexion than were the short Jews.[2] This was not sustained by investi-

---

[1] Otto Ammon, *Die naturliche Auslese beim Menschen*, p. 134, Jena, 1893.
[2] I. I. Pantiukhof, "Semitic Types," *Proc. Russian Anthropolog. Society*, St. Petersburg, vol. ii., 1889.

gations made by others who have taken measurements of large numbers of Jews. The present author has found that the contrary is true among the immigrants of New York. The shorter Jews have larger chests than the taller ones. It has also been found that among the Jewish conscripts those who were affected with consumption were taller than those who were healthy. Observations of Jewish consumptives in New York City made by the author show that this condition prevails also here. Consumption appears to select its victims preferably among the taller Jews. Judt thinks that this factor, by a natural elimination of the taller Jews, exerts a great influence on their average stature.[1]

[1] J. M. Judt, *Die Juden als Rasse*, p 85; Berlin, 1903.

CHAPTER V.

TYPES OF JEWS.

The "indelibility" of the Jewish type—The type of the ancient Hebrews—The characteristics of the Jewish face—The artist's conception of the Jewish type—The novelist's conception of the Jewish face—The anthropologist's conception of the Jewish type—Prepotency of the Jewish type—The Sephardi type of Jews—The Ashkenazi type of Jews—The Slavonic type—The Turanian type—The Teutonic type—The Mongoloid type—The Negroid type—Other types of Jews.

WHILE all acknowledge that the Jewish type cannot be distinguished by separate physical traits, such as stature, complexion, head-form, nose, etc., it is nevertheless the prevailing opinion that the Jew's physiognomy is typical, that his cast of countenance is uniform, and that one can pick out a Jew from among a thousand non-Jews without any difficulty. Indeed, it has been stated by many ethnologists that the facial features of the Jews are the best proof of the purity of their race. Nott and Gliddon, in their book on the *Races of Mankind*, speaking of the constancy of the Jewish type, bring, in substantiation, two pictures of mummied heads, one from the time of Moses and another the origin of which "is fixed between the reign of Sennacherib and the fall of Nineveh, about the seventh century B.C." They comment on these two reproductions by saying that after 2,500 years the type is so indelible in the Jew that their city's most honoured Jewish citizen looks to-day in Mobile (Ala.) exactly like this Chaldean effigy. These authors conclude as follows:—" The monuments of Egypt and Assyria, history and the Bible, have enabled us to ascend to the age of Abraham, first historical progenitor of the Israelitish line, and demonstrate the indelibility of the Jewish type from his era downwards. . . . The Jews themselves are living testimonies that their type has survived every vicissitude; and that it has come down, century by century, from Mesopotamia to Mobile (Ala.)

Fig. 33.—Ancient Races Portrayed on the Egyptian Monuments 3000 Years Since.

Amorites.
King of Hittites (With Pigtail).
Judean (Chief of Canata).

Philistine.
Hittite Soldiers.
Judean (Pseudo-Rehoboam).

[From Sayce's *Races of the Old Testament*.]

for at least 5,500 years, unaltered and, save through blood-alliance with Gentiles, unalterable." [1]

Other authors, especially archæologists who have devoted their studies to the discernment of the remains of ancient Assyrian, Babylonian, and Egyptian monuments (Rawlinson, Layard, Maspero, Delitzsch, and others), bring many reproductions of *bas reliefs* which tend to show that the cast of countenance of the Jews of to-day is practically the same as it was 4,000 years ago. Centuries of dispersion in all the countries of the habitable globe among the various races of mankind, under the influence of nearly every variety of climatic conditions, are said to have been powerless to obliterate the characteristic facial features of the Jews. Even the adoption of the diet, dress, habits, customs of life, and language of the people among whom his unhappy lot has thrown him, it is alleged, have not altered the Jew's countenance.

That the Jewish face is characteristic, and that a Jew can be singled out from among a thousand Christians, is a recent opinion. In mediæval ages the tormentors of the Jews did not place much confidence in the so-called "Jewish" type as a safe distinguishing mark. It seems they knew that appearances are often deceptive, that one who has a hook nose, black eyes and hair, thick lips, etc., may be a Christian, Mohammedan, or heathen as well as a Jew, and that one devoid of these traits is not necessarily a Gentile. They were, however, determined to know a Jew when they met one, and to avoid mistakes, many enactments were promulgated compelling Jews to wear badges in order that they may be easily distinguished from non-Jews. In 640 the Jews in Islam were ordered by the Pact of Omar to wear a yellow seam in their garment; in 1005 the Jews of Egypt were ordered to wear badges on their coats, and in 1301 they were forced to wear yellow turbans. In France, Spain, Italy, England, and Germany similar laws prevailed, and Pope Innocent III., in the preamble to the law enforcing the badge, complains that Jews were being mistaken for Christians.[2] Even to-day

---

[1] Nott and Gliddon, *Types of Mankind*, Philadelphia, 1854, pp. 116-17, 141.

[2] See Ulysse Robert, "Étude historique sur la Roue des Juifs," *Revue des Études Juives*, vol. vi., pp. 80-95; vol. vii., pp. 94-102. Also his *Les Signes d'infamie*, Paris, 1891.

TYPES OF JEWS. 93

there are similar laws in force in certain oriental countries, like Persia and Morocco. In the latter place the law provides that Jews must wear dark-coloured gaberdines

Fig. 34.—Jewish Doctor (Sephardi Type).
[*Rembrandt.*]

and black skull caps and slippers, in order that they may be distinguished from their Mohammedan neighbours.

It appears that to-day things have changed materially in this regard. Even as distinguished an ethnologist as

Andree, among many others, writes, "We all know the 'Jewish type;' we easily distinguish the Jew by his facial features, by his manners and habits of life, by the manner in which he holds his head, his gesticulations; or when he opens his mouth and begins to speak we always discover some characteristic trait which betrays his origin." He adds, however, that when we are asked to define this type, to give a formula which will identify a Jew, we remain helpless, for our terminology and our descriptive powers are of no avail in this respect. "But this by no means excludes the existence of a peculiar racial type, many other races of mankind are easily distinguished one from another, although most writers agree that the types do not lend themselves to easy definition of their characteristic traits."[1]

It appears to the present writer that in this case, just as in the case of many other alleged peculiarities of the Jews, the opinion is based on observations of Jews in the Ghettoes, or such who have just emerged from the Ghettoes, and have not yet had sufficient time to adapt themselves to their new *milieu*. All those who have taken the Ghetto factor into consideration have found that there are many types of Jews, and, also, that Jews who have for a few generations been out of the Ghetto are hardly to be distinguished from the races and peoples among which they live.

It is nevertheless important to study those physical peculiarities which are usually considered "Jewish." The best sources for such a study are the works of artists who have painted Jewish faces, of writers of fiction in which Jewish life is portrayed, and of ethnologists, who in addition to measurements, have also described the Jewish physiognomy as a racial trait. Figs. 18-20, 34-40, reproduce some Jewish faces painted by well-known artists. I have purposely refrained from reproducing on these pages the so-called "Jewish types" made by illustrators of fiction treating of Jewish life. It is a remarkable fact that whenever an artist, even one who is sympathetic to his people, makes an attempt to depict the Jewish face in all its details, the result is almost invariably a caricature. When the artist is not over zealous in his attempt to

---

[1] R. Andree, *Zur Volkskunde der Juden*, p. 37; Leipsic, 1881.

bring forth all real and alleged facial features, the types he produces could be taken for any racial or national type. Of the few painters who have produced excellent Jewish

Fig. 35.—Jewish Face.
[*Drawing by Lilien.*]

faces, Rembrandt is to be mentioned first. The portraits he made of Spanish Jews in Holland can hardly be duplicated in point of truthfulness of racial type. In addition

Fig. 36. [*Hirszenberg.*]

Fig. 37. [*Pasternack.*]

Fig. 38. [*Sichel.*]

Fig. 39. [*Gottlieb.*]

Figs. 36-39.—Artists' Conception of Jewish Face.

to his types we have also reproduced some faces of Jews painted by Hirszenberg, Gottlieb, Kaufmann, Lilien, and Pasternack, showing Russian, Polish, and German Jewish types as conceived by artists of high rank (Figs. 18-20, 34-40).

A study of these heads reveals that artists paint the Jewish face oval in shape, with a narrow and receding forehead. The hair is thick, dark, often jet black and curly. The eyes are almond-shaped, the upper eyelid excessively large; the eyebrows thick and bushy, and almost meeting over the root of the nose. The eyeball, though deeply set in the socket, is large as a whole and unusually protruding, or at least appearing so. The expression of these dark eyes is very difficult to describe. On the whole they are strikingly brilliant and radiant, and

Fig. 40.—JEWISH FACES.

[*Drawn by E. M. Lilien.*]

in some they appear sleepy or dreamy, have a weary, tired appearance; in others they are piercing, blinking or lurking, while in those portraits in which the upper eyelid is especially large—which gives the eye a half-closed appearance—there is a suggestion of what Ripley calls suppressed cunningness. The strength of expression in the eyes of most of these portraits is much augmented by the dark rings around them representing excessive deposition of pigment in the skin of that region. The nose is narrow at the root, but large and prominent as a whole; aquiline, but not decidedly hooked, the *bec d'aigle* nose is not seen in any of these paintings. The most an artist permits himself is a slight curve at the extreme tip. The wings are large and well developed in every painted face. The mouth is rather large, the lips—especially the under lip—thick, often negroid-like (Fig. 39), and the chin receding. The line formed by the fold running from the wings of the nose to the angles of the mouth is very much accentuated. In those portraits in which the ears are not covered by the hair they are seen to be unusually large and prominent.

Such is generally the Jewish face as painted by artists of the first rank. Another class of artists, the caricaturists, draw the Jewish face on entirely different lines. They give full sway to their pen when drawing the abovementioned characteristics. As might be expected, they exaggerate every feature in unmistakable terms, and the result is invariably an ugly, repulsive picture. Thus while the painter, as has just been shown, usually paints the Jewish face with a straight or an aquiline, commonly known as a Roman, nose, the caricaturist pictures it invariably as large and bulky, with fleshy wings, convex and hooked, in profile appearing like the beak of a parrot. The head is covered with curly and oily hair, often carelessly disarranged. The under lip is very large and the ears protruding, the neck short, the shoulders round and elevated, so that the head appears sunken in between them. A stooping, often cringing attitude of the body is never omitted by a caricaturist when he attempts to bring out prominently the repulsiveness of the Jewish type.

It appears that the carricaturist's conception of the Jewish physiognomy is the one which writers of fiction have often adopted in their descriptions of the cast of countenance of Jews who figure in their novels. To mention only one, Thackeray, who thus describes the Jews in the London Ghetto in his sketch "Codlingsby:" "Smiling faces . . . Ringlets glossy, and curly, and jetty—eyes black as night—midsummer night—when it lightens; haughty noses bending like beaks of eagles—eager quivering nostrils—lips curved like the bow of love—every man or maiden, every babe or matron in that English Jewry bore in his countenance one or more of these characteristics of his peerless Arab race." Most other writers of fiction picture the Jew as invariably swarthy or brunette, with a long hooked nose, with thick "sensuous" lips, and a long beard. It appears that

Zangwill is, perhaps, the only one who in his novels recognizes the fact that there is more than one type of Jew to be met with in various countries. In his description of the International Zionist Congress at Bâle he speaks of the variety of the Jewish types in the following manner. He says that "no two of the leaders are alike," and that the "rank and file fail to resemble one another," that they present "a strange phantasmagoria of faces. A small, sallow Pole, with high cheek-bones; a blonde Hungarian, with a flaxen moustache; a brown hatchet-faced Roumanian; a fresh-coloured Frenchman with eye-glasses; a dark, Marrano-descended Dutchman; a chubby German; a fiery-eyed Russian, tugging at his own hair with excitement, perhaps in prescience of the prison awaiting his return; a dusky Egyptian, with the close-cropped, curly black hair, and all but the nose of a negro; a yellow-bearded Swede; a courtly Viennese lawyer; a German student, first fighter in the University, with a coloured band across his shirt-front; a dandy, smelling of the best St. Petersburg circles; and one solitary caftan Jew, with ear-locks and skull-cap, wafting into the nineteenth century the cabalistic mysticism of the Carpathian Messiah. Who speaks of the Jewish type? one can only say negatively that these faces are not Christian. Is it the stamp of a longer, more complex heredity? Is it the brand of suffering?" asked Zangwill justly. As will be seen hereafter, there is considerable truth in the supposition that the hard fate of the Jew has had a great deal to do with the evolution of his racial type.

Very little attention has been given to the Jewish type by ethnologists,[1] beyond speaking of either the uniformity or plurality of the ethnic type. In general, there are two diametrically opposed opinions. Some, like Jacobs, Andree, Elkind, Judt, and others speak of a "Jewish" physiognomy which is typical and uniform. Jacobs even speaks of the "prepotency" of the Jewish type, by which he understands some mysterious power possessed by

[1] John Beddoe, "On the Physical Characters of the Jews," *Transact. of the Ethnological Society*, vol i. pp. 222-237, London, 1861; A. D. Elkind, "Evrei," in *Trudi antropol. otdiela*, Moscow, 1903; Weissenberg, "Die südrussischen Juden," *Archiv fur Anthropologie*, vol. xxiii. 1905; discuss the Jewish cast of countenance.

COMPOSITES.

D

B

Jewish blood which transmits the type uninterruptedly from generation to generation. Even in non-Jewish families "into which there has been an infusion of Jewish blood this tends to appear in a marked and intensely Jewish cast of features and expression. . . . Now as reversion is mostly towards the side of greater prepotency, this curious fact confirms our conclusion as to the superior prepotency of Jewish blood."[1] How this prepotency works, so as to eliminate all the foreign blood from Jewish veins and to reappear in a marked and intensely Jewish cast of features and expression when mixed with non-Jewish blood, is not explained by Jacobs, and one is at a loss to account for the many non-Jewish faces met with among Jews in every country, if prepotency is considered a potent factor in maintaining ethnic purity and eliminating every drop of foreign blood.

Jacobs is one of the few who wrote from the scientific standpoint in attempting to define the Jewish type. He says that it is not a correlation of definite anthropological measures or characteristics, but consists principally in a peculiar expression of the face, which is immediately and unmistakably recognized as "Jewish" in a large number of cases of persons of the Jewish race. He admits that it is difficult to determine the precise nature of the "Jewishness" with any degree of certainty and accuracy In a very ingenious manner he attempted to determine this type by a series of composite photographs which were prepared according to Galton's method. The results are reproduced here on p. 100-101, showing A the composite portait of five boys of the Jewish Free School, London, and B of another five, and C a composite of A and B. Jacobs thus describes these portraits[2]: "The result is remarkably Jewish in appearance, and it will be found that this character is given by the eyebrows, eyes, nose and lips, while the position and contour of the cheek-bone also serve to determine it. The eyebrows are generally well defined, somewhat bushy toward the nose, and

---

[1] J. Jacobs, "On the Racial Characteristics of Modern Jews," *Journal Anthropolog. Institute*, vol. xv. pp. 31 of reprint, 1885. Hellwald also speaks of the tenacity of the Jewish physical type, *Culturgeschichte*, p. 503, Augsburg, 1875; Andree, *Zur Volkskunte der Juden*, p. 46.
[2] Article, "Types," *Jewish Encyclopædia*, vol. xii., p. 294.

tapering off toward the extremities. The eyes themselves are generally brilliant, both lids are heavy and bulging,

Fig. 42.—Spanish Jewess, Jerusalem.

and it seems to be the main characteristic of the Jewish eye that the upper lid covers a larger proportion of the pupil than among other persons. This may serve to give a sort of nervous, furtive look to the eyes, which, when the pupils are small and set close together with semistrabismus, gives keenness to some Jewish eyes. The lymph sac beneath the eye is generally fuller and more prominent than among non-Jews. The high cheek-bone gives, as a rule, the hollow cheek that adds to the Jewish expression, while the nose in full face can be discerned only by the flexibility of the nostrils, the chief Jewish characteristic of this organ. The upper lip is generally short, the lower projects, giving a somewhat sensual appearance to the face. The chin almost invariably recedes from the lip, leaving an indentation beneath it in the great majority of instances. The ears of many Jewish persons project, and in boys increase the impression of Jewishness." A glance at the composite portraits herewith reproduced shows that very few of the above characteristics are discernible, notwithstanding the fact that the boys were carefully selected as such who look more Jewish than the average. As a matter of fact, it can be observed in public schools of the East Side of New York City in which the majority of the pupils are Jewish, that the vast majority of the boys and girls hardly look like Jewish children should look, according to the standard of those who believe in the prepotency of Jewish blood. Many who visit these schools are often surprised to find that only few of the pupils have the traditional Jewish cast of countenance; indeed, the Jewish expression is much more frequent among adults than among the young Jews, which goes far to support the opinion of the present author, that it is an acquired trait.

Elkind is also of the opinion that the Jews, irrespective of their wide geographical distribution, are distinguishable more or less by a certain uniformity of physical and physiognomical type, and that we may speak of the existence of a Jewish physiognomy common to all the scattered representatives of the race, and which unites them into a distinct ethnic group. He enumerates shortness of stature, a comparatively long face, mesocephalic skull, dark hair and eyes, etc., as the main characteristics. The hook nose he does not consider a Jewish trait, because only a small proportion of Jews have this form of nose. But he admits that it is difficult to describe the characteristics which will identify a Jew as a member of his

Fig. 43.—GALICIA. Fig. 44.—EUROPEAN TURKEY.

Figs. 45, 46.—JERUSALEM.
Figs. 43-46.—SEPHARDI TYPES OF JEWS.

race, and even mentions that the peculiar Jewish articulation of spoken language is often alone sufficient to identify one as belonging to the Chosen People.[1] The illustrations of his book, however, show various types of Jews.

It is the consensus of opinion among anthropologists to-day that there is more than one type of Jews. Even Jews who, for obvious reasons, are loath to acknowledge that any foreign blood flows in the veins of any of the Chosen People, acknowledge two types among the modern followers of Judaism, the *Ashkenazim* and the *Sephardim*. Karl Vogt, in his *Lectures on Man*, first gave a detailed description of these two types of Jews. The first are said by this author to be found mostly in Northern Russia, Poland, Germany, and Bohemia. Their chief characteristics are red hair, short beard, a short concave nose, small and grey lustrous eyes; their body is inclined to stoutness, the face is round with broad cheek-bones. On the whole they are physically very much like the Northern Slavonians. The second type is mostly found in the Orient, and around the Mediterranean, also in Portugal and Holland. Their special features are long black hair and beard, large almond-shaped eyes, a melancholy cast of countenance, with an oval face and a prominent nose,—in short, the type of Jews represented in the paintings of Rembrandt.[2] Similar descriptions of two types of Jews are given in the works of Broca, Stieda, Blechman, Topinard, Maurer. The last-mentioned author speaks of the *Turanian* and the *Semitic* types, while Deniker speaks of the *Arab* and the *Assyroid* types, and adds that sometimes these types are modified by the addition of elements from the populations in the midst of which they dwell.[3] Ikoff speaks of the Slavonic, Hellenic, Roman, and other types of Jews,[4] while Weissenberg describes in detail "fine," "coarse," North European, Caucasian, Mongoloid, and Negroid types of Jews.[5] And all these types this author found among the Jews of one city in South Russia, Elisabetgrad.

[1] A. D. Elkind, "Evrei," *Trudy antropolog. otdiela*, vol. xxi., pp. 328-329; Moscow, 1903.
[2] K. Vogt, *Vorlesungen uber den Menschen*, vol. ii., p. 238.
[3] J. Deniker, *The Races of Man*, pp. 423-425; London, 1899.
[4] K. N. Ikoff, "Neue Beiträge zur Anthropologie der Juden," *Archiv für Anthropologie*, vol. xv., pp. 369-389; 1884.
[5] S. Weissenberg, "Die südrussischen Juden," *Archiv für Anthropologie*, vol. xxiii.; 1895.

TYPES OF JEWS.

The two main types, known among the Jews as those following the *Ashkenazi* and those following the *Sephardi* rites, are acknowledged to exist by nearly everybody who writes on the subject. Some even go so far as to say that they are not only different types, but they constitute two distinct races, and the only thing they have in common is the religion of Judaism. The *Ashkenazim* are by far the more numerous; more than ninety per cent. of the Jews of to-day are included in their midst. Their name is derived from the word *Ashkenaz*, the son of Gomer, grandson of Noah.[1] The Talmud, and also mediæval rabbinical literature, identify Ashkenaz with Germany and Teutons, while according to Saadia the Slavs are meant.[2] At the present all the Jews from Russia, Poland, Germany, and Austria are called *Ashkenazim*, partly because of the *Yiddish* or German jargon which is employed by most of them as their mother tongue. The name *Sephardi* has its origin in *Sepharad*, the Biblical name of an unknown land in which the Jews exiled from Jerusalem were brought.[3] The mediæval rabbis believed that Sepharad referred to Spain and Portugal, hence the name *Sephardim* for the Spanish and Portuguese Jews. When banished from Spain in 1492, over 200,000 Jews were dispersed in various parts of the world; some wandered to North Africa, others to Italy, France, Holland, England, Germany, Austria, Hungary, Turkey, Asia Minor, etc. Many wandered to North and South America. The first Jews who came to the United States were of this class. The remnants of these Jews who live at the present time in the Balkan States, as Bosnia, European Turkey, Roumania, etc., are also known by the name *Spagnuoli*, probably because of the Spanish dialect which they still employ. There were many of them in the United States and in England, but they are rapidly disappearing through intermarriage with non-Jews, and to a lesser degree with *Ashkenazim*. These two groups of Jews differ in their traditions, rites, ritual, and also in physical type. The Sephardim are very proud, and consider themselves as that branch of Israel which has succeeded in maintaining

---

[1] Genesis, x. 3; Chronicles, i. 6.
[2] *Jewish Encyclopædia*, vol. ii., pp. 191-193.
[3] See *Abadias*, 20.

itself to the present day in its original Semitic purity, and has not suffered foreign infusion as the *Ashkenazim*. "The many sufferings which they had endured for the sake of their faith had made them more than usually self-conscious; they considered themselves a superior class, the nobility of Jewry, and for a long time their co-religionists, on whom they looked down, regarded them as such."[1] They have their own synagogues, cemeteries, etc., in any place where they find themselves in reasonable number, and refuse to share all this with their Ashkenazi co-religionists. They also refuse to intermarry with the German and Russian Jews, whom they consider beneath themselves. They have an old tradition, which was credited by Mediæval Jews, that they are descended from the tribe of Judah, while their Russian and German co-religionists, the Ashkenazim, were alleged to have descended from the tribe of Benjamin. This legend had considerable influence in keeping these two groups of Jews from intermarrying one with the other.

The Sephardi Type of Jews.—There are significant differences between these two types of Jews when considered anthropologically, although there is hardly any justification for speaking of two distinct races as has been done by some writers. Neither of the two types can claim special racial purity. The Sephardi type (Figs. 42-46) is the one which conforms most to the ideal Jewish type, and anthropologically corresponds to the "Mediterranean" race of Ripley, or the "Race Ibero-Insulaire" of Deniker. They have generally black or brown hair, occasionally red and rarely blonde; large black or brown eyes, seldom grey, and rarely blue. In addition to their dark complexion, they are short of stature and either dolichocephalic or mesocephalic. The face is oval, the forehead receding, the eyes almond-shaped with the outer extremity very

---

[1] *Jewish Encyclopædia*, vol. xi., p. 197. "If they have suffered more than the *Ashkenazim*," says Leroy Beaulieu, "they have, at any rate, been less humiliated. Honour did not always present itself to them in the guise of a pinnacled castle with a drawbridge, over which no Jews were allowed to pass. They were sometimes permitted to bear arms within the castle walls, and they often associated with Arab knights and Christian hidalgos. Despite their four centuries of exile, we can at times detect in them what seems like a reflex of Castilian pride or Oriental dignity." *Israel Among the Nations*, p. 205.

pointed, while the dark eyebrows are very bushy at the inner end, where they tend to unite over the root of the

Fig. 47.—Jewish Rabbi, Oran.

nose. The traditional Semitic beauty, which in women often assumes an exquisite nobility, is generally found among these Jews, and when encountered among Jews in

Eastern or Central Europe is always of this type. Indeed, it is hard to imagine a beautiful Jewess, who looks like a Jewess, presenting any other physical type. It appears that in addition to the delicacy and the striking symmetry of the features which are often met with, it is also the brilliant, radiant eyes which give these Sephardim their reputation for bewitching elegance and charm. The Spanish and Andalusian women are said by some to owe their charms to these beautiful eyes, which are alleged to have their origin in the small quantities of Semitic blood which flows in their veins. Their long, narrow heads often have prognathous faces, the upper and lower jaws protruding forward. The nose is generally narrow, prominent, often convex, but only rarely of the kind popularly considered "Jewish." Many of them have a rather large mouth with thick lips, especially the under-lip. They are medium-sized, slender, narrow-shouldered, but graceful people, with a somewhat melancholy and thoughtful expression. Only very rarely is to be seen a Spanish Jew displaying a servile or cringing attitude in the presence of superiors, as is often to be seen among German and Polish Jews. The Sephardim are very proud, and their sense of dignity manifests itself even in their dress and deportment, to which they pay scrupulous attention. These traits, which they acquired while living for centuries among the Castilians, have been transmitted to their descendants of to-day. As has already been mentioned, they look down on their German co-religionists and consider them of an inferior race. As will be noted from the reproductions of Sephardi portraits on pp. 62 and 93, Rembrandt has painted this type of Jews exclusively. He met them in Amsterdam, where many settled after their expulsion from Spain and Portugal. But it must not be taken for granted that this type of Jews is only met with among those who can trace their ancestry back to Spain and Portugal. Many of the Russian, Polish, German, and English Jews are of this type. Considering that during their dispersion at the end of the fifteenth century they scattered in all these countries, we have a clue as to the origin of the Sephardi type among all other Jews.

It is also important to mention in this connection that the Sephardi type is not as uniform and homogeneous, even among Spanish Jews, as is generally supposed. Many Sephardim look like the Spanish among whom they have lived for long centuries; others remind one of the Moors who suffered the same fate as the Jews in Spain. The Sephardim of to-day in various European countries have taken on many somatological traits of the races and peoples among which they live. Thus the Jews in Italy are hardly to be distinguished from the Italians of the region in which they live, and the same is the case with the French, especially the Southern French Jews. In Algeria, Tunis, Morocco, etc., they have acquired many of the characteristics of the Arabs, Berbers, Kabyls, etc., as can be seen from the portraits reproduced on pp. 138-144. Indeed the term Semitic, or Arab type, which some have applied to these Jews, only holds good when applied to those who live among these races. The Sephardim of Holland, England, Germany, etc., have changed physically to a marked degree by intermarriage with their Ashkenazi co-religionists, or with Christians.[1]

The Ashkenazi Type of Jews.—The Jews of Germany, Russia, Poland, etc., known as the *Ashkenazim*, are generally of a type which differs much from the one just described. Their features are not as elegant, not as graceful as those of the Sephardim. Indeed, as has already been stated, most of the beautiful Jewesses, irrespective of the country in which they are encountered, are of the Sephardi type. A blonde Jewess, no matter how charming she may be, is not in conformity with what one would expect a Jewess to look like. It is true that the majority of Ashkenazim are also brunette, but, as has been shown already (Chap. IV.), around thirty per cent. of them are blonde, and fifty per cent. have fair eyes. They are brachycephalic, and in the Caucasus they are even hyperbrachycephalic. They correspond on the whole to the "Alpine" race of Ripley. Their face is round, with prominent cheek bones, and the nose medium-sized, broad,

[1] These intermarriages were more often with Christians than with German Jews. The Sephardi congregation of London, for instance, passed a resolution in 1776 that a Sephardi marrying an Ashkenazi forfeited his claim on congregational charity; in 1772 a Sephardi petitioned the Board for permission to marry a *Tedesca*, but was refused. *Jewish Chronicle*, p. 8, June 28, 1901.

with fleshy wings, often narrow and depressed at the root, appearing generally somewhat pear-shaped. The aquiline

Fig. 48.   Fig. 49.

Fig. 50.   Fig. 51.

FIGS. 48-51.—ASHKENAZI TYPES OF JEWS, EASTERN EUROPE.

nose is found only to the extent of twelve to fourteen per cent. among these Jews, excepting those who come from Germany, especially Bavaria. The chin is heavy, the

TYPES OF JEWS. 113

mouth large, and the lips thick, all of which give a rather heavy expression to the countenance (Figs. 8-11, 13-16, 48-53).

Fig. 52.   Fig. 53.

Fig. 54.   Fig. 55.
POLISH JEWESS, MONGOLOID TYPE.
FIGS. 52-55.—ASHKENAZI TYPES OF JEWESSES.

What has been said about the diversity of type of the Spanish Jews applies with more emphasis to the German,

8

Polish, and Russian followers of Judaism, who are even less uniform physically. Besides the Sephardi, or Mediterranean type which is quite frequently encountered among them (Figs. 43, 132), other types are met with even by the casual observer. Most prominent among the various types is the *Slavonic* which is met with among the Russian, Polish, Austrian, Roumanian, and German Jews. They have usually grey or beer-coloured eyes deeply set in the sockets, a very broad face, prominent cheek-bones, and an abundant beard. They are of medium height and brachycephalic. In fact, many of these Jews are hardly to be distinguished from their Slavonic neighbours, especially when they don the national costumes of the countries in which they live. This is particularly true of the Jewesses of Poland and White Russia. It is also a striking fact that anthropologically they conform to certain ethnic types encountered in this region of Europe, which Deniker called *race orientale*, and *race vistulienne*, and the chief characteristics of which are medium stature, round head, fair or flaxen hair, square face, and a retroussé nose.[1] Several portraits of this type are reproduced (Figs. 29-30, 60-63, 68-71).

The *Turanian type* is akin to the last and is encountered very often among the Jews in South Russia and Austrian Galicia, Bukowina, and Roumania. Jews of this type are slightly above the median height, have a short square face with very prominent cheek-bones with some depression immediately below. The nose is short and thick, with a deep indentation at the root; it is straight, never hooked, often retroussé or snub. It has been suggested that this type has its origin in the *Chozars*, a Turanian tribe in South Russia which adopted Judaism during the eighth century of the present era. Whether they are the sole descendants of the Chozars is difficult to say. One thing is certain: this type of humanity is often seen among the non-Jewish population of this region.

The *North European*, or *Teutonic* type, is often found among the Russian, Polish, German, and English Jews. They have the usual characteristics of North Europeans: they are tall, or above the medium height, often dolicho-

---

[1] J. Deniker, "Les six races composant la population actuelle de l'Europe," *Journ. Anthropol. Institute*, vol. xxxiv., 1904, pp. 181-206.

cephalic, have blonde hair and blue eyes; the face is narrow and oval in shape, the nose delicate, narrow, long, and straight, rarely aquiline, and the lips of medium size.

Fig. 56.—POLISH JEW.   Fig. 57.—GALICIAN JEW.

Fig. 58.   Fig. 59.
Figs. 58, 59.—RUSSIAN JEWESS, MONGOLOID TYPE.

While some authors attribute this type among Jews to ancient intermixture with the Amorites, who are said to have been Teutons, others are equally certain that it is due to more recent intermixture with Europeans. It is, however, important to mention in this connection that

Fig. 60.   Fig. 61.
Figs. 60, 61.—POLISH JEW, SLAVONIC-MONGOLOID TYPE.
[*Photo lent by Elkind.*]

Fig. 62.   Fig. 63.
Figs. 62, 63 —GALICIAN JEW, RUTHENIAN TYPE.

blonde Jews are not often tall and dolichocephalic ; on the contrary, most of them are, on the average, of medium height and brachycephalic, conforming to the *race orientale* of Deniker. This would tend to indicate that the blonde-

Fig. 64.

Fig. 65.

Figs. 64, 65.—POLISH JEW, MONGOLOID TYPE.

[*Photo lent by Elkind.*]

Fig. 66.

Fig. 67.

Figs. 66, 67.—GALICIAN JEWS, NEGROID TYPES.

ness was acquired in Europe while living among these races (Figs. 72-73).

THE JEWS.

The most curious is the *Mongoloid type* of Jews, often seen in Russia, Poland, and Germany, especially among women and children. The portraits reproduced here are fair illustrations of this type as met with among Jews (Figs. 54-55, 58-59, 60-61, 64-65). Their chief characteristics are long, smooth, black hair, which is very thick. It grows very long on the head, but only sparingly on the body and face. In fact the Mongolian beard is often seen among Jews. The most distinguishing trait, however, is the Mongolian eye, which is placed obliquely, or slanting, so that its external angle is higher than the inner angle, and the aperture is much narrower than in ordinary eyes. Instead of being almond shaped, it has rather the appearance of a triangle. In general the face of these people is square or lozenge-shaped, and the nose small, short, slightly depressed at its upper half, while broad at its lower half. Many Jewesses of this type are easily taken for Japanese, and in Russia for Tartars.

It is difficult to estimate the proportion of frequency of Mongoloid traits among the Jews of Europe. According to Weissenberg it is quite frequent. He observed among 100 adult male Jews, 23 had more or less strongly protruding cheek-bones, and 13 had slanty eyes. But the epicanthus, which is probably the most distinguishing sign of Mongolian eyes, has not been observed by him in adult male Jews. Among children it is, however, very frequent.[1] This type is very often seen among the immigrant Jews in New York City, especially among women and children. As to its frequency, the present author can state that in East Side Schools in nearly every class at least one pupil, usually more than one, is to be seen with Mongolian features.

Those who believe that the ancient Hittites were Mongolians are inclined to believe also that the Mongoloid Jews of to-day are cases of atavism, reverting to their ancestors who intermarried with the Hittites.[2] But con-

---

[1] S. Weissenberg, *Die südrussischen Juden*, pp. 119-120, 1895.
[2] See M. Alsberg, "Rassenmischung im Judenthum," *Sammlung gemeinverst. wissensch. Vortrage*, New Series, Serie v., Heft 116, pp. 1-40, Hamburg, 1891; Sayce, *The Races of the Old Testament*, chap. vii.; Wright, *The Empire of the Hittites*, and others are inclined to regard the Hittites as Mongolians, but the proofs they bring forward are not convincing. See also G. Sergi, *The Mediterranean Race*, pp. 144-149, London, 1901.

sidering the large number of Russians who have Mongolian blood in their veins, one is inclined to attribute this type to the same source as that which gave origin to the

Fig. 68.

Fig. 69.

Figs. 68, 69.—SOUTH RUSSIAN JEW, SLAVONIC TYPE.

Fig. 70.

Fig. 71.

Figs. 70, 71.—JEW, NATIVE OF WARSAW, POLISH TYPE.
[*Photo lent by Elkind.*]

Slavonic type among the Jews,—to intermixture with their Slavonic neighbours.

The *Negroid type* among Jews is yet to be mentioned. One occasionally meets with a Jew whose skin is very dark, the hair black and woolly, the head long with a prominent occiput. The face is prognathous, the two jaws are projecting in the form of a muzzle. The lips are large, thick, and upturned, and the nose flat, broad, and the wings upturned so that the nostrils can be seen in profile. This negroid type can be singled out in any large assembly of Jews. They are often mistaken for mulattoes, and the author knows of one who had considerable difficulty to get along in one of the southern states of America. As with all the other types of Jews, some Biblical scholars are inclined to attribute the origin of the negroid Jews to intermarriage with the Cushites of Biblical times. It is indeed remarkable that this type is met with among Jews who have not come in contact with negroes for centuries, as for instance the Jews of Eastern Europe. Among the Jews in North Africa, Egypt, etc., there are many who look like mulattoes (see Fig. 106), but here the native population, like the Berbers, Arabs, etc., have a considerable negroid infusion, and the Jews have probably derived it from the same source. Among the European Jews no such explanation is tenable, unless it be attributed to immigration from Southern Europe and North Africa. In fact, many Jews driven from Spain and Portugal, and scattered among the European Jews, may have had some negroid elements which they obtained by intermarriage with the Moors, who are known to have a considerable infusion of negro blood.

These are the main types of Jews in Europe. In addition, one can observe local types in various parts of the continent, which are interesting, inasmuch as they resemble more or less closely the types of mankind among which they live. Every country has its special variety of Jews, which differ not only intellectually and socially but also physically, as every one who has travelled and carefully observed the Jews has seen. Outside of Europe, in Asia and Africa, entirely different types may be met.

CHAPTER VI.

TYPES OF JEWS IN VARIOUS COUNTRIES.

Jewish types in Palestine—The Samaritans—Yemenite Jews—Jews of Bokhara—The Persian Jews—The Jews in the Caucasus—The Daghestan Mountain Jews—The white and the black Jews in India—Chinese Jews—The Various types of Jews in North Africa—Berber Jews—Jewish cave-dwellers in Tripolis—Falashas in Abyssinia—Other Negro Jews—In Jamaica and Surinam—The Karaites—Crypto-Jews—The distinction between Jews by race and Jews by religion—The Dönmeh—The Chuetas—The Annussim.

IN Palestine and Asia Minor there are several types of Jews. There are the Ashkenazim, consisting of immigrants from Europe, who came to die in the holy land and to be buried in the sacred soil of Jerusalem. They do not differ from the Eastern European Jews who have just been described. There are also the Sephardim, or the Spanish Jews, who came thither at the end of the fifteenth century. They also do not materially differ from the Sephardim who have already been spoken of. In the interior towns and villages of Palestine there are also communities of Jews who have been there since the destruction of the second Temple. Weissenberg found them in El-Buke'a, Safed, and Schefa'amr as well as in some parts of Galilee, and is convinced that among them many a *Judæus primigenius* is found. They are mostly agriculturists, and in language, dress, habits, and customs are not easily distinguished from the Fellaheen around them. Their physical type is different from that of the European Jews. They are dolichocephalic, of dark complexion, and above the medium height. Whether they are the pure unadulterated descendants of the ancient Hebrews is problematical, but they are of the same anthropological type as the Mohammedan population of that district, who, according to Weissenberg, are probably direct descendants of the Canaanites.¹ Each of these three groups of Jews in Asia Minor and Palestine avoids associating closely with the others. Each has its own synagogues, cemeteries, etc.

The most interesting type of Jews is that of the Samaritans, the sect which was once quite numerous, but has so dwindled that in 1901 Huxley found only 152 of them in Nâblus, and of these there were only 55 females to 97 males. They are despised and repudiated by the Jews, who do not permit them to marry with their daughters, so that there is hardly any prospect of the Samaritans

Fig. 72.   Fig. 73.

Figs. 72, 73.—Jews, Teutonic Type, United States.

maintaining themselves much longer as a distinct group. The reports as to their physical type differ widely according to the personal equation of the observer, and serve as excellent illustration of the caution needed in accepting the description of various authors as to "Jewish" features. Thus Wackernagel states that the family of the high priest at Nâblus is derived from the tribe of Levi, while the rest of the Samaritans are ascribed to the tribes of Ephraim

¹ Weissenberg, "Die autochtone Bevölkerung Palestinas," Zeitschr. Demographie u. statist. d. Juden, pp. 120-139, 1909; "Peki' in und seine Juden," Globus, vol. xcvi., No. 3, 1909.

and Menasse. "Only the first house is, however, of the Jewish physical type, while the facial features of the others

Fig. 74.—Polish Jew in Jerusalem.

unmistakably show a non-Semitic origin." On the other hand, Professor von Orelli says that the high priest "has noble facial features, but not of the Jewish type."[1] Leroy Beaulieu says of them that he "must confess that I found nothing peculiarly characteristic in the faces of these Samaritans... They appear to me taller, sturdier, of more robust health, than the neighbouring orthodox Jews. From a physical point of view these Samaritans... are indisputably superior to their hostile brothers in Israel; perhaps for the reason that, having been spared the bitter exile of the latter, they have had to endure less suffering and degradation."[2] Huxley, who studied this sect from the anthropological point of view,[3] finds that "the general type of physiognomy of the Samaritans is distinctly Jewish, the nose markedly so... They have preserved the ancient type in its purity, and they are to-day the sole, though degenerate, representatives of the ancient Hebrews." But his photographs do not bear out this contention. Their type of physiognomy can easily be taken for nomadic Arabs. Most of them appear prognathous, a trait, while not unknown, uncommon among European Jews. The measurements taken by Huxley also show that they diverge widely from the physical type of the Jews in Europe, and that they approach the type met with among their Syrian neighbours. They are very tall, averaging 173 cm. in height; in fact they are the tallest people in Syria. They are dolichocephalic, with an average cephalic index of 78.1, corresponding to the type of the Bedouin nomads of that neighbourhood. The predominant complexion is brunette, but many have blonde and red hair and grey and blue eyes (see Figs. 75, 76, 141).

In Yemen, South-Western Arabia, there are about 40,000 Jews who, according to Burchard, are racially Arabs who have adopted Judaism. Weissenberg's recent measurements confirm this view. He describes them as of short stature, of dark complexion, with jet black hair and eyes. Among 92 men and women he did not meet with one who had fair hair or eyes (Figs. 78, 79, 139). They are dolichocephalic (index 74.3), and among two-thirds the index

---

[1] See W. Wackernagel in *Daheim*, p. 440, 1871; Orelli, *Durch's Heilige Land*, Basel, 1879. Quoted from Andree, *loc. cit.*, pp. 214-215.
[2] A. Leroy-Beaulieu, *Israel Among the Nations*, New York, 1896, p. 115.
[3] "Anthropology of the Samaritans," in *Jewish Encyclopædia*, vol. x. pp. 674-676.

was less than 75; the prominent occiput accentuates their dolichocephaly. The nose is mostly straight, but few had

Fig. 75. —SAMARITAN.

[*Photo, Weissenberg.*]

the so-called "Semitic" hook. Weissenberg is of the opinion that they diverge widely from the European Jews and racially have more affinity with their Arab neighbours than with the Jews of other countries. It appears that their history is in agreement with the opinion that they have been converted to Judaism some two thousand years ago.[1]

The Jews of *Bokhara* also differ from their European co-religionists. All travellers agree that they are fine specimens of humanity, particularly the women are said to be charming. They speak a Persian dialect, which

Fig. 76.—SAMARITANS, NÂBLUS.
[*Photo, Weissenberg.*]

would indicate that they have come thither from Persia. They, however, consider themselves descendants of the Ten Tribes. But as they are Talmudic Jews, E. N. Adler suggests that they are probably descended from the Babylonian Jews who migrated eastward after the conquest of Jerusalem by the Romans[2] (Figs. 4, 17, 80).

[1] See S. Weissenberg, "Die jemenitische Juden," *Zeitschr. f. Ethnologie*, pp. 309-327, 1909; H. Burchard, "Die Juden in Jemen," *Ost und West*, pp. 337-341, 1902; Maltzan, *Reise nach Südarabien*; Brunswick, 1872.
[2] *Jewish Encyclopædia*, vol. iii. p. 295.

TYPES OF JEWS IN VARIOUS COUNTRIES. 127

The Jews in *Persia* have been in that country since the earliest times. Many writers state that they have main-

Fig. 77.—SYRIAN JEWESS.

tained the Jewish type very tenaciously, and that a Jew can easily be distinguished from a Mohammedan. That they cannot be easily distinguished, however, there can-

128   THE JEWS.

not be any doubt, because they are compelled to wear certain kinds of dress so as to be easily recognized, and they are not permitted to wear the *Kolah* or Persian head

Fig. 78.—YEMENITE JEWS.
[*Photo, Weissenberg.*]

dress.[1] From Persian Jews seen by the present author, it appears that they differ physically very little from the rest of the population of Persia, and are not at all of the

Fig. 79.—YEMENITE JEWS.
[*Photo, Weissenberg.*]

type which we are wont to call "Jewish" The photograph on page 129, taken in New York, shows a group of

[1] Lord Curzon's *Persia and the Persian Question*, vol. ii. pp. 510-511; London, 1892.

TYPES OF JEWS IN VARIOUS COUNTRIES. 129

Fig 80.—JEWESS FROM BOKHARA.   Fig. 81.—SYRIAN JEWESS.

twelve Jews, all natives of Persia, who emigrated to the United States. It cannot be said that they all look like Jews.

Fig. 82.—PERSIAN JEWISH IMMIGRANTS IN NEW YORK.

The Jews of the Caucasus are very interesting. Historically it has been proven that they have been there for

Fig. 83. Fig. 84.

Fig. 85. Fig. 86.
Figs. 83-86.—Jews in Kutais, Georgia, Caucasus.
[*Photo lent by Weissenberg.*]

more than two thousand years. They claim that they are the descendants of those ubiquitous Ten Lost Tribes, and many missionaries are inclined to believe them. The most curious, both from an anthropological and ethnological standpoint, are the mountain Jews of Daghestan. They have diverged completely from the ethnic type of the Jews in every other country. According to the measurements obtained recently by Kurdoff, they are tall, averaging 166.0 cm. in height, and 57 per cent. of them were above the average height. Very few blondes are met with among them, 87 per cent. have both dark hair and eyes. Their head-form is hyperbrachycephalic, the average cephalic index being 86.35, and not one dolichocephalic individual was found among 160 measured by Kurdoff. Their face is broad, the forehead straight, the aperture of the eye horizontal; the cheek-bone somewhat protruding, the nose straight and of medium size; only thirty per cent. have "Semitic" noses. The mouth is broad, the lips thick, and the ears large. That author concludes that the Daghestan mountain Jews are physically far removed from all other Jews, and have nothing in common with them. They are a product of mixture of the mountain tribes of Daghestan on the one hand, and some other races, especially the Kirghis Mongolians, on the other.[1] Their language, dress, and manners are the same as those of the other mountaineers among whom they live. All who have observed these Jews agree that they are of a totally different type from the one generally known as "Jewish." It is impossible to distinguish them from the Tats, Lesghians, and Circassians, among whom they live, says one who has studied the races of the Caucasus,[2] and most other ethnologists agree with this view (Figs. 3, 87-88, 138).

In India several types of Jews are encountered. First, there are the recently arrived Jews, who do not differ at all from the types of Jews in the countries whence they came from. Then there are the native Jews, whose first settlement in India dates back to antiquity. Their parents have come thither from Persia, Yemen, and Southern Arabia, and some from Europe during mediæval times. Those of Cochin, on the Malabar coast, appear to repre-

---

[1] K. Kurdoff, "Gorskie Yevrei Dagestana," *Russian Anthropological Journal*, 1905, Nos. 3-4, pp. 57-87.
[2] C. Hahn, *Aus dem Kaukasus*, pp. 161, 232; Leipzig, 1892.

sent the earliest settlers, and the original colony is alleged to have come to the Malabar coast from Jerusalem, after the destruction of the second temple. In the presidency of Bombay are found the "Beni-Israel," another group of native Jews. Both groups are divided into two classes, the *white* and the *black* Jews. The white Jews keep aloof and do not associate with their black co-religionists, who are said to be descendants of slaves owned by them. It is also stated that slaves in times bygone used to have to undergo ablutions, and the males circumcision, before being admitted into the fold of Israel.

Fig. 87.   Fig. 88.
Figs. 87, 88.—DAGHESTAN MOUNTAIN JEW.
[*Photo lent by Weissenberg.*]

The physical type of these two classes of Jews has been described by Schmidt,[1] who found that the white Jews do not materially differ in physical type from European Jews. Although they have lived for centuries in the tropics, they appear to have remained unaffected by the external environment. It must, however, be mentioned that their number has been often augmented by new arrivals from Europe, thus renewing their blood to some extent. The colour of their skin differs in different

[1] Emil Schmidt, *Reise nach Südindien*; Leipzig, 1894. *Idem.*, "Die Anthropologie Indiens," *Globus*, vol. lxi., pp. 17-20, 1892.

TYPES OF JEWS IN VARIOUS COUNTRIES. 133

individuals, from the white of the North European to dark, like that of the South Europeans; in other words, their complexion is that of the European Jews. Some are of a strikingly fair complexion, so that in contrast with the dark complexion of the natives of Southern India, their whiteness is accentuated, appearing somewhat in the nature of a sickly pallor. The hair and beard is mostly black, but blonde hair, with grey and blue eyes, is also met with among them. The beard and hair are of abundant growth, somewhat curly or wavy. Schmidt stated that the specific Jewish cast of countenance is

Fig. 89.   Fig. 90.
Figs. 89, 90.—CIRCASSIAN JEWS, CAUCASUS.
[*Photo lent by Weissenberg.*]

very much accentuated among the white Jews. He distinguished two types among them, corresponding to our Ashkenazim and Sephardim, which he describes in detail.

The black Jews are of a totally different type. Schmidt observed that the colour of their skin is of various shadings, ranging from fair, like that of the European Jews, to dark, like that of the Dravidians, among whom they live. Occasionally one meets among them persons with a white colour of the skin which is hardly a shade darker than that of the Southern European. Such persons also have a Jewish physiognomy, which is so specific that one would be inclined to believe that they are of mixed Jewish blood, were they not so cruelly maltreated by their white co-religionists and treated as "black" Jews. On the other hand, most of the black Jews are hardly to be distinguished from the native Hindus living on the Malabar coast. In the majority of cases it can be easily discerned that they are of a mixed origin; traits of both types are evident among these black Jews. They are kept at a respectable distance, and not even permitted to enter the synagogues of the whites, nor do they bury their dead in

Fig. 91.   Fig. 92.

Figs. 91, 92.—BLACK JEWS OF INDIA (Natives of Jhelin, Punjab District).

the same cemetery. The Beni-Israel dress like the natives, though formerly they used to wear turbans, which they have now largely abandoned for the Turkish fez. Their women wear nose rings and anklets, and dress like the Hindu women. The two black Jews reproduced here (Figs. 91-92) were photographed in New York.

The most curious are the *Chinese Jews*, who, as can be seen from the photographs on p. 137, do not look like Jews at all, but can easily pass as Chinamen. It has been known for many years that there are native Jews in China, from the reports of Jesuit missionaries who visited them during the seventeenth century. Recently Jews in

TYPES OF JEWS IN VARIOUS COUNTRIES. 135

Shanghai have made a more or less successful effort to study and also to "rescue" the remnant of Israel which

Fig. 93.—WHITE JEW, COCHIN, EAST INDIA.
[*Photo E. Schmidt.*]

Fig. 94.—BLACK JEW, COCHIN, MALABAR.
[*Photo E. Schmidt.*]

Fig. 95.—JEW, SAMARKAND.
[*Photo, Anthrop. Mus., Moscow.*]

Fig. 96.—TURKESTAN JEWESS.

was left in K'ai-Fung-Foo. Berthold Laufer, who studied their history, is of the opinion that the Chinese Jews emigrated from Persia and Central Asia during the reign of the Han dynasty, or the second century of our era. He believes that the remnants of the Jews in K'ai-Fung-Foo represent many other colonies of Jews who lived in various parts of China, but who in the course of time were absorbed by the indigenous population and left no trace behind.[1] It is interesting in this connection again to point out how unreliable some of the superficial observations of travellers are when an attempt is made by the untrained ethnologist to determine the type of a people. While most of the photographs taken of Chinese Jews show conclusively that they are pure Mongolians, some writers have spoken of "Jewish" physiognomies as met with among them. Andree says that one of the two Chinese Jews who came in 1851 from K'ai-Fung-Foo to Shanghai had a real Jewish cast of countenance. Excepting the fact that they were circumcised and retained their Jewish religion, they were Chinese in everything; their language, dress, habits, and customs were those of real Chinamen. About the Jews in Tchin-Kiang, on the Yang-tse-Kiang, it has recently been said that their physiognomy and bent noses remind one of the Jews on the ancient Egyptian monuments. "They have a somewhat yellowish skin, which is similar to that of the Chinamen, but otherwise their faces are real Jewish," says the *Overland China Mail* (Hong-Kong, September 13th, 1873). Andree also quotes Dr. Martin to the effect that he saw a young man in K'ai-Fung-Foo who pretended to be a Jew, and "whose face confirmed it." All this Andree holds as good proof of the Semitic origin of the Chinese Jews.[2] But the recent photographs of Chinese Jews by no means show any "Jewish" facial features, and it all goes to show how easily persons who look for Jews can find the Jewish cast of countenance among any race or people in the world.

In Africa there are other types of Jews found in various

---

[1] B. Laufer, "Zur Geschichte der Chinesischen Juden," *Globus*, vol. lxxxvii., pp. 245-247; 1905. He points out that there is at present in Hong-Kong and Shanghai a considerable colony of so-called Oriental Jews speaking Arabic, who came thither directly or indirectly from India. This confirms the belief that the process of immigration, which dates back to the ninth century, has continued to date.

[2] R. Andree, *Zur Volkskunde der Juden*, pp. 247-248; Leipzig, 1881.

TYPES OF JEWS IN VARIOUS COUNTRIES. 137

Fig. 97.   Fig. 98.
Figs. 97, 98.—CHINESE JEWS.

Fig. 99.—FAMILY OF CHINESE JEWS IN K'AI-FUNG-FOO.

138 THE JEWS.

parts of the continent. Here, instead of being physically Asiatic, as is the case with the jews of Asia Minor,

Fig. 100.—Tunisian Jew.

Central Asia, China, etc., the Jews are of distinctly African appearance. Their complexion varies from white in North Africa to black in Abyssinia. In North Africa there are

TYPES OF JEWS IN VARIOUS COUNTRIES. 139

several types of Jews in Morocco, Algeria, Tunis, and Tripoli. There are seen there: First, the Sephardim,

Fig. 101.—FAT JEWESS IN TUNIS IN NATIVE COSTUME.

descendants of the Jews expelled from Spain and Portugal at the end of the fifteenth century. They do not materially differ from the same class of Jews living in Europe and Asia Minor, already described. Then there are the indigenous Jews, who differ in physical type, dress, habits, and customs, according to the region they live in. In the cities of Algiers, Tunis, Oran, Constantine, Biskra, etc., the native Jews are quite interesting from an ethnological standpoint. They dress almost exactly like the indigenous Moors, excepting that the colour of the clothing is somewhat different, and the women do not wear veils. In general the Algerian and Tunisian Jewesses are pleasing;

Fig. 102.—Tunisian Jewess.

many can even be called beautiful. Their big black eyes are full of expression, their long black hair and vivacious features give them a charming appearance. But their size is appalling; most of them are rather over than under two hundred pounds, and they have absolutely no shape. But this is in accordance with the Oriental notion of feminine beauty. A young lady who is not fat cannot find a husband.

From anthropological investigations of these Jews made by the present author, it was elicited that they are taller than the Jews of Europe, and that only five per cent. have fair hair, as against nearly thirty per cent. among the Jews in Europe. They are dolichocephalic, especially the

Fig. 103.—FAT JEWESS, SFAX, TUNISIA.

Tunisian Jews, whose cephalic index is 77.56, thus corresponding to the type of head among the Mohammedans

142   THE JEWS.

Fig. 104.—JEWESS IN CONSTANTINE.

of that region of Africa.[1] The author was unable to distinguish a Jew from a Mohammedan while passing

[1] M. Fishberg, "North African Jews," *Boas Anniversary Volume*, pp. 55-63, New York, 1906; *Idem*, "Beiträge zur Anthropologie der nordafrikanischen Juden," *Zeitschrift fur Demographie und Statistik der Juden*, No. II, 1905.

TYPES OF JEWS IN VARIOUS COUNTRIES. 143

along the streets of Algiers, Constantine, and Tunis. It is remarkable that among the non-Jewish natives there

Fig. 105.—TATTOOED JEWESS IN BISKRA, ALGERIA.

are seen many Jews of negroid type, showing a decided negro infusion.

On several of the oases of the Sahara there are many

nomadic tribes of Jewish faith. They are known as "Berber Jews," or "Daggatuns." They are described as a people living in tents, and in their mode of life, language, dress, habits, and customs resemble much the

Fig. 106.—SAHARA JEWESSES.

Tuaregs and other Berber tribes among whom they live. Physically they are hardly to be distinguished from their Mohammedan neighbours, excepting by the colour of their skin, which is said to be somewhat fairer. It is also stated that they do not intermarry with the Tuaregs, although they are subjected to them.¹

The Jews on the oasis M'zab, to the south of Algeria, are a very interesting type, because they have there been isolated for centuries, having hardly had any relations with Jews outside this oasis. There they live among the Berber tribes, dress like their non-Jewish neighbours, and are only to be distinguished from the latter by the ear-locks which they wear and by the fact that the women wear no veils.² Huguet obtained measurements of Jewish, Mzabite, Arab, and negro children on this oasis. All have dark hair and eyes. The cephalic index was 72.9 in the Jews, 75.5 in the Mzabites, 77.2 in the Arabs, and 79.3 in the negroes. These Jews are thus the most dolichocephalic of all that have been measured in any part of the world. The stature and chest measurements of the Jewish children showed that they are below all the other groups. The general type is that of the Mzabites and Arabs, from whom they are hardly to be distinguished.³

The most interesting of the North African Jews are the cave-dwellers of Tripoli and its adjoining districts of Southern Tunisia. From the recent descriptions of Slousch and Hesse-Wartegg we learn that in the rocky fastness of Tripoli and South-Eastern Tunisia, on the slopes of which is the caravan road from the Mediterranean to the Sudan, there are found many Jewish Troglodytes.⁴ They live in caverns, built three or four stories underground. Wartegg describes several of these buried cities and villages—Beni Abbas, Yehud Abbas, Tigrena Dschebel Iffern, Dschebel Nifussia, etc.—in which the homes, the schools, synagogues, shops, etc., are all underground. The dwellings are hardly visible to the traveller unless his attention is drawn to the crater-like openings which serve as entrances. On entering it is found that these caverns

---

¹ See I. Loeb, *Les Daggatouns*, Paris, 1880; R. Mordecai abi Sarur, in *Bull. de La Soc. de Géographie*, Dec., 1895.
² J. Huguet, "Les Juifs du M'zab," *Bulletin et Mémoires de la Soc. d'Anthropologie de Paris*, V. series, Tome III.; Paris, 1902.
³ J. Huguet, in *Revue de l'École d'Anthropologie*; Paris, January, 1906.
⁴ N. Slousch, "Hebræo-Phœniciens et Judéo-Berbers," *Archives Marocaines*, vol. xiv., 1908; Ernest von Hesse-Wartegg, "Die jüdischen Hohlenbewohner der nordafrikanischen Sahara," *Ost und West*, vol. x., pp. 225-236, 1910.

run zig-zag fashion ten metres in diameter and about the same depth until the dwelling rooms are reached. In each cave is found a family consisting of father, mother, sons and daughters with their spouses, children and grandchildren. Each pair has its den, which is practically devoid of any furniture. The donkeys, fowls, dogs, and other domestic animals are also sheltered there. Wartegg observes that apparently this subterranean existence has no deleterious effects on the health of these Jews, because they appear lively, their faces beaming with large bright eyes. He says that in his opinion these troglodytes are not only Jews by religion, but also by descent, especially the women are of a pronounced Jewish type. "I emphasize this," says Wartegg, "because I found among the Riff Berbers in Northern Morocco a large number of Jews whose forefathers were converted to Judaism many centuries ago. They hold on to their religion, although physically they are decidedly of the Berber race, having blonde hair and blue eyes."

In Abyssinia there is a large colony of Jews called *Falashas*, who are of pure African type. They claim to have come thither in the retinue of Menelik, the son of King Solomon and the Queen of Sheba. They are described as a tall, muscular people, with a dark brown skin, like that of the Abyssinians in general. Their hair is black and frizzly, or woolly, as is also the beard, which they never shave, but only cut with scissors. Many of them are black, and have thick lips, which are upturned, and are practically negroes. They speak the same language, live in similar houses, and have most of the habits of life and customs of the non-Jewish Abyssinians, from whom they differ only in religion. It is curious that they not only circumcise their male children, but their female children are also subjected to a similar barbaric operation.[1] Of the latest travellers who studied them was M. Faitlovitch, who was delegated by the Alliance Israélite Universelle of Paris to visit them and to report in detail. From his report we quote the following as of interest:—"The Falashas say that they belong to the Jewish race, and are descendants of our ancestors, Abraham, Isaac, and Jacob. Their African colour, their

---

[1] See Flad, *Kurze Schilderung der abessinischen Juden*; Konthal, 1869.

TYPES OF JEWS IN VARIOUS COUNTRIES. 147

more or less dark skin, appears to contradict this relationship. However, their fine traits, their strong intelligence, which manifests itself in their physiognomy, the obstinate resistance which they displayed during thousands of years to the surrounding population, the persistence of their religious convictions, justify their pretensions. The nobility of their origin is affirmed also by their compatriots, Christian, Mussulman, and Pagan, who respect them greatly for this very reason. The religion which they profess is a pure Mosaism, modified by their religious literature.[1]

Fig. 107.   Fig. 108.
Figs. 107, 108.—FALASHAS.

M. Faitlovitch brought along with him two young Falashas to Paris. Their portraits, which are here reproduced, show that physically they are of the negro type. According to the description given of them, they are dark, but not as black as African negroes. They are said to resemble the dark Hindus of India in complexion. But the large lips, prognathism, and frizzly hair, all point to negro origin.[2] M. de Castro, physician to the Italian

---

[1] "Israélites Falachas," *Bulletin de l'Alliance Israélite Universelle*, 3 serie, No. 30, pp. 96-104; Paris, 1905.

[2] While some writers speak of the "Jewish" cast of countenance as met with among the Falashas, many Jews resented the idea that there are negro Jews. M. Joseph Halvéy, who also brought home a Falasha to Europe about thirty years ago, was accused of fraud. Some members of the Alliance Israélite Universelle maintained that he was a negro whom Halvéy bought in a slave market in the Soudan. See *Revue Sémitique*, January, 1906.

Legation at Addis-Ababa, has made a study of the different races of Abyssinia, and says that the Falashas have all the physical characters of the indigenous population to such a degree that they may be mistaken for them.

The latest description of these Jews is from the pen of H. Nahoum, another representative of the Alliance Israélite. He believes that they were converted to Mosaism by a group of Judaizers who came from Egypt around the second or third century B.C., probably during the epoch of Ptolemy Euergetes, and gives good reasons

Fig 109.—Falashas in Abyssinia.

for this opinion. In former times their number was quite large, but since the wars between the Christians and Mussulmans of the sixteenth century the severe persecutions, as well as forced conversions, have reduced their number, and at present there are from seven to eight thousand of them. Physically Nahoum finds them akin to other Abyssinians, of medium height, slender, with relatively long extremities. The colour of their skin varies according to the altitude, being fairer in the mountainous districts and darker in the plains. Like other Abyssinians, they have frizzly hair. Because of the

TYPES OF JEWS IN VARIOUS COUNTRIES. 149

mixture of race, he was unable to define the physical types of the Falashas.[1]

It is stated that the Falashas are not the only Jews of negro race. Bastian speaks of negro Jews living on the *Loango Coast* in Western Africa. They are called there "Mavambu" or "Judeos." "They are, on the whole, a fair looking race," says Bastian. "They are more serious and restrained than the rest of the negroes. Although in other places they are despised, here they take a dominating position, or at least such as to be respected and partly even feared, because they are rich and have most of the commerce in their hands."[2] The same author claims that though they are of negro race, still he detected Semitic facial features in their physiognomies. Even in Madagascar a traveller has discovered Jews. Sibree mentions that in Ambohipeno, on the east coast of that island, he met natives who called themselves "Zafy Ibrahim," or descendants of Abraham, and who claim to be altogether Jews. "But I could not detect any difference in colour, features, or dialect between them and the other people of the eastern coast," comments the author.[3]

The most curious class of negro "Jews" is said to have existed in Jamaica and Surinam. In Jamaica there was a very large degree of intermarriage of the Spanish and Portuguese Jews with negroes, and to-day there is said to be there a very large coloured population bearing Jewish names, but nearly all of whom have, however, lapsed from Judaism. About one hundred and fifty years ago a new half-breed colony was constituted in the neighbourhood of Surinam, which was the result of intermarriage between Jews and negroes. They developed their own peculiar language, "Djoe-tongo," or "Jew language." Dr. Lotze describes this dialect in detail. The first settlers were partly English, and partly Jews who came from Brazil and Cayenne, and who spoke Portuguese. Both spoke to their slaves their own languages, which

---

[1] Haim Nahoum, "Mission chez les Falachas d'Abyssinie," *Bull. de l'Alliance Israélite Universelle*, 1908, pp. 100-137.

[2] A. Bastian, *Die Deutsche Expedition an der Loango-Küste*, vol. i., p. 43, 277.

[3] Sibree, *The Great African Island*, quoted from Andree, *Volkskunde*, p. 91.

were not well understood by the latter. In this manner two new languages, negro-English and negro-Portuguese, were developed, which in time coalesced, and new terms and expressions common to both were developed. The Jew negroes at first spoke a corrupted Portuguese combined with Hebrew and native words. At the time when Dr. Lotze visited them this language was yet spoken by some negroes who worked on Jewish plantations, but it was being replaced by the negro English dialect.[1] This class of negro "Jews," if visited by some dilettante who cares little for making sure about his facts, might have been described as "the remnants of the Ten Lost Tribes," or as Semitic negroes or what not. It shows how careful we must be with descriptions of Jews found in various parts of the world.

There remains yet to be described another group of Jews, the *Karaites*, who, though they are considered only partly Jews, yet claim that they are the real descendants of the ancient Hebrews. These people are now found mostly in Russia, while small colonies are also found in Galicia, Turkey, and Egypt. They are followers of pure Mosaism, and do not consider the Talmud as authoritative. The founder of this sect was one Anan, who lived at the end of the eighth century. They were at first called *Ananites*, but later adopted the name *Karaites*. In Russia they enjoy all rights in common with all the Russian subjects of the Czar, and do not suffer the disabilities of the Jews, because, not following the Talmud, and claiming to have been in South Russia for two thousand years, their ancestors could not have participated in the crucifixion of Christ, which is not in agreement with the fact that this sect was only established at the end of the eighth century. Some have suggested that most of the Karaites are the descendants of the Chozars, a Turanian tribe in South Russia which adopted Judaism during the eighth century, though the Chozars were Rabbinic Jews, and followed the Talmud as well as the other Jews. But it may be true that many of the Chozars, after the destruction of their kingdom, may have joined the Karaites.

---

[1] For information on this point the author is indebted to Mr. Max J. Kohler, secretary of the American Jewish Historical Society. See also *Ztscht. deu'sch. Morgenl. Ges.*, p. 324, 1857.

TYPES OF JEWS IN VARIOUS COUNTRIES.

Anthropologically it has been ascertained that the modern Karaites are quite a distinct ethnic group, and are more akin to the Tartar tribes of South-eastern Russia than to their Jewish rabbinic neighbours. From the studies of these people made by Ikoff, Weissenberg, and Talko-Hryncewicz,[1] it appears that they are more brachycephalic than the Eastern European Jews. Their cephalic index is about 85 according to measurement of skulls and living Karaites. They are brunettes; only five per cent. of blondes have been found among them by Weissenberg.

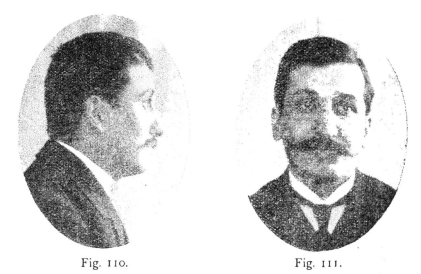

Fig. 110.   Fig. 111.

Figs. 110, 111.—KARAITE, CRIMEA.

[*Photo, Weissenberg.*]

This author also finds that they are a very mixed race, and have a large quantity of Mongolian blood in their veins, which he attributes to intermarriage with the Bashkirs, a Turkoman tribe in South Russia. From the photograph reproduced (Figs. 110, 111) it is seen that they look more like Tartars than like Eastern European Jews, although many Jews coming from Eastern Europe are of

---

[1] C. Ikoff, "Neue Beiträge zur Anthropologie der Juden," *Archiv für Anthropologie*, vol. xv., pp. 369-389; S. Weissenberg, "Die Karaer der Krim," *Globus*, lxxxiv., pp. 139-143, 1903; *idem*, "Karaimi," *Russian Anthropological Journal*, Nos. 1 and 2, pp. 66-75; 1905.

the same type. Weissenberg assures us that many Karaites are of the coarse Jewish type. From those seen by the present author it appears that many of them do look like Russian Jews, but the Sephardi type is not met with among them.

This by no means exhausts the number of types of Jews met with in various parts of the world. A careful study reveals that every civilized country has its own type of children of Israel, who differ in one way or another from all the other Jews. Some writers speak of three classes of Jews. First, *Jews by religion and by race*, and include among these the Ashkenazim, Sephardim, and the Samaritans; second, *Jews by religion, but not by race*, including in this class the Falashas, the Karaites, the Daggatouns, the Black Jews, and Beni-Israel of India, and the Negro Jews of the Loango coast; and third, *Jews by race but not by religion*, which include several groups of so-called "crypto-Jews," such as the *Dönmeh* or *Maiminim* in Saloniki, the *Chuetas*, or *Anussim* of the Balearic Islands, and the *G'did al Islam* of Khorassan, who were forcibly converted to Islam half a century ago. This classification of Jews is by Jacobs, and many others have also followed with similar divisions of the Sons of Abraham in modern times.[1] At present this classification is untenable, because it is impossible to determine exactly which class of Jews represents the true, pure, original "race." If it is said that the Ashkenazim are the true ethnic representatives of the Jewish race, then besides the fact that there are many among them who do not at all conform to a true type, it is also to be considered that all the Sephardim are excluded. The diversity of the anthropological type among the Jews which has just been described excludes a classification of the kind.

Of these "Crypto-Jews," or Jews by race but not by religion, the *Dönmeh* are the most interesting. They are at the present mostly found in Salonika, European Turkey. They are the descendants of Spanish Jewish exiles, who followed the false Messiah, Shabbethai Zebi, who appeared

---

[1] See J. Jacobs, "On the Racial Characteristics of Modern Jews," *Journal Anthropological Institute*, vol. xv., 1886; *idem*, article "Crypto Jews," *Jewish Encyclopedia*, vol. iv., pp. 379-380. Also R. Andree, *Zur Volkskunde der Juden*, Leipzig, 1881.

during the seventeenth century, pretending to have a message to deliver the Jews. He was finally, with some of his followers, converted to Mohammedanism. Those left to-day are outwardly Mohammedans, but secretly observe certain Jewish rites. They are said to keep apart from their Mohammedan neighbours, with whom they do not intermarry, and to have secret synagogues. According to Struck, the Dönmeh, from the ethnographic standpoint, diverge from the people of the Ural-Altaic linguistic stock. They display all the characteristics of an unadulterated Semitic race stock, retaining all the physical and moral peculiarities of the Semites in their complete purity. The men are of medium height, but robust, and have a sharp characteristic cast of countenance. Their forehead is broad, the nose slightly bent, the eyes large, dark, and sparkling. Their hair is mostly curled, only rarely smooth, of a dark tint; the beard somewhat lighter in colour, and grows abundantly. When old and grey, the Dönmeh have an upright and venerable appearance. The women are of about the same type; they are somewhat smaller than the men, but physically well developed, as is true of all Oriental women. The women are somewhat fairer of complexion than the men.[1] It is thus pointed out that the so-called "Semitic" physical type is still retained by these people, although they have for several centuries kept apart from the Jews. Similar descriptions have been given of other "Crypto-Jews" in Spain and Portugal.

These "Crypto-Jews" have often been described by authors as proof that the sons of Jacob can never be anything else but Jews; that when compelled to abjure their faith and for centuries professing officially Christianity or Mohammedanism, their descendants still adhere, under stress, secretly to the religion of their ancestors; in short, that Judaism is purely a matter of race. The inference that they can never be expected to assimilate or merge with the population around them, but are destined to remain indefinitely an alien element of the population of western countries, was but natural under the circumstances. Many Hebrew writers have expressed great pride in the

[1] A. Struck, "Die verborgenjüdische Secte der Donme in Salonik," *Globus*, vol. lxxxi., 1902, pp. 219-224.

natural persistence of Jews and Judaism even under the most adverse conditions; and many anti-Semites of the type of Stöcker, Drumont, Goldwin Smith, and others never fail to emphasize that Jews cannot fuse with "Aryans," even if they wanted to commit race suicide. Of late the Jewish Nationalists have revived this problem, and state that all attempts to assimilate the Jews in Europe and America are bound to prove a failure for this reason, and that for this reason also they must look for repatriation and renationalization in their natural home, Palestine. Herzl stated that assimilation was possible, and instanced the Huguenots in Germany, who became thorough Germans,[1] but few Zionists agree with him on this point. Nordau knows of only one possible way to destroy Judaism —by killing all the Jews. But "should the Jews stoically decide to commit suicide," he says, "this desperate act will prove of no use. They will find that they are insoluble in Aryanism. They will no more be Jews, but they will become Jewish-Christians, and anti-Semitism will treat the Jews in Christian garb in the same manner as it does when they retain their Jewish exterior." The Dönmeh, the Marranos, the Chuetas, etc., are cited as proof for his assertion that "whenever a large number of Jews have simultaneously changed their religion they remained an isolated group, who in the midst of their new co-religionists are as easily and surely distinguishable as the water of the Gulf Stream in the midst of the Atlantic Ocean. At the borders there is a gradual crumbling which slowly wipes away the sharp line of demarcation, but the centre remains unmixed for an indefinite time."[2] It is indeed noteworthy that here as well as in many other points Zionists agree with such enemies of the Jews as Goldwin Smith, Arnold White, Drumont, Stöcker, and their like. But it seems that anthropologists and ethnologists have also considered this an ethnic trait. Andree, speaking of the Dönmeh, the Anusim, and the Marranos, says that they are good proof that with the Jews "race is stronger than religion," and that no mixture of blood takes place even after they convert to Christianity. "Historical

---

[1] *Minutes of Evidence taken before the Royal Commission on Alien Immigration*, 6353.
[2] Max Nordau, *Zionistische Schriften*, p. 193.

evidence proves that it is simply impossible for the Jews to fuse with other races."[1]

Careful study of historical facts does not support these views. The cruel persecutions of the Jews in the Iberian Peninsula during the fourteenth and fifteenth centuries brought about a large number of conversions to Christianity. It has been estimated by various historians that between 1391 and 1492 about 100,000 Jews were thus brought to the Church, and at the time of the final expulsion from Spain these were augmented by about 50,000 more. They were known in those days as *Christãos Novos* in Portugal and *Conversos* in Spain. The bulk were converted forcibly by the well-known methods of the Inquisition, but no mean number changed their faith voluntarily. The latter consisted mostly of the rich and cultured, who, like Jews at all times during periods of prosperity, discarded their faith and tradition, and, as is to be seen to-day in Germany, Austria, France, etc., began to assimilate, many to the extent of joining the Catholic Church. "Whether their conversion was sincere or not," says Lea, "they had broken with the past, and, with the keen intelligence of their race, they could see that a new career was open to them, in which energy and capacity could gratify ambition, unfettered by the limitations surrounding them in Judaism. That they should hate, with an exceeding hatred, those who had proved true to the faith amid tribulation was inevitable. The renegade is apt to be bitterer against those whom he has abandoned than is the opponent by birthright, and in such cases as this consciousness of the contempt felt by the steadfast children of Israel for the weaklings and worldlings who had apostatized from the faith of their fathers gave a keener edge to enmity. From early times the hardest blows endured by Judaism had always been dealt by its apostate children, whose training had taught them the weakest points to assail, and whose necessity of self-justification led them to attack these mercilessly."[2] These New Christians were met with in every walk of life. Even the clergy had a large share of them, while in the Govern-

[1] R. Andree, *Zur Volkskunde der Juden*, p. 56.
[2] Henry Ch. Lea, *A History of the Inquisition in Spain*, New York, 1906, vol. i. p. 113.

ment service they held many of the highest positions. In short, as Lea says, they filled the highest places in the courts, in the universities, in the Church, and in the State. They intermarried with the noblest houses in the land; the clergy at first recommended marriage between converts and Christians as the surest means of obliterating all differences between the Old and the New Christians.

As long as this policy lasted there were no intimations that the New Christians were not on the way of fusing with the rest of the population. But the persecution of those who remained true to Judaism was kept up by the clergy and agitators, as well as by the converts who wanted to prove that they were good Christians, and in their denunciations of the Jews they soon began to attack the New Christians. "The hatred and contempt which, as apostates, they lavished on the faithful sons of Israel reacted on themselves," says Lea. " It was impossible to stimulate popular abhorrence of the Jews without at the same time stimulating the envy and jealousy excited by the ostentation and arrogance of the New Christians. What was the use of humiliating and exterminating the Jew if these upstarts were not only to take his place in grinding the people as tax gatherers, but were to bear rule in court, camp, and church?"[1] Thus extreme tension was generated between the Old and New Christians. Agitators accused the *conversos* of all kinds of crimes, and insisted that they were not sincere Christians, but that they secretly practised Judaism. The New Christians were ostracized just as the Jews were; they were isolated from Christian society, with the results which are the usual concomitants of isolation. These *conversos* were the main cause of the Inquisition and the final expulsion of the Jews from Spain in 1492, according to the opinion of the best historians.[2]

The persistence of habits, customs, and superstitions is

---

[1] Lea, *loc. cit.*, p 121.
[2] Salomon Reinach is quite explicit on this point. He says: "L'Inquisition n'a jamais été dirigée contre les Juifs, qui étaient des infidèles, mais contre les Chrétiens qui professaient des opinons hérétiques; c'est, enfin, que l'Inquisition espagnole elle-même n'a pas persécuté directment les juifs, mais les juifs convertis au catholicisme, auxquels elle reproachait de pratiquer en secret la religion juive, c'est à dire d'être des catholiques apostats." *Cultes, Mythes et Religions*, vol. ii. p. 401 ; Paris, 1906.

well known to ethnologists. Social traits hold on even after a change of religion, language, and even the external environment, including the country, in which a given social group lives. In every population these traits, sometimes called survivals, are met with in abundance. Naturally these *conversos* held on to certain habits and customs which were their cultural heritage for centuries. Lea speaks justly of Rabbinical Judaism, which so entwines itself "with every detail of the believer's daily life and attaches so much importance to the observances which it enjoins, that it was impossible for whole communities thus suddenly Christianized to abandon the rites and usages which, through so many generations, had become a part of existence itself. Earnest converts might have brought up their children as Christians, and their grandchildren might have outgrown the old customs, but the *conversos* could not be earnest converts, and the sacred traditions handed down by the fathers from the days of the Sanhedrin were too precious to be set aside."[1] The Inquisition was very zealous to detect any deflection, and succeeded in promulgating laws against these converts which made their existence more miserable than when they were Jews. The names under which they were known show clearly that they were an ostracized lot. *Marrano* is derived from the New Testament phrase *maran atha* ("our Lord hath come"), and in Spanish denotes "damned," "accursed," "banned," and "hog;" in Portugal they were known as *Chuetas*, because in order to convince the Christians of their sincere allegiance to the Church they ate pork publicly ("Chuya," diminutive "chueta.")[2] That they were even then kept in the Ghetto is known from many historical documents, and the fact that they were also known as *Individuos de la Calle*, "Ghetto People," confirms it. They were held in abhorrence by their Catholic neighbours. In church they were compelled to sit apart, and in the cemetery their bodies were interred in separate sections. There is ample historical evidence that it was not only the

---

[1] Lea, *loc. cit.*, p. 145.
[2] Sofer says that he read in a Spanish novel that the Marranos used to greet each other with the word *Chitton*, caution, and suggests that Chueta might have been derived from this word. *Politisch-anthropologische Revue*, p. 102, 1906.

conversos who abstained from intermarriage, but that the Catholic Church has done its best to discourage and even prohibit such unions. For centuries the Spanish had an actual mania for *Limpieza*, or purity of blood, and prohibited marriage with any one who had the fatal *mancha* or Jewish stain, setting no limit to the number of generations in which the stain is wiped away. Many individuals, moved by zeal or malignity, compiled books from all kinds of sources and circulated them under the name of *Libro verde* or *del Becerro*. No one in the upper or middle classes was so safe that an investigation might not reveal some unfortunate *mésalliance* of a distant ancestor. In fact, only those could feel secure whose obscurity precluded prolonged research into their ancestry.[1] These prohibitions of intermarriage came rather late to keep Jewish blood out of the Spanish. "We hear of marriages with Lunas, Mendozas, Villahermosas and others of the proudest houses. As early as 1449 a petition to Lope de Barrientos, Bishop of Cuenca, by the *conversos* of Toledo, enumerated all the noblest families of Spain as being of Jewish blood, and among others the Henriquez, from whom the future Ferdinand the Catholic descended, through his mother, Juana Henriquez"[2] The Catholic Church, whose greatest dignitaries were of Jewish descent, as was Santa Maria Torquemada, Cardinal of San Sisto; Diego Deza, the second Inquisitor General; Hernando de Talavera, Archbishop of Granada, and many others, was more responsible for the abstinence from intermarriage between the Marranos and Catholics than the so-called Jewish blood which is alleged to be incapable of mixing with that of other "races." Yet, no claim has been made that "Catholic blood" cannot mix with "non-Catholic blood."

This isolation of the *conversos* was hard to bear, and it was difficult to convince the clergy that the conversion was sincere. They were constantly spied upon, and whenever discovered in practicing Judaism brought before the Inquisition and punished in the most atrocious manner. In a law issued for the guidance of the clergy in their efforts to discover backsliding Marranos, thirty-seven signs

---

[1] See Lea, *loc. cit.*, vol. ii., pp. 285-314.
[2] *Ibid.*, vol. i, p. 120.

are given by which a Jew may be recognized. Any Marrano who changed his linen, put on better garments or spread a new table-cloth on Saturday; ate no pork, gave his children Old Testament names; while dying turned his face to the wall, and similar crimes, was to be considered a backslider. In a description of the torture by the Inquisition of a young woman, given by Lea, we read that her entire Judaism consisted in refusing to eat pork because it made her sick. It is easily understood that such signs of Judaism could prove that it is impossible for a Jew to part with his religion.

The persecutions, especially the sequestration of the Marranos, were enough to keep alive among them certain habits and customs indefinitely, and some writers thus see evidences of racial characteristics of the "Semites." Only as late as 1782, about three hundred years after their baptism, a royal decree was issued to the effect that the Chuetas in Palma were permitted to live in any part of the Balearic Island or in any street in the city, and were no more to be called Jews, Hebrews, or Chuetas. Three years later they were declared eligible to the army and navy as well as to public office. The *Jewish Encyclopædia*[1] mentions also that on May 2nd, 1768, the lists containing the names of the New Christians were ordered to be suppressed; a law of May 25th, 1773, decreed that all disabilities based on descent, chiefly directed against the Marranos, should cease. But in various cities in Spain and Portugal, even as late as the nineteenth century, lists were displayed in churches naming the families which were descendants of those *conversos* of the fifteenth century, and warning devout Catholics to abstain from intermarrying with them.[2]

---

[1] Vol. x., p. 140.

[2] Annette M. B. Meakin, *Galicia, the Switzerland of Spain*, p. 268; London, 1909. That the Christians have not ceased to isolate these conversos is shown by a book which appeared in 1857 under the title *La Sinagoga Balear. Historia de los Judios de Majorca*, by Juan de la Puerta Vizcains. It appears that the descendants of the Chuetas were scared because they practically bought up the whole edition for destruction. At a stormy session of the Spanish Parliament in the spring of 1904, the Prime Minister Maura, politically an ardent clerical, was called by one of his opponents "Chueta." Maura is a native of Majorca, where the population is supersaturated with the *mala sangre*. According to a writer in the *Kolnische Zeitung*, the descendants of those converts, notwithstanding the

Under such circumstances it is problematical whether we are justified in attributing the alleged avoidance of intermarriage of the *conversos* with Christians to racial causes. Everything appears to point to a willingness on the part of the New Christians to mix with those around them, but that the Church prevented fusion by the isolation it imposed on these unfortunate people. It was only under such severe sequestration that habits and customs could survive for generations. Moreover, considering that more than 150,000 were baptized during the fifteenth century in Spain, and if they really held on tenaciously to their faith and traditions there should at present be an enormous number of Crypto-Jews in that country. As a matter of fact the evidence that there are any is practically nil. Borrow, in his fanciful book *The Bible in Spain,* mentions that he met one who told him that there were other secret Jews. Some other writers speak of having met some Crypto-Jews in Spain and Portugal, but their descriptions are rather inconclusive. On the other hand, Kayserling,[1] who studied the problem more thoroughly than any other writer, comes to the conclusion that time has obliterated all differences between the "new" and the "old" Christians in that region. We met a Sephardi in Bucharest, a scholar of eminence, whose ancestors were Marranos, who fled to European Turkey during the sixteenth century. He showed letters from people in Spain who were bearing the same name and were derived from the same family as our friend. They write that there are no Crypto-Jews in Spain at present, excepting many who know that their forbears were Marranos.

The other Crypto-Jews, known as Dönmeh, live in

fact that they are at present devout Catholics, are still called Chuetas, are even now not admitted as members of religious and fraternal orders, and when one is ordained for the priesthood he is not allowed to preach in a church. (See Leo Sofer, "Chuettas, Maiminen und Falascha," *Politisch-Anthropologische Revue*, pp. 100-105; 1906.) T. B. Soler (*Un Milagro y una Mentira*, Valencia, 1858) writes in 1858 that the New Christians were even then persecuted, compelled to live in the *calle*, and to marry among themselves, for no one would contract alliance with them, nor would the clergy grant licences for mixed marriages. Even as late as 1877 Padre Taronji (*Estado religioso y social de le Isla de Mallorca*, Palma, 1877) was disqualified from the priesthood because of his Chueta origin.

[1] *Geschichte der Juden in Spanien und Portugal*, vol. ii. p. 335.

European Turkey, and everything known about them tends to show that they constitute a Jewish sect. That their abstinence from intermarriage with the Turks is by no means due to ethnic causes is attested by the fact that they have not intermarried with Jews up till recent times, and also because they consisted of three groups, each of which abstained from marrying into the two other groups.[1] Of course no one will claim that these groups do not intermarry because of racial differences. M. J. Cohen described them as a dwindling sect, and of late they have been compelled to seek wives among the Jews, because a Turk will under no circumstance permit his son or daughter to marry a Dönmeh. It may be curious to note what will become of this Jewish sect under the new regime in Turkey, with its religious liberty.

It is evident that the so-called Crypto-Jews are the product of social conditions having no ethnic basis. With a change in social conditions, especially as soon as they are no more persecuted by the majority around them, they cease to be peculiar and are lost in the multitude.

[1] For details see W. M. Leake, *Travels in Northern Greece*, vol. iii., London, 1835, who appears to have been the first to describe these peculiar people. Also J. T. Bendt, "Die Donmes oder Mamin in Salonichi," *Ausland*, pp. 186-190, 206-209, 1888; E. N. Adler, *Jews in Many Lands*, pp. 146-147, London, 1905; Leo Sofer, *loc. cit.*

CHAPTER VII.

ORIGIN OF THE VARIOUS TYPES OF JEWS.

Dress and deportment as contributary causes of the distinctive type of the Jews—The attitude of the body—The psychic type of the Jew—The Ghetto face—The Jewish eye—The ubiquitous Ten Lost Tribes of Israel—Jewish type as met with among many races and peoples in various parts of the world—Isolation and selection as factors in the production of the Jewish type.

WHILE it is true, as has been shown in the preceding chapter, that there is no single type of Jew, but that there are many types, still it must be acknowledged that, in certain countries, the Jews are easily distinguished from the non-Jewish population. This is especially true of Eastern Europe, Russia, Austria, Roumania, etc., and also of certain Oriental countries, like Turkey, Palestine, Persia, the Barbary states, etc. It is remarkable that in some of these countries one can point out a Jew among a crowd of non-Jews, even if the Jew be blonde, although the vast majority of Jews are brunettes. It is this so-called "Jewish type" which makes them an ethnic unit, apart from all other peoples. It is also this "Jewish type" which the Jews point at with pride, and the anti-Semites are not slow to exploit as something peculiar and to beware of. What is that "Jewish type," that Jewish physiognomy, which characterizes the Jew?

It is the opinion of the present author that it is less than skin deep. Primarily it depends on the dress and deportment of the Jews in countries where they live in strict isolation from their Christian or Moslem neighbours. A striking example is furnished by the side-locks of hair which most oriental and semi-oriental Jews allow to grow on their temples. In Austrian Galicia one of Jewish faith may be of any ethnic type; he may be a Slavonian pure and simple, as many of them are, still as long as he wears side-locks any one can distinguish him as a follower of Judaism, because nobody of any other creed wears side-locks. The same is true of the Jews in Bokhara, Tripolis, Palestine, and even India. Jewesses are in the same manner distinguished by their bewigged heads, which no other people of Eastern Europe has, or by the fact that they wear no veils in Mohammedan countries, while all Moslem women do wear them; or the caftan and the slippers of the Polish Jews will at once mark one, because the Christian population of that country are differently dressed. A man in Galicia dressed in a long caftan or frock-coat, an undercap (skull-cap), a hat pushed to the back of the head, and two spiral locks hanging down in front of his ears, can only be a Jew, no matter what his face looks like. If the same individual should one day shave off his beard, cut his ear-locks, and don the dress of his Christian neighbours, the change might be magical. All the so-called "Jewishness" might disappear, and a Slavonian pure and simple might be evident to any one who knows the physical type of the Eastern European races. This can best be seen among the Jewish immigrants to the United States. Here they discard all their Jewish peculiar garb, and as a result the "Jewishness" disappears together with the dress in a large proportion of cases. During his last journey in Eastern Europe the present author could point out nearly every Jew in the smaller towns in Poland, Russia, and Roumania, because of their peculiar dress and deportment. A similar attempt made in New York City among Jewish immigrants from those countries meets with failure in many cases. It is often difficult to say whether some female domestic servant in New York City, seen in the home of a Jew, is a Jewess or a Slavonian. At least the writer has often been in doubt whether the girl who met him at the doors of Jewish houses was a Jewess, a Ruthenian, or a Pole. To the Americans all immigrants look "foreign," but an analysis shows that many who profess Judaism are not at all of the traditional Jewish type, but look like Russians, Poles, Roumanians, or other Eastern Europeans.

Next to dress and deportment the Jew in Eastern Europe has often a peculiar attitude of the body which is distinctly characteristic. The inferior hygienic, economic, and social conditions under which he was compelled to live in the Ghettoes have left their mark on his body; he is old prematurely, stunted, decrepit; he withers at an early age. He is emaciated, his muscles are flabby, and he is unable to hold his spinal column erect. That this peculiar attitude of the body has a great influence on the type of the Jew can be seen from the drawing by Ismael Gentz, reproduced on this page (Fig. 112), which shows graphically that it is not always the face that betrays the religious belief of the man in the case of the Eastern European. This decrepit condition of the body is one of the most important stigmata of the Jew's long confinement in the Ghetto. It must, however, be emphasized that this is not an ethnic trait of the Jew; it does not depend on any peculiarities of an anatomical or physiological nature. As an acquired character, due to adverse social and economic conditions, it is not transmitted by heredity. In fact the Jew displays a remarkable capacity to rid himself of this cramped attitude of the body when given a fair chance to recuperate. In Europe it can be seen that the Jew's spine becomes more erect, his muscles more developed, and his gait more elastic, as one proceeds from east to west, and when

Fig. 112.—The Ghetto Bend.
[*Drawing by Ismael Gentz.*]

France, Belgium, and especially England, is reached, it is seen that among the native Jews this trait has disappeared entirely. The same is the case with the native Jews of the United States. On the East Side of New York City it can be seen that a fair proportion of the older immigrant Jews are stunted and more or less hunched. But their children, who have had the benefit of Western education, walk erect and cannot be distinguished by the attitude of their bodies. It is the more remarkable when we consider that this metamorphosis is apparent in the first generation of American Jews. The same can be seen in London, where many Jewish immigrants from Eastern Europe have settled.

While dress and deportment, and also the attitude of the body, determine the type of the Jew in many cases, yet Jews are often met with who do not have these peculiarities, and can still be pointed out as children of Israel. Indeed there are many individuals of Jewish faith who physically do not have any of the traits which we are wont to associate with the Jewish type; persons who are of tall stature and are of excellent musculature have blonde hair and blue eyes, straight or even snub noses, delicate lips, and even clean shaven, still they can be pointed out as Jews. In contrast with these individuals one often meets persons who are short of stature and of poor physique; brunettes have long, hooked noses, thick lips, and other "Jewish" traits, yet every one will say, without being able to give any special reason for the assertion, that these persons are not Jews. The causes which mark the one class as Jews and the other as Gentiles are of immense interest to study. In these cases a careful study reveals that it is not the body which marks the Jew; it is his soul. In other words, the type is not anthropological or physical; it is social or psychic. It is not the complexion, the nose, the lips, the head which is characteristic; it is his soul which betrays his faith. Centuries of confinement in the Ghetto, social ostracism, ceaseless suffering under the ban of abuse and persecution have been instrumental in producing a characteristic psychic type which manifests itself in his cast of countenance which is considered as peculiarly "Jewish." As a matter of fact, the Jews are not alone in having this peculiar expression.

Physiognomies akin to that of the Ghetto face, as it may be called, are encountered among many other races and peoples who, as religious minorities, have been subjected to cruel treatment for many generations. The Armenians, whose lot has not been better than that of the Jews, are hardly to be distinguished from Jews by their facial features. The native Christians of Egypt, called the Kopts, and also the Basques in France and Spain, are said to "look like Jews." Many scientists have spoken of a special psychology of religious minorities, but none have studied the effects of religious isolation, which often involves also social isolation, on the facial features. But it is well known that the mental state has a great influence on the features of an individual. Emerson, in his *English Traits,* says—"Every religious sect has its physiognomy. The Methodists have acquired a face, the Quakers a face, the nuns a face. An Englishman will point out a dissenter by his manners. Trades and professions carve their own lines on faces and forms." It is also well known that occupations have a remarkable influence on physiognomy. We often say one looks like a butcher, a carpenter, a tailor, a waiter, a coachman. Each one possesses a peculiar cast of countenance which easily betrays his vocation in life, and it by no means depends on the race stock to which he belongs. There are special varieties of facial expression which at once tell the profession of a man. Who does not know the actor's face, the ecclesiastical, the musical, the artistic, the legal, the military face?[1]

The "Ghetto face" is not the result of the complexion, nor of stature, nor is it due to the size, prominence, or form of the nose, cheek-bones, lips, or chin. It is purely psychic, just like the actor's, the soldier's, the minister's face. This is best proven by the fact that illustrations in books on Jewish life, made by second-rate artists, usually do not show any "Jewish" faces. Only great artists are able to represent the soul of the persons they draw. On the other hand, in those cases where the mediocre artists are zealous to portray "Jewish" faces at all events, they usually produce caricatures. The stereotyped stage Jew is also rare in real life. One would have to search very hard in the lower east side of New York or the East

---

[1] See P. Mantegazza, *Physiognomy and Expression,* chap. xviii.

ORIGIN OF THE VARIOUS TYPES OF JEWS. 167

End of London to find a type corresponding to the average burlesque Jew, or the type of Jews shown often in the comic press. The stage and the press have produced other "types" which are not seen in real life, for instance, the German professor, the lieutenant, the ward politician, the stage Irishman, Scotchman, German, etc. They are all the creation of the pen of the cartoonists or the burlesque actors.

All the illustrations in this book which portray the Jewish type, and which can be recognized as portraits of Jews, show the psychic type of the Jew. The portrait of

Fig. 113. Fig. 114.
Figs. 113, 114.—JEW, TETUAN, MOROCCO.

the immigrant Jew from Morocco (Figs. 113, 114) shows this point to an advantage. His physiognomy is that of an Italian or a Spaniard, and because of this he has found it difficult to convince his unsophisticated co-religionists on the East Side of New York City, where he lives, that he is a Jew. They all consider him an Italian who pretends to be a member of the "chosen people." But a careful study of his countenance reveals that his large, bright eyes cannot be anything else but Jewish. That "haunting sadness and mystery" which they express can only be found in one who, according to the prophet, is "despised and rejected by men, a man of sorrows." His fate has been that of the proverbial wandering Jew. Born in Tetuan, Morocco, he went to Jerusalem at the early age of sixteen, where he soon married, and emigrated with his wife and children to Gibraltar. Not finding comfort, he changed his location to London, England. Here he spent ten of his best years in poverty and misery, and then proceeded to France and afterwards to Holland, both of which places failed to give him satisfaction. Cuba was the next country in which he tried to find happiness for himself and his growing family, and after, with his wife and children,

Fig. 115.

Fig. 116.

Figs. 115, 116.—Jew, Moscow. Great Russian Type.

working in a cigar factory on starvation wages for eight years, he was compelled to move again because he could not make a living during the Cuban war. In New York City he has been selling Yiddish newspapers, and has a hard struggle with his co-religionists, who claim that an Italian ought not to compete with them in this line. It is not surprising that his eyes bear the imprint of his unhappy fate, which has been a miniature repetition of the fate of his people.

The portrait of the Jew of Great Russian type (Figs. 115, 116) tells the same story. Every part of his physiognomy shows that he is a Muscovite. But no Muscovite could be the possessor of such melancholy, thoughtful, and piercing eyes. He also has been "on the move" from the interior of Russia to the Pale of Settlement, where during an anti-Jewish riot he has been reduced to poverty. He then proceeded to Germany, then to France, then to England, and finally to the United States. A well-to-do merchant in Russia, he has been compelled here to sell fruit from a push-cart for a living, and constantly be on the alert for the policeman who keeps him "on the move." All these hardships were not potent enough to destroy any part of his anatomy. He remained, as he was, a Slavonian, who, through the irony of fate, worships in the synagogue with the orthodox Jews. But the mirror of his soul bears the imprint of his ceaseless sufferings, his eyes show the effects of the hard and cruel fate of both his people and his individuality.

It seems that the most characteristic trait of the "Ghetto face" is the eye. It is not the nose, because only twelve to fifteen per cent. of Jews have so-called "Jewish" noses, while it is often met with among non-Jews in a more accentuated form, with a larger hook, and still it does not make its possessor look "Jewish" in the least. On the other hand the eye, which has been described by various authors as bright, thoughtful, sleepy, weary, lurking, etc., appears to be typical of the Ghetto face. Beddoe describes it as generally full and prominent, though the brow is well marked. He denies that it is recognized because it is almond-shaped, because this is common to several Oriental peoples. The expression he describes as of meditative mildness, with a degree of cunning, or sometimes of timidity, which appears almost always to accompany it in the Israelite, and which seems to speak of centuries of oppression patiently endured by a people of great intellectual powers. This, Beddoe believes, is not observed in other people with eyes of that form.[1] The best description of this eye has been given by Ripley:—"The eyebrows, seemingly thick because of their darkness, appear to be nearer together than usual, arching smoothly into the lines of the nose. The lids are rather full, the eyes large,

[1] John Beddoe, "On the Physical Characters of the Jews," *Transact. of the Ethnological Society*, London, vol. i., p. 222; 1861.

170   THE JEWS.

Fig. 117.

Fig. 118.

Figs. 117, 118.—IMER. CAUCASUS, WITH JEWISH EXPRESSION.
[*Photo, Pantiukhof.*]

Fig. 119.
TARTAR FROM TIFLIS, WITH
JEWISH PHYSIOGNOMY.
[*Photo, Pantiukhof.*]

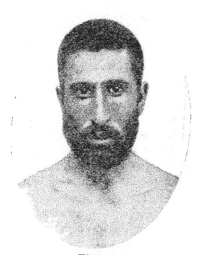
Fig. 120.
GEORGIAN, CAUCASUS, WITH
JEWISH PHYSIOGNOMY.
[*Photo, Pantiukhof.*]

dark, and brilliant. A general impression of heaviness is apt to be given. In favourable cases this imparts a dreamy, melancholy, or thoughtful expression to the countenance, in others it degenerates into a blinking, drowsy type; or, again, with eyes half-closed, it may suggest suppressed cunningness. The particular adjective to be applied to this expression varies greatly according to the personal equation of the observer."[1] But that this is a psychic trait, and does not depend on any anatomical peculiarities, is shown by the fact that it is only met with among the Jews in the Ghetto or their immediate descendants. Jews who have been out of the Ghetto for two or more generations do not have this peculiarity. Among the Jews in the southern states of the United States, or among the native English, Italian, French, or Scandinavian Jews, only a few are found with this Ghetto expression of the eyes. Professor Schleich, speaking of the Jewish type, says that it is more of a functional character than a formative. It depends more on the soul of the individual than on his morphology. The activity of the muscles of the face, due to mental anxiety, arterial tension, deposition of fat in various parts of the face, are greatly influenced by the above conditions; and, finally, all those things which depend on the psychic state of the individual. He also shows that it depends more on imitation or mimicry, children acquiring the Jewish expression by imitating their parents, than on heredity.[2] "Continued hardship, persecution, a desperate struggle against an inexorable human environment as well as a natural one, could not but write its lines upon the face," says Ripley. "The impression of a dreary past is deep sunk in the bodily proportions. . . Why not in the face as well?"[3] This explains why the peculiar Jewish expression disappears in Jews who have been out of the Ghetto for a few generations.

The so-called "Jewish" cast of countenance is a phenomenon not exclusively met with among Jews. It is seen among various races and peoples in different parts of the

[1] Wm. Z. Ripley, *The Races of Europe*, New York, 1899, p. 396.
[2] C. L. Schleich, "Jüdische Rassenköpfe," *Ost und West*, vol. vi., 1906, pp. 227-239.
[3] Wm. Z. Ripley, *The Races of Europe*, p. 397.

172   THE JEWS.

globe. It is no more a sign that its possessor or his parents have worshipped in the synagogue than blondeness is proof that one is a German or than brunetteness is proof that one is an Italian. The "Jewish" type has been met with among various races, among many nations, and in places where one would least expect Jewish influence. In fact, it seems to be ubiquitous, met among peoples among which Jews have never lived. All interested in the Bible know how assiduous some theologians have been in their search for the "Ten Lost Tribes." In their zealous

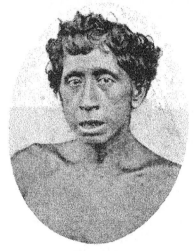

Fig. 121.   Fig. 122.

Figs. 121, 122.—Bakairi Indian with Jewish Cast of Countenance.

[*From a Photo by Ehrenreich.*]

search for these Lost Tribes of Israel, students of the Bible, missionaries, and dilettantes, have positively identified nearly every nation on the habitable globe as descendants of these mysterious tribes. Successive investigators have discovered that the English, the Irish, the Basques, the Spanish, the Franks, the Hunns, the Romans, the Greeks, the ancient Peruvians and Mexicans, the dead peoples of Central America, the Japanese, and many others are the descendants of those carried by Shalmaneser into a distant land. Many Biblical quotations are cited in support of the positive identification of each and every one

ORIGIN OF THE VARIOUS TYPES OF JEWS. 173

of the above-mentioned peoples as being "Jews." That they "look like Jews" goes without saying. Recently the theory that the Japanese are the true descendants of these ubiquitous tribes was revived. Some similarity between Shintoism and Judaism is shown to exist, and the Scriptures and Japanese traditions and customs are stated to conjoin to prove that the Japanese are the real

Fig. 123.—JAPANESE WITH JEWISH PHYSIOGNOMY.
(From Hutchinson's *Races of Mankind*.)
[*Photo by Messrs. Kajima & Suwo*]

descendants of the Ancient Hebrews.[1] One of the main supports of this theory is the fact that many Japanese often "look exactly like Jews," and the aristocracy are often hardly to be distinguished from European Jews. Even expert anthropologists testify that many Japanese have a Jewish appearance. Ten Kate[2] speaks of Semitic physiognomics among Japanese men and women; also

[1] N. McLeod wrote a book on the subject, which passed through three editions. See *Epitome of the Ancient History of Japan*; Tokio, 1879.
[2] *Internationales Zentralblatt für Anthropologie*, Heft, 5; 1902.

Baelz, who studied the Japanese thoroughly, describes the "Jewish" type in Japan, and brings excellent illustrations in proof of its existence. From the photograph reproduced (Fig. 123) it is evident that there is considerable truth in Baelz's statement. Others who have been identified as the Ten Lost Tribes are the Kareens of Burmah, "because of their Jewish appearance," the American Indians, because of the "common cowardice and want of charity of the Israelites and Indians," according to Garcia, in his "Origen de los Medianos."[1]

In addition to these absurd identifications of the Lost Tribes, many ethnologists who have devoted their work to the study of types of mankind speak of the "Jewish" facial expression as encountered among various races of mankind. Ten Kate[2] speaks of "Semitic physiognomies found among various races in which near relationship with Semites is excluded." In addition to the Japanese already mentioned, and who remind him often of Spanish and American Creoles, and Spaniards of the dark type, he also found these features among the North American Indians, as the Creeks and Choctaws, and among the Indonesians, while among the Papuans they are repeatedly noted. Ratzel states that many negroes in Africa have "typically Jewish physiognomies," and the Kaffirs "look like Jews."[3] Von den Steinen describes and illustrates the Jewish type among the Bakaïri tribe of South American Indians. The illustration (Fig. 121-122) bears out the assertion that it was "typically Jewish."[4] "To most observers the Afghan has a most remarkably Jewish cast of features," says Pennell, "and often in looking round the visitors of our out-patient department, one sees some old greybeard of pure Afghan descent and involuntarily exclaims: 'That man might for all the world be one of the old Jewish patriarchs returned to us from Bible history!'"[5] Of the natives of

---

[1] See "Ten Lost Tribes," *Jewish Encyclopædia*, vol. xii., pp. 249-253.
[2] *Loc. cit.*
[3] F. Ratzel, *Volkerkunde*, vol ii , p. 8 ; Leipzig, 1887.
[4] Von den Steinen, *Unter den Naturvölkern Zentralbraziliens*, fig. 16.
[5] T. L. Pennell, *Among the Wild Tribes of the Indian Frontier*, p. 32, London, 1909.

Afghanistan and Baluchistan it is said: "In physiognomy there is a striking resemblance, both possessing a decidedly Jewish type of countenance."[1] Of the Hindus of Kashmir it is stated that "the men are of a square, herculean build, well proportioned, and with a frank expression, while the women are fresh looking and often decidedly beautiful, with an almost Jewish cast of

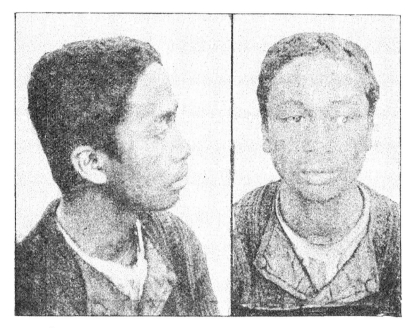

Fig. 124.—HOVA OF TANANARIVO WITH JEWISH CAST OF COUNTENANCE. [*Photo by Collignon.*]
(From Deniker's *Races of Man.*)

countenance.[2] It is well known that the old Incas frequently presented Jewish facial features. Stratz says that he can testify from personal experience that he encountered fine Jewish faces among the noble families of Java, and also among the old German and old French aristocratic families, and again among the old Netherland patrician families. He also points out that

[1] H. N. Hutchinson, *The Living Races of Mankind*, p. 212; New York, 1902.
[2] *Ibid*, p. 196.

among the many busts of Cæsar not a few are seen which present a Jewish countenance, and shows that various writers have found the same "Semitic" type among Japanese, North and South American Indians, Papuans, Todas, Indonesians, Negroes, Incas, Javanese, Germans, Frenchmen, and Dutch. Particularly often is this type met with, in a more or less striking manner, in old noble families.[1] He agrees with Ten Kate, who considers these Jewish traits as an isomorphism—*i.e.*, as physical peculiarities which are met with everywhere, and they are not at all a racial trait, but common to all races, like, for instance, red hair. It must be emphasized, again, that there is not any single part of the anatomy of the Jew which marks him as a follower of Judaism, or determines any other person as being of the "Jewish" type. This is not peculiar to the Jews. No other race or people can be judged by any single physical criterion. Galton, speaking of features, says:—"The general expression of a face is the sum of a multitude of small details, which are viewed in such rapid succession that we seem to perceive them all at a single glance. If any one of them disagrees with the recollected traits of a known face the eye is quick at observing it, and it dwells upon the difference. One small discordance overweighs a multitude of similarities, and suggests a general unlikeness; just a single syllable in a sentence pronounced with a foreign accent makes one cease to look upon the speaker as a countryman." Watching an artist painting a portrait, Galton calculated that 24,000 separate strokes of the brush, or separate traits which each stroke attempted to bring out, were necessary to complete the portrait, to bring all the features out completely.[2] It is easily understood that most of these features are not of an anatomical nature, but rather functional. They are, consequently, not hereditary.

I am inclined to agree with Ripley to the effect that the physiognomical type of the Jew is a product of artificial selection. It appears that many other groups of people, who for one reason or another have been isolated for centuries, develop a peculiar cast of countenance. The

---

[1] C. H. Stratz, *Was sind Juden*, pp. 25-26; Wien, 1903.
[2] Francis Galton, *Inquiries Into Human Faculty and Its Development*, pp. 3-4; London, 1907.

ORIGIN OF THE VARIOUS TYPES OF JEWS. 177

Basques, as Ripley points out, "by long continued and complete isolation and in-and-in breeding primarily engendered by peculiarity of language," have developed a type differing from that of the French and Spanish among whom they live. "It is easy to conceive of artificial selection in an isolated society, whereby choice should be

Fig. 125.—Yoro Combo, fAIrlY pure FulAh of KaYor (Futa-Jallon), with Jewish Cast of Countenance. [*Photo by Collignon.*]
(From Deniker's *Races of Man.*)

exercised in accordance with certain standards of beauty which had become generally accepted in that locality. . . . A primary requisite is isolation—material, social, political, linguistic, and at last ethnic."[1] The Jews have been isolated from the peoples among which they lived, in a manner unprecedented among other civilized peoples. In

[1] Wm. Ripley, *The Races of Europe*, p 204.

addition they were always keenly sensible of their social individuality. They, in fact, kept aloof, and the ideals of their non-Jewish neighbours were rarely or never in accordance with their own standard. How could they be expected to idealize anything characteristic of their tormentors? They particularly abhorred anything not in conformity with their own ideals of Jewishness, especially concerning physical appearance. To the strictly orthodox Jew in Eastern Europe, a strong muscular person is an Esau. The ideal of a son of Jacob was during the centuries before the middle of the nineteenth century, "a silken young man." This was a delicate, anæmic youth with flabby muscles and above all with a Jewish facial expression. A young man of well-developed physique, of blonde complexion and non-Jewish appearance, one who "looked like a *Goi* (Gentile)," stood less chance to be acceptable to the parents of a young Jewess than the proverbial "silken young man." This is true even to-day of the sect of Chasidim in Galicia and Poland. Such a conception of the ideal of physical beauty could not but have a strong tendency to perpetuate the Jewish type, and by in-and-in breeding accentuate it. The fact that among many Jews who have left the Ghetto, who are no more isolated from the general population, and whose ideal of beauty is about the same as that of their non-Jewish neighbours, this peculiar cast of expression disappears, as has already been stated, is also proof of artificial selection being an important factor. In Western Europe and America there is at the present a strong tendency in the opposite direction. Many Jews are proud of the fact that they do not look like Jews. "If you want to compliment a Jew," says Israel Zangwill, "tell him that he does not look like one. What a depth of degradation for a people to have reached!"[1] Considering this, it must be acknowledged that there is hardly a glowing future for the so-called "Jewish" cast of countenance.

[1] Israel Zangwill, "Zionism and East Africa," *The Menorah*, Dec. 1904.

CHAPTER VIII.

PROSELYTISM AND INTERMARRIAGE AMONG JEWS.

The Jewish race—Mixtures during the period of consolidation of the Hebrews—Intermarriage of the Patriarchs and Kings of Israel with other races—Intermarriages during the Babylonian captivity—Ezra's admonition about the purity of the race—Intermarriages during the Greco-Roman period of the Jews—Extent of proselytism—Graetz's and Reinach's estimate of the extent of intermarriage and proselytism of the Jews during that period—Intermarriages prohibited by Church edicts—Intermarriages in Gaul and Spain—In Slavonic countries—The Chozars—Origin of the Eastern European Jews.

WHILE speaking of the various types of Jews in the preceding chapters it was briefly indicated that the origin of some types is due to intermixture with races and peoples with whom they came in contact. Some writers have stated that the history of the Jews is against any such supposition, because Judaism is an exclusive religion, and also that the laws of most countries where they lived prohibited intermarriage, while proselytism was always discouraged by the Jewish law. This is, indeed, the crucial point in the anthropology of the Jews: are they of pure race, modified more or less by environmental influences, or are they a religious sect composed of racial elements acquired by proselytism and intermarriage during their migrations in various parts of the world? In other words, are the various types of Jews the result of difference in *milieu*, or are they due to the admission of non-Jewish blood into the fold of Judaism?

As far as our present knowledge of the origin of racial traits can teach us, we know that the *milieu* cannot change dark hair into blonde, or the reverse, nor can a residence in any country transform a hook nose into a snub nose, or a long head become round by a change of climate. Somatic traits are known to be influenced only by heredity. The negroes in the Western States of North America bring forth only black children as long as no mixture with whites takes place; the offspring of the blondes in the southern states are of fair complexion; the children of the English immigrants in Australia look like their parents, and not at all like the native tribes of that continent. By analogy it may be concluded that if the Jews had been a pure race

Fig. 126.—Young Woman of Arles with Jewish Physiognomy. Mixed Littoral Race(?).
[*Photo lent by School of Anthropology, Paris.*]
(From Deniker's *Races of Man.*)

originally, and then throughout their migrations had refrained from intermarriage with others, they would to-day present quite a homogeneous physique. There would not have been dark Jews and fair Jews; black Jews and white ones; brachycephalic, mesocephalic, and dolichocephalic Jews; tall, medium, and short Jews, etc.

It is remarkable that history confirms the fact that there is no such thing as a Jewish race. As a people with a written history dating back about five thousand years, it should be an easy matter to investigate this problem from the historical standpoint. And, in fact, beginning with Biblical evidence and traditions, it appears that even in the beginning of the formation of the tribe of Israel they were already composed of various racial elements. One has only to look carefully into the evidence of archæological research and Bible criticism to find that the ethnology of Canaan was not simple. We find in Asia Minor, Syria, and Palestine at that time many races—the Amorites, who were blondes, dolichocephalic, and tall; the Hittites, a dark-complexioned race, probably of Mongoloid type; the Cushites, a negroid race; and many others.[1] With all these the ancient Hebrews intermarried, as can be seen in many passages in the Bible. The prohibition alone is good proof of the frequent occurrence of cross marriages between Jews and Gentiles. If it had not been so, it would have been needless to enumerate the Hittites, Girgashites, Amorites, Canaanites, Perizzites, Hivites, and Jebusites, and to order that "neither shalt thou make marriage with them; thy daughter thou shalt not give unto his son, nor his daughter shalt thou take unto thy son."[2] Intermarriages were quite common if we consider that the patriarchs had Gentile wives: Abraham cohabited with Hagar, an Egyptian; Joseph also had an Egyptian wife, Asenath, the daughter of Potipherah, priest of On. Moses married a Midianite woman, Zipporah,[4] and was the first to be rebuked for this act: "Miriam and Aaron spoke against Moses because of the Ethiopian woman whom he had married."[5] In addition we may mention the mixed multitude that went along with the Hebrews when they left Egypt, and undoubtedly intermarried with them.[6] There were many others, as Elimelech's sons, who married Moabites;[7] Samson, a Philistine;[8] and King David, the son of the Moabite Ruth, married Maccah, daughter of the King of

---

[1] A readable description of the races of that region is to be found in A. H. Sayce, *The Races of the Old Testament*; London, 1893.
[2] Deuteronomy, vii. 1, 3.
[3] Genesis, xli. 45.
[4] Exodus, ii. 21.
[5] Numbers, xii. 1.
[6] Exodus, xii. 38.
[7] Ruth and Orpah.
[8] Jud. xiv.

Geshur.[1] Of Solomon, himself the son of a Hittite woman, the Bible says he "loved many strange women, together with the daughter of Pharaoh, women of the Moabites, Ammonites, Edomites, Zidonians, and Hittites "[2] Bathsheba married Uriah the Hittite;[3] the mother of King Hiram, a Syrian;[4] Ahab to Jezebel, a Sydonian Princess;[5] and many others, including State functionaries, teachers, and warriors.[6] There can be no question that such intermarriages with Gentiles by the great patriarchs and Kings of Israel were imitated and practised by many of the ancient Hebrews. It all goes to show that the Biblical prohibition to intermarry with the Canaanites mentioned above was never followed religiously. At any rate, the Bible distinctly permitted the Hebrews to marry captive women during the time of war.[7] Even conceding that it was followed implicitly, and Canaanite women were tabooed, it still permitted the infusion of non-Jewish blood into the veins of the Chosen People. That they did intermarry is seen from the above-quoted examples, and these led to idolatrous practices, which the interdiction was intended to prevent.

These marriages with Gentiles were continued by the Hebrews during their Babylonian captivity, although they considered themselves "a holy people unto their Lord God." Ezra's admonition shows that " the holy seed have mingled themselves with the people of those lands,"[8] and the prophet Malachi also bewails the profanity of " marrying daughters of a strange God."[9] Ezra's revival movement urging the Hebrews to leave their Gentile wives and children, to preserve the seed of Abraham in its purity, had not been a complete success. Many were opposed to such a procedure and interpretation of the law. The books of Jonah and Ruth testify to the views held by those who, against Ezra, pleaded for a non-racial and all-embracing Israel.[10]

But all these intermarriages are stated by some to be of little significance from the anthropological standpoint, because they could not have influenced the Jewish physical type. "The distinction between Jews and other Semites

---

[1] II. Sam. iii. 3.
[2] Kings, xi. 1.
[3] II. Sam, xi. 3.
[4] I. Kings, vii. 14.
[5] I. Kings, xvi. 31.
[6] Jud., iii. 4-6.
[7] Deuteronomy, xxi. 10-13.
[8] Ezra, ix. 1, 2.
[9] Malachi, ii. 11.
[10] E. G. Hirsch, in *Jewish Encyclopædia*, vol. x. p. 221.

was religious, not racial," says Joseph Jacobs. Modern archæological research has, however, shown that ethnic conditions were not as simple as Jacobs would lead us to believe. It appears that the diversity of physical type of mankind in Egypt, Syria, Palestine, Mesopotamia, etc., was at least as great as that seen to-day in Europe. And judging by the small extent of the region under consideration and the small number of inhabitants, racial mixtures should leave a profound impression on the type of the Hebrews. One has only to recall that there were the tall, blonde and dolichocephalic Amorites, the negroid Cushites, the Hittites, who are held by some to have been a Mongoloid race, and an Armenoid race by others, but at all events not of the type considered Semitic, etc. That intermarriages with all these should not have left any impression on the Jewish physical type can not even be imagined.[1]

The greatest mixtures of which there are any historical records have taken place during the Greco-Roman period of the Jews. Notwithstanding the fact that Judaism is such an exclusive religion, and thought always to discourage proselytism, still during that period it made many converts. Everything points to an intense activity in spreading Judaism among the pagans. "Modern researches have shown positively that Judaism has sent forth apostles," say E. G. Hirsch.[2] That they have succeeded is shown by the fact that many important personages were gained, as, for instance, the Royal family of Adiabene, a province on the banks of the Tigris Another instance was Flavius Clemens and his wife Flavia Domitilla; he was a cousin of the Emperor Domitian, a member of the Senate and Consul, and his wife was also a near relative of the Emperor. Another important proselyte was Fulvia, the wife of a highly respected senator. This last proselyte gave the Jews considerable trouble; the Senate promulgated a law that the Jews must leave Rome.[3] During the last ten years which

[1] Feldman says that up to the time of Ezra "intermarriage between Jew and alien went on on a scale sufficiently large to silence for ever the claim of racial purity for the Jew."
[2] *Jewish Encyclopædia*, article "Proselytes," vol. x., p. 222.
[3] H. Graetz, *History of the Jews*, vol. ii., pp. 136-137.

preceded the destruction of the Judæan State," says Graetz, "there were more proselytes than there had been at any other time. Philo relates from his own experience that in his native country many heathens, when they embraced Judaism, not only changed their faith but their lives, which were henceforth conspicuous by the practice of the virtues of moderation, gentleness, and humanity."[1] It appears that the Jews gained more women to their creed than men. Perhaps the fact that women had not to undergo circumcision made it easier for them to enter, while men might have been kept away for just this reason. In Damascus the greater part of the women were converted to Judaism, and in Asia Minor there were also many female proselytes, according to Graetz. In Palestine, too, there must have been many proselytes, and they must have had an important social position, otherwise the Tannaim would have no reason to discuss their status and the conditions of their reception. One Judah ben Ezekiel, fearing lest his son might marry a woman who is not of pure seed of Abraham, kept on delaying his marriage long after he reached maturity. Upon this his friend Ulla pertinently remarked: "How do we know for certain that we ourselves are not descended from the heathens who violated the maidens of Zion at the siege of Jerusalem?"[2]

There were two kinds of converts at that time, complete converts and "half converts." The latter class consisted of men and women of non-Jewish birth, who, forsaking their ancestral pagan and polytheistic religions, embraced monotheism and adopted the fundamental principles of Jewish morality, without, however, submitting to circumcision or observing other ceremonial laws. Their number was very large during the centuries immediately preceding and following the fall of Jerusalem.[3] Complete converts were those who also submitted to circumcision. It appears that the Rabbis were not unanimous as to the standing of each of these classes of proselytes in the Jewish community. Some insisted that the half converts are not to be considered Jews at all,

---

[1] H. Graetz, *History of the Jews*, vol. ii., p. 215.
[2] *Ibid*, p. 551.
[3] Article "Proselytes," *Jewish Encyclopædia*, vol. x., p. 221.

PROSELYTISM AND INTERMARRIAGE. 185

Fig. 127.—THE RAW MATERIAL.

Fig. 128.—WHAT BECAME OF THEM.
Figs. 127, 128.—JEWISH LADS' BRIGADE, LONDON.
Showing the Effects of the Environment on the Type of the Jew.

while others were more lenient, and were ready to accord them full equality with the Jews as soon as they had solemnly forsworn idolatry. The "via media" was taken,[1] and they had to be regarded by the Jews as brothers, although later, during the third century when Christianity had grown, conditions changed, and half converts were again looked at with suspicion. Theodore Reinach, one of the best authorities on the history of the Jews, says about these conversions: "The fervour of proselytism was indeed one of the most distinctive traits of Judaism during the Greco-Roman epoch—a trait which it never possessed in the same degree either before or since." He enumerates various methods which were employed to increase the flock of Irsael. "The most brutal was that of forced conversion—that is to say, circumcision—such as had been imposed by John Hyrcanus on the Idumeans and by Aristobulus upon a portion of the Itureans (Galileans). Next was the conversion of slaves owned by Jews as their individual property. But it was especially the moral propaganda, by word, example and book which was the most productive of success throughout the whole extent of the Diaspora."

Reinach points out that Judaism possessed prudence and tact in dealing with the proselytes. It did not exact the complete adoption of the Law immediately. The neophyte was simply a "friend" to the Jewish customs and observed only some of the laws. His sons frequented the synagogues and deserted the temples, and contributed their *oboli* to the treasury of Jerusalem. At last the proselyte took the decisive step: he received the rite of circumcision and the bath of purity. In the third generation, according to Deuteronomy, xxii. 8, there existed no distinction between Jew by race and Jew by adoption,[2] unless the latter belonged to the accursed races.[3] "It cannot be doubted that Judaism in this way made numerous converts during two or three centuries. . . .

---

[1] E. G. Hirsch, *Ibid.*, p. 222.

[2] According to the Talmud proselytes held an inferior position in the Jewish community (*Kiddushin*, 4, 1). They were, however, admitted to intermarriage with all social grades below the highest—*i.e.*, the priests. Most Hebrews were not better situated (*cf. Sanhedrin*, 4. 2).

[3] These accursed races were the Canaanites—*i.e.*, Semites, who could not alter the Jewish physical type, according to Jacobs.

PROSELYTISM AND INTERMARRIAGE. 187

It is an indisputable fact that proselytes were found in large numbers in every country of the diaspora. The

Fig. 129.—JEWESS IN ASIA MINOR.

pagan authors, struck by this phenomenon, carefully distinguish the Jews by race from Jews by adoption. In Antioch a large portion of the Greek population was

Judaized in the time of Josephus; and although they turned Christians in the days of Chrysostom, they had not forgotten the way to the synagogues. The same holds true of certain districts of Spain. In Damascus 'almost all the women' observed the Jewish usages. Paul met with proselytes in Antioch of Pisidia, in Thyatira, in Thessalonica, and in Athens. In Rome, where the Jewish propaganda had taken the first step at the time of the embassy of Numenius (139 B.C.), its efforts and success are indicated by Horace, Persius, and Juvenal." "The enormous growth of the Jewish nation in Egypt, Cyprus, and Cyrene," says M. Reinach, "cannot be accounted for without supposing an abundant infusion of Gentile blood. Proselytism swayed alike the upper and the lower classes of society. The great number of Jews passing through the state of slavery must, of course, have catechized their comrades rather than their masters." It is true that the State, and later the Jews themselves, discouraged proselytism, and under Domitian, Nerva, and others, placed heavy penalties for converting Gentiles to Judaism. It is also true that the evangelical preachers met with ready ears among the half-proselytes, and that it was among them that Christianity made its first and its most numerous conquests.[1] But to say that this removed all the foreign blood from Judaism, and left the flock of Israel in its original purity, is absurd.

With the spread of Christianity in Europe the Church did its best to discourage intermarriage between Jews and Christians. That it was not always successful is attested by the fact that it was often necessary to repeat the edicts at various Church Councils. Andree enumerates the following edicts of the Church directed against intermarriages[2]:—The first prohibition was enacted by the Eastern Church at the Council of Chalcedon in 388. In the West the third *Concilium Aurelianese* issued the following prohibition:—"*Christianis quoque omnibus interdicimus ne judæorum conjugiis misceantur: quod si fecerint,*

---

[1] For further information on this subject see Th. Reinach, article, "Judæi," in *Dictionnaire des Antiquités;* also, article, "Diaspora," *Jewish Encyclopædia,* vol. iv. pp. 569-571; E. Renan, *Le Judaïsme comme race et comme religion;* Paris, 1883.

[2] R. Andree, *Zur Volkskunde der Juden,* p. 48; Leipzig, 1881.

PROSELYTISM AND INTERMARRIAGE. 189

usque ad sequestrationem, quisquis ille est, communione pellatur." At the Council of Toledo, held in 589, the clergy was admonished "*ut Judæis non liceat Christianas habere uxores.*" The Council of Rome, held in 743, ordained "*si quis Christianus filiam suam Judæo in conjugio copulare præsumserit — anathema sit.*" Many other prohibitions of this sort were issued both by the Church and State in various parts of Europe. In Hungary, for instance, according to Grætz,[1] the Jews lived in friendly relations with their German brethren. Mixed marriages between Jews and Christians also occurred frequently, as the Church had not yet established itself in the country. King Ladislaus prohibited such marriages in 1092. But that his prohibition did not bring the desired result is seen from the fact that the Archbishop Robert von Gran complained in 1229 to the Pope that many Jews in Hungary are married to Christian women, and that the latter are often converted to Judaism; that Christian parents are selling their children to Jews, and some, out of greed for money, permit themselves to be circumcised, and that within a few years many thousands of Christians were lost to the Church.[2]

Another focus of intermarriage of immense significance in relation to the ethnic type of the Jews was in Southern Europe, especially in Spain, Portugal, and Gaul. In Gaul, during the sixth century, Graetz says that the Jews lived on the best of terms with the people of the country, and intermarriages occurred between Jews and Christians,[3] and in Spain "intermarriages between Jews and Christians occurred quite as frequently as in Gaul."[4] King Reccared in 589 was the first to prohibit these marriages, and to order that children born to such mixed couples should be forcibly baptized.[5] That slaves were converted to Judaism is shown by the same edict which ordained that slaves initiated into Judaism, and especially circumcised, should be forfeited to the State. That the desired effect was not achieved in this case as well as in others is shown by the

---

[1] *History of the Jews*, vol. iii., p. 521.
[2] V. Czeernig, *Ethnographie der Österr. Monarchie*, vol. ii. pp. 113-114.
[3] H. Graetz, *History of the Jews*, vol. iii. p. 36.
[4] *Ibid.*, p. 44.   [5] *Ibid.*, p. 46.

fact that mixed marriages continued to take place. Thus, in the thirteenth century, according to Graetz, "among the Jews in Southern Spain the lukewarmness towards the law went so far that not a few contracted marriages with Christian and Mohammedan women,"[1] and it is also stated that Rabbi Moses of Coucy, a kind of Jewish revivalist, in the thirteenth century "succeeded in influencing those who had contracted mixed marriages with Christian and Mohammedan women to divorce themselves from their strange wives."[2] It seems that mixed marriages kept on occurring, because, in King

Fig. 130.—Jew, Jerusalem. Mongoloid Type.

Fig. 131.—Hungarian Jewess.

Alfonso's code, we meet again an interdiction of such unions as well as against conversions of Christians to Judaism.

A large proportion of the blondes encountered among the Jews of to-day may have been acquired into the fold of Judaism in the following manner, which is but one of many instances which can be quoted from the history of the Jews: "The Jews of Germany are to be regarded as colonies of the Frankish Jews," says Graetz, "and such of them as lived in Austrasia, a province subject to the

[1] H. Graetz, *Ibid.*, p. 527.   [2] *Ibid.*, p. 546.

Merovignian kings. . . . From the vast horde of Jewish prisoners, the Vangioni had chosen the most beautiful women, had brought them back to their stations on the shores of the Rhine and the Main, and had compelled them to minister to the satisfaction of their desires. The children thus begotten of Jewish and German parents were brought up by their mothers in the Jewish faith, their fathers not troubling themselves about them. It is these children who are said to have been the founders of the first Jewish communities between Worms and Mayence."[1] Such violent infusion of Gentile blood into the veins of the flock of Israel has been especially frequent in Slavonic countries. One of the favourite methods of the Cossacks to wring out money from the Jews was to take a large number of prisoners, knowing well that the Jews would ransom them. That the women thus ransomed were violated by these semi-savage tribes goes without saying. In fact, the "Council of the Four Lands," at its session in the winter of 1650, had to take cognizance of the poor women and children born to them from Cossack husbands during captivity, and thus restore order in the family and social life of the Jews.[2] Similar outrages were recently again perpetrated on Jewish women in Russia during the massacres in 1903-05. While at the present it may be stated to have practically no effect on the type of the Jews, it must be recalled that during the middle ages the number of Jews was comparatively small, and any infusion of foreign blood surely had its impress on the future physical type of the Jews.

The most important infusion of non-Jewish racial elements into the veins of Eastern European Jews took place in the eighth century when the Chozars adopted Judaism. These Chozars were of Turanian origin and their kingdom was firmly established in South Russia. For about two hundred years, until subdued by the Russians, these Jews flourished and were considered a power in that region.[3] There is considerable historical evidence that after the destruction of their kingdom many of them

[1] H. Graetz, *History of the Jews*, vol. iii., pp. 40-41.
[2] See *Jewish Encyclopædia*, vol. iv., p. 286.
[3] For details see H. Rosenthal, article "Chozars," *Jewish Encyclopædia*, vol. iv.

mingled with the Jews in that region and in other countries. It is stated by many authorities that the Jews in South Russia, Hungary, Roumania, and part of Poland are mainly descendants of Chozars who intermarried with Jews. It is, in fact, one of the most important questions on which historians are not in agreement—How have the Jews entered Russia, Poland, etc.? The contention of some that they all came from the West, from Germany where they were cruelly persecuted during the time of the Crusaders, and that Poland offered them an asylum, is only partly borne out by facts. Historical evidence goes to show that there were already Jews in South Russia before the destruction of the Temple. This has been attested by inscriptions unearthed in various parts of the northern shore of the Black Sea. They are said to have come thither mostly from the Byzantine Empire and also from the Caucasus. In the latter country they have been even before the present era, and there is considerable evidence showing that many Jews have migrated from the Caucasus to South Russia. This puts a completely different aspect on the question of the origin of the Jewish types met with in Eastern Europe. It must also be mentioned in this connection that the number of Jews who entered Poland from Germany could not have been so great as to transfer the centre of gravity of the Jewish population in Europe from Rheinish Franconia to Poland. To-day about three-fourths of all the Jews in the world are found in Eastern Europe. It is more likely that the stream of Western European Jews met with a large number of native Jews, and also with a stream coming from the East. These, together with the Chozars, who commingled with them after the fall of their kingdom, contributed to make Eastern Europe the centre of the Jews in Europe. In addition to this must also be mentioned that there is no lack of proof of proselytism in Russia. The sects known as "Judaizing Heresy," and the "Subbotniki" prove that Judaism has been active there in making converts. Many of these sectarians are practising circumcision, keep the Sabbath, deny the divinity of Christ, and of the Trinity, etc. According to some Russian historians it appears that the first to preach their doctrines was a Jew, Zechariah, who came from Kief to Novgorod during the last quarter of the fifteenth century. These sectarian Russians have been as cruelly persecuted as the Jews in any country in Europe, and still there are said to be more than two millions of them in the Empire of the Czar to-day. Many of them have become Jews.[1] It is true that to-day a few converts to Judaism would have but little influence on the type of 5,500,000 Jews in Russia, but during the fifteenth to the eighteenth centuries, when the number of Jews there was quite small and the number of proselytes was larger, such infusion

Fig. 132.
JEW, BUKOWINA.

Fig. 133.
JEWESS, ORAN, ALGERIA.

must have left its impression on the physical types of the Jews. That they did mingle with the Jews is attested by the fact that the Russian government always did its best to keep them apart from the Jews. In the districts where

[1] Even to-day many Subbotniki adopt Judaism. They usually leave Russia for the purpose, because there it is an offence punishable severely. I know of two families who came to New York in order to embrace Judaism. Here they, as well as their male children, submitted to circumcision, etc. They said that they do it because of the conviction that they are "Jews." Many of them go to Palestine. In 1907 about 100 families of Russian peasants migrated to Jemma, Galilee, and were converted to Judaism. Their children attend Jewish schools, study Hebrew, and learn to speak Yiddish. The Jews call them "Gerim," *i.e.*, strangers. See F. Theilhaber, "Gerim in Palestina," *Die Welt*, No. 27, 1907.

they are met with no Jew is permitted to live. They, on the other hand, compelled to keep their religious views secret, are very careful to conceal their opinions when they come in contact with Russians of the Greek Orthodox Church, while with the Jews they are rather communicative. They have often asked Jews for prayer-books, explanations of some religious matters, etc.

The history of the Jews in Russia furnishes ample evidence that in the south of the Empire, especially in Kief, there were Jews long before the Jews came thither from Poland and Germany. Some historians even say that during the eighth century the majority of the population of Kief was made up of Jews of Chozar descent. Many of these Jews, after the fall of the Chozar kingdom and their subjugation by the Russians during the eleventh century, have spread all over the country, and made up the nucleus of the future Jewry of Eastern Europe. Later, when the German Jews came, both these classes commingled, and their descendants constitute the millions of Jews living to-day in Eastern Europe.[1]

History thus confirms the observations made by anthropologists to the effect that many of the types of the Jews in that region are hardly distinguishable from the types of mankind met with among the Christians in Eastern Europe, and that this is due to intermarriage and proselytism.

[1] K. N. Ikoff, "Neue Beiträge zur Anthropologie der Juden," *Archiv für Anthropologie*, vol. xv., pp. 369-389, 1884, discusses this question.

CHAPTER IX.

MIXED MARRIAGES IN MODERN TIMES.

The legal status of intermarriage between Jews and Christians—What is a "mixed" marriage?—Number of mixed marriages—In Scandinavia—In Germany, France, Italy, England, Australia, and the United States—The opposition of the Church and the Synagogue to intermarriage between Jews and Christians—Mixed marriages between followers of various Christian denominations—The Ghetto is the best preventive of intermarriage.—Fertility of mixed marriages—Distinguished persons of half-Jewish origin—The loss sustained by Judaism through intermarriage—Frequency of divorce among mixed couples—Decrease of the Jewish population as a result of intermarriage—Intermarriage and missionary work among Jews—Ethnic effects of mixed marriages—Jewish theological attitude toward intermarriage.

THE intermarriages between Jews and non-Jews during the time preceding the middle of the nineteenth century cannot be statistically established for obvious reasons. We had to rely on statements in various historical records for the determination of its extent. At the present time some countries in Europe publish the data collected from the registration of marriages, and especially as regards the religious denomination of the parties entering matrimony. From these statistics it is more or less easy to determine the proportion of Jews who marry Christians. It must be stated at the outset that intermarriages are not permitted in every country where the Jews reside. Thus in Russia no Jew is permitted to marry a Christian unless he is first baptized; in Austria it is also prohibited, but one of the ways out of the dilemma is that one or both of the couple seeking a marriage licence declares himself or herself a "Freethinker" (Konfessionslos). So that in these two countries, where more than one-half the total number of Jews in the world reside, intermarriages cannot take place at all. Similarly in the Orient, in Turkey, Persia, Morocco, etc., no mixed marriages can take place for the same reason. In some other countries intermarriages are permitted, yet it is impossible to determine their frequency because the registrar's offices do not publish denominational statistics on the subject. This is the case in France, Italy, Belgium, England, the United States, etc.

But it must be borne in mind that even in countries where mixed marriages are recorded as such, and the statistics of their frequency published in the official publications, the records show only the faith of the consorts. A mixed marriage is considered one in which the creed of the consorts is different at the time the marriage is contracted. It has only a religious basis. The result is that a marriage in which the bridegroom is a baptized Jew and the bride a Jewess is considered a "mixed" marriage; the marriage of a Christian woman who shortly before entering matrimony adopted Judaism is considered a "pure" Jewish marriage, and the like. It is thus evident that it is not in the ethnic sense, as the marriages between the white and coloured in the United States, that the term "mixed marriage" is here used. For those who believe in the various race theories which have of late become fashionable this definition of mixed marriages will not be satisfactory. But it must be recalled that if we adhere strictly to race distinctions, we must necessarily consider the union of a blonde Jew with a Christian woman of the same complexion as "pure," while a marriage between a dark-complexioned Protestant and a blonde of the same creed must be considered a "mixed" marriage.

A study of available statistics shows that there are more mixed marriages contracted between Jews and Christians than is generally supposed. In some places, as Scandinavia, Hamburg, Berlin, etc., mixed marriages are almost as frequent as pure marriages. It appears that in Scandinavia the largest proportion of Jews marry Christians. From a recent paper on the subject[1] it is seen that during the twenty-four years, 1880-1903, there were contracted 358 pure Jewish marriages and 234 mixed, or 65.36 per cent. of the pure Jewish marriages were contracted with Christians. How far in that city these mixed marriages are in vogue is seen from the fact that

[1] J. Salomon, "Eheschliessungen zwischen Juden und Christen in Kopenhagen," *Zeitschrift fur Demographie und Statistik der Juden*, 1905, No. I.

MIXED MARRIAGES IN MODERN TIMES. 197

MArrIAges between Jews and Non-Jews in certaIn Coun1Ries.

Country or City.	Period.	To 100 Pure Jewish Marriages. Jews Married.		
		Christian Husbands.	Christian Wives.	Total Mixed Marriages.
German Empire	1901-04	8.01	9.26	17.27
,,	1905-07	9.98	11.57	21.55
Prussia	1875-84	5.23	4.52	9.75
,,	1885-94	6.06	6.39	12.45
,,	1895-99	7.91	9.04	16.95
,,	1900-07	9.85	11.32	21.17
Bavaria	1876-84	1.67	1.95	3.62
,,	1885 94	2.50	2.77	5.27
,,	1895-99	3.17	5.28	8.45
,,	1900-04	4.00	4.71	8.71
,,	1905-07	4.38	4.55	8.93
Elsass-Lorraine	1905-06	7.05	3.30	10.35
Hesse	1906-07	4.42	3.87	8.29
Baden	1903-05	5.21	4.00	9.21
Hungary	1895-1904	3.03	3.18	6 20
,,	1908	4.93	4.38	9.31
Copenhagen	1880-90	——	——	55.17
,,	1891-1900	——	——	71.07
,,	1901-05	——	——	96.05
Berlin	1875-79	16 43	19 64	36.07
,,	1895-99	13.07	21.05	34.12
,,	1905-06	18.65	25.40	44.05
Breslau	1905	7.25	6.52	13.77
Munich	1891-95	13.33	20.00	33.33
,,	1896-1900	10.00	27.50	37.50
,,	1901-05	13.46	17.31	30.77
,,	1906 08	15.27	22.13	37.40
Hamburg	1905-06	26.37	34.82	61.19
Frankfort	1905-06	10.87	12.42	23.29
,,	1907-08	12.54	12 22	24.76
Charlottenburg	1905-07	11.62	23.26	34.89
Brandenburg	1905-06	15.81	24.15	39 96
Budapest	1896-1900	7.22	6.11	13.33
,,	1903-04	8.22	8.84	17.06
,,	1907	7.78	10.62	18.40
Trieste	1887-1903	——	——	36.01
Vienna	1906	——	——	12.97
Bucharest	1904-05	2.89	0.83	3.72
Amsterdam	1899-1903	——	——	12.22
,,	1904-08	——	——	10.30

from 1880 to 1890 the percentage was only 55.17; it rose to 71.07 per cent. during 1890 to 1900, and from 1901 to 1905, inclusive, there were 76 pure and 73 mixed, both classes about equal.¹ Similar conditions are reported in other Scandinavian countries. In Sweden, according to Samter, the number of mixed marriages exceeds the number of pure Jewish marriages.² In former years, we are told by Salomon, the Rabbis revolted and refused to solemnize mixed marriages or to admit the children born to such couples into the fold of Judaism, but of late years the Jewish community authorized several physicians to

Fig. 134.
AMERICAN JEW.

Fig. 135.
AMERICAN JEWESS.

circumcize such new-born boys. But as will appear later very few such children are in need of this operation, because most of them are baptized at birth.

The statistics of the German empire are particularly reliable in this regard, because they have been collected for many years with great care, with a view to elicit the degree of assimilation of the Jewish population. During the seven years 1901-1907 there were contracted in Germany

¹ Cordt Trap, "Die Juden in Kopenhagen nach der Volkszahlung von 1906," *Zeitschr. Demographie und Statistik der Juden*, pp. 97-101; 1907.
² N. Samter, *Judentaufen im 19 Jahrhundert*, p. 82; Berlin, 1906.

27,672 marriages between Jews and Jewesses and 5,300 between Jews and Christians. The mixed marriages constituted consequently 19.15 per cent. of the pure Jewish marriages; nearly one marriage out of five was contracted with a non-Jew. It was also found that 8.86 per cent. of all the Jewesses and 10.29 per cent. of all the Jews in that country married Christians during these seven years. In other words, every twelfth Jewish bride and every tenth Jewish bridegroom married a Christian.

The Jews in the various states of Germany have different proclivities in this respect. In Prussia a very large number marry Christians. Statistics are available here for 33 consecutive years, since 1875, when this sort of marriages was legalized. The growth of the proportion of mixed marriages has been remarkably steady. The proportion of mixed marriages has more than doubled within these 33 years, and still keeps on increasing. The absolute number has also doubled. During 1875 to 1879 the average number of such marriages was 239, and in 1908 the number was 742; while the number of pure Jewish marriages has diminished from 2,675 in 1875 to only 2,623 in 1908, notwithstanding the fact that the Jewish population has somewhat increased during that period. The larger number of these marriages in Prussia are contracted in the city of Berlin, where the proportion is about double that observed in Prussia. Here the increase was as follows:—In 1875-1879, 36.26 per cent., while in 1905 it was already 44.4 per cent. of the pure marriages. During the last-mentioned year 17 per cent. of all the Jewesses, and 27 per cent. of all the Jews who entered matrimony in Berlin married Christians. In other words, every fourth Jew and every sixth Jewess married outside of their faith.[1] Conditions are similar in Hamburg, where the increase has been as follows during the three years 1903-1905:—

	Husband Christian.	Wife Christian.	Total.
1903	23.64	17.27	40.91%
1904	26.47	23.53	50.00
1905	25.00	33.65	60.65

[1] See A. Ruppin, "Die Mischehe," *Zeitschr. f. Demograph. Statistik der Juden*, pp. 17-23; 1908. *Idem., Die Juden der Gegenwart*, pp. 78-96.

The conditions here are about the same as in Scandinavia. In other German states the proportion is not so great as in Prussia or Hamburg, but still there is everywhere shown a decided tendency to intermarriage. In Bavaria the increase has been from 3.86 per cent. in 1876-80 to 10.26 in 1905, and in Hesse from 0.5 per cent. in 1866-70 to 7.33 in 1901-04,[1] and even 10.30 per cent. in 1905. In Baden the percentage was, during 1903-05, 9.2, and in Elsass-Lorraine, during the same period, 8.2 per cent.[2]

It is remarkable that even in the most orthodox Jewish communities, where mixed marriages would be least expected to occur, there are evidences that the tendency is in this direction. Thus, in Amsterdam, where up to about fifty years ago hardly any Jew ever married out of his faith, there are to-day quite a considerable number of such unions. During 1899-1901 the mixed marriages constituted 9.45 per cent., and during 1902-03 the proportion increased to 15.08 per cent.—*i.e.*, one out of six Jewish marriages was contracted with a Christian.[3] In Austria, as has already been intimated, mixed marriages are prohibited. Jews who want to marry Christians have to proceed in a roundabout way: one of the couple either joins the religion of 'the other, or declares himself a Freethinker. While in Austria the number of marriages of Jews with Freethinkers is comparatively small, conditions are different in the city of Trieste. Between 1887 and 1903 there were contracted 472 marriages between Jews and Jewesses, and 170 between Jews and Freethinkers—*i.e.*, the mixed constituted thirty-six per cent. of the pure Jewish marriages. This does not, however, give a complete picture of the state of affairs. Many mixed couples both declare themselves as Freethinkers, while in other cases one accepts the religion of the other. "This shows that, like

---

[1] J. Thon, "Die Bewegung der jüdischen Bevölkerung in Bayern, etc.," *Zeitschr. fur Demographie und Statist. der Juden*, No. 8, 1905; Knopfel, "Stand und Bewegung der jüdisch. Bevölker. in Hessen," *Ibid.*, No. 6, pp. 81-85, 1906.

[2] Calculated from figures given in the *Zeitschrift fur Demographie und Statistik der Juden*, No. 4, 1905; p. 158, 1906; p. 79, 1907.

[3] *Statistisch Jaarboek der Gemeente Amsterdam*, vol. viii.; Amsterdam, 1905. There was a decrease during 1904-08 to 10.30 per cent. (*Statistique Annuelle*, Amsterdam, 1908.)

MIXED MARRIAGES IN MODERN TIMES. 201

Denmark and Australia, the integrity of Judaism is here in danger."[1] The conditions in Hungary, while not as acute as in Trieste, are also interesting in this respect. In that country mixed marriages were not permitted until 1895, when they were legalized. Since then they have been growing in frequency and were 9.31 per cent. in 1908,[2] and in Budapest the proportion even reached 18.40 per cent. during 1907. Even in Roumania, where the social and intellectual conditions of the Jews have remained rather backward, there are mixed marriages contracted. Most of them are contracted in Bucharest,

Fig. 136.—RUSSIAN JEWISH RABBI.
SLAVONIC TYPE.

Fig. 137.
CAUCASIAN JEW

where during 1904-05 3.52 per cent. of the pure marriages were mixed.[3]

France and Italy publish no denominational statistics, but it is well known that intermarriages between Jews and Christians are very prevalent there. In France it has been said that most of the Jewish rich families have

[1] *Zeitschrift für Demographie und Statistik der Juden*, pp. 60-61; 1907.
[2] L. Schick, "Eheschliessungen zwischen Juden und Christen in Ungarn," *Zeitschrift für Demographie und Statistik der Juden*, No. 4, 1905. He shows that during the nine years 1895 to 1903, 3,590 Jews married Christians in Hungary.
[3] A. Ruppin, "Die Bewegung der jüdischen Bevölkerung in Rumanien," *Zeitschrift für Demographie und Statistik der Juden*, p. 12, 45-46; 1907.

intermarried with the decadent aristocracy of that country. Indeed, Jewish heiresses in various European countries have often married with men of the highest grade of nobility, and some have stated that the majority of the mixed marriages are of this nature—*i.e.*, somewhat like the marriages of American heiresses with European nobility. This is decidedly not the case with the bulk of mixed marriages. The fact that more Jews marry Christian women than Jewesses marry Christians is good proof against this statement.[1] Conditions in Italy are most interesting in regard to the assimilation of the Jews. It has been stated by many who are well informed that there is hardly a Jewish family in that country with no Christian relatives through intermarriage. The number of mixed marriages is said to be much in excess of the number of pure Jewish marriages.

In English-speaking countries conditions are about the same as in Western Europe among the native Jews. Although the immigrant Jewish population of London do not marry with Christians as often as the native Jews do, still such unions are not as rare as is generally supposed, and the number is growing.[2] The Spanish and Portuguese Jews in England have practically disappeared; they were absorbed through intermarriage with Christians.[3] In New

---

[1] See table on p. 197. This phenomenon is not peculiar to the Jews. In the United States intermarriages between aliens and natives are mostly contracted between foreign-born men and native women. Among five million children who had but one parent native-born, it was ascertained by the census of 1900, that in two-thirds it was the father who was an alien. Ripley attributes it to the ambition to rise among men, tending inevitably to break down racial barriers. The woman is always the conservative element in society, and tends to cling to the old ways long after they have been discarded by the men. The result is, that in intermixture of various peoples, it is more commonly the man who marries up the social scale. Even colour lines are more often crossed by men; more negroes have white wives than white men coloured wives. See Wm.° Z. Ripley, "The European Population of the United States," *Journal Royal Anthropol. Institute*, vol. xxxviii., pp. 221-240, 1908.

[2] I believe that the decrease of the number of Jewish marriages recently observed in England is in a great measure due to this cause.

[3] The orthodox Jews have recently been alarmed at the increase of this sort of marriage in England. The Chief Rabbi preached a special sermon admonishing his flock: "Be steadfast in your separateness, so that your wedded state may bring you true happiness," *Jewish Chronicle*, pp. 10-11; September 27th, 1907.

South Wales, where denominational statistics are published, it was found, while collecting the census statistics of 1901, that of all married Jews, 781 were married to Jewesses, and 360—*i.e.*, 46.1 per cent., were married to Christians.[1] In Western Australia 157 Jews married with Jewesses, and 62 married Christians; again, 39.5 per cent. of Jews were married to Christians.

Intermarriages between Jews and Christians were already quite common in the United States in colonial times. According to Hollander, the well-known "Ye Jew doctor," Jacob Lumbrozo in Maryland married a Christian woman about 1660.[2] Dembitz shows that "there is no frequenter of the synagogue who either lived in Kentucky or whose ancestors lived there before 1836," and he gives as a cause that the early Jewish settlers disappeared through intermarriage with Christians, "and the descendants of the early settlers are known only by their Jewish family names and their Oriental (?) features."[3] One has to read detailed accounts of several Jewish families in New York, Pennsylvania, Connecticut, Massachusetts, etc., to be convinced as to the extent of mixed marriages in pre-revolutionary times; the reason for the disappearance of the Sephardi Jews is then evident.[4] This process can be seen now with the German Jews, who are frequently marrying out of their faith. There are even Rabbis who are not loath to officiate at such unions, although the strictly orthodox condemn them. For lack of denominational statistics it is impossible to state accurately the number and proportion of this sort of marriage. It is, however, known to be very common in the Western and Southern States, and less in the Eastern States. Rabbi George Zepin, the director of circuit preaching of the Central Conference of American Rabbis, estimates that in the northern part of the United States five per cent. is the maximum proportion of mixed marriages, while in the south the proportion ranges

---

[1] *Results of Census of New South Wales*, Part V., p. 449; 1901.
[2] *Publications American Jewish Historical Society*, vol. i., p. 29.
[3] *Ibid.*, pp. 99-101.
[4] See for details, *Publications American Jewish Historical Society*, vol. i., pp. 57-58; vol ii., p. 91; vol. vii., p. 43; vol. xii., pp. 68-69; vol. vi., pp. 92-93.

between twenty and fifty per cent., thirty-three per cent. being the most nearly correct. Similarly, an investigation made by the Superintendent of the Jewish Orphan Asylum in Cleveland revealed that the graduates of that institution are very much prone to marry Christians: 175 girls and 122 boys were married; of the boys ten and of the girls twenty-four are married to Christians.[1]

Fig. 138.—DAGHESTAN MOUNTAIN JEWS.
[*Photo, Kurdoff.*]

There are no available statistics as to the frequency of intermarriages in New York City to-day. They are not so rare as is generally supposed. A Rabbi informs me that he is often called to circumcize children born to such parents. Curious as it may appear, it is not of very rare occurrence for the Christian woman to embrace Judaism in order to obtain permission from the parents of the man

[1] *American Israelite*, p. 4; October 18th, 1906.

she loves, while occasionally a man even submits to circumcision for this reason. In a Jewish hospital, located in the east side of the city, I have myself witnessed this operation performed by a *Mohel*, in the presence of physicians, thus initiating a Christian into the fold of Judaism, and incidentally making him acceptable to the parents of the Jewess he longed for. Many such cases are met with by the *Mohalim*. One informs me that he circumcizes two to three adults a year, and many more children born to mixed parents. But the vast majority of mixed marriages taking place in New York City are devoid of any of these ceremonies. Most of them are satisfied with a civil ceremony, while the rich have either a Rabbi or a Christian clergyman.

From the facts and figures just presented it appears that the Jews do intermarry with people of other faiths in every country where the law permits such unions. The assumption of many authors that Jews and Christians refrain from intermarriage because of an inherent racial antipathy existing between the Aryan and the Semite is disproved by the large number of mixed marriages in Western Europe, America, and Australia.[1] All the facts go far to prove that the main reasons why they have not intermarried to any large extent during mediæval times, and even as far as the middle of the nineteenth century, were the opposition of the state laws and the difference of religious belief. Even to-day, in countries where the law does not permit such marriages, as, for instance, Austria, and especially Russia, intermarriages are next to impossible. Both the Church and the Synagogue are against mixed marriages. Not only has the Church prohibited intermarriage with Jews, Mohammedans, and heathens, but even the adherents of the different Christian denominations have thus been enjoined. Moreover, in the past and to-day in Russia, the Church could enforce such

[1] Andree says: "It is impossible for Jews to mix completely with other peoples" (*Zur Volkskunde der Juden*, p. 56). The German philosopher, Eduard von Hartmann, also says that no intermarriage takes place between Jews and Christians, because of the instinctive repulsion existing between the Semites and Aryans, although he is of the opinion that such intermarriage would prove beneficial for the Jews, and more so for the Germans. —See *Das Judenthum in Gegenwart und Zukunft*, pp. 6-28; Leipzig, 1885.

a prohibition in unmistakable terms.¹ It must be recalled that in the beginning of the nineteenth century intermarriages between Catholics and Protestants were comparatively rare in Europe and America. It was only with the change of conditions characteristic of our age, with the spirit of toleration which has become dominant in some countries, that intermarriages have become more or less frequent in those countries.

That religion is often a bar to intermarriage can be seen from statistics published in some countries on the subject of intermarriage between the followers of various religious denominations. In Hungary it appears that the Unitarians are more apt to marry persons of other denominations than the Protestants, Catholics, or Jews. The percentage of mixed marriages in 1903 was as follows:—Unitarians, 167.73; Protestants, 49.39; Reformed Church, 48.52; Greek Catholic, 42.79; Greek Oriental, 16.88; Jews, 7.21.² Here it is seen that two factors are determining the frequency of intermarriage: the degree of religious toleration and the number of persons who profess the religion. The Unitarians, who are only few in Hungary, must search for mates among the majority who follow other creeds; they are also the most tolerant religion, nothing is consequently in their way to marry out of their faith. There are more mixed than pure marriages among them. Next come the Protestants, with nearly fifty mixed to one hundred pure marriages. The large proportion of mixed marriages among the Greek Catholics is due to intermarriage with adherents of the Roman and Greek Oriental Churches; comparatively few marry Protestants. The Jews and Roman Catholics have the lowest percentage of mixed marriages in Hungary, because their clergy does its best to oppose such unions. In the capital of that country, in Budapest, where the Rabbis are not exerting as great an influence on the Jews, who are on a higher

---

[1] Angelo Sovia was, in 1712, arrested in Turin and sentenced to seven years on the galleys, because he married a Christian woman and had two children with her.—*Allgemeine Zeitung des Judenthums*, p. 678; 1867. In Vienna such a marriage, contracted in New York, was declared void by the court when the parties returned to their native land.—*Neue Freie Presse*, p. 11; May 22nd, 1906.

[2] Compiled from figures given in the *Ungarisches Statist. Jahrbuch*, 1903.

economic and intellectual plane than their co-religionists in the province, the rate of intermarriage is more than double, reaching 18.4 per cent. in 1907, although it is only thirteen years since they have been legally permitted to marry with Christians. In Germany similar conditions prevail. Of a total number of 468,329 marriages contracted during 1901, only 41,014 were between persons of different faith—*i.e.*, only 9.59 per cent. mixed to 100 pure marriages. Among the Jews in that country the percentage of mixed marriages was 16.97 during that year. This shows a larger tendency to marry outside of their faith than among the Christians in Germany. A study of conditions in the various German provinces in this respect shows that the religion which has the larger following exerts a powerful influence on the minority, and always tends to absorb by intermarriage the few who follow other creeds.[1]

Intermarriage between persons of different creed is a recent phenomenon; only one hundred years ago it was quite rare. It is only since civil marriage has been recognized in some countries that such marriages have become possible. In some countries, like Russia, Austria, Spain, Portugal, etc., the civil marriage is not yet recognized, and matrimonial affairs are left entirely to the clergy. Intermarriages between persons of different creeds are there not tolerated even to-day. "In no respect has modern civilization acted more beneficently than as a promoter of religious toleration," says Westermarck. "In our time difference in faith discourages sympathy to

[1] Detailed statistics on the subject can be found in H. A. Krose, *Konfessions-statistik Deutschlands;* Freiburg, 1904. See especially pp. 132-168. Some of the figures are reproduced by the author in the *Popular Science Monthly*, pp. 502-505; December, 1906. A somewhat similar phenomenon has been noted among the immigrant population in the United States. The Tenth Census made the interesting deduction that in those portions of the country where a single nationality was numerously represented, as, for instance, the Irish in New York City, there was little intermarriage with other nationalities. But where the nationality was not numerously represented, as the Irish in St. Louis, there was a greater tendency among the men to marry native women, or women of other nationalities.—See R. Mayo-Smith, *Statistics and Sociology*, pp. 111-112. The same holds true of the Jews in the United States. Only few marry Christians in New York City, while in the Western and Southern States intermarriage is common.

208 THE JEWS.

a much less extent than it did in former ages."[1] In Prussia the number of mixed marriages has quadrupled within the last fifty years, while the number of marriages

Fig. 139.—YEMENITE JEWS.
[*Photo, American Colony.*]

in general has increased only 70 per cent. during that period. In Bavaria the increase has been even more

[1] E. Westermarck, *History of Human Marriage*, p. 376.

pronounced. During the first half of the nineteenth century mixed marriages constituted less than three per cent. of the total number, while to-day more than one in ten are contracted between persons of different faiths.

All this goes to show that it was not difference in race, or instinctive antipathy between the so-called "Aryan" and "Semite," which kept Jews in former days from marrying with Christians. There were few mixed marriages, excepting clandestinely, among persons of different religion in mediæval days, when the Church and the Synagogue had full sway over the people. Indeed, before the Church had such great power, intermarriages between Jews and Christians did take place, as can be seen from the instances cited in the preceding chapter about Spain, Gaul, Hungary, etc. To-day again the clergy has been losing its influence in this respect, while the State has not been helping them, and the number of mixed marriages has been increasing among persons belonging to all creeds, including the Jews.

The best preventive of intermarriages of Jews is the Ghetto, as has been aptly pointed out by Ruppin. In Galicia, Russia, the East End of London, and the East Side of New York, they are infrequent; but in countries where the Jews participate in the social and economic life of the general population as equals, mixed marriages occur, and are steadily increasing in frequency, as is the case in Prussia, Scandinavia, France, Italy, etc. The largest proportion of mixed marriages in Europe is contracted in large cities, as was shown to be the case in Copenhagen, Berlin, Budapest, etc. This is because in large cities the population, Jewish as well as Christian, is less apt to be influenced by the clergy, and there are better opportunities offered for people of different faith to come into intimate social contact with each other.

Effects of Intermarriages between Jews and Christians.— Intermarriages have been welcomed by many Jews and Christians, who have claimed that they are the best means of solving the Jewish question, which is acute in some European countries. Some have maintained that racial intermixture is of advantage for both Jews and "Aryans," because the fusion of the two "races" will be beneficial by giving the progeny the higher intellectual and moral qualities of the original people.[1] On the other hand, some have discouraged intermarriage. The orthodox have their religious scruples. Others again state that no good can be expected from the children born to such couples; they inherit all the vices of their parents, but hardly any of their virtues. Moreover, it has been stated that most of the mixed marriages are infertile, that a large proportion remain sterile, and that the average number of children born to each marriage is much below the average of pure marriages. In fact, it has been repeatedly stated, as one of the best proofs of the racial purity of the Jews, that intermarriage with "Aryans" produces no progeny.

The fertility of mixed marriages has been discussed especially by Joseph Jacobs, who calculated that even if one-tenth of all the Jews and Jewesses married outside of their faith only a little over two per cent. would be left of the original ten per cent. within six generations or two hundred years. Of course, if this was the case, it would tend to show that, in spite of intermarriages, the Jewish race remains pure. It purges itself of all foreign blood in time, and the seed of Abraham again becomes as pure as it was originally. This idea of the infertility of mixed marriages prevailed until, recently, Arthur Ruppin, after a thorough study of Prussian statistics, showed conclusively that there is no real basis for any such assertion. The fertility of mixed marriages in Prussia is not much below that of pure marriages.[2]

It is true that, superficially, statistics do show a lower

---

[1] Bismarck even said that he favoured intermarriages. He tersely expressed the wish to see that "Christian stallions should be mated with Jewish mares." M. Busch, *Graf Bismarck und seine Leute*, vol. ii., pp. 218; Leipzig, 1878. W. T. Stead says: "The Jews are to the human race very much what the pure-bred Arab steed is to the equine world. But whereas the Arab thoroughbred is used freely to improve other breeds of horses, the Jew obstinately objects to be utilized in the same way for the purpose of raising the intellectual level of the human race. He is afraid, he says, of debasing the purity of his blood. But the Arab strain of blood runs through the veins of a million European horses without impairing the purity of the desert stock. If half the Jews of the world intermarried with other races the other half would keep the original fount free from debasement" (*Review of Reviews*, p. 217, March, 1910).

[2] Arthur Ruppin, "Die sozialen Verhaltnisse der Juden in Deutschland," *Jahrbücher für Nationalokonomie und Statistik*, vol. lxxviii., pp. 760-767; *Idem, Die Juden der Gegenwart*, pp. 78-96.

birth-rate among Jews married to Christians than among such as are married to their co-religionists. Thus, in Bavaria, statistics of the number of births per marriage during thirty years may lead one to believe that there is a smaller fecundity among mixed than among either pure Jewish or Christian couples[1]:—

	Pure		Mixed.
	Christian.	Jewish.	
1876-1900	2.64	3.54	1.58
1902	4.40	2.20	1.38
1903	4.31	2.31	2.11
1905-1906	4.11	2.24	1.37

In Prussia and Hungary the same is shown to be the case, while in Berlin the fertility of mixed marriages appears to be even lower. It has also been stated that the number of couples who are completely sterile was much larger among the mixed-married. Evidence collected during the census of New South Wales seems to substantiate this statement. There 13.41 per cent. of all the Jews married to Jews were sterile, while among the Jews married to Christians 30.55 per cent. were sterile. The average number of children was 3.48 among the general population, 4.06 among the Jews, and only 2.01 among Jews married to Christians.[2]

But all these figures are no safe criterion as to the fertility of mixed marriages. They are calculated by a fallacious method—namely, by dividing the number of births in a given year by the number of marriages contracted during the same year. It is known that only very few of the births during any one year are due to the marriages during that year; the vast majority are born to couples married within the preceding twenty-five years. If the number of marriages would, within reasonable limits, remain stationary, such a division would more or less accurately give us the average marriage fecundity.

[1] J. Thon, "Die Bewegung der judischen Bevölkerung in Bayern," Zeitschr. Demogr. Stat. d. Juden, 1905, No. 7.
[2] Results of Census of New South Wales, 1901, pt. iii., 1902; pt. v., 1903.

But as has already been shown, the number of mixed marriages has been increasing steadily in every country considered. It is evident, consequently, that the births of the year considered represent a smaller number of marriages than have been contracted during the year. The smaller fertility of mixed marriages is thus only apparent. We will illustrate this point by figures compiled by Ruppin about conditions in Prussia. During 1901 there were 4.2 births to each Christian marriage, 2.8 to each Jewish marriage, and only 1.8 to each marriage of a Christian to a Jewess and 1.53 to each marriage of a Jew

Fig. 140.
SOUTH ARABIAN JEW.
[*Photo, Hildebrandt.*]

Fig. 141.
SAMARITAN GRAND RABBI.

with a Christian woman. But recalling that few of these births were the result of marriages contracted during 1901, but represent marriages for about twenty-five years, we are led to investigate further. In 1876 only 256 mixed marriages were contracted in Prussia, and during the twenty-five succeeding years they increased annually, reaching 455 in 1901. If we accordingly calculate the birth-rate for 1901 on the basis of the average number of marriages during these twenty-five years (1876-1901), the result is entirely different. Ruppin shows that the rates calculated by this method are 5.07 births to each Christian marriage, 2.96 to each Jewish marriage, and 2.5 to each marriage of a Christian to a Jewess and 2.35 to each marriage of a Jew with a Christian woman. The difference is thus not much in favour of pure Jewish marriages when compared with mixed marriages. But it must be added that even this does not give a clear picture. In many mixed marriages one of the partners subsequently accepts the religion of the other, or declares him or herself "*Konfessionslos*," and the births henceforth are recorded not as the issue of a mixed marriage, but of a pure Christian or Jewish marriage, as the case may be. Many of these births are therefore missing from the official records, thus reducing the number of births from mixed marriages perceptibly. Considering this and, in addition, the fact that most of the mixed marriages occur in cities, where the birth-rates are much lower than in the country, and also that the tendency to a low birth-rate is very strong among the Jews in Western Europe in any case, one is bound to agree with Ruppin that Prussian official statistics do not support the theory that mixed marriages are less fertile than pure marriages.

There is very little to be said about the alleged physical deterioration of the offspring of mixed marriages, because it has not been proven by any reputable author.[1] Some have attempted to prove the lack of vitality of the offspring from mixed marriages by stating that immediately at birth the chances of such infants surviving is less. It has been stated that the proportion of still-births is much higher among such infants than among infants born to parents who are both Jewish. This would tend to show even an ante-natal unfavourable influence. As a matter of fact, however, the number of still-births in Prussia was found during 1875-99 as follows:—Christians, 3.59 per cent.; Jewish, 3.21 per cent.; and mixed, 3.45 per cent. The rates of the mixed are thus about midway between the pure Jewish and pure Christian.

---

[1] One writer, Maretzki, says that criminality is very common among children born to mixed couples, and he believes that there is a relation between criminality and intermarriage. His main reason is that persons who are as careless about their religion as to marry out of the pale of their faith cannot expect to have decent children. Quoted from Samter, *Judentaufen im 19. Jahrhundert*, p. 84.

Intellectually the offspring of mixed marriages cannot be said to be below the average of Jewish and Christian in Europe. In fact, some have even maintained that a large number of persons of half-Jewish origin have achieved distinction in various walks of life. Grant Allen[1] even thinks that the number of such distinguished people is rather extraordinary. To mention only a few makes quite a fine list: Montaigne; Sir John Herschel, the astronomer; Paul Lindau and his brother; G. Ebers, the Egyptologist; Ludovic Halévy, the musician; Paul Heyse; Francis Turner Palgrave, the critic; W. Gifford Palgrave, the traveller; Sir H. Drummond Wolff; Prévost Paradol; Edwin Booth, the actor; Bret Harte, the novelist; Elie Metchnikoff, the biologist; David Manin; Léon Gambetta; Sir John Millais, the British painter; Mrs. Keeley, the actress; Joseph Salvador; Sir A. Sullivan, the musician; Sidney Sonnino, the Italian sociologist, and many others. This can hardly be called intellectual degeneration.

Mixed marriages were objected to for other reasons. The Church in many countries often complained that they are a net loss to Christianity, because the children born to Christians married to Jews are more apt to be raised in the tenets of Judaism. The Jews, on the other hand, have always maintained that each marriage of this kind is a distinct loss to Judaism. Indeed, some have even stated that because most of the children of mixed couples are raised as Christians, the Jews are the gainers. The purity of Israel's breed is thus maintained by purging itself of all foreign blood.

All statistical evidence on the subject shows that about seventy-five per cent. of all the children born to Jews married to Christians are baptized immediately at birth, and only twenty-five per cent. are raised as Jews. This is best seen in Hungary, where the law permitting mixed marriages stipulates that a person intending to marry one of another religion may make a provision at the time of making the application for a marriage licence as to the religion of the children which may be born to them in the future. They may also leave the question open if they so desire. In the latter case it is provided that the boys

---

[1] *Mind*, vol. viii., pp. 504-5.

should follow the religion of their father, and the girls that of their mother. Of the 4,069 mixed marriages contracted in that country during the ten years 1895 to 1904, only 915 have taken advantage of the provision of the law and decided at the time they applied for their marriage licences about the religious affiliation of their future children. Of these 779, or 85.13 per cent., declared that they desired to bring up their children as Christians, and only 136, or 14.87 per cent., decided in favour of the Jewish religion. It is a striking fact that even in cases where the parents registered themselves as Freethinkers married to Jews one-half declared their intention to raise their children in the tenets of the Christian Church. The Jews thus lose 85 per cent. of this kind of children, which is a gain to Christianity.

In New South Wales it was also found that most of the children born to mixed marriages are raised as Christians. In cases where the husband was Jewish only 25.99 per cent. were Jewish; in cases where the mother was Jewish the percentage of Jewish children was larger, 36.36 per cent. It is noteworthy that here the mother has more influence than the father in determining the religion of the children.

In Copenhagen it was found that among 370 families of Jews married to Christians only 61 raised their children as Jews, 284 as Protestants, 4 in other religions (probably Catholic, etc.), and 21 without any religion at all.[1] The same conditions prevail in Italy,[2] France,[3] etc. In Prussia the census has especially enumerated the inhabitants who have married out of the pale of their faith, and published statistics on the religious affiliations of the children of mixed couples.[4] From these figures it appears that in

---

[1] Cordt Trap, *loc. cit.*, p. 98.

[2] See Guiseppe Cammeo, "Del matrimonio misto e sue consequenze," *Vessilo Israelito*, p. 357; 1903. He shows that the children are mostly raised as Catholics.

[3] A correspondent writes:—" For the most part the children, whatever be the religious indifference of the parents, are brought up in the dominant religion, whichever of the two spouses was born in the ranks of Judaism." *American Hebrew*, p. 655; May 1, 1908.

[4] *Zeitschrift des königl. preuss. statistischen Landesamts*, Heft 4; 1907. For an excellent compilation see A. Ruppin, " Die bestehende Mischehen in Preussen und die konfessionelle Erziehung der Kinder," *Zeitschr. Demogr. u. Statist. d. Juden*, pp. 74-76; 1908.

1905 the census officials enumerated 5,117 mixed couples living in Prussia, of which 2,931 were Jews married to Christian wives and 2,186 Jewesses married to Christian husbands. Altogether there were returned 7,016 children living with these parents, and the inquiry as to the religious affiliations of the children gave the following results:—

	Children raised as :		
	Jews.	Christians.	Dissenters.
Husband Jewish	24.61	73.36	2 03
Wife Jewish	20.18	76.04	3.78
Total	22.67	74.53	2.80

Only 22.67 per cent. of the children were raised as Jews; in cases where the husband was Jewish the percentage was 24.61, while with Jewish mothers the proportion was only 20.18 per cent. Jewish, and the rest a complete gain to the dominant religion. It is also noteworthy that the inroads thus made by Christianity are becoming stronger in recent years. At previous censuses it was ascertained that in 1885 24.78 per cent. were raised as Jews, in 1890 25.48 per cent., in 1895 24.47 per cent., in 1900 24.21 per cent., and in 1905 only 22.67 per cent. The decrease has been steady and in favour of Christianity. It is also interesting that in cases in which the non-Jewish parent was Protestant only 20.39 per cent. of the children were raised as Jews, with Catholics 24.03 per cent., and with Dissenters and Freethinkers 48.04 per cent. Protestantism, as the dominant faith, exerts the greatest absorbing influence. It must, however, be mentioned that the highest percentage of Jewish children in cases where one of the parents was a Freethinker is only apparent. The law of Prussia provides that parents cannot register their children as Freethinkers before they have reached their fourteenth year.

It must be mentioned that this does not represent the entire loss sustained by Judaism through intermarriage. A person who has one parent of Christian origin, even if raised as a Jew, is more likely to marry a Christian than a Jew, because socially he comes in intimate contact with his Christian relatives and their friends. It is also not as difficult for him to be baptized, because he considers himself as much of Christian as of Jewish origin. It is Ruppin's opinion that hardly ten per cent. of the children resulting from mixed marriages remain Jews for any considerable length of time. Of these it is doubtful whether any Jews are left after two or three generations.

Mixed marriages have been objected to by both Jews and Christians on the score of the problematical felicity of the parties married. One of the ways to determine marital felicity is the frequency of divorce. It has been shown that mixed marriages are more liable to dissolution than pure marriages. In Prussia it was found that during 1905 140 mixed marriages were divorced by the courts. The following are the figures of divorce to the number of marriages contracted during that year[1]:—

Husband and wife Protestant	26.7	Divorces per 1000 marriages.
,, ,, Catholic	9.6	,, ,, ,,
,, ,, Jewish	40.9	
Husband Protestant, wife Catholic	37.2	,,
,, Catholic, wife Protestant	40.8	,,
,, Christian, wife Jewish	56.1	
,, Jewish, wife Christian	52 0	,, ,, ,,

Divorces, which are more common among the Jews than among the Christians, are most common among mixed couples, especially among Jews married to Christians. The same is the case in Berlin where during the ten years, 1892 to 1902, to each 1,000 marriages there were divorces as follows: Jews, 3; Christians, 3.91; Jews married to Christian women, 10.09; Christians married to Jewesses, 11.16. Mixed marriages are thus three to four times more likely to be dissolved than pure marriages. Marriages between Christians and Jewesses are more often dissolved than marriages between Jews and Christian women. That the excessive friction incidental between married couples of different faith is one of the causes of divorce among them, is seen from the fact that marriages between Protestants and Catholics have also a high rate of divorce. In addition it must be recalled that mixed

[1] *Zeitschrift für Demographie und Statistik der Juden*, pp. 110-111; 1907.

marriages are taking place mostly in large cities, where divorces are more common than in small towns and in the country. Another factor which may have an influence is the fact that mixed marriages have lately been increasing, as was shown above, and divorces are more frequent among couples recently married than among those who have passed successfully several years of marital life. Statistics of divorce among mixed couples for a small number of years are, therefore, likely to be fallacious, and for a long period of years there are no available data.

The most noteworthy effect of these mixed marriages is the resulting diminution of the number of Jews in countries where they are at all common. "The loss sustained by Judaism through mixed marriages," says Ruppin, "is not to be considered a negligible quantity. In 1901, after five years of legalized intermarriage in Hungary, the proportion of children born to mixed parents was 1.23 per cent. of the total number of Jewish births; in Prussia, after twenty-five years of intermarriage, it was found to be 10.47 per cent. (in 1908, even 12.4 per cent.); and in Berlin, as high as 15.15 per cent. of all the Jewish births were of mixed origin. Between 1875 and 1902 14,536 children were born in Prussia from mixed marriages." Indeed Ruppin points out that the loss is much greater than the loss sustained through baptism, which is very much in vogue in Prussia. He shows that in that country only about 400 Jews are converted annually to Christianity, as against 700 children of half-Jewish blood becoming Christians. Only about 25 Christians are annually converted to Judaism and 75 children of half-Jewish blood are gained by Judaism through intermarriage.[1] It is of interest to mention in this connection the enormous sums spent annually by various Christian missions to the Jews, maintained mostly by moneys contributed by English-speaking people. It is well known that they meet with little, if any, success. From some reports published it appears that it costs between £600 to £3,000 for the conversion of a single Jew, which makes a converted Jew a rather costly article. It appears from the figures given above that intermarriages bring much better results for the promotion of Christianity among the Jews than

[1] A. Ruppin, "*Die Juden der Gegenwart*, pp. 92-94.

missions with their "costly converts," who only rarely, if ever, prove desirable acquisitions to Christianity.

The ethnic effects of intermarriage between Jews and Christians must not be under-estimated. We have shown that comparatively few of the offspring born to "mixed" parents remain within the fold of Judaism,—in the long run hardly more than ten per cent. But it must be borne in mind that the number keeps on increasing and is cumulative. It is consequently to be expected that in the course of years new anthropological types are being introduced among the children of Israel. We do not realize on superficial examination the significance of fusion unless it involves the total population of given groups of people. Professor Franz Boas has calculated that in a population in which two types intermingle, and in which both types occur with equal frequency, there will be in the fourth generation less than one person in ten thousand of pure descent. When the proportion of the two original types is as nine to one, there will be among the more numerous part of the population only eighteen in one thousand in the fourth generation of pure blood.[1] It is thus evident that both the Jewish as well as the Christian populations of the countries in which mixed marriages take place to any considerable extent are bound to show their effects from the anthropological standpoint. When, in this connection, it is again mentioned that in some cities in Europe, America, and Australia the proportion of "mixed" marriages is between twenty-five and sixty per cent. of the number of "pure" Jewish marriages, it is clear that even with the small number of children that are left within the fold of Judaism the Chosen People cannot maintain themselves ethnically in that state of purity which they claimed to date. It will, indeed, be a very fertile field for anthropological study to follow up the new generation of Jews in Berlin, Munich, Copenhagen, Sydney, etc., and watch the effects of this fusion on the number of blondes among them, as well as on the stature, head-form, and other stable physical traits. We know from biology that, as a result of intercrossing of two or more types, no new or middle types are originated as a rule. From investiga-

[1] Franz Boas, "Race Problems in America," *Science*, vol. xxix., pp. 839-849; 1909.

tions made by Franz Boas on Half-breeds of American Indians[1] it was evident that they revert to either of the original types of the parents; in other words, there is a tendency in the offspring of red and white parents to revert to either the paternal or maternal type. Investigations on Eastern Jews in New York City have confirmed the above by showing that, as regards the head-form, there is an alternating heredity, largely a reversion to the type of the father and mother, but also to a remote ancestral type.[2]

We are under the impression that the effects of this law of alternating heredity is responsible for the claim made by several authors that Jewish blood is more prepotent than the non-Jewish.[3] When among some of the offspring of a mixed marriage the "Jewish" cast of countenance is very pronounced, it is pointed at as a proof of the greater power of survival of Jewish blood, without taking the trouble to find out how many of the other children look like their Christian parent. Indeed, we have read somewhere a statement that just as among animals and plants there is by intercrossing a tendency to revert to a more primitive type, so may it be expected that as a result of Jewish-Christian marriages the reversion will be toward the Jewish racial type, which is alleged to be the older of the two. In other words, there will be no progression, but reversion. The alleged "prepotency" of Jewish blood was thus used both by the Jews, who were proud of the superior tenacity of their blood, and by their enemies, who claimed that Jewish survival under such circumstances was merely a reversion to a more primitive and inferior type. However, all available evidence, quite meagre to be sure, tends to point in the opposite direction. Investigations made on a large scale on Jewish immigrants in the United States show that the taller, the fair-complexioned, and the dolichocephalic have more chances to survive and leave a progeny. This is evident from measurements taken of the second and third generation of

---

[1] *Verhandl. d. Berliner anthrop. Gesellsch.*, pp. 367-411; 1895.
[2] F. Boas, "Heredity in Head Form," *Amer. Anthropologist*, N.S. vol. v., pp. 406-409; "Heredity in Anthropometric Traits," *Ibid.*, vol. ix., pp. 453-469.
[3] See p. 99, *supra*.

American Jews. Whether this is due to environmental influences or to a natural elimination of the darker, shorter, and brachycephalic types in the United States is difficult to determine with our present limited knowledge as to the origin of these traits in general.

It remains yet to speak of the Jewish attitude toward intermarriage. Of course the orthodox are altogether opposed to such unions. They follow implicitly the Biblical prohibition as regards the seven nations of Canaan, "Neither shalt thou make marriage with them; thy daughter thou shalt not give unto his son, nor his daughter shalt thou take unto thy son."[1] From the facts just brought together it is evident that the reason, "for they will turn away thy son from following Me, that they may serve other gods," holds good to-day as it did in Biblical times. Ezra for the same reasons extended this prohibition to all other idolatrous nations, and the Talmud to all Gentiles. A modification of this prohibition was interpreted in cases of converts to Judaism; when a Gentile says like Ruth: "Thy people shall be my people, and thy God shall be my God." A Rabbi interprets in the Talmud the Biblical law relating to a captive woman not being tabooed provided she "shall bevail her father and mother," as meaning that she shall bevail her ancestral religion.[2]

It is interesting that at some periods of their history Jews were inclined to look at intermarriage without scorn, some Rabbis even going so far as to exclude only the seven nations of Canaan, or idolaters in general, or to condemn only such marriages "by which the offspring is turned into idolatry," while Christians being regarded as "proselytes of the gates" might be permitted to marry with Jews. But here the Church intervened. Emperor Constantinus prohibited such marriages in 339 under the penalty of death, and this prohibition has been repeated at various Church Councils throughout the Middle ages.[3]

[1] Deuteronomy, vii. 3.
[2] For details see article, "Intermarriage," *Jewish Encyclopædia*, by K. Kohler.
[3] The texts of the ecclesiastical canons prohibiting friendly intercourse and intermarriage between Christians and Jews are given by Prof. B. Feldman, "Intermarriage Historically Considered," *Year Book Centr. Confr. Amer. Rabbis*, 1909, pp. 271-307.

In 1807 Napoleon I. convened the Assembly of Jewish Notables, known as the *Sanhedrin*, with the object of inquiring into the Jewish view-point on many questions relating to Jews as citizens of European countries. One of the questions propounded by the Government read as follows: "May a Jewess marry a Christian, or a Jew a Christian woman? or does the Jewish law order that the Jews should only intermarry among themselves?" The answer given by the representatives of the Jews, among whom were many great Rabbis of that time, was to the effect that "marriages between Israelites and Christians when concluded in accordance with the civil code are valid, and though they cannot be solemnized by the religious rites of Judaism, they should not be subject to rabbinical anathema (*Cherem*)." Of course the orthodox Jews have never accepted this resolution as binding. But the reform synagogues of Germany have not condemned intermarriage. At its session in Brunswick the Rabbinical Conference in 1844 declared that "the marriage of a Jew with a Christian woman or with any adherent of a monotheistic religion is not prohibited if the children of such issue are permitted by the State to be brought up in the Israelitish religion." While I am convinced that it was the secularization of marriage by the law of Germany that has been the most important factor in popularizing this kind of unions, yet it must be conceded that the liberal attitude of the Rabbis has also been a factor in increasing the number of mixed marriages in Germany, France, and other countries.

The American Rabbis, who follow closely the German reform movement, have for years looked at intermarriages with equanimity, and some have even not refused to officiate at such functions. But the number has of late increased to such a degree that an alarm was sounded in Jewish circles and an agitation started against them. At their conference held in 1909 in New York City, the General Conference of American Rabbis took up the problem for discussion. While many rabbis strenuously opposed intermarriage as threatening the integrity of Judaism, yet the following mild resolution was passed by a large majority: "Resolved, that the General Conference of American Rabbis declare that mixed marriages are contrary to the tradition of the Jewish religion and should therefore be discouraged by the American rabbinate." An amendment to the effect that a rabbi "ought not to officiate" at a mixed marriage was lost when put to a vote. In the discussion it was stated by several rabbis that if a rabbi will refuse, the couple will surely go to a Christian minister, showing that the rabbis are powerless to counteract the tendencies of the times. Indeed, this was the most logical way to look at the matter. American rabbis do not grant divorces and remarry persons who were divorced in the state courts; they do not insist on the restrictions imposed on the *Cohanim* in the choice of a wife[1]; they do not insist on the Levirate marriage (*Chalizah*), the practice of marrying a dead brother's widow, and the like. If intermarriage was not as dangerous for the integrity of Judaism as it practically proves to be, the rabbis would undoubtedly do away with the restriction as they did away with other traditional ordinances.

In England, where the synagogue followed strictly the orthodox precepts, the rabbis never countenanced intermarriage. During recent years the Jewish Religious Union, which declares Judaism essentially a universal religion and its doctrines not merely suited to one race, has not declared in favour of such unions. "We agree with our orthodox brethren in rejecting and deprecating intermarriage, for the simple and adequate reason that only by this means can Judaism as a distinct and separate religion be preserved," says Claude Montefiore in a dissertation on the principles of the religious reform of the English Jews. It is noteworthy that although French Judaism has been strictly orthodox during the nineteenth century, German reform not having had any influence till recent years, still the number of mixed marriages has been very large, as already shown. This again confirms our contention that at the present time religion is powerless to keep the Jews away from marrying with Christians as long as the State does not interfere. But since the final act of the separation of the Church and State of 1905 a reform synagogue has been established in Paris which is very lax in this regard, inasmuch as it permits mixed

[1] The plot of Zangwill's *Children of the Ghetto* is based on this peculiar Jewish restriction.

marriages, makes circumcision optional, has a "solemn service on Sunday," and the like.

In Russia, Austria, and the Orient the rabbis need not take any action in this matter, because the laws of these theocratic countries prohibit intermarriage between Jews and Gentiles. It is noteworthy that with such laws some statesmen in those regions complain that the Jews will not assimilate. Of course, these legal prohibitions are more effective barriers in the way of fusion than the religious prohibitions. Thus, while practically all the rabbis agree with the American rabbi, Einhorn, that every mixed marriage is a nail in the coffin of Judaism, yet they find themselves powerless to counteract the tendencies of the times, and they submit to the inevitable. Just as they find that it is practically impossible for the majority of the Jews to obey the Sabbath in a country where the majority of the population rests on Sunday, and they therefore have Sunday services in their temples; just as they find that dietary laws cannot be obeyed by Jews who come in intimate social contact with their Christian neighbours, in just the same manner they acknowledge that social intimacy must often result in intermarriage. Dr. Emil G. Hirsch,[1] the leading rabbi in the reform movement in the United States, speaking of the problem, points out that intermarriage is inevitable under present conditions; he says that he cannot agree with the opinion that the increase of mixed marriages will seal the doom of Judaism. He considers Judaism a philosophy of life and an interpretation of history, surviving without the racial or national substratum of Jewry. He points out that social intercourse between Jew and non-Jew is responsible for intermarriage, and from the standpoint of those opposed to it, anything which prevents social intimacy between Jew and Christian must be regarded as providential. "Let us cease protesting against our being socially ostracized, against the refusal of private schools to receive Jewish pupils. They who exclude us work for the preservation of Judaism. For social intercourse is very apt to result in mixed marriages."

[1] E. G. Hirsch, "An Historic Resolution," *Reform Advocate* (Chicago), Nov. 27th, 1909.

CHAPTER X.

DEMOGRAPHIC CHARACTERISTICS.

The alleged superior fecundity of the Jews—Birth rates of Jews in various countries—In Eastern Europe—In Western Europe—The decline in the procreating capacity of the Jews—The marriage fecundity of the Jews in eastern and western countries—Causes of the low birth rates of the Jews—Sex at birth—The enormous excess of males is only apparent—Proportion of still-births—Illegitimacy among the Jews.

Natality.—The vulgar errors often made by writers on the racial characteristics of various peoples become evident when a study is made of the demographic phenomena of the Jews. Most recent authors, drawing upon antiquated sources of information which deal with conditions in the Ghettoes, assume that the Jews in Western Europe and America are possessed of the same traits. The birth-rates of the various populations in Europe were very high during the Mediæval centuries, and only began to abate about the middle of the nineteenth century. The death-rates, especially the infant mortality, were high almost everywhere. The Jews at that time also had high birth-rates, but their general, as well as their infant mortality, was comparatively low, for reasons which will be stated hereafter. Owing to this lower mortality, their natural increase, the excess of births over deaths, was much higher than that of the non-Jews among whom they lived. Moreover, the economic, social, and especially the political conditions of the non-Jewish inhabitants of various countries, differ according to the country in which they lived, and according to the social group or caste to which they belonged. As might be expected, the demographic phenomena were heterogeneous, depending on various social and intellectual factors. With the Jews conditions were different. They were isolated by law from the general population and segregated in

Ghettoes; their religion, to which they strictly adhered both to the spirit as well as to the letter of the law, was just as strong as the civic law, often even stronger, in keeping them apart from their non-Jewish neighbours. These conditions could not but result in a totally dissimilar *milieu*, which carried with it as a concomitant demographic phenomena which differed in no small degree from those observed among the Christians.

What is of most importance in this connection, and which must always be borne in mind, is that the conditions of the Jews in the various countries of Europe were, up to the beginning of the nineteenth century, more or less the same. They were everywhere isolated from the non-Jewish population, engaged everywhere in similar occupations, adhered to their religion with as much fervency in every country to about the same degree, etc. Homogeneity of environment produced homogeneity of demographic phenomena. They were everywhere prolific, their birth-rates were high, their mortality low, and the excess of births over deaths was large almost everywhere. Seeing that these characteristics were evident among Jews in various countries, it was at once explained as a racial trait, as inherent in the Jews to "increase and multiply and replenish the earth."[1] It is also mentioned that excessive fecundity is not a new phenomenon among the Jews, it had already been observed among them in ancient times. In Egypt, "the children of Israel were fruitful, and increased abundantly, and multiplied, and waxed exceedingly mighty; and the land was filled with them."[2] Those who consider ancient statistics as reliable as those carefully collected to-day, even point to the Biblical census

---

[1] "The demographic phenomena are very favourable among the Jews, as is attested by the investigations of many statisticians. This is to be considered as a characteristic trait of the Semitic race, as against the Aryans, who are less favoured. Not only are the Jews, by virtue of these racial characteristics, able to prosper in climates which are detrimental to the Aryans, but by greater fertility and longer duration of natural life, they multiply much faster."—Schimmer, *Statistik des Judenthums*, p. 5. Andree also speaks of the demography of the Jews as partly differing from that of the Aryans, and says that these differences have been elicited in every country in which sufficient statistical evidence has been collected on the subject (*Zur Volkskude der Juden*, p. 70). But he bases his opinion on statistics gathered during the first half of the nineteenth century.

[2] Exodus, i. 7.

according to which Jacob emigrated to Egypt only seventy strong, and after remaining there for about four hundred years the descendants of these seventy persons left the country under the leadership of Moses, their number amounting to 611,730 males over twenty years of age and capable of bearing arms, thus implying a population of over three millions.

If a racial characteristic of the Jews, this fecundity should be stable, persistent, and only little if at all influenced by external conditions such as climate, economic and social conditions. Inasmuch as the census offices of many European countries inquire also into the religious belief of the population, it makes it an easy matter to determine whether at the present there are any differences in this respect between Jews and the races and peoples among which they live. On the whole, it must be stated at the outset that from the enormous mass of vital statistics collected during the past century nothing definite has been established as to the influence of race on the birth and death rates. All the evidence indicates that the influence is negative, and that standards of comfort, intellectual, social, and economic conditions are the sole determining factors. Race, *per se*, has nothing to do with the demography of Europe; and as regards the Orient and the peoples in a state of nature, there are no censuses made among them, so that no opinion can be formed on their birth and death rates. Judging by European conditions, there is positively no race influence to be observed. On the one hand, one would be led to believe that the Teutons have a high birth-rate, when the rates of the peoples in the German Empire are considered. But on the other hand, more than one-half of the population of that country is not at all Teutonic in origin, while in Scandinavia, where the Teutons have preserved themselves in much greater purity, the birth rate is comparatively low, as it is also in England. The Slavonic races in Eastern Europe have a very high degree of fertility, but the differences in the various provinces of Russia, Poland, and Austria are so great as to disprove directly the contention that race is necessarily the cause. In the same manner the differences in the rates in Italy and Southern France are striking. The racial elements are about the same in both countries, as are climatic conditions, yet the birth-rates of Italy are much higher than those of France. These and other examples which are to be observed in Europe and America are definite proof that race has nothing at all to do with fertility.

With such a complex problem, however, it is always best to consider every factor which may have an influence. Inasmuch as it is difficult and often impossible to include every essential factor and to exclude everything which is not essential, when speaking of other races and peoples, the Jews in Europe, owing to their isolation and alleged abstinence from intermarriage with Christians, should offer good material for the solution of the question of the influence of race on fertility. The vital statistics of several countries where the birth, death, and marriage certificates include questions as to the religious belief of the parties concerned, give excellent information on the subject. This is the case with the vital statistics of Russia, Germany, Austria, Hungary, Bulgaria, Roumania, Servia, and partly also Holland and Italy. It is to be regretted that in France, England, Belgium, and the United States no such information is to be obtained from the census and registrars' reports.

As is the case with many other alleged characteristics of the Jews, their demography is not uniform in every country. From statistics collected in various parts of Europe it appears that there are just as many differences among the Jews as there are among the various races and peoples of that continent. Those living in Eastern Europe are very prolific, while those in Western Europe and America have quite low birth-rates, and between these two extremes there are Jews who stand in this respect in an intermediate position. In other words, the Jews who live among people with high birth-rates also have the same characteristic, and the reverse. Thus the highest birth-rates recorded among the Jews is in Algeria, where the rate was in 1903, 44.67 per 1,000 population; next to these are the Jews in Bulgaria with a rate of 38.2 per 1,000, while among the Greek Orthodox in that country the rate was 41.4. The Jews in Austrian Galicia are also very prolific, in 1900 their birth-rate was 38.01 (as against 45.85 among the Christians of that country), as are also the Jews in European Russia, where the rate during the census year 1897 was 35.43 and 53.36 among the Greek Catholics, who seem to be the most prolific people in Europe. Austria with a birth-rate of 33.89 among the Jews in 1900 (Christians 38.01), and Roumania with rates of 36.63 among Jews in 1897-1902 and 40.72 among Christians, come next.[1] Finally, Hungary also shows high Jewish birth-rates, 30.09, as against 37.0 among the Christians in 1907. It is thus seen that in countries where the birth-rates of the non-Jewish population are high, the same is to be seen among the Jews, although as a whole they are slightly lower than those of the Christians among whom they live. The reason for this will appear later in this chapter.

In Western Europe, where the rates among the general population are either low, or have been falling during recent years, the birth-rates of the Jews are also low, in fact lower than among their neighbours. Thus in Hesse their birth-rate was in 1901-04, 19.0, while among the Christians it was 34.0 per 1,000 population; in Bavaria during 1906 it was, Jews, 18.17, and Christians, 35.91; in Prussia, in 1908, Jews, 17.01, and Christians, 32.89; and Bohemia in 1900, Jews, 17.85, Christians 34.88. In some cities the rates among Jews are even lower ·

	Jews.	Christians.
Berlin (1905)	17.73	25.54
Frankfort-on-Main (1905)	16.19	29 08
Prague (1901)	15.85	31.31

It is thus seen that everywhere the birth-rates of the Jews are lower than those of the Christians among whom they live. In some countries and cities, like Prussia, Bavaria, Bohemia, etc., they are only one-half as fertile as the Christians. While, as has already been stated, some authors consider the Jews a very prolific race, there are other authors who speak of the lower Jewish birth-rates as a racial peculiarity, common to all Jews living in different countries, and having a definite physiologic or ethnic basis as its cause. Instead of looking into the social environment, which is the most potent factor in the reduction of the birth-rate of most European peoples,

[1] A. Ruppin, *Die Juden in Rumanien*, p. 65; Berlin, 1908.

instead of inquiring into the occupations, standards of comfort, economic prosperity, age at marriage, etc., which would give reasonable explanations of this phenomenon, many writers have been satisfied with "race" as a satisfactory interpretation of conditions. But the figures cited above directly disprove the ethnic theory of the low birth-rates of the Jews. If it was a physiological characteristic of the Jews, we should expect that the rates in every country would be about the same. As a matter of fact, however, there are wide limits of variation, as wide, in fact, as for the whole population of Europe, extending as they do, from 44.67 per 1,000 population, in Algeria, to as small a rate as 15.85 in the city of Prague. Ethnic conditions are never known to display such wide limits of variation.

An attempt has been made by several statisticians to find some geographical differences in the birth-rates of Europe. Sundbärg, studying the rates during the entire nineteenth century, finds that 38.2 births took place on the average annually per 1,000 population, but that there were significant differences when Eastern Europe is compared with Western Europe. He calculated an annual rate per 1,000 population for Eastern Europe, 46.1; Western Europe, 33.6; South-west, only 32.3; and North-west, 34.7.[1] On the whole his calculations are well-founded, although there are some exceptions which are to be attributed to social conditions of a local nature. A careful analysis of the figures given above shows that the Jews, in a measure, follow the rule laid down by Sundbärg, excepting the fact that their birth-rates are everywhere lower than those of the Christians. Russia, Poland, Galicia, and Roumania are typical of Eastern Europe, and there the Jews are the most prolific in Europe. As there are no statistics obtainable for the extreme west of Europe, we must consider some Central European countries instead. Taking Bavaria as typical of conditions among Western European Jews, we find here a very low birth-rate, only 18.02 per 1,000 Jews. Amsterdam is intermediate between these two extremes, only 24.82, corresponding roughly to the North-west of Europe.

[1] Sundbärg, *Statistika Ofversiktstabeller*, ix., Stat. Tidskrift, H. 130, 1904, p. 278.

For the south of Europe there are no available statistics of recent date, because the census inquiries do not ask any questions about the religious affiliation of the people.

It thus appears that the Jews follow quite closely the rates observed in Europe. The highest rates are observed in the east, the lowest in the west, etc. It is also known that in Denmark the birth-rate of the Jews is very low, corresponding to the rates in the north, and in France it is at least as low as that of the French. In general, it can be stated that Sundbärg's rule holds as good for Jews as non-Jews in Europe.

The fall in the birth-rates among Europeans, which has engaged so much attention of recent years, is also seen among the Jews. Indeed, the decline is much more decided among them than among the Christians. In Poland, for instance, the birth-rate of the Jews was, in 1891, 36.98, sinking in 1901 to 30.85, while among the Catholic population of that city it remained stationary, 41.58 and 41.59 respectively. In Roumania it decreased among the Jews from 40.17 in 1896 to 32.36 in 1902, while among the Christians it actually increased during that period from 41.49 to 42.86; and in Hungary also the rate sank from 36.86 in 1891-95 to 28.00 in 1908, and in Budapest during 1901-05 it was only 22.8.[1] This decline in the fertility of the Jews is remarkable, because it has been taking place in Eastern Europe, where the fertility of the Christian population is very great, and is indicative of great and important changes in the social conditions of the Jews of that region. But in Western Europe the decline in the birth-rates among the Jews is actually appalling. In Bavaria the difference between 1876 and 1906 is nearly one-half against the Jews:—

	Annual Birth-rate.	
	Jews.	Christians.
1876	34.40	45.90
1904	18.02	38.56
1906	18.47	35.91

The birth-rate of the Christian population was, in 1906, only 78 per cent. of the rate in 1876, while among the Jews the decline during these thirty years was greater,

[1] Auerbach, "Die Sterblichkeit der Juden in Budapest," Zeitschr. Demogr. Stat. d. Juden, p. 152; 1908.

sinking to 52 per cent. That this is not due to any special cause operating in 1906 is shown by the fact that the rates have been steadily going down in Bavaria. The average annual birth-rates were as follow:—

1876-1880	35.5
1888-1890	26.3
1890-1900	19.9
1906	18.5

Bavarian Jews are not unique in this respect. In Prussia the decline in Jewish fertility has been much more pronounced. In that country the available vital statistics for eighty-six consecutive years, 1822-1908, show a condition alarming to all who have any regard for the future of Judaism. The rates among the Christians were in 1822-40, 40.01; in 1888-92, 37.03; in 1908, 32.89. Among the Jews the rates dropped from 35.46 in 1822-40 to 23.75 in 1888-92 and 17.01 in 1908.

The decline among the Christians has not been very great during the eighty-four years; the rate was, in 1908, 83.4 per cent. of the rate of 1822-40. Among the Jews it sank to only 48.0 per cent. of the rates in 1822-40; less than one-half the number of children are proportionately born to Jews in 1908 than eighty-four years ago. This is not specially due to mixed marriages, which are very common in Prussia, as will be seen from the next chapter. In the above figures the factor of intermarriage has been provided for in the following simple manner:—One-half the number of children born from such unions have been credited to Christians and the other half to Jews. This shows that it is an actual decline in the procreating capacity of the Jews in Prussia, as well as in Bavaria, which is responsible for the low birth-rates.

The immigrant Jews in London have quite high birth-rates. Dr. S. F. Murphy testified before the Royal Commission on Alien Immigration that while the birth-rate has been falling in London it rose in Whitechapel from 35.7 to 39.2 between 1886-90; in St. George-in-the-East it rose from 39.9 to 43.3; in Limehouse it fell from 35.3 to 33.4; in Mile End Old Town it rose from 37.5 to 38.2.[1] Dr.

[1] *Minutes of Evidence*, 3957.

Joseph Loane testified to the same effect and showed that the rate of the English in that district was 31 to 35, and among the Jews it goes up to 48.¹ This is confirmed by the figures in the *Annual Report of the Public Health Committee* of the London County Council for the year 1906, which shows that the birth-rate in Stepney was 35.3 in 1906 and 36.7 during the period 1901-05. Both these figures are the highest recorded in London for the years named. In 1906 the nearest figure to that of Stepney was the 34.5 in Bethnal Green, and the next highest the 34.2 in Shoreditch. The Stepney rate compares with 17.2 in Westminster and 19.2 in Kensington. A high birth-rate is characteristic of immigrants for various reasons, particularly because they have a higher proportion of persons of child-bearing ages. Among the native Jews in England the rates are much lower, probably the same as among the Christians of the same social and economic status.

For the Jews in the United States there are no available vital statistics, excepting those collected in 1890, and published by Dr John S. Billings, containing information about 10,618 Jewish families, including 60,630 persons living in the United States, December 31st, 1889.² From this census bulletin it is evident that the birth-rate of the Jews is only 20.81 per 1,000, which is at least 10 per cent. lower than among the general population. A fairer means of comparison, however, is the ratio of births with reference to the number of women of child-bearing age present—viz., those between 15 and 49 years of age, inclusive. This rate was found to be 72.87 per 1,000, as against 82.9 in Massachussets and 86 in Rhode Island. During the six years in which this investigation was made by the census officials the rates among the Jews were decreasing perceptibly, showing the same tendency as is being observed among their European co-religionists. It must be mentioned that the majority of the Jews enumerated in the above inquiry were immigrants or children of immigrants. It is well known that among the native Jews of the United States conditions are almost the same as among the native population of Massachusetts.

¹ *Minutes of Evidence*, 4557-59.
² *Census Bulletin, No. 19;* Dec. 30, 1890, Washington, D.C.

Indeed, the large families, in which up to a dozen and even more children were seen, which were not uncommon among the Jews of Europe before the middle of the nineteenth century, are almost unknown among the American Jews. Among the immigrant Jewish population large families are not rare, just as is the case with most other immigrant populations; but even their fertility is declining. Physicians who practise their profession among the immigrant Jewish population of New York City all agree that its fertility is decidedly on the wane. Those who have been for some time in the United States are only too frequently inquiring as to the best means of "prudentially" limiting the size of the family. In Eastern Europe the same Jewesses have never known of the possibility of doing any such thing. This metamorphosis goes hand-in-hand with other habits and customs which the Jewish immigrants are acquiring from their American neighbours.

From all that has been said, it appears that in no country in the civilized world is there to be seen such a formidable decline in fertility as among the Jews in Western Europe. In Germany the birth-rates among the Christians have, with slight fluctuations, remained about the same since the beginning of the nineteenth century; since 1840, the rates have been about 36 births per 1,000 population, and have remained about the same in the beginning of the twentieth century. In some provinces it has decreased, but the decrease was comparatively slight, as in Prussia from 37.8 in 1841 to 36.5 in 1900. The reduction of the birth-rate in Germany is chiefly shown in its great cities, while the rural population has not yet been affected to any great extent.[1] In other countries, like Scandinavia, England, Italy, Austria, etc., the decline has been more pronounced. The most striking decline in the procreative capacity has been observed in France; there it was 27.3 in 1841-50, and it sank to 22 in 1900. This is considered by statisticians the most appalling decline in Europe. But among the Jews in Western Europe racial self-effacement has been much more pronounced. In Prussia it was in 1906 less than one-half of what it was

[1] Newsholme and Stevenson, "The Decline of Human Fertility," *Journal Royal Statist. Society*, vol. lxix., pp. 34-87; 1906.

eighty-four years ago. In Bohemia, Bavaria, etc., the rates are even lower than in Prussia, only 17 per 1,000 Jews. In large urban centres, like Berlin, Prague, etc., it is yet lower, almost reaching vanishing point. The effects of this violent race suicide are evident in the censuses of the Jewish population in those countries. The number of native Jews is decreasing in rapid strides to an extent unknown in the history of any civilized people. If there were no immigration of Eastern European Jews to the West the future of the Jews in Western Europe would not be an encouraging one. They could hardly hold their own as a religious minority.

It has been suggested that notwithstanding the low birth-rate the Jews have a higher marriage fecundity or fruitfulness than the Christians. But this is not borne out by facts as recorded in various censuses. When judged by the number of children to a marriage, they show the same characteristics as when the crude birth-rate is taken as criterion. In the Orient and in Eastern Europe their marriage fecundity is very high, while in Western Europe it is low, even lower than among their Christian neighbours. Thus in Bulgaria there were during 1897-1902 5.67 births recorded to each marriage among Jews, while among the Christian population of that country the rate was only 4.68. In Austria it was in 1901, Jews, 5.37; Christians, 4.59; in Algeria in 1903, Jews, 4.74; Europeans, 3.86 (the native non-Jewish population cannot be compared with the Jews because they are polygamous); in Warsaw, Poland, in 1901, Jews, 4.59; and Catholics, 2.95; in European Russia in 1897, Jews, 4.33; and Greek Orthodox, 5.63; and in Roumania in 1902, Jews, 3.22; and Christians, 2.15. It is thus seen that with but two exceptions the Jews have a higher marriage fecundity than their non-Jewish neighbours. However, in the named countries the native populations are very fertile, while the Jewish rates are also high, but somewhat lower than those of Gentiles. But in Western Europe the fruitfulness of the Jews is alarmingly low. In Prussia, where there were recorded in 1905 4.11 births to each Christian marriage, the Jews only had a rate of 2.48. This condition had not been observed among the Jews of thirty years ago. The following are the figures showing the marriage fecundity of the Jews in Prussia since 1820.[1] It was 4.33 per 1,000 in 1820-30, and 4.11 in 1905 among the Christians; among the Jews it fell during that period from 5.19 to 2.48 per 1,000, showing that while the decline in fruitfulness among the Christians in Prussia has been insignificant during the mentioned eighty-five years among the Jews it has been reduced to nearly one-half. Similar conditions have been observed among Jews in other Western European countries. In Bavaria, the number of children per marriage was during 1876-80, 4.75; it decreased during the next five-year period to 4.15; during 1886-90 to 3.49; then a further fall was observed to 3.01 during 1891-95; during 1896-1900 it was only 2.50, and it did not stop here, but kept on sinking till it reached in 1904 a rate of only 2.11 births per marriage. Similar conditions have been reported about the province of Hesse and in several other European countries.

The traditional large families of the Jews are matters of the past, and are only seen among Jews living in the state in which the forefathers of the Western European Jews lived fifty years ago. To-day in their "march of progress" they have outstripped the Christians in regard to the tendency to "prudentially" limiting the size of the family. Indeed, if their death-rate was not so favourable, as will appear in a later chapter, there would hardly be left any Jews in Western Europe within the next fifty years.

The causes of this decline in the procreating capacity of the Jews of Western Europe and America are not of a physiological or pathological nature. It is not due to physical degeneration affecting the reproductive powers, or the procreative capacity of the Jewish people. The etiology is the same as the etiology of the decline in human fertility among other peoples in Europe and America. It is mainly due to the late marriages, high proportion of celibacy, and the determination of modern people to improve the standard of comfort in their daily life. With the Jews there are some special causes, which are also seen among others, but which act for various reasons more intensely among the descendants of Israel.

[1] A. Goldscheider, "Die Entwicklung der jüdischen Bevolkerung Preussens im 19 Jahrhundert," *Zeitschr. Demog. Statistik der Juden*, pp. 70-75; 1907.

The Jews are city dwellers *par excellence*, as has already been shown. The fertility of city populations is almost everywhere lower than that of the rural population. The agricultural people of all nations are to-day swelling the birth-rates of every European country, and in Russia, Austria, the Balkan States, etc., where the proportion of persons engaged in agricultural pursuits is very great, the highest birth-rates are to be seen. The Jews have practically no agriculturists, hence a cause for a lower fertility. It has also been shown that the birth-rate is lowest among the rich, highest among the very poor, and that the mass of the population which lies between these two social extremes occupies an intermediate position in regard to preventive measures taken against conception.[1] This is well confirmed by conditions among the Jews. In the Orient and in Eastern Europe, where the bulk of the Jews live in poverty and want, their birth-rate is high, and they are very prolific; in Western Europe, where the majority of the Jews are economically prosperous, mostly engaged in mercantile pursuits and in finance, their birth-rate is low, even lower than that of their Christian neighbours. The latter have a higher birth-rate, because among them there are many agricultural and industrial labourers whose high fertility raises the general birth-rate. If Jews in Germany were compared with Christians in that country, who are merchants, manufacturers, professional people, bankers, etc., there would hardly be any difference between the two groups in regard to fertility. It is absurd to compare the Jews with the millions of agriculturists with their high fertility found in that country. The Jews, who are on a high economic, social, and intellectual plane, cannot, according to modern standards of comfort, afford to marry early; and after marriage are anxious to limit the size of the family at all events, for reasons known to-day in every large city.

The lack of religious restraint among the Western European Jews is well known. In Eastern Europe and in the Orient they are intensely religious, and as a result marry earlier, and after marriage know little or nothing about keeping their families within "prudent" limits. It is considered a sin to remain unmarried, an old maid

---

[1] Newsholme and Stevenson, *loc. cit.*

is considered a disgrace to the family, and sterility is a valid cause for divorce by the Rabbis. The result is that these Jews are having a very high birth-rate. It is remarkable, however, that when these Jews leave their native country and emigrate to Western Europe or America, where religious restraint is either weakened or, as is often the case, almost entirely lacking, their fertility also declines. As has already been intimated, the methods of prevention of conception are sought for by immigrant Jews, and especially by their descendants, to the same extent as by other peoples living in the United States, and probably more often than by Catholics, among whom religion plays a greater rôle.

The lower birth-rate of the Jews is not then a sign of physical degeneration, but solely due to the practice of artificial prevention of child-bearing. In this they have outdone the Christians, even those of France, where conditions are considered alarming. The outlook for the Jews in Western Europe and America is gloomy; it is a question how long they can hold their own as a religious minority with a low birth-rate which keeps on sinking.

Sex at Birth.—The number of boys at birth exceeds the number of girls among nearly all European races and peoples. From an exhaustive statistical study on the subject made by Nichols, it appears that among nearly seven million births in all parts of Europe the average ratio was 1,057 boys to every 1,000 girls born, and that in most countries in Europe the ratios range in the neighbourhood of the average. Only in the southernmost countries of Europe is there a decided general tendency toward a much higher ratio of boys, as is the case in Greece, Roumania, Bulgaria, etc. The highest proportion of boys has been found among the Mussulman population of Algeria, 1,191 boys to 1,000 girls.[1] Among the Jews it has been found that in certain countries this excess of male births is more pronounced than among the non-Jewish population. Inasmuch as at the present state of our knowledge we do not know the cause of the preponderance of males at birth, this excess has been

[1] J. B. Nichols, "The Numerical Proportion of the Sexes at Birth," *Memoirs American Anthropological Association*, vol. i., pp. 247-300; Washington, 1907.

considered a race trait of the Jews. What else can be the cause if not "race"? The social and physical environment is not known to exert any influence. Some have attributed it to the smaller proportion of illegitimate births,[1] others to the fact that they are mostly town dwellers, and to many other causes which by no means explained the case.

From the vital statistics of European Russia it appears that there is a very excessive number of male births reported among the Jews. During 1897 there were recorded 121,031 Jewish births, of which 69,089 were males and 51,942 were females, or 1,331 boys to 1,000 girls. But a careful study of these figures brings forth some strong suspicion as to their accuracy. Thus when we examine the various provinces we find great variations. In Taurida the ratio was only 1,016 boys to 1,000 girls; in Cherson, 1,112; in Poltava, 1,128; while in Wilna it reached the unprecedented ratio of 1,774; in Grodno, 1,706, and in Minsk, 1,654. In general it can be stated that in the south of Russia the excess of male births is not much larger among the Jews than among the Christians, while in the north-western provinces the excess is enormously high. That climatic conditions are not the cause is shown by the fact that the excess is not more pronounced among the Christians in the north-western provinces than in the southern. Two provinces not far distant from each other, like Wilna and Curland, show great differences in the proportion of male births among Jews—1,774 in the former and only 1,154 in the latter Climatic conditions cannot therefore be considered.

If the excess of males were really as large as the above figures would indicate, we should expect that the number of male infants below one year of age would also be excessive among the Jews. But from the census statistics of 1897 it is shown that it was only 1,042 boys to 1,000 girls below one year of age. The higher mortality of male infants is not sufficient to account for the loss of so many boys during the first year of their life.

[1] See C. Lombroso, *Le Crime Politique et les Révolutions*, vol. i., p. 149; E. Nagel, "Der hohe Knabenüberschuss der neugeborenen der Judinnen," *Statistische Monatschrift*, pp. 183-186, 1884; J. Jacobs, article, "Births," *Jewish Encyclopædia*, vol. iii., pp. 223-226.

The only plausible explanation for this apparent excess is that a large number of female births are not reported to the authorities by the midwives and Rabbis, who are expected to register each birth. This finds its explanation in certain features of Jewish life in Eastern Europe. The birth of a boy in a Jewish family is accompanied by important festivals and ceremonials. It is very dangerous in later life for a boy, who has not been registered at birth: he cannot obtain a passport when he wants to leave his native city; he cannot prove his identity, which is often of vital importance in Russia; he can be drawn into military service unjustly, etc. All this brings it about that practically all the male births are registered, while a large number of female births is missing from the registry books. A female birth among Jews in Russia is easily overlooked, because among the poorer classes no ceremonial is attached to its appearance. The father merely mentions its occurrence when visiting the Synagogue on Saturday, and the Rabbi confirms the name selected for the newcomer. That this is the true explanation is seen from the fact that in 1893 the ratio of recorded male births among the Jews in Russia was 1,459, while in 1901 it was only 1,295 to 1,000 females, indicating a more complete registration of female births in recent years.

If the excessive proportion of male births was a racial trait of the Jews it would be expected that the same phenomenon should be observed among the Jews in all countries. But this is not the case. In Warsaw, Poland, the ratio was in 1897 only 106 boys to 100 girls. Ethnically there is hardly any difference between Polish and Lithuanian Jews, still the latter show a ratio of 177 in Wilna, which again confirms the opinion that the excess in Wilna is due to neglect in reporting female births. In Bulgaria also the ratio is excessive, 1,224 boys to 1,000 girls during 1897-1902, but in Prussia, where the reporting of births is more thoroughly done, the proportion was, in 1893-1902, 1,062 (1,059 among the Christians); in Austria, in 1900, it was 1,078 (1,060 among the Christians). In Prague the number of male births among the Jews in 1901 was equal to that of the female births, although among the Christian population there was an excess of males

DEMOGRAPHIC CHARACTERISTICS. 241

amounting to 104.1 per cent.[1] In the United States the excess of male births among the Jews was not large, only 103.16, while among the general population of Massachusetts and Rhode Island it is much higher.[2]

It is thus seen that the Jews do not at all differ in this regard from other peoples. Only in countries where the registration of females is neglected there appears to be a larger excess of male births. But this is not the case in countries where the registration is properly done.

Proportion of Still-births.—In many works on the demography of the Jews it has been stated that not only is the Jew more long-lived than his neighbour of other creeds, but even at birth he has already an advantage. Indeed, before his birth he was said to be endowed with a peculiar vitality which renders him less liable to lose his life during parturition. This vitality can only be measured by the proportion of still-births, which were said to be less frequent among Jews than among Christians; even when only one of the parents is a Jew, the chances of death during parturition were alleged to be somewhat less than when both parents are non-Jews, though not as good as in cases where both parents are children of Israel. All this was based on imperfectly collected statistics of the first three-quarters of the nineteenth century. More recent data on the subject show that this is not the case with the Jews in every country,[3] and that only in two out of ten instances are the Jews more favourably situated in respect to the proportion of still-births. Only in Amsterdam and in Frankfort-on-Main is the percentage smaller among them than among the Christians, while in Bulgaria, Warsaw, and Bucharest they have even a larger proportion of still-

---

[1] Thon shows that in Galicia and Bukowina, where the registration of girls is as defective as in Russia, the excess of male births also appears high; while in Silesia, Moravia, and Bohemia, where the registration is more or less complete, there is hardly any excess. J. Thon, *Die Juden in Oesterreich*, pp. 23-27; Berlin, 1907.

[2] *Census Bulletin*, No. 19; 1890.

[3] See J. Segal, "Die Vitalitat der jüdischen geborenen," *Zeitschr. Demogr. Stat. d. Juden*, pp. 76-79, 1910. He finds that in two countries, Bavaria and Austria, the vitality of the new-born is about the same among Jews and Christians; in two other countries, Russia and Galicia, the vitality is inferior among the Jews; and in Hungary they have a smaller proportion of still-births.

births. In all the other places mentioned the percentage s about the same among both groups, Jews and Christians. It should be mentioned in this connection that the smaller number of illegimate births among the Jews would lead one to expect a smaller percentage of still-births, because the proportion of still-births is very large among illegitimates. The suggestion made by some that the large ratio of males born among Jews is due to the fact that the percentage of still-births is small is also not to be seriously considered, simply because the proportion of still-births is not smaller among them. It must, however, not be overlooked that the percentage of still-births among the Jews varies roughly with the conditions observed among non-Jews in a given country. It is high in Austria, Warsaw, Bucharest, etc., and low in Bulgaria, Frankfort, Bavaria, Prussia, etc., as it is among the Christians in these places.[1] In other words, in Eastern Europe, where child-birth is attended by ignorant midwives, the proportion of still-births is larger than in Western Europe, where either physicians or trained midwives are, as a rule, in attendance. Still-births are, after all, dependent on economic and social conditions. They are very frequently met with among people in the lowest social and economic strata, and rarely among the prosperous. An apparent exception appears to be the Jews in Berlin. But there the high percentage of still-births is probably due to the high proportion of illegitimacy among them.

Illegitimate Births.—Illegitimacy has often been taken as an index of the morality of a community. While it may be a true index in some countries, yet in others, owing to special marriage laws, an excessive proportion of illegitimate births is not necessarily an indication of vice. A good illustration is presented in Austria. There, a child is considered illegitimate when the parents have not registered their marriage with the civil authorities. It

[1] It appears that in Austria the rates of still-births are larger in Lower Austria, Bohemia, and Silesia, where the Jews are economically on a superior plane when compared with their co-religionists in Galicia and Bukowina. But considering that the predominant religion in Galicia and Bukowina is Catholic, we have an explanation for the low still-birth rates among the Christians. They are said to often declare a child to have been born living when it was really born dead, in order that it should be baptized. See J. Thon, *Die Juden in Oesterreich*, pp. 26-28.

appears that the Jews in Galicia and Bukowina very often neglect to register their marriages, and consider their religious ceremony as sufficient for all purposes. As a result of this special law, it is found that while nowhere else is the proportion of illegitimate births among the Jews over four per cent. of the total number of births, it reached in Austria 61.37 per cent. In Galicia and Bukowina the percentage is about 80, and in one small town in Galicia the records even show 99.61 per cent. of illegitimate births among Jews, which is manifestly absurd. For similar reasons the percentage of illegitimacy in Bucharest, Roumania, during 1904-05 is reported to be 22.99, and only 3.82 among others; while in Hungary, and particularly in Budapest, the statistics are worthless for the same cause. In other countries, where conditions are not disturbed by this factor, it is evident that illegitimacy is less frequent among Jews than among others. I find that about five illegitimate children are born to Christians in Bavaria to one among Jews; in Amsterdam and Warsaw, seven to one; in Frankfort, four to one; in Berlin, about three to one; and in Russia, five to one. With the exception of Bulgaria and Amsterdam, it is seen that the percentage of illegitimacy among Jews increases as we proceed from east to west of Europe. It is very low in Russia, about one-half of one per cent.; higher in Bavaria, 2.5 per cent.; and is nearly four per cent. in Prussia, while in Berlin it is even six per cent. This indicates that where the Jews are not affected by modern "civilized" conditions the chastity of the women is much superior, the family ties are much stronger, and girls only rarely go wrong. In small towns in Russia, Poland, and Galicia, one only rarely hears of a Jewish child born out of wedlock. Unmarried women seldom associate, even socially, with men before marriage. The absence of alcoholism, particularly among Jewesses, who never drink, is another factor in keeping the sexes apart. But in the large cities in Eastern Europe, where the separation of the sexes is not so strict, illegitimacy is frequently encountered. In Western Europe it is more frequent for the same reason. It was shown by Ruppin that in Germany illegitimacy is rarer among the Jews in Eastern Prussia (Posen, Pomerania, East and West Prussia), where they adhere strictly to their orthodox religion, while in large cities, where they have adopted many of the habits and customs of their Christian neighbours, the percentage of illegitimacy is much higher, though still smaller than among non-Jews. He concludes that "a higher percentage of illegitimate births among Jews is quite a good sign that the orthodox Jewish life has weakened, and paradoxical as it may appear, it is also not a bad index of the degree of assimilation of the Jews in general."[1]

It is well known that illegitimate births are very rare among women living with their parents, while agricultural servants, domestics, factory hands, etc., show a high proportion of births out of wedlock. The Jewish women in Eastern Europe only rarely live away from their parents or relatives, comparatively few are engaged in domestic service, and practically none as agricultural servants. In the small towns, Jewish girls rarely work outside of their own homes. In Western Europe the social conditions of the Jews are nearer those of the Christians among whom they live, and illegitimacy is more frequent than in the East. But inasmuch as the economic conditions of the Jews in Western Europe are superior to those of the average non-Jewish population, the women receiving a better education and being taken care of by their parents and relatives to a much higher degree, illegitimacy is less common than among non-Jews.

[1] Arthur Ruppin, *Die Juden der Gegenwart*, p. 245; Berlin, 1904.

CHAPTER XI.

DEMOGRAPHIC CHARACTERISTICS (*continued*).

Marriage rates among modern Jews in various countries—Differences in marriage rates between eastern and western Jews—Age at marriage Proportion of celibates—Causes of low marriage rates of the Jews—Consanguineons marriages—Divorce.

Marriages.—One of the most important causes of the low birth-rate of the Jews is their low marriage rate. Especially the Western European Jews are marrying later in life than Christians, thus diminishing the period of the married state, and increasing the interval between generations. Only about fifty years ago an unmarried Jew was rare in Europe, while an old maid was hardly to be met with in the Ghetto. In every large settlement of Jews in Europe there was a special society for the purpose of assisting poor young men and women to enter the marriage state. Even to-day one can see Jewish women in Russia, Galicia, Roumania, etc., going around from house to house collecting money for dowry, trousseau, and furniture for a poor girl whom they intend to lead to the altar. I am under the impression that one of the causes of the large number of defectives found among the Eastern European Jews is the fact that the Jewish communities have always been doing their best to marry every defective man and woman, who among other peoples would hardly have a chance to propagate their kind.

Up to about fifty years ago the Jews closely followed the Rabbinical ordinances: "It is the duty of every Israelite to marry as early in life as possible." Eighteen years is the age set by the Rabbis; any one remaining unmarried after his twentieth year is said to be cursed by God Himself. Some Rabbis urge that children should marry as soon as they reach the age of puberty—*i.e.*, the fourteenth year. A man who, without any reason, refuses to marry after he has passed his twentieth year was frequently compelled to do so by court.[1] These Talmudical laws were observed by the Jews during the Middle Ages, and in Eastern Europe even as late as the middle of the nineteenth century. To-day it appears that they are more or less disregarded by the bulk of the Jews in Europe and America. Their marriage rates are as a result much lower than those of the Christians, among whom there is a large agricultural class who marry early.

A study of the crude marriage rates—*i.e.*, the annual number of marriages per 1,000 population—shows among Jews and Christians in some countries that, with the exception of Algeria and Bavaria, the rates are lower among Jews than among others. But it must be emphasized that even registrar's figures do not give an adequate idea of the low marriage rates of the Jews, because the Jewish population, especially in Western Europe, contains a smaller number of children and larger proportion of adults of marriageable ages. If statistics of the number of marriages per 1,000 Jews over fifteen years of age, and especially of unmarried adults, were obtainable, the rates for the Jews as compared with the Christians in Europe would show that they are yet less apt to marry than available statistics indicate. Thus it was found in Berlin during the Census of 1900 that of all persons over twenty years of age the following percentage were married[2]:—

	Men.	Women.
Jewish	51.62 per cent.	52.51 per cent.
Christian	60.38 ,,	53.83 ,,

This shows that there are more celibates among these Jews than among Christians. And even those who marry do so later than Christians, which has an important influence on their birth-rate. In Berlin it was found in 1900 that of married persons there were the following percentages under thirty years of age:—

	Men.	Women.
Jewish	6.89 per cent.	20.41 per cent.
Christian	15.56 ,,	24.34 ,,

---

[1] *Jewish Encyclopædia*, vol. viii. p. 347.
[2] A. Ruppin, *Die Juden der Gegenwart*, p. 49.

Similar conditions have been found in Hesse and also in Bulgaria.[1] The Jews have a larger proportion of celibates and marry at a more advanced age than the Christians. In Hungary only twenty-five years ago marriages at the early age of fifteen or even less were quite common among Jews. To-day conditions have changed. In that country young men under eighteen and women under sixteen must obtain special permission from the authorities before they can procure a marriage licence. It appears that the Christian population by no means often apply for such special permission to marry at an early age—during 1904 2,673 young women and three young men received this special permission to marry. That the Jews only rarely marry so young is to be seen from the fact that only seven Jewesses and not a single Jew are included in the above, and the Jews constitute nearly five per cent. of the total population of that country.[2]

It is interesting that even in Russia, where the bulk of the 5,500,000 Jews live to-day under strict adherence to their faith and traditions, early marriages are less frequent than among the Christians. From the census taken in 1897 it was found that the Jews marry later than their neighbours of Greek Orthodox faith. Only 5.95 per cent. of all the Jews who married in 1897 were less than twenty years of age, while about five times as many (31.22 per cent.) Christians married at this youthful age. Even among the Jewesses only 27.76 per cent. married before reaching twenty, as against double that number, 55.01 per cent., among Christian women. On the other hand, marriages between twenty and thirty years of age are more frequent among the Jews—77.78 per cent. as against only 54.58 per cent. among Christians, and 63.91 per cent. among the Jewesses and 38.53 per cent. among Christian women. Finally, marriages between persons at advanced ages, over thirty, are contracted in about the same proportion in both groups. In general Russia has an extraordinarily large number of youthful marriages. Nowhere

---

[1] See A. Ruppin, "Zur Statistik der Juden im Grossherzogtum Hessen," *Zeitschrift für Demographie und Statistik der Juden*, p. 171, 1907; "Bewegung der Bevölkerung in Bulgarien," *ibid.* p. 134-137.

[2] *Ungarisches Statistisch. Jahrbuch*, 1904, Budapest, 1906; *Zeitsch. Demographie u. Statistik d. Juden*, p. 61, 1907.

in Western Europe are there to be found more than four per cent. of bridegrooms under twenty years of age. This, of course, is due to the numerical predominance of agricultural workers with a communistic arrangement of the village community. The Jews in that country live mostly in cities, are either merchants, manufacturers, etc., or skilled artisans. Marriage among such people has to be postponed till business assures a secure income, or till the individual has attained skill in his trade or profession. The low birth-rate of the Jews in Russia (compared with the non-Jewish population of the same country) is thus partly explained. The later an individual marries, the shorter is the period of the married state, and the number of children to be expected is smaller. In fact, during the census of 1897 it was found that there were five per cent. more unmarried Jews than unmarried Christians.

In this connection it is interesting to note that the percentage of protogamous marriages is smaller among Jews in Russia than among the general population. The marriages of bachelors and spinsters constituted 83.73 per cent. among the general population and only 80.72 per cent. among the Jews. Second marriages are more frequent among the Jews in Russia, though in Western Europe the reverse appears to be the case. Contrary to the almost general experience that widowers are more likely to marry maids than widows, the Jewish widowers in Russia more often marry widows. These peculiarities are to be explained by social customs.

The marriage statistics of the Jews confirm the conclusion that marriage is purely a social phenomenon, unaffected by any racial affinities. The Jews in Eastern Europe marry earlier and have a smaller proportion of celibates than their co-religionists in Western Europe, because the latter enjoy on the average higher social and economic prosperity, and find it advisable to postpone marriage till they have attained proficiency in their callings. It is a case of "prudential forethought," as it has often been described. When compared with their non-Jewish neighbours in Eastern Europe, the Jews have a lower marriage rate, because they have only few agricultural labourers, and have, on the other hand, a larger number of merchants, skilled mechanics, professional men, etc., whose marriage and birth-rates are lower among all the peoples of Europe. In Oriental countries like Palestine, Turkey, Persia, Morocco, Algeria, Tunis, etc., where the Jews live under a primitive culture, and are almost entirely unaffected by any occidental influences, the Jews to-day marry very early. Husbands at fourteen and wives at the same age are not uncommon. Their birth-rate is also above that of the Christian population in those countries, as was shown to be the case in Algeria. Of course, when compared with the Mohammedans of these countries, their marriage and birth-rates are lower, because the former are polygamous.

In Western Europe and America, owing to the intense influence exerted on the Jews by the occidental social environment, their marriage rates are low.[1] But even here the conditions have not always been the same as we find them to-day. Statistics of marriage rates in the beginning of the nineteenth century show conclusively that then the Jews married earlier and had fewer celibates than the Christian population in Germany. Their economic, social, and intellectual condition at that time was about the same as that of the Jews in Eastern Europe to-day. Even as late as 1861 to 1870 Austrian statistics show that 34.3 per cent. of all the Jews who married were less than twenty-four years of age, as against only 17.6 per cent. of Christians who married thus early; 23.5 per cent. of Jewesses were married at this early age, and only 15.1 per cent. of Christian women. Conditions have changed recently, as

---

[1] According to statistics published in the *Report of the Registrar-General* for the year 1908, there has been a remarkable decline in the number of Jewish marriages in England and Wales. They show that the proportion of Jewish marriages, which had, with slight fluctuations, steadily increased for many years, until, in the year 1906, it reached 8.3 per 1,000 marriages solemnized, fell in 1907 to 7.2, and in 1908 to 6.6 per 1,000. The Jewish population has during that period increased, as is evident from the number of dead interred in Jewish cemeteries. In London the percentage was 39.5 in 1906, and it fell to 32.6 in 1908. Some Jewish writers were inclined to attribute this to hard times, but the decrease was noted in the rich West London Synagogue of British Jews, at Hampstead and Bayswater Synagogues, where such a cause cannot be operative to any extent. I am inclined to the opinion that it is mainly due to the increase of civil marriages as well as to mixed marriages, which have both been on the increase among the Jews in England.

we have seen, going hand-in-hand with the change in the sum total of the social, economic, intellectual, and particularly political conditions in which the Jews find themselves at the beginning of the twentieth century.

Consanguineous Marriages.—The extraordinarily large number of physical and mental defectives among Jews in Europe has been in part or wholly attributed to the frequency of marriage of near kin among them. Thus most writers on the pathology of the Jews say that the excessive proportion of deaf mutes, blind, insane, idiotic, and imbecile, diabetics, etc., is the result of breeding in-and-in, which has been going on for centuries among the Jews in Europe. It is of interest to determine the extent to which such unions are observed among Jews in order to be in a position to judge some of their pathological traits.

All available statistical evidence shows that consanguineous marriages are much more often contracted among Jews than among others. Joseph Jacobs, adopting Sir George H. Darwin's method, found that 7.5 per cent. of all Jewish marriages in England are between cousins, while among Englishmen only 2 per cent. are of this class.[1] Stieda found that in Lorraine the proportion of consanguineous marriages is 1.86 per 1000 ordinary marriages among Protestants, 9.97 among Catholics, and 23.02 among Jews.[2] In Hungary this kind of marriage is prohibited by law, but a dispensation is usually given to those who apply to the civil authorities for permission to marry cousins. The data collected on the subject and published annually in the *Ungarisches Statistisches Jahrbuch* are therefore very reliable in showing the extent of marriages of near kin in that country. During 1901-06 such permission was granted to 1,570 Jews and to 5,952 Christians. On a basis of population it thus appears that the Jews obtained proportionately about five times as many permits to marry relatives as Christians. According to the census of 1900, the Jews constituted only 4.4 per cent. of the total population of Hungary, but 27.55 per cent. of all the consanguineous marriages contracted in that country during 1901-06 were between Jews. It must, however, also be

[1] J. Jacobs, *Studies in Jewish Statistics*, pp. 1-9; London, 1891.
[2] Schmidt's *Jahrbücher des gesammten Medicin*, vol. clxxxi., p. 89.

mentioned in this connection that the majority of the Christian population of Hungary is of the Catholic denomination, and the Catholic Church prohibits such marriages.[1]

There are similar statistics available for Prussia and other countries. In Russia, especially in the small towns, this kind of marriage is very frequent among the Jews, although there are no available data collected on the subject.

It is doubtful whether this in-breeding is the sole cause of most of the diabetes, idiocy, deaf-mutism, etc., encountered among Jews. It is at present the consensus of opinion that consanguineous marriages contracted between healthy individuals are not at all detrimental to the offspring. "If the parents are perfectly healthy and exempt from all commencing degeneracy, they can only give birth to children at least as healthy as themselves. . . . But if the same degeneracy has already tainted both the parents, the offspring will show it in a greater degree, and will tend toward entire disappearance."[2] But when such marriages are contracted by defectives, the physical or mental defect is likely to appear in a more accentuated form in the progeny. It must, in this connection, be mentioned that consanguineous marriage among the European population rarely exceeds one per cent. of all marriages, and is more frequent as a rule in the country than in the city. The Jews as city dwellers ought to have a still smaller proportion of marriage of near kin.

Dissolution of Marriage.—The frequency of divorce among the Jews is difficult to estimate with any degree of accuracy. In the first place there are great differences between Jews in various countries. In the Orient and even in Eastern Europe the Jews have perfect autonomy in matters pertaining to marriage and divorce; the civil authorities do not interfere at all in these matters. Divorces are granted in these countries by the Rabbis. Any trivial cause often suffices before some Rabbis to obtain a divorce. The husband can even send a divorce

---

[1] *Zeitschrift für Demographie und Statistik der Juden*, vol. iii., p. 46; 1907.
[2] Pouchet, quoted from Westermarck, *History of Human Marriage*, p. 337.

to his wife by proxy through a messenger. While not uncommon, considering the ease with which they can be obtained, divorces are not very frequent. Family ties are very strong among the Oriental and Eastern European Jews, and only rarely is advantage taken of the Rabbinical law to dissolve marriage. The extent to which these rabbinical divorces are being made use of is difficult to determine, because the Rabbis do not keep nor publish statistics on the subject. Moreover, in the Slavonic countries, the Christians very rarely go to a divorce court, because there is very little chance of obtaining the separation sought for. The Church in Russia is averse to divorces. So that even if statistics were available they could not be compared with similar figures about the non-Jewish population.

The Western European Jews consider dissolution of marriage more of a civil procedure, and even in cases when they want to have a Rabbinical divorce, they first apply to the civil authorities for it. From the few statistical data available on the subject it appears that during the middle of last century divorce was less frequent among the Jews than among the Christians of Bavaria. The same is the case in Berlin, where the proportion of divorces granted to Jews is somewhat smaller than to Christians, but it has been increasing of late years, so that in 1905 Jews almost approach non-Jews in this respect.[1] In Prussia there appear to be more divorces among Jews than among Christians. During 1905 there were the following proportion of divorces granted, counting the ratio per 1,000 marriages:[2]

        Protestants ... ... 26.7 per 1,000 marriages.
        Catholics ... ...   9.6 ,, ,, ,,
        Jews .. .. 40.9 ,, ,, ,,

Similarly in Hungary the number of divorces is more frequent among the Jews than among the rest of the population, and while the evil has been increasing in that country among all classes, still the Jews seem to show a

[1] See A. Ruppin, *Die Juden der Gegenwart*, p. 246; *idem*, in *Jahrb. für Nationalökonomie u. Statistik*, vol. lxxviii., p. 385; *Zeitschr. Demogr. u. Statist. d. Juden*, p. 172, 1907.
[2] *Zeitschrift für Demographie und Statistik der Juden*, pp. 110-111; 1907.

much larger increase in the number of divorces than the Christians. Thus when it is remembered that the proportion of Jews in Hungary is 4.4 per cent. of the total population, the following figures are important in this respect. Of all the divorces granted by the courts in that country during 1901, 8.75 per cent. were granted to Jews; in 1902, 9.12 per cent.; in 1903, 9.29 per cent.; and in 1904, 9.98 per cent.[1] The Jews thus have more than twice as many divorces as the Christians. It must, however, be mentioned that the majority of the population in Hungary is Catholic, which partly explains the divergence. In Roumania also the number of divorces is larger among the Jews than among the rest of the population, 5.83 per cent. of all the divorces granted during 1897 were granted to Jews, while only 4.55 per cent. of the total population was Jewish.[2] Even in Algeria it appears that the Jews are much given to divorce, although since the native population is mostly polygamous, it is difficult to make comparisons.[3]

There are no denominational statistics of divorce in the United States, but it can be stated, without fear of serious contradiction, that it is not uncommon among the Jews. The divorce courts in New York City are quite often asked by Jews to dissolve their marriage. I am inclined to believe that it is in New York at least as frequent among the Jews as among the rest of the population. On the east side of the city the immigrant population very often takes advantage of the Rabbinical law, and easily obtain divorces. But among the native Jews this never happens; they go to the civil courts for the purpose, and London conditions are about the same.

From all the evidence available it appears that the causes of divorce among the Western Europe and American Jews are about the same as those among the Christians. In Berlin, Ruppin mentions that infidelity on the part of the husband is more frequently a cause among the Jews than among Christians. Wife-desertion is also more

---

[1] *Zeitschrift für Demographie und Statistik der Juden*, pp. 93-94, 1906; *Ungarisches Statist. Jahrbuch*, 1904.
[2] *Zeitschr. Demogr. Statist. d. Juden*, No. 3, p. 15, 1905.
[3] See *Annuaire Statistique de la France*, 1903; *Zeitschr. Demogr. Statist. Juden*, pp. 15-16, 1906.

frequent among Jews than among Christians in Berlin.[1] In New York City only infidelity on the part of one of the parties is a valid cause, and the fact that so many divorces are granted to Jews indicates that it is not infrequent, thus showing that the traditional family ties are breaking down among the Jews. In Eastern Europe, where Rabbinical divorces are granted, the causes are only rarely of this nature. Wife desertion is also very common among the immigrant Jews in New York and London. The United Hebrew Charities and the London Jewish Board of Guardians find it one of their most difficult tasks to deal with this problem.[2]

Divorces among Jews make evident the influence of the social environment. In the Orient and in the small towns in Eastern Europe, where the Jews live in strict adherence to their faith and traditions, participating but little in the tendencies of modern life, the sacredness of the family ties is strictly guarded. Divorces, though easily obtainable from the Rabbis, are rather uncommon, and those granted are very rarely for infidelity. In Western Europe and America, where the Jews are completely under the influence of modern city life, divorces are frequent, and are growing in frequency.

[1] A. Ruppin, *Die Juden der Gegenwart*, pp. 245-247.
[2] See *Annual Reports of the United Hebrew Charities* for the years 1903-1907.

CHAPTER XII.

DEMOGRAPHIC CHARACTERISTICS (*concluded*).

Mortality of the Jews in various countries—Tenacity of life of the Jews Jewish infant mortality—Expectation of life of the Jews—Causes of the low death-rates of the Jews—Effects of the demographic phenomena on the Jews—Excess of births over deaths—Differences between Eastern and Western Jews—The recent decline in the natural Increase of the Jews.

Mortality.—The bulk of the Jewish population in the Orient and Eastern Europe live mostly in the oldest and most congested parts of cities, amid squalid and unsanitary surroundings, where the mortality rates are by general experience known to be excessive. In England and the United States the immigrant Jews also live, as a rule, under similar conditions, as can readily be seen in the East End of London and the East Side of New York. Physically, we have seen, the Eastern Jews are appearing weak, anæmic, and decrepit when compared with the Christians among whom they live; and, in addition, they are engaged mostly in indoor occupations. These peculiarities would lead one to expect *a priori* that the mortality rates among them would be much higher than among other people who live mostly under better hygienic and sanitary conditions, have a large proportion of agriculturists who live in the open country and are more often engaged in outdoor occupations, and to all outward appearances are more robust and healthy.

Paradoxical as it may appear, however, the contrary is true. Statistics, wherever available, show that the general mortality of the Jews is lower than that of the Christians among whom they live. It appears that while among the general population the mortality of infants and children is very high, during adolescence much lower, and among the dead only a small proportion are found who are over sixty years of age, among the Jews the proportions are different. Their infant mortality is lower; during adolescence they also lose less through death, and many more die at an advanced age. From the sociological standpoint the Jewish rate of mortality is more advantageous. The high infant mortality among the Christians means an enormous drain on the national resources spent in procreation and rearing of infants and children. Among the Jews more children reach maturity and even old age, and during their lifetime are in a position to return to society the investment made on their rearing and education.

In every country in which vital statistics have been collected, classifying the material in accordance with the religious belief of the inhabitants it is found that the death-rates of the Jews only rarely exceed twenty per 1,000 population. In Galicia, Poland, Russia, and Austria the rates are between seventeen and nineteen; in Holland and Bavaria and in some German cities the rates are even as low as twelve per 1,000. From figures presented before the Royal Commission on Alien Immigration it appears that in London the mortality rates of the immigrant Jews are rather low. Dr. J. Loane showed that the rate of aliens in Whitechapel was 14 to 16; of natives, 20 to 26.4, according to the sanitary condition of the home. He also showed that the rates have declined since Jews settled in that district from 26 to 18 per 1,000 between 1880 and 1900.[1]

A yet lower mortality was found among 10,618 Jewish families, including 60,630 persons living in the United States, December 31st, 1889. In the figures published by the United States Census Bureau it appears that the death-rate was only 7.11 per 1,000, "which is but little more than half the annual death-rate among other persons of the same social class and conditions living in this country."[2]

When compared with the non-Jewish population of the countries in which they live, the Jews have a much lower mortality. In Algeria their death-rate is only eighty-nine per cent. of that of the Europeans in that colony; in

[1] *Minutes of Evidence*, 4519, 4538-44.
[2] *Census Bulletin*, No. 19, Dec. 30; Washington, 1890.

Poland it is less than seventy-five per cent.; in Bavaria, about fifty-eight per cent., while in European Russia less than one-half the number of Jews die proportionately than Christians. In other words, the death-rates of the Jews are from eleven to fifty-two per cent. less than those of the Christians.

These favourable mortality rates are not a recent phenomenon among the Jews. At all times when statistics on the subject were compiled it was found to be the case. The censuses of Prussia, which are very reliable, give some interesting figures in this connection, showing that the mortality has been sinking in recent years among both Jews and Christians, decreasing about thirty-four per cent. since 1822 in both groups. This is, of course, to be attributed to advancement in the social, economic, hygienic, and sanitary conditions characteristic of the age. But it is remarkable that there is only a slight change in the ratio of Jewish to Christian mortality during the eighty-three years under consideration; it was in 1822-40 about seventy-three per cent. of the Christian mortality, and increased to seventy-seven per cent. in 1906. When it is considered that the average of economic prosperity of the Jews in Prussia during the last twenty-five years is much superior to that of the Christians, it is evident that the decrease in the mortality was not commensurate with the economic comfort they attained. But bearing in mind that the Jews had already a very low mortality in 1822, which could not sink much more, the explanation is at hand. Among the Christians in Prussia, the lowering of the mortality is a recent phenomenon, which began to manifest itself only during the middle of the nineteenth century. But there is yet an enormous difference in mortality in favour of the Jews, which will not be wiped out soon, even if we admit that the longevity of the Jews in Prussia has reached its limit.[1] Hungary is another country where reliable statistics are available for fifteen years. In 1891-95 the mortality of the Jews was 19.07 per 1,000; it went down to 16.95 in 1901, and in 1906 it fell to 16.7; among the Christians it was 33.12 in 1891-95, 25.94 in 1901, and 25.7

---

[1] See A. Goldscheider, "Die Entwicklung der jüdischen Bevölkerung Preussens im 19. Jahrhundert," *Zeitschrift fur Demographie und Statistik der Juden*, pp. 70 75; 1907.

in 1906. The decrease has consequently been more marked among the Christian population. In 1891 the Jews' mortality was 57.58 per cent. of the Christian mortality, while in 1906 it was 63.8 per cent., which indicates that they are approaching the mortality rates of their non-Jewish neighbours on the one hand; and on the other, with the improvements of sanitary and hygienic conditions, the rates among the Christians are getting lower and approaching those observed among the Jews. This, as well as evidence available for other countries, all tends to show that in recent years the differences between Jews and Christians in this respect are being obliterated.

Death, as a biological phenomenon, cannot be influenced by purely ethical or metaphysical factors, such as, for instance, religion, when Jews are compared with Christians. Viewed from this view point, differences in religious belief are not sufficient to explain the differences in the mortality rates between Jews and followers of other creeds. Nor can racial affinities explain this "absolutely unprecedented tenacity of life," as Ripley calls it. It has already been shown that there is no uniformity of racial traits to be noted among the Jews, but on the contrary, physically they bear a striking resemblance to the non-Jews among whom they live. Besides, racial uniformity would imply also demographic uniformity, which is by far not the case. The differences in the rates of mortality are too large when Jews of one country are compared with Jews of another country, to admit the racial factor as the main cause. It appears that a study of differences in social and economic conditions is more fruitful of reasonable results. Thus in Budapest the death-rate of the Jews has been only about seventy per cent. of that of the Christians. But, as is aptly pointed out by Körösi, according to the census of 1891, out of every 1,000 inhabitants there were 118 common labourers among the Catholics, among the Lutherans 125, and among the Jews only 67; 95 domestic servants were found among 1,000 Catholics, among Lutherans 98, and among the Jews only 17; 20 merchants were found among 1,000 Catholics, among Lutherans 36, while among the Jews the figure was 131. These social differences are of sufficient importance to influence perceptibly the death rates, and to account for the favourable showing made by the Jews. As is well known, certain occupations are more deadly than others. When to this are added other social factors which differentiate the Jews from the Christians, such as the rarity of alcoholism and illegitimacy among the former, and the proverbial care bestowed by them on their offspring, thus contributing to a low infant mortality, the effect of the social factors becomes apparent. The influence of poverty is evident. Recent statistics by Dolgopol show that in the richer districts of Odessa the Jewish mortality was 12.5 as against 35.6 in the poorer districts.

Infant Mortality.—All this is depicted in a striking manner when the infantile mortality among Jews is considered. It appears, namely, from all available data, that the Jews do not have any advantage over others when deaths of adults, particularly persons over fifty, are compared. It is only during infancy and childhood that fewer deaths occur among them. In Prussia, where the mortality rates are classified in the official reports according to the age of the individual, whether he is less or over fifteen years old, it was found that the mortality of Jews under fifteen years of age was less than one-half that of the Christians. In 1906, 53.1 per cent. of all the deaths among the latter in Prussia occurred in individuals less than fifteen years of age, while among the Jews only 18.58 per cent. of all the deaths were in persons of these ages. In Berlin it was in 1905, among Christians, 42.28 per cent., and Jews, 13.45 per 1000 population, less than one-third. In some cities in Germany, where detailed statistics of infant mortality are published, this point is yet better illustrated. Thus in Frankfort-on-Main in 1905 the mortality was as follows among infants under one and under five years of age :—

	Under One.	Five years of age.
Among Protestants	29.27	39.09 per 1000
Among Catholics	30.11	40.72 ,,
Among Jews	12.33	14.33 ,, [1]

The infant mortality among the Jews is here also less than one-half that of Christian infants. In Amsterdam

[1] *Zeitschrift für Demographic und Statistik der Juden*, pp. 61-62; 1907.

the deaths recorded in 1900 were distributed by ages as follows:—

Age.	Christians.	Jews.
1	25.23%	18 76%
1-13	15.68	11.72
13-64	33.58	33.38
64 and over	25.51	36.14 [1]

The mortality during infancy and childhood is here also smaller among the Jews than among the Christians; between the ages of 13 and 64 it was equal among both classes, while among the old it was more frequent among the Jews. The same condition has been observed in Hungary, where the mortality of children below seven years of age was 49.5 per cent. among the Christian population, and only 43.69 per cent. among the Jews.

Objections may justly be raised against this method of calculating the infant mortality, because it must first be ascertained whether the distribution of the population by age classes is the same in both groups. This is especially important when we deal with Jews, whose birth-rate is known to be lower than that of the Christians with whom they are compared. The smaller the number of births, the smaller the number of infants liable to die. The best way to compare the mortality of Jews and Christians is to calculate the ratios of deaths at each age period—*i.e.*, to ascertain the death-rates at each age in both classes, Jews and Christians. But this is difficult, because there are no available data published in the census reports. The exact infant mortality is, however, easily computed by finding the ratios of deaths of infants below one year, excluding still-births. From available figures it is evident that the Jews have an enormous advantage over their Christian neighbours when the infant mortality is investigated in this manner. In Hungary the rates per 1,000 births during 1901-05 was among the Catholics 166.5 as against only 98.2 among the Jews;[2] in other words, of 1,000 new-born infants 834 survive the first year of life among the

---

[1] Statistisch Jaarboek der Gemeente Amsterdam, Jaargang, 1900, quoted from *Zeitschrift für Demographie und Statistik der Juden*, No. 8, p. 15; 1905.

[2] E. Auerbach, "Die Sterblichkeit der Juden in Budapest," *Zeitschrift für Demographie und Statistik der Juden*, p. 152; 1908.

Catholics, while among the Jews 902 survive. In Amsterdam the survivals were in 1900 among Jews, 907, and among Christians only 861. In Russia the figures stand as Jews, 849, and Christians, 726. In Frankfort, Jews, 903; Christians, 830. In Galicia, where they live in poverty and want to an extent not seen among Jews in other countries, and in Wilna, Russia, conditions appear not to be so favourable. In Lemberg, during 1901-02, the number of surviving infants was even less than among the Christians, 866 and 870 respectively. In Wilna also Abramowitsch shows that the infant mortality among the Jews is much higher than among the Catholics in that city,[1] which goes far to show that economic conditions have a great influence on the mortality of children among Jews as well as among others. Even in Whitechapel, London, under the most unsanitary conditions, the infant mortality is very low. Dr. Murphy testified before the Royal Commission on Alien Immigration that while the infant mortality has increased in London between 1886-1900 from 153 to 161 per 1,000 births, the Whitechapel district showed a decline from 170 to 144; in St. George-in-the-East, from 195 to 181; in Limehouse it rose from 191 to 204, etc. E. W. Hope, Health Officer of Liverpool, testified that in his city also the infant mortality is lower among the Jews than among the Christians; and Niven, who held the same office in Manchester, showed that there it was lowest in Cheetham, the Jewish district, 104 per 1,000 births, as against 205 for the city.[2]

But some Galician and Russian towns only prove to be the exceptions to the rule that the Jewish infant mortality is lower than among others. This has a great bearing on their expectation of life. According to calculations presented in *Census Bulletin*, No. 19, 1890, the expectation of life of the Jews is much more favourable than that of the Christians in the United States. Assuming 100,000 Jewish individuals to have been born on the same day (among which there would probably be 50,684 males and 49,316 females), 45,680 males and 44,995 females will survive the first year; 41,731 males and 42,326 females

---

[1] M. Abramowitsch, "Die Bewegung der jüdischen Bevölkerung in Wilna," *Ibid.*, pp. 23-29; 1909.
[2] *Minutes of Evidence*, 3,960, 214,11-17, 21,749-57.

will survive the fifth year, etc. At the end of about seventy-one years one-half of them will be dead. Taking the data for Massachusetts for 1878-82, of 100,000 American infants born (among whom there would probably be 51,253 males and 48,774 females), only 41,986 males and 41,310 females would survive the first year; 36,727 males and 36,361 females would survive the fifth year; and half of them would be dead at the end of about forty-seven years.

While these figures are open to criticism, for, as has been pointed out by Hoffmann, the method adopted for the calculation of the life-tables is not stated in detail, still it may be said without any hesitation that the longevity of the Jews in the United States and Europe is superior to that of non-Jews.[1] The insurance associations of the Jews in the United States have never made known the results of their experience, but the published data as to the average ages at death, average duration of membership, mortuary cost, death-rate, etc., support the conclusion that the Jews in this country, as well as abroad, enjoy a longevity superior to that of the Christian populations.

I can add that this superiority is mainly due to the lower mortality during infancy and childhood. It is doubtful whether there are any differences in mortality rates during adolescence and middle life between Jews and others. Among persons of advanced age the rates are higher among the Jews, simply because a larger number of Jews reach that age.

The lower mortality of Jewish infants is not due to any special inherent vitality, but finds its explanation in certain social causes. Jewesses in Eastern Europe and the United States almost invariably nurse their infants at the breast, and it is rare to find among them an infant brought up by artifical feeding, unless the mother is physically incapable of suckling, which is comparatively rare among them. The mortality of breast-fed infants is much lower than of hand-fed. A large proportion of lives is thus saved. Jewish mothers only rarely go to work after marriage, and can, therefore, bestow all possible care on their infants, which cannot be said to be invariably true of the poorer classes of the population in Eastern Europe and America. In

---

[1] F. G. Hoffmann, article, "Expectation of Life," *Jewish Encyclopædia*, vol. v. pp. 306-308.

Western Europe the Jews are economically on a higher plane than the general population, and when causes of infant mortality are considered, it must be recalled that it is much lower among the economically prosperous than among the poor. The native Jews of the United States and Western Europe should be compared with the wealthier classes of population, and not with all classes; the majority of the general population being more or less poor and at the same time very prolific, swell the infant mortality. To these social factors there must also be added the fact that the birth-rates of the Jews are, on the whole, lower than those of Christians, and a high mortality cannot be expected when fewer children are born. Indeed, where the birth-rates of the Jews are very high and economic conditions are bad, as is the case in Galicia and some parts of Russia, their infant mortality is also higher. As has repeatedly been pointed out by various authors, illegitimate children of Jewish mothers have a much higher mortality than the same class of Christian mothers, thus indicating that the lower mortality of Jewish infants generally is not due to any inherent tenacity of life, but to the care bestowed on them by their mothers. That this is the case is confirmed in another way. Auerbach points out that in Budapest, as well as in Vienna, the infectious and contagious diseases which have a favourable prognosis in children who are carefully nursed, such as measles and its sequelæ, pneumonia, bronchitis, diphtheria, and croup, kill comparatively fewer Jewish than Christian children. On the other hand, diseases in which the prognosis is not very much influenced by the care taken during an attack, such as scarlet fever, meningitis, etc., give about the same rates among both Jews and Christians.[1] This, as well as the fact that more Jewish infants in Budapest die from congenital debility than Christian children, tends to disprove any theory of an extraordinary vitality of the Jews.

Arthur Ruppin, who has studied this problem thoroughly, insists that the superiority of the expectation of life of the Jews is mainly due to the higher infant mortality among the Christians, which drags down the average duration of life. "To use a coarse illustration, the expectation of life of a Christian child on the day of its birth is, roughly

[1] E. Auerbach, *loc. cit.*

stated, about forty years, as against sixty years of the Jewish child; at the tenth birthday the probable duration of life of the Christian child is fifty-five, while that of the Jewish child is sixty-five; and at the twentieth birthday the probable duration of life is, for both, seventy years—*i.e.*, the expectation of life of the Christian is equal to that of the Jew as soon as the Christian has passed his years of infancy and childhood and reached adolescence."

"The best illustration," Ruppin goes on to say, "of this condition is perhaps seen when we take definite statistical data of a given city, say Budapest, Hungary. The mortality during 1902 was 14.17 per 1,000 Jews and 21.81 per 1,000 Christians. The Jews were favoured by the following factors:—

1. *A Low Infantile Mortality.*—The proportion of deaths of infants under one year was during that year 9.52 per cent. of all the births from Jewish mothers and 16.46 per cent. of all the births from Christian mothers. If the infant mortality was as high among the Jews as among the Christians, the number of Jews who died during that year would have been larger by 320, and through that the general mortality would have increased by 1.89—*i.e.*, the death-rate would have been 16.06, instead of 14.17.

2. *The Lower Birth-rate of the Jews.*—The birth-rate per 1,000 population was, namely, 27.29 among the Jews and 32.74 among the Christians. If the Jews had relatively as many births as the Christians had, the mortality rate, on the basis of the Jewish infant mortality just determined above, would have been larger by 0.48 per 1,000; their general death-rate would have been increased to 16.54 from 16.06.

3. *The Smaller Mortality of Children under Ten Years of Age (excepting Infants under One Year).*—The proportion of deaths of children between one and ten years old was 2.15 per 1,000 among the Jews and 3.73 among the Christians. If the Jewish mortality at these ages were as high as that of the Christians, 266 more Jews would have died during that year, and the general mortality rates would have increased by 1.57 per 1,000, or, instead of 16.54, it would have been 18.11.[1]

In this manner one-half the difference in death-rates

[1] A. Ruppin, *Die Juden der Gegenwart*, pp. 54-57.

between Jews and Christians in Budapest is wiped out. It stands now as 18.11 for Jews and 21.81 for Christians. The remaining difference in the rates of 3.7 per 1,000 in favour of the Jews can also be accounted for by other social factors, and no special physiological tenacity of life of the Jews need be considered as a cause. One has only to recall that alcoholism is very rare and that the Sabbath is a day of rest among the orthodox Jews in Eastern Europe, and not of drink and dissipation, to find a reason for being spared by certain diseases and a lesser liability to accidental death. Their occupations are mainly of the kind in which accidental or violent deaths are not of frequent occurrence. There are, relatively, very few Jews engaged in shipping, mining, and dangerous trades generally. The deleterious effects of the indoor occupations which they prefer mostly manifest themselves in the anæmia and poor physique which are characteristic of them. But, on the other hand, they are only rarely exposed to the inclemencies of the weather, and thus acute articular rheumatism, pneumonia, etc., are less often a cause of death among them than among others. In fact, diseases of the respiratory organs, including tuberculosis, have been observed to be less commonly a cause of death among the Jews in Russia, Hungary, Austria, England, United States, etc., as will be shown in a later chapter.

Effects of Demographic Phenomena on the Jews.—From the statistical evidence presented in the preceding pages it is evident that the birth, marriage, and death-rates of the Jews are everywhere in Europe and America more or less lower than among their non-Jewish neighbours. But a low birth-rate does not always mean a low degree of fertility. It is of importance to inquire what effect these low rates have on the increase of the Jews. Are they gaining in strength, are they losing, or are they merely holding their own? This is of supreme importance, because, as a religious minority, their future depends largely on numbers; if they keep on losing it is only a question of time when they will be swallowed up by the majority amongst whom they have lived. Population increases, as is well known, by the excess of births over deaths, and it is important to determine whether the small birth-rates are everywhere compensated by the low death-rates, leaving a substantial surplus, or whether their low birth-rate is insufficient to replace all those who die and leave an excess which keeps them, after all, on the increase. These are problems of greater importance than appears at first sight.

In general terms it can be stated that there are two ways in which a population may replace its losses by death: first, by a higher birth-rate much in excess of the death rate. This is usually the rule in communities in a low state of culture, among agricultural classes, and also among the poorer and labouring classes in European and American industrial centres. It is an extravagant way of keeping up the population. The death rate, especially the infant mortality, is very high; early marriages and an excessive prolificacy are actively engaged in replacing in the community the losses sustained by death, and leave yet a substantial surplus. On the whole the average duration of life is in such communities comparatively short; the population is being replaced at frequent intervals. Life insurance societies do not consider members of such communities as good risks.

The second is the more economical way. It is usually seen in communities in a higher state of culture, where the birth, marriage, and death-rates, especially the infant mortality, is much lower than in the first-mentioned communities. It requires a longer period of time to renew its population, because the average duration of life is superior. This is observed generally among the upper ten thousand of modern civilized states, particularly in large cities. From a sociological and economic standpoint this method of perpetuation of population, if kept within certain limits, has its advantages over the former method. To use Spencer's terminology, it decreases the expenditure on genesis, leaving sufficient for individual evolution. In other words, the smaller number of children born has as a concomitant a smaller infant mortality, and also gives the parents an opportunity to raise their offspring on a more desirable standard. It appears that the second method is seen in various degrees of intensity among the Jews, especially those in Western Europe and America. "The Jews have thus a twofold advantage over their fellow-countrymen of different religions: they multiply more rapidly and with less waste. They bring fewer children into the world, but they bring more of them to maturity. It would seem as if, with their characteristic cleverness at calculations, they had instinctively solved the difficult problem of population in the manner most advantageous to themselves and most satisfactory to the economists."[1]

But the Jews are not everywhere "clever at calculation" in this respect. In some countries they are quite wasteful in their efforts to maintain their numbers. It is after all, with the Jews as well as with others, a matter of social and economic environment. In the East their birth-rates are high, and their mortality is high, though not as high as among their non-Jewish neighbours. The result is that their natural increase—*i.e.*, the excess of births over deaths per 1,000 population—is much above that seen among Christians in the same country.

In Oriental and Eastern European countries, where the birth-rates of the Jews are lower than those of non-Jews, they nevertheless increase in number much more rapidly than the Christians. The excess of births over deaths is larger among them, excepting in Roumania. In Algeria the natural increase is very great. The social conditions of the native Jews in that country are purely Oriental. Early marriages are the rule and celibacy almost unknown. I have seen in Constantine a married couple with the combined age of twenty-nine years, which was not considered anything unusual or of special significance. The result of these conditions is a high rate of fertility. Their birth-rate was 44.67 per 1000, with a correspondingly high mortality rate of 20.58. But, after all, the excess of births over deaths was large, reaching annually 24.09 per 1000. In European Russia, where the social conditions of the Jews are somewhat more occidental, the excess of births over deaths is smaller, only 17.61; in Austria 16.63, in Roumania 12.34, etc. They all show the characteristics of Eastern people in this regard.

Conditions in Western Europe are diametrically opposite to those just seen. Here the natural increase is much lower than among the Christians. The rates of proliferation are

[1] A. Leroy Beaulieu, *Israel among the Nations*, p. 155; New York, 1896.

low, owing to the low marriage and birth-rates; even their favourable mortality rates are insufficient to leave a substantial excess of births over deaths. Thus in Bavaria the natural increase is 4.81, as against 13.96 among the Christians; in Prussia it was only 3.34 among the Jews, and in Prague even lower, only 2.59. Conditions in Scandinavia are even worse.[1] The influence of social and economic conditions on the natural increase is well displayed in the various provinces of the Austrian Empire. In Galicia, where the bulk of the Jews live in poverty and want, and are rigidly devoted to their religion and traditions, their natural increase was during 1900 17.92 (Christians 16.61); in Bukowina, where the conditions are about the same, it was 12.66 (Christians 15.83); but in Lower Austria, where their social, economic, and intellectual conditions are much superior, almost the same as in any Western country, it was only 7.69; while in Bohemia, which is on the Bavarian border, and the Jews live on about the same standard, the natural increase is very low, lower even than in Berlin, only 1.35 per 1,000 Jews, as against 10.76 among the Christians. There are good reasons to believe that in Italy, France, England, and the United States the same conditions prevail among the native Jews.

This is a recent phenomenon among the Jews in Western Europe and America. During the first half of the nineteenth century the excess of births over deaths was equal, and even superior, to that of the Christians. In Prussia, for instance, the average natural increase during 1822-40 was 14.02 per 1,000 Jews, as against only 10.40 among the Christians. This excess began to sink gradually but steadily, as can be seen from the following figures[2]:—

---

[1] See Cordt Trap, "Die Juden in Kopenhagen," *Zeitschrift für Demographie und Statistik der Juden*, No. 7, pp. 97-101; 1907. In some cities the number of deaths actually exceeds the number of births among the Jews Thus, in Breslau, in 1906-07 there were 581 births and 694 deaths. *Breslauer Statistik*, vol. xxvii., 1907.

[2] Fuller details on this subject can be found in A. Ruppin, "Das Wachstun der jüdischen Bevölkerung in Preussen," *Zeitschrift für Demographie und Statistik der Juden*, vol. i., 1905, No. 6; A. Goldscheider, "Die Entwicklung der jüdschen Bevölkerung Preussens," *Ibid.*, No. 5, pp. 70-75, 1907.

DEMOGRAPHIC CHARACTERISTICS. 269

	Natural Increase.	
	Jews.	Christians.
1885	10.33	12.29
1890	7.64	12.58
1895	6.66	15.12
1900	4.52	14.57
1905	3.34	12.93
1908	3.33	14.97

The Christian population has held its own during these years; in fact the excess of births over deaths was in 1908 much superior to the average attained in 1822-40. It is different with the Jews. From 14.02 in 1822-40 it slowly dropped to 10.33 in 1885, and kept on falling, reaching the negligible excess of 3.33 per 1,000 population in 1908. There is hardly any doubt that this is not the lowest mark attained.

The excess of births over deaths has thus dwindled to about one-quarter in Prussia since 1822, and to a little over one-third in Bavaria[1] since 1876. This decline in the natural increase is not only characteristic of Western European Jews, but is beginning to be noted in Eastern Europe. In Hungary, where the rate was among the non-Jewish population only 9.69 during 1891-95, and with slight fluctuations rose to 12.2 in 1904, the tendency among the Jews was decidedly in the opposite direction. It was 17.79 during 1891-95, and sank to 16.07 in 1901, and even to 14.4 in 1904,[2] and in 1908 it went further down to 12.8. Similar conditions have been observed among the Jews in Russia, Austria,[3] Roumania, etc. It will probably not take very long before the Eastern Jews will catch up with their western co-religionists. In fact the Jewish immigrants to the United States, who are mostly from Eastern Europe, show a decided tendency in this direction. While in their native homes they hardly knew anything about "prudential" limitation of the size of the family, they know all about it in New York City. Their children are hardly to be distinguished in this regard from native Americans of any origin.

[1] J. Thon, "Die Bewegung der jüdischen Bevölkerung in Bayern, seit dem Jahr 1876," *Zeitschrift für Demographie und Statistik der Juden*, No. 6, pp. 6-9, 1905, shows that it sank from 15.8 to 4.8 during that period.
[2] Hugo Hoppe, "Zur Statistik der Juden in Ungarn," *Zeitschr. f. Demographie und Statistik der Juden*, No. 12, pp. 8-13; 1905.
[3] See J. Thon, *Die Juden in Oesterreich*, pp. 40-42.

CHAPTER XIII.

PATHOLOGICAL CHARACTERISTICS.

Race and disease—Effects of social conditions on the incidence of pathological processes—Alcoholism—Contagious diseases among Jews—The black death—Typhoid fever—Cholera—Endemic diseases—Causes of differences in the frequency of certain contagious diseases among Jews and non-Jews—Tuberculosis—Causes of the infrequency of tuberculosis among Jews.

THE external causes of disease, such as climate, condition of the soil, habits and customs of life, state of culture, which find their expression in the sanitary and hygienic condition of the person, home, and city, have all been more or less thoroughly studied. It is known to-day that infectious and contagious diseases find their best opportunity to spread among the poor, underfed, and ignorant; that those who are on a higher plane economically and intellectually are more or less spared during epidemics of contagious disease, though they are more liable to suffer from organic and functional derangements of the nervous and circulatory systems. It is also known that certain diseases require a special *milieu* for their development and propagation among people. Malaria is mostly found in marshy and swampy regions where mosquitoes are numerous; tuberculosis, among the poor who live in overcrowded dwellings, and among persons who work in dusty shops and factories. But after discounting these and many other external factors in the production of disease, it is found that there are also certain internal factors which render people either excessively predisposed or immune to certain pathological processes. In the past, physicians have attributed these differences in the susceptibility to disease to differences in temperament of various persons or peoples.

Among anthropologists there is to-day a tendency to ascribe these differences in proneness to disease to somatic or racial differences. It is shown that plants and animals react differently to organic and inorganic poisons. The dog and the cat, and carnivora generally, are distinguished by a marked degree of resistance to anthrax and septic infection, which is almost equivalent to exemption; chickens are immune to tetanus, or lockjaw, and the white rat to diphtheria. Other animals display an excessive susceptibility to certain diseases. Guinea pigs, mice, rabbits, etc., are especially susceptible to anthrax; the camel, the horse, the ass, and the ox are less resistant to tropical fevers; while the cat and the hog are relatively immune. It has also been observed that among animals of the same species differences occur in this respect. The Algerian sheep is immune against anthrax, an infection fatal to other sheep; and the Holland cow is easily stricken by peri-pneumonia, while other sub-species are only rarely affected.

Among men certain differences in susceptibility or immunity to disease are observable which can only be due to internal or racial causes. The Negro is only rarely affected by yellow fever, and he resists malarial fever much better than the white man. Such racial immunity is at present explained, to a great extent, as having been acquired by a process of natural selection and heredity. These diseases were in the past probably very prevalent among these races, and all individuals who were susceptible have perished, while the most refractory members of the race have survived. And since the properties to which they owe their survival are of benefit to the species, it is assumed that they are readily transmitted by heredity. On the other hand, populations which have not been subject to this kind of selection are violently affected when a new disease is introduced among them. Thus, when measles, scarlet fever, diphtheria, etc., are imported on islands where they were unknown before, the population is actually decimated in a short time. Their ancestors have not acquired any immunity and have not transmitted it by heredity. But this kind of special vulnerability to contagious disease cannot in the strict sense of the word be called ethnic, because after a few epidemics—*i.e.*, after most of the susceptible persons have succumbed,—those who either were not affected or who have acquired immunity by an attack of the disease, transmit these properties to their progeny, who are not as susceptible. Other so-called racial susceptibilities or immunities to disease are also interpreted easily without resorting to race theories. Thus sleeping sickness, a disease endemic in western equatorial Africa, was up to recently considered peculiar to the negro race, and Europeans were thought to be perfectly immune. But recent investigation has shown that the immunity of the white race is due to the fact that there are only few Europeans living in Western Africa, that those who do live there are under much better hygienic and sanitary conditions than the natives, and that this is the reason why they usually escape. In fact, many cases have recently been reported in whites. All this proves that when racial immunities or susceptibilities to disease are spoken of, many circumstances which may contribute to the observed peculiarity must first be ascertained. "Race" alone may often be only a cloak for our ignorance, unless all the conditions of the *milieu* have been excluded.

By committing this common error—forgetting the environmental influence in the etiology of disease—the Jews have repeatedly been described as the best example of a race which shows striking immunities or susceptibilities to certain diseases. It was, namely, found that they suffer less than Christians from certain contagious diseases, that they are especially prone to derangements of the nervous system and of the metabolism. Some have found in this a confirmation of the alleged differences existing between the "Semites" and the "Aryans." Buschan says that, in spite of all the arguments brought by those who believe in the heterogeneity of the Jewish type, he is convinced of the purity of the Jewish race. He has always gained the impression that the Jews are physically, as well as psychologically, in a great measure different from the Aryans. He insists that racial pathology confirms this view, showing that the Jews, in contrast with the Aryans, display a racial influence in their susceptibilities or immunities to certain pathological processes.[1]

[1] G. Buschan, "Einfluss der Rasse auf die Form und Häufigkeit pathologischer Veränderungen," *Globus*. lxvii., pp. 21-24, 43-47, 60-63, 76-80; 1895.

While discussing the pathological characteristics of the Jews, we shall in the following pages always first inquire into the facts as they present themselves, investigating, in accordance with statistical data obtainable from publications of registrars' offices of cities where many Jews live, the causes of death among both Jews and Christians; we shall also make use of scattered literature in medical books and journals bearing on the morbidity of the Jews. If in certain respects it is found that the Jews show either a tendency to an excessive susceptibility or a relative immunity to a certain pathological process, we shall not be satisfied with the easy explanation of "race influence." We shall go into detail as to other causes that may contribute to the differences displayed. Particular attention has to be paid to the distribution of the population by ages, because people with a lower birth-rate have a lower infant mortality, which means also a lower morbidity and mortality from contagious diseases of childhood. The habits and customs of life must receive due attention, with especial reference to the consumption of alcoholic beverages, because this plays a great *rôle* in the etiology and particularly in the prognosis of many diseases. Occupations, distribution of population in cities and in the country, and their influence on the morbidity and mortality, will receive their proper share of attention. Only after the social and economic environment has been studied and found to be inadequate to explain a phenomenon can it be attributed to race influence.

Before going into details of the pathological peculiarities of the Jews it is important to speak of the rarity of alcoholism among them. It is a well-known fact that a drunken Jew is rarely met with in any part of the world. Indeed, many physicians state that in their professional experience they have never treated one for inebriety. Even among the poor and dependant Jews drunkenness is extremely rare. In the capacity of physician to the United Hebrew Charities of New York City, I see thousands of applicants for relief annually, and during the last ten years I have hardly seen more than a dozen Jews whose poverty was due to drink. This is also true of conditions in London, Paris, Berlin, and especially Eastern Europe. In this connection it is important to mention that between twenty-five and sixty per cent. of the dependency and pauperism among people of other faiths are directly or indirectly ascribed to alcoholism. The problem recently discussed in sociological literature whether alcoholism is a cause or an effect of poverty cannot be applied to the Jews either way. Among them it has been neither a cause nor an effect of adverse sanitary, hygienic, social, or economic conditions.

On the other hand their abstinence is responsible for many of their pathological, social, and economic peculiarities. It is well known that alcohol reduces the vitality of the body and increases the susceptibility to infectious and contagious diseases, and as a result we find that during an epidemic drunkards are usually the preferred victims of the scourge. Alcoholic mothers are apt to neglect their children, in addition to begetting inferior offspring, and thus expose them to the ravages of disease. Many diseases are known to be caused directly or indirectly by the abuse of drink, especially Bright's disease, cirrhosis of the liver, arterio-sclerosis, etc. The experience of life insurance companies shows that the expectation of life is greater in those who are total abstainers or only moderate drinkers than in those who indulge in it excessively. In spite of their abstinence, the Jews are great sufferers from nervous diseases, especially insanity, but alcoholic insanity is extremly rare among them. A case of delirium tremens in a Jew is seldom seen in European and American hospitals.

As has been the case with many other peculiarities of the Jews, their abstinence has been spoken of by many authors as a racial trait. Some have even maintained that Jews are immune to alcohol. Thus, Norman Kerr[1] had never in his professional intercourse with Jews been consulted by one of them for inebriety. He believed that it is due more to racial than to religious influences, considering, as he thought, that they are sober in all climes and under all conditions. He "cannot help thinking that some inherited racial insusceptibility to narcotism, strengthened and confirmed by the practice of various hygienic habits, has been the main reason for their superior temperance." G. Archdall Reid, who never

[1] *Inebriety*, London, 1889.

treated a Jew for alcoholism and never heard of one being so treated, also believes that it is not superior moral teachings, education, or environment that keeps them back from drinking, but is purely due to inclination, "because deep indulgence, so far from being delightful, is disagreeable to them."[1] His theory is that alcohol eliminates in course of years a great number of people so constituted that intoxication affords them keen delight, leaving the perpetuation of the race, in a great measure, to those on whom intoxication confers little or no delight. Alcoholism is thus a strong agent of selection and transmissible to the offspring. He finds evidence that the ancient Hebrews drank excessively, and their contemporary descendants are therefore not inclined to excessive drinking.

This is not in agreement with the true conditions of the Jews. There are practically no total abstainers among them. Those who follow implicitly their religious precepts drink regularly, at least every Friday and Saturday and at every festival, including marriages, births, etc. The followers of the sect known as the *Chasidim*, who are very numerous in Eastern Europe, indulge in drinking quite freely, often to intoxication.

On the whole, total abstainers are rare among them, moderate drinkers quite common, while dipsomaniacs are very rare. That this is all due to social conditions is evident, for as soon as they leave the Ghetto atmosphere their "racial" immunity to alcohol vanishes.

In England and the United States the immigrant Jews are quite temperate, and a drunkard is rare among them. But among their descendants drunkenness is becoming more and more common. The same is reported to be true of the Jewish immigrants to Paris.[2] Their reputation in this regard is in fact waning. While in former times it was rare for a Jew to be seen in a hospital for the treatment of dipsomania, there are many cases seen at present in the United States and in Germany. It was the Jew of the Ghetto, isolated from his non-Jewish neighbour, who abhorred drunkenness as a sin, a disgrace, only fit for a *Goi* (Gentile) but not for one of the Chosen People. In

---

[1] G. A. Reid, *Alcoholism*, pp. 99-100, 117-118; London, 1902.
[2] L. Cheinisse, "La race Juive, jouit-elle d'une immunité a l'égard de l'alcoholisme?" *Semaine Médicale*; Dec. 23, 1908.

mediæval times, everywhere, and recently in Eastern Europe, he had a profound contempt for everybody and everything not Jewish. He considered himself on a higher plane of culture. But as soon as the barriers of the Ghetto are broken down and he comes in more or less intimate contact with non-Jews, he learns much from them which is not always good for him. Drinking is one of those acquirements which is beginning to show itself among the Sons of Jacob in recent times.

There is no doubt that many of their biostatic social and economic peculiarities have been changing of late as a result of their drinking. That the change is not to their advantage does not alter matters. As will be seen in subsequent chapters, this is responsible for the change in their proclivity to commit certain forms of crime. It also influences their demographic characteristics as well as the diseases from which they are liable to suffer. Many of the immunities which they enjoyed in former times, and which the Jews who live at present in a Ghetto atmosphere still enjoy, are bound to disappear with this change, so that no differences between them and others may be evident in the future in regard to these characteristics.

Contagious Diseases.—According to many observers, the Jews enjoy a remarkable immunity to most of the contagious and infectious diseases. In medical literature there are many articles dealing with the subject, and nearly all of them record the testimony of physicians in various countries to the effect that most epidemic diseases kill, proportionately, a lesser number of Jews than non-Jews. This peculiar resistance of the Jews to the noxious effects of contagious disease had already been noted in mediæval times, especially during the great epidemics in Europe of the plague, known then as the "Black Death." At that time it appears that the immunity had not done them much good; on the contrary, they suffered severely because it was thought that the pestilence affected them to a lesser degree than it affected their Christian neighbours. The Jews were accused of being special emissaries of Satan in causing the plague. It was said that their immunity was due to a special protection conferred on them by Satan, as a compensation for the services they rendered him by their wholesale poisoning of the wells.

The use of this poisoned water was thought to be the cause of the Christians being attacked by the plague. The Almighty had to be propitiated before he could be expected to move in the direction of lessening the severity of the plague, and, by torturing and murdering the Jews, and especially by confiscating their tainted property, Satan was expected to be thwarted and the terrible scourge driven from Christendom; and, in fact, after thousands of Jews were burned at the stake, or otherwise done away with, the plague finally disappeared, but not before killing twenty-five millions of people, a quarter of the population of Europe at that period.

That this legend was not based on fact is evident when we read in Graetz that the Marranos who fled to Naples, Genoa, and other Italian cities, in 1492, were severely attacked by the pestilence, to which thousands succumbed. Then, their enemies accused them of spreading the plague among the Christians and demanded that they be expelled for this reason.[1] G. Deutsch[2] quotes a contemporary author, Conrad von Meyenberg, to the effect that the Jews of Vienna had to enlarge their cemetery to find room for their dead during the epidemic of the plague. In Worms, during the plague of 1666, 136 Jews died within four months, a death-rate equal to that of ten years under normal conditions. In a study of the causes of death among the inhabitants of the Ghetto in Vienna during 1648-69 Schwartz finds that many died from contagious diseases, such as plague, typhus, dysentery, small-pox, etc., and can find no evidences of immunity.[3]

Medical literature of the last century mentions many instances showing a complete immunity of the Jews during epidemics. In an article by Dr John Stockton Hough[4] the following data are collected from ancient books:— Tschudi, in speaking of the plague of 1346, says that this malady did not affect the Jews of any country. Fracastor mentions the fact that the Jews escaped completely the

[1] Graetz, *History of the Jews*, vol. iv., pp. 359, 363, 486.
[2] *Jewish Chronicle*, July 9th, 1909.
[3] I. Schwartz, *Das Wiener Ghetto*, Leipzig, 1909; "Zur Mortalität der Wiener Ghettobewohner, 1648-69," *Zeitschr. Demogr. Stat. d. Juden*, pp. 49-61, 1910.
[4] "Longevity and Other Biostatic Peculiarities of the Jewish Race," *Medical Record*, vii., pp. 241-245; 1873.

epidemic of typhus of 1505. Rau mentions the same immunity from typhus observed at Langeons in 1824. Ramazzini insisted on the immunity of the Jews from intermittent fevers observed at Rome in 1691. Degner says the Jews escaped in 1736 the epidemic of dysentery at Nimègue. Michael Levy makes the remark that this immunity was manifest at the same time in the French and in the Israelites. M. Eisenmann insists on the extreme rarity of croup in Jewish children. In addition to all the above immunities, Cohn also reports that between 1856 and 1865 the proportion of deaths due to typhoid fever in Posen, Prussia, was 9.96 per 1,000 deaths, due to all causes among the Protestants, 9.4 among the Catholics, and only 5.26 among the Jews.[1] In recent years no such immunities are observed among the Jews, although it appears that the mortality from typhoid fever is slightly less than among others. In the United States, according to the special census of the Jewish Vital Statistics[2] the mortality rates from typhoid fever per 1,000 deaths due to all causes was, among the Jews, 27.64, as against 32.16 among the general population of this country. In Vienna, Rosenfeld[3] reports also that there is hardly any difference in the mortality from this disease between Jews and Christians. The rates in 1901-03 were: Jews, 3; Protestants, 3; and Catholics, 4 per 100,000 population.

Between 1896 and 1900 the mortality from typhoid in Cracow was slightly less among the Jews, 28.1, and among the Christians, 29.8 per 100,000 population; in Lemberg, in 1897-1902, the mortality of the Jews was even higher, 24.2 and 20.6 respectively. Similar statistics are available for Budapest.[4] And it must be borne in mind that a low mortality does not necessarily mean a lower morbidity, because the prognosis of typhoid fever is more favourable among Jews than among Christians, mainly

[1] "Sterblichkeitsverhältnisse der Stadt Posen," in *Vierteljahrsschrift für Gerichtliche Medicin*, p. 292; 1869.
[2] Report on Vital Statistics, *Census Bulletin No. 19*; 1891.
[3] S. Rosenfeld, "Die Sterblichkeit der Juden in Wien," *Archiv für Rassen und Geselschaftsbiologie*, heft 1 and 2; 1907.
[4] See M. Fishberg, "Die Angebliche Rassenimmunität der Juden," *Zeitschr. Demogr. der Juden*, pp. 177-188, 1908; also E. Auerbach, "Die Sterblichkeit der Juden in Budapest," *Ibid.*, Nos. 10-11, 1908.

because of the sobriety of the former. It is reasonably evident that in mediæval times the Jews may have been spared during some epidemics of typhoid fever, not necessarily because of some physiological or ethnic advantage, but mainly because they lived apart from the Christian population, segregated in closed Ghettoes, and usually having a separate water supply. During epidemics of this disease among the Christian population, it could easily happen that the wells which supplied the Ghetto-dwellers with water were not contaminated. Such things occur quite often in recent years, when the population of one part of a city suffers from an epidemic of typhoid fever while a neighbouring part is spared, mainly because it has a separate water supply.

Cholera.—Medical literature abounds with many instances of the Jews being spared during epidemics of Asiatic cholera. According to all etiological factors of cholera, excepting alcoholism, the Jews should suffer from this disease much more frequently than, or at least as often as, other peoples. Yet there are records showing that during many epidemics they were affected to a lesser degree than non-Jews; indeed, during some epidemics they are said to have displayed a perfect immunity. According to Boudin, the Jews of Algiers, notwithstanding the fact that they lived overcrowded in small and dark dwellings, very often in cellars, showed a lesser morbidity and mortality during the epidemic of cholera in 1844-45.

Similarly, while cholera was raging in Budapest, Hungary, in 1851, the mortality among the Christian population was seven times as great as among the Jews, and during the epidemic of 1866 there were, in every 100 deaths in the general hospital, 51.76 deaths from cholera, and in the Jewish hospital only 34.0.[1] From a pamphlet published in 1869 by Dr Scalzi, Professor of Medicine in the University of Rome, it appears that the case mortality of cholera was in 1866, among the Catholics, 69.13 per cent.; among the inhabitants belonging to other non-Jewish cults, 42.13 per cent.; and among the Jews only 22 per cent. In proportion to the population, the mortality from this disease was 0.45 per cent. among the Jews and 1 per cent. among the Christians—more than double.

[1] Tormay, *Die lebens und sterblichkeitsverhältnisse der Stadt Pest;* 1866.

Dr. Mapother of Dublin,[1] in one of his lectures on public hygiene, stated that there was observed a surprising immunity of the Jews in Whitechapel, London, during epidemics of cholera; and Mr. Wolff, surgeon to the poor of the Spanish and Portuguese Synagogues in London, thus refers to the immunity of the London Jews in 1849:— "They do not suffer from the depression caused by habitual intoxication. These circumstances in their favour enabled them, during the epidemic of 1849, to enjoy almost an immunity from the disease, which raged with frightful violence in the immediate neighbourhood of the district where they most congregate, and the sanitary conditions of which, as regards cleanliness, ventilation, etc., were decidedly unfavourable.[2]

But the Jews have not always enjoyed such immunity from cholera. During some epidemics of this disease they are said to have suffered severely. Thus, Hirsch states that the Jewish population of Algiers and Smyrna suffered more from cholera during the epidemic of 1831 than the rest of the population, and the same was observed in 1831 among the Jews in Poland, Roumania, and in many other places.[3] Boudin also collected evidence showing that the cholera attacked the Jews during 1831 much more often, and their mortality was much higher, than among their non-Jewish neighbours, although thirteen years later the exact opposite was the case.

During the most recent epidemic of cholera in Europe in 1891-96 it appears that in some places at least the Jews were less often affected by the disease. In Hamburg, Germany, during the months of August and September, 1902, there were buried in the non-Jewish cemeteries 6.4 times the average number of dead for the three previous years; in the Jewish cemetery only 3.5 times as many.[4] George Buschan also states that there are evidences that in Berlin, Breslau, etc., the Jews suffered from the recent epidemic of cholera in Germany to a lesser degree, and

[1] *Revue Scientifique*, p. 625; 1881.
[2] *Medical Times and Gazette*, vol. vii., p. 356; London, 1853.
[3] A. Hirsch, *Handbuch der Historisch-geographischen Pathologie*, vol. i. Haesar, in his *History of Medicine*, brings many instances showing that the Jews are often greater sufferers from cholera than the Christians among whom they lived.
[4] *Deutsche Medizinische Wochenschrift*, p. 193, 1893.

had a lower mortality, than the Christians.[1] Similar evidence is brought showing that in Nikolayeff, South Russia, the Jews had a lower morbidity and mortality during the cholera epidemic than non-Jews. In that city there were at that time about 75,000 inhabitants, of whom about 15,000 were Jews—*i.e.*, one Jew to four others. Among the latter the scourge attacked 756, of whom 382 died, while among the former only 36 were attacked, and but 13 of these succumbed.[2] Dr. Barazhnikoff reported to the St. Petersburg Medical Society that during the epidemic of this disease in 1894 in the province of Mohileff the morbidity among the Jews was greater and the course of the disease much more severe than among the Christians, but the rate of mortality was much smaller among the Jews. He adds that it must be borne in mind that the Jews in that locality, although generally poorer, are more intelligent than their neighbours, and take better care of their health.[3]

In this disease it is again evident that the immunity of the Jews has no ethnic basis, but is solely due to their social conditions. Their abstemiousness in the use of alcoholic liquors spares them quite often from infection, because it is well known that cholera attacks much more often alcoholics than those who abstain from excessive drinking. In the Middle Ages, when they were segregated in Ghettoes, the disease often did not penetrate the walls of their quarters, and they remained as a result completely unaffected during an epidemic. Since they commingled with the general population during the nineteenth century, it is seen that they are often affected, occasionally more severely so than non-Jews. But recalling that they take better care of their health, that they believe in infection as a cause of certain diseases, and more readily take proper precautions to prevent the spread of contagious disease, while in Russia and in many other places the poor and ignorant are likely to attribute epidemics to acts of Providence, it can only be expected that the Jews should be less often affected, and the prognosis in those who are stricken be much more favourable.

[1] *Globus*, vol. lxvii. p. 47.
[2] *Vratch*, xiv. p. 115; 1893.
[3] *Proceedings of the St. Petersburg Medical Society*, p. 206; 1895.

Endemic Diseases.—A considerable amount has been written on the prevalence among Jews of the more common contagious diseases which are endemic in all civilized countries. Many authors have mentioned that the contagious diseases of infancy and childhood, such as measles, scarlet fever, diphtheria, whooping-cough, etc., are either less among the Jews or that they have entirely been spared during certain pandemics. Considering the poverty, overcrowding in dark and ill-ventilated dwellings, and the unhygienic surroundings in which a large proportion of Jews live, this peculiar resistance to the noxious effects of contagion on the part of Jewish children was surprising, and could only be ascribed to an inherent or racial characteristic, which gives them an invaluable advantage in their struggle for existence among the nations of Europe.

These opinions prevailed as long as the testimony of individual physicians on local conditions was relied upon. But since registration of contagious disease has been inaugurated in various countries in which many Jews live, and since the registration of the causes of death has been enforced almost everywhere in Europe, the data accumulated by these processes have shown conclusively that things are not as simple as was supposed. The most important point elicited from the statistics of registrars' offices is that the Jews do not show any uniformity in this respect, but that there are great differences in the rates of Jewish morbidity and mortality from contagious diseases according to the time, place, severity of the epidemic, etc. In fact it was shown that some contagious diseases are more often a cause of death among Jews than among others. Diphtheria and croup particularly appear to affect Jews much more often than Christians, or at least have more often a fatal issue. Stokvis reports that in Amsterdam during 1856-62 the death-rates from diphtheria and croup among Jewish children was 13.7 per cent., among the non-Jewish poor only 4.04 per cent., whereas it was 5.88 per cent. among the rest of the population of the city. Similarly, according to Census Bulletin No. 19, 1891, the Jews in the United States are also more liable to diphtheria and croup than the rest of the population, although in New York City it appears from statistics collected by the author[1] that the mortality from these diseases in the four wards largely inhabited by Jews was during 1897-99 5.95 per 10,000 population, as against only 6.42 among the general population of the city. But it must be recalled that the Jewish population of these wards consists mainly of immigrants, with an excessive proportion of adults, especially males, and a lesser proportion of children than among the general population.[2] So that the slightly lower mortality from diphtheria and croup may be ascribed to the difference in the age distribution of the population. But according to the careful statistics collected by Rosenfeld[3] of the mortality in Vienna during 1901-03, the mortality from this disease was more favourable among the Jews than among the Christians of that city. There the mortality was as follows:—Catholics 27, Protestants 19, and Jews only 13 per 100,000 population. But in Cracow, Galicia, the Jews are at a disadvantage when compared with the Christian population in this respect. In 1896-1900 the death-rates from diphtheria were—Jews 57.6 and Christians 49.0 per 100,000 population, and in Lemberg during 1897-1902 Jews 27.1 and Christians 35.5, showing that there is no uniformity.

That the mortality and possibly also the morbidity of the Jews from this disease depends on the severity of the epidemic, and not on any inherent ethnic peculiarity, is well illustrated by statistics from the city of Budapest, Hungary. Glatter[4] reports that during 1863 the mortality of the Christians from diphtheria and croup was only 2.6 per cent., as against 4.2 per cent. among the Jews, while Körösi[5] found the exact opposite during 1886-90, as the following figures show:—

---

[1] M. Fishberg, *Health and Sanitation of the Immigrant Jewish Population of New York City*; New York, 1904.

[2] In fact, in 1906 it was found that the mortality from diphtheria of the Russians (mostly Jews) in New York was 71 per 100,000 population, as against 39.9 among the general population. Gilfoy, "The Death-rate of New York," *Medical Record*, vol. lxxiii., pp. 132-135.

[3] *Loc. cit.*

[4] "Das Rassenmoment in seinen Einflus auf Erkrankungen," *Caspers Vjsch*, t. xxv. pp. 32-45; 1864.

[5] "*Einflus der Confession, des Wohlstandes und der Beschäftigung auf die Todesursachen*, p. 11; Berlin, 1898.

	Diphtheria.	Croup.
Catholics	559	265 deaths per 100,000 children under 10 years.
Protestants	509	286 ,, ,, ,, ,,
Jews	345	215 ,, ,, ,,

And in 1901-05 Auerbach[1] also found a lower proportion of deaths among Jews—16.5 per 100,000, as against 33.7 among Catholics.

It cannot be imagined that in 1863 the Jews in Budapest were more susceptible to diphtheria and croup because of their ethnic characteristics, but within twenty-five years their racial traits have changed so that they gained a comparative immunity from the diseases. The most reasonable explanation is that in 1863 the disease invaded the part of the city largely inhabited by Jews with greater severity, while in 1886-90 and 1901-05 the Christian parts of the city was more severely invaded.

Conditions are the same with other endemic diseases, such as measles, scarlet fever, whooping-cough, dysentery, etc. In some places the Jews appear to suffer less from these diseases, while in others the contrary is true. I have shown elsewhere that in Vienna and in Budapest the Jews have more favourable mortality returns from scarlet fever, measles, diphtheria, croup, whooping-cough, and dysentery than the Catholics and Protestants. But in Cracow, Lemberg, and New York quite the opposite is the fact[2]; these diseases claim more victims from among the Jews than from among the Christians of these cities. Conditions in many other cities could be cited showing similar differences, which all go to prove that there are no racial proclivities among the Jews in this respect, but that they are, under similar conditions, just as liable to be affected as others.

Smallpox has repeatedly been mentioned as a contagious disease which only rarely affects Jews. Cohn reports that in Posen, Prussian Poland, the mortality from it among children during the period 1856-65 was 31.3 per 1000 deaths due to all causes among Catholics, 22.6 among Protestants, and only 9.0 among Jews. Similarly in

---

[1] Elias Auerbach, "Die Sterblichkeit der Juden in Budapest," *Zeitschr. Demogr. Statis. d. Juden*, p. 167; 1908.

[2] M. Fishberg. "Die angebliche Rassen-immunität der Juden," *Zeitschr. Demogr. Stat. d. Juden*, pp. 177-188, 1908.

Budapest, during the epidemic in 1886 and 1887, the mortality per 100,000 population was as follows: Catholics, 106; Protestants, 81; Calvinists, 74; and Jews only 33. Nearly all who quoted these figures were satisfied that the Jewish "racial peculiarities" have given them an advantage in this respect, forgetting that vaccination has a much greater influence on the prevalence of smallpox than racial proclivities. As a matter of fact, it is well known to every physician of experience among the Jews that they are always ready to take advantage of any new measure to prevent or cure disease. There are practically no anti-vaccinationists among them[1]; nor are there any other kind of cranks among them to urge them on to resist the attempts on the part of the authorities to vaccinate them. The Jewish clergy also is always in favour of placing medical matters in the hands of the physicians, and is not in favour of leaving such things solely to Providence. As a result of this the Jews in Eastern Europe have been almost universally vaccinated during the first half of the nineteenth century, while the general population of that region have not even to-day submitted completely. Indeed, since vaccination has been adopted on a grand scale in Russia, Austria, Hungary, etc., both Christians and Jews are only rarely affected by this disease, and there are hardly any differences between both groups. In Cracow and Lemberg, according to Thon, the mortality from smallpox was the same among Jews and Christians during 1901-03, and in Vienna Rosenfeld reports that during 1901-03 neither Jews nor Christians died as a result of this disease.

It must be emphasized in this connection that the Jews in Eastern Europe, superstitious as they are undoubtedly, believe in infection as a cause in the transmission of certain diseases; they believe that disease may be transmitted from the sick to the healthy by personal contact, by fomites, dwellings and food, and are willing to follow the advice of medical men in these matters. This cannot be said of the poorer and more ignorant parts of the

---

[1] According to Dr. Ward, Whitechapel is the best vaccinated district in the whole of London; the Jews seek vaccination. Dr. Niven reports the same for Manchester. See *Minutes of Evidence taken before the Royal Commission on Alien Immigration*, 18,314, 21,792.

population in Eastern Europe, especially of the Slavonian peasantry. The Russian government is always helpless in times of epidemics when attempting to check the progress of a scourge. No assistance can be obtained from the general population, in fact they resist all sanitary and hygienic orders of the medical men. Living in separate parts of a city, and obeying the sanitary orders, the Jews may occasionally be spared during an epidemic. But this cannot by any means be considered an ethnic trait of the Jews.

Tuberculosis.—The *habitus phthisicus*, which was described in great detail by ancient medical writers, and which can also be found mentioned in many recent monographs on tuberculosis, is very common among Jews. The phthisical chest described by Hippocrates and Galen is to-day found in a large proportion of Jews. Indeed, that frail, undersized, emaciated body, with a long, narrow, flat chest, in which the ribs stand out promiuently, the chest-bone is depressed, and the shoulder blades project in the back like two wings, may be considered as characteristic of a large number of Jews. The capacity of the chest, considered by some as the "index of vitality," is also at a minimum in the Jew when compared with non-Jews. This is especially noted if we take into consideration only one criterion about which a consiberable amount of evidence has been accumulated, namely, the relative size of the chest. As was shown before (Chap. IV.), the circumference of the Jew's chest is usually less than one-half his height, while among others it is almost invariably more than one-half the height in healthy persons. Physically, the Jews can, under the circumstances, be considered predisposed to pulmonary diseases, especially consumption.

Considering their economic and social conditions, it is also evident that everything favourable for the development and spread of tuberculosis is found among them. They are pre-eminently town-dwellers, and in cities the bulk of the Jews reside usually in the most densely overcrowded sections of the city; and lacking proper ventilation, fresh air, and sunshine, they are thus in an atmosphere favourable for infection with tubercle bacilli. Their occupations, which are usually of the indoor variety, such as tailoring, shoemaking, fur, etc., also enjoy the evil distinction of supplying a greater number of consumptives than outdoor occupations. When to this are added poverty, grief, anxiety, and excessive mental exertion, want of proper exercise, fresh air, and sunshine, conditions under which the majority of Jews live in various parts of the world, it would be expected that they should be attacked more often by this disease than others; indeed, *a priori* they should actually be decimated by the White Plague.

Investigation of the prevalence of tuberculosis in various countries has, however, revealed the amazing fact that this disease is less frequent among the Jews than among their Christian neighbours. In Italy, Lombroso has found that the Jews of Verona have a lower mortality from tuberculosis than the Catholics of that city; in London it was found that the Jews in the Whitechapel district have relatively only about one-half as many deaths due to this disease as the general population of the city; and similar evidence is available for Eastern Europe, Russia, Austria, Hungary, and Roumania, as well as for New South Wales, Tunis, and the United States.[1] The most recent statistics on the subject are given about Budapest, where, during 1901-05 the mortality from pulmonary tuberculosis was 44.15 per 10,000 Catholics, 20.06 among Jews, and 39.27 among persons of other faiths.[2] Also in Vienna the mortality from all forms of tuberculosis during 1901-03 was, per 100,000 population, among Catholics, 496; among Protestants, 328; and among Jews only 179. To pulmonary tuberculosis alone succumbed 388 per 100,000 Catholics, 246 Protestants, and only 131 among Jews.[3] Tuberculosis of the lungs, the brain membranes, or of the bones among adults and children is here less frequent among Jews than among either Catholics or Protestants. The same has been the fact in New York City. Here the bulk of the

---

[1] For detailed statistical evidence, see M. Fishberg, "The Relative Infrequency of Tuberculosis among Jews, *American Medicine*, Nov. 2nd, 1901; *idem*, Transactions Sixth International Congress on Tuberculosis, 1908.
[2] E. Auerbach, in *Zeitschrift für Demographie und Statistik der Juden*, No. 11, p. 164; 1908.
[3] S. Rosenfeld, "Die Sterblichkeit der Juden in Wien," *Archiv für Rassen-und Gesellschaftsbiologie*, Nos. 1 and 2; 1907.

immigrant Jewish population lives mostly in the lower East Side, the streets of which have the unenviable reputation of being the most insanitary in the United States; the tenement houses in which they mostly live are overcrowded and ill ventilated; the size of the rooms is proverbially small, and they each accommodate many inhabitants. The majority of these people work in the well-known "sweat shops" for long hours daily, at tailoring and the allied industries. But in spite of all these unfavourable conditions, the mortality from tuberculosis is much lower in these streets inhabited by Jews than in any other part of the city. Lower yet is the mortality from this disease in the Harlem district, where a large number of more prosperous Jews live.

How far adverse hygienic and sanitary conditions, *per se,* are from being always conducive to the development and spread of tuberculosis is illustrated by conditions in Tunis, North Africa. The Jews in that city live in very narrow streets, such as can only be seen in Oriental countries. Their conditions are there to-day only slightly different from those in which they could have been seen several hundred years ago, and although they are no more compelled to live in a closed Ghetto, still the poorer class, which constitute the majority of Jews, even now live often more than one family in one room. The Europeans, who have only recently immigrated into Tunis, live in the European part of the city, which hardly differs, from the standpoint of sanitation, from the average provincial town in France. Still, according to Tostivint and Remlinger, the mortality from tuberculosis in that city during 1894-1900 was 11.3 per 1,000 Arabs; 5.13 per 1,000 Europeans; and only 0.75 per 1,000 Jews.[1]

The cause of this relative immunity of the Jews to the white plague has been differently interpreted by different writers. The race element has been given attention by many authors who state that here the vitality of the Jewish race, its tenacity of life, and its power of resistance to the noxious effects of contagious disease is evident. Others have argued that no ethnic factors are at work in this

---

[1] Tostivint and Remlinger, "Note sur la rareté de la Tuberculose chez les Israélites Tunisiens," *Revue d'Hygiène et de Police Sanitaire,* vol. xxii., p 984. Paris, 1900.

respect, but that it is a question of a peculiarity of the Jewish *milieu,* which often spares the Jews from infection by the tubercle bacilli. Lombroso, who holds the latter view, attributes this immunity to the fact that the Jews are engaged in occupations which require no exposure to the vicissitudes of the weather; in fact, all other acute pulmonary diseases, particularly pneumonia, are also infrequent among them, and their lungs are thus left in a condition fit to resist infection by tubercle bacilli. But this does not hold good for the Jews in Eastern Europe, nor for those in London or New York. These Jews' occupations, while not exposing them to frequent changes of temperature, still being mostly of the domestic and indoor variety, and the workshops in which they are generally employed for long hours being of the "sweat shop" kind, should rather render them more liable to be affected with this disease than others who have a large number of agriculturists in their midst and work outdoors.

Drs. Tostivint and Remlinger also do not regard it likely that ethnic peculiarities of the Jews explain this immunity, because they are just as "Semitic" as the Tunisian Arabs, yet the latter suffer much from tuberculosis. These authors are also unable to discover any disparities as to nourishment, clothing, etc., which might reasonably be held to explain the situation, because both eat about the same kind of food and are dressed in the same Oriental fashion. Moreover, the poor native Jews occupy a portion of the town common to them and the Mussulmans, while the few rich live in the European section of the city. There is, however, one thing to which these writers attribute the lesser liability of the Jews to tuberculosis. The Jews abhor the dusting-brush, and instead of using it they wipe all surfaces, in some instances several times daily, with damp cloths. By this means very much less dust is raised than by brushing, and the risk of inhaling air laden with tubercle bacilli is lessened. Moreover, the Jews have but little furniture as compared with the French or Italian immigrants living in Tunis, and consequently the opportunities for collecting dust are correspondingly diminished.

This explanation, which is in accordance with our present knowledge of the spread of this disease, may hold good for the Jews in Tunis, but as regards the Jews in other countries is hardly tenable. The dusting-brush is not abhorred by Jews all over the world, unless in some parts where neither dusting nor wiping with moist rags are brought often enough in operation to remove dust at all. To meet this situation several authors have attributed their lesser liability to succumb to tuberculosis to a special inherent vitality of the Jewish "race," which saves them not only from this but from all other contagious and infectious diseases. Some have even maintained that the "Semitic" blood which flows in their veins renders the Jews immune to the virus of infection and gives them an advantage in the struggle for existence when they meet the "Aryan" in Europe. But this argument is fallacious, not only for the reason that, as we have already seen, the Jewish "race" is not as pure as is generally believed, but for various other valid reasons. Tuberculosis is known to attack without any racial preferences. The small differences observed among the various divisions of mankind in regard to their liability to tuberculosis are traceable to social and economic causes. Moreover, the variations displayed by the different social groups of white humanity, such as the differences in the incidence of the disease between city and county dwellers, rich and poor, those engaged in indoor or outdoor occupations, persons active in a dusty atmosphere as compared with such as are working in clean, airy shops and the like, are just as great, often greater, than the differences observed in the white, black, red, or yellow races. It is also a fact that intermarriage of Jews with Christians does not increase their susceptibility to tuberculosis. In Berlin, where the proportion of mixed marriages is over forty per cent. of the pure Jewish marriages, the mortality rate from tuberculosis is the lowest recorded, 9.81 per 10,000, while in Cracow and Lemberg, where intermarriages are practically not taking place, the rates were 20.49 and 30.64 respectively.[1]

The ritual dietary laws practised by the Jews have also been given credit for their lower tuberculosis mortality.[2]

---

[1] M. Fishberg, "Tuberculosis among the Jews," *Trans. Sixth Intern. Congress on Tuberculosis*, vol. iii., pp. 415-428; 1908.
[2] See especially Behrend, *Nineteenth Century*, September, 1889.

As is well known, Jews, before pronouncing meat as fit for human consumption (*kosher*), subject every carcass to a thorough examination by an expert. Special attention is paid to the condition of the viscera, particularly the lungs, pleura, liver, and spleen. Those animals whose lungs present any adhesions to the thoracic walls or adhesions between the lobes of the lungs, or in which small nodules are discovered scattered over the surface of the lungs, are pronounced *terefa*—*i.e.*, unfit for human consumption. It has been stated that bovine tuberculosis is thus prevented from gaining a foothold among the children of Israel. In the light of our present knowledge of the origin and spread of tuberculosis, some of the foremost authorities (Behring, Calmette, and others) being of the opinion that tuberculosis is more often acquired by ingestion than by inhalation, the Jewish dietary laws should be an excellent preventive when strictly adhered to. But as a matter of fact, all the available evidence is against this view. In Eastern Europe, where the Jews follow the dietary laws, strictly adhering both to the letter and spirit of the sacred ordinance, there is more consumption among them than among their co-religionists in western countries who disregard the dietary laws in part or completely. In Germany, France, England, Italy, etc., where the majority of the native Jews are constantly met with eating in Christian restaurants, and many are not particular to procure *kosher* meat at home, there is less consumption among them than in Eastern Europe, the East End of London, or the East Side of New York City, where the poor, as they generally are, pay exorbitant prices for meat which is, or is alleged to be, *kosher*. The incidence of this disease among the Jews depends more on their social and economic conditions than on racial or ritual affinities. In Berlin, where they are economically prosperous, there is but little tuberculosis among them, only 9.81 deaths per 10,000 population; in Vienna, where a large proportion are on a high economic plane, but still many poor artizans of Jewish faith are met with, the rate is somewhat higher, 13.1 for pulmonary and 17.9 for all forms of tuberculosis; in Budapest and Bucharest, where the bulk of the Jews are poor, the rates were 21.93 and 25.6 respectively; in Galicia, where their poverty is appalling, it even reaches 30.93 per 10,000 Jews. The influence of the social and economic conditions is also illustrated by the tuberculosis mortality of the Jews in various parts of the city of New York. In those districts where the poorer class of artizans and labourers live the mortality rates are quite high, while in the districts in which the richer class of Jews have settled it is very infrequent as a cause of death. The Jews in the East Side are more orthodox, more strictly adhering to their faith and traditions, and still have proportionately a higher rate of morbidity and mortality from tuberculòsis than their co-religionists in the Harlem district, who, as is characteristic of the Jews generally, with their prosperity have more or less discarded many of their religious practices, and the first change consists usually in consuming meat not prepared according to the dietary law.

It must also be mentioned in this connection that the rarity of alcoholism and syphilis among the Jews has a salutary effect in this respect. It is well known that chronic alcoholics are very prone to be attacked by tuberculosis; the alcohol lowers the vitality of the tissues and thus enables the bacilli to develop and grow more readily. It must also be borne in mind that the centuries of life in the confines of the Ghetto might have adapted Jews to indoor life by a selective process. The bulk of the European population were agriculturists before the advent of the industrial development of the nineteenth century, and even at the present, from sixty to ninety per cent. of the population of the various countries are engaged in agricultural pursuits. It is a matter of general observation that races not adapted to indoor life quickly succumb to consumption as soon as they attempt to live in modern dwellings or to work in mills and factories. When alcoholism is added to the indoor life, the morbidity and mortality from tuberculosis is actually appalling. Savage tribes, as long as they live in their villages and do not know anything about alcoholic drinks, are only rarely attacked by this disease, but so soon as they come in touch with our civilized life, which, in most cases, means they learn to drink, tuberculosis becomes quite common among them. Among the wild or "blanket" Indians of the western plains of North America the disease is almost unknown, but upon the reservations, where, though prohibited by law, yet whisky is consumed quite freely, they are almost being exterminated, chiefly by tuberculosis. The same is true of the Indians of Peru, of the Khirgiz Tartars, and of the savage tribes of Africa and Australia. How far this is true of the modern city populations of Europe, which are mostly drawn from the loins of the country people who are not adapted to urban life, has not been investigated to the extent it deserves. We do know, however, that the progeny of the tuberculous, when reared in a hygienic and sanitary environment, are not more predisposed to the disease than others; in fact, there is evidence tending to show that they display some degree of immunity. The Jew, living for centuries in the Ghetto, could under the circumstances have adapted his organism to an adverse *milieu*, to overcrowding, to dark and ill-ventilated dwellings, etc. Those Jews who could not adapt themselves to a confined atmosphere succumbed to various diseases which thrive in such a *milieu*, chief among which is tuberculosis, and they were eliminated from their midst, having had slight chances to perpetuate their kind.

Contrary to the generally accepted notion, the mortality of the Jews in the mediæval Ghettoes was appalling, due to the overcrowding, lack of ventilation in the dwellings, etc. Hanauer shows that the death-rate in the Ghetto of Frankfort during 1624-1800 was always higher than that of the Christians in that city.[1] Schwartz finds from a study of the mortality of Vienna during 1648-69 that among 883 registered deaths in the Ghetto 92 were attributed to "Schwindsucht," 124 to "Dorr," and 62 to "Lungensucht"—*i.e.*, nearly one-third of all the deaths were due to tuberculous conditions.[2] Living under such conditions for eighteen hundred years has had the effect of weeding out a large proportion of those Jews who were excessively predisposed to tuberculous infection.

This gives a reasonable theory why they do not have a very high mortality from tuberculosis in the East End

---

[1] W. Hanauer, "Geschichte d. Sterblichkeit, etc., in Frankfurt-am-Main," *Deutsches Vierteljahrsschrift f. offentl. Gesundheitspflege*, 1908.

[2] I. Schwartz, "Zur Mortalitatsstatistik der Wiener Ghettobewohner, 1648-69." *Zeitschr. Demogr. Stat. d. Juden*, pp. 49-61, 1910.

of London and the East Side of New York.[1] The immigrant Jew has not made a material change in his removal from Eastern Europe to London or New York. He lived there in a city and settled again in a city; he worked before at some indoor occupation, and does again the same in his new home; he lived there in an over-crowded home, and moves again into an American tenement or a London slum dwelling. He has paid the price for urbanization already for several hundred years. With other immigrants to the United States, such as the Italians, Irish, Syrians, Slavonians, and Hungarians, the case is different. At home they were mostly farmers, living in the open country, and when they come to the United States or England they meet for the first time with urban conditions to which their organism is not adapted, and they must pay an exorbitant price while trying to adapt themselves to the new conditions. The tuberculosis mortality among them is actually appalling.

The effects of the thorough urbanization of the Jews are manifesting themselves in many other ways. It has been observed by many physicans that even when infected by the tubercle bacilli the prognosis is more favourable in the Jew than in other people. The course of the disease is slower. We have seen very few cases of tuberculosis of the fulminant or galloping type among several thousand cases of consumption in Jews. Acute miliary tuberculosis is very rare indeed among them. The cases in which the victim is stricken with high fever and rapid extension of the disease with cavity formation within a few weeks or months are also rare. But cases of the extreme chronic type, running on for years, and still permitting the victim to make himself useful at some occupation, are common, more so than among other people of the same social status. Of course this is due to a certain extent to the infrequency of alcoholics among them, but this alone does not explain the condition. It appears that thorougly urbanized humanity does not offer a good soil for the growth and development of the tubercle bacilli, while the inhabitants of the plain, and less so the peasant or farmer in modern European and American villages, offer a virgin soil for

[1] For conditions in London see *British Medical Journal*, April 25th, 1908.

these parasites. This is the only reasonable way we can explain the high rates of morbidity and mortality from tuberculosis of the rural dwellers who emigrate to cities. Being more predisposed to infection, they also more often supply cases of the acute fulminant or galloping type, as well as acute miliary tuberculosis. Among the Jews it is just the reverse.

CHAPTER XIV

PATHOLOGICAL CHARACTERISTICS (*continued*).

General diseases—The diatheses—Diabetes as a "Jewish disease"—Diseases of the respiratory organs among Jews—Diseases of the circulatory organs—Diseases of the digestive organs—Goitre—Cancer—*Fœtor Judaicus*—Skin diseases among Jews—Syphilis—Leprosy—Eye diseases among Jews—Blindness—Colour blindness—Myopia.

General Diseases.—Certain pathological processes of obscure causation have been attributed to a peculiar diathesis of the persons affected. With the advance of our knowledge of the etiology of disease, most of these diathetic disturbances are disappearing from the terminology of medicine. In fact, many disease proclivities which have previously been considered as racial, or as due to somatic characteristics, have been proven to have their origin in certain habits of life, diet, climate, or the social environment. The ethnic factor in the causation of these pathological processes has been in most cases eliminated in recent years, especially after it was demonstrated that with a change of the social environment the liability to the diseases has diminished or disappeared. One of the best examples in this respect is the so called "nervous diathesis" of the Jews, which, as has been shown, is solely due to their peculiar mode of life, their occupations, and especially their past history of martyrdom; no peculiarity of the structure of the nervous system has been found among the Jews to account for their excessive number of neuropathics and psychopathics.

French medical writers, like Charcot, Lancereaux, Féré, and others, have stated that the rheumatic and gouty diathesis is more widespread among Jews than among people of any other European race. The group of diseases, called by French medical men by the terms *arthritisms* and *herpetisms*, are also said to be more common among Jews. By arthritisms these authors understand a certain group of diseases which are usually due to disturbances of the normal metabolism, and manifest themselves primarily as chronic rheumatism and gout; they also include other morbid processes, such as diabetes, gall-stones, stone in the kidneys, obesity, and some diseases of the skin. By herpetism is understood a group of diseases which manifest themselves in various forms of vasomotor disturbances, as some skin eruptions, neuralgia, migraine, gastralgia and nervous dyspepsia, various forms of trophoneuroses, pulmonary emphysema and arterio-sclerosis, with their sequelæ—apoplexy, softening of the brain, paralysis, etc.[1]

Of these pathological disturbances only diabetes has been found to be more frequent among certain classes of Jews than among non-Jews. The testimony of many physicians who have had a large experience with this disease goes to show that it occurs from two to six times as frequently as it does among the people around them. Indeed, diabetes has been called by some German physicians a *Judenkrankheit*, a Jewish disease. Reliable statistical evidence as to its excessive prevalence among the Jews is, however, not abundant, just as it is difficult to estimate its extent among people of other creeds. It has been stated to be extremely common among the educated classes of natives of India and Ceylon, but almost unknown among the negroes in Africa, though many cases have been observed in coloured people in the United States, which tends to show that their immunity in Africa is by no means absolute or due to ethnic causes. There is abundant evidence that the Jews in Germany are very subject to the disease. In Hungary, also, their mortality from this disease has been excessive. From Auerbach's analysis of the demography of the Jews in Budapest it appears that of the 487 deaths reported as due to diabetes during 1902-07, 238, or more than one-half, occurred in Jews, although they only constituted 23.6 per cent. of the population. The rates were 5.9 deaths due to diabetes

[1] See on this point, "Discussion on the Pathology of the Jews before the Paris Academy of Medicine," *Bulletin de l'Académie de Médecine*, Sept. 8, 1891.

per 100,000 Catholics and 21.4 per 100,000 Jews.[1] In Frankfort, Wallach found that the number of Jews who died from diabetes during 1872-90 was proportionately six times as large as the number of Christians who died from the same cause.[2] In Prussia, Singer finds the mortality was six and a half times larger among the Jews than among the general population, and in ratio to the total mortality it was even nine times more frequent among the Jews.[3] Specialists in diseases of the metabolism who meet many cases of diabetes all agree that the Jews supply an extremely large quota of patients suffering with this disease. Thus Frerich found that twenty-five per cent. of his diabetics were Jews[4]; Kulz[5] found 17.8 per cent., and Carl v. Noorden even 38.8 per cent.[6] But these statistics cannot be accepted without reservation. They are mostly taken from patients treated in German bathing resorts and sanatoriums, where well-to-do patients from all parts of the world are apt to flock for relief. While of other Europeans mostly the rich and prosperous come to these health resorts, it is different with the Jews. Besides the prosperous, there also come numerous diabetics who are quite poor, as any one who has been at Carlsbad or Marienbad can testify. Hundreds of poor and destitute Jews are there every season, coming from Russia, Poland, and Austria, all seeking a cure from the hands of some famous physician at these resorts. It is clear that they thus swell the proportion of Jewish diabetics on the books of the physicians at these resorts. Dr. Arnold Pollatschek of Carlsbad, finding that fifty-six per cent. of his diabetic patients were Jews, is inclined to partly agree with the view just expressed. In the first place, about fifty per cent. of all his patients were of Jewish origin, which would lead one to expect that fifty per cent. of the diabetics should be Jews. He is inclined to believe that the slight excess of Jewish diabetics is only

---

[1] E. Auerbach, "Die Sterblichkeit der Juden in Budapest," *Zeitschr. Demogr. Stat. Juden*, p. 164; 1908.
[2] Wallach, "Notizen zur Diabetessterblichkeit in Frankfurt-a.-M.," *Deutsche Medizinische Wochenschr.*, p. 779; 1893.
[3] H. Singer, *Krankheitslehre der Juden*, p. 81; Leipzig, 1904.
[4] F. T. Frerich, *Über den Diabetes*, p. 185; Berlin, 1884.
[5] *Klinische Erfahrungen über Diabetes Melitus*, pp. 2-3; Jena, 1899.
[6] *Die Zuckerkrankheit und Ihre Behandlung*, p. 44; Berlin, 1901.

apparent. He indicates that the circumstance that Jews apply oftener than Christians to the sanatoriums for treatment is due to their greater wealth, and that consequently as a bath physician in Carlsbad he saw more patients of Jewish origin. He also draws attention to the fact that the mortality from this disease in England is quite high, although there are comparatively few Jews there, and states that it is doubtful whether Thomas, Willis, Dobson, and Rollo, who first observed and described diabetes, had Jewish material for their researches.[1] It is hardly justifiable to speak under the circumstances of diabetes as a *Judenkrankheit*.

In New York City it has also been found that the Jews suffer from this disease more often than others. Stern has found that the mortality from diabetes during 1899 was relatively more than double that among the non-Jewish population.[2] Rudisch has investigated the morbidity from this disease in the Mount Sinai hospital of New York City, and compared it with four non-Jewish hospitals in the city, and comes to the conclusion that, after making all allowances for the chances of error, diabetes is nearly three times as prevalent among Jews as among Christians.[3]

It has been stated by several physicians of experience that the course of the disease is to a certain extent different among Jews from what it is among others. It is also stated that they bear diabetes better than other people. Von Noorden observes that it is remarkable how some patients will endure glycosuria for years without much discomfort, succumbing finally—perhaps after decades—to what is supposed to be heart failure. This peculiar type of diabetes, and this remarkable endurance of the human body of the disturbance of the metabolism are more frequently observed among women, and almost exclusively among Jews.[4] This peculiarity may be explained by the rarity of alcoholism among the Jews.

---

[1] A. Pollatschek, "Zur Aetiologic des Diabetes Melitus," *Zeitschrift für Klinische Medizin*, vol. xxxii., pp. 478-482; 1901.
[2] Stern, "The Mortality from Diabetes Mellitus in the city of New York during 1899, *Medical Record*, lviii., pp. 766-774.
[3] *Mount Sinai Hospital Reports*, pp. 26-29; 1898-99.
[4] Von Noorden, *loc. cit.*, p. 176.

It is well known that diabetes in alcoholics is much more severe, and the course is more rapid than among those who abstain from the abuse of alcoholic drinks. Another peculiarity, which was pointed out by Dr. Stern, is that Jewish diabetics succumb to coma more often than others.

On the whole there is no justification for considering diabetes a racial disease of the Jews. It has not been observed to be more frequent among the Jews in every country than among their non-Jewish neighbours. Dr. Sée is emphatic in his statement that it is no more prevalent among the French Jews than among the rest of the population of France.[1] In New York City it is met with in an excessive proportion only among the German Jews, and is hardly more frequent among the Russian Jews than among any other class of people of the city. This may be due to the fact that the German Jews in New York City are mostly of the prosperous business and professional class, among whom diabetes is always more frequent, while the bulk of the Russian Jews are working men, a class which is not often affected with this disturbance of metabolism.

Many reasons have been assigned for the excessive prevalence of diabetes among the German Jews. Von Noorden[2] thinks that the frequent racial intermixture of Jewish with "Indo-Germanic" blood is the cause, but he does not state how such racial intermixture can produce diabetes. Racial intermixture is quite frequent among civilized peoples, and it has never been considered to have any etiological relations to the disease. Most writers have attributed diabetes to the frequency of consanguineous marriages among Jews, but these, provided they are contracted between healthy individuals, have by no means been proven to be detrimental to the metabolism of the offspring.

It must be borne in mind that diabetes is a disease of the wealthier classes, and is more frequent in cities than in the country. Bertillon has demonstrated that it is more frequently a cause of death in the wealthy districts of Paris than in the poorer districts. Persons of a nervous

---

[1] *Bull. de l'Academie de Médecine*, Sept. 8, 1891.
[2] "Ueber Diabetes Mellitus," *Berliner klinische Wochenschrift*, p. 1117; 1900.

temperament are very often affected, and it is not uncommon to elicit a history of insanity, consumption, and gout among the blood relatives of diabetics. Sudden emotional excitement, grief, terror, worry, and anxiety may each and all be followed so closely by diabetes that there is no room to doubt as to their having been the cause of it. It is well known as a result of commercial disaster "When stocks fall diabetes rises in Wall Street," says Dr. Kleen. For the same reasons engine drivers are especially subject to this disease, the excessively anxious nature of their occupation being the etiological factor. It is also more frequent among the class that is given to high living, to overfeeding, lack of proper exercise, etc. All these etiological factors are found among the Jews in Germany owing to their superior economic status. Their nervous temperament, their occupations, their high living, etc., are just the etiological moments in the causation of diabetes.[1] We know of no ethnic causes for the frequency of this disease, and among the class of Jews who live moderately, it is no more frequent than among others of the same class. The case is similar with gout, which is extremely rare among the poorer Jews in Eastern Europe, and among the immigrant Jews in the United States and England, while it is very often met with among the wealthier Jews in all parts of the world. Chronic rheumatism, however, is very frequent, even among the poorer classes of Jewish immigrants in the United States. But this can be considered as due more to their nervous disposition than to disturbed metabolism. There are no data published to show that acute articular rheumatism is more frequent among Jews than among others, as was found to be the case with the Jews in the United States. In Vienna and in Cracow, Rosenfeld and Thon[2] have found no difference between

[1] Auerbach points out that in Budapest, where the diabetes mortality of the Jews is very high, among the deaths during 1902-05, one out of 296 artizans, one out of 128 professional persons, and one out of 65 commercial persons died from diabetes. The diabetes mortality of the professionals was consequently two-and-a-half times and that of the merchants even four-and-a half times as high as that of the artizans. It is true that one-half of all these deaths was of Jewish origin, but it nevertheless tends to show the great liability of merchants to this disease. *Loc. cit.*, p. 165.
[2] *Loc. cit.*

the Jewish and Christian mortality from this disease. Considering that their occupations are mostly of the indoor variety, and they are not so often exposed to the inclemencies of the weather, it may be expected that they should suffer less than others.

Diseases of the Circulatory and Respiratory Systems.— The acute respiratory diseases appear to be less often a cause of death among Jews than among the Christians around them. This is particularly the case with pneumonia, which claims less victims in the districts largely inhabited by Jews in New York City than in districts where the Jewish population is scarce. In Budapest, also, Körösi notes a lower mortality of the Jews from pneumonia. During 1886-90 the mortality per 100,000 population in that city was, among the Catholics, 405; among Protestants, 307; and among Jews only 186.[1] And during 1901-05 Auerbach found the mortality among Jews 89.1, and among Catholics 176.9 per 100,000. Similarly Rosenfeld finds that during 1901-03 the mortality from pneumonia and pleurisy was in Vienna as follows per 100,000 population: Catholics, 218; Protestants, 183; and Jews only 113.[2] Other respiratory diseases, such as acute and chronic bronchitis, etc., were also less often a cause of death among the Jews in Vienna than among either the Catholics or Protestants of that city. Altogether diseases of the respiratory system were the cause of death to the extent of 355 per 100,000 among Catholics, 291 among Protestants, and only 176 among Jews. And in Budapest Auerbach reports that the Christians die from these diseases more than twice as often as the Jews. Lombroso also reports that in Verona, Italy, the mortality from pneumonia among the Jews was eight to nine per cent., as against fifty per cent. among the Catholic population of that city.[3]

The lesser liability to die from pneumonia and other acute respiratory diseases does not at all mean that they

---

[1] J. von Körösi, *Einfluss der Confession, des Wohlstandes und der Beschäftigung auf die Todesursachen*, p. 14; Berlin, 1898.
[2] S. Rosenfeld, "Die Sterblichkeit der Juden in Wien," *Archiv für Rassen-und Geselschaftsbiologie*, Nos. 1 and 2; 1907.
[3] C. Lombroso, *L'antisemitismo e le scienze moderne*, Appendix; Torino, 1894.

have also a lesser morbidity from these causes. In fact it can be stated that the chronic respiratory diseases, such as chronic bronchitis, pulmonary emphysema, and asthma, are very common among them, perhaps even more common than among others. This peculiarity has been brought out in the discussion on the pathology of the Jews held before the Academy of Medicine in Paris in 1891.[1] Among the immigrant Jews in New York City the author has observed a very large number affected with these chronic respiratory diseases, especially asthma and pulmonary emphysema. Their life in cities, as well as their indoor occupations, are to be considered the most important causes. In New York and London, and also in Russia and Austria, a large number of Jews are furriers, and asthma is as a result very common among them. Chronic bronchitis with emphysema is also frequent among tailors, a favourite occupation of Jews.

Their indoor occupations, however, are to be considered a cause of the infrequency of the acute respiratory diseases, especially pneumonia. They do not expose themselves too often to the inclemencies of the weather and to frequent chillings of the body. Besides, it must be recalled that alcoholism is an important factor in the etiology and prognosis of pneumonia. Chronic drunkards are more liable to be attacked by this disease, and when attacked, the prognosis is more grave than in moderate drinkers or total abstainers. The Jews, not being addicted to the abuse of alcoholic beverages, are placed in a more favourable position as regards liability to acute respiratory diseases, and when attacked are more likely than others to recover. It is clear from all this evidence that no ethnic peculiarities are to be discerned in this respect. The determining factors are the mode of life, occupations, etc.

Lombroso, investigating the vital statistics of the Jews in Verona, Italy, found that they have a very high mortality from heart disease. Nine per cent. of the total number of deaths among the Jews were due to this cause, while in the Catholic population only four per cent. of deaths from heart disease were recorded. He explains this phenomenon by the fact that in Verona the Jews live in

[1] *Bulletin de l'Academie de Médecine*, September 6th, 1891.

high buildings, often on the seventh and eighth floors. He tersely remarks that they thus have "all the disadvantages of mountaineers without any of the hygienic benefits of a mountain climate." He also points out that the Jews in Verona have among them a larger proportion of old persons, and heart disease is the "privilege" of old age. Finally he considers as other factors their passionate temperament and the anxious struggle for existence to which they are exposed by reason of constant persecution. Lombroso believes that the fact that Jewesses are affected with heart disease to a much lesser extent than Jews proves that his contentions have a firm basis.

But a careful study of other literature on the subject does not confirm the above observations. In other countries the Jews do not suffer more than the Christians from heart disease, and the percentage of mortality is even less among them. Thus in Budapest Körösi shows that in 1886-90 the mortality from the diseases of the circulatory system was, per 100,000 population, as follows: Lutherans, 198; Catholics, 134; Calvinists, 100; other Protestants, 104; and Jews, 106. Here the Jews had about the same mortality from this class of disease as the Calvanists and Protestants, and a much lower mortality than the Lutherans and Catholics.[1] Auerbach also found that the mortality of the Jews was quite as low as regards diseases of the circulatory system, 18.86 as against 22.93 among the Catholics during 1901-05.[2] In Vienna Rosenfeld did not find any differences between Jews and Christians in this respect.[3]

Of the diseases of the circulatory system which have been stated to be more common among the Jews than among others may be mentioned arterio-sclerosis, varicose veins, hemorrhoids, and hemophilia. The old adage that a man is as old as his arteries may be applied to the Jew as regards his liability to arterio-sclerosis; he is often mentally and more often physically precocious, and displays a tendency to grow old prematurely. All precocious persons have this characteristic, and early physical decay is one of the penalties the Jew pays for the rapid pace he makes in life—for the excessive care, worry, and anxiety he displays in his business pursuits. Many "climbers"

[1] Körösi, *loc. cit.*   [2] Auerbach, *loc. cit.*   [3] Rosenfeld, *loc. cit.*

suffer from arterio-sclerosis. As a matter of fact it is not observed with great frequency among the Jewish artizans and labourers, though among the small traders it is quite common.

Aneurism is very rare among Jews. Dr. Arpad G. Gerster, of Mount Sinai Hospital in New York, who for a long period of years has had many Jewish patients, says that during a service of twenty-five years in a large Jewish hospital he has met with only one case of aneurism, and this was in a gipsy. He believes that the rarity of this disease among Jews is due to the rarity of syphilis among them, which again he ascribes to the toughened glands, the result of ritual circumcision, which makes the danger of syphilitic infection less than in those not circumcized. He adds that the majority of the Jews are not employed in occupations which require severe physical exertion, and this may be an important factor.[1]

Varicose veins are very common among Jews, especially among Jewesses. It may be attributed to their indolent habits, deficient muscular development, and in women to frequent pregnancies. The results of these varicose veins are to be seen in surgical clinics frequented by Jews, in eczema and ulcers of the legs, which heal with great difficulty. Another manifestation of varicose veins is hemorrhoids, which are probably more common among Jews than among any other people. Indeed, in Eastern Europe "the Jew with the hemorrhoids" is proverbial, and among the sect of Chasidim in Galicia and Poland a Jew without piles is considered a curiosity. Physicians of experience among Jewish patients all agree that it is rare to find a Jew who has passed middle age without having his hemorrhoidal veins more or less enlarged. The Eastern European Jews attribute this condition to the habit of sitting during the greater part of the day on the hard benches of the synagogue school while studying the Talmud, and to constipation of the bowels, from which they suffer very much. Hemorrhoids in young persons, which are only rarely observed among non-Jews, are very prevalent, and Jews under twenty-five years of age have often to be treated for piles.

Hemophilia appears to have been known to the Jews in

[1] *New York Medical Record*, vol. lxxiv. p. 167; 1908.

ancient times, since there is an ordinance in the Talmud that in case two children of the same mother die as a result of circumcision, the third child born to her shall not be circumcized. The reason given is that in some families the blood does not clot readily, and any wound inflicted may prove fatal. Among the Jews of to-day bleeders appear to be more common than among others. Jewish boys are mostly affected, girls only rarely. The reason may be that in boys circumcision reveals it eight days after birth, when they are circumcized, while in girls it may pass off unnoticed till a wound is accidentally inflicted. Meanwhile many of these female bleeders may die in infancy from some other causes, thus reducing the number actually observed. In fact there are evidences that there are many bleeders among Jewesses.[1]

Diseases of the Digestive Organs.—It appears that during infancy the Jewish child has some advantage over his non-Jewish neighbour, because the disturbances of digestion, which claim so many victims during infancy, especially during the summer months, do not affect him to the same extent as others of the same social status. Infantile diarrhœa is mostly prevalent among the poor who live amid insanitary surroundings, in overcrowded dwellings; just the conditions under which the bulk of Jews in large cities live in Europe and America. But it appears from the vital statistics of many cities that the mortality of Jewish children from diarrhœal diseases is about one-half to one-third that of non-Jewish children. In Budapest Körösi reports the death-rate from infantile diarrhœa during the period 1886-90 to have been as follows per 100,000 children under five years of age[2]:—

Catholics	4,143
Lutherans	3,762
Calvinists	3,293
Other Protestants	3,498
Jews	1,442

---

[1] See N. Rothschild, *Ueber das Alter der Hæmopilie*, Munich, 1882; Grandidier, *Die Hæmophilie*, Leipsic, 1877; Julius Moses, *Die Blutkrankheit*, Greifswald, 1892.

[2] Körösi, *Einfluss der Confession des Wohlstandes und der Beschäftigung auf die Todesursachen*, p. 10; Berlin, 1898.

And during 1901-05 Auerbach finds the infant mortality from diarrhœa among Jews 17.9, and among Catholics 24.7 per 100 deaths of children under two years of age.

The mortality here is about one-third that of the mortality of non-Jewish children. In Vienna also Rosenfeld found that the mortality caused by infantile diarrhœa among children less than two years of age was as follows: Catholics 186, Protestants 137, Jews only 61 per 100,000 population—*i.e.*, the mortality of the Jewish children was only one-third of that of the Jewish children.[1] The same conditions have been observed in the United States and in England. In New York City, where the immigrant Jews live in the most overcrowded sections of the city, the author has calculated from the reports of the Department of Health that during 1897-99 the annual mortality from diarrhœal diseases in the entire city was 125.54 per 100,000 population, whereas in the four wards largely inhabited by Jews it was only 106.79, notwithstanding the insanitary surroundings and overcrowding in ill-ventilated tenements.[2] And in London, where the sanitary and hygienic *milieu* of the Jews is not superior to that of the east side of New York City, the same conditions have been observed. The Jewish infants suffer from diarrhœal diseases to a much less extent than others of the same social status. Several physicians testified to this effect before the Royal Alien Immigration Commission, and stated that it is their opinion that the lower mortality of Jewish children is due in a measure to their great power of resistance to contagious diseases and gastro-intestinal derangements during infancy.

The lower mortality of Jewish children from gastro-intestinal derangements of early life is not due to inherent or congenital vitality giving them an advantage over other children. As has been shown (Chap. XII.), the mortality of the Jews is lower mainly because of the favourable mortality rates of their children under ten years of age. It is not only that they have a favourable mortality in the case of infantile diarrhœa, but the infantile mortality

---

[1] S. Rosenfeld, "Die Sterblichkeit der Juden in Wien," *Archiv für Rassen-und Gesellshaftsbiologie*, No. 1 and 2 ; 1907.

[2] M. Fishberg, *Health and Sanitation of the Immigrant Population in New York* ; 1907.

due to all causes is lower than among others. In general this is due to the great devotion of the Jewess as a mother. The care bestowed by the Jewish mother on her children, even when labouring under severe stress of poverty and privation, is proverbial. The anxiety displayed by the parents, even in cases of slight illness of their children, is well known to every physician who practises among them. What is of most importance, however, is the fact that only rarely does a Jewish woman go to work in the mill or factory after she is married. The large number of married women who leave their children at home or in the nursery, and work the whole day in the factories and mills, which are to be seen among the proletariat of other peoples, are only rarely seen among Jews in every country, although in New York and London this class of Jewesses is already beginning to be seen. The result of this is that the Jewish mother nurses her children at the breast, and artificial feeding is rare among them, and among healthy Jewesses almost unknown. Infantile diarrhœa, which is chiefly caused by improper artificial feeding, is as a result less common among them. Indeed, this gives these Jewish children an advantage over other children of the poor in many other ways. Their general health is superior to that of infants of the slums of other nationalities. Rickets, atrophy, malnutrition, scrofula, etc.,[3] which undermine the vitality of the children of the poor and make them ready victims of contagious diseases or of some acute diseases of childhood, are less common among Jewish infants as compared with children of others of the same economic and sociologic condition. This was brought out by testimony given before the Inter-Departmental Committee on Physical Deterioration in London, England, in 1904. Dr. Hall stated that in Leeds he found 50 per cent. of children in a poor school affected with rickets, and only a percentage of eight in a school attended by children of the better classes. In a school of poor Jewish children he found only seven per cent. affected with rickets. It has been affirmed by

---

[1] But this is not true of all the Jews. In Wilna, where their poverty is appalling, rickets and scrofula are more common among them than among Christian infants. (S. Kowarsky, in *Wrachebnaia Gazeta*, No. 20, 1908.) I observed the same among the poorer classes of Jews in Russia and Austria.

Drs. Eustace Smith, Eichholz, and others that this superiority of Jewish children in England, in spite of their inferior sanitary and hygienic environment and their overcrowded dwellings, is due to the fact that Jewish mothers bestow more care upon their children during infancy and childhood, and also because it is exceptional to find a Jewish mother acting as breadwinner.[1]

As might be expected, considering that there are no anatomic or physiological peculiarities to be discerned in the Jews, there are no differences in the morbidity and mortality from gastro-intestinal diseases among adult Jews. Lombroso[2] reports that in Italy these diseases are more frequently a cause of death among Jews than among the Catholics, and Glatter[3] states that the same obtains in Hungary, though Auerbach's statistics of more recent date show that in Budapest the contrary is true. Lombroso attributes these conditions to the overcrowding in badly ventilated dwellings, and also to the fatty foods which Italian Jews are wont to eat and which are unsuitable for people living in a warm climate. But the statistics recently compiled by Rosenfeld[4] about the Jews of Vienna, and by Körösi[5] about Budapest, and many others, show, on the contrary, that the Jews have either about the same rate of mortality from gastro-intestinal disorders, or even less than the non-Jewish population among which they live. The same is true of diseases of the liver, which show no peculiarity among Jews, excepting in the case of cirrhosis, which is quite uncommon. This is due to the infrequency of alcoholism and syphilis, which are the most important etiological factors in the production of cirrhosis of the liver.

Nervous dyspepsia is a very common disease among Jews, and acid dyspepsia (hyperchlorhydria) is also more frequently met with among them.[6] Physicians who have experience among them find that acute indigestion is particularly met with among orthodox Jews on Sundays,

---

[1] *Jewish Chronicle;* August 19, 1904.
[2] *Loc. cit.*
[3] *Loc. cit.*
[4] *Loc. cit.*
[5] *Loc. cit.*
[6] A prominent clinician, a specialist in diseases of the stomach in Berlin, states that three-fourths of the Russian Jewish patients who consult him belong to the class of neuropaths and hypochondriacs. See H. Oppenheim, *Journal f. Psychologie u. Neurologie*, vol. xiii., 1908.

due to the consumption on the Sabbath of food which has been prepared on Friday and kept in the oven from twelve to twenty-four hours. This is seen mostly in Russia and Poland, but rarely among the Jews in Western Europe and America, because here, as a rule, they do not prepare their Sabbath food on Friday to be kept in the oven till Saturday. But chronic dyspepsia is very common. It is due to the fact that Jews generally, owing to deep absorption in their business, rarely have regular hours for meals, and can hardly spare time to masticate their food properly. Among the Jews living in Slavonic countries, excessive tea-drinking, a habit acquired from their Slavonic neighbours, is much to blame for the frequent occurrence of chronic indigestion. It must be mentioned, however, that alcoholic gastritis is, for obvious reasons, quite rare among them.

Of many other diseases which various physicians have stated that the Jews are either relatively free from, or more predisposed to, than non-Jews, are to be mentioned Bright's disease, exophthalmic goitre, cancer, various forms of skin disease, etc. But it appears that there are hardly any special peculiarities to be noted when everything connected with the etiology and diagnosis of these diseases is taken into consideration. Thus Bright's disease was found to be more frequent among American Jews than among the general population of the United States.[1] But when it is recalled that the Jews are largely town-dwellers, and that this disease is mostly prevalent among this class of people, it is evident that they are only to be compared with city population. Indeed, when this is done it is elicited that there are hardly any differences between Jews and non-Jews in this respect; a slightly lower mortality of the Jews from this disease is then found and can be explained by the fact that there are very few alcoholics among them, since alcoholism is an important factor in the etiology of this disease. Among the Jews in Vienna the mortality from Bright's disease is about the same as among the Christian population of that city,[2] and in Budapest it is slightly lower among the Jews.[3] It is

---

[1] *Census Bulletin No. 19*, 1890.   [2] Rosenfeld, *loc. cit.*

[3] Körösi, *loc. cit.*; also Auerbach, *loc. cit.*, who found the rates: Jews 37.2, Catholics 55.2, and others 53.3 per 100,000.

PATHOLOGICAL CHARACTERISTICS. 311

thus seen that no ethnic factors are at work; it all depends on the complex etiology of the disease.

G. Lagneau states that Jewish women are hardly ever afflicted with goitre, and mentions that the medical society of Metz handed out the question in one of its competitive examinations of 1880: "Why are Jewesses exempt from goitre?" Bordier also says that this disease is rare among them.[1] On the other hand, G. Buschan states that he finds that Jews are more strongly inclined to this disease than non-Jews.[2] The present author has seen many cases of goitre among Jews, and can find no differences between them and non-Jews in this respect. This is merely cited as an example, showing how some diseases are either stated to be very frequent, or less common among Jews, or one physician states emphatically that Jews are exempt from a certain disease, while another finds the Jews more inclined to suffer from it.

In his investigations of the demography of the Italian Jews Lombroso found that while the mortality from cancer was among the general population only two per cent. of the total mortality, the cancer mortality of the Jews was 3.3 per cent. He also found that Jewesses are more often attacked by cancer than Jews, which is in agreement with the observed fact that women are more apt to be affected than men.[3] On the other hand, in England, Dr. James Braithwaite noticed that cancer of the uterus was seldom or never encountered among the numerous Jewesses attending the outdoor department of the Leeds General Infirmary. Only one case was met with in ten years. He points out that the experience of the London Hospital, where there is a special Hebrew department, is the same, only one case was seen in a Jewess during a period of five years, against 178 among Gentile women. Dr. Braithwaite considers that the only possible explanations are difference in race or difference in diet, especially the absence of pork in the Jewish diet.[4] On the other hand, a writer in the *British Medical Journal*[5] states that in his experience cancer of the breast has often been met with among Jewesses in London, and while examples of

---

[1] A. Bordier, *La Géographie médicale*, p. 529, Paris 1884.
[2] *Globus*, vol. lxvii., p. 46; 1895.
[3] Lombroso, *loc. cit.*
[4] *Lancet*, vol. clxi., p. 1578.
[5] March 15, 1902, p. 681.

nearly every form of cancer have been seen, there seemed to be a special tendency to the development of intestinal malignant growths. Of the patients dying between forty and sixty-five years of age, a large percentage have been suffering from cancer. The writer then brings figures from the records of the United Synagogue Burial Society of London, showing that during 1898-1900 the percentage of deaths from cancer to deaths due to all causes among persons over twenty years of age was as follows:—

	1900.	1899.	1898.
Jews	6.1	6.5	5.02
General population (Registrar-General's report)	8.4	8.8	6.1

It thus appears that the Jews in London are by no means free from cancer. In the United States also it is found that deaths due to cancer and tumour are just as common among Jews as many others.[1] In New York City the present author found that the mortality from cancer among the Russian Jewish emigrants is much below that of the non-Jewish population. But it must be borne in mind that the Jewish immigrants are mostly young men and women, a class among which cancer is uncommon.[2] And a study of the reports of a large Jewish and one Christian hospital in New York elicited that Jews affected with cancer are by no means rare in this city, although less common than among non-Jews. Sarcoma appears to be more frequent among the Jews, while cancer of the breast, and especially of the uterus, is less frequently met with among them. They appear, however, to be more often affected with cancer of the gastro-intestinal tract, with the exception of the rectum, though they are great sufferers from other rectal diseases, such as hemorrhoids, fistula, etc. In other cities also it has been found that Jews are not exempt from cancer. Rosenfeld finds a mortality per 100,000 of 129 among Catholics, 108 among Protestants, and 130 among Jews. Auerbach gives figures for Budapest as follows:—Cancer, excepting of the uterus— Jews, 66.2, and Catholics, 73.7; cancer of the uterus— Jewesses, 8.6, and Christians, 24.0 per 10,000 population. In Berlin, 8.6 per cent. of all deaths among Jews were, in

[1] *Census Bulletin No. 19;* 1890.
[2] See article, "Cancer," *Jewish Encyclopædia,* vol. iii., pp. 529-531.

1905, due to cancer, as against only 6 per cent. among the general population. This may be due to the low infant mortality among the Berlin Jews, and thus a larger proportion of dead are adults.

The rarity of cancer among Jewesses has been observed not only in London, and confirmed by the mortality rates in Budapest, but also by gynecologists generally, who have an extensive Jewish *clientéle*. Auerbach and Theilhaber mention that the experience of German surgeons confirms this rarity of cancer among Jewesses, and several gynecologists in New York have given me information to this effect.[1] Moreover, it is well known that caricinoma of the uterus is more often met with in women who have given birth to children than in sterile women, and Jewesses only rarely remain single. What the cause is of this peculiarity, whether it is due to some peculiarity of the ritual dietary laws, or anything else, cannot even be conjectured as long as we are ignorant of the cause of cancer. At any rate this seems to be an important field for investigation, which may throw some light on the etiology of cancer.

Skin Diseases.—Popular fancy has for centuries known of many skin eruptions which were alleged to have been very common among Jews. In the European Christian folk-lore we find many fairy tales about the causes of these alleged skin eruptions of the Jews. Each tribe of the Jews was said to be afflicted with a special disease, which was meted out as a punishment for certain sins they have committed against Christians. Thus the tribe of Simeon, for nailing Christ to the Cross, had to be punished by the Almighty, and the punishment inflicted was that four times a year their descendants have bloody sores on their hands and feet. The tribe of Reuben was alleged to have laid hands on Christ, and, as a result, their hands

---

[1] It cannot be stated, however, that this is the case with Jews everywhere. Dr. Kalgut reports an "epidemic" of cancer in a small town in Russia containing 900 Jewish and 600 Christian inhabitants. In a single year he met with eight cases, of which seven were in Jews and but one Christian was the victim. (*Vratchebnaïa Gazeta*, June 29th, 1908.) See also R. de Bovis, "Du rôle des principaux facteurs accessoires dans l'étiologie du cancer," *Semaine Médicale*, September 24th, 1902; L. Cheinisse, "Die Rassenpathologie u. d. Alkoholismus bei den Juden," *Zeitschr. Demogr. Stat. d. Juden*, pp. 1-8, 1910.

dry up anything they touch. The tribe of Zebulon was accused of disposing by lot of the garments of Jesus (although in the New Testament the Roman soldiers are said to have done it), and therefore the descendants of Zebulon have sores in their mouth and spit blood. The men of the tribe of Asher have their right arms shorter than the left, and the women of the tribe of Joseph have their mouths full of worms, after their thirty-third year onward, etc.

All these legends had a wide circulation during mediæval times, and contributed by no small means to the hatred displayed against the Jews. The most remarkable fairy tale, which some who have pretensions to ethnologic knowledge have accepted without question, is the alleged peculiar odour which the Jews exhale, and which is considered as a marked characteristic which betrays the Jews when any other sign fails. The origin of this legend of the *fœtor Judaicus* dates back to Fortunatus, who was first to speak of it, and is chiefly due to either a blunder or a malicious trick of the copyist of the Middle Ages, of the passage from Ammianus Marcellinus (xxi., 5) of Marcus Aurelius, who substituted "*Judæorum fetentium*" for "*Judæorum petentium*"—*i.e.*, ill-smelling, for turbulent. This *fœtor Judaicus* was in mediæval times considered of importance in this respect: some Christian theologians stated that the baptismal waters are the best remedy to remove this objectionable odour from any Jew, while others claimed that even this will not help.[1] It is to be regretted that these able theologians were not possessed with any special knowledge of "races" and "race traits," in the sense some are using these terms to-day. If they had been imbued with the "scientific spirit" they would surely have claimed that this is one of the racial traits of the Jews which cannot be obliterated. Yet the consensus of opinion appears to have been that even baptismal water

[1] Fortunatus, however, was of the opinion that the baptismal waters were effective. He said:

"Abluitur judæus odor baptismate divo,
Et nova progenies reddita surgit aquis,
Vincens ambrosios suavi spiramine rores,
Vertice perfuso chrismatis efflat odor."

—*Venantii Fortunati Carm.*, v. 5, 109-112.

leaves this peculiarity unchanged, because it was sometimes discovered by the odour that this or that high dignitary of the Church was of Jewish extraction. Many recent writers have expounded this nonsense and given it a kind of a scientific air.[1] Gustav Jaeger of Stuttgart constructed a complete theory of odours which human beings exhale, and which are characteristic of each age, sex, race, and even the mental and emotional state of each individual. He pretends to be able easily to recognize any Jew by his odour, and that even an "Aryan" who has the least drop of Jewish blood in his veins can thus be distinguished. It appears that he has not experimented much to test his theory, and he says that the fact that some Jews have placed some obstacles in his way when he attempted to give his teachings a wide circulation has not influenced his opinion against them. He mentions a certain Dr. M., who visited Pope Pius IX. in 1847 at Rome. When he was allowed to kiss the Pope's slipper, he claims that he at once perceived by the odour that the Pope was of Jewish origin. That this Dr. M. was right, Jaeger thinks, is confirmed by the fact that Cardinal Consalvi had said a long time before *E un Ebreo*, although Dr. M. knew nothing about it. Finally, he assures us that Pius IX. confirmed this fact while confidentially speaking to certain brothers Cahn from Lyon, two baptized Jews.[2]

Racial odours have been described by many writers. In addition to the well-known odour of the negro, it has also been stated that every other coloured race has its characteristic smell.[3] Recently a Japanese anthropologist has even described the smell of the Europeans, and says that it is very pronounced to the Japanese, and that ablebodied adults smell most. The odour is local, chiefly in the armpits, and is not removed by soap and water, while Japanese armpits are practically odourless. Indeed,

---

[1] See also R. Kleinpaul, "Alt-in Neu-Jerusalem," *Ausland*, No. 25-26, 1874; M. Reich, *Die Einheit des Menschengeschlechts*, pp. 90-92, Augsburg, 1873.
[2] Gustav Jaeger, *Entdeckung der Seele*, vol. i., pp. 246-248; 1884.
[3] See R. Andree, "Volkergeruch," *Ethnographische Parallelen*, New Series, pp. 213-222, 1889. H. Ellis, *Studies in the Psychology of Sex*, vol. iv., "Smell," pp. 59-90, gives a good summary.

Adachi states that an armpit odour disqualifies a Japanese from military service and makes it difficult to enter matrimony.[1] How far this is true cannot be stated. At any rate, it has not been confirmed by any other investigator. But one thing is sure: no ethnologist believes at present that the Jews exhale a characteristic odour discernible to other Europeans. Even Richard Andree, who cannot be considered biased in favour of the sons of Jacob, says:—"No matter how the theory of special race odours may be substantiated by incontrovertible evidence, yet it is difficult to prove a special Jewish odour, in spite of Professor Jaeger's assertions." Andree believes the origin of this myth is to be sought for in the filthy and malodorous conditions of the mediæval Ghettoes of Europe, and also in the fact that the Eastern Jews love to consume large quantities of garlic, a tendency which they displayed already in ancient times.[2] But he points out, justly, that there are many other races who indulge in excessive consumption of garlic, as, for instance, the Italians, the Provençals, etc.[3] It must be mentioned in this connection that the Jews were not the only ones who were accused by ancient theologians of exhaling a special disagreeable odour from their skin. There were many so-called "accursed races," about whom it was stated that they emit offensive odours, which wither fruits when held in the hands of one of these accursed ones; and many others unfit to mention.[4]

It is noteworthy that skin diseases, which might have given a reason for the allegation of a special *Fœtor Judaicus*, are no more common among Jews than among others. Hardy[5] stated that eczema is more frequent among Jews than among Christians, but many other dermatologists with extensive experience among Jews assert the contrary. In the dispensaries of New York City, where large numbers

---

[1] B. Adachi, "Geruch der Europäer," *Globus*, vol. 83, pp. 14-15.
[2] "We remember the fish, which we did eat in Egypt freely; the cucumbers, and the melons, and the leeks, and the onions, and the garlic." Numbers, xi., 5.
[3] Richard Andree, *Zur Volkskunde der Juden*, pp. 68-69; Leipzig, 1881.
[4] See a curious book by Francisque Michel, *Histoire des races maudites de la France et de l'Espagne*; Paris, 1847.
[5] *Bulletin Medical*, p. 851; 1901.

of Jews are being treated daily, it is not observed that they have an excessive proportion of eczematous persons; and when compared with other immigrants—for instance, the Italians, Greeks, or Hungarians—it would appear that the disease is even less common among them. In Chicago, Dr. Fishkin also found that among the immigrant Jews the number of patients suffering from eczema is not much above the usual proportion.[1]

Parasitic diseases of the skin and scalp are said to be more common among the Jews in Eastern Europe and the Orient than among non-Jews. This is particularly emphasized in reference to scabies and favus (*plica Polonica* and *plica Judaica*).[2] In the United States this is not observed to be the fact when the immigrant Jews are compared with non-Jews of the same social status. In the Russian army, on the other hand, there is statistical evidence that the Jews are the greatest sufferers from favus. It must be mentioned, however, that the Jews in the Russian army are mostly recruited from the lowest and poorest classes, as was shown by Weinberg, while the robust and also the richer classes of Jews escape military service in some manner.[3] It is a fact that in order to escape conscription, Jews often submit to certain treatment by quacks who, by the use of some acids, produce artificial eruptions on the scalp, thus simulating favus. Of late, favus is not considered by the authorities a sufficient cause for liberating Jews from military service, and the number of cases of this disease has decreased considerably in the military hospitals of Russia. Parasitic diseases of

---

[1] *Journal of the American Medical Association*, August 23rd, 1902.

[2] *Plica Polonica*, or *Weichselzopf* in German is, as its name implies, a disease, mostly met with in Poland along the banks of the Vistula, characterized by the agglutination of the hairs which are infested with vermin. It was quite common in Slavonic lands during the Middle Ages when the comb was not used as often as it should be. Lafontaine (*Traité de la Plique Polonaise*; Paris, 1808) shows that not only the peasantry, Jews, and beggars were attacked, but even the nobility and the burghers were not free from it in Poland, Lithuania, etc. The Jews appear to have acquired it in those regions, and at present since it disappeared among the Christian population it is also very rare among the Jews. Its synonym, *Plica Judaica*, is as unjust as the accusation of the *fœtor Judaicus*. See also Gould and Pyle, *Anomalies and Curiosities of Medicine*, p. 848.

[3] R. Weinberg, "Zur Pathologie der Juden," *Zeitschrift für Demographie und Statistik der Juden*, p. 10; 1905.

the skin are mostly seen among the poor and degraded; in fact, they are filth diseases, pure and simple. In Western Europe and America, where the social and economic conditions of the Jews are superior, these diseases are uncommon among them. The same is true of impetigo contagiosa, which is quite as common among Jews as among the poor of all nations. Syphilitic dermatoses, on the other hand, are very uncommon among the children of Israel, who strictly adhere to their religion and traditions and maintain strict purity of the family, as is to be observed in Eastern Europe and the Orient. This is not true, however, of the Western European and American Jews, among whom this disease is tolerably frequent; thus disproving the theory that the Jewish "race" possesses a peculiar immunity to venereal diseases, which was entertained by many physicians. It appears that even circumcision, which was considered one of the reasons for their immunity to venereal diseases, is not of material avail when they expose themselves to the dangers of infection. Of course certain complications of gonorrhœa, such as balanitis and posthitis, and also phimosis, are unknown in circumcised persons of Jewish as well as of any other creed. But no other specific immunity has been established.

It is immaterial for our purposes whether the disease mentioned in the Bible as *Zaraat* is the same as leprosy of to-day, or includes various diseases which have as their chief characteristic some skin eruption. To-day it appears that leprosy is uncommon among Jews, the numerous photographs of leprous Jews sent out by missionaries in Palestine notwithstanding. Most of the physicians who practise in Palestine and Asia Minor speak of the rarity of this disease among the Jews in those countries. Dr. Nicholas Senn reports from Jerusalem that "most of the lepers are Arabs, and the Jews are singularly free from the disease... Among the forty-seven inmates of the Jesus Hilfe Hospital there is only one Jew. Dr. Einsler, during his long and extensive practice in Jerusalem, has seen only five Jews affected with leprosy; and of these one came from Salonica, and of the remainder two from Morocco. It seems that the Jerusalem Jews have in the course of time acquired an immunity from this disease, notwithstanding the increase of poverty and unsanitary surroundings."[1] Only one physician in the Orient mentions leprosy as common among Jews; Zombacco[2] found it to be very frequent among them in Constantinople. Buschan, quoting this statement,[3] argues that the predisposition of the Jews to leprosy is a racial characteristic hereditarily transmitted from the ancient Hebrews to the modern Jews. In support of this he mentions that the Karaites of Constantinople are entirely free from the disease, as attested by Zombacco during twenty years of medical practice among them. These Karaites are only Jews by religion, according to Buschan, but ethnically they are not Semites.[4] They are of "Finnic" origin, derived from the Chozars who accepted Judaism during the eighth century of our era. The other Jews of Constantinople, those who follow the Talmud, are, on the other hand, derived from the "Syro-Arabic-Semitic" race, and they are the ones who are racially predisposed to leprosy. He further asserts that the Mohammedans, Christians, Greeks, Armenians, and other non-Jews in Constantinople are free from it, notwithstanding the fact that they frequently come in contact with the Jews. For Buschan this is sufficient proof that the predisposition of the Jews to leprosy is of a racial nature, and also that the modern Jews are a pure race. But as a matter of fact there are many Turkish, Greek, and Armenian lepers in Constantinople whom Zombacco has not met, while among Jews in other countries no excessive number of lepers have been met with. Thus in Russia, where in some provinces leprosy is endemic, Jewish lepers are only seldom seen; while in Palestine they seem to be entirely rare, as has already been mentioned.

Pathology of the Eye.—"We know of certain eye diseases," says Singer, "which are met with among the Jews in an unusually high proportion, so that it can be admitted that the Jewish race in all probabilities has a special predisposition to these diseases."[5] Many specialists emphasize

---

[1] N. Senn, "The Hospitals in Jerusalem," *American Medicine*, vol. iv., pp. 509-512.
[2] *Bulletin de la Société d'anthropologie de Paris*, October 1891.
[3] *Globus*, vol. lxvii., p. 61.
[4] "About the Karaites," see p. 150 *supra*.
[5] H. Singer, *Krankheitslehre der Juden*, p. 100; Leipzig, 1904.

that the Jews are the greatest sufferers from certain eye diseases, especially conjunctivitis and trachoma. There is no doubt that the Jews living in Eastern Europe and in the Orient are often attacked by trachoma, or granular lids. But it must be borne in mind in this connection that this disease is endemic in the large cities of these regions. It was, for instance, found that a large proportion of the population, both Jewish and Christian, of Hungary, Prussian Poland, certain provinces of Russia, suffers from trachoma; and in Egypt, Syria, and other countries in the near East an appalling number of children and adults are thus affected.[1] As is well known, this disease is practically a filth disease, which is mostly found among people living under adverse hygienic surroundings. It is especially prevalent among the poor, who live in overcrowded dwellings and who are careless as regards personal cleanliness. Considering the social conditions under which the Jews in Eastern Europe live, it is to be expected that they should more often be affected with trachoma and follicular conjunctivitis than their Christian neighbours, who are materially better off. That there are no racial peculiarities in this respect is evident from the fact that it is only among the poor Jews that these pathological conditions are met with, while among the more prosperous classes of Jews it is just as rare as among the prosperous classes of Christians.

Many specialists also have observed that glaucoma is more prevalent among Jews than among others, but it appears that not all ophthalmologists have found it to be the case. Sichel could not confirm this in his experience in Vienna and Paris. In the eye clinics in New York City the proportion of Jews treated for glaucoma is also not unusually excessive. This disease is not ascribed to any ethnic peculiarity of the Jews, but is usually attributed to their intense nervousness, of which this is only one of the manifestations.

Retinitis pigmentosa, a hereditary disease of the eye characterized by the deposition of pigment in the retina, which leads to contraction of the field of vision and ultimately to total blindness, is said to be mostly seen

---

[1] For the geographical distribution of trachoma, see J. Boldt, *Das Trachom*, pp. 21-81; Berlin, 1903.

among Jews. The cause of this disease is unknown, beyond the fact that it occurs mostly in males, is hereditary, and in a very large proportion of cases the parents of the patients are cousins. Its prevalence among Jews is attributed to the frequency of consanguineous marriages among them.[1]

All the sequelæ of trachoma, such as entropion, pannus, etc., are met with among the Jews in Eastern Europe and the Orient. The same is true of simple conjunctivitis, and especially blepharitis. All this is due to their poverty and the concomitant huddling together in unhealthy dwellings, among miserable sanitary conditions. Indeed, among the well-to-do Jews in every country these pathological conditions are very rare.

It is curious that, notwithstanding the fact that from twenty-five to fifty per cent. of blindness in the new-born is due to gonorrhœal infection from the mother during parturition, and in spite of the fact that gonorrhœa is rather uncommon among Jews, especially in Eastern Europe, still the number of blind among them is abnormally excessive. Statistics gathered by the Census offices in Germany and Hungary show more blind persons among the Jews than among the Christians around them. In Prussia the census of 1895 showed that, per 100,000 population, there were 104.8 Jewish and 65.3 Christian blind; in Hungary the ratio was, in 1890, Jews 85.83, and Christians 76.66 per 100,000.[2] There is no evidence that this is also true of the Jews in Russia, Poland, and Roumania. In fact, if the enumeration of the defectives made in Russia during the census of 1897 is to be considered reliable, it appears that the number of Jewish blind in that country is proportionately less than that of non-Jewish blind. There were, namely, enumerated, 101 Jewish and 197 non-Jewish blind per 100,000 population.[3] As causes of the excessive blindness among the Jews in Germany were assigned the frequency of consanguineous

---

[1] R. Liebreich, "Abkunft aus Ehen unter Blutverwandte als grund von Retinitis Pigmentosa," *Deutsche Klinik*, No. 6, 1860.

[2] A. Ruppin, *Die Juden der Gegenwart*, p. 104. For other statistics see article "Blindness," by the author, *Jewish Encyclopedia*, vol. iii., pp. 251-252.

[3] B. Goldberg, "Die Gebrechlichen unter den Juden Russlands, *Zeitschr. Demogr. Stat. der Juden*, pp. 72-74; 1908.

marriages and the excessive number of Jews who suffer from various nervous diseases, as well as diseases of the eye, especially the cornea and the uveal tract.

It is also found that Jews are more often colour-blind than the races and peoples among which they live. In Breslau, Cohn found that 4.1 per cent. of the Jews and only 2.1 per cent. of the Christians are colour-blind.[1] In London it was also found that 4.9 per cent. of the Jewish boys and 3.1 per cent. of the girls were colour-blind, as against only 3.5 and 0.4 per cent. respectively among non-Jewish children.[2] Among adults in London, Jacobs even found 12.7 per cent. of male Jews and 2 per cent. of the women were colour-blind.[3] But that this is not a racial proclivity is evidenced by the fact that among the West End Jews, who are richer and more cultured, the percentage was only 3.4, while among their poorer co-religionists in the East End the proportion reached 14.8 per cent. Similarly, in Italy Ottolenghi found that the proportion of colour-blind children was about the same among both Jews and Christians, 2.9 per cent. in the former and 2.7 per cent. in the latter.[4] As is well known, colour-blindness is more common among the poor and destitute, and the bulk of the Jews in Eastern Europe and England, where tests have been made in this regard, are just of this class, while among their more prosperous co-religionists in Italy and England the number of this class of defectives is not at all excessive. Jacobs justly attributes the colour-blindness of the Jews to the fact that they are town-dwellers, where comparatively little colour, and especially so little green, is to be met with. To the high proportion of colour-blindness he also attributes the absence of painters of great ability among the Jews, and the want of taste shown by Jewesses of the lower grades of society, which manifests itself in the preference of bright primary colours for wearing apparel. It is difficult to agree with this view, because the absence of painters of

---

[1] *Centralblatt fur Augenkunde*, p. 97; 1873.
[2] *Transact. Ophthalm. Society*, vol. i., p. 198.
[3] J. Jacobs, "On the Comparative Anthropometry of English Jews," *Journal Anthropological Institute*, vol. xix., p. 83.
[4] *Gazetta Clinica*, 1883, quoted from J. Jacobs, "Racial Characteristics of the Modern Jews," *Journ. Anthrop. Institute*, vol. xv., p. 15 of reprint.

great ability is better explained by the religious prohibition to engage in and to foster the fine arts, especially painting and sculpture, under which the Jews have been brought up for centuries. In recent years there are many good Jewish painters, and even a few who may be considered among the category of great artists. The preference Jewesses give to bright, primary colours in their wearing apparel is also explained by the fact that they have lived among the Eastern Europeans, who also prefer bright colours, and have thus learned it from their Christian neighbours. Excepting among the *parvenus,* it is not at all common among Western European and American Jews.

As town-dwellers and as people who have very few agriculturists in their midst, the Jews also have an abnormally large proportion of near-sighted persons. This has been found to be the case by Jacobs among the English, and by Botwinick[1] among the Russian Jews. The same is true of the Jewish children in the public schools of New York City.

[1] *Vratch*, No. 42; 1899.

CHAPTER XV

PATHOLOGICAL CHARACTERISTICS (*concluded*).

Nervous and mental diseases—Hysteria and neurasthenia—Locomotor ataxia — Paralysis agitans — Intermittent claudication — Epilepsy Apoplexy—Causes of the nervousness of the Jews—Frequency of idiocy and imbecility among Jews—Deaf-mutism—Insanity among the ancient Hebrews—Insanity among modern Jews—Forms of insanity among Jews—*Psychosis Judaica*—Causes of the excessive incidence of insanity among Jews—Suicide among Jews—Recent increase in the tendency to self-destruction among Jews.

Nervous and Mental Diseases among Jews.—Nearly all physicians who have practised among the Jews agree that derangements of the nervous system are very frequently met with among them. This impression has been largely gained by observing the intense worry and anxiety displayed by relatives and friends of patients in cases of even slight illness; and in cases of death among Jews, the profound impression made on all relatives, friends, and neighbours is hardly to be observed among other Europeans. Fits of hysterical crying and wailing are the rule, and beyond control by reasonable interference. In most monographs on hysteria and neurasthenia the authors never omit to state that these diseased conditions are most frequently observed among the Jews, and Charcot spoke in his lectures of the *Juif errant*, poverty-stricken and destitute, yet finding his way from Poland to Paris to consult a famous physician about his imaginary ailment. Tobler claims that all the Jewesses in Palestine are hysterical; and Raymond says that in Warsaw hysteria is very frequent among both Jews and Jewesses. The Jewish population of that city alone is almost exclusively the inexhaustible source for the supply of specimens of hysterical humanity, particularly hysteria in the male, for all the clinics of Europe.[1] Other specialists of nervous diseases speak in the same vein. In London and New York City the clinics of nervous diseases can be seen daily to be overcrowded with Jews, and most physicians have noted that no matter what their Jewish patient complains of, his malady is usually coloured by the nervous strain which is predominating over all other symptoms.

It is difficult to estimate the vital effects of the nervousness of the Jews, because it is almost impossible to determine the mortality from these diseases. While the morbidity from the so-called functional derangements of the nervous system is undoubtedly very great among them, still it must be mentioned that these diseases hardly ever shorten the life of the sufferer, and they are only rarely, if at all, a cause of death. Besides this, it is also a fact that certain chronic organic nervous diseases are as a rule only rarely registered as a cause of death. This is the case with locomotor ataxia, in which the victim often succumbs to an intercurrent disease, like pneumonia and the like, and the death is registered as caused by the last ailment. The result is a disagreement among physicians as to the question whether Jews are only subject to functional nervous diseases to a greater extent than non-Jews, or whether they also suffer more from the organic diseases of the brain and spinal cord. Dr. Minor,[2] of Moscow, analyzing 3,214 cases of nervous diseases which came under his observation, comes to the conclusion that, as far as he could discover, the Jews are not any more predisposed than Christians to nervous diseases. On the contrary, the most serious organic diseases of the brain and spinal cord, chronic inflammations of the cerebral blood vessels, etc., are far more often met with among the Christians in Moscow than among the Jews. This author is satisfied that the main, if not the only, reason lies in the fact that the Jews are not alcoholics, and that they only rarely suffer from syphilis. The only disease from which Minor found the Jews to suffer more often than non-Jews was hysteria, especially hysteria in the male.

[1] *L'Étude des maladies du système nerveux en Russie*, p. 71; Paris, 1889.
[2] L. S. Minor, "Contribution à l'Étude de l'Étiologie du Tabes," *Archives de Neurologie*, vol. xvi., pp. 183, 362.

Locomotor ataxia, one of the most important nervous diseases, is the best example in this respect. It has been stated by several physicians that it is very rare among Jews. Stembo reported to the Eleventh International Medical Congress that in Wilna, Russia, this disease is as rare among the Jews as is syphilis. Among 200 inmates of the hospital in Wilna who suffered from nervous diseases, he has not met one affected with locomotor ataxia. It is true that he has seen forty Jews suffering from the disease, but all had syphilis.[1] Gajkiewicz also found among 400 Jewish patients affected with nervous disease only thirteen with locomotor ataxia, three per cent., which is very low.[2] Minor found that among his patients the Christians suffered proportionately four times as often from locomotor ataxia as the Jews, and that all his Jewish tabetics gave a history of syphilis. All this goes to show that there are no racial factors to be discovered among the Jews in regard to their morbidity from locomotor ataxia. It all depends on the frequency of syphilis among them. In New York City, where syphilis is not infrequent among them, there are many Jewish tabetics. It appears more frequently on the list of diseases of the inmates of Montefiore Home than any other single nervous disease. This may be explained by the fact that patients affected with this disease remain in the institution for a long time, and consequently accumulate in large numbers, thus annually appearing on the reports for many years. It is also a fact that nearly every poor Jew affected with this disease is likely to seek admission to this institution, and thus the number in that Home is representing the majority of poor Jewish tabetics in New York City. A Christian institution drawing upon as large a population as the Jewish of New York City would surely have a yet larger number of tabetics. Still, it all goes to show that the Jews are by no means free from this disease.

Another nervous disease said to be very frequent among the Jews is *Paralysis agitans*, or shaking palsy. Minor[3] found that in Russia it is met with three times more often

---

[1] L. Stembo, "Psychiatria," *Atti dell' XI. Congresso Medico Internationale*, vol. iv., p. 119; Roma, 1898.
[2] *Syphilis du Système Nerveux*, p. 158; Paris, 1892.
[3] *Loc. cit.*

among the Jews than among Christians. Krafft-Ebing found that among 100 of his cases, thirty-two were Jews. He remarks that at the time when he observed these cases the Jews of Austria-Hungary constituted only four per cent. of the total population. Their morbidity was consequently eight times greater than their proper proportion.[1]

Of the few diseases which are said to be most frequently met with among the Jews is *Intermittent claudication*, a nervous disease of obscure causation, which has its origin largely in the constriction of the arteries of the lower limbs in nervous individuals suffering from arterio-sclerosis. Physicians in Russia have especially reported many cases among Jews of that country, and it is quite often seen among the immigrant Jews of New York City. Higier found that among eighteen cases seventeen were Jews.[2] Christians in Russia and Poland are only rarely affected with this disease. W. Erb[3] also observed that a large proportion of his patients were of Russian Jewish origin, fourteen out of forty-five being Jews. The cause of this disease is unknown. It occurs mostly in males between twenty and forty years of age, and generally in individuals in the higher walks of life. As to why it occurs more often among Jews cannot be said as long as the etiology of this disease remains obscure.

As has been already mentioned, it is difficult to state whether the life of the Jew is shortened by nervous diseases. Judging from the mortality returns published by registrars of some cities with large Jewish populations, it appears that in some cities their mortality from nervous diseases is higher than among the surrounding people, while in other places the contrary is to be noted. Thus, from statistics collected by the Eleventh Census of the United States we gather that the mortality from diseases of the nervous system was among Jewish men 121.22 and among women 120.62 per 1,000 deaths in which the cause

---

[1] R. v. Krafft-Ebing, "Zur Etiologie der Paralysis Agitans," *Arbeiten aus dem Gesamtgebiet der Psychiatrie und Neuropathologie*, Part III., p. 6.
[2] *Deutsche Zeitschrift für Nervenheilkunde*, xix. ; 1901.
[3] *Münchener Medicinische Wochenschrift*, No. 21, p. 905; 1904. Oppenheim found among 48 patients suffering with this disease 38 were Russian Jews, and he attributes it to their neuro-psychopathic diathesis. (*Jour. f. Psychol. u. Neurologie*, vol. viii., 1908.)

was known, as against a rate among the general population of 118.62 among men and 108.61 among women.[1] The mortality from nervous diseases is thus higher among the Jews, and the high mortality of the Jewesses, almost equalling that of the men, is striking, and is in agreement with the high frequency of insanity among Jewesses. Similarly, Lombroso found that the mortality of the Jews in Verona is almost double that of the Catholics in that city,[2] and the same was found to be the case in Cracow, Austrian Galicia.[3] On the other hand, in Budapest Auerbach found that the mortality from nervous diseases during 1901-05 was among the Christians 22.42 per 10,000, as against only 16.31 among the Jews,[4] and the same was found to be the case in Vienna, where Rosenfeld gives the rates as—Jews 123, Protestants 156, and Catholics 160 per 100,000,[5] while in Lemberg there were no differences to be discerned between Jews and Christians.[6]

These contradictory mortality rates may be due to differences in the *milieu* in which Jews in various countries live, or to differences in the classifications of the many varieties of nervous disease as registered in the vital statistics. On the whole, we cannot place considerable reliance on this kind of test as to the prevalence of nervous disease among Jews, or even as to the proportion of deaths caused by nervous derangements. Better results may be had by investigating the morbidity of the Jews as compared with the people among which they live. A study of this character shows no uniformity in every class of Jews, but tends to confirm our previous observation that there is no racial factor concerned in the etiology of these diseases, but that it all depends on many and complex causes, such as degree of culture, prevalence of alcoholic intemperance, syphilis, accuracy of diagnosis, and the like.

[1] *Census Bulletin*, No. 19; Washington, 1890.
[2] C. Lombroso, *L'antisemitismo e le scienze moderne*, Appendix; Torino, 1894.
[3] J. Thon, *Die Juden in Oesterreich*, pp. 34-36.
[4] E. Auerbach, "Die Sterblichkeit der Juden in Budapest," *Zeitschr. Demographie Statist. Juden*, p. 163; 1908.
[5] Rosenfeld in *Archiv für Rassen u. Gesellschaftsbiologie*, Nos. 1 and 2; 1907.
[6] J. Thon, *loc. cit.*

Epilepsy is a disease usually met with in families of a neurotic taint, which would lead us to expect it among the Jews with greater frequency than among others. But on the other hand, it is mostly met with in the offspring of parents who suffer from syphilis or alcoholism, conditions only rarely met with among Jews. It appears from the available evidence that epilepsy is, in fact, rather infrequent among them. In the discussion on the pathology of the Jews in the Paris Academy of Medicine in 1891, Charcot stated that at the Salpêtrière only thirty-nine Jewish epileptics came under observation during a period of thirteen years; Worms stated that at the Rothschild Hospital in that city it was also infrequently met with.[1] Minor in Moscow found it less often among his Jewish than among his Christian patients; and from information I obtained from the physician in charge of the Craig Colony for Epileptics in New York, it seems that the percentage of Jewish inmates is lower than their percentage in the population.[2] Among Jewish insane it appears that epilepsy is rather infrequent. Pilcz found it less often among Jewish lunatics in Vienna,[3] and Sichel also found it one-half as frequently among the Jewish inmates of the insane asylum of Frankfort as among the Christians.[4] All available evidence tends to show that their neurotic taint has not been sufficient to produce among them a large number of epileptics. The rarity of alcoholism and syphilis was more potent in preventing this disease than their predisposition to neuroses.

Taking another common disease, apoplexy, which is quite common and is usually diagnosed properly, no racial preference of either Jews or others can be discovered. Lombroso,[5] analyzing the vital statistics of the Italian

---

[1] Discussion sur la Pathologie de la Race Juive, *Bull. de l'Académie de Médecine de Paris*, vol. xxvi., pp. 238-241.

[2] Among the applicants for relief in the United Hebrew Charities in New York I only rarely meet with an epileptic. During ten years' service in that institution, examining over 3,000 Jews annually, I have not met with more than six cases of epilepsy on the average per year.

[3] A. Pilcz, "Ueber Geistesstörungen bei den Juden," *Wiener Klinische Wochenschrift*, Nos. 47-48; 1901.

[4] M. Sichel, "Ueber die Geistesstörungen bei den Juden," *Neurologisches Centralblatt*, pp. 351-367; 1908.

[5] *Loc. cit.*

Jews, found that deaths due to apoplexy were about twice as common among them as among the general population of that country, and assigns as reasons the emotional temperament of the Jew, his avarice, his constant struggle against adverse conditions of life, and the sufferings caused by the ceaseless persecution to which he has been subjected. Consanguineous marriages and the greater development and use of their brain are also assigned as predisposing causes. But an inquiry into the question in New York City showed that the proportion of patients suffering from apoplexy admitted to two large Jewish hospitals was proportionately about the same as in two non-Jewish hospitals in the city, and the mortality of the Jews from this disease does not materially differ from that of the general population.[1] In Vienna, on the other hand, Rosenfeld found that the mortality from apoplexy was as follows:—Catholics 62 per 100,000 population, Protestants 71, and Jews only 51; and in Budapest Auerbach found the rates—Jews 35.2, and Catholics 41.7 per 100,000 population.

All the evidence so far brought forward shows distinctly that when the Jews are compared with the non-Jewish population among which they live, it is found that they are no more liable to die from diseases of the nervous system than others. The mortality rates from these diseases are different in different times and places, and depend on a multiplicity of causes of a complex nature which are difficult to unravel. One thing is certain, the Jews are more affected with the so-called functional nervous affections, especially neurasthenia and hysteria, and most of the physicians who have an extensive experience among the Jews testify that hysteria in the male is a characteristic privilege of the children of Israel.

The causes of this nervousness of the Jews are apparent to every one who knows the conditions under which they have laboured for the last two thousand years. In the first place, they have been town-dwellers for centuries, and only rarely engage in agricultural pursuits. Neurasthenia is known to be a disease of large urban centres, where the hurry and bustle of life is an appalling drain on nervous energy. These diseases are also most frequently seen

[1] See article "Apoplexy," *Jewish Encyclopædia*, vol. ii., pp. 11-12.

among commercial people, speculators, and bankers; and considering the large number of Jews who depend on commerce for a living, and their ways of doing business often with a small capital, it is not surprising that many break down under the strain of speculation. It is, however, to be remembered that neurasthenia and hysteria are not only encountered among the richer classes of Jews. They are just as frequent among the poorer Jews, the artisans and labourers. In fact, one can almost daily meet with numerous Jews in the clinics for nervous diseases in New York City, many of whom are seeking relief from several physicians during the same week, and whose chief complaints are the symptoms of neurasthenia and hysteria in their various manifestations. But the Jews are not the only ones who have overstrained their nervous system in the keen struggle for existence. A large proportion of the inhabitants of modern large cities are known to be in the same plight. Leroy Beaulieu, speaking of this nervousness of the Jews, concludes as follows:—" It is well known that the increase of cerebral diseases and the exacerbation of nervous disorders is one of the distinctive marks of our age and our civilization. It is due to the feverish intensity of modern life, which, by multiplying our sensations and efforts, overstrains the nerves and rends the delicate network of the cerebral fibres. The Jew is the most nervous and, in so far, the most modern of men. He is by the very nature of his diseases the forerunner, as it were, of his contemporaries, preceding them on that perilous path upon which society is urged by the excesses of its intellectual and emotional life, and by the increasing spur of competition. The noisy army of psychopathics and neuropathics is gaining so many recruits among us that it will not take the Christians long to catch up with the Jews in this respect. Here, again, there are probably no ethnic forces in operation."

Many authorities on nervous diseases have blamed the frequent consanguineous marriages among them for the nervousness of the Jews. While on the whole facts are against them, because marriage of near kin when contracted between healthy individuals has not been proven to be detrimental to the offspring, still, considering that the inbreeding among them has been going on for the long centuries of their dispersion, often in small communities the members of which had unstable nervous systems, it is not surprising that this has at least partly contributed to their nervousness of to-day. People who "owe their existence less to their hands than to their brains," and who have to tax their ingenuity severely in order to subsist, in a manner unknown among any other human beings, cannot be anything else than nervous, and the children they bring into the world cannot but inherit these characteristics.

The present author has seen many of the Jews who have survived the recent "pogroms" in Russia. The stories each of these men, women, and children had to tell were sufficient to explain why they, as well as the children they may bring forth in the future, should be psychopathics and neuropathics. No physician can expect that children who have witnessed the slaughter of their parents, the violation of their mothers, sisters, and friends, should remain with a stable nervous system. The Jews, who for centuries had been maltreated or at least harassed, have had their nervous system shattered, hence their nervousness to-day.

Mental and Physical Defectives among Jews.—Statistics obtained by German censuses tend to show that there is an excessive number of feeble-minded Jews. It is difficult to say whether this is the case with the Jews in other countries, because the available data on the subject for Russia and Roumania, where about one-half of the total number of Jews in the world live, are rather defective. The German censuses give a special enumeration of all defectives according to their religious affiliation. One of the most important results of these investigations is that figures were obtained tending to show that idiocy and imbecility are more frequently met with among the Jews than among the Christians in that country, and various theories were advanced to explain this phenomenon. In Hanover[1] it was found that in 1855-56 there was one idiot to 1,528 Lutherans, 1,473 of the Reformed Church, 1,143 Catholics, and 763 Jews, which shows that the Jews have nearly twice as many of this kind of defectives as the Protestants. Similarly, in Baden and Bavaria, according to Mayr, the number of Jewish defectives is larger than of

[1] G. Brandes, *Der Idiotismus und die Idiotie mit Besonderer Berücksichtigung der Verhältnisse in Kgr. Hanover*; 1862.

Christian. In 1880 there were 260.7 idiots per 1,000,000 Jews, and only 158 per 1,000,000 Christians; and in Bavaria the rates were 207.3 and 144 respectively. But in other German provinces the excess of feeble-minded of Jewish faith is not as large. Thus, in Würtemberg it is reported that there was one idiot among 3,003 Jews, as against one among 3,207 Protestants and one among 4,113 Catholics. The difference between the Jews and Protestants is so small as to be of no significance, while the difference between the Protestants and Catholics is quite large; still nobody would say that there is a racial basis for this advantage of the Catholics. In Silesia also there is hardly any difference between Jews and non-Jews in this respect. There is, it was found, one idiot to 580 Catholics, one to 408 Protestants, and one to 514 Jews, which is rather unfavourable to the Protestants. From the reports of the asylums for mental defectives in Prussia, I compiled the following table, showing the number of idiots admitted per 1,000,000 population:—

	Christians.	Jews.
1882-1885	25.9	95.5
1886-1890	28.6	88.1
1891-1895	53.4	122.7
1896-1900	62.1	140.2

The disparity between the number of male and female idiots and imbeciles was greater among the Jews than among the Christians. Thus, of the total number of patients in the Prussian asylums it was found that 9.9 per cent. of the males and 8.9 per cent. of the females were idiots and imbeciles, while of the Jewish patients the ratio was 11.1 per cent. male and 6.6 per cent. females. The enormous number of Jewish idiots and imbeciles in Prussia is only appreciated when it is recalled that the birth-rate of the Jews has only been one-half that of the Christian population, and that the number of Jewish children is comparatively small, especially when compared with the Germans, whose rate of increase has been remarkably high. The number of mentally feeble and defective Jews is, when looked at from this view-point, not only double, but more than triple the number met with among the Christian population in that country. Pilez found that in the clinic for nervous diseases in Vienna no less than 17.7

per cent. of the male and 15.3 per cent. of the female idiots and imbeciles who applied for treatment were of Jewish extraction. Considering that the Jews in Vienna constitute only 8.86 per cent. of the total population, it appears that they are twice as liable to idiocy as the Christians.[1] But it must be borne in mind that Vienna is a veritable Mecca for the sick and afflicted Jews of Austria, and particularly Galicia and the Bukowina, and to a certain extent also from South Russia and Roumania. Many who suffer from some intractable disease or defect go to consult some famous specialist in Vienna; even some who are very poor often beg their way to Vienna in hope to obtain relief. The patients in that clinic do not include only Viennese Jews, but also a large number of strangers; so that this by no means proves that idiocy is twice as common among the Jews of Vienna as among the Christians.[2]

There is one more point to be considered. Jews are well known, as a rule, to take more care of the health of their children than the poor classes of the Christians among whom they live. They are thus more likely to send their defective children to institutions. This is especially true of Prussia, where their economic condition is superior to that of the non-Jewish population. The Jews are town-dwellers almost exclusively, and a feeble-minded child cannot be kept at home in the city; while the Christians, the majority of whom live in the country, can, and do often, keep a large proportion of their defectives at home. The result is that a larger proportion of Jews reach the institutions for the care of mental defectives, thus showing an apparent excess when admissions to asylums are taken as a criterion. To this must be added the fact that, as the result of the enormous care bestowed by Jews on their children, their defectives have more chance to survive than defectives of the slum population of non-Jews, and the differences between Catholics and Protestants

[1] A. Pilcz, "Geistesstörungen dei den Juden," *Wiener Klinische Rundschau*, vol. xv., pp. 888-890, 908-910; 1901.
[2] According to Thon, there were in Austria, during 1898-1892, per 100,000 population: Idiots, Jews 0.98, Christians 0.70; imbeciles, Jews 3.53, and Christians 2.05. This indicates a higher ratio for the Jews. See *Die Juden in Oesterreich*, p. 157.

in this respect are often just as large as between Jews and Christians. No theory of race influence is advanced in this case, and the complex causes at work are obscure. There is consequently no good reason for attributing the excess shown in the relative number of idiots among the Jews in some countries to ethnic causes.

It is difficult to estimate the number of idiots among the Jews in the United States. In New York City the number of feeble-minded Jews in the hospitals for these diseases is quite considerable. But then, the Jewish population of this city is also very large. It must be mentioned in this connection that the immigration authorities are very strict in regard to the exclusion of feeble-minded aliens when they attempt to enter the United States.

One form of idiocy, known as *Amaurotic Family Idiocy*, a rare and fatal disease of children, is mostly found among Jews. The largest number of cases have been observed among the Jews in the United States. At first it was thought that here an exclusively Jewish disease was at last found, because all the cases first reported were in Jewish children. But later on many cases have been observed among non-Jews. The chief characteristics of this disease are progressive mental and physical enfeeblement of the child, weakness and paralysis of all the extremities, and marasmus. These symptoms are associated with changes in the *macula lutea*, the yellow spot in the retina. An investigation of the etiological factors has left pathologists in the dark as to the causation of this disease. It has been found that neither syphilitic, alcoholic or nervous antecedents in the parents, nor consanguinity, have anything to do with the disease. No preventive measures have as yet been discovered, and no treatment has been of any benefit. All reported cases have terminated fatally.

The *Mongolian type of idiocy* has also been frequently observed among Jews. Its chief features are shortness of stature, broad, protruding cheek-bones, flattened bridge of the nose, rounded pinna of the ears, enlarged tongue, and the obliquely-placed Mongolian eyes. As to why this form of idiocy occurs more frequently among the Jews is impossible to say, as long as the etiology of the disease remains obscure.

Deaf-mutism is another defect which appears to be more

frequent among Jews. The latest census of these defectives in Germany shows that in 1902 there were the following proportions of deaf-mutes in that country[1]:—

Protestants	83 per 100,000 population.
Catholics - - - -	92 ,, ,, ,,
Jews -	136 ,, ,, ,,

The Jews in Germany are thus shown to have over one-third more deaf-mutes than either the Catholics or Protestants. In Bavaria it was found that in 1871 there were 8.6 deaf-mutes per 10,000 Catholics, 9.5 among Protestants, and 18.5 among Jews. A new census in 1901-02 showed that the proportion among the Christian population remained about the same—8.3 among 10,000 Catholics, and 9.1 among 10,000 Protestants. Among the Jews the number of deaf-mutes decreased during these thirty years from 18.5 to 12.6 per 10,000.[2] In Hungary also it was found in 1890 that there were, per 100,000 population, 100.93 Jewish and 88.51 Christian-deaf mutes; and in Prussia in 1895 the proportions were, Jews 129.8 and Christians 85.8.[3] It has been stated that the number of Jews who are congenital deaf-mutes is about the same as among the Christians, and that it is only the acquired form which is more prevalent among them. Thus, the census of Germany in 1902 shows that there 77.5 per cent. of the Protestant, 77 per cent. of the Catholic, and 79.2 per cent. of the Jewish deaf-mutes were disabled since early infancy; while in Prussia in 1895 it was found that 46.88 per cent. of the Christian and 57.40 per cent. of the Jewish deaf-mutes were such since infancy. This would tend to confirm the opinion that congenitally, or racially, there are not many more Jewish than Christian deaf-mutes, and that only in later life, as a result of disease, a larger number of Jews acquire the defect. If this could be confirmed by further evidence, then the explanation might be this: deaf-mutism is usually acquired as a result of some febrile disease, particularly scarlet fever, measles, diphtheria, or meningitis in early

---

[1] *Medizinalstatistische Mitteilungen aus dem Kaiserlichen Gesundheitsamt*, vol. viii., p. 21; 1905.
[2] Papratz, *Allgemeine Statistik über die Taubstummen Bayerns;* München, 1906.
[3] A. Ruppin, *Die Juden der Gegenwart*, p. 104.

life. Considering the great care taken by Jews in cases of illness, and that the number of children who survive attacks of acute ailments is larger than among the poor of other peoples, a larger proportion of those who survive may remain deaf-mutes. Congenital deaf-mutism, which constitutes the great majority of these defectives, has usually inheritance as a potent cause, and it has been stated that consanguineous marriages are at the bottom of many cases. Among the deaf-mute children admitted to the institutions for the care of these defectives in Holland it was found that 24.3 per cent. of all the Jewish deaf-mutes had a history of marriage of near kin in their parentage, as against only 9.7 per cent. among the Protestants, and 3.7 per cent. among the Catholics.[1] But it must be again mentioned in this connection that the number of consanguineous marriages among Jews is much larger than among Christians, and that any class of Jews will therefore show a larger proportion of consanguinity.

On the whole, it appears that no ethnic factors are the cause of the larger number of deaf-mutes among the Jews. The larger number of survivals from acute febrile diseases during early life, the fact that they are town-dwellers, and are subject to nervous diseases much more than others, give us hints as to the complex etiology of this peculiarity.

Insanity among Jews.—From statistics collected in various parts of the world it appears that insanity is much more frequent among Jews than among the Christians among whom they live. Some authors, like Buschan, consider this predisposition of the Jews to mental derangement an ethnic trait. They point to the Bible, in which it is frequently mentioned that the ancient Hebrews were already great sufferers from mental alienation.[2] The number of people "possessed with devils," "lunatics," "men with unclean spirits," etc., mentioned in the New Testament as having called on Christ for relief, and that He had cured them, are other

[1] *Zeitschrift für Demographie und Statistik der Juden*, p. 63; 1907.

[2] W. Ebstein, *Die Medizin im Alten Testament*, Stuttgart, 1902, gives details; see especially pp. 114-117. Bordier says: "Les songes, les hallucinations, le don de prophétie jouent en effet un grand rôle dans l'Ancien Testament et montrent la fréquence considérable, chez le peuple juif, des phénomènes cérébraux d'excitation," *Géographie Médicale*, p. 530; Paris, 1887.

indications of the frequency of insanity among them.[1] In modern times it was shown that the Jews in various countries are from two to four times more liable to insanity than the non-Jews among whom they live. This was especially noted in Germany, where careful statistics are published on the subject of insanity, and the religious faith of the patients is stated in the reports. During 1895-97 it was found that the insane asylums, both public and private, contained, proportionately, about three times as many Jews as Christians. There were, namely, 23 insane per 100,000 Catholics, 33 per 100,000 Protestants, and 92 per 100,000 Jews.[2] The census of the insane in Prussia taken in 1895 showed that there were, per 100,000 population, 491.9 Jewish and 253.0 Christian lunatics.[3] During 1898-1900 it was found that the Jews made up 3.42 per cent. of all admissions to the insane asylums in Prussia. Inasmuch as they constitute only 1.14 per cent. of the total population, it follows that the Jews have about three times as many lunatics as the Christians.[4] Per 100,000 population the admissions to the asylums in Prussia were as follows[5]:—

	General population.	Jews.
1881	29.7	92.9
1890	39.7	120.4
1895	58.0	145.6
1900	68.3	163.1

These statistics are to be taken with a certain amount of reservation. They are based on the asylum population of the country, as most statistics of this nature are. But it is a question whether the Jews are not more likely to send their mental defectives to asylums than Christian's. As city dwellers they find it difficult to keep lunatics at home, while the Christian population, over one-half of

[1] See particularly St. Matthew, viii. 16, ix. 32, xii. 11, xvii. 15; St. Mark, v. 2; St. Luke, viii. 27, xiii. 11, and many other places. Ebstein in his *Medizin im neuen Testament und im Talmud* (Stuttgart, 1903); also Sichel, "Psychiatrisches aus der Literatur und Geschichte der Juden," *Neurologisches Centralblatt*, Nos. 5-6, 1909, give details.
[2] Statistics for earlier years in the various German States, also for Italy, Denmark, etc., are given in the article "Insanity," by the author, in the *Jewish Encyclopædia*, vol. vi., pp. 603-605.
[3] A. Ruppin, *Die Juden der Gegenwart*, p. 104.
[4] *Ibid.*, p. 103.
[5] H. Singer, *Krankheitslehre der Juden*, p. 91; Leipzig, 1904.

which live in the country, may not send all their insane, especially those of the milder forms, to institutions. Moreover, insanity is mostly met with among adults and is comparatively rare among the young. As already understood, the birth-rate of the Jews in Germany is phenomenally low, and the composition of the Jewish population is consequently peculiar in regard to the small number of children, especially when compared with the Germans, whose birth-rate is remarkably high. It is thus evident that much of this heavy proportion of insanity may be only apparent. In fact, in some cities in Germany the number of Jewish lunatics is not above their proportion in the population. In Frankfort, Sichel has recently investigated the problem and found that, "contrary to the general impression, the number of Jewish lunatics corresponds altogether to the proportion they make up of the general population"[1] They constituted 6.8 per cent. of the total population and made up 6.5 per cent. of the insane asylum population in 1906-07, and an investigation of the number of admissions during the period 1897-1907 gave the same result. From statistics of other German cities it appears that in cities the divergence between the rates of insanity of Jews and Christians is not at all great. In Berlin, 3.4 per cent. of the insane are Jews, while they constitute 4.8 per cent. of the population; in Leipsic the proportions are 1.3 and 1.5, and in Breslau 4.3 and 4.0 respectively. This is probably due to two factors: The large proportion of alcoholic insanity among the Christians, which is rare among the Jews, and also because in the cities the Christians as well as the Jews cannot keep their demented at home and must commit them to institutions.

In Austria it is seen from statistics compiled by J. Thon, that during the twenty years 1882-1902 the number of Jewish lunatics was in excess of their proportion of the population. During 1898-1902 there were confined in the insane asylums 49.35 per 100,000 Christians and 67.89 per 100,000 Jews.[2] In the city of Vienna alone the proportion

[1] Max Sichel, "Ueber die Geistesstorungen bei den Juden," *Neurologisches Centralblatt*, pp. 351-367; 1908.

[2] See detailed statistics in J. Thon's *Die Juden in Oesterreich*, pp. 151-160; also N. Weldler, "Die Geisteskrankheiten unter den Juden Oesterreichs in den Jahren 1882-1902," *Zeitschr. Demogr. Statistik der Juden*, pp. 61-63; 1908.

seems to have been higher. During 1903 it was found that 13.2 per cent. of all admissions to the insane asylums were Jews, while they constituted only 8.86 per cent. of the population of that city.[1]

In Hungary also the birth-rate of the Jews is quite high, and the disproportion in the incidence of insanity among Jews and Christians is not very great. During 1890 it was found that there were 91.01 insane per 100,000 Jews and 87.94 per 100,000 Christians.[2] In Russia, where the birth-rate of the Jews is the highest in Europe, the returns of the census of 1897 showed that the number of Jewish insane is not at all excessive. It was found that 4.23 per cent. of all the insane enumerated in that country were Jews, which is about the same as the proportion they made up of the total population. Some special classes of Jews in Russia have, however, been found to be more liable to mental derangement than the Christians around them. Thus, among the troops stationed in Kieff, Maximoff and Sikorski found the following proportions of insane:—Russians, 0.91 per cent.; Poles, 0.92 per cent.; Mohammedans, 1.06 per cent.; and Jews, 2.19 per cent.[3] Even in Algeria it has been found that the Jews have a larger quota of insane. Marly, the physician to the hospitals in Constantine, shows the following proportion per 1,000 population:—Jews, 1.7; French, 1.5; and Arabs, 0.07.[4]

The only statistics about the Jews in the United States were collected by Dr. Hyde.[5] He found that the admissions of Jewish insane to the asylums of New York City, during the period extending from December 13, 1871, to November 30, 1900, amounted to 1,722, among a total number of 17,135 patients. The Jews thus constituted 10.05 per cent. of the total number of insane admitted. While at present the proportion of Jews in Greater New York is about twice ten per cent., it must be recalled that

---

[1] *Bericht über die niederösterreich. Irrenanstalten für 1902.*
[2] A. Ruppin, *Die Juden der Gegenwart*, p. 104.
[3] *Proceedings of the Twelfth International Medical Congress*, vol. iv., Part I., p. 661. See also M. A. Ryazansky, in *Vrachebnaia Gazeta*, ix., pp. 438-442, 1902, for further evidence in Russia.
[4] *Zeitschr. für Demographie und Statistik der Juden*, No. 4; 1907.
[5] Frank G. Hyde, "Notes on the Hebrew Insane," *American Journal of Insanity*, lviii., pp. 469-471.

up to 1882 there were fewer Jews there, and that this indicates a higher proportion than 10 per cent. for the twenty-nine years. Indeed, an analysis of the figures given by Dr. Hyde for the five years ending November 30th, 1900, shows that the proportion of Jewish insane in New York City is much larger. During these five years 3,710 insane were admitted to the asylums of New York City, and of these 573 were Jews. However, it again makes a smaller proportion than the estimated Jewish population of this city, for indeed it constituted only 15.44 per cent. Whether there is an error in these figures somewhere, or the Jews in New York are not as liable to mental alienation as in their native countries in Europe, is impossible to say, as long as there are no available data about other cities in the United States. Perhaps the care taken by the immigration authorities to exclude defective aliens has some influence.

As to the forms of insanity most frequently met with among Jews, alienists are not in agreement. Dr. C. F. Beadles, basing his assertion on the experience he gained in the Colney Hatch Asylum in England, stated that there appears to be a great preponderance of general paralysis among Jewish males; twenty-one per cent. of all the male Jews admitted to that institution being subjects of this disease, while the proportion of cases of general paralysis among all the males admitted to the hospitals for the insane in England and Wales is only thirteen per cent. "It is evident," says Dr. Beadles, "that among the Jewish males, admissions for general paralysis are sixty per cent. more frequent than among the non-Jewish English and Welsh."[1] No such disparity has been observed in the case of Jewesses. Other observers also found an excessive proportion of general paralysis among Jews. Thus, Pilcz found a large number of paretic Jews among his patients in Vienna. He is impressed that the so-called circular course of this disease is not to be noted among Jewish paralytics.[2] Hirschl also found among 200 of his paretic patients that 40—*i.e.* twenty per cent.—

[1] C. F. Beadles, "The Insane Jew," *Journal of Mental Science*, xxvi., pp. 731-737.
[2] A. Pilcz, *Beitrag zur vergleichenden Rassen-Psychiatrie*, p. 17; Leipzig, 1906.

were Jews.[1] Both these last two alienists state that the classic pictures of the disease with abundant megalomania, wonderful exaltation of ideas, etc., are most commonly observed among Jews, although many authors agree that of late this form of the disease is becoming rare among other peoples.

Further investigation, however, shows that general paralysis is not very frequent among the Jews in other countries. Minor found that in Moscow it is six times more often met with among Christians than among Jews, and Sichel found only 12.5 per cent. among Jews as against 8.3 per cent. among Christians.[2] Minor compiled statistics of his own with Dr. Kajewnikoff's observations, and found that among 4,700 Christian patients affected with nervous diseases 2.6 per cent suffered from general paralysis, while among 696 Jewish patients only 0.8 per cent. suffered from this disease. He points out that it is all a question of the prevalence of syphilis. Among syphilitic Jews this disease is just as frequent as among syphilitics of other creeds, and inasmuch as syphilis is comparatively rare among the Jews in Russia, general paralysis is also infrequent. This is confirmed by the observations of Dr. Savage of London, who says· "In my experience there has been very little general paralysis either among the Jewish men or women. Just as other races are affected, general paralytics among Jews have nearly all some history of syphilitic degeneration."[3]

The infrequency of syphilis among Jewish insane, as among Jews generally, has been observed repeatedly. In the insane asylums of New York city, as Hyde reports, only 4.18 per cent. had syphilitic antecedents, which is very low. The same is the case with the alcoholic form of insanity. Among 205 patients suffering from alcoholic form of insanity, Pilcz did not find a single Jew, and only 5.51 per cent. of the Jewish patients of the New York insane asylums were alcoholics, according to Hyde. Indeed, it is very rare to meet with a Jewish patient suffering from delirium tremens in the alcoholic ward of

---

[1] Hirschl, "Zur Aetiologie der progressiven Paralyse," *Jahrbüch. für Psychiatrie*, vol. xiv. p. 429.
[2] Sichel, *Neurologisches Centralblatt*, p. 356; 1908.
[3] *Journal of Mental Science*, 1900, p. 735.

Bellevue Hospital, although of late cases have been becoming more frequent. But in Algeria, where the Jews are more addicted to the abuse of alcoholic beverages, Trenga found that 17.6 per cent. of Jewish insane were affected with alcoholic insanity.[1]

Many other peculiarities have been attributed to the Jewish insane by various authors, but most of them, being based on only a small number of observations, are of doubtful value; in fact, many authors contradict each other. Thus Pilez states that among the Jewish insane in Vienna moral insanity is very rare, while Savage saw a large number of cases of "moral depravity" among Jewish insane in London, and Sichel, in Frankfort, says that he met with many Jewish lunatics of this class, and he observed that they often came in early life in conflict with the law.[2] It is also stated that melancholia is more common among Jews than mania, and Pilcz is under the impression that melancholia has a preponderatingly hypochondriac colouring among the Jews, and also that the prognosis is most unfavourable among them, very few cures being attained. In London, Beadles observed that insanity following childbirth is more common among Jewish women than among others; that insanity appears earlier in both sexes; and that relapses occur twice as frequently among Jewish patients discharged from insane asylums as in Christians. Pilcz's experience among Jewish insane in Vienna leads him to believe that paranoia, or delusional insanity, is more frequently met with among Jewish males, while Jewesses are only rarely affected, but those Jewesses who are affected by this disease suffer from a very rapid and unfavourable course and they soon succumb. Dementia præcox claims an exorbitantly high proportion of Jewesses, and dementia senilis produces very often peculiarly fine pictures of a hypochondriac character among Jews. The same author also finds that the epochal insanities are predominant among Jews.[3] While only 8.86 per cent. of the total population of Vienna was Jewish, he found that 26.08 per cent. of his patients

---

[1] Trenga, *Sur les psychoses chez les Juifs d'Algérie*; Montpellier, 1902.

[2] *Neurologisches Centralblatt*, p. 357; 1908.

[3] Pilcz, *Die periodische Geistesstörungen*, p. 19; Jena, 1901.

suffering from the epochal insanities were of this creed.[1] This agrees with Beadles' observation of the unusual number of Jewesses who suffer from puerperal insanity in London. It appears that, predisposed as they are to mental derangement, the least exciting cause, such as reverses in family life or in business, pregnancy, childbirth, lactation, etc., will often be the determining factor. Considering the unusual prevalence of hysteria and neurasthenia among them, it is clear why such a large proportion of insane Jews are of this type.

The observations made in insane asylums in various parts of the world indicate that men are more liable to insanity than women,[2] and this is confirmed by statistics of Jewish insane. Thus among the annual admissions to both public and private insane asylums in Prussia there were the following proportions of women[3]:—

	Jews.	Christians.
1881	46.15 %	40.67 %
1890	45.31	42.84
1896	46.47	42.06
1900	50.00	41.62

Both Jews and Christians show a lesser liability to insanity of the women, but the proportion is higher among Jewesses than among Christian women. The percentages among the former were from 46 to 50, while among the latter they were only from 40 to 42 per cent. It is important to note, however, that a census of the asylum population in that country, taken in 1895, showed that there were confined in asylums for the insane 43,448 men and 39,402 women, of which 995 were Jews and 894 Jewesses—*i.e.*, that in both groups there were 47 per cent. of women. This may be due to either a higher recovery or mortality rate of the male lunatics, especially the Christian. In Frankfort, also, Sichel found that while among the Christian lunatics only 28 per cent. were women, among the Jewish the proportion reached 49 per

---

[1] Pilcz, "Ueber Geistesstörungen bei den Juden," *Wiener Klinische Rundschau*, Nos. 47 and 48; 1901.
[2] See Havelock Ellis, *Man and Woman*, 4th ed., pp. 389 *et seq.*
[3] Compiled from figures given in H. Singer, *Krankheitslehre der Juden*, pp. 90-91; Leipzig, 1904.

cent.[1] In Austria, where careful statistics are published, it is also found that the proportion of Jewish female lunatics is larger than that found among Christians, as can be seen from the following figures, giving the results of censuses of the asylum population[2]:—

	Per cent. of Women.	
	Jews.	Christians.
1882-85	47.00	45.95
1886-89	47.46	44.92
1890-93	48.25	45.30

The results are not materially different when only new admissions are considered. During 1894-97 the proportion of women was, among Jewish insane admitted to the asylums of Austria, 47.35 per cent., while of Christian women it was only 42.21 per cent.; during 1898-1902 the percentages were 49.25 and 44.59 respectively. The proportion of female Jewish insane is here from 47 to 49 per cent., as against only 42 to 46 per cent. This striking liability of Jewesses to insanity is interesting from another view-point. Havelock Ellis has shown that the increasing tendency of women to insanity may be compared with the varying frequency of criminality among them. "Roughly speaking, both tend to go together, and to reach a maximum in the restless industrial centres of civilization; everywhere insanity and criminality follow in the wake of progress and prosperity, though insanity is probably a more certain and well-marked sign of the tension of civilization than criminality."[3] This is confirmed by the figures just quoted, especially when considered in connection with the figures collected by the Russian census of 1897. The returns showed 67,755 male and 49,954 female lunatics in that country, of which 2,905 were Jews and 2,075 Jewesses—*i.e.*, the proportion of female insane was 44.25 per cent. among the Christians and 41.66 per cent. among the Jews. Considering that the life of the Jewess in Russia is more simple and primitive when compared with that of her sister in Germany and Austria, this is to be expected. It is also noteworthy that criminality is

---
[1] M. Sichel, "Ueber die Geistesstörungen bei den Juden," *Neurologisches Centralblatt*, pp. 351-367; 1908.
[2] J. Thon, *Die Juden in Oesterreich*, p. 154; Berlin, 1908.
[3] *Man and Woman*, p. 403.

much rarer among Jewesses than among Christian women in Europe, and their greater liability to insanity may be said to be due more to their greater prosperity and "tension of civilization," to which they as town-dwellers are exposed more than Christian women.

The best summary as to the differences in the forms of insanity observed among Jews when they are compared with Christians has been compiled from the figures published in the *Oesterreichische Statistik* by N. Weldler.[1] From these figures I gather the following table, showing the average annual number of insane during 1890-1902 per 100,000 population, as well as the forms of insanity with which they were affected:—

	Christians.	Jews.
Congenital idiocy	0.70	0.98
Congenital imbecility	2.05	3.53
Melancholia	2 97	3.89
Mania	1.61	3.87
Amentia	7.62	13.44
Paranoia	5.41	5.96
Psychosis periodica	1.99	4.86
Dementia	6.79	10.79
Progressive paralysis	7.77	11.07
Epileptic insanity	3.10	2.22
Hysterical insanity	1.35	2.04
Insanity, with neurasthenia	0.71	1.78
Psychosis cum cerebropathia circumscripta	0.45	0.62
Psychosis cum pellagra	0.50	0 16
Alcoholism	5.44	0.68
Alcoholism, with drug addiction	0.14	0.28
Other forms	0.65	1 42

It will be observed that these figures give an excellent summary as to the differences between Jews and others in Austria in respect to the forms of insanity to which they are liable. Alcoholism is rare among Jews, though addiction to drugs is more frequently met with than among Christians. Both melancholia and mania are more frequent among Jews, while amentia is nearly twice as often met with as among Christians. Paranoia is met with in about the same proportion among both classes, while progressive paralysis, dementia, and periodic insanity, as well as hysterical and neurasthenic forms of mental derangement, are more frequent among the Jews.

[1] See *Zeitschr. f. Demographie u. Statistik der Juden*, pp. 59-63; 1898.

Epileptic insanity is rarer among Jews, which is to be expected, considering that epilepsy is comparatively infrequent. These differences between Jews and Christians have never been studied as regards their causation. The infrequency of syphilis and alcoholism among the Jews, while explaining some phases of the problem, does, however, not explain all that may be important in this connection.[1] It is important to inquire why the psychoses of an hereditary and degenerative nature are so often met with among the Jews, and also the frequency of idiocy and imbecility, as well as dementia and progressive paralysis, irrespective of the prevalence of syphilis.

It has been stated that the prognosis of insanity is more unfavourable in Jews than in others. During 1902-03 the proportion of admissions of Jewish patients to the asylums in Vienna was 11.6 per cent., and only 7.5 per cent. of those who were discharged as cured and 15.4 per cent. of those who died were of this creed.[2] Similarly, in the Austrian insane asylums the number of Jewish patients discharged as cured is smaller than the number admitted. Here, however, the number of deaths is smaller among the Jews.[3] On the other hand, Sichel[4] could discover no differences between Jewish and Christian lunatics in Frankfort as regards their chances of recovery. It must also be borne in mind in this connection that the number of alcoholic insane is very small among the Jews, and among Jewesses almost unknown, and the prognosis of alcoholic insanity is rather favourable. The higher death-rates of the Jewish insane merely indicate that they are more often affected with the more dangerous and incurable forms of insanity.

---

[1] The influence of modern conditions on the Jew is noteworthy in connection with the number of drug fiends met with among them. In Russia, Roumania, the East End of London, and New York, a Jew addicted to the morphine or cocaine habit is very rare. In Austria such Jews are twice as often treated in institutions than Christians. The same is true of Germany with greater force. Singer mentions that in one institution there were 970 Jewish among 3,200 drug habitues—*i.e.*, they made up 30 per cent.— *Kranheitslehre der Juden*, p. 92. The frequency of neuralgia, gall stones, stone in the kidney, etc., among Jews may be the cause of the large number who have to resort to drugs for the relief of pain.

[2] *Zeitschr. Demogr. Statist. u. d. Juden*, No. 1; 1907.

[3] *Ibid*, No. 10; 1907. J. Thon, *Die Juden in Oesterreich*, 1908.

[4] Sichel, *Die Umschau*, No. 26; 1908.

On the whole, it can be stated that the so-called *psychosis Judaica*, spoken of by some writers,[1] is not recognized by most authorities. The talkative and quarrelsome proclivities of many Jewish lunatics are not a specific Jewish trait, and are met with among most lunatics who suffer from the mania stage of circular insanity and among certain cases of paranoia. Sichel[2] could not find any specific Jewish form of insanity, and Pilcz[3] shows that there is no justification for speaking of *Judenpsychosen*. The only differences to be observed between Jews and others are in the frequency of insanity and in the forms most often met with among the two classes. The symptomatology of a given disease is, however, about the same in both Jews and Christians. Altogether there are no racial peculiarities to be observed in the forms of mental derangement which affect the Jews. It must be borne in mind that "religion, as part of the civilization of a nation, plays some part in the colouring of insanity, and to a smaller extent has an influence in producing it; the Protestant religion, for instance, has its special mode of colouring melancholic feelings." "The position and the profession of the individual will colour the nature of the insanity: a doctor tends to hypochondriasis, a parson to remorse; a man is more egotistical, a woman more altruistic in her morbid bent, etc."[4] Considering the peculiarity of the social and economic environment of the Jew, there is little wonder that his peculiar *milieu* should lend a certain colouring to the manifestations and course of his malady, when his mind gives way to the excessive strain under which he labours so often.

Causes of the Frequency of Insanity amongst Jews.—Many authors believe that the frequency of insanity among the Jews is but another manifestation of the neurotic strain running through the Semitic race. Some like Erb, Buschan, and others, state that even in Biblical times the Hebrews were already neurotics, and since then this

---

[1] Brosius, "Die psychose der Juden," *Allgem. Zeitschrift für Psychiatrie*, etc., vol. lx., p. 269.
[2] *Neurologisches Centralblatt*, p. 364; 1908.
[3] A. Pilcz, *Beitrag zur vergleichenden Rassen-Psychiatrie*, p. 31; 1906.
[4] G. H. Savage, in Allbutt's *System of Medicine*, vol. viii., p. 184 and 186.

ethnic peculiarity has been transmitted by heredity from generation to generation. The fact that the Jews in every country are more liable to mental derangement than their non-Jewish neighbours would speak in favour of racial peculiarity in this respect. But it must not be overlooked that up to recent years the Jews have for centuries lived in every part of the world under almost identical social and economic conditions, and have been engaged in about the same occupations, subjected to the same kinds of abuses, persecutions, and disabilities. Identity of environment could not but produce the same pathological results. Altogether, it is questionable whether certain races are more liable to insanity than others. Neurologists have so far not yet determined that race influence is the cause of the differences in frequency of insanity among the various peoples in the world. While it is true that insanity occurs more frequently than is generally supposed among primitive races, still they suffer much less than the civilized and cultured. But this does not indicate that there is an ethnic basis for these differences. The complexity of modern life, the violent increase of mental work, the variety of social and economic requirements which are very difficult to satisfy, are each and all well-known causes of insanity among civilized peoples. It is well known that the differences in the incidence of insanity between the various social classes of a modern community is much larger than between the various races of Europe. Indeed, mental alienation is not at all more common among the dark-complexioned, excitable southern peoples than among the blonde and phlegmatic northerners. The *milieu* is more of a determining factor in this respect than ethnic origin.

Marriage of near kin, which is very common among Jews, has also been considered a potent cause of the great frequency of insanity among them. In fact, all the other physical, mental, and intellectual peculiarities of the Jews have been ascribed by many authors to this cause. Being very neurotic, consanguineous marriages among Jews cannot but be detrimental to the progeny. In one generation the neuropathy may manifest itself as hysteria, in another as some other functional or organic nervous disease, then as insanity, etc. The chances of thus perpetuating a nervous strain in families by consanguineous marriages are much greater among the Jews than among other peoples in whom nervous derangements are less frequently encountered.

The Jews, as town-dwellers *par excellence*, cannot be compared with the general population of any European country in regard to the incidence of insanity. About two-thirds of the European non-Jewish population live in the country, and are engaged in agricultural and allied pursuits which entail, comparatively, but little care and worry. With the Jews it is the exact opposite; three-fourths of them live in cities, and hardly five per cent. of them are engaged in agricultural pursuits. The populations of the cultured states in Europe, as has been repeatedly proven, keeps on renewing itself by intermarriage of the city-dwellers with the immigrants from the country. It has been calculated by Ripley that in thirty of the principal cities of Europe only about one-half of the population increases from their own loins, the overwhelming majority being of country stock. For eighteen centuries the Jews have been at a disadvantage in this respect. As town-dwellers, they degenerated physically like all others, but could not drain pure, healthy, fresh country blood for the rejuvenation of their own, which has been deteriorated by the deleterious effects of urban life. The evil effects of the strained, nerve-shattering city life has thus been deeply rooted in their bodies and minds, and is kept up by hereditary transmission. With each new generation the nervous vitality of the Jews lessened, and one of the results of this mode of life is that most of the diseases which increase with the advance of civilization, especially the neuroses and psychoses, are more common among them than among others.

Suicide among Jews.—One of the most peculiar traits of the Jewish pathology and psychology was once considered to be the infrequency of self-destruction. It is well known that mental alienation is the most potent factor in the etiology of suicide. The Jews having such a large proportion of insane, would, *a priori*, be expected to have also a large proportion of suicides. But most writers on the subject, relying on statistics collected about fifty years ago, found that the Jew only rarely kills himself. Various explanations were offered for this phenomenon. Some have attributed it to their proverbial cowardice, others to their abstemiousness, others again to the great tenacity of life of the Semitic blood which flows in the veins of the Jews.

The fact is that suicide is a purely social phenomenon, and has hardly anything to do with ethnic origin. The Jews are the best example illustrating the influence of the environment on the rates of self-destruction among men. Statistics collected by Morselli[1] show that during the middle of the nineteenth century Jews only rarely committed suicide. From the table given by Morselli on the influence of religion on the tendency to suicide, it appears that in Central Europe, Austria, Hungary, and Transylvania, the most frequent order in which the various religions follow each other in their tendency to self-destruction is this: Protestants, Catholics, and Jews; and the next order of frequency is Protestants, Jews, and Catholics. "This peculiar position occupied by Jews in relation to Catholics deserves attentive investigation," says Morselli. "Jews in general are more subject to mental alienation than either Catholics or Protestants." He does not, however, attribute this characteristic entirely to race influence, because he finds that Jews of various countries differ more among themselves than Catholics from Protestants, who maintain a certain relative proportion with little variation. He justly lays great stress on the influence of religious fervency, and maintains that individuals ardently devoted to religion, especially women (nuns and lay sisters), only rarely commit suicide. Jews intensely devoted to their religion are similarly less apt to self-destruction.

A study of more recent statistics about the Jews confirms this view. In Eastern Europe and the Orient, where they follow the religion of their fathers fervently, a Jewish suicide is very rare; in some cities in Russia, Galicia, or Roumania, with over 20,000 Jews, more than ten years often pass without a Jew taking his own life. During the first half of the nineteenth century, when the social and economic condition of the Jews in Western Europe was

[1] *Suicide*, p. 122; New York, 1882.

not much different from that of their Eastern European co-religionists of to-day, self-destruction was also rare among them. With the decline of the intensity of religious belief which is characteristic of the contemporaneous Jews in Western Europe and America, an adoption of the habits and customs of the Christian population has been noted, among which suicide may be mentioned as a social fact important for the study of the effects of the *milieu* on certain human traits.

In Eastern Europe suicide is even to-day less frequent among the Jewish than among the Christian population. In Cracow, for instance, one per cent. of all the deaths during 1895-1900 was self-inflicted among the Christians, as against only 0.4 per cent. among the Jews,[1] and the same is true of Lemberg. In Budapest, Hungary, the rates during 1901-05 were per 100,000 population: Jews, 21.1; Catholics, 28.8; and others, 25.7.[2] Suicide is here less frequent among the Jews than among others. But proceeding to Western Europe, where the Jews are affected by what Morselli characterizes as the " universal and complex influence to which we give the name civilization," the proportion of suicides is at present much larger among the Jews than among Christians, although but fifty years ago it was quite uncommon. Thus in Vienna, where both the orthodox and the liberal Jews are about equally common, the rates in 1901-03 were, according to Rosenfeld,[3] 28 per 100,000 Catholics; Protestants, 38 per 100,000; and Jews, 32 per 100,000 Jews. Here the Jews have more suicides than the Catholics, and less than the Protestants. In Würtemberg, the Jews also had but few suicides during 1846-69, only 65.6 per 1,000,000 population, as against 77.9 among Catholics, and 113.5 among Protestants. But the rate for the Jews kept on increasing, and during 1898-1902 it was 252, as against only 162.7 among the Christian population of that country.[4] In Bavaria the rates for the Jews were already higher than those of the

---

[1] J. Thon, "Die jüdische Bevölkerung in Krakau," *Zeitschr. für Demographie und Statistik de Juden*, No. 11; 1905. Also *Die Juden in Oesterreich;* Berlin, 1908.
[2] Auerbach, *loc. cit.*
[3] *Loc. cit.*
[4] *Zeitschr. für Demographie und Statistik der Juden*, No. 4; 1905.

Catholics, during 1844-56, when it was Jews: 105.9; Protestants, 135.4; and Catholics, 49.1 per 1,000,000 population. Since 1870 a steady increase was noted as follows:—

	Catholics.	Protestants.	Jews.
1870-79	73.5	194.6	115.3
1880-89	95.3	221.7	185.8
1890-99	92.7	210.2	212 4

It is evident from these figures that the increase of suicide has been more pronounced among the Jews than among the Christians in that country. Among the Protestants the rate during 1890-99 was 156 per cent. of the rates in 1844-56, among the Catholics it was 189 per cent., while among the Jews it was 200 per cent., actually an appalling increase in fifty-five years.

The greatest increase in self-destruction among the Jews is to be seen in Prussia, where it was rather uncommon in the first half of the nineteenth century. During 1849-55 the rates were: Jews, 46.4; Catholics, 49.6; and Protestants, 159.9 per 1,000,000 population. Then an increase began to be noted among the followers of each of these three denominations, and during 1869-72 it was: Jews, 96; Catholics, 69; and Protestants, 187; the Jews then outstripping the Catholics, though still having fewer suicides than the Protestants. But they did not stop at that. The latest figures available are for 1907, which show that the rates were for Catholics 104, for Protestants 254, and for Jews 356 per 1,000,000 population.[1] For each suicide among the Catholics in 1849-55, there were in 1907 about two; for each suicide among the Protestants in 1849-55, there were in 1907 one and a half, while among the Jews the increase was eight-fold during these fifty-eight years. Such an appalling increase has not been noted among any other civilized people.

All these figures show conclusively that the rates of self-destruction among the Jews are not at all influenced by ethnic factors. The social environment is solely responsible for the infrequency of suicide among the Jews in Eastern Europe, where they live in strict adherence to their faith and traditions; while in Western Europe, where

[1] *Preuss. Statistik*, vol. cxxiv.

they commingle with their Christian neighbours, adopting their habits and customs, the rates of suicide increase. Considering that there is a lesser number of children among the Western European Jews, and suicide is rare among the young, and that they are mostly town-dwellers, and have a larger proportion of persons engaged in mercantile, financial, and professional pursuits, than people of other creeds, there is good reason for the higher rates among them than among others. A curious illustration of the influence of occupation on the suicide rates of the Jews is afforded from data obtained in Baden, where the rates among both Jews and Christians were about the same during 1896 to 1901, excepting 1900, when the rates were 19 per 100,000 Christians (about the average for the six years) and 50 per 100,000 Jews. During that year there was a commercial depression in Germany, and many merchants and bankers were ruined. The Jews, owing to their unusual participation in commerce and banking and other hazardous occupations, have suffered more than the Christians, hence the enormous increase in suicides among them during the year 1900.[1]

Further proof of the influence of the environment on the suicide rates of the Jews may be adduced from the fact that with a change of the *milieu* there is an immediate change in their suicide rates. The Jewish immigrants to the United States are much given to self-destruction, although in their native homes suicide is very rare. There are no available statistics as to the exact number of Jewish suicides in New York City, but judging from the newspaper reports it appears that it is of frequent occurrence. An editor of a Jewish daily writes as follows:—"About fifteen years ago suicide was uncommon among the immigrant Jews, so much so that I always gave each case reported a prominent place in my paper. To-day, conditions have changed. There are so many cases of suicide among my co-religionists that, unless it is a pro-

---

[1] L. Wasserman, "Aufbau der jüdischen Bevölkerung in Baden, etc.", *Zeitschrift für Demographie und Statistik der Juden*, pp. 22-29; 1906. During the commercial crisis in the winter 1907-08 in the United States the number of Jewish suicides in New York was extraordinary. Hardly a day passed but one or more Jews were reported in the press as having put an end to their existence, and one day I knew of as many as six.

minent person, or there are special news features connected with the case, I do not at all mention it in the columns of my paper." He estimates that there are about six cases of Jewish suicides on the average weekly in New York City. If this figure is near the truth, and I am inclined to believe it is, then the suicide rate of the Jews in New York is appalling, constituting about forty per cent. of all the suicides, while only about twenty per cent. of the population is Jewish.

The aversion to suicide of the Eastern European Jew is thus seen not to be racial. As soon as he is brought face to face with a more complex life in New York City, as soon as his devotion to the religion of his fathers more or less dwindles, any serious reverse in life is liable to discourage him to the extent of causing him to terminate his existence.

CHAPTER XVI

SOCIAL AND ECONOMIC CONDITIONS.

Factors influencing social and economic conditions—Distribution of the population by ages—Differences between Eastern and Western Jews—Poverty—Absence of the pauper element—Economic conditions depend mostly on their political status—Poverty of the Jews in Russia, Poland, and Roumania—Prosperity of the Western Jews—Differences in the economic conditions of the native and immigrant Jews in the United States—Capacity for regeneration of the Jewish immigrant.

THE social characteristics of a community depend on a variety of factors of a very complex nature. It is often impossible to disentangle the different elements at the bottom of a social phenomenon, to select those which are important as social facts and to eliminate those which are of little or no significance. Indeed, cause and effect are often so inter-related as to make it impossible to distinguish one from the other. When it appears, for instance, that a very large proportion of Jews are engaged in commercial pursuits, it is questionable whether the fact that they have been town-dwellers for nearly two thousand years is not a sufficient reason, because an inhabitant of a city cannot engage in agriculture for obvious reasons. On the other hand, some authors have argued that his aversion for agriculture, and for manual labour in general, has brought the Jew to the city and made of him a merchant *par excellence*. There are many similar problems to be discussed while speaking of the social conditions of the Jews, most of which have been explained by various authors in a different fashion. What we must guard against, however, is the danger of finding a ready explanation of many complex social and economic phenomena by attributing them to racial characteristics. "Race" has been used recently as a cloak to cover a large number of facts which are more correctly and truthfully explained by a careful inquiry into the composition of the population as regards age and sex, education and facilities for educating the young generation, occupations, economic well-being, poverty and pauperism, etc.

The distribution of the population by age classes is of vast sociological importance, and before speaking of differences between Jews and Christians in a given place, we must make sure that there are no differences between the two classes in this respect. From an economic standpoint, a community with an excessive number of children and aged persons who are incapable of self-support, has its productive members highly burdened with the task of supporting these dependents. Age distribution has also an important effect on the rate of criminality observed in a given place. A community with a high proportion of children under twelve years of age will show a smaller ratio of criminality when calculated on a basis of the total population. Occupation will also have an important bearing in this regard, especially as to the species of crime most often observed. Thus, labourers, agricultural workers, etc., cannot become bankrupts, nor defraud in business. On the other hand, crimes of violence occur more often among labourers than among merchants. The political status of the members of a community is of special interest to us while studying the social conditions of the Jews. It must be recalled that at the present time the majority of the Jews live under legal restrictions which hinder them in many of their undertakings, aspirations, and ideals. This is the case with the Jews in the Orient, in Russia and Roumania, representing about 7,000,000 out of a total of 12,000,000 Jews in the world. As will soon be evident, the social conditions of these Jews are different from those who live in Western and Southern Europe, America, and Australia, where they are politically on an equal plane with the population around them.

These factors are to be considered when speaking of the social conditions of the Jews, and the differences noted when they are compared with the Christians among whom they live. In addition it must be emphasized that religion has more bearing in this respect among the Jews than among the Christians. The separativeness which Judaism exacts from its faithful followers, the Sabbath, the dietary laws, etc., have had a profound effect on their social conditions. In fact, as will appear later, this exclusiveness of Judaism has been the cause of many of the Jews' disabilities, perhaps to a greater extent than many Jews are willing to admit.

Age Distribution of the Population.—That the social conditions of the Jews are not alike in every country, that there are differences in this respect just as we have seen that there are differences in the physical types of Jews, is evident when we consider the distribution of the Jewish population according to age classes. Considering those below fifteen years of age as unproductive, we find that there are material differences in the burden carried by the productive class of fifteen to sixty years of age while attempting to provide for their dependents. In Eastern Europe they are prolific, as was already shown. The result is that they have a large number of children. In Russia, 51.9 per cent. of male and 52.6 per cent. of female Jews are under twenty years of age, as against only 48.4 per cent. among the general population. Under ten years of age there were enumerated 40 per cent. of all the Jews, and only 38 per cent. of the Russians. This, of course, is the result of a high fecundity coupled with a low infant mortality. Old persons are found less among the Jews than among the Christians: 2.0 per cent. of males and 1.6 per cent. of the female Jewish population were over seventy years of age, as against 2.5 per cent. among the Russians. Similarly, in Servia the census of 1900 showed that 38.99 per cent. of the Jews were under 15 years of age, and 4.56 per cent. over 60 years. In Western Europe conditions are different. In Frankfort-on-Main only 21.42 per cent. of the Jewish population is under 14 years of age, while among the Christians the proportion was 25.2 per cent. In Hamburg there were under fifteen years of age, Jews 22.27 per cent., and Christians 29.45 per cent.; in Bâle, Switzerland, Jews 26.2 per cent., Christians 27 per cent.; in Denmark (under 20), Jews 24.9, and total population 43.6 per cent.; in Hesse, Jews 25.8 per cent. (under 15), and Christians 32.9 per cent.; in Italy, Jews 26.45 per cent., and Christians 34.5 per cent. In the United States the Tenth Census showed that the proportion of children under five years of age was less among the Jews than in the general population in the proportion of 9 to 13, while from five to fifteen years of age it is greater in the proportion of 29 to 23.[1]

It is thus evident that the Western European Jews have fewer children than their Eastern co-religionists, or than the Christians among whom they live. The proportion of persons of the productive ages—*i.e.*, between fifteen and sixty years of age—is larger among the Jews in Western Europe than in Eastern Europe, and they are in this respect also at an advantage when compared with their Christian neighbours. This advantage is the more valuable economically because they have another advantage when compared with non-Jews. They are, namely, mostly engaged in mercantile pursuits which do not incapacitate them at sixty. On the contrary, a business man is usually reaping a great reward with the advance of age and experience. The Jews in Eastern Europe, engaged as they are to a large extent in industrial pursuits, at which a man is often quite incapacitated at sixty, are at a disadvantage in this respect. In addition, these facts also confirm our observations regarding the decadence of the Jews in Western Europe. A smaller number of children implies that in the near future there will be a smaller number of adults. The numerical strength of Judaism is thus by no means hopeful. On the other hand, it must be borne in mind that the Jews in Eastern Europe, with their large number of children, will remain for some time to come the vast reservoir whence Jews will keep on streaming by immigration into western countries, thus replacing those who disappear under modern conditions.

Poverty.—There is a widespread tradition that in spite of disabilities to which they have been subjected, Jews are always successful in every walk of life, and, as a class, economically prosperous. "As rich as a Jew," is a common saying. This, however, involves, as Jacobs aptly says, one of the popular fallacies in destroying which statistics perhaps do their most useful work.[2] The reasons for this popular fallacy are evident to all students of the economic conditions of the Jews. As town-dwellers,

[1] *Census Bulletin No. 19*, p. 5; 1890.
[2] Joseph Jacobs, *Studies in Jewish Statistics*, p. 11; London, 1889.

and engaged to a large extent in mercantile pursuits, they are looked at by the people around them as prosperous. A large proportion is engaged in money exchange. The unsophisticated peasant in Eastern Europe, beholding the Jewish money-changer sitting in the market place behind a small desk on which a display of money in various denomination is exhibited, is convinced that he sees one of the richest men in the world. As a matter of fact many of these dealers in money are by no means prosperous, often even poor. The comparatively large number of Jews seen in the stock exchanges of Western European cities also gives an impression that all the Jews are rich.[1] If to this is added the fact that a Jew only rarely applies to a Christian for assistance, the impression that there are no poor Jews is gaining credence. Indeed, the Jews take great pride in the fact that they take care of their own poor, and in former times they always promised that under no circumstances would they permit their co-religionists to fall a burden on the community in which they lived.[2] It must also be mentioned that there are comparatively few vagrants and paupers among Jews, considering a pauper one who is able-bodied, but has lost all ambition to work for himself and his own. Among the Jews there are many poor, but they mainly consist of the sickly, the infirm, and the defective. When nearly every vestige of the traditional Jewish

[1] The participation of Jews in the stock exchanges has been very much overestimated. According to Mr. Percy M. Castello, M.P. (*Jewish Chronicle*, June 17th, 1910), there are at most 330 Jewish among 5,100 members of the Stock Exchange in London. The great American Market contains several Jews, but the Consol Market has but a single Jewish jobber, while the Home Rails Market has also a solitary Jewish operator. In continental European *Bourses* the proportion is not much higher, while in Wall Street in New York there are many Jewish jobbers, but their proportion in the Stock Exchange is not very high.

[2] When the Jews came first to New Amsterdam in 1655 they had great difficulty in obtaining permission to land. After several negotiations the Dutch West India Company wrote to Governor Stuyvesant that "after many consultations, we have decided and resolved upon a certain petition made by said Portuguese Jews, that they shall have permission to sell and to trade in New Netherland and to live and remain there, provided the poor among them shall not become a burden to the Company, or to the community, but be supported by their own nation." Similar promises were often exacted from Jews who sought refuge in European countries during the Middle Ages.

solidarity has vanished, as is the case in some communities in Western Europe, charity apparently remains, and the Jewish poor are kept from the door of the Gentile.

It can be stated, without fear of meeting competent contradiction, that there are more poor among the Jews than among the Christians in Europe. This is especially true of Eastern Europe, where they are subjected to political and economic disabilities. There, the number of Jewish poor is abnormally high. Thus, in Russia there are thousands of Jewish families who never know where they will obtain their next meal, who are never sufficiently fed, nor have a human habitation to rest their bodies at night, or adequate clothing for protection during the hard winters. A glance at conditions in the Pale of Settlement reveals privation and want not seen in any other part of Europe. The number of hungry-looking, pale, emaciated and debilitated persons met with in Wilna, Odessa, Lemberg, and Jassi is actually appalling. We concur with Jacobs, who says that if we choose to regard them as a nation, it is probable that they are the poorest of all that can claim to be civilized; and if we were to capitalize their wealth and distribute it among the twelve millions of Jews, they would dispute with any poor nation for the lowest place in the scale of wealth.

There are significant differences in the economic conditions of the Jews according to the country in which they reside. It appears that wherever they enjoy political equality with the rest of the population they are on the whole prosperous; the bulk of them is well-to-do, and the number of poor and dependent is below that observed among the people around them. On the other hand, in the Orient and in Eastern Europe, where they are subject to political and economic disabilities, they are generally poor. It seems that the degradation into which they have been submerged by the laws of those countries, while not effective in checking their increase in number, is very effective in harming them economically. The proverbial paradox of the Jew's prosperity in spite of abuse, persecution, and degradation does not hold from the standpoint of economic well-being; and limitations as to the choice of the place of residence and of occupation, education and the like, work economic havoc even among the Jews who have adapted themselves to an unfavourable *milieu* during the long centuries of residence among a hostile majority.

It is very difficult to ascertain the exact, or even the approximate, number of dependents in any community. The usual method is to determine the number of inmates of the poor and almshouses, and to add to these the number of persons who receive assistance from outdoor relief agencies, both public and private. With the Jews this would by no means give an adequate idea of the number of dependents. They only rarely, and in some communities never, enter public almshouses in Europe and America. In New York City there are very few Jews in the poorhouse, although many are poor and dependent. They do not even seek relief in the public and private non-Jewish relief agencies. If an attempt were made to ascertain the number of Jewish poor from the records of the Charity Organization Society, the Society for the Improvement of the Condition of the Poor, and similar organizations in New York City, we would be misled into believing that there are no poor Jews, because practically none have received assistance. The same is true of conditions in Germany, France, and England. Jews always apply to their own co-religionists in case of need, and their poverty can therefore be ascertained only by a study of the records of the Jewish charitable and relief societies which exist in almost every community where the sons of Jacob are in substantial number. But few of these societies, especially those in Eastern Europe, publish any reports as to their activity. However, there is an excellent report on the economic condition of the Jews in Russia, based on a special investigation made by representatives of the Jewish Colonization Association.[1] Facing immense difficulties in the attempt to determine the extent of poverty of the Jews in Russia, the authors of this work have determined to ascertain the number of Jews who

---

[1] This work was originally published in the Russian language. A French translation was issued under the title *Recueil de matériaux sur la situation économique des Israélites de Russie*, vol. i.; Paris, 1906. An English abstract of this work has been made by I. Rubinow, "On the Economic Conditions of the Jews in Russia," in *Bulletin of the Bureau of Labour*, No. 72, pp. 487-583; Washington, 1907.

SOCIAL AND ECONOMIC CONDITIONS. 363

applied for unleavened bread (*Matzos*) for Passover. Jewish communities in every city have a special fund for the purpose of providing unleavened bread for Jews during the Passover week. Inasmuch as the relief thus given is very small, it can be stated that only the very poor apply for it, and the number of destitute represented in these figures give an adequate idea of the minimum proportion of Jews who live in dire poverty. From this investigation, which was quite thorough and painstaking, it appears that 132,855 Jewish families in Russia applied during 1898 for this form of relief. Inasmuch as the total number of Jewish families in that country can be estimated, counting five persons to a family, at 709,248, it appears that 18.8 per cent.—*i.e.*, nearly one-fifth of all the Jews—were in need of charitable relief. In some provinces the proportion even exceeded twenty-five per cent. Such an appalling number of poor is not at all to be seen in any civilized community, and will hardly be given credence by the critical reader. But a study of the data obtained by the same organization about another form of relief fully confirms the above conditions. As may be conjectured, one of the most important problems of the poor in Russia is the heating of the homes during the cold winters. Some Jewish communities have special societies with the object of providing fuel for their poor co-religionists. It was found that in the small towns 18.2 per cent., in the medium-sized towns 19.4 per cent., and in the large cities 20.3 per cent. of the total Jewish population were assisted with fuel during the winter of 1898. Another confirmation of these deplorable conditions is given in an investigation made by Brodowski about the poverty of the Jews in Odessa during 1899, based on the records of the Jewish charity society.[1] During the year mentioned 8,500 Jewish families received assistance from the charity society. These families comprised 48,500 souls—*i.e.*, 32.36 per cent. of the total Jewish population of that city. That this is rather the minimum number of poor can be appreciated when it is considered that all the relief these poor creatures received consisted of either 120 to

---

[1] J. Brodowski, *Jewish Poverty in Odessa* (in Russian), Odessa, 1899. See also "Das jüdische Elend in Odessa," A. Nossig, *Jüdische Statistik*, pp. 287-292; Berlin, 1903.

180 pounds of coal to keep warm during the entire Russian winter, or forty pounds of unleavened bread to feed a family of eight persons during the Passover Week. It is understood that those who could manage in any way to get along without this pitiable relief did not apply. Brodowski estimates that there were in addition to the above about 30,000 Jews in Odessa who manage with great difficulty to obtain a daily supply of nourishment without applying for charity, and who are in constant danger of sinking lower into the category of paupers. It is his opinion that fifty per cent. of the Jews in that city live in dire poverty and privation. This is confirmed by the fact that sixty-three per cent. of their dead are buried free of charge, and another twenty per cent. have to be buried at a reduced price. It must be recalled that Odessa is one of the chief industrial cities in Russia, and that it is the largest centre for the garment industry in that country. But the wages paid there are below any in Europe, excepting perhaps Roumania. Skilled artisans receive from eight to twenty-five shillings weekly wages; the majority receive less than sixteen shillings, and female labour is much cheaper. Girls working at cigarettes, or as packers of tea, receive from eight to twenty shillings per month. The Jewish labourers at the docks, who toil at loading and unloading vessels, receive less than two shillings per day. On such wages, coupled with unsteady employment, it is not surprising that such a large proportion is destitute.

The economic conditions of the Jews in the smaller towns of Russia is even more appalling. They cannot even earn such pitiable wages as those in Odessa, because there are very few industrial activities in these small towns. Very few mills and factories are found in the Jewish Pale, and even in these few not many Jews find employment. They are left to exist on what can be derived from commerce, petty trading, and domestic industries. The result is the state of poverty which has already been spoken of. I have seen as many as three families living in one room in Warsaw and Wilna. As to how some manage to make a living the following case will show. When walking in the main street of a small town of the province of Kovno in the summer of 1905, I noticed that several Jewesses were selling herring which were sliced into small pieces. Inquiring of one of these "merchants" about her business, I elicited the following information. She is a widow, with five children to support. She buys every morning four or six herrings, and cuts each one into six or eight pieces, each of which she sells at a kopeck, or about a farthing. If she succeeds in selling a half-dozen herrings in this manner, she can manage to exist with her family. Her "standard of life" is by no means that of the kind we are accustomed to associate with paupers. She pays for the Hebrew education of her children, and is anxious to teach them also to read and write Russian, but Jews are not admitted to public schools. The "staples" in their diet are herring, potatoes, and buckwheat; of vegetables very few are consumed by the bulk of poverty-stricken people; beets, carrots, cabbage, onions, garlic, horseradish, and a few others are all called ironically "Jewish fruits" in Russia and Galicia. Conditions of misery seen in the Russian Pale can hardly be exceeded in destitution and starvation in India during a famine year.

Conditions are not much better in Galicia and Roumania. When I visited the latter country during 1907 I was struck with the low wages paid to Jewish artisans. A good tailor works for eight to sixteen shillings a week, and is compelled to support a large family on these wages. Female labour is paid about one-third of what is paid to men. While rent for dwellings is comparatively cheap, still two or even more families in one room are often seen. In Galicia conditions are even worse. It is from these regions that most of the Jewish emigration is derived. Indeed, it is difficult to find a man, woman, or child who has not at least a remote relative in the United States or England, where the majority are reputed to have become rich.

In Western Europe the economic conditions of the Jews are diametrically opposite those just detailed. In Germany, Switzerland, France, Italy, England, etc., the *native* Jews are on the whole more prosperous than the non-Jewish population, while the Jews in Eastern Europe cannot at all be compared with them from the standpoint of economic well-being. It is evident, when observing the Jews in western countries, that when the legal barriers are removed, when they are permitted to choose their place of residence, occupation, education, and the like, the poverty in which they live is not at all irretrievable. Only seventy-five years ago the social and economic conditions of the Jews in Western Europe were not superior to those observed to-day among their co-religionists in the East. Indeed, considering that there were very few skilled mechanics among them, they were even in a worse plight than the modern Jews in Russia, Poland, and Roumania. But what a change within less than a century of freedom from legal disabilities! There are very few, hardly any, poor among the Jews of Western Europe in the strict sense of the word. Most of the money raised for charity among these Jews is for the purpose of relieving the miserable conditions of their Eastern co-religionists. A visit to the Jewish relief societies of Paris, Berlin, or London shows clearly that nearly all the applicants are immigrants.

For lack of denominational statistics it is impossible to state definitely the economic conditions of the Jews in Western Europe. An exception in this respect is Germany, where the census of occupations, taken in 1895, gives some details about the Jews. The German census in its classification of occupations has a class "independent, without occupation," corresponding in part to the English term "retired," and including mostly persons who live on an income. It was found that in 1895 8.76 per cent. of the Christians, and nearly double, 16.3 per cent. of the Jews, were of this class.[1] From the income-tax statistics of Germany it also appears that the Jews are more prosperous than the Christians in Germany. In Berlin, where they constitute 4.88 per cent. of the total population, it was found in 1904 that fifteen per cent. of those who paid twenty-one marks tax annually and over,—*i.e.*, who had an income of over 1,500 marks yearly,—were Jews.[2] In Frankfort it was found that in 1900, 11.54 per cent. of the Protestants, 5.79 per cent. of the Catholics, and 32.4 per cent. of the Jews paid on an income of over 6,000 marks annually.[3] If statistics about the native Jews in England, France, Italy, Belgium, and other western countries were

---

[1] A. Ruppin, *Die Juden der Gegenwart*, p. 179; Berlin, 1905.
[2] *Zeitschrift für Demographie und Statistik der Juden*, p. 32; 1906.
[3] *Ibid.*, No. 4; 1905.

obtainable they would without any doubt show similar conditions. The Jews are economically prosperous, more so on the average than the Christians in those countries.

Speaking of economic conditions of the Jews in England and the United States, it is absolutely essential to bear in mind the distinction between the native and the immigrant. The differences in the economic and social conditions of these two classes are enormous, more so than in Continental Europe. Of the thousands of applicants for relief seen in the Jewish charitable organizations, very few are native born. Only two per cent. of the applicants of the United Hebrew Charities in New York City were born in the United States, and the experience of the relief societies in other large cities is not materially different. "Of these (the native applicants) the majority of heads of families were of the first generation. Jewish dependents who have an ancestry in the United States of more than two generations are practically unknown."[1] It is noteworthy that the so-called "pauper" element so often met with among others is very rare among the immigrant Jews in the United States. The vast majority of Jewish dependents are recruited from the diseased and defective classes, who are physically incapable of helping themselves; from among the widows, with small children to support; and also from among the aged and infirm. The able-bodied require assistance only during commercial and industrial crises. The absence of the pauper element is to be attributed to the rarity of alcoholism among them. My personal experience as physician to the United Hebrew Charities of New York City convinces me that alcoholism is a negligible quantity in the etiology of poverty and dependency among Jews. Among many thousands of applicants for relief whom I have examined, I have met with less than a dozen whose misfortune has been due directly or indirectly to an excessive consumption of alcoholic beverages. Among non-Jewish applicants for relief the proportion of persons whose descent in the social scale is due directly or indirectly to alcoholism has been estimated at twenty-five per cent., and even more.

[1] Lee K. Frankel, "Jewish Charities," *Annals of the Amer. Acad. of Polit. and Social Science*, p. 49; May, 1903.

This also is mainly the reason for the remarkable capacity for social regeneration of the Jew when the law puts no unreasonable obstacles in his way. The Western European Jews, who, but seventy-five years ago, lived in a condition of poverty and want, due to legal degradation, have recuperated within the last five decades, after their disabilities have been removed. The same process is repeated at present with the Jewish immigrants in the United States and England. The vast majority leave their native home for economic reasons, and arrive at their new home in a very poor condition. The fact that they bring less than fifteen dollars per head on the average when landing, while not necessarily proving that they are of the poorest class, because the cost of transportation is no mean sum in Eastern Europe, still goes to show that they are quite poor while setting their foot on the soil of the United States. But the social and economic metamorphosis wrought within a few years is astonishing. Their standard of life is decidedly superior to that of many other immigrants. Some may be surprised to hear that, in a large proportion of the tenements in the East Side of New York City, pianos are to be seen in the dingy rooms. We have seen in some tenement houses several homes with pianos. Excepting among the recent arrivals, most of the Jewish tenement-dwellers have fair and even good furniture in their homes. The rooms with only a few cots, a kitchen table and several cheap chairs, which are seen among the non-Jewish tenement-dwellers are uncommon among the Jews of New York. They are very ambitious, and remain in the so-called *Ghetto* on the East Side a comparatively short time, and move up town as soon as they can afford.[1] It is difficult to estimate the prosperity of the Eastern European Jewish immigrants who have come to the United States within the last thirty years. While it is true that it has been much exaggerated by many writers, still it must be acknowledged that their social and economic regeneration has been astonishing to both their friends and enemies.

---

[1] In London also the immigrant Jews move from the East End to the West End as soon as they can afford, according to testimony brought before the Royal Commission on Alien Immigration. See *Minutes of Evidence*, § 20644-58.

They undoubtedly control the garment industry of the United States, and are represented in enormous numbers in nearly all the important branches of commerce and industry, as both employers and employees. There is no doubt that sobriety and thrift are the main factors in the remarkable regeneration of the Eastern European Jew on the American soil. It is also because of these qualifications that he rarely sinks to the low level of the non-Jewish European and American slum population, with its appalling misery, resulting from drink, hereditary vice, shiftlessness, and degradation.

The social and economic conditions of the Jews are thus seen to depend on their political status. Wherever they are oppressed and legally limited in their choice of residence, occupation, and the like, they are on very low social and economic level. But soon after the barriers placed in their way by the law had been removed, as was the case in Western and Southern Europe, their social and economic conditions improve in a most astonishing manner. This capacity for regeneration is of immense importance for those who are troubled about the problem of immigration in England and the United States, and who are horrified by the thought of the invasion of the "alien pauper" and the resulting consequences. It appears that, when given the opportunity to advance himself, the Jew is not at all doomed to eternal poverty and degradation. This by no means indicates that all their poverty in the East is due to external causes. It must be mentioned, also, that wherever they assimilate— *i.e.*, adopt the language and habits and customs of the people around them—they are more or less prosperous, as is the case in Western Europe and America and Australia. On the other hand, in Eastern Europe, where they keep apart from the general population, where they differ in language, dress, manners, and habits from their non-Jewish neighbours, they are generally poor and destitute. The same Jews, after emigrating into Western countries, discarding the most separative ritualism of their religion, which is just as effective in keeping them backward as the legal restrictions, and assimilating to their new neighbours, are, on the whole, sooner or later, successful.

CHAPTER XVII.

EDUCATION OF THE JEWS IN VARIOUS COUNTRIES.

Facilities for education an important factor—Illiteracy among the immigrants—Illiteracy in Russia—Superiority of Jews in countries where the public schools are open to them—Higher education—Jews in high schools and universities—Disabilities in Russia—Preference for the study of medicine and law—Jewish students of philosophy and applied science—Languages spoken by Jews—There is no Jewish vernacular—Chaldaic displaced Hebrew at an early age—Greek, Arabic, and the Romance languages used by the Jews during the Middle Ages—Effects of Isolation—Characteristics of Jewish jargons—*Spagnuoli*—*Yiddish*—Its centre of diffusion—English displacing Yiddish—Language as a test of social contact—Alleged inability of Jews to pronounce European languages.

IT is obviously difficult, and often impossible, to determine the intelligence and education of the members of a community. It all depends on the point of view as well as the standard of intelligence which the writer on the subject has set for himself. What one observer will consider intelligent and educated another will condemn as ignorant and illiterate. This is in fact seen in many writings about the Jews. Some speak of them as lowly, ignorant, and illiterate, especially as far as the Eastern European and Oriental Jews are concerned, while others speak of the " people of the Book" as clever, cultured, well-informed, and even wise. Of course both opinions are due to bias. The fact of the matter appears to be that it all depends, just as is the case with all other civilized peoples, on the facilities they have for the education of their children, as well as on their economic condition—*i.e.*, on their ability to keep their children in school. It appears that these factors are of more significance for the Jews in Eastern Europe than for any other people. While the schools are open for all the children who want to avail themselves of a State education, the Jews are either not at all admitted, or only a small proportion are permitted to attend educational institutions, as is actually the case in Russia, Roumania, etc.

The only available test of the education of a people is the proportion of persons who can read and write. In a community where the public schools are available or even compulsory for every child this would certainly give a fair index of the education of the people, or at least of their desire for education. But the vast majority of contemporary Jews live in countries in which the public school system is not general, and even the schools which are available for the Christian population are more or less closed to the Jews, although they are obliged to pay taxes for the maintenance of schools. An excessive proportion of illiteracy among the Jews in Russia or Roumania, or in the Orient, may be due more to the lack of educational facilities than to their unwillingness to learn.

I believe that the proportion of Eastern European Jews who can read and write is best shown in the *Report of the Commissioner-General of Immigration* of the United States of America, in which definite statistics are given about the illiteracy of the immigrants of each nationality who arrived in the United States. In the Report for 1897 I find that there were admitted 149,182 Jews, 111,486 of whom were over fourteen years of age. Of the latter it was found that 31,885, or 28.6 per cent., were illiterate. It is interesting to mention in this connection that in Russia the returns of the census of 1897 showed that 61.1 per cent. of the Jews were illiterate. The difference in favour of the immigrants is due to several causes—viz., the Russian census gives the ratio of illiteracy to the total population, while the Report of the immigration authorities enumerates only those who are over fourteen years of age; among the immigrants there are also Jews from other countries, especially from Austria-Hungary, where they have all the public schools open to them. But even with this high percentage of illiteracy the Jews in Russia make a favourable showing, considering that seventy-nine per cent. of the total population of that country has been found unable to read or write; and of the Russian immigrants to the United States during 1907, 43.5 per cent. of those over fourteen years of age were illiterate.

If it is recalled that all the schools are open to the Christians, but in a measure closed to the Jews, it appears that they are even superior in this respect to the non-Jewish population. It must also be mentioned in this connection that the Eastern European Jews, like all Eastern people, are more apt to educate their boys than their girls. The fact is, that 51.6 per cent. of the Jews and 71.1 per cent. of the Jewesses were illiterate in Russia, according to the census returns.

The differences between Eastern and Western Jews in this regard is well exemplified in London, where, according to the *Annual Report of the Registrar General* for 1908, the proportion of bridegrooms who could not sign their names in the marriage register was 1.3 per cent., and of brides 1.9 per cent. But this illiteracy is practically confined to the group of Eastern Registration Districts, where a large proportion of the signatures by mark occur in the marriages of foreign Jews. The native Jews, on the other hand, rarely have illiterates in their midst.

How far the education of the Jews depends on the educational facilities offered to them can be seen from the statistics of illiteracy in other Eastern European countries. In Bulgaria, where they do not suffer from the disabilities characteristic of Russian conditions, they also have a smaller proportion of illiterates. Thus, of the persons who applied for marriage licences during 1902, it was found that 95.9 per cent. of the Jews and 78.7 per cent. of the Jewesses could read and write, which was much superior to conditions among the general population, among whom only fifty-eight per cent. of the men and only seventeen per cent. of the women were thus qualified.[1] In Servia also the Jews appear to have a smaller proportion of illiterates than the Christian population. In 1900 it was found that fifty-seven per cent. of the Jews and only twenty-one per cent. of the general population could read and write.[2] But that this superiority of the Jews is not due to any inherent thirst for knowledge is shown by the fact that the illiteracy in that country is mainly found among the peasants. In the cities fifty-five per cent. of the general public could read and write.

[1] *Zeitschrift für Demographie und Statistik der Juden*, p. 136; 1907.
[2] A. Wadler, *Zeitschrift für Demographie, etc.*, p. 170; 1906.

Further confirmation of the influence of public schools on the education of the Jews is seen from the conditions found in Galicia. In Cracow the persons who applied for marriage licences during 1901-02 showed the following percentages of illiteracy[1]:—

	Jews.		Christians.	
	Men.	Women.	Men.	Women.
1901	2.5	2.5	18.6	24.9
1902	2.2	2.2	15.1	20.6

The Jews have thus only 2.5 per cent. of illiterates as against twenty to twenty-five per cent. among the Christians in Cracow, which is also, at least partly, due to the fact that many of the Christians who married in that city were agriculturists from the country districts who came to the city to solemnize their marriages. In Budapest it was found in 1904 that 18.2 per cent. of the Jews, 23.6 per cent. of the Catholics, and eighteen per cent. of the Protestants could neither read nor write.[2] No differences are to be seen between Jews and Protestants in that city as to the percentage of illiteracy; both of these classes are superior to the Catholics.

In Western and Southern Europe there are practically no differences between Jews and Christians in this respect. But inasmuch as the Jews are generally town-dwellers, with greater facilities for education when compared with the Christians, among whom there is a very large proportion of agriculturists, it is to be expected that the former should have a smaller proportion of illiterates. This is best shown by the returns of the census of Italy, where it was found that among the Jews under fifteen years of age 39.5 per cent. of males and 41.4 per cent. of females could not read, as against 67 and 68.4 per cent. respectively among the general population. Of the adults over fifteen years of age three per cent. of men and 7.5 per cent. of the women among the Jews, and 42.6 per cent. of men and 57 per cent. of the women among the general population were illiterate. The difference is here due to the enormous percentage of illiteracy among the southern Italian peasantry. In the western countries

---

[1] A. Wadler, *ibid.*, p. 160.   [2] *Ibid.*, No. 11; 1907.

the native Jews are rarely unable to read and write, while in the United States it is well known that almost every child of Jewish parentage who is physically able attends the public school. The truant officers in New York City have less trouble with the immigrant Jews than with immigrants of other faiths. From conditions in Australasia, where the facilities for education are about the same as in the United States, we can judge as to the salutary effects a free and compulsory education has on Jewish children. The census enumerates there the population by religious confession, and the results are more or less exact. In New South Wales the census of 1901 has shown that 3.15 per cent. of the Jews and 3.81 per cent. of the Christians of fifteen years of age and over were illiterate; and in Victoria the proportion was—Jews 6.81 per cent., and general population 10.6 per cent. The advantage shown by the Jews is undoubtedly due to the fact that they are mostly town-dwellers, while many of the Christians live in outlying agricultural and mining districts where the school facilities are defective.

Algeria is an excellent example of the effects of educational facilities on the Jews. Only thirty years ago hardly any Jewish child attended a secular school, and the Alliance Israélite Universelle had great difficulty in inducing them to send their children to the Jewish schools established by this organization. Since the French Government has established a public school system, conditions have gradually changed, so that at the present a large proportion of Jews give their children a French education. It was found in 1903 that 16.75 per cent. of the French Europeans, 20.74 per cent. of the other Europeans, 6.21 per cent. of the native Mohammedans, and 26.65 per cent. of the Jews attended the *Écoles Primaires et Naturelles*. It must, however, not be concluded that the Jews in Algeria are more apt to send their children to school than the Europeans who live there. The latter are mostly colonists, who have fewer children than the native Jews. But the Jews do take better advantage of the educational facilities than the Mohammedans. Even their daughters are often sent to secular schools, which was very rare about twenty-five years ago.[1]

[1] *Annuaire Statistique de la France*, 1903. Also *Ibid.*, pp. 15-16; 1906.

We often hear of the "thirst for knowledge" of the Jews. Not only do books and articles on the children of Israel devote an unusual amount of space to discussing it, but the press and pulpit as well often remind non-Jews of this Jewish proclivity to seek knowledge, and wish that all others would emulate them. There is indeed a very large proportion of Jews who take up higher studies more or less successfully. They are represented as students in universities and high schools far more strongly than their number would warrant. Up to about one hundred years ago it was very difficult, often impossible, for a Jew to gain admission to a higher school of learning, no matter what his qualifications might have been. But since the road for higher education has been opened to them all over Europe, excepting Russia, they have flocked to these seats of learning in a number which has astonished everybody, even the Jews themselves. Thus, in Prussia, where the Jews constitute only 1.14 per cent. of the total population, they make up 8.11 per cent. of the students in the universities.[1] In Baden, the Jews have 35.93 students per 10,000 population, as against only 10.93 per 10,000 Christians in the two universities, Heidelberg and Freiburg, and in the technical high school in Karlsruhe. The Jews have thus proportionately about 3.5 times as many students as the Christians.[2] In Austria over twenty-five per cent. of the students of the universities are Jews, although they constitute less than five per cent. of the population. In 1851 there were altogether 641 Jewish students in the Austrian universities and technical high schools; since then their number has been growing, so that in 1904 there were 4,485 Jewish students. Their number has thus been increased sevenfold within fifty-three years, while the number of Christian students has hardly trebled within this period.[3] In Hungary, where the Jews constitute 4.9 per cent. of the population, they were in 1904 represented in the universities and the polytechnicum and law school to the extent of 30.27 per cent. of the total number of students, or six times as

---

[1] A. Ruppin, *Die Juden der Gegenwart*, p. 206.
[2] L. Wasserman, *Zeitschrift für Demographie und Statistik der Juden*, p. 25; 1906.
[3] J. Thon, *Die Juden in Oesterreich*, pp. 98-104; Berlin, 1907.

many, proportionately, as the non-Jews. It is difficult to state the exact number of Jewish students in American universities and high schools, because the reports of these institutions do not publish any data about the religious confession of their pupils. A private investigation was, however, made recently by Professor Morris Loeb, which gives some figures which are fairly approximate to the real number.[1] He found that 32.6 per cent. of the students in the Collegiate Division of Columbia were Jews during the session 1904-05. In the New York City College 73.7 per cent., in the New York University College 20.5 per cent., and in the Washington Square Division of this institution 19.6 per cent. were Jews. Considering that the Jewish population of New York City constitutes about 20 per cent. of the total population, it is evident that the number of Jewish students in Columbia College, and especially in the City College, is very excessive. This excess comes mostly from the poorer and middle class of Jews in the lower and upper east side of the city, a class which, among people of other faiths, only rarely sends its children to college. In the post-graduate courses the Jews are not represented in as high a percentage as in the undergraduate colleges. Only 14.7 per cent. of the post-graduate students in Columbia and 33.6 per cent. in the New York Univerity Graduate School were Jews. Perhaps the reason is that the post-graduate courses have students from all over the country, and also from foreign lands, while nearly one-half of all the Jews in the United States live in New York City. Only in Russia the number of Jewish students in univer sities and high schools is rather small. This is because they are legally barred from entering these institutions; only a small percentage of the total number of students are permitted to attend. In 1899 it was found that in the nine Russian universities 16,170 students were enrolled,

[1] The method pursued by Professor Loeb was to go over the list of students in the annual reports of the institutions, and to select those who have Jewish names as Jews. Of course, many Germans and Poles have names which can be taken for Jewish. But this is more than counterbalanced by the large number of Jews who have names suggestive of American origin. On the whole, I believe that, as an approximation, these figures are as good as can be obtained, and that they are rather below than above the real number.

1,757 of whom were Jews. They thus constituted 10.9 per cent. of the total number of students, or 3.5 per 10,000 population. When compared with conditions in the rest of Europe, where 25 to 30 per cent. of the students are Jewish, it appears that Russia has succeeded, in a great measure, in keeping them out of her own universities. But it seems that the Jews are not to be baulked. Many leave for Germany, Austria, Switzerland, France, and Belgium, where they enter the universities. According to Ruppin, there are about 3,000 Russian Jewish students in the universities of the countries just mentioned.[1] If America and England are added, the number of Russian Jews compelled to seek a higher education abroad would be found to be enormous.

It is interesting to note the kind of studies preferred by Jews. From reports of European and American universities, it is evident that medicine and law are given preference. Thus, during the session 1899-1900, the attendance in the medical departments of the Prussian universities was made up of 14.6 per cent. Jews and 85.4 Christians; in the department of jurisprudence, Jews 8.67 per cent., and Christians 91.33 per cent.[2] Recalling that the Jews constitute only slightly over one per cent. of the total population of Prussia, it is evident that they are represented in the medical department of the universities about thirteen, and in the department of jurisprudence about seven times stronger than their number would warrant. In Austria, where they constitute less than five per cent. of the total population, they furnished, in 1904, 27.1 per cent. of the medical and 18.2 per cent. of law students,[3] while in Hungary the proportion was even higher—46.77 and 27.55 per cent. respectively. In New York City the above-mentioned investigation by Professor Loeb determined that, in 1904-05, 33.8 per cent. of the medical students in Columbia, 35.1 per cent. in Cornell, 49 per cent. in the University and Bellevue, 44.5 in the Long Island College, and 48.5 per cent. in the Eclectic Medical School were Jews. Among 1,871 medical students in the

---

[1] For details, see *Zeitschr. f. Demogr. u. Statistik d. Juden*, No. 11, 1905; No. 3, 1906.
[2] A. Ruppin, *Die Juden der Gegenwart*, p. 206.
[3] J. Thon, *Zeitsch. für Demographie und Statistik der Juden*, p. 34; 1907.

above-mentioned institutions, 732, or 39 per cent. were Jews—*i.e.*, about twice as large as the ratio of the Jewish population in New York City. In several other medical schools located in Illinois, Louisiana, Massachusetts, Missouri, Ohio, and Pennsylvania, Professor Loeb calculated that 10.7 per cent. of the students were Jews. If to this should yet be added dentistry and pharmacy, the number of Jewish students in medicine and allied branches would be enormous. Similarly, in the law schools of New York City, the number of Jews is very large. During the session, 1904-05, Professor Loeb found that of the 1,931 law students enrolled in the schools of this city, 659, or 34 per cent., were Jews. The percentages were as follows:— Columbia, 26.8; New York Law School, day and evening classes, 23; University Law School, day, evening, and women's classes, 52.5. I do not know of any enumeration of the number of lawyers of Jewish faith in New York City, but it may be stated that it is very large, by far larger than their number would lead us to expect.

The preference shown by the Jews for the study of medicine is not a recent phenomenon. All through the Middle Ages we meet with many famous Jewish physicians. Many conditions have been favourable to them to excel as medical men. Their knowledge of anatomy, because of the ritual slaughter of cattle and fowl in accordance with the Jewish law, may have had some influence in this regard. But the most important factor was the discouragement of the practice of the healing art by the Christian Church, which left the field practically clear for them.[1] Several of the Popes and many kings have had Jewish physicians, who enjoyed special privileges. On the other hand, the study of jurisprudence is rather recent among the Jews. Up to their emancipation they could neither study nor practise law in any court in Europe. Even to-day it is very difficult for a Jew to be admitted to the bar in Russia or Roumania.

[1] Abrahams (*Jewish Life in the Middle Ages*, p. 236) says "the Church never reconciled itself to the reputation won by Jewish physicians, and the influence which it gave them over their patients. Efforts were constantly made to suppress these doctors, but the kings and popes themselves disobeyed the Church canons on the subject. When, however, the Christian Universities taught medicine scientifically, the Jewish and Arabian predominance died a natural death."

It must be said, however, that medicine and law are not the only professional studies in which they engage. Thus, in Austria 12.5 per cent. of all the students of the philosophical faculty and 20.2 per cent. of the technical high schools were Jews in 1904. In other words, during 1898-1902 the proportion of Jewish students per 10,000 population in Austria was 7.0 among the Christian, and 32.2 among the Jewish population.[1] In Hungary, 20.95 per cent. of the students in philosophy and 45.27 per cent. of the students in the polytechnicum in 1904 were Jews. In New York, Professor Loeb found that, in 1904-05, 12.2 per cent. of all the students in the Teachers' College, 22·5 per cent. in the University School of Pedagogy, 20.6 per cent. in the Schools of Mining, Engineering, and Chemistry of Columbia University, and 18.3 per cent. in the New York University School of Applied Science were Jews. In other countries, as in England, France, Germany, etc., the proportion of Jewish students in the departments of philosophy, applied science and arts is also very large. Indeed, it cannot be said that they are in any way one-sided in regard to studies, as has been stated by some authors. It is about the same as with their occupations. As long as they were kept out of certain trades by the guilds and by the law generally, they were compelled to confine their activities to but a few trades. To-day they are to be seen in almost every trade and occupation in which they are permitted to engage. Similarly with studies pursued by Jews. Since they are allowed to select their studies, they are met with in every department of the universities of Europe and America.

Languages spoken by Jews.—Of immense sociological importance are the languages spoken by the Jews in various countries. As a religious minority, segregated in separate parts of a city as the Mediæval Ghetto, or in separate parts of a country as the Pale of Settlement of Russia, they have often been deprived of opportunities for social intercourse with the people among whom they have found a resting-place. If in addition to their separate day of rest, their dietary laws, etc., they also spoke a foreign tongue, as was often the case, there is little wonder that they have been considered an alien element in race,

[1] *Zeitschr. f. Demograph. u. Statistik der Juden*, p. 35; 1907.

religion, traditions, and language. But, peculiar as it may appear to the uninformed, it is nevertheless a fact that there is no such language as could properly be called "Jewish." There is no language which is, or has been, the mother-tongue of the Jews in every country, or at least understood by all Jews. The language called by many writers "Hebrew," "Jewish," and the like, is either not used at all by any Jews in their daily intercourse with their co-religionists, and understood by very few Jews, as is the case with the Hebrew language; or when used as the mother-tongue by some Jews, as is the case with *Spagnuoli, Yiddish, Judæo-Persian*, etc., it is not at all a Jewish language in the strict sense of the word, as will soon be seen. At any rate, each of these dialects is not understood by all Jews, as German is understood by all Germans, or English by all Englishmen. The Yiddish-speaking Jew does not understand his Spanish-speaking co-religionist, the Persian does not understand either; while very few indeed understand Hebrew.

The use of the Hebrew language in their daily intercourse with each other was given up by the Jews long before their dispersion among the nations. Since their Babylonian captivity, and even before, Chaldaic, or East Aramaic, displaced Hebrew as a vehicle for interchange of thought. In addition to several fragments of the Bible and the Apocrypha being written in that language, the Jews at that time found it necessary to prepare a translation of the Bible into Chaldaic in order that the bulk of the Jews should be able to understand it. Ever since their dispersion the rule has been that the Jews adopted the language of the country they lived in. During the Hellenic period Greek completely displaced Hebrew and Chaldaic, and became the vernacular of the Jews. When Arabic culture spread in the countries around the Mediterranean, the Arabic tongue displaced Greek among the Jews, and for about five centuries it was their vernacular in Southern Europe. Later, when Arabic was fading away in Southern Europe, and the Jews came under the rule of the Latin-speaking peoples, such as the Spanish and the French, they adopted these languages as their mother-tongue.

Hebrew was, however, never entirely forgotten, at least

by cultured Jews. It has been, ever since their dispersion, the language of literary composition, of sacred literature, and of prayer. It was *Loshon Hakodesh*, the holy language, understood only by the minority. But there were many exceptions in this respect. The Babylonian Talmud and the Jewish literary productions of the first ten centuries of the present era were written in Syrian, or Western Aramaic, and not in pure Hebrew. The prayer-books of the modern orthodox Jews are mostly written in Hebrew, although only very few understand them. In Jewish synagogues the majority of Jews merely read their prayers without having any idea as to the exact meaning of the words.

All the facts of history show conclusively that the Jews living among various nations have always made strenuous efforts to assimilate linguistically with their neighbours of other faiths. In Rome they spoke Latin; in Spain, Arabic and later Spanish; in France, French; in Italy, Italian; in Germany, German; etc. As long as the Church and State which in mediæval times worked hand-in-hand, did not interfere, as long as they were permitted to associate freely with the general population, "they spoke Arabic, Spanish, Italian, German, or French with accuracy, though they probably employed Hebrew characters."[1]

An important change took place during the eleventh to the sixteenth centuries. Persecutions were then the order of the day. The most important and far-reaching consequences as regards the languages spoken by the Jews were the frequent expulsions to which they were subjected. Even when they were allowed to remain in a country they were only tolerated in certain parts of the city assigned to them, in the Ghetto. "There was hardly a congregation in which a large foreign element had not been forced to settle by continued expulsion from their native land." This was in itself sufficient to introduce foreign words and phrases and thus affect the language. Hebrew, of course, being the language understood by many Jews of every country, was therefore used on such occasions, and thus many Hebrew expressions were introduced into the vernacular of both the native and foreign Jews. Social ostracism, which was part and parcel of

[1] J. L. Abrahams, *Jewish Life in the Middle Ages*, p. 359.

Ghetto life, also contributed to the development of peculiar jargons. Isolation among all nations is the chief cause of the development of dialects and languages, which remain permanent once there is the proper soil, especially political unity, which was lacking among the Jews. The result is that the dialects which they thus developed were only evanescent, as I will soon show.

Thus, the peculiar Jewish dialects known as Judæo-Spanish, or *Ladino, Judæo-Persian, Judæo-German*, etc., have developed as a result of emigration and social isolation. The chief characteristics of these dialects are that foreign words are often treated as Hebrew, or Hebrew words treated as foreign words, or they are marked by the use of words which have long since disappeared from the ordinary speech of the country, or by the retention of the ancient pronunciation of the language.[1] Another peculiarity was the singular proclivity of the Jews to write these languages with Hebrew or Syriac characters in correspondence among themselves, and even in literary compositions. Arabic, Persian, even Provençal, and to a lesser extent Italian, were at various periods of Jewish history written by Jews in Hebrew script, modified by the incorporation of some Hebrew words.

The most important of these dialects, even at the present employed as the vernacular of a large number of Jews, are *Spagnuoli* and *Yiddish*. The former is known under various names, as Espanol, Spaniolic, and Ladino. It was acquired by the Jews during their long residence in Spain and when expelled from that country at the end of the fifteenth century, they continued to speak Spanish in the various places where they found a resting-place. Spanish is still the mother-tongue of a large proportion of the Jews in European Turkey, Servia, Bulgaria and Bosnia, North Africa, Palestine, etc., although more than three hundred years have passed since they have been mercilessly expelled from Spain. This Spagnuoli dialect is essentially the old Castilian language of the fourteenth and fifteenth centuries, into which many Hebrew words were incorporated by the process already mentioned, and also some Arabic expressions which they acquired from the Moors who lived with them and shared their fate in

[1] *Jewish Encyclopædia*, vol. iv., p. 557.

Spain. In addition, new words and expressions were admitted from the languages of the people among whom they have lived during the last three hundred years. In Turkey many Turkish words, in Bulgaria and Servia, many Slavonic words, and in North Africa, Arabic and Berber, and recently also French words became part and parcel of the dialect. Even to-day many Jews write Spanish by transliterating it into Hebrew characters, but occasionally also in Latin script. Quite a rich literature was developed, which is still being cultivated, and several periodicals are published in Ladino. An important peculiarity, to which I will revert later, is that up to the end of the first half of the eighteenth century nearly all the descendants of the Spanish Jews employed this language in speaking and writing. Of late it has remained the mother-tongue only of some Jews in Oriental countries, as Palestine, Turkey, Morocco, and also Servia, Bulgaria, etc. In Western and Southern Europe, as in Holland, England, France, Italy, Germany, and America, it has completely disappeared, and has been replaced by the languages of these countries.[1]

The most widespread of the Jewish dialects is *Yiddish*, which is the vernacular of about three-fifths of all modern Jews. During mediæval ages the Jews in Germany spoke the same language as the Christians in that country. When later they were restricted by law to the Ghetto, and thus deprived of the opportunity for social intercourse with the people around them, the German spoken by the Jews assumed certain characteristics which are the usual results of isolation. In addition, many Hebrew words and phrases were incorporated by the usual process already indicated. When the Jews began to emigrate during the fourteenth century from Germany into Poland and Russia they brought their German vernacular along with them. The native Jews of Eastern Europe who lived there before the invasion of their German co-religionists spoke Polish, Russian, Lithuanian, etc. It appears, however, that the German Jewish immigrants, with their superior religious culture, succeeded in imposing their language on the natives. It must be emphasized that up to the end of the

[1] For further details about Spagnuoli see A. Hebraus, "Die Spaniolische Juden," *Ost und West*, vol. x., pp. 351-367.

Middle Ages the Jews employed the archaic German vernacular of that time. A considerable number of French words found their way into the German spoken by them when persecutions in France brought a large number of Jewish immigrants from the Rhine district, where they originally spoke French. A curious feature of this linguistic chaos is the fact that while the Crusaders harassed them they were compelled to flee into Poland, where they were welcomed. There they preserved the various dialects of Northern and Southern Germany for about three hundred years, and when they returned to Germany during the seventeenth and eighteenth centuries they brought along with them the German language of the fourteenth century, modified by the inclusion of a large number of Hebrew and Slavonic words and expressions. In Germany this dialect has at present entirely disappeared among the native Jews, who now speak a pure German. But in Eastern Europe nearly all the Jews speak Yiddish, which is archaic German, but also contains a large number of Hebrew words, introduced into the dialect through the religious instruction to children, which is entirely in Hebrew. It is quite natural that Slavonic words of the peoples among whom they lived should have been introduced by social contact, as well as in business pursuits, among the Russians and Poles.

More than one-half of all the Jews in the world speak Yiddish in their daily intercourse with each other. According to the census of Russia, 97 per cent. of all the Jews in that country speak "Jewish"—*i.e.*, Yiddish. A curious feature is that 8,856 non-Jews were enumerated as Yiddish-speaking. Among them were 4,841 who professed to be Greek Orthodox, 2,129 Roman Catholics, 861 Protestants, and even 12 Yiddish-speaking Baptists and 304 Mohammedans were found in Russia. All these were converted Jews who still considered Yiddish as their mother-tongue.[1]

Another focus of Yiddish-speaking humanity is Austria, especially Galicia, where two-thirds of all the Austrian Jews live. According to the census of 1900, 34.7 per cent.

---

[1] For details see B. Goldberg, "Ueber die sprachlichen Verhaltnisse der Juden Russlands," *Zeitschrift für Demographie und Statistik der Juden*, Nos. 6 and 7; 1905.

of all the Jews spoke "German," which is practically Yiddish, especially in Galicia and Bukowina; 50.8 per cent. considered Polish as their mother-tongue; 4.7 per cent. spoke Bohemian, Moravian, and Slavonic, and 3.4 per cent. spoke Ruthenian.[1] In Hungary, where Yiddish was as widespread among the Jews as in Russia and Galicia, it appears that they are giving it up in favour of Hungarian. According to the census of 1900, 70.32 per cent. spoke Hungarian, and only 25.45 per cent. German. In Croatia 35.22 per cent. spoke Croatian, 41.92 per cent. German, and 21 per cent. Hungarian.[2] In contrast with Hungary may be mentioned Servia, where the Jews, who are mostly of Spanish origin, do not as yet part with their Spagnuoli dialect. According to the census of 1900, 80.35 per cent. of the Jews spoke this dialect, 12.56 per cent. German, and only 2.79 per cent. Servian and Slavonic.[3]

Up to the middle of the nineteenth century the Yiddish speaking Jews were concentrated in Poland, Russia, Roumania, Austria-Hungary, and parts of Germany. These Jews only rarely emigrated, and therefore Yiddish was seldom heard outside of that region. But since they began to wander away from their native lands during the last fifty years, they have carried this dialect into all parts of the globe. Over two million Eastern European Jews have within the last thirty years settled in England, France, Germany, Switzerland, Palestine, America, South Africa, and Australasia. It is natural that the first generation should employ this dialect as their vernacular. One can hear Yiddish in every part of the globe to-day; but it is not the same dialect as employed by the Jews in Russia and Austria. In the western countries new changes have taken place by the introduction of new words, expressions, and even phrases borrowed from the languages with which they came in contact among their new neighbours, and incorporated into the dialect. Thus, according to the best authority on the Yiddish language

[1] J. Thon, *Die Juden in Oesterreich*, pp. 108-112, gives details about the languages spoken by the Jews in Austria.
[2] See H. Hoppe, "Zur Statistik der Juden in Ungarn," *Zeitschr. Demogr. Statistik. der Juden*, No. 12; 1905.
[3] A. Wadler, "Die Juden in Serbien," *ibid.*, pp. 145, 168; 1906.

and literature, L. Wiener, the various Yiddish dialects in Eastern Europe contain about seventy per cent. of German, twenty per cent. of Hebrew, and ten per cent. of Slavic words.[1] In the United States and in England they have dropped a considerable number of the Slavic words, and incorporated a large number of English words into the Yiddish vocabulary. In England, North America, and Australia many words and expressions among the Yiddish-speaking inhabitants are exclusively English. Thus they practically employ no Yiddish equivalent for the words "chair," "broom," "suit," "skirt," "sleeve," "curtains," "car," "carriage," "ceiling " "floor," "picture," " rent," " roof," " potatoes," " dinner," " supper," and many others. The Yiddish equivalents for these words have practically been forgotten by the Jews who have been here for several years. Similarly in France many French words have been made part of the Yiddish dialect, and when we spoke recently to some Eastern European Jews in Paris we found a considerable proportion of Gallicisms in their Yiddish. Even in the Yiddish newspapers published in New York and London the language is so changed that Jews in Eastern Europe find it difficult and often impossible to decipher some of the English words and phrases. Most of the Slavonic words have been dropped.

Professor G. Deutsch has calculated that Linetzky, in his *Poilische Yingel*, written in the middle of the nineteenth century, used 84 per cent. German words, 13 per cent. Hebrew, and 3 per cent. Russian; Peretz, a contemporary Yiddish writer, uses 92 per cent. German, 7 per cent. Hebrew, and less than one-half per cent. Polish. The editorials of the *Yiddische Tageblatt* in New York contain even more German words, 95 per cent., over 1 per cent. Hebrew and 3 per cent. English; I. Zevin, popular Yiddish writer in New York, uses 90 per cent. German, 5 per cent. Hebrew, over 4 per cent. English, and less than 1 per cent. Russian. The Yiddish language is thus seen to undergo radical changes both in Russia and America.

As is the rule in Western Europe, the Jews in England and the United States give up Yiddish in favour of the

[1] *Jewish Encyclopædia*, vol. vii., p. 305. Also *History of Yiddish Literature*; New York, 1899.

English language. The children of the immigrants, compelled to speak to their parents in Yiddish, learn somewhat of this dialect. But they practically never speak it among themselves, especially in the street. A walk through the East End of London or the East Side of New York City will convince one that all the children speak English among themselves, excepting of course such as have been only a short time in the country. It may also be mentioned that there are very few native English or American Jews, even descendants of Eastern European immigrants, who read Yiddish, and practically none who write it. Attempts made by some parents to teach their children to read and write Yiddish meet with no response. The numerous Yiddish newspapers published in England and the United States have a very wide circulation, but only among immigrants, and are practically never read by their descendants. This process of rapid adoption of the English language within one generation is seen, not only in the United States and England, but also in Canada, South Africa, Australasia, etc.; while in France, Germany, Switzerland, Argentine, etc., the children of Jewish immigrants from Eastern Europe acquire just as quickly the French, German, or Spanish tongue respectively. This fact has a great bearing on the question of the assimilation of the Jews. Intimate social intercourse with the people around them is difficult, perhaps even impossible, when a majority speaks an alien tongue. Social isolation is furthered by difference in language at least as much as, and I believe much more than, by difference in religious confession.

This is not a recent phenomenon among the Jews. Throughout their history, with few exceptions, they have adopted the language of the people among whom they lived. As has already been mentioned, even before their dispersion in Europe Chaldaic replaced Hebrew as the vernacular of the Jews. They spoke Greek in Greece, Arabic and later Spanish in Spain, French in France, German in Germany, etc. The exceptions are noteworthy. In countries of low culture, as in Turkey, North Africa before its French occupation, in the Balkan States, etc., Jewish immigrants, coming from a more civilized country, have not adopted the language of their new hosts. In these countries they speak and write Spanish even to-day, after remaining there over three hundred years. On the other hand, in France, Germany, Italy, England, United States, etc., where many of the same Spanish Jews found refuge after their expulsion from Spain, they have given up Spagnuoli in favour of the local vernacular. The reason is simple. In Oriental countries, where the Church reigns supreme, the Jews are kept in isolation and not permitted to come into intimate social contact with their neighbours. The Jewish religious hopes, aspirations, and practices, which are so exclusive and separative among the faithful, always become intensified after each misfortune that befalls them. Especially is this the case when they are expelled from a country in which they considered themselves at home for a long period. Under such circumstances we have a union of both Jewish exclusiveness on the one hand and the Christian or Mohammedan sequestration of all who have a different religion on the other. While their "Loshen Hakodesh," or holy language, always remains sacred, still their secular vernacular which they acquired in their last place of residence also assumes a certain amount of sanctity. This was the case with German among the Polish Jews, and Spanish among the Sephardim. Only twenty-five years ago the Jews in Poland considered it a sacrilege to study any language outside of Hebrew and Yiddish. Language is, after all, a test of social contact, as has been affirmed by several ethnologists. Linguistic conditions among the Jews confirm it. Wherever they are permitted to come in social contact with their non-Jewish neighbours they soon acquire the language of the people around them.

A curious phase of the study of the ethnic characteristics of the Jews is the allegation made by some authors to the effect that they are incapable of acquiring the spoken language of any European country. This is based on the assumption that articulate speech can serve as an excellent basis for the classification of the races of mankind.[1] It is argued that differences in pronunciation observed among various peoples are due to differences in the anatomical structure of the organs of speech, and even of hearing.

[1] See H. Hale, "Language as a Test of Mental Capacity," *Trans. Royal Society of Canada;* 1891.

This is said to be the reason why negroes cannot acquire the English or Spanish language to perfection after several hundred years of sojourn among English and Spanish-speaking peoples. "Language is rooted half in the bodily and half in the mental nature of man," says Huxley. "The vocal sounds which form the raw materials of language could not be produced without a peculiar conformation of the organs of speech. The enunciation of duly accented syllables would be impossible without the nicest co-ordination of the action of the muscles which move such organs; and such co-ordination depends on the mechanism of certain portions of the nervous system. It is therefore conceivable that the structure of this highly complex speaking apparatus should determine a man's linguistic potentiality; that is to say, should enable him to use a language of one class and not of another. It is further conceivable that a particular linguistic potentiality should be inherited and become as good a race mark as any other."[1] Keane also urges as an important subject for investigation why the European languages continue to be "shibboleth" to the Jews residing for hundreds of years amid Europeans, and why no Ephraimite could frame to pronounce this very word right, whence

"so many died,
Without reprieve adjudg'd to death
For want of well pronouncing *shibboleth*."
Samson Agonistes.[2]

Andree says that no matter how readily Jews acquire the language of the country in which they live and, finally, even consider it their mother-tongue, yet most of them lack proper pronunciation, which is one of their distinguishing marks. Even the majority of the cultured Jews have a peculiar lisping or unpleasant enunciation,

---

[1] Th. Huxley, "The Aryan Question," *Nineteenth Century*, Nov., 1890.
[2] A. H. Keane, *Ethnology*, p. 194; London, 1901. Similar tests were applied on the night of the Sicilian Vespers: the French fugitives, with swords at their throats, were bidden to say the word *ciciri*, and if the *c* was pronounced as *s*—if they said *sisiri* instead of *chichiri*—they were recognized as Frenchmen and killed. Again, when the Mamelukes in Egypt exterminated the Arabs of the Said, they made them say the word *dakik* (flour) in order to ascertain whether the guttural was pronounced as a *k* or a *g*. I. Taylor, *The Origin of the Aryans*, pp. 273 *et seq*., gives other examples.

that author goes on to say, which is so characteristic that when one closes his eyes so as to be unable to see the physiognomy of the speaker, the Jew will at once be recognized. The Germans had coined a special word, "mauscheln," to designate this peculiar Jewish pronunciation, and which designates both Jewish as well as vulgar speech. This *mauscheln* is, according to Andree, an ethnic trait of the Jews which disappears no more than their physical type, and he brings evidence to the effect that it has been observed in various parts of the world.[1]

Here again we see conclusions based on observations made of conditions of the Jews before the middle of the nineteenth century, when they lived apart from the general population. Sequestrated and locked up in Ghettoes, it could not be expected that the Jews should acquire a perfect pronunciation of the language. There are differences in this respect among others, and it is by no means due to race influence. The differences between the German spoken in Berlin, Vienna, and Zurich are striking, not to mention the various dialects of Southern Germany. Then the differences in the spoken English among the inhabitants of London, Edinburgh, Dublin, New York, and Louisville are well known. Yet there are no anatomical differences in the organs of speech between the average Londoner and New Yorker. As a matter of fact, children of Boston parents raised in New York schools speak like the average New Yorker; the descendants of the English immigrants raised in the United States acquire the American pronunciation beyond recognition. The fact that the negroes do not learn to speak English or Spanish perfectly is another confirmation that language is primarily a test of social contact, while pronunciation is entirely dependent on social intimacy. There is no necessity to mention the well-known fact that the coloured population of the United States are kept at a respectable distance from the whites. A white man or woman considers it below his or her dignity to teach coloured children in the schools of the Southern States. The negroes are thus left to learn English speech from other negroes, and they thus acquire the articulation and enunciation which has been

[1] R. Andree, *Zur Volkskunde der Juden*, pp 116-118.

handed down to them—a heritage of their extreme isolation during slavery. "I do not think that there is any good ground for the supposition that an infant of any race would be unable to learn and to use, with ease, the language of any other race of men among whom it might be brought up," says Huxley. "History abundantly proves the transmission of languages from some races to others; and there is no evidence, that I know of, to show that any race is incapable of substituting a foreign idiom for its native tongue."[1] It is noteworthy that there are great differences between the Jews in various Eastern European countries in the pronunciation of the Yiddish language. Those in Lithuania cannot pronounce the letters "sh" or "zh," both of which are common in Russian, and thus a Russian can recognize a Jew by this trait. But the Polish and South Russian Jews pronounce these letters perfectly, and even the Lithuanian Jews who have been educated in Russian or English, French or American schools, pronounce these sounds excellently. In London, New York, Paris, etc., we meet with thousands of Jews who cannot pronounce the English or French *j*, *ch*, *sh*, *z*, while their children pronounce these sounds as well as Englishmen or Frenchmen.

There is one thing to be remembered in this connection. During the Middle Ages the Jews were not instructed by Christian teachers. After being segregated in Ghettoes by the iron law of Church and State, they were as far from the general population around them as if they lived across an ocean. They thus often retained the pronunciation and articulation which they learned while coming freely in contact with the Christians before the age of the Ghetto. As a result of this, the Yiddish of to-day, "in its many dialectic variations, closely follows the High German dialects of the Middle Rhine, with Frankfort for its centre."[2] Spagnuoli bears the same relation to Castilian of the fourteenth to the sixteenth centuries. Since they have been treated differently during the last seventy-five years the Jews in Germany speak a good German, those of France are not to be distinguished from the French in this regard, and the same is true of England, Italy, and the

[1] Huxley, *loc. cit.*
[2] L. Wiener, *History of Yiddish Literature*, p. 17; New York, 1899.

rest of Western Europe. In Russia the Jews who live in the Pale of Settlement, which is a remnant of the mediæval Ghetto as regards isolation from the non-Jewish population, speak a defective Russian. Those, however, who live in Moscow, St. Petersburg, Kief, etc., and have been educated in schools with Christians, speak as perfectly as any Russian, and are not all to be distinguished by the linguistic test. One has to see conditions in New York City, where so many Jews teach in the public schools, to be convinced that they can acquire the English language in the same manner as any other class of people. Then the large number of Jewish actors and actresses in various European countries, as well as in the United States, where they are represented on the stage in very large numbers, prove that they can acquire European languages and speak them with perfect pronunciation and articulation.

CHAPTER XVIII.

OCCUPATIONS.

Effects of political disabilities on the occupations pursued by Jews Influence of the Jewish religion on the choice of occupation—Preference for the garment industry—Jews in various trades—Commercial pursuits—Changes observed in the occupations of the American Jews —Jews as agriculturists in Russia, Palestine, and America.

IN addition to the usual conditions which are the determining factors in the choice of occupation among civilized people, there are special causes which have limited the Jew in his sphere of productive activity. The most important drawback he encountered in this respect during his sojourn among the nations was his political status. He could not become a farmer, because he was nowhere permitted to own or lease land. Moreover, considering his precarious position, always liable to expulsion from a country without warning, it would be dangerous for him to own land, which cannot be taken along when one must move quickly. The trade guilds of the Middle Ages were practically Christian organizations, into which persons of other faiths could not gain admission. This excluded the Jews from nearly all industrial occupations. It is thus evident that the only occupations left open for them were trading in merchandise and money. Mediæval conditions were often very favourable for them in this respect. Under the feudal system the nobility hardly ever engaged in mercantile pursuits, while of the common people very few were capable or inclined to act as middlemen. Here the Jew filled a gap in mediæval society.[1] As a wanderer

[1] Lecky (*Rationalism in Europe*, vol. ii., p. 283) says that the Jews succeeded in making themselves absolutely indispensable to the Christian community by organizing a system of exchange which was then unparalleled in Europe. Abrahams (*Jewish Life in the Middle Ages*, p. 216) points to the fact that they were the only great merchants, practically without rivals in Christian circles, until the great Italian republics reorganized themselves on a commercial basis.

all over Europe, he knew conditions of trade in various countries. He could be the best international salesman, because wherever he came he met his co-religionists, who were ready and anxious to co-operate with him. The proverbial solidarity of the Jews, which is quite natural among a religious minority, came in here in good stead. This is the most important reason why they were often invited to some countries in order to develop their commerce. Under such circumstances, they were given special privileges and immunities which were not enjoyed by the common people of Christian faith. They usually did not enjoy these privileges very long. Once they had accomplished the pioneer work of developing the commercial possibilities of the country, they were curtailed in their prerogatives, or even persecuted and expelled. Finding the Jew a formidable rival, Christian merchants organized themselves into municipal corporations or trade guilds for competition. But even this was not sufficient. The Christian guilds often applied for and secured legal decrees against the Jews, which excluded them from various trades and industries. Often nearly all occupations were in this manner barred to them, excepting money-lending and peddling. It appears that money-lending by Jews was only rarely interfered with, excepting occasionally by declaring all debts to Jews as void. The Roman Catholic Church prohibited usury. But in the Middle Ages, just as to-day, commerce could not prosper without a system of credit. The Jews, exempt from the Church prohibition, filled this gap in mediæval commerce and industry. In many cases they only acted as agents of the rich Christians while lending money; but, nevertheless, this was a peculiarly Jewish function, which has left its impress on the Jews of to-day.

That religious belief may have an influence on the selection of an occupation by most of its devoted followers is a fact which is not generally appreciated. Few understand that the Jews engage in the so-called domestic industries, such as tailoring, tobacco, etc., largely because of their religious belief. Joseph Jacobs, who was the first to point out this peculiar characteristic of the Jews, says:—
"It will be found, I think, that in a large majority of instances the occupations are determined by their religious

needs. Thus, butchers are required for *Kosher* meat, and many Jews are, therefore, found in a trade seemingly alien to their general character, and generally adopted by persons born in country neighbourhoods. Printing and bookbinding are also branches where the sacred has led to the secular applications of those industries. The opportunities given by the fruit and tobacco trades for avoiding a second Sabbath account for a large predominance of Jews in these trades. And, as a general principle, those trades are most favoured by Jews which afford them opportunities for arranging their own time for work and leaving them free for their festivals and religious duties generally. Piece work rather than time work, domestic industries rather than factory work; in fact, occupations in which they can be, to a certain extent, masters, would naturally be chosen by a people whose holidays differ from those of their neighbours. Add to this certain natural tendencies, heightened by historic causes, towards private banking and international exchange, and the chief occupations of the Jews are accounted for."[1]

The place of residence is also often a determining factor in the choice of occupation. Thus, persons living in cities only rarely engage in agricultural pursuits. Indeed, there is no instance in history showing a large number of town-dwellers to have either themselves engaged, or raised their children, as workers of the soil. It is only the rural population which perpetuates agricultural labourers, notwithstanding the heavy drain of their children who go the cities, which is counter-balanced by enormous birth-rates. The mills and factories in our large urban centres derive their workmen principally from the city population, and partly also from the excess of rural population which constantly emigrates to cities. As urban-dwellers for nearly two thousand years, the Jews could not be agriculturists for the reason just stated. Even to-day, when they are permitted in Western Europe and America to own land, they do not turn in substantial numbers to the soil, because they have been thoroughly urbanized.

When their political position changed in Western Europe at the beginning of the nineteenth century, when they were

[1] J. Jacobs, *Studies in Jewish Statistics*, pp. 24-25; London, 1891.

at last permitted to engage in any occupation they might choose, they did not change at once. For a time, by the restrictions imposed by their religion, and by force of inherited instinct, they refrained from engaging in industrial pursuits. They still continued to derive their livelihood from commerce and usury. Most writers on the social conditions of the Jews, basing their assertions on conditions observed at that period, speak even to-day of the incapability of the Jew to engage in occupations which require vigorous muscular exertion; that he is unfit for military service; that there are no Jewish sailors because they prefer trading to hard labour, etc. Gradually the Jews have changed in this respect. It cannot be said of the modern Jews that they are all merchants, traders, money-lenders, etc. There are to-day significant differences in the occupations preferred and followed by Jews according to their religious and social position. Even in Russia, where about fifty years ago very few Jews were engaged in industrial pursuits, there is to-day a large number of Jewish artisans and labourers. According to the census of 1897, 34.63 per cent. were dependent on industrial pursuits for a living. They prefer the garment industry, and 202,417 Jews and 51,670 Jewesses were actively engaged in the manufacture of wearing apparel.[1] In other words, 782,454, or one-seventh of the total number of Jews who are gainfully employed and those dependent on them, were dependent on the garment industry for subsistence. In this class are included tailors, shoemakers, hatters, cap-makers, milliners, glove-makers, etc. In the Pale of Settlement these industries are almost exclusively in the hands of Jews; 1.94 per cent. of all the Russians, 2.36 per cent. of all the Poles, 2.62 per cent. of all the Germans living in Russia were engaged in these industries,

---

[1] Tailoring appears to have been a favourite occupation of the Jews in the Middle Ages. Ramazzini in his *De morbis artificum diatriba* (2nd edition, 1703) describes in detail the deleterious effects of this occupation on the health of the Jews in Italy. According to Berliner (*Geschichte der Juden in Rom*, vol. ii., p. 86) three-fourths of the Roman Jews by the beginning of the eighteenth century were tailors. Abrahams says that tailoring became in time the most common Jewish occupation, and in the Ghettoes on a summer day the Jews might be seen seated by hundreds at their doors plying their needles and shears. (*Jewish Life in the Middle Ages*, p. 224.)

as against 15.45 per cent. of all the Jews.[1] In Roumania, where according to the census of 1899 the Jews made up less than 4.5 per cent. of the total population, an investigation of the number of artisans in 1908 showed that of 45,682 persons engaged in the garment industries 13,740 were Jews. In other words, nearly one-third of all garment-workers were of Jewish origin. Of the tailors 43 per cent., of the shoemakers 15 per cent. were Jews.[2]

Another industry in which the Jews are well represented is the preparation and sale of foods and provisions. The rigid observance of the dietary laws implies that their foods must be prepared and handled by Jews exclusively; 183,310 Jews in Russia were engaged in these industries. But most other industries have a fair proportion of Jews. The census officials enumerated in 1897 152,678 Jews in the building industry, including masons, joiners, etc.; 148,329 metal-workers, such as plumbers, tinsmiths, locksmiths, iron-workers, etc.; 139,476 in the wood industries, such as cabinetmakers, wood-turners, etc. In general, the Jews appear to have a higher proportion of artisans in certain trades than the Christians, as can be seen from the following figures, giving the number employed at certain trades per 10,000 population:—

	General Population.	Jews.
Mining	32	1
Animal products	32	142
Wood industry	87	276
Textile industry	131	185
Metal industry	134	293
Chemical industry	13	41
Distilling and brewing	10	51
Food and provisions	71	362
Tobacco industry	4	35
Printing and paper industry	13	82
Scientific instruments, watches, toys	5	42
Garments	220	1545
Building industry	150	302
Wagon and carriage industry	3	2

[1] A. Ruppin, *Die sozialen Verhältnisse der Juden in Russland*, pp. 58-66; Berlin, 1907.
[2] *Ancheta en privire la mesriasi si la carea legii pentru organizorea meseriilor*, Partea I.; Bucharest, Dec. 1908.

It appears from these figures that the Jews are represented in all these industries, excepting mining and the wagon and carriage industries, in a higher proportion than the Christian population. Russia is principally an agricultural country, and most of the Christian population depends on the soil for subsistence. The Jews, for reasons which have been already stated, do not have many agriculturists, and most of the working population is therefore industrial. The figures also confirm the observation made above, that the domestic industries are preferred by the Jews, as are those of the preparation of foods, printing, etc., for obvious reasons.

Similar conditions have been found in Austria during the census of 1900. In the garment industry there were engaged: Jews 81, and Catholics only 40 per 1,000; in the food industry: Jews 35, and Catholics only 17 per 1,000, which is again due to the exigencies of the dietary laws.[1] The prevailing opinion that the Jews never do any work which requires strong muscular exertions has many important exceptions.[2] Thus, in Russia, during the census of 1897, there were enumerated 5,254 Jews engaged in mining; in Austria the census also found a fair number of Jews similarly employed. The cab drivers, carriers, and diggers in the cities of the Pale of Settlement are mostly recruited from among the Jews; even farm hands come from these ranks, as far as the Government permits them to work outside of the cities. According to investigations made by the Jewish Colonization Association, it appears that 105,000 Jews, or two per cent. the total number in Russian Pale, are unskilled labourers.[3] In Odessa, Libau, and other harbour cities an enormous number of Jewish longshoremen are found. Many of the reports of special government commissions contain evidence showing that a large number of Jews are engaged in loading and unloading vessels. Russia is not the only country where Jews do

---

[1] J. Thon, *Die Juden in Oesterreich*, pp. 118-127.
[2] An observation made recently by the author was to the effect that many Jews worked in the shafts when the new bridges and tunnels were made in New York City. I have also met with several Jewish sailors on transatlantic steamers, not only as stewards, but even as firemen. Formerly it was said that a Jew has never been seen to work as a miner or a sailor.
[3] *Recueil de Matériaux sur la Situation Économique des Israélites de Russie*, vol. i., p. 423; Paris, 1906.

this kind of work. In Salonica, Beyruth, etc., most of the labourers at the harbour are Sephardi Jews.

In New York City many can also be seen working as labourers at new buildings, as far as such work can be procured by persons who are not of Italian origin. According to a compilation of the statistics published by the Commissioner-General of Immigration of the United States, Rubinow finds that of 330,573 Jews who were admitted during 1901-06 sixty-three per cent. were industrial workers. The list of occupations of these Jewish immigrants includes almost every kind of manual labour.[1] Considering that most of these immigrants come from Eastern Europe, the largest percentage is engaged in the garment industry, including 78,502 tailors, 13,123 shoemakers, 22,875 cabinetmakers and carpenters, 4,882 blacksmiths, 374 iron workers, 1,381 workers at metal other than iron or tin, 4,401 tinners, etc. In the United States the Jews also work at similar trades. The number of skilled artisans of Jewish faith is very large. While most of the tailoring industry is practically in Jewish hands, they are also found in nearly every kind of both skilled and unskilled labour.

Commercial Pursuits.—However, historic conditions are not so easily wiped out. The number of Jews engaged in mercantile pursuits remains greater, relatively, than among the people around them. In Russia the census of 1897 showed that 386.4 per 1,000 Jews were dependent on commerce for subsistence, as against only 39.3 among the general population. In other words, the Jews are about ten times as strongly represented among those who derive their livelihood from commercial pursuits as the Christian population. Bearing in mind that they are barred by law from Government employment, which in Russia includes railroads, steamships, postal, telegraph, and telephone service, it is amazing that 39.8 per 1,000 Jews derived their subsistence from transportation, as against only 15.4 per 1,000 among the general population. Most of these Jews are engaged in what the census calls "wagon transportation," and nearly all the cabmen and the majority engaged in wagon transportation of merchandise in the

[1] See I. M. Rubinow, "Economic Condition of the Jews in Russia," *Bulletin of the Bureau of Labour*, No. 72; Washington, 1907.

Pale are Jews. As an agricultural country Russia offers excellent opportunities for trading in agricultural products, such as grain, cattle, etc. Here the Jew comes in as very useful for the peasant. Most of the dealers and exporters of agricultural products in that country are Jews. According to the census enumeration, 887,280 Jews, or 45.35 per cent. of all the Jews dependent on commercial pursuits, are trading in this branch of commerce. But this by no means exhausts their activity in business. They are represented in nearly all commercial branches, often in a higher proportion than the Christians.

The same conditions prevail in Austria, where the Jews constitute only about one-twentieth of the total population, though, according to the census of 1900, they constitute about one-fifth of all those engaged in commerce and transportation. While only eighty-three per 1,000 of the Christian population depended on these branches for subsistence, more than five times as many Jews, 437 per 1,000, are thus engaged. In fact, nearly one-half of all the Jews depend on commerce.[1] Similarly, in Roumania it was found in 1904 that 21.1 per cent. of all the Jewish inhabitants were engaged in commercial pursuits, while they constitute only 4.55 per cent. of the population.[2] In Hungary also the census shows the same conditions.

In Western and South Europe, as well as among the native Jews in England and America, the proportion of Jews engaged in mercantile pursuits is even higher. In Italy it was found, during the census of 1899, that 50.35 per cent. of all the male Jews over fifteen years of age were engaged in commerce and transportation,[3] as against only 8.32 per cent. of the general population, and in Germany the census of 1895 showed that 54.56 per cent. of all the Jews, and only 9.18 per cent. of the Christians were actively engaged in commerce.[4] Recalling that the Jews constitute less than 1.5 per cent. of the population of Germany, it is interesting to note that 38.89 per cent. of all the persons engaged in banking, exchange

---

[1] For details see J. Thon, *Die Juden in Œsterreich*, pp. 118-128; Berlin, 1907.
[2] *Zeitschrift für Demographie und Statistik der Juden*, No. 8; 1905.
[3] *Ibid.*, No. 1.
[4] A. Ruppin, *Die Juden der Gegenwart*, p. 184.

and credit were Jews; 13.14 per cent. of all those who were engaged in the sale of manufactured goods and products, 8.16 per cent. of all traders in domestic animals, and 7.16 per cent. of all engaged in insurance were Jews.[1]

As there are no denominational statistics published by the Census Bureau, it is impossible to state the exact proportion of Jews in the United States who depend on mercantile pursuits for subsistence. A few observations can, however, be made without fear of meeting contradiction from those who are well informed on conditions. The native Jews, mostly descendants of Polish and German immigrants, are almost exclusively engaged in mercantile pursuits; those who are active industrially are engaged more in the capacity of employers that employés. Very few native and German Jewish artisans are met with in the United States. The vast majority of the Jews who are engaged in banking and money-lending are German Jews, and they have had a practical monopoly of the garment industry for the last fifty years, though lately they are being displaced by their Russian co-religionists. They are excellent speculators in Wall Street and merchants *par excellence*: many of the large department stores have been organized by them and brought to a stage of perfection. The more recent Jewish immigrants, those who came from Russia, Poland, and Austria-Hungary, have a very large proportion of artisans, just as in their native countries. Here they engage in the same trades as in their native homes. It is they who have been doing most of the garment work during the last twenty-five years, first in the capacity of employés of their German co-religionists, and later also in the capacity of employers. They have practically pushed out every other nationality from the garment industry, though of late the Italians are coming in for a good share of the more common work. They are also well represented in the wood industry, especially as carpenters, joiners, cabinetmakers, turners, etc., and also as house painters, masons, bricklayers, etc. A large number of them are ironworkers, tinsmiths and locksmiths, and also tanners, having received their training in the large tanneries of Western Russia. It can be stated that there is hardly an industry in New York City in

[1] A. Ruppin, *ibid.*, p. 193.

which many Jews are not employed, though those just enumerated seem to be preferred.

Significant changes are to be observed among the children of these immigrant Jews. Very few of them are to be met with in the garment industry, excepting as employers. Having facilities for education, they often take full advantage of the opportunities, and, after graduating at public schools, take courses in high schools and universities, and thus swell the ranks of the so-called liberal professional class. A large number of them are public school teachers, or engaged in the various departments of the city, State, and nation in the ranks of the civil service. The number of Jewish male and female school teachers is enormous in New York City, while nearly all the city departments have Jewish clerks and officials; some are actually crowded with Jews. They also make up a very large proportion of the physicians and lawyers of New York, Philadelphia, Chicago, Baltimore, etc. Of late a large number have become civil and electrical, as well as mining, engineers. In this respect the Russian Jews excel their German co-religionists very much in the United States. The latter, who at home produced so many scholars and scientists, have hardly brought forth any scholar of first magnitude, educating their children as good business men. Nearly all the scientists, artists, litterateurs, and even famous Rabbis of German Jewish origin were born and educated abroad. Their Eastern European co-religionists appear to be more idealistically inclined, and are to a great extent giving preference to education.

The vast majority of the descendants of Eastern European immigrants, however, are also merchants and manufacturers. As has already been stated, they have practically displaced their German co-religionists in the garment industry. But they are also found in almost every branch of industry. Many of the large architectural ironworks in New York City are conducted by them. In Wall Street they do not play the rôle of the German Jews, but a considerable number are found even there. Their preferred method of speculation appears to be real estate. They have practically rebuilt the East Side, replacing the old private and tenement houses with the latest models of double-deckers, and more recently have built more than their share of flats of Harlem and the Bronx. Most of them do not build for purposes of investment, but for speculation, and in their feverish way of working many have made fortunes, and again lost them within a few years. On the whole, there is to be noted a great change in the character of the Jew in this respect. After he has remained in the United States for some time, he approaches the type of mechanic, artisan, merchant, and speculator, which is characteristic of the native population. After two generations there are hardly any differences between Jews and Christians of the same social status in the United States. The Jewish parents are, as a rule, very ambitious, and do their best to equip their children with an education which fits them for higher callings than workers at the garment industry. Similar conditions have been observed in London among the Eastern European immigrants.[1]

Jews as Agriculturists.—There remains yet one important phase of the social and economic activity of the Jews to be discussed—namely, the rarity of agricultural workers among them. In their home in Palestine the Hebrews were distinctly agricultural; few persons mentioned in the Bible were following mercantile pursuits. The attempt made by Solomon to develop a merchant class was not of a lasting nature. After their dispersion they began to engage mainly in commerce, but not to the complete exclusion of farming. In States where the Government did not prevent them from owning or leasing land they did work the soil. According to Kohler, many Jews in Syria, Africa, and Arabia were engaged in agriculture. "The Jews of Southern France pursued an agricultural life, and were possessed of ships for their wine trade from the sixth to the ninth century. In Languedoc many were owners of the vineyards. In the time of Charlemagne, Jews used to farm large tracts of land for their Christian neighbours, who had no experience in agricultural life, but the legislative measures of the King, intended to render the Jews as a merchant class more serviceable to the State, prohibited this. It was especially the wine trade which

[1] See *Minutes of Evidence taken before the Royal Commission on Alien Immigration*, 1902-1903.

they controlled. In Spain, in the early Middle Ages, the Jews were the chief agriculturists, and remained such, notwithstanding the Visigoth legislation, prohibiting them from working in the field on Sunday and buying slaves and the like . . . In Portugal the Jews were always allowed to cultivate the land and produce wine, while they were forbidden to do so in Spain under Christian rulers. In Greece the Jews, during the twelfth century, were most prosperous as agriculturists. Benjamin of Tudela found Jews inhabiting the vicinity of Mount Parnassus occupied in tilling the soil. In Italy the Jews were encouraged by Pope Gregory V. to be owners of land, though he would not countenance their having Christian slaves. The Jews, first of Greece, then of Italy, devoted particular care to the culture of silk, which involved the plantation of mulberry trees, and helped toward the improvement of land and commerce."[1] When, however, during the Middle Ages the Jews were declared aliens in every Christian state, and not permitted to own or lease land, nor to own slaves, they were not allowed to live in the country and to work the soil. The result was that within the last eight centuries they could not, even if they preferred it, engage in agriculture. Being thoroughly urbanized in this manner, they now find it difficult to become farmers. It is not an impossibility, however. In Russia the Government made an attempt at the beginning of the nineteenth century to encourage them to work the soil, and thus divert them from petty trading, which was declared not beneficial for themselves nor to the people around them.[2] Many of them were given Government land, and, in addition, many privileges and immunities. Since 1881, however, no Jew is permitted to own or lease land, or even to live outside of incorporated towns and cities of the Pale of Russia, so that, even if they desired to work the soil, the law has been in their way. But of the original colonists many have remained. The

---

[1] K. Kohler, article "Agriculture," in *Jewish Encyclopædia*, vol. i, pp. 262-266.

[2] For details see *Recueil de Matériaux sur la Situation économique des Israélites de Russie*, vol. i. pp. 47-58. A good English abstract has been made by Rubinow in *Bull. of the Bureau of Labour*, No. 72, pp. 506-509.

census enumerators found in 1897, 192,721 Jews, or 3.81 per cent. of their total number in Russia, as dependent on farming, forestry, fishing, etc., for subsistence. "In the character of their agricultural methods," says Rubinow, "the kind of implements they use and the crops they grow, the Jewish peasants differ little from their Russian neighbours, from whom they received their first lessons in agriculture. Like the Russian peasants, the Jews plant more than two-thirds of their land in cereals, the rest being left for grazing purposes."[1] It must also be emphasized that the majority of these Jewish farmers till the land with their own hands, very few use hired labour. They thus proved themselves capable of pursuing agriculture when encouraged.

During the last thirty years many Russian Jewish idealists have begun a propaganda in favour of encouraging their co-religionists to till the soil, especially in their ancient home, Palestine. As a result of this agitation many Russian Jews have emigrated to Palestine and established colonies, which are reported to be quite successful, in a measure. According to the most recent enumeration made by Ruppin, about 6,500 Jews in Palestine are thus engaged in agricultural pursuits.[2] In the United States many efforts have been made by philanthropists to induce Jews to engage in agricultural pursuits. Of the various colonies established within the last thirty years, a number have proved a failure for various reasons. Nevertheless, there are at the present time many Jewish farmers in the United States. According to the most recent investigation made by the Jewish Agricultural and Industrial Aid Society,[3] there were found 3,040 Jewish farmers in the various states of the Union. The largest number was located in New Jersey, 703; in Connecticut, 575; in New York, 847; in North Dakota, 216; the rest are scattered all over the states. This number does not by far represent all the Jews in the country who till the soil. According to those in authority, it hardly represents seventy-five per cent. of their total number. In Canada also there are many Jewish farmers, and their number has

---

[1] Rubinow, *ibid.*, p. 510.
[2] *Zeitschrift für Demographie und Statistik der Juden*, p. 191; 1907.
[3] *Annual Report for the Year 1909.*

been on the increase during recent years. But there are no available statistics as to their exact number, which is much less than that in the United States.

In Argentine also there are many Jews engaged in agriculture. Most of them have been brought thither by the Jewish Colonization Association. According to the last report of that organization, there were in 1909 15,771 Jews under the care of the Baron de Hirsch Fund; they were cultivating 84,000 hectares (one hectare = 2 acres, 1 rod, 35 perches); and had 178,000 head of cattle. They work with the assistance of their adult children and of labourers, nearly all of whom are Jews. The total harvest of the winter 1907-08 amounted to 436,926 cwt. of produce, the approximate value of which was 2,185,000 dollars. On the whole they make successful farmers, especially considering that most of them have been merchants or traders in Russia and Roumania, and they again prove that the assertion that Jews are, for one reason or another, incapable of tilling the soil is without foundation.[1]

[1] For details of the Hirsch Colonies see *Rapport de l'administration centrale* of the Jewish Colonization Assn. ; Paris, 1909.

CHAPTER XIX.

CRIMINALITY.

Differences between Jews and Christians in regard to the number of arrests—Number of convictions—Effects of occupation on criminality —Criminality of the Jews in Germany, Hungary, and Holland— Differences in the nature of crimes committed by Jews and Christians —Infrequency of crimes of violence among Jews—Recent changes among the Jews in England and America.

So many contradictory statements have been made about the criminality of the Jews, most of them based on general impressions of the writers, that it must be stated at the outset that in this chapter only statistical evidence will be relied on in our consideration of the subject. Such data are available for several European countries, where the official publications take cognizance of the religious faith of the offenders. But even these figures do not afford a thorough understanding of the difference in the criminal proclivities of the Jews as compared with the Christians around them. As an illustration it may be mentioned that the total number of arrests or of convictions cannot be taken as a criterion, because the Jews would in most cases appear in a more favourable light than may actually be the case. The large number of arrests and convictions for drunkenness observed among Christians is altogether lacking among the Jews. On the other hand, in some places, as in the large cities of the United States and England, where many Jews are engaged as pedlars and street vendors, many are often arrested and convicted for violation of city ordinances, such as selling in the streets without a licence or for obstructing traffic. Here it will appear that the Jews are more liable to arrest and conviction than others, although the transgressions with which they are charged are trivial and not essentially anti-social. Similarly, violations of the Sunday laws of some states will more often be committed by Jews for obvious reasons, but this will not make them a criminal element of the community in the strict sense of the word. It must also be added that in certain countries the Jews are at a disadvantage as regards the punishment meted out for transgressions of the law. In Russia and in Roumania a Jew is more liable to arrest and to conviction to a long term of penal servitude than a Christian. This is especially true in respect to political offences, which are dealt with by the Russian authorities more severely in cases in which Jews are the culprits. The result is that the number of Jews confined in penal institutions may appear larger than their real criminal records would warrant.

The Jews have always taken great pride in the reputation they have acquired as being law-abiding citizens of the communities in which they live, and that comparatively few of their co-religionists find their way into prison. Statistics of crime in various countries seem to confirm the assertion that the Jews are less likely than the Christians to get into conflict with the law. Thus, in Germany during the four years 1899-1902 the average annual number of convictions was 78.87 per 10,000 Jews and 86 per 10,000 Christians;[1] in Holland during 1898-1902 the number of convictions per 10,000 was—Christians 29.78, and Jews 18.27;[2] in Austria, Jews 107.4, and Christians 134.8 per 100,000.[3] On the other hand, in Russia the number of persons confined in prisons was as follows:—[4]

	Men.	Women.					
Russians	19	2	per 1,000 persons over 10 years of age.				
Poles	23	5	,,	,,	,,	,,	,,
Letto-Lithuanians	17	2	,,	,,	,,	,,	,,
Jews	22	2	,,	,,	,,	,,	,,

The larger number of Jews and Poles in Russian prisons is the result of their intense participation in the revolution-

---

[1] *Zeitschr. f. Demogr. u. Statist. d. Juden*, No. 1; 1905. Blau (*ibid.*, pp. 49-54, 1909) gives detailed figures for 1903-1906, which do not materially differ from the above.
[2] *Ibid.*, No. 2.
[3] *Ibid.*, p. 6; 1906.
[4] R. Weinberg, "Psychische Degeneration Kriminalität und Rasse," *Monatschr. f. Kriminal Psychologie*; February-March, 1906.

ary movement. If a census of the prison population were taken to-day, it would be found that there are even more Jews imprisoned, because of late there have been arrests and summary convictions of Jewish political offenders in appalling numbers. As will soon be evident, excluding political prisoners, the proportion of Jewish offenders in Russia is smaller than of prisoners of other religious denominations. In the United States the relative number of Jewish prisoners appear to be less than of the general population. Bushee's investigations in Boston lead him to believe that they are more law-abiding than other immigrants, and even the native Jews are less liable to get into conflict with the law than others.[1] An investigation made by the Commissioner-General of Immigration has shown that 559 alien Jews were confined in penal institutions of the United States, constituting 6.5 per cent. of all the aliens confined in prisons. Considering that over ten per cent. of the aliens admitted into the United States are Jewish, it appears that there are less Jewish prisoners than of other immigrants. Similarly, the reports of the Boards of Magistrates of New York, Philadelphia, Boston, Chicago, etc., show that the number of Jewish offenders brought before them is less than their proportion in the general population. Of course it must be recalled that the number of "drunks" is practically *nil* among the Jews, but on the other hand a larger number get into trouble for peddling without a licence, for obstructing traffic, for violation of the Sunday laws, and similar insignificant offences. The experience of the police courts in London is about the same as in New York. Evidence presented before the Royal Alien Immigration Commission was to this effect. The report of the United Synagogue shows that during the six years ending 1909 there has been a very material diminution in Jewish criminality in London. In 1904 the number of Jews and Jewesses imprisoned was 717, but this number decreased steadily, reaching 433 in 1909—*i.e.*, there was a decrease of forty per cent. Jewesses were singularly rare in prisons, and not one remained in Holloway on December 31st, 1909. For a population of

[1] F. A. Bushee, "Ethnic Factors in the Population of Boston," *Publical. American Economic Association*, No. 2, vol. ix. pp. 98-121, Third Series; New York, 1903.

over 150,000, 433 in prison shows a rather low rate of criminality, and it is noteworthy that the terms of imprisonment inflicted were mostly short, indicating that the offences committed were not as a rule of a serious character.[1]

A considerable literature has been produced within the last fifty years on the subject of the criminology of the Jews. Most of the articles and pamphlets are, however, of no scientific value, because they are either apologetic, prepared for the purpose of showing that the Jew has an advantage over others in this respect, or they are anti-Semitic, showing that the Jew is a dangerous member of a community. It is a matter of course that friends of the Jews are not slow to point to such figures as those just cited, showing that the Jews have a slighter proclivity to act in an anti-social manner, as confirmed by the lesser number of Jews sentenced for offences against the law and the smaller proportion of Jews in penal institutions. On the other hand, anti-Semites have maintained that the Jew is very clever, and by various tricks succeeds in keeping out of the clutches of the law, while the unsophisticated "Aryan" gets into trouble as soon as he commits the least offence. As regards certain crimes, it is shown that the Jew is more liable to get into conflict with the law. Many authors have even been inclined to attribute the Jews' alleged shortcomings in this regard to race influence, and consequently as beyond redemption by environment, education, and the like. He is therefore a dangerous element in a European community.

The subject can best be studied by a consideration of the kinds of crimes for which Jews and Christians are convicted in countries where the official publications classify the population by religious faith. It must be borne in mind that evidence is necessary for a long number of years, otherwise the chance element may enter to large extent. The factors of place of residence, occupation, education, and the like are to be considered in connection with the kinds of crimes, because each of these has an immense influence. A good illustration is the violation of the game and fishing laws of Germany. During the four years 1899-1902, only one Jew was annually con-

[1] *Jewish Chronicle*, March 11th, 1910.

victed for evading this law, as against 5,695 Christians convicted for this offence. Relatively it appears that, per million, there were 2 Jews and 102 Christians convicted for the violation of this law. But this by no means indicated that the Jews are so law-abiding as to carefully obey the game and fishing laws. The fact of the matter is that very few Jews indulge in the sports or derive their livelihood from fishing and hunting. On the other hand, we find that convictions for fraudulent bankruptcy in Germany during 1899-1904 were among Jews 1.4, and among Christians 0.2 per 100,000—*i.e.*, seven times more frequent among Jews than among Christians.[1] But when we learn in this connection that of the persons who are engaged in the money and credit business in Germany 38.89 per cent. were Jews, although they only constitute a little over one per cent. of the total population, we have a reason for the larger number of failures among the Jews. It must be borne in mind that agricultural labourers, factory workers, and artisans are not as a rule liable to fail in business. All this indicates that, considering the large proportion of Jews engaged in banking and in commercial pursuits, there is little wonder that a larger number of failures are shown among them. Only by comparing the number of failures among all the Christians engaged in financial and commercial pursuits, with a similar class of Jews, can we determine which class is more unscrupulous in its dealings. Business men cannot be compared with farmers and labourers in this respect.

Uniformity of political and social conditions for centuries have been effective in determining to a certain extent the choice of occupations of the Jews. As has already been shown, they have everywhere a large number of persons

[1] To dispel the idea that bankruptcy is a peculiarly Jewish crime, only rarely committed by "Aryans," it is only necessary to mention that during 1899-1906 there were convicted for fraudulent bankruptcy 11 Jews and 192 Christians. In cases like this the absolute figures are often to be preferred to the relative. Proportionally it appears that Christians hardly ever commit transgressions of this kind. But, dealing with such small numbers, we must be careful. While among a population consisting of ninety-nine per cent. of Christians and one per cent. of Jews a few more Christian bankrupts will not show an excessive relative rate of criminality, a couple more of Jewish bankrupts will make it appear that they are the only ones who are committing this kind of crime.

engaged in commercial pursuits. It has also been shown that they are everywhere thoroughly urbanized, and as such have all the social attributes of the city population. The result is that, with slight variations due to special local causes, the criminology of the Jews is about the same in every European country and in America. This is, however, difficult to demonstrate, because the laws, and particularly the zeal which the police and judiciary display in suppressing lawlessness, are not the same in every country. There are no crimes which can be called political in the greater part of Western Europe and in America, while in Russia, where nearly one-half of all the Jews live, such offences are most zealously prosecuted. Even specific crimes are treated differently in different countries, and any attempt to make comparisons will meet with failure immediately upon attempting to adjust the terminology. I will therefore simply take the classifications of crime adopted in three European countries as a basis of comparison, and consider them as types of Jewish criminality. Germany, with its excellent official publications on the subject, may serve as an illustration of conditions in Western Europe, and Hungary of conditions in Eastern Europe. Divergencies from these types of criminality shown in other countries will have to be explained in accordance with special causes.

The following figures show the proportion per 100,000 population of persons convicted for the mentioned classes of offences during 1899-1902:—

	Jews.	Christians.
Crimes against the State, public order and religion	221.7	136.4
Crimes against the person	265.5	373.1
Crimes against property	299.1	348.1
Crimes in public office	2.4	2.4

It appears from these figures that the Jews are more often convicted for transgressions against the State, public order and religion, while for crimes against the person and against property they are less often punished. It is interesting to point out some of the specific crimes which are included in these four mentioned classes in order to gain a more comprehensive understanding of the differences in criminality between Jews and Christians in

Germany. Some of the offences in the first group are the following:—

	Jews.	Christians.
Treason, lese majesté, etc.	0.3	0.6
Resistance against the State authorities	9.7	33.4
Violations of the Sunday laws	90.7	12.7
Violations of the trade ordinances	44.7	21.0
Disturbing the peace of the home	22.3	40.5
Other disturbances of public order	7.9	4.0
For evading military duty	38.4	17.1

It is seen from these figures that the Jews are especially often convicted for violations of the Sunday law. Considering that many keep the Sabbath and are not inclined to take two holidays during the week, and also that many Jews are small traders, just the class tempted to make some sales during hours legally set apart for rest, there is no surprise that they are often found guilty of this offence. For the same reasons we find that there are also more Jews liable to take the risks involved in violations of the trade ordinances, which agriculturists and artisans are not at all in a position to do. Because Jews are more liable to emigrate there are more evasions of military conscription among them. In addition, it must be mentioned that Jews as a class cannot see any bright prospects for themselves in a military career in Germany, and there is little wonder that many see fit to evade it. On the other hand, disorderly conduct, or disturbing the peace of the home, is less often punished among the Jews than among the Christians. There is no doubt that the rarity of alcoholism is the main reason.

Crimes against the person, for which the Jews are less often convicted, include primarily crimes of violence. The ratio of murder, homicide, manslaughter and infanticide is four to one, when Christians are compared with Jews. Assault among Christians was also 228.3 and among Jews only 94.6 per 100,000, while duelling was more than twice as often punished among Jews as among Christians. Perhaps the reason for this is the fact that there are comparatively more Jewish than Christian students in the universities, where differences of opinion are, in Germany, often settled in this manner. Slander is another crime for which Jews are more often punished than Christians. I do not think that their alleged excitable temperament is to be blamed for this shortcoming. It appears to me that the comparatively large proportion of Jews engaged in journalism and often sued for libel, and also the large number of petty traders who will stop at nothing when trying to promote their business, amply explains it. Indeed, slander appears to be more often punished among business men in other countries, where the Jewish element is insignificant.[1]

Among the crimes against property, burglary and larceny are less frequently a cause for conviction among Jews than among Christians. The proportion stands as 64.9 among Jews and 175.4 among the latter, and the same is true of other crimes consisting in the violent appropriation of property which belongs to others. The case is different with fraud, forgery, embezzlement, bankruptcy, etc. During the four years mentioned there were convicted annually 82 per 100,000 Jews for fraud, as against only 43.6 per 100,000 Christians; for forgery the ratio was Jews 21.1, and Christians 9.9 per 100,000; fraudulent bankruptcy, Jews 1.4, and Christians 0.2; simple bankruptcy, Jews 18.9, and Christians 1.1; and other offences relating to bankruptcy, Jews 1.2, and Christians 0.2 per 100,000. To these crimes may also be added offences in dealings with lotteries and other games of chance, for which Jews were convicted, 9.4, and Christians only 2.6, while convictions for usury were 0.04 among the Jews and 0.5 among the Christians. On the other hand, "damaging property" is more often a cause for conviction of Christians, 33.9, than of Jews, 7.3 per 100,000. Other dangerous crimes, such as arson, malicious mischief, etc., also are more often committed by Christians than by Jews. The convictions were 5.8 among the former and only 2.0 among the latter, while the reverse is true of crimes in connection with adulteration of food and evasions of the laws regulating the sale of diseased animals and meats, which is explained by the fact that,

[1] That the larger number of convictions for slander is not due altogether to their excitable temperament is confirmed by the following figures:— In Germany, convictions for slander were per 10,000 as follows: Merchants 49.3, employers in industrial pursuits 27.8, other occupations 20, domestic servants 9.8, and farmers only 2.4 See Prinzig, "Soziale Factoren der Kriminalitat," *Zeitschr. d. gesamt. Strafrechts-wissenschaft*, vol. xxii., p. 551.

constituting one per cent. of the population, they made up 8.16 per cent. of all who deal with domestic animals.

Conditions are about the same in other countries where many Jews live. From Thon's compilation of the official Hungarian records of crimes committed during 1904 it appears that Christians are more often convicted for the following offences[1]:—

Manslaughter	10 5	times more often than Jews.
Robbery	9.0	,, ,,
Homicide	7	
Assault	6.3	
Arson	4.83	,,
Disturbance of the peace of the home	2. 8	
Violence against authorities	2. 6	
Larceny	1 7	
Crimes against morality	1.71	
Receiving stolen goods	1.30	,, ,,

For the most violent crimes, such as premeditated murder and infanticide, no Jews at all were convicted. But there are crimes for which they are more often punished. Some are the following:—

Bankruptcy	62.50	times more often than Christians.
Duelling	11.10	,, ,,
Usury	4.40	,,
Fraud	4.02	,,
Perjury	4.00	
Forgery	1.66	
Slander	1.39	
Counterfeiting	1.15	

Similar statistics are available for other countries, especially Austria,[2] Russia,[3] and Holland.[4]

It appears from all these figures that up to a certain point the criminality of the Jews is about the same in every country. They are less liable to commit crimes of violence, and also certain crimes against property, such as larceny, burglary, etc., while crimes against property

[1] J. Thon, "Die Kriminalität der Christen und Juden in Ungarn im Jahre, 1904," *Zeitschr. Demographie und Statistik der Juden*, pp. 104-107; 1907.
[2] See J. Thon, "Kriminalität der Christen und Juden in Oesterreich," *ibid.*, No. 1; 1906.
[3] P. Kovalevsky, *La psychologie criminelle*, pp. 21, *et seq.*; Paris, 1903.
[4] *Zeitschr. Dem. Statistik d Juden*, p. 190; 1907.

committed through fraud, forgery, bankruptcy, etc., and also slander, are more often committed by Jews than by the people around them. Ruppin thus generalized on this point: "The differences in the criminality of the Jews as compared with Christians can be summarized as follows: *The Christians commit crimes with their hands, while the Jews use their reason for these evil purposes.*"[1] The Jewish immigrants to England and the United States show the same tendency. Crimes of violence have been rare among them, although a change, to be noticed among their descendants in America, will soon be mentioned. Testimony given before the Royal Commission on Alien Immigration in England shows that in London the immigrant Jews are only rarely brought to courts for crimes against the person and against property. Certain parts of the East End, which were formerly the most dangerous in London, where the display of a shilling at night endangered the person of its owner, and where the whole day long there were constant brawls and fights among drunken men and women, have actually been pacified since the Jews have displaced the natives of the district. The police have very little trouble with the present inhabitants.[2]

The chief annoyance these immigrants are apt to give the London police is their aptitude for street vending and their passion for gambling. The same conditions are observed among the Jews in the United States. In New York City certain parts of the lower East Side, like Water, Cherry, and neighbouring streets, were quite dangerous three decades ago. The police found it difficult and hazardous to preserve order in that neighbourhood, where brawls and fights were the rule and not the exception. To-day this is one of the most peaceful districts in the city. The occasional robberies and assaults, which the police of that district have to deal with, are mostly committed by non-Jews. One of the chief characteristics of this district is the small number of liquor shops, but gambling resorts are perhaps more numerous than in any

---

[1] A. Ruppin, *Die Juden der Gegenwart*, p. 233.
[2] See *Minutes of Evidence taken before the Royal Commission on Alien Immigration.* Also *Report on the Volume and Effects of Recent Immigration from Eastern Europe into the United Kingdom.*

other part of the city. It appears, however, that an important change in the character of the people of that neighbourhood is taking place, especially with their descendants. While about thirty years ago it was practically unknown that a Jew should commit murder, several Jews have been punished within the last fifteen years for this crime. Crimes of violence, such as assault and battery, are becoming more and more common among the native Jews of the United States. This may be due to either the increase in the consumption of alcoholic beverages or the acquisition of the knowledge of the importance of physical force in the struggle for existence, both of which they have learned from their American neighbours. The number of excellent prize fighters which are met with among the descendants of the Jewish immigrants shows that they have of late begun to cultivate their muscles, which have been neglected for centuries. The gymnasiums in the various large cities also have a very large proportion of Jewish patrons. This gives them the power to exercise brute force when occasion arises, and those of criminal tendencies apply it for evil purposes. New York Jews are not unique in this respect. It appears from the figures reproduced that in Amsterdam also the Jews are apt to commit crimes of violence; 18.7 per cent. of all the Jews convicted during 1901-04 were brought to justice for this sort of offences, as against only 15.2 per cent. among the general population. This has been explained as due to the fact that the majority of the Jews in that city are artisans, working at the diamond industry, and are not averse to the abuse of alcoholic beverages. Among such persons differences are often settled by fights and brawls.[1] In Germany, Austria, and Hungary, where these crimes are rare among the Jews, it may be due to the fact that there is a smaller proportion of artisans and labourers, and a larger proportion of merchants among them. It is also significant that the proportion of Jews in Amsterdam who were convicted for fraud was smaller than among the Christians, 1.7 per cent. among the former and 1.9 per cent. among the latter. This is the exact opposite of conditions in Germany, Austria, and Hungary. It again confirms the influence of occupation on criminality. Russia

[1] *Zeitschr. Demogr. u. Statis. d. Juden*, p. 190; 1907.

offers an excellent illustration on the influence of external causes on the criminality of the Jews. In all other countries Jewish vagrants are very rarely seen. The well-known type of tramp is seldom a son of Jacob. Still, in the statistics of convictions in Russia given in an official compilation we find the following percentages of convictions for " vagrancy and violation of the laws concerning passports":—Jews 6.5, Greek Orthodox 4.5, Protestants 3.7, Catholics 3.1, Mohammedans 2.6, and followers of various sects 1.8.[1] This by no means indicates that there are more Jewish tramps and vagabonds in Russia than of other faiths. In fact it is well known that a Jewish tramp is very rare in that country. The large number of convictions for vagrancy is merely due to the limitation of the rights of residence of Jews to the Pale of Settlement, and any Jew discovered outside of the Pale without special permission is arrested and transported back to his native city as a vagrant. Thousands of well-to-do Jews are thus annually treated as vagabonds.

The criminology of the Jews, inasmuch as it differs from conditions among others, can be summarized as caused by the special conditions under which they live. The differences are mainly due to the fact that they are town-dwellers, whose chief occupations are commerce, industry, and finance, and in some countries to their political disabilities. Discounting these social differences between Jews and the people around them, there is hardly any difference in the criminology of Jews as compared with Christians. One author has recently proven mathematically that most of the phenomena under consideration, at least as far as concerns the Jews in Germany and Austria, are due to the fact that they have such a large proportion of merchants and traders.[2] The same could be demonstrated for other countries by the application of the same method of study, and would prove one of the most valuable contributions to the subject of the influence of the *milieu* on criminality.

[1] *Itogi russkoĭ ugolovnoi statistiki za 120 liet*, p. 167-8; St. Petersburg.
[2] See R. Wassermann, *Beruf, Konfession und Verbrechen*; Munich, 1907.

CHAPTER XX.

POLITICAL CONDITIONS OF MODERN JEWS.

Proportion of emancipated Jews—Effects of the union of the Church and State on the political conditions of the Jews at various periods of their history—Political status in ancient Greece and Rome—Effects of the spread of Christianity—Effects of the separative tenets of Judaism—Aims of the Mediæval legislation against the Jews—Political condition of the Jews in Roumania—Conditions in Russia—Summary of restrictions imposed on the Jews by the Russian laws—Causes of Russian persecutions—Political conditions of the Jews in Western countries—First admission to citizenship in France—Emancipation in England, in Holland, Austria, Germany, Italy, Switzerland, etc.—Analogy between conditions of the Jews in Russia and Roumania and those in Mediæval ages—General effects of the recent political disabilities—Migrations of modern Jews—The United States the point of destination of the vast majority of the Jewish immigrants.

FEW in Western Europe and America realize that less than one-half of the total number of contemporary Jews enjoy the civic and political rights of the non-Jewish inhabitants of the countries in which they live. Only England, France, Italy, Germany, Austria-Hungary, Holland, Belgium, Switzerland, Scandinavia, Servia, and Bulgaria, as well as America and Australasia, consider the Jews citizens more or less on an equal basis with the Christian population. We find that of the twelve million Jews in the world only five millions, a little over forty per cent., can be considered in that category. The rest, sixty per cent. of all the Jews, are to-day being treated by the nations among which they live as aliens, and, in some countries, as even beyond the law.

A study of the history of European legislation concerning the Jews shows that during the last eighteen hundred years the most important factor in determining their legal status in a given country has been the relation of the Church to the State. In countries where the Church has been part and parcel of the machinery of the State the fate of the Jews has been more or less deplorable, while wherever the Church has been divorced from the State the Jews have enjoyed some degree of civic and political liberty. "All the Mediæval States were moulded by the Church," says Bernard Lazare. "In their essence, in their very existence, they were permeated with the ideas and doctrines of Catholicism. The Christian religion gave to the numerous tribes which were segregating into nations that unity which they lacked."[1] The Jews who would not adopt the prevailing religion placed themselves on an equal basis with foreigners. The same is true to-day of the Christians and Jews in Mohammedan countries—Turkey, Persia, Morocco, etc.—where those who are not followers of the State religion are considered aliens and enemies of the social order. In Morocco the natives cannot imagine a citizen who is a follower of any but the dominant faith. Similarly the Mediæval European could not conceive a citizen who denied the divinity of Christ, even one who denied the authority of the Pope, as was the case with the Protestants.

During the first centuries of the present era the Jews, barring some insignificant exceptions, were politically treated on a level with the rest of the population. In fact, while in pre-Christian Rome and Greece they were opposed on account of their monotheism, when Christianity began to spread the Pagans treated both the Jews and the early Christians with the same suspicion as aliens— as opponents of the prevailing order. Under Caracalla, 211-217, they were full-fledged Roman citizens, enjoying all political and civic rights, even holding public office. But inasmuch as their dietary laws prohibited them from eating food prepared by non-Jews, and the obligations of the Sabbath precluded their service in the army, they as a rule abstained from military service. But with the spread of Christianity, after the Emperor Constantine yielded to that religion, the conditions of the Jews changed. On the one hand, the Jewish religion sought separation from Christian and Pagan, and exerted its utmost to keep apart the holy seed from those who believed differently; on the other hand, the Church, being in its formative stage,

[1] Bernard Lazare, *L'Antisémitisme, son Histoire et ses Causes*, chap. v.; Paris, 1892.

welcomed this separativeness of the Jews, and promulgated laws with the object of preventing Judaizing, which was not infrequent in those days. On the whole, the Jews also welcomed separation, but though originally granted as a special privilege, later it became a terrible burden. "During the first seven centuries of the Christian era, anti-Judaism originated exclusively from religious causes, and was led only by the clergy," says Bernard Lazare. "One must not be misled by evidences of popular excesses and legislative repression; they were never spontaneous, but were always inspired by bishops, priests, or monks. It was only in the eighth century that social causes supervened over the religious causes, and it was only after the eighth century that real persecution of the Jews began to manifest itself. This coincides with the universal spread of Catholicism."[1] A study of the history of the Jews in Spain, France, Italy, etc., shows that their fate depended mainly on the influence exerted by the Church on the State. As long as the State was independent of the Church they enjoyed political rights and often even greater privileges than the bulk of the non-Jewish population. The origin of the Ghetto was, in fact, Jewish. Before Christendom made it compulsory the Jews themselves preferred to live in separate parts of the cities. This was not due to the alleged clannish proclivities of the Jews, but was the best way of following their religious precepts, of preparing food, especially meat, in accordance with the dietary laws, of being near the synagogue where they could pray three times a day, etc. Indeed, as Abrahams well says, "the Ghetto was rather a privilege than a disability, and sometimes was claimed by the Jews as a right when its demolition was threatened."[2] But later Christian States began to enforce that isolation by various legal decrees. The seventy-sixth paragraph of the decisions arrived at by the Cortes of Toledo in 1480, held after the union of the crowns of Aragon and Castile, opens with a clause which proves that up to that date the attempt to isolate the Jews had utterly failed. "As great injury and inconvenience results from the constant society of Jews and Moors being intermixed with Christians, we

[1] Bernard Lazare, *ibid.*, chap. iv.
[2] Abrahams, *Jewish Life in the Middle Ages*, p. 65; London, 1896.

ordain and command that all Jews and Moors of every city, town, and place in these our kingdoms shall have their distinct Jewries and Moories by themselves, and not reside intermixed with Christians, nor have enclosures together with them, etc."[1]

As has been pointed out by Scherer, the legislation concerning the Jews in mediæval ages was mainly based on two different conceptions of the civic function of those who were not of the dominant faith. The Jews, followers of an alien faith, opposed to the established Church and State, must be suppressed in order to prevent them from gaining converts to their religion. They must be kept apart from the general population, segregated in separate quarters, and their civil rights must be restricted, though their life, property, and liberty must be protected to some extent. This principle, traces of which are perceptible in heathen Rome, permeates the Christian-Roman, Germanic-Roman, and Mohammedan systems of law. The second basic principle of mediæval law concerning the Jews has its foundation in the conception that the Jews are members of a foreign nation, and must accordingly be treated as aliens.[2] Early Teutonic law held that foreigners did not share in the rights accorded by the nation to its members; they might at any time be expelled from the country in which they had settled, and their property, which was regarded as belonging not to them but to the sovereign, might be taken away from them. Rights were secured by them only through grants from the sovereign, and were limited by such grants. Such were the principles of law applied to the Jews in Germany, in the Carolingian empire, in most portions of Austria, and in Aragon, Castile, Portugal, England, France, and South Italy till the thirteenth or fourteenth century.

The only two countries in Europe in which similar treatment is being accorded to the Jews of to-day are Russia and Roumania. In the Orient, in Persia, and Morocco the Ghetto is as well an institution at the present as it was in Mediæval Europe. In Europe, Roumania alone treats her

---

[1] Abrahams, *ibid.*, p. 66.
[2] J. E. Scherer, *Die Rechtsverhältnisse der Juden in den Deutsch-Oesterreichischen Landern*; Leipsic, 1901. Cf. *Jewish Encyclopædia*, vol. iv., p. 609.

266,000 Jews as aliens. The only difference between the mediæval way of considering Jews aliens and the modern way adopted by Roumania is this: Mediæval statesmen candidly stated that the reason why the Jews are discriminated against was their refusal to adopt the dominant faith, while in a modern constitutional government inhabitants cannot be discriminated against because of their creed, especially when the basic principle of the constitution has been framed and guaranteed by the "Powers," as was the case with the Roumanian Constitution. With chicanery characteristic of Oriental statesmen, the Government of Roumania went around the Treaty of Berlin by declaring all the Jews aliens and framing laws against all those who were not citizens. The ridiculousness of the laws discriminating against the Jews in Roumania is evident when it is realized that they have all the duties of citizens without enjoying any of their rights and privileges. They are not only taxed excessively when compared with the Christian population, but, though "aliens," they are compelled to serve in the national army just as all other inhabitants, excepting that they cannot rise from the ranks under any circumstances. This injustice has been perpetrated by classifying the Jews as "aliens not subject to alien protection" (*Nesupusi nici unei protectiuni*). All those who cannot prove that they have to serve a foreign state must, on reaching twenty years of age, enlist in the army. But after his service, no matter with what distinction, the Jew, in common with his co-religionists, remains an "alien." He must not live in the rural districts, nor can he own land outside of towns or work as an agricultural labourer. The humour of the situation is that whenever the Jewish problem is discussed in the Parliament of that country some of the deputies point with disdain at the Jews who refrain from working on the soil. The Jew in Roumania cannot vote for public office, nor hold a position in the civil service. All the liberal professions are closed to him; he cannot even open a pharmacy; his presence in the Chamber of Commerce is not tolerated, though his main support is derived from commercial pursuits, and he has done much for the commercial and industrial development of that backward country. Factories and mills must not employ more than twenty-five per cent. workmen who are of Jewish persuasion.

The analogy of this treatment of the Jews with that accorded them in Mediæval Europe is plain. Just as many other survivals are to be noted in Eastern Europe, the political situation of the Jews may be considered a political survival. The effects of this anomalous political situation on the social and economic conditions of the Jews may be conjectured. Ostracized as pariahs, subjected to abuse and persecution at the hands of petty officials who receive pitifully low salaries, without any hope of receiving just treatment, even in the highest courts, unless bribes are freely used, they have of late despairingly begun to emigrate in large masses. Many settle in Western Europe, especially France and England, while the vast majority go to North and South America.

The causes of these persecutions have been discussed rather extensively. Lazare, who studied the problem quite thoroughly, is inclined to attribute it to the separativeness of the Jews, manifesting itself in their special garb, their Yiddish language, their preference to live in separate parts of the cities, thus proving that they are aliens. "They were the victims of an isolation which was due to the influence of their guides, the Rabbis. The patriotic passions were particularly aroused in that country, which was in a nascent state, and striving to acquire a nationality and unity. There has been a pan-Roumanism, just like pan-Germanism or pan-Slavism. There were discussions on the Roumanian race, on its integrity, its purity, the danger threatening it by adulteration. Associations were formed to counteract foreign encroachment in particular. Schoolmasters and university professors were the soul of these societies; just as in Germany they were the most active anti-Semites. They looked upon the Jews as agents and apostles of Germanism, and they became the instigators of restrictive legislation in order to repel and restrain them. They reproached the Jews with forming a State within a State, which was true, but—and this is the everlasting inconsistency of anti-Judaism—they passed laws to retain them in the condition they considered dangerous. They asserted that the Jewish education crippled the brain of those who received it, which was but too correct, and yet they proposed to shut the Jews out completely from obtaining the education given to Christians, exactly the kind that would lift them from degradation."[1]

We cannot agree with this view. While it is true that about thirty years ago the separativeness of the Jews in that region was very marked, that they differed from the Christian population in language, dress, habits, and customs, etc., conditions have recently changed. When we studied the Jewish problem in Roumania during the summer of 1907 we were surprised to find that practically all the young Jews speak Roumanian, even in their intercourse among themselves; that the Talmud is hardly studied in that country, as the Rabbis deplored when speaking of it; their dress, especially among the Jews living in Valachia, does not at all differ from that worn by the other city population; the majority of the young men shave, and one with side locks is rather uncommon, even in Moldavia. These and many other changes in the habits of the Jews indicate that they are doing their best, in spite of all the laws to keep them isolated, to assimilate with the general population. Indeed, the anti-Semites in that country point to the dangers of the assimilated Jew, showing that while the bulk of the Christian population is submerged in ignorance and about ninety per cent. are illiterate, the Jews, especially the younger generation, are showing a very small percentage of persons unable to read and write. They point to the fact that the simpleminded and ignorant Roumanian cannot compete with the clever Jew. Roumania is an agricultural country, but most of the land is owned by a comparatively few landlords, all Christians, who spend most of the money in Western Europe. The bulk of the peasantry is exploited in a manner unknown in other parts of Europe, and, fearing revolt, the authorities not only keep them in ignorance and illiteracy, but also continue agitating against the Jews, and thus divert the attention of the peasants from the real causes of their poverty. The causes are purely economic, and could only be solved by opening public schools for the education of the peasantry,

---

[1] Bernard Lazare, *L'Antisémitisme, son Histoire et ses Causes*, chap. viii.; Paris, 1892.

as well as by a more just distribution of the land, which has been appropriated by a few landlords.

It appears that, though on the whole the political position of the Jew in Russia is not better than that just described in Roumania, there is one feature which indicates that Russia is somewhat advanced in the manner she treats her inhabitants of Jewish faith. While in Roumania they are considered absolute aliens. in the land of the Tzars they are permitted to vote and even to be elected as deputies to the Duma. This would indicate citizenship, with the highest rights and privileges of citizenship. Russia practically never permitted Jews to settle on its sacred soil, yet has at present about one-half of all the Jews under its flag. This large number of the children of Israel was acquired by Russia while annexing Poland, White Russia, etc. It appears that at the time of annexation of these provinces the Jews were promised all the rights and privileges of subjects of the Tzar. In a manifesto published at the time of the invasion of White Russia in 1772, the Empress Catherine, through Governor-General Tschernyschew, promised the Jews freedom of religion and rights of property, on an equal basis with the rest of the population. In a later Ukase the Empress ordained that "the Jews, on the strength of former Ukases, have been raised to an equality with others, and that it is imperative to observe always the fundamental principle of equality of the Tzar's subjects, without distinction of religion or nationality." It will be understood that these promises were never kept. Even at the end of the reign of Catherine, in 1794, the Jews were compelled to pay higher taxes than the Christians.

The political status of the Jews in Russia at the present time is most peculiar, and cannot be duplicated in any other country. They are acknowledged subjects of the Tzar, and have all the duties of such subjects, such as military conscription, taxation, etc.; they can also vote for deputies to the Duma, and several have even been elected as deputies. But, on the other hand, their rights and privileges have been curtailed by certain administrative orders and "temporary laws," which do not even apply to aliens living in Russia. Especially severe are the so-called "temporary laws" or "May laws," promulgated

May 3rd, 1882, for the repression of the Jews. The restrictions under which they labour in Russia can be thus summarised:—The Jews have no right to live outside of the so-called *Pale of Settlement*. This Pale is, on the whole, not Russia at all, but consists mainly of provinces which Russia has annexed within the last 200 years, and where Jews have lived for centuries before that annexation. The fifteen provinces of Western and South-Western Russia, embracing White, Little, and New Russia, as well as the ten provinces which make up the part of Poland which Russia has sliced off for itself during the division of that country, are the "Pale." Outside of these provinces, in the interior of Russia and Siberia, only some special privileged classes of Jews may live, such as merchants of the first guild, who pay about 1,000 roubles annually for a licence; Jews who have graduated from the highest educational institutions; and some artisans. That very few of these can avail themselves of these privileges is seen from the fact that only six per cent. of all the Jews in that country live outside of the Pale. A peculiar feature of these restrictions of habitation is the fact that no Jew may live in Siberia unless convicted for a serious crime. But, after the term of his banishment has ended, he may not remain in Siberia, unless he commits another crime.

Within the Pale there are other restrictions as to residence. The Jews are segregated in cities and incorporated towns, and are not permitted to live in the rural districts; they are not even allowed to live in many health resorts located in villages. This segregation in cities and towns, most of which are commercially and industrially unimportant, has worked economic havoc among them, because it virtually prevents them from working at agriculture, and especially in many factories and mills, metal smelting, and glass works, which are usually located in rural districts. Some of the most important harbour cities, as Nikolayeff, Sebastopol, etc., are also closed to them. By prohibiting them from owning or even leasing land outside of cities in the Pale, they are cut off not only from working the soil, but also from trading in agricultural implements or products, and agriculture is the staple industry of seventy-five per cent. of the population of Russia. In addition to this, they are excluded completely from the civil service and public office in any capacity. When, several years ago, the railroads in Russia were monopolized by the Government, 100,000 Jews suddenly lost their employment at vocations for which they were best fitted by education and special training. Nor are they permitted to teach in public schools, excepting Jewish religious schools, or to hold any academic position in high schools and universities. Many a Jewish scholar of international eminence had to leave Russia in search of emoluments in foreign countries. Among the university professors in Germany, Italy, and France there have been many Russian Jews who could not advance in their native country.

The public schools in Russia are mostly found in cities, while the agricultural districts hardly have any schools worth mentioning, and the result is that about eighty per cent. of the population is illiterate. It is a notorious fact that the Government has never been in earnest as regards the education of the peasantry. The Jews, with their universal eagerness for knowledge, are anxious to give their children proper school training. Indeed, the only way to assimilate those portions of the Jewish population in the Pale that has remained foreign in Russia, and is still ignorant of the Russian language, traditions, customs, and habits, is to give them a Russian education. As taxpayers in cities, they pay even more for such purposes than the Christian population. They are kept out of the common and high schools and universities. Bearing in mind that in many cities in the Pale they constitute from thirty to eighty-five per cent. of the total population, it will be evident that the law permitting only ten per cent. of the pupils in educational institutions to be of Jewish faith is a great hardship for those who have an intense desire for education. Moreover, the Christian population in some cities is not at all eager for education, and comparatively few seek admission to the schools. The result is that the total number of pupils is quite small, and of this small number only ten per cent. may be Jews. It often happens that Jews hire some Christian children to enrol in a school, in order to increase the total number of pupils, and thus secure a chance for their own children in the schools.

These and many other political restrictions, coupled with special taxation, have had a terrible influence on the social and economic condition of the Jews in Russia. In addition to the usual taxes paid by the Christians, they are compelled to pay extra taxation on the rents they receive from their property, on inheritances, on the meat they consume (*Kosher* meat is therefore about double the price of non-*Kosher*), on the candles their women light every Friday for ritual purposes, and even for the skull-caps some Jews wear during religious ceremonies. They pay excessive municipal taxes, but still they are not admitted to hospitals, schools, and public functions which in the Pale are maintained from funds mainly derived from Jewish taxation. In addition to this, they are the constant prey of petty officials, as well as the higher ones who subsist on the bribes regularly collected from the Jews. Indeed, it appears that almost everything a Jew may do can be arbitrarily declared illegal by the police, or the governor, and the only way of conducting his affairs without molestation is by oiling the machinery of the State with bribes. It is a notorious fact that the Jews consider a governor or chief of police as bad in case he proves to be incorruptible, which is, however, rare. According to Harold Frederick, and Weber, and Kempster, half the income of the Jews of the middle-classes finds its way to the police.

The causes of these political and civic disabilities of the Jews in Russia are mainly religious, in spite of many assertions to the contrary. While Roumania as a constitutional monarchy cannot limit the rights of any of its citizens because of their faith, the case is different in Russia. There the union of the Church and State is to-day just as intimate as it was during the Middle Ages in the rest of Europe. While the Chauvinist agitators and press of Russia are constantly clamouring for Pan slavic supremacy on racial grounds, yet it cannot be denied by any of them that the so-called Slavonic race is a composite of many racial elements, and that a considerable portion of its blood is Asiatic, or Mongolian. The tendency of the Government has always been to strive for religious unity, and the followers of Christian sects other than the Greek Orthodox have been persecuted more or less. Russian statesmen of influence, such as the late Pobiedonostzeff, are convinced that homogeneity of religious confession is indispensable for the maintenance of the unity of the State. The Tzar is not only the head of the nation, but of the Church as well. It is a fact that Russia has always kept the Jews out of the interior of the empire for fear of Judaizing, which in former centuries was not at all rare. The Subbotniki, a sect of Russians which denies the divinity of Christ and keeps the Jewish Sabbath, etc., are said to have been organized by Jews. There are several other sects with similar tendencies, and the Church has always done its best to suppress them just as the Jews were suppressed. Another proof of the religious character of the persecutions of the Jews in Russia is the fact that baptism at once removes all disabilities. All kinds of efforts have been made by the Government to encourage them to abjure their faith. Every convert has been given a bonus of thirty silver roubles; a convert who was married to a Jewess before baptism is divorced as soon as he is immersed in the holy waters, and the same is true in case a Jewess adopts Christianity, while the non-converted consorts are considered married by the law. Judaism has also been persecuted as a religion. The Rabbinical seminaries have been closed, the number of synagogues limited, and in Moscow the synagogue had been closed altogether since 1892 as "an indecent thing," and only re-opened since the constitution was granted by the Tzar in 1905. That these attempts to bring the Jews of Russia nearer to Christianity have utterly failed can be seen from the fact that Judaism has lost numerically less in Russia during the nineteenth century than in Prussia, although there are about twelve times as many Jews in the former as in the latter. During recent years some Jews, especially those who sought admission to universities, have adopted Mohammedanism in the hope of gaining permission to live outside of the Pale, or to enroll as students in the university, but the decision of the Government was to the effect that only by conversion to Christianity can a Jew remove the disabilities which the law places on him.

Excepting Finland, where but few Jews reside, and

Spain and Portugal, where their number is also insignificant, the civil and political rights of the Jews in the rest of Europe are more or less the same as those of the non-Jewish population. It was within the territory which was soon to become the United States of America, where, for the first time since their dispersion among the nations, the Jews were placed on a basis of absolute equality with people of other creeds. Roger Williams, founding Rhode Island, welcomed the Jews on the same terms as Christians. But their number was rather small and insignificant. The first admission of the Jews to citizenship was accomplished in France, September 27th, 1791, one day before the closing of the Constituent Assembly. Although some of the minor political and civil disabilities were yet enforced for years thereafter, still this was the first act of emancipation of the Jews in Europe, and was sooner or later adopted by all other European nations excepting Russia, Roumania, Finland, Spain, and Portugal. In England repeated attempts to emancipate the Jews were made during preceding centuries, but without success. In 1753 Pelham introduced a bill permitting the naturalization of Jews who applied to Parliament, which passed the House of Lords without much opposition. But when it came before the Commons the Tory party made a great outcry against this "abandonment of Christianity," as they called it. It was only after the Roman Catholics of England were in 1829 freed from all their civil and political disabilities that the Jews and their friends began an active agitation in favour of emancipation. Bills were repeatedly introduced to that effect, but they usually died before reaching the third reading, though a Bill permitting Jews to hold municipal office was passed on July 31st, 1845, and the following year the Religious Opinion Relief Bill removed a certain number of minor disabilities, which affected, not only the Jews in England, but also other dissenters from the Established Church. It was only in 1858 that a Jew was permitted to enter as a member of Parliament by allowing him while taking oath to omit the words, "on the true faith of a Christian." The difficulties in the way of a Jew becoming a scholar or a fellow in an English university were removed as late as 1870 by the University Test Act. Since then the political and civil position of the Jews in England does not at all differ from that of persons of other creeds. In all the English colonies, as well as in the United States, the Jews are at present politically equal with the population of other creeds.

In Holland the Jews have enjoyed for centuries a certain amount of freedom, and when in 1795 the emancipation was proclaimed in France, Holland followed suit. The National Convention on September 2nd, 1796, proclaimed this resolution: "No Jew shall be excluded from rights or advantages which are associated with citizenship in the Batavian Republic, and which he may desire to enjoy." This, as well as the later removal of some minor disabilities, solved the Jewish question in the Netherland.

In the rest of Europe the naturalization of the Jews came slower. In Austria, Emperor Joseph I. (1780-90) was the first to remove some of the restrictions placed by law on the Jews. The laws requiring Jews to wear distinctive dress was first abrogated, then the poll tax, and finally attempts were made to assimilate them by encouraging them to enter schools. But it remained for the revolution of 1848, when the new constitution of April 25th was adopted, providing freedom of religion and the abolition of the special Jewish taxation, to remove the major political disabilities. However, they still laboured under important restrictions till the constitution of December 21st, 1867, was adopted which completely naturalized the Jews and made them citizens in the full sense of the word. Similarly in Germany it was only during the middle of the nineteenth century that most of the states admitted Jews to citizenship. In Prussia, Hanover, and Nassau this occurred in 1848; in Würtemberg, in 1861; in Baden, in 1862; in Holstein, in 1863; in Saxony, in 1868; and it was only after the establishment of the North German Confederation by the law of July 3rd, 1869, that all the existing restrictions imposed upon the followers of different creeds, and among them the Jews, were abrogated. Moreover, and this is important in relation to the question of assimilation, mixed marriages were only legalized in 1875. In Austria they are not even at present permitted.

In Italy all the papal states became the United Kingdom

in 1859, and, except in Rome, where oppression lasted until the end of the papal dominion (September 20th, 1870), the Jews obtained full emancipation. In Switzerland political equality for the Jews was advocated by many of the Liberals of the Great Council of Helvetia (1798-99), but without avail. In 1860 and 1861 some Cantons—Graubünden, Zurich, etc.—granted them civil rights but refused to naturalize them. Only as late as 1874 the revised Confederate Constitution proclaimed religious liberty, and all the Jewish inhabitants became full fledged citizens. In some countries emancipation was even slower in coming. In Bulgaria and Servia they were naturalized as late as 1878 and 1879 respectively.

It is thus evident that comparatively few of the Jews have had human rights for more than one hundred years; the majority of those who are politically free have enjoyed this freedom for between one to three generations, while more than one-half the total number of Jews in the world are to-day in about the same position from the civil and political standpoint as their grandfathers during the dark Middle Ages. Of the 12,000,000 of Jews, 5,500,000 in Russia are at present segregated in a Ghetto in the Russian Pale of Settlement, which does not materially differ from the Mediæval Ghetto in Prague, Rome, or Venice. That the Russian Pale is a Ghetto in the true sense of the word can be realized when it is considered that it is not at all as large as one would be led to believe from its extent. It is true that the extent of the Pale is about 950,000 square kilometres, or one twenty-third of the Russian Empire. But the Jews are only allowed to live in cities and incorporated towns, which reduces to a minimum the space on which they are permitted to dwell. Bearing in mind that fully 5,500,000 souls are thus segregated in several cities, the analogy with the Mediæval Ghetto is evident. When to this is added the fact that they are exposed to frequent attacks on their lives and property, as well as to expulsions from certain parts of the country, or ordered to leave the country altogether, as is often the case in Roumania, we can see no difference between the modern and former Ghetto. The words written in 1781 by Dohm about the civil disabilities of the Jews can be applied to the modern

Jew in Russia and Roumania. He says: "This unfortunate being, who is countryless, whose activities are everywhere circumscribed, who is nowhere permitted to exercise his talents untrammelled, in whose virtue no one places credence, for whom scarcely one attainable distinction exists—for him no path leads to the enjoyment of a dignified and independent existence, or even to self-support, other than the path of trade. But here also discriminatory limitations and imposts beset him, and but few of these people have sufficient property to engage in wholesale trade. They are, therefore, mostly confined to a petty retail trade, in which only the constant duplication of small profits suffices to sustain a needy existence; or they are compelled to lend to others the money they cannot employ themselves . . . Many kinds of trade are wholly closed to them; others are open only under legislative regulations concerning time, place, and person; the permitted trades are beset by so many imposts, hampered by so many investigations, and dependent on the caprices of so many petty officials, that the earnings of the Jews are extremely small, and can attract only such as are accustomed to the most miserable existence."[1] The differences between the Jews of mediæval times and those of to-day in Russia and Roumania vanish when these words are read.

These political disabilities of the Jews in Russia and Roumania have made themselves felt not only in those countries, but also in Western Europe and America, and, to a certain extent, also in Australasia and South Africa. The segregation in the Pale of Settlement, and within that Pale in cities and towns, has brought about social and economic conditions which cannot be paralleled in any other region in Europe. The Jewish misery and poverty, which has been described in one of the preceding chapters, has become unbearable. The number of artisans and small traders who cannot find opportunities to earn a living has been growing. Their only salvation at present appears to be emigration to more hospitable countries. Thus it was brought about that the centre of gravity of the Jewish population, which has till recently been in

[1] C. W. von Dohm, *Ueber die bürgerliche Verbesserung der Juden*, pp. 9-11; Leipsic, 1781.

Poland, has been shifting westward, not in Europe, but across the Atlantic—in the United States of America.

In Roumania, where anti-Jewish legislation reached its climax in 1899, emigration of the Children of Israel has removed over thirty per cent. of their total number in the country. Up to that time very few Jews left that country, while many have emigrated from Russia, Austria, and Hungary. But the hostile legislation since 1899, added to the disabilities of previous years, has made their existence unbearable, and large hordes of poverty-stricken Jews have began to wander westward to France and England, the vast majority, however, going to the United States, and of late also to Argentine and Canada. According to the *Moniteur Officiel* (August 13th, 1906), the Minister of the Interior has issued during 1899-1904 passports to 42,968 Jews who left for America. From statistics published in the *Annual Reports of the Commissioner-General of Immigration*, it is seen that there arrived during 1884-1910, 65,000 Jews from Roumania. England also was a point of destination of many Roumanian emigrants, and an estimate of 12,000 Jews having settled in that country during that period will be nearly correct. If to these be added the number who have gone to France, Switzerland, Argentine, Canada, etc., it is evident that over 85,000 Jews have left Roumania within the last sixteen years. Bearing in mind that the returns of the census of 1899 showed a total of 266,000 Jews, the removal of 85,000, or nearly one-third of all, is enormous. But it must be mentioned in this connection that the total number of Jews in that country has not diminished to the same extent. Their natural increase has been very high, as was already shown. It amounts to about two per cent., indicating that during these years the greater part of the number who left have been replaced by new-born Jews.

The emigration from Russia is just as great relatively. Before the inauguration of the "Temporary Laws" in 1881 few Jews left Russia for Western countries. From the official reports of the United States Immigration Service, it is seen that during 1821-70 very few Russian Jews came to this country, only 7,550 during these fifty years. During 1871-80, 41,057, or 4,100 annually on the average reached the United States from Russia. But then the number of Jewish immigrants began to swell, and during 1881-90 the annual average reached 20,700. Especially marked has been the increase after 1882. The available statistics show that during 1884-1903 there came 406,657 Russian Jews to the United States, and during the seven years, 1903-10, 600,000, or over 85,000 annually. That persecution is the main cause is evident from the fact that during the two years following the bloody massacres in 1905 the number of Russian Jewish immigrants to the United States was over 125,000 and 115,000 respectively. To these must be added the large number who went to Western Europe, as well as to other parts of North and South America, and also to Australasia, South Africa, and Palestine, which can only be estimated. I believe that an estimate that during the thirty years, 1880-1910, over 1,500,000 Jews have left Russia for Western countries will be rather conservative. Of these over one million went to the United States, and the rest were scattered in various parts of the globe. Since no religious data have been collected in England, it is impossible to state the number of Jews from Russia who have permanently settled in the British Isles. Moreover, it is well known that a fairly large proportion of those whose first destination is England subsequently find their way to the United States and Canada. This is evident from the American official statistics of immigration, showing a large number of English Jews arriving annually, and it was also proven during the investigation of the Royal Commission on Alien Immigration. Of the Jews who go to Argentine and Palestine many afterwards go to the United States.

That these migrations are mainly caused by the political oppression of the Jews in Russia and Roumania is evident from the fact that comparatively few Jews from other European countries emigrate. The only exception appears to be Austria and Hungary. But there the economic factor is predominating. The Christians as well have been emigrating to the United States in much larger numbers.

The Jewish problem in some Western European countries, which should have been settled, considering the remarkable manner in which Jews have assimilated since their emancipation, is again raised by the arrival of these new immigrants. They serve the purpose of keeping up Judaism, which has been undergoing a process of disintegration through the adoption by the native Jews of the culture, habits, and customs of their non-Jewish neighbours. Their low birth-rates, frequent baptisms, and mixed marriages have been decimating the Jews in Western countries. They have not been increasing in number, and in some countries their number has so much decreased as to threaten their existence. But this loss sustained by Western Judaism has been more than compensated by the arrival of their co-religionists from the East. They bring along with them a more intense religious feeling, and adherence to the faith of their ancestors, which is only after a couple of generations' residence in the West more or less weakened or obliterated. The general effects of these conditions on the Jews and Judaism have been discussed in detail in other parts of this work.

CHAPTER XXI

SOCIAL DISABILITIES AND THEIR EFFECTS—BAPTISM.

The entry of the emancipated Jew into modern society—Discrimination in the armies and navies of Europe—Social ostracism in the United States—Discrimination in German academic circles—Number of Jewish professors in German Universities—Baptism the usual prerequisite for academic appointment—Fear of the "Semite" by "Aryan" jingoes—Baptismal waters the specific means of clearing the "Semite" of his objectionable racial traits—Singular position of the emancipated Jews—Causes of baptism—Baptism in ancient and Mediæval times—Prominent modern Jewish converts to Christianity—Number of baptisms during the nineteenth century in Russia, in Austria—Social conditions of Jews baptized in Vienna—Freethinkers from the Jewish fold—Infrequency of baptism in Galicia—Baptisms in Hungary—Social conditions of the Jews baptized in Berlin—Marriage and advancement, the two main causes of baptism—Effect of baptisms on the social status of those who remain within the fold of Judaism—Excessive proportion of Jewish parvenus—Eastern European Jews replacing those lost through baptism in Western countries.

THE removal of political and civil disabilities has had a profound effect on the social and economic conditions of the Jews in Western countries. They have been freed from restrictions which have weighed heavily upon them for centuries. They began to feel like human beings and act as such, participating in all the civil, political, and intellectual movements of the age, and have in their march of progress even outstripped, to a certain extent, the Christians among whom they live. This was but natural, considering that they are mostly city-dwellers among whom all great movements, economic, social, political and intellectual, originate and are maintained. Thus we find them to-day represented, not only in commercial and financial pursuits, activities in which they have been trained for centuries, to a certain degree far beyond their proportion in the population, but also in all the political and intellectual movements of the nineteenth and twentieth centuries. They have been among the leaders of the Liberal and Socialist movements in Germany and Austria, of the anti-Royal movement in France, in the revolutionary movement in Russia; many have been elected to the parliaments of various countries; they are leading journalists in Western Europe; in the theatre they lead as players, authors, managers, and patrons; in the Salons and other places of exhibition of works of art they are represented far beyond their proportion in the population, and in the scientific laboratories their number is amazingly large, both as teachers and students. They have achieved this in the space of two to four generations of liberty.

But all this has by no means freed them from the peril of social ostracism to which they have been subjected in Western countries. Free as they are to-day in Germany, France, Italy, England, the United States, etc., to live wherever they choose, to engage in any occupation or profession, to own property of any kind, to publish any newspaper, magazine, or review, to study in any school or university, and the like, they are checked when they attempt to reap the harvest of social position to which they consider themselves entitled. Thus in Germany no Jew can advance in the army or navy; even if he abjures his faith he finds it exceedingly difficult, often impossible, to receive a military appointment. There are practically no Jewish officers in the German army and navy as a result of this discrimination, in spite of the fact that many have made strenuous efforts in this direction. Even the recent suggestion of the Kaiser to the effect that religious belief should not debar a citizen from serving his fatherland when otherwise qualified has not had any influence. In Austria-Hungary, on the other hand, although great efforts are being made to keep them out of the army, the discrimination has not been so complete as in Germany. As early as 1855 there were 157 officers in the Austrian army, the majority probably in the medical corps. In 1893 Austria-Hungary had as many as 2,179 Jewish military and 2 naval active officers, exclusive of those in the reserve contingents.[1] Recently, a Jew was even advanced to the rank of major-general, after being requested to be baptized, which he refused. In France

[1] *Jewish Encyclopædia*, vol. ii., p. 127.

many Jews have advanced in the army and navy to the rank of captain, major, colonel, and even general. Their number is, in relation to the total number of Jews in France, even larger than that of non-Jewish army officers. In Italy they have been emancipated much later, and they are comparatively few in number, but no distinction has been made in appointing army officers. The result is that many have achieved distinction in military service, and several have become generals. In England also Jews are not discriminated against in this regard, and in January 1902 there were 12 naval and marine officers of the regular English army, 17 officers of the British militia, and 66 officers of British volunteers. Adding colonial Jewish officers of militia and volunteers, Canada provided 2, Fiji 2, Jamaica 2, Australia 27, New Zealand 8, South Africa 43, and India 1, making a total of 239 Jewish officers in the British forces.[1] In the United States conditions are about the same; many Jews have been army and naval officers with distinction. All this tends to prove that the discrimination against Jews in some European armies and navies is based on mere prejudice. In fact, in Russia, where no Jew can advance in the army beyond the grade of private, many Jews are permitted, and during war compelled, to serve in the army in the medical corps. In this capacity many have achieved distinction and been promoted to the grade of colonel and even general. This, of course, is due to the fact that Russia has comparatively few physicians for her large army, and from sheer necessity during war they are compelled to ask the Jews' services.

The army is not the only institution which discriminates against Jews in Western countries, where they are politically equal with the rest of the population. In the United States, where Jews have held the highest offices, elective as well as appointive, such as mayors of cities, governors of states, and judges in the high courts, there is hardly a social club pretending to an exclusive set of members which admits Jews. Even clubs in which an academic degree is a pre-requisite to eligibility for membership, rebuff Jewish applicants for admission. The same is true of the college and university fraternities, some of which reject Jews because they are distinctly "Christian" organizations, but

[1] *Jewish Encyclopædia*, vol ii., p. 127.

the majority do so on general principles. It often happens that a student is not known as a Jew, and invited to enter, but meanwhile his origin is in some manner ascertained, and he is suddenly dropped. It has been stated that the few Jews who, for one reason or another, have slipped into some of the college or university fraternities in the United States have not found it very comfortable, the treatment they received being by no means fraternal. Similarly, in many boarding schools, some Jewish children have been admitted by "mistake," and the result was disastrous as soon as the principal discovered the faith of these pupils' ancestors. This social discrimination against Jews, while not unknown in Europe, appears to be more especially an American institution. There are many health and pleasure resorts which have no vacant room for Jews, no matter what their social or intellectual standing. A large number of the hotels on the Atlantic sea coast thus discriminate against Jews, and many proprietors of such hotels have stated that while personally they would welcome Jewish guests, by admitting them they run the danger of losing most of their non-Jewish patrons. Thus it happens that the majority of first-class hotels harbour either Jews or non-Jews. According to an eminent Rabbi, thousands of his co-religionists are compelled to flee from America during the summer months and spend their vacations abroad, because of the prejudice against them at practically every attractive resort on their side of the Atlantic. Moreover, a Jewish child with a distinctly Jewish name, such as Goldberg, Cohen, Silverstein, etc., finds it almost impossible to gain admission to any first-class boarding-school, even into the few that do admit a limited number of "Hebrew" children. They draw the line at Jewish names. The result of this condition of affairs is that nearly every city in the United States with a considerable Jewish population has its own Jewish clubs, Jewish boarding-schools in which no Judaism is taught, Jewish summer resorts, which do not serve *Kosher* food, etc. The isolation of the Jew is in this respect as stringent as it was within the gates of the Mediæval Ghetto, and it prevents assimilation, especially intermarriage, more effectively than laws of the Church, Synagogue, or State.

It is true that there are in Europe also *Judenreine Haeuser* in Germany, and restaurants in Berlin, Vienna, and elsewhere, in which a Jewish patron is frankly rebuffed with the phrase *wir bedienen keinen Juden*[1]; it is also true that recently such a restaurant made its appearance in Manchester, where the proprietor attempted to segregate his Jewish patrons in a special room, and was upheld by the courts; still, on the whole, they are rare and far between. Nor are clubs as severe on the Jew in Western Europe; excepting to the Royalist Clubs in France and some clerical institutions, Jews are freely admitted. Even in Russia, where persecution of the Jews is open and merciless, Jews are members of the most exclusive clubs. They are excluded from some resorts not because they are considered undesirable, but because the Government does not permit their sojourn in certain places. As soon as the necessary permission has been granted they are admitted into any hotel or resort, and are socially entertained on a basis of equality.

This ostracism does not stop with the exclusion of the children of Abraham from hotels, resorts, and social clubs, but goes much farther. In Germany, where, as I just stated, their social disabilities are not as stringent as in the United States, they suffer from discriminations imposed on them in academic circles. Superficially, it appears that Germany is overcrowded with professors of Jewish origin. It must, however, be recalled in this connection that there is a great difference between the "ordinary" and "extraordinary" professor and the "Privatdocent" The bulk of the Jewish teachers in the German universities are "Privatdocenten," few are extraordinary professors, and an ordinary professor of Jewish origin is very rare; most of those who have thus been honoured, not in their case through what is known as "influence," had to abjure their faith. In a recent article on the subject of Jews in the medical faculties in German Universities[2] some interesting figures are given on the subject. The idea that the Jews carry off most of the medical

---

[1] For a detailed description of Jewish ostracism in Germany see Mrs. Alfred Sidgwick's instructive book, *Home Life in Germany;* London, 1910.

[2] *Berliner Tageblatt*, Oct, 22, 1908.

academic honours is dispelled. There are altogether only four Jews holding regular professorships in the medical departments of the German universities; five more who have been appointed have died or retired. It is further stated that two of the greatest authorities in the medical world have resigned their lectureship in the Berlin University because they could see no prospect for merited promotion. Several others of international eminence in their specialities are merely honorary professors. The most noteworthy fact is that none of the regular medical professors in the Berlin University is a Jew, although of the 11 honorary professors 3 are Jews, of the 43 extraordinary professors 9 are Jews, and of the 113 " Privatdocenten " 44 are Jews. This clearly indicates that in academic circles even the Jew who has attained great distinction in his branch of medicine cannot advance very high. Appointments which are remunerative and carry with them certain privileges are almost entirely out of his reach. Even the appointment of a Jewish " Privatdocent " is very difficult, and is only given to one who has attained great eminence. In spite of all these disabilities, there were some Jewish professors in Berlin, as Traube and Remak, the physicians; Levin Goldschmidt, the jurist; and Kronecker, the mathematician. The last-named, however, was baptized, although it is said on good authority that he continued to pay his dues to the Jewish congregation until his death. There are several more Jewish professors in various German Universities holding the highest academic rank, as Julius Bernstein, the physiologist, in Halle, who is also a *Geheimer Medizinalrath;* Rosanes and Pasch, the mathematicians, in Breslau and Giessen respectively; Jacob Firedrich Behrend, the jurist in Greifswald, served a term as dean (*Rector Magnificus*); and Rosanes was also elected in 1903 to this high office of his alma mater. There are several more, but nearly all have been baptized before even aspiring to an appointment.[1]

[1] A most recent case in point is that of Professor Oscar Minkowski, one of the greatest living authorities on internal medicine, who has been called to fill the chair left vacant in Breslau by the transfer of Professor Strumpell to Vienna. In spite of his great attainments, he remained for years an assistant in the Strassburg clinic. One day he decided to change his faith, and his conversion was soon followed by the appointment to the Professorship in Greifswald.

In academic circles in Germany a Jew who devotes his life to science and expects merited advance is compelled to do either one of these two things: he must be baptized or emigrate. Germany has lost many eminent Jewish savants who emigrated in search of emoluments in foreign countries. To mention only a few: Gustav Gabriel Valentin, the eminent physiologist, had to go to Berne, where he even became dean; another physiologist, Moritz Schiff, and Max Budinger, the historian, also went to Switzerland; Lazarus Loewe, the Orientalist, and many others, went to England; Gottlieb Gluge, the physician, to Belgium; Salomon Munk and Joseph Dernburg, the eminent Orientalists; Heinrich Weil and Louis Benloew, the philologists; Philip Koraleck, the mathematician; Wilhelm Wertheim, the physicist; Maurice Loewe, the astronomer; Julius Oppert, the Assyriologist, and many others, went to France. They could not expect to progress very far in their native land. Salomon Munk, before leaving Germany, applied at the Ministry of Public Instruction for an academic position. Altenstein, the Minister, answered him that the Ministry could not see its way clear to help him in his scientific researches as long as he professed the Mosaic religion.[1] Maurice Loewe was asked by a Minister, Count Leo Thun, "directly and personally," whether he would not change his faith if a professorship were promised him.[2] He refused the offer, and went to Paris, where he became the Director of the Observatory, and even corresponding member of the Academy of Sciences of the country which could not find a place for him unless he passed through the Church. The curious part is that in a country where the Constitution provides that religious belief should not bar any one from any rights, the Minister of Public Instruction (*Kultusminister*) does not conceal his aversion to Jews who seek academic positions. Gossler, who was Minister up to 1891, always asked Jewish candidates whether they were inclined to sacrifice their religious belief,[3] but his successor, Von Bosse, is reported to have acted differently;

---

[1] *Jahrb. f. jüdische Geschichte und Literatur*, vol. ii., p. 181; 1899.
[2] *Deutsche Rundschau f. Geographie und Statistik*, vol. xvii., p. 277; 1895.
[3] N. Samter, *Judentaufen im 19, Jahrhundert*, p. 33.

he once said to a newly-appointed Jewish professor, "Do me the favour not to be baptized."[1]

The first step of a Jewish savant in his career is baptism. He must pass through the Church before he can ascend an academic chair. The reasons given for this condition of affairs are peculiar. The Chauvinists and Jingoes, who are exalted with the alleged "Aryan" culture, believe that modern civilization is distinctly Christian, and the Jew, the "Semite," as an alien in race, traditions, culture, religion, etc., endangers the progress of the modern world. Schleiermacher, the eminent German philosopher, was of the opinion that "Jews who refuse to accept Christianity are Frenchmen who refuse to learn German."[2] Mommsen, Treitschke, Paulsen,[3] and many others have stated that before becoming perfect Germans the Jews must first become Christians. Hartmann is of the opinion that the only way to bridge the gulf which separates the Jews from the Christians is for the former to adopt Christianity, and that they will thereby prove that they are willing to become real Germans.[4] It appears that the separation of the Church from the State in Germany has as yet not been so complete as some would believe. Even in the United States a resolution was recently carried by a board of Christian ministers, urging on the Jews that, in exchange for the liberty and equality which they enjoy at present in Christian countries, they should give up their Sabbath and other religious traditions and customs. That inferior "Semite," or *Homo Syriacus*, is said to have contributed nothing of value to our culture and civilization; H. Stewart Chamberlain is even convinced that Jesus was an "Aryan" or Teuton, and says that "whoever maintains that Christ was a Jew is either ignorant or a liar."[5] Professor Haupt, of

---

[1] *Allgem. Israelit. Wochenschrift*, p. 184; 1898.

[2] W. Dilthey, *Leben Schleiermachers*, vol. i., appendix, p. 112.

[3] See Th. Mommsen, *Auch ein Wort über unser Judenthum*, pp. 15, 1889; H. Treitschke, *Deutsche Geschichte im 19. Jahrhundert*, vol. iv., p. 455, Leipzig, 1889; F. Paulsen, *System der Ethik*, vol. ii., p. 526.

[4] Eduard von Hartmann, *Das Judenthum in Gegenwart und Zukunft*, pp. 29-48; Leipzig, 1885.

[5] H. St. Chamberlain, *Grundlagen des 19. Jahrhunderts*, p. 218; Munich, 1900. Those who like to speculate in race theories have recently discussed the racial affinities of Christ quite extensively. Adolph Harnack

Johns Hopkins University, repeated the same opinion at the Orientalist Congress of 1908. It is curious that some "scientific" jingoes have even identified Jesus as a German,[1] and Max Bewer knows even that He was of Rhinish-Westphalian origin.[2] These and similar assertions have been repeatedly made by pseudo-scientists who gave their writings a scholarly veneer. The effect on those who have been imbued with the idea that their "race" or nation has a great destiny, the Pan-Germans, Pan-Slavists, etc., can well be imagined. The absurdity that the baptismal waters can magically convert the alien Semite into a pure-blooded "Aryan" German, Slav, Anglo-Saxon, etc., and imbue him with the spirit, ideals, aspirations, etc., of European "races" is never touched upon. As soon as he is baptized all his Jewishness disappears, and he is admitted to the most exclusive club, given a chair in the university, if he proves otherwise fit, and permitted to hold the best political, civil, or military honour.

It may appear incredible at first sight that this ostracism brings many more Jews to the Church than mediæval massacres or the Russian pogroms of the twentieth century. Still, it is a fact. The position of the emancipated Jew is most singular. He succeeded, through two to four generations of freedom, in acquiring wealth; from a small trader who peddled his wares on the highroads, or sold second-hand clothing in the dingy streets of the Ghetto, or lent small sums of money on high interest, he became a great merchant, a manufacturer, a banker, a stock-jobber. Only one hundred years ago he was not permitted to pass the threshold of a university as a pupil, and within that short space of time he succeeded in becoming a scholar, a scientist, a painter, sculptor, musician, actor, and the like;

---

aptly points out that if Jesus were no Jew his Jewish antagonists would undoubtedly not have omitted to mention it. But, on the other hand, if it were proven that the supposed lineal descent of Jesus from David is a myth, then His claims to Messiahship, upon which the New Testament rests largely, would receive a heavy blow. Furthermore, the alleged direct descent of the modern Jews from the ancient Semites, as well as the purity of their race, is shattered, if it is agreed that 1900 years ago the Hebrews had "Aryan" elements in their midst. The ethnic theory of antisemitism is then without foundation.

[1] J. W. Binzerbach, *War Christus ein Deutsche?* Berlin, 1900.
[2] *Oesterreichische Wochenschrift*, p. 588; 1902.

but he is repulsed when he attempts to break into the drawing-room of modern society; repulsed when he attempts to enter a social club or college fraternity; or when he desires to teach in a university the science to which he has devoted the best years of his life. In the Ghetto he did not invite social intercourse with the non-Jews around him. In fact, his separate religion precluded social intimacy with those who had not a Jewish table; he could not eat with his Christian or Mohammedan neighbour, nor could he share with him his joys and sorrows. The reputation of the pride and aloofness of the Jew has its origin in these separate traits of his religion, which he followed implicitly. But with the emancipation not only were the portals of the Ghetto opened to him, but he also began to discard most of those tenets of his creed which made an unsocial being of him in former times. He eats now at any table, he does not rest on the Sabbath but on Sunday, he is even not averse to marry out of his faith. Under the circumstances, he desires, and often craves, social intercourse with the people of other faiths. When rebuffed he feels it more keenly than he felt the blows given him during the massacres of Mediæval Europe, or the frequent expulsions to which he was subjected; indeed, Jews are more sensitive about social discrimination than about political and civil discrimination. "Contempt is worse than hatred," says an American Rabbi; "social discrimination attacks a man's personality, where legal discrimination only robs him of his civic rights."

The causes of the social ostracism of the Jews are to be sought for in the centuries of oppression of the Children of Israel in Europe. The prejudice of ages cannot be obliterated in one or two generations of freedom and political equality. Social sympathy and intimacy are not gained in a short period of time. One has to consider that some text-books used in schools speak of Jews and gypsies as accursed and inferior races[1]; even books on ethnology and anthropology refer to the Jew as an Asiatic,

---

[1] The analogy between Jews and gypsies is quite often drawn in text-books on geography and history, but it is unjust to the Jews. The Jews have a history to which they look back with pride, and which Christendom has adopted as part and parcel of their past; the gypsies have played no rôle in the history of the world. The Jews have a religion to which they

a stranger in Europe. These teachings leave their impression on the average pupil, who accepts them usually without further investigation, and thus they become deeply-rooted prejudices. If to this be added the modern teachings of a certain class of pseudo-scientists, who believe that the "Aryan" is the superior race, we can readily understand why liberal and educated people should often be imbued with the alleged inferiority of the "Semite," and look at him with suspicion. An excellent illustration is to be seen in a recent work by Shaler, an American author of note, who says that he has investigated the problem personally, and asked some twenty of his friends for introspective investigation, and the conclusion he arrives at is the old idea of "race" differences between the "Aryan" and the "Semite," and not at all mere differences in faith. His "fair hypothesis" is that "the trouble is attributable mainly to something which takes place in the intercourse between individuals of diverse stocks." He sees a confirmation of this hypothesis in the repugnance of the whites against the blacks. He forgets, however, that baptism often helps a "Semite" to remove all his objectionable traits, while the negro cannot by any known means reconcile his white neighbour. His suggestion that it is a "spontaneous instinctive contact dislike" and an "emotional and instinctive state, being in effect the same as that which is always excited by contact of racially different men," is rather vague, and admits of no proof for or against.[1]

have adhered tenaciously under the severest stress of persecution, and the greater part of which makes up the main principles of Christianity and Mohammedanism; while the gypsies are heathens, and often adopt the religion of the people around them, at least giving the impression that they do. The Jew adopts the language of the dominant people as his vernacular; the gypsy holds on to his Romany. The Jew is plastic, and accommodates himself to the social environment in which he lives as soon as the laws of the state are not in his way; the gypsy looks down with disdain on every ideal of those who differ from him. The Jew is an active worker, thrifty and persevering, trying to amass wealth, power, and to become a factor in the social and political life of the country in which he lives, while the gypsy is shiftless and lazy, never caring for the future. The Jew is a settled inhabitant, maintains a home and is a citizen, while the gypsy remains a nomad, caring little for the advantages of citizenship. The Jew has participated and contributed to the civilization and progress of the world, while the gypsy has done nothing of the kind.

[1] See N. S. Shaler, *The Neighbour*, pp. 107-111; Boston, 1904.

This alleged instinctive dislike for the Jew is differently explained by Max Nordau, in an essay on the psychological causes of Anti-Semitism,[1] as caused by misoneism, which he, in common, with Lombroso, considers one of the most fundamental and general traits of human and animal psychology. Every creature endowed with consciousness bears a certain animosity toward every other creature which differs from itself in appearance, habits, and disposition. Especially is this the case when the differing group constitutes only a small and weak minority, and we find no need for suppressing or concealing our aversion to the stranger. He can then be used as the scapegoat for all the shortcomings, mistakes, and misfortunes of the majority around him. This was undoubtedly true in former ages, and to a certain extent the Jew differs in habits, in customs, from his neighbours in Eastern Europe at present. But as we have shown elsewhere in this work, there is no ethnic difference of great significance to sustain such a theory. Social causes are more operative in this direction. Indeed, the baptismal waters remove all disabilities in one, or at most two, generations, proving that it is not altogether the Jew who is disliked, but it is his Judaism.

We believe that Leroy Beaulieu is nearer the truth in his explanation. " Religious differences and mutual intolerance," he says, "are forces strong enough to separate men of the same blood into hostile and almost foreign tribes. And the old lines of division are often visible in social customs long enough after the hatreds which produced them have passed away. Consider by way of example the position of the French Protestants. Even at the present time, when the dividing walls of governmental ordinances and the barriers of prejudice between them and us have been levelled, and in every school their children sit side by side with ours, it seems at times to us, Catholics, as if the French Protestants still retained a certain Puritan stiffness foreign to the French nature. There appears to be in their manners, their speech, and their turn of mind something strange, something Swiss, something Genevese, I might say, for want of a better

[1] *La Vita Internationale*, 1897; *Zionistische Schriften*, pp. 199-201, 360-367.

word. I have known Parisian Freethinkers who, having accidentally fallen in with Protestant fellow-countrymen, felt themselves entirely out of place, having no ear for what has been humorously called the 'Patois of Canaan.' And yet, although many of them have come to us, or come back to us, from the beyond the Rhine or the Jura, our Protestants are often as thoroughly French in blood as our old Catholic families, and woe to him who would dare to question their patriotism. Similar illustrations might be drawn from the Irish Presbyterians and the Catholics of the Netherlands, the Hungarian Calvinists, the Piedmontese natives of Vaud, and certain *Raskolniks* of Russia."[1]

The bulk of the Jews, those who live in poverty and have a hard struggle to make both ends meet, are not affected by this social discrimination. It is mostly the emancipated Jew who is disappointed by meeting obstructions on the way he lays out for himself. Nothing but a reaction could be expected under the circumstances. Some have despairingly given up the struggle against such great odds and returned to certain aspirations of the Jews which have consoled them during centuries of oppression, abuse, and persecutions among the European nations. They again begin to dream of a Jewish kingdom or republic in Palestine, their own home, where they will not be exposed to political and civil disabilities, to massacres, or to social discriminations at the hands of those who believe differently. They look forward to a revival of the national consciousness of the Jews, and do their best to assert themselves as Jews at every opportunity. These are the Zionists, Territorialists, and other nationally-conscious Jews who have been ardently advocating their cause within the last twenty years. As will be seen in a subsequent chapter, they are not in the majority, and do not include in their ranks many of the prominent Jews in any country. On the other hand, the Jews who have since their emancipation attained eminence in any walk of life have taken an entirely different view of the situation and adopt radical methods for the solution of the Jewish problem. Having discarded most of the separative tenets of Judaism, and finding nothing in the

[1] *Israel among the Nations*, pp. 303-304.

way of intimate association with their fellow-men who profess Christianity, they often take the decisive step which removes all the disabilities from which they, as well as their ancestors, for generations have suffered. Even if they themselves are not to be the gainers, they at least hope that their children will not be handicapped by that heavy load of Judaism. This voluntary baptism, which is so prevalent among certain classes of Jews, is an interesting social phenomenon in the history of the Children of Israel, and deserves to be treated in detail. Its causes and effects are of more than passing importance in regard to the present condition as well as the future of the Jews among the nations. Indeed, it appears from all available data that while it is mainly used by Jews who wish to remove the social disabilities from which they suffer, and that in each individual case of baptism it has, sooner or later, the desired effect, it makes the burden harder for those who remain within the fold of Judaism by removing from their midst the most assimilated as well as the best elements among them, elements in which they have taken great pride. The result is that an excessively large proportion of Jews are upstarts, or *parvenus*, who, in their attempts to gain recognition, often cast discredit on their co-religionists.

In his study of the problem of baptism, Ruppin arrives at the conclusion that the Jews are the more inclined to change their faith for Christianity the more they participate in the intellectual life of modern times.[1] Samter, in his study of the baptism of Jews, also says that the modern estrangement of the Jews from their religion is mainly due to their emergence from their isolated life heretofore, and their participation in the general culture of the peoples among which they live.[2] It is a fact that as long as the portals of the Ghetto are bolted and he remains unaffected by the life, habits, and customs of the surrounding peoples, the Jew remains faithful to his creed, and even prefers martyrdom in case severe measures are taken to bring him to the Church. As soon, however, as the gates of the Ghetto are thrown open, and he begins to come into intimate contact with his non-Jewish neigh-

[1] A. Ruppin, *Die Juden der Gegenwart*, p. 69.
[2] Samter, *loc. cit.*, p. 94.

bours, he is affected by their civilization, culture, ideals, and aspirations; and finding that his march of progress is more or less impeded, or even checked, he often displays no hesitation in passing through the gates of the Church on his way to success. During preceding ages it was usually political and civil disabilities, expulsions, confiscation of property, massacres, and the like that have convinced some Jews of the superiority of the Christian or Mohammedan religion. Often thousands of Jews have been "converted" *en masse* by these methods.[1] But making all allowances it appears that Judaism lost just as many, perhaps even more of its adherents during prospering periods than during massacres and expulsions. To mention only two periods in Jewish history which bear out this assertion: during the Hellenic period, when they adopted the Greek language, habits, and customs, they soon began to discard Judaism, and were even ashamed to be recognized as children of Israel. Particularly offensive was it to some to appear nude in the gymnasium, and thus expose themselves to be recognized as circumcised. Judaism lost at that time many of its followers. Similarly in Spain they assimilated the current mode of thought and action and began to discard Judaism. A Jewish savant wrote the following about their condition at that period:

[1] An active missionary in Spain, Vincent Ferrer, afterwards a saint, is said to have converted 35,000 Jews into devout Christians by his preaching and miracles. Milman (*History of the Jews*, vol. ii., p. 387) quotes from his biography that "the Jews, before the insurrection in July 1391, were assembled for worship in a noble synagogue, afterwards the Monastery of St. Christopher. A voice was heard three times, 'Ye Jews, depart from my house.' The Jews took no heed. On the ninth of the month, when they were again in prayer, the holy martyr spoke once more, rebuked their obstinacy, and threatened them with condign punishment. The perverse and blind race were not moved by this celestial monition. In the middle of the day a procession of boys, with crucifixes and white banners, appeared at the gates of the Jewry, crying out to the Jews to be converted to the faith of Christ and be baptized. The Jews, dreading popular fury, closed their gates, some of the boys and some men remaining within; the men raised a cry that the Jews were murdering the boys; the rabble rose, burst the gates, slew 300, and sacked the whole quarter. At the sight of this carnage, the eyes of many Jews were opened; they fled to the Cardinal Archbishop of Valencia, Don Jayme of Arragon, and, relating the marvels about St. Christopher, demanded baptism." Such marvels often convinced the mediæval Jews in various countries of the superiority of the Christian religion.

"I know Jews in whose homes no co-religionist is ever admitted; they keep themselves aloof as if their gold had ennobled them. The word Jew must not be mentioned in the presence of their servants; in fact, they are not ashamed to deny everything Jewish, and even to scoff at Judaism. The children are not given presents on *Purim*, as our sacred laws and customs ordain, but on Christmas. Jewish holidays are not at all kept. Those who still pray in Hebrew are frightfully alarmed when a non-Jew enters at the time, and drop their prayers at once. The girls do not pray in Hebrew at all. Indeed, nothing Jewish remained in these families; during my youth they were all baptized."[1] Samter, quoting the above, aptly remarks, "Does this author speak of Berlin? No, he deals with the conditions of the Spanish Jews of the fourteenth and fifteenth centuries." To those well acquainted with Jewish history it appears that the persecutions to which they were at that time subjected rescued Judaism among a great number of its followers who, had they peacefully remained in Spain, would have sooner or later become assimilated to such an extent as to be lost to their co-religionists.

Similar phenomena affecting a yet larger number of Jews are seen to-day in every country where they have been emancipated, and even in Eastern Europe among the richer children of Abraham. The spirit engendered by the Talmud, that spirit of exclusiveness which held them together for centuries, is vanishing wherever the Jew is admitted freely into the modern schools and universities. Abandoning most of the ritual and ceremonial tenets of their religion, there is very little left for which to struggle and uphold. The result is that most of these Jews can hardly be considered Jews; they are mostly Rationalists and altogether Freethinkers. For such it is often not difficult to submit to baptism when they find that it will give them important advantages or remove some obstacle in their way. Those who for one reason or another do not care to abjure the faith of their ancestors themselves often baptize their children at birth. This has been done by many Jews in Germany, Austria, and France. "In the Strassburg University we can count more Jewish professors than is necessary for a Jewish prayer meeting,"

[1] L. Zunz, *Ges. Schriften*, vol. ii., p. 177; Berlin, 1876.

writes a correspondent. "None of them have been baptized, but not one of them has neglected to baptize his children."[1] Even Cremieau, the late president of the Alliance Israélite Universélle, who has done so much for his co-religionists, has baptized his children with a view of assuring them a smoother road in their future life. As Gutzkow says, the majority of Jewish baptisms are the result of their intense love for their children.[2] Even in France and England, where the Jew does not suffer as much as in other countries from the exclusion from social and political advantages, baptism has been decimating the higher classes of Jews, and, together with mixed marriages, has prevented the accumulation of aristocratic families among them. In a list of prominent converts to Christianity given in the *Jewish Encyclopædia*, which does not include living converts, and is not by any means exhaustive, it is seen that the majority of Jewish-German savants and litterateurs of first and second rank have been sprinkled with holy water. French Jews are rare, "which is probably owing to the fact that conversion was not necessary to a public career in that country."[3] Even England has been affected. Many of the most prominent Spanish and Portuguese Jewish families whose parents fled from Spain, sacrificing everything while refusing to abjure their faith, have during the nineteenth century voluntarily adopted Christianity. The Bernals, Furtados, Ricardos, Disraelis, Ximenes, Lopezes, Uziels, and many others have been lost to Judaism in this manner.

From statistics compiled by several authors,[4] taking as their sources either governmental documents or reports of the Jewish communities or of missionary societies, it appears that during the nineteenth century there have been baptized in Europe about 224,000 Jews. Of these 84,000 exchanged Judaism for the Greek Orthodox Church in Russia. It is noteworthy that among the Russian Jews

[1] *Allgemeine Israelitische Wochenschrift*, p. 640; 1898.
[2] K. Gutzkow, *Ges. Schriften*, vol. vi. p. 323; Frankfort, 1845.
[3] *Jewish Encyclopædia*, vol. iv. p. 253. A more recent list of "celebrities of Jewish birth or descent" is given in the *Jewish Year Book*, pp. 279-291; London, 1909.
[4] See Joh. de le Roi, *Judentaufen im 19 Jahrhundert*, Leipzig, 1899; N. Samter, *Judentaufen im 19 Jahrhundert*, Berlin, 1906; A. Ruppin, *Die Juden der Gegenwart*, pp. 62-77, Berlin, 1904.

nearly 4,000 have joined the Protestant Churches. The reason is that many cultured Jews who decide that the only way to get along on the path of progress is baptism give preference to the Protestant ministers to escort them to salvation from disabilities which became unbearable. In the Greek Orthodox Church they have to submit to certain ceremonials which are distasteful to them. The English clergymen are the preferred class of Christian ministers for the purpose, because, without subjecting the nascent Christian to any rituals or ceremonials, they simply issue a certificate to the effect that the bearer has been admitted to the Church and is to be considered a "Christian" henceforth. Many Jews in St. Petersburg, Moscow, Kieff, etc., where they are not permitted to live, when asked how they succeeded in remaining there, answer, "I reside here on a baptismal certificate."[1]

That the more cultured as well as the richer Jews more often abandon Judaism than their poorer as well as their uncultured co-religionists is seen from conditions in Austria. There they are politically free, and many Jews have even been elected to Parliament. Socially they are, however, ostracized and maltreated in every conceivable manner. Moreover, in that country we have about 900,000 Jews living in the provinces of Galicia and Bukowina, who, in spite of their emancipation, have remained backward and live in their primitive way, strictly adhering to their faith, traditions, customs, and habits, hardly affected by modern conditions. In other provinces, in Lower Austria, Moravia, Bohemia, etc., there are 300,000 Jews who have more or less abandoned their separative practices, who speak the language of the country, dress like the rest of the population, and attend the same schools, thus coming in more or less intimate contact with their non-Jewish neighbours. It appears from statistics compiled by Thon that in Galicia and the Bukowina baptism is exceedingly rare, while in

---

[1] Major W. Evans Gordon repeats a characteristic story of a Jew whose business interests required that he should reside in St. Petersburg, and he determined to be baptized. He was prepared for the rite, and at the end of his instruction in the tenets of the Orthodox Church his preceptor asked him, "What do you believe?" "I believe," he replied, "that now I shall not be driven out of St. Petersburg." "Ah, Jewish brain—Jewish brain!" said the tutor, and, beckoning the pupil to his side, he whispered, "I, too, am a Jew."—*The Alien Immigrant*, p. 63; London, 1903.

Lower Austria, Moravia, and Bohemia it is quite frequent. This is evident when the city of Vienna is compared with the two largest Galician cities, Cracow and Lemberg.[1]

In Vienna the social conditions of the Jews are about the same as those in Berlin, Paris, London, etc. They are cultured, and a large proportion are economically prosperous. From statistics of baptisms in that city, it appears that during the thirty-seven years, 1868-1904, Judaism lost to the Church in that city 9,675 adherents, of which 5,426 were men and 4,249 women. In 1868, before their emancipation, only seven Jews were baptized; during the five years, 1868-72, the annual average was but thirty-two baptisms. But then emancipation came, with its impetus to assimilation, and the number of baptisms began to increase steadily, so that during the five years, 1900-04, the annual average was 577, and in 1905-06, 610 annually. This does not include cases of baptism of children whose parents remain within the fold of Judaism. The social conditions of the baptized Jews are an interesting topic for inquiry, because they throw a sidelight on the causes which are operative in the direction of the defilement of Judaism. From Thon's figures it appears that three-fourths of all the Jews who join the Church are unmarried, showing that one of the important causes of baptism is marriage with a Christian consort, especially since mixed marriages are not permitted in Austria. The fact that about one-half the number are of marriageable age, between twenty and thirty tends to confirm this view, but it also shows that the fact that a Jew is impeded in the advancement of his vocation is another factor. The vast majority of the population of Austria being Roman Catholic, it is natural that most of the Jews who abjure their faith should join this Church. It is, however, noteworthy that only a little over one-half of the converts become Roman Catholics; and, although only a little over one per cent. of the general population of Austria is Protestant, 23.1 per cent. of all the baptized Jews became Protestants, while 19.9 per cent. declared themselves Freethinkers (*Confessionslos*). These last are an interesting

[1] See J. Thon, "Taufbewegung der Juden in Oesterreich," *Zeitschr. Demogr. u. Statistik der Juden*, pp. 6-12, 1908; also *Die Juden in Oesterreich*, pp. 69-81.

class. It must be mentioned that in Austria Dissenters or Freethinkers do not enjoy any advantages, probably less than the Jews, because the clericals, who have great power, will rather stand for a Jew than a Freethinker. The Jews who declare themselves Freethinkers, while abandoning Judaism, do so consequently for no purpose of material advancement; in the vast majority of cases it is done in order to be permitted to marry a non-Jewish consort, because mixed marriages are not allowed in Austria.[1] It is also noteworthy in this connection that one-third of all those who declared themselves Freethinkers during 1868-1903 in Vienna were of Jewish origin. This, in connection with the fact that so many, when abandoning Judaism, prefer the Protestant Church in that clerical Roman Catholic country, shows that they want to slip away as quietly as possible, without having to undergo various ceremonials characteristic of Roman baptism. The large number of Freethinkers from the Jewish fold may also be explained in another way. Jews who discard the religion and traditions of their ancestors often do so because of their rationalist tendencies, and in such cases the Trinity does not appeal to them. A similar phenomenon is to be observed among the Jews in the United States, where the Ethical Culture movement has attracted a large number of former Jews. The majority of the baptized Jews in Vienna were by occupation engaged in the liberal professions, such as physicians, lawyers, students, teachers, civil and military functionaries of the State; in short, vocations in which the social disabilities of the Jews are most acute. Very few were labourers and artisans, because these hardly suffer in that city from disabilities of the kind mentioned, nor do they often need a baptismal certificate in order to obtain employment.

In contrast with Vienna may be taken Cracow and Lemberg, two cities where the Jews have enjoyed emancipation for exactly the same period of time, but, for various reasons, have remained backward, keeping themselves isolated from the Christian population around them, and thus remaining unaffected to a large extent by modern conditions. These two cities have a combined Jewish population of 69,928 (Census, 1900), among which mis-

[1] See Chapter IX.

sionaries have been hard at work propagating their faith, not even stopping at taking children from the bosom of their mothers and thus bring them to salvation. In Lemberg, during the six years, 1897-1902, only 157 (77 Jews and 80 Jewesses) were baptized; 68 per cent. joined the Roman Catholic Church, 12.7 per cent. the Greek Catholic, and 15.3 per cent. the Evangelical Church. The vast majority, 115, were unmarried, and 137 between the ages of 14 and 40. From Cracow there are available statistics for 16 years, 1887-1902, showing that Judaism lost during that period 444 adherents in this manner. Among them were more women than men, 302 and 142 respectively; 412, or 92.8 per cent., were unmarried; and 395, or 89 per cent., were less than 30 years of age. It is interesting to note that only 10 per cent. of these backsliders were natives or inhabitants of Cracow, 66 per cent. came from various parts of the country for the purpose, 18 per cent. came from Russia and Poland, and 5.4 per cent. from other countries. It thus appears that Cracow forms some kind of a central point for Galician Jews who want to abjure their faith, and even some from other countries are often attracted thither under such circumstances.

From all available statistics it appears that in Austrian Galicia and Bukowina baptisms are comparatively rare, about one out of 10,000 is lost to Judaism in this manner annually. In Vienna it is much more frequent, about one out of 200 Jews is baptized annually. The causes of this disparity have been indicated already. It mainly depends on the extent to which Jews come in contact with their neighbours.

Hungary also publishes some details about the baptism of Jews. Excluding those who, after deserting Judaism, do not join any other Church, but declare themselves Freethinkers, the average annual number of baptisms was, during 1896-1900, 261; since then the number has swelled so that in 1908 there were registered 510 baptisms, 255 men and 255 women. During 1896-1908 Judaism lost in that country through baptism 5,790 persons, or 482 annually on the average. On the basis of the natural increase during 1908 it made up 4.3 per cent. of the Jewish excess of births over deaths. The majority joined the Roman Catholic Church.¹ Budapest seems to be here the central point for baptism. During 1896, 120, Jews were baptized in that city, and the annual number kept on increasing, reaching 206 in 1904.²

Stronger yet than in Budapest has been the movement of baptism in Berlin. In that city there was a great rush of Jews in the direction of the Church during the first decade of the nineteenth century, when they began to emerge from the Ghetto; still, the movement soon ceased, and but few backsliders were recorded. During 1872-76 the average number of baptisms was 26 annually, or one in 1,700 Jews. But soon the anti-Semitic movement began to make its appearance, social ostracism was acutely felt by the Jews, and the number of those who found it to their advantage to change their faith, in order to clear the way of all obstructions which kept them back in their march of progress, began to grow entirely out of all proportion to the growth of the Jewish population. During the five years 1899-1903 it reached an average annual number of 153, and in 1908 186 baptisms, or one to 535 Jews.³ From a study of the social conditions of the baptized Jews in Berlin, made by Blau,⁴ it is shown that 70 per cent. were between twenty and forty years of age, mostly unmarried. The occupations of these baptized Jews were most varied, but the largest contingent was derived from among the mercantile class—43 per cent. were merchants, agents, manufacturers, bankers, etc. Next in frequency to these merchants come the physicians, who made up 11.81 per cent., not including students of medicine; while the jurists were a close second, 11.1 per cent. More than one-third, 35.88 per cent., of the Jews who were baptized in Berlin had a liberal education, not including the authors and editors, who made up 3.4 per cent. of the total number.⁵

---

¹ *Ungarisches Statistisches Jahrbuch*, vol. xvi. ; also *Zeitschr. Demogr. Stat. d. Juden*, vol. iii., p. 45, vol. vi., p. 112.

² Samter, *Judentaufen im 19, Jahrhundert*, p. 148.

³ Samter, *Ibid.*, p. 147.

⁴ Bruno Blau, *Austritte aus dem Judenthum in Berlin* ; Berlin, 1908. Also *Zeitschr. Demogr. Sta. Juden*, pp. 145-153, 1907 ; pp. 87-90, 1909.

⁵ From Jewish history it appears that it was always the richer and the more cultured who were more apt to desert Judaism than the poorer classes of Jews. According to a Hebrew writer, Joseph Jabez, himself one of the

All these facts point to two main causes of baptism among the Jews in countries where they have been emancipated—marriage and advancement. In Austria, where mixed marriages are not permitted by law, marriage appears to be as great a factor as advancement in life. In Germany the most important factor is not marriage, because mixed marriages are allowed. Here it is mostly the well-to-do merchant, as well as the physician and lawyer, who suffers from the disabilities which emancipation has not removed. In the case of the Jew with an academic education, we have already seen that the only road to advancement in his profession is baptism, and the same is true of many who look for an appointment in any of the government bureaux. Having been freed from the ancient political disabilities, and having abandoned most of the separative tenets of his religion, the wealthy and the cultured Jew has of late become either a ceremonial deist or altogether a Freethinker. Under the circumstance, in case he finds that modern society is not inclined to forget and forgive that his parents were Jews, or that an appointment in a university is withheld because of the faith of his ancestors, which he has practically discarded, he, often against his inner self, visits a Christian clergyman and buys a baptismal certificate, with the hope that even if he personally should not be much of a gainer, his children at least will be freed from the stigma of Judaism. Many have nothing to lose, while nearly all believe, often with truth, that they have everything to gain, be it social advancement, a position in a government bureau, an appointment as teacher in a school, college, or university, and the like.

That these are the main causes of baptisms in countries where the Jews have been politically emancipated is confirmed by the fact that in those countries in which religion

refugees at the time of their expulsion from Spain in 1492, it was mostly those who were known for their riches or culture who submitted to baptism, while the poor and humble sacrificed everything for their faith. (Cf. Samter, *Judentaufen*, p. 78). The same is seen among the Poles in Russia and Germany: the prosperous and learned more often desert Romanism for the Greek Church or Protestantism than their poorer compatriots, perhaps because the latter have little to gain by the change. Lecky (*The Leaders of Public Opinion in Ireland*, 1871) shows that similar conditions prevailed among the Irish Catholics during the eighteenth century.

is not always a hindrance to advancement, as is the case in England, France, Italy, the United States, etc., very few baptisms are taking place.[1] In these countries, as has already been shown, Judaism suffers defilement from other causes, mainly mixed marriages, which work in the same direction—namely, removing from Judaism the wealthiest, the most cultured, and the best assimilated.

The general effect of these factors on the social status of the Jews in Western Europe and America cannot be overestimated. In the first place, the number of native Jews either remains stationary or is actually decreasing, as a result of the large number of baptisms and of mixed marriages, coupled with a vanishing birth-rate. The loss sustained by Judaism includes Jews who, had they remained true to their faith during several generations of prosperity and culture, would have formed a nucleus of Jewish aristocracy endowed with the attributes requisite for membership in the society for which they crave. But as conditions prevail at present, they are removed in the manner indicated, and their places are filled by large hordes of Jews from Eastern Europe, driven away from their native lands by political persecution, with its concomitant misery and poverty, and attracted to France, Switzerland, England, the United States, etc., by the freedom as well as by the superior economic prospects. Their adaptability is well known: they display a remarkable power of regeneration, and in a short period of time these immigrants ascend in the social, economic, and intellectual scale, and demand recognition, which their Christian neighbours are often slow to extend. "The metamorphosis was often too sudden to be complete," says Leroy Beaulieu. "There seems, at times, something incongruous in the French and English (and I may add

---

[1] I am aware that the missionary societies publish reports showing that in England and the United States many Jewish souls are annually saved by baptism. But most of the Jews who are baptized in these countries at present belong to the poorer classes, who are actually bribed to declare themselves Christians, and thus justify the endowments of the missionary societies by pious Christians. I have known Jews who have been baptized many times in several cities in England and the United States and received payment on every occasion. One assured me that a missionary in New York, an apostate of Jewish origin, knew all about the trick, and did not mind it as long as he could show that he gained a soul for the Church.

American) Israelites whose fathers have emigrated from Poland and Germany. A glance, a word, a gesture, all of a sudden lays bare the old Jews at bottom. 'Scratch an Israelite,' said a friend to me, 'and you will find the Jew of the Ghetto.'"[1]. The final result is that the number of *parvenus*, or upstarts, is abnormally large among the European and American Jews.

People of other faiths have also upstarts, but the children of these *parvenus* remain within their fold; and having received superior breeding and education, they are fit for the society in which their parents were more or less tabooed. One has to consider the large number of upstarts in the United States who do not at all differ from the Jewish upstarts. Their arrogance, ostentation, and self-assertion, their lack of manners, want of tact and distinction are notorious. They also crave for display, jewels, horses, and anything that may excite comment; and will go to any extreme to gain recognition in European "noble" society, or give away their hard-earned fortunes to some scion of European family with a title. Persons of this type of *parvenu*, so common in America but not unknown in any other country, also have hotels in Europe which are shunned by the native rich. The higher classes of English ladies and gentlemen, excepting such as have some special interest to meet these Americans, avoid many hostelries in London for fear of coming in intimate contact with these upstarts, who are characterized as noisy, ostentatious, pompous, lacking manners and tact—exactly what is said of the Jew. But eccentric or even repulsive as this class of people is, their children, or at least their grandchildren, will acquire the manners, tastes, the bearing, reserve, moderation, and distinction which go to make up a gentleman, and as such will redeem the good name of the American people. This is actually the case with a large number of Americans, especially in New England, who have had behind them a couple of generations of prosperity and culture.

With the Jews this is often not the case. A large proportion of the rich among them, as we have just seen, are either baptized or have entered into matrimony with Christians; and their descendants, no matter how refined,

---

[1] Leroy Beaulieu, *Israel among the Nations*, p. 218.

are no more considered Jews. In addition, having in their midst a large number of rich merchants, bankers, authors, journalists, etc., who have been self-made, they are everywhere in evidence, and are judged by their conduct, which is often unfavourable, just as is the case with other upstarts. As a matter of fact, Jews who have remained true to their faith during a few generations of material or intellectual success are admitted into the social life of the *haute société* of Europe, as is the case in England, France, Germany, and Italy. Even in the United States, where the line of demarcation is quite distinctly drawn against the Jew in "Society," exceptions are often made in cases of Jews who have been here for several generations. But there are comparatively few of this class, which again illustrates vividly the causes of their social disability. Here there were about 2,000 Jews at the beginning of the nineteenth century. Had they not been absorbed by the surrounding Christians, we should have now between 25,000 and 30,000 Jews who could trace back their ancestry as residents of the United States for more than a century. But as a matter of fact there is hardly one-fifth that number, and the few who have remained Jews do enjoy all the social advantages to which their position entitles them, in spite of the drawbacks placed in their way by the conduct of their German and Polish co-religionists who have come since. Confirmation in other countries is not wanting. Max Nordau summarizes conditions in France: "Of the descendants of the French members of the Synhedrion, not half are now Jews; and even of those who have not abjured Judaism many have Christians in their families. There is not a single Jewish house of more than half a century's standing which has not become related by marriage to Christians. Yet another generation and not one of these old families of French Jews will any longer adhere to Judaism. The poor, the young, and the uneducated have remained true to Judaism; but no sooner had a Jewish family attained wealth and culture, entered into higher careers, and been seized with ambition, than it was at once, or in the next generation, lost to Judaism."[1]

[1] Max Nordau, "The Decadence of Judaism in France," *Jewish Chronicle*, p. 10; London, January 10, 1907.

Similar conditions are known to exist in other countries, especially in Italy, Germany, England, and even in Russia and Poland. According to Samter, there are to be seen on the walls of the Jewish community (*Israelitische Kultus-gemeinde*) in Vienna portraits of former representatives, communal workers and philanthropists, of the Jews in that city. Their descendants are mostly Christians. In Berlin the descendants of the great Itzig family of the eighteenth century are now known as Christians under the name of Hitzig, the Ephraims are now Ebers and Ebertys, etc.; in Breslau the privileged Jews of former times have all been baptized, and in Königsberg conditions are not different.[1] In Italy we have already shown that there is hardly a Jewish family of note that has no Christian relatives, and their children are practically lost to Judaism; while in England the best and most distinguished Sephardic and many of the once prominent Ashkenazi families have been lost in this manner.[2] The statement made by a Jewish author that Judaism cannot withstand a couple of generations of prosperity is confirmed by modern conditions observed in Europe and America.

It is thus evident that there is hardly anything like a hereditary Jewish aristocracy; only few of those who have acquired wealth, culture, and social position, with their concomitant advantages in modern society, can trace back their ancestry for several generations as belonging to the same class. The vast majority of the Jews who have attained eminence in any walk of life during the first half of the nineteenth century have left descendants who are not any more within the fold of Judaism. Their places have been filled by a yet larger number of their former co-religionists who have risen from the lower social strata, or

[1] Samter, *Judentaufen im 19 Jahrhundert*, pp. 78-79.
[2] The Old Portuguese Congregation in Philadelphia offers an excellent example of the disintegration of the Jews in the United States after several generations in this country. They recently built a synagogue, a member having left the necessary funds for it as a legacy. But the nephew of the testator, who was the executor under the will, was a member of the Episcopalian Church. Rabbi Hirsch was called to officiate at the funeral of a well-known Jew, where he found that the whole family had either intermarried or gone over to Christianity. (*Jewish Chronicle*, May 27th, 1910.) Most rabbis in the United States have had similar experiences. Some call such persons "Cemetery Jews."

have immigrated from Eastern Europe. It is this last class that is usually discriminated against in the *haute société* of western cities. But they, just like their forerunners, adopting the habits, manners, and customs of the people among which they live, leave a progeny which is not averse to intermarriage with Christians, or to abjure their faith in case they find it to their advantage, and will sooner or later be lost to Judaism to give place to new upstarts, who again may create a "problem." Whether this means the complete absorption of Judaism in the near future is a question which cannot even be answered by conjectures. Lazare says that "the Jewish religion itself is in its death agony. It is the oldest of all existing religions, and it would seem right that it should be the first to disappear."[1] This cannot be taken seriously as long as there are such large numbers of Jews who, under stress of abuse and persecution, hold on steadfastly to their faith and traditions. As long as the six millions of Jews in Russia and Roumania are compelled to live under cruel discriminatory laws, segregated in Ghettoes or Pales of Settlements, isolated from their neighbours of other faiths, they will keep on increasing in numbers more than ample to replace those who are lost through intermarriages and baptisms in Western Europe and America.

[1] Bernard Lazare, *loc. cit.*, Chap. xiv.

CHAPTER XXII.

ASSIMILATION *versus* ZIONISM.

Tendencies among the modern Jews—Georg Brandes' view of his relation to Judaism—Causes of revival of Jewish Nationalist aspirations—The Zionist's programme—Zionism and assimilation—The Zionist's assumption of a distinct Jewish nation—Attempt to avert disintegration of Judaism—Are the Jews a nation?—The Jews were a nation before their emancipation in Europe—Judaism and the laws of Christian States have kept them apart from their neighbours—Assimilation of the Western Jews—Causes of denationalization of the modern Jews—Religion and nationality—Language and nationality—There is no national Jewish vernacular—Adoption of culture and civilization of the countries in which they live by modern Jews—The failure of the Nationalists in their efforts to revive the Jewish national spirit—What is Jewish art?—Is there a Jewish literature?—Absence of a specific Jewish spirit in painting, sculpture, music, and architecture—There is no Jewish folk-lore, folk-tales, folk-medicine, etc.—Professor Lazarus on Jewish nationalism—Why Palestine is inadequate to shelter all the Jews—Christendom would not favour renationalization of the Jews in the Holy Land—The fertility of Palestine—The difficulties in the way of developing Palestine industrially and commercially—Repatriation offers no solution of the Jewish problem—Zionism has not attracted the cultured Jews—Objections to an autonomous territory—The two tendencies observed among the modern Jews.

I<small>T</small> is evident from all available facts that Judaism thrives best when its faithful sons are isolated from the surrounding people, segregated in Ghettoes or Pales of Settlement, excluded from educational institutions frequented by people of the dominant faith, and thus prevented from coming into intimate contact with their non-Jewish neighbours. As a religious minority it is difficult for the Jews to preserve their identity after coming into close social contact with the majority around them; social intimacy means danger of losing many, I may say most, of their best elements. Anti-Semitism on the one hand and tendencies to assimilation and even fusion with the Christians among cultured Jews on the other, have made some thoughtful

Jews take note of the dangers threatening Judaism of to-day. The result is that two diametrically opposed tendencies are to be noted among the leading modern Jews, each working in a different direction, while aiming at the solution of the perennial "Jewish question." The leading Jews who have adapted themselves to the culture, customs, and manners of the countries in which they live begin to discard the separative tenets of Rabbinical teaching. They demand assimilation and adoption of the culture, ideals, and aspirations of the peoples among which they live. Those of them who still claim adherence to Judaism are of the opinion that they can best fulfil the mission of their religion by being good Englishmen, Frenchmen, Italians, Germans, Americans of Jewish faith. Most of these do not disdain fusion with the Christians through intermarriage. Their Rabbis teach that the Biblical interdiction of intermarriage was really intended for the priests of Israel, originally for the High Priest,[1] and not for all the Jews; or that only the "seven nations" of Canaan were tabooed by the Bible in order to prevent idolatrous practices among the Chosen People. The Christians are not tabooed, because they are not idolaters. This class of Jews also points to the impossibility of holding on to tenets of Judaism while living among Christians, and advocate and practise certain reforms which make their position more tenable. These are the reformed Jews of Western Europe and America. A large proportion of them go much farther, and join many of the rationalist movements, such as that of ethical culture in the United States[2] and the Freethinkers in Europe. The latter type of Jew is best represented by Georg Brandes, the eminent Scandinavian critic, who, in an article published in the *Frankfurter Zeitung* concerning his relation to Judaism, says:—"As a rule, writers when speaking of me refer to my Jewish origin. I may remark *en passant* that there is no danger that I should overlook in which

---

[1] Leviticus, xxi. 14.
[2] More recently many Jews in the United States, especially women, have joined the Christian Science churches, many of them, however, not deserting the synagogues, The Rabbis, just like the Christian ministers, have raised a stormy protest against the Jewish "Christian" Scientists, and point to its dangers to Judaism.

religious community I was born. I confess that if all my life I were not constantly reminded of the fact by others, I should have forgotten it, so little significance has it had for me. . . . As soon as any one puts his pen to paper to write about me, for or against me, invariably the first thing he says is that I am a Jew! How funny! If there is anything I am not, it is this. The whole of Denmark and the whole of Finland are impregnated with Judaism; their God is Jewish; their religion is reconstructed, developed Judaism, with a few mystic additions. The Old Testament in both lands is a holy book; and the New, which is still holier than the Old, was written by Jews. Half the Danish culture originates from Palestine; half its literature is thence inspired. Even the real Danish names, Petersen, Hansen, Jensen, etc., are Jewish names, Biblical names. If, then, a solitary young man succeeds for a short time in cutting adrift from the prevalent Judaism, he falls back again on all fours; returns, like so many Danes, to one of the many representatives of Jerusalem, to the Pope, or to Grundtvig, or (like Strindberg) to Swedenborg. There was a time when I was about the only man in the whole country who was not a Jew. Nevertheless I might almost say that the sole thing that everybody in the country knows about me, and the sole thing that they communicate to the whole world, is that I am one. They all live and breathe in Jerusalem's atmosphere. All the churches are full of it. It was not long since it was pumped into the universities. And he among the Danes who earliest, most zealously, and most obstinately in his spiritual life strove towards Athens they are never tired of dragging back to Jerusalem, which they can never eliminate from their own minds."

A large proportion of the intellectual Jews in Europe and America of to-day entertain the same view as to their relations to Jews and Judaism. In fact it can be stated that if on the one hand the Jews should not claim them, and on the other Christendom should not push them back to breathe the atmosphere of Jerusalem, they would like to forget it; they would like their children to remain in entire ignorance of it. It is from these that the *confessionslose* in Germany, the Ethical Culturists, "Christian Scientists," and most of the Reform Jews in England, France, and the United States draw their followers among Jews. It is this class of Jews that go down into the "melting pot" of Western countries, as Zangwill calls it, and alloy with their non-Jewish neighbours. Their effect on the social and political position of the Jews has already been indicated in a preceding chapter. But it remains yet to speak of that class of intellectual Jews who express an unwillingness to dissolve in the "melting pot" of Europe and America; who see in this tendency to assimilation real race suicide, and adopting the Chauvinistic ideas of their Christian neighbours, make strenuous efforts to revive a racial and national spirit among their co-religionists. Living in Eastern Europe, where the struggle of the oppressed nations is most acute, where minorities and often majorities are seen endeavouring to assert themselves against their oppressors, some Jews were inoculated with the nationalist tendencies and began to dream of the renationalization and repatriation of their people. Seeing that on the one hand their emancipation in Western Europe has brought new perils in the shape of Anti-Semitism and social ostracism; and that assimilation threatens their survival as Jews among people of other faiths, they in their discouragement begin to look for a specific remedy which will surely cure Judaism. Considering that for centuries the Jews, dispersed among the nations, never forgot Zion, *Eretz Israel*, the land of Israel, and awaited the Messiah to reappear and reassemble the Jews from various countries in which their fate has dispersed them, lead them back to Palestine and re-establish a Jewish kingdom, it is not surprising that the dreamers among the modern Jews have again turned their eyes toward Palestine. The orthodox Jews of to-day expect yet that Messiah will come at any time, in spite of the fact that Christian missionaries have been industriously at work to convince them that he had already appeared in the person of Jesus Christ; but the more enlightened Jews, having lost confidence in supernatural redemption, have been imbued with the idea that the only way to relieve their people from all political and social disabilities is to "obtain for the Jewish people a legally secured, publicly recognized home in Palestine," as the Zionists demand, or "to acquire a territory in any place of the world upon an autonomous basis for those Jews who are unable or unwilling to remain in the lands in which they live at present," as is demanded by Zangwill's "Jewish Territorial Organization." As the best means of attaining their object the Zionists have adopted the following programme:—1. To promote the settlement in Palestine of Jewish agriculturists, handicraftsmen, industrialists, and men following professions; 2. To centralize the Jewish people by means of general institutions agreeably to the laws of the land; 3. To strengthen Jewish sentiment and national self-consciousness; and 4. To obtain the sanction of governments necessary to carrying out the object of Zionism. "Zionism is an ideal," according to Max Nordau, "a wish, a hope, just as Messianic Zionism was and is. But the new Zionism, which is called political, is distinguished from the old religious Messianic Zionism in this, that it repudiates all mysticism and does not rely upon the return to Palestine to be accomplished by a miracle, but is resolved to bring it about through its own efforts. The new Zionism has partly arisen out of the inner impulses of Jewry. . . . It is also partly the effect of two influences that have come from without: first, the national idea that has dominated European thought and feeling for half a century and determined international politics; secondly, Anti-Semitism, under which the Jews of all countries have to suffer more or less." "Doubtless many an educated Jew has been constrained only through Anti-Semitism to attach himself again to Judaism," Nordau goes on to say, "and he would again fall away if his Christian compatriots would welcome him as a friend."[1]

To the Zionists the Jews are a distinct, non-European race which has preserved itself in its original purity in spite of the Jews' wanderings all over the globe. They hold that the Jews can never merge with the European races, and are bound to remain distinct from their Christian or Mohammedan neighbours. The Jewish problem can therefore not be solved by emancipation, as is evident in Western Europe, where they still have troubles after one hundred years of freedom and political equality. Nor

[1] Max Nordau, *Zionism: its History and its Aims*, pp. 6-7; London, 1905.

ASSIMILATION *versus* ZIONISM.

will emigration solve the problem of the Jews in countries where they suffer from political oppression. "Like previous migration of Jews, it has produced fresh trouble," say the Zionists in an "Official Statement to the Christian World." "These large numbers of poor Jews are, at best, not welcome in the places to which they migrate. Their immigration is not that merely of an alien people who, whatever temporary inconvenience may be caused by their arrival, will soon merge in the general population of their new home. The immigration of Jews is different. They form or augment a body differentiated from the general population."[1] They object to assimilation. "With whom is the Jew of Eastern Europe to assimilate if he is to assimilate at all? Clearly not with the Russian Moujik or the Galician or Polish peasant. But this is a proposal that a superior race shall become absorbed by a greatly inferior, a stronger by a weaker, a sober by a particularly unsober one, and is altogether contrary to the course of race absorption. The Jew has no mean opinion of the status of his race in the world. Purer than most, it is one of the oldest; its preservation is part, a great part, of his religious belief. He does not readily yield it even to advance civilization."[2]

To the Zionists the Jews are not only bound together by a common religion, differing from others only in creed; they are not only a race having a common origin; but a nation with a distinct history, traditions, aspirations, ideals, etc. "The hypothesis upon which political Zionism is based is that there is a Jewish nation," says Nordau,[3] and "whoever maintains and believes that the Jews are not a nation cannot in truth be a Zionist." Says another Zionist, in reply to a question whether the Jews cannot completely identify themselves with the English nation: "They (the Zionists) feel that as Jews this is not possible. They cannot be as entirely English in thought as the man who is born of English parents and descended from ancestors who have mingled their blood with other Englishmen for generations. Jews must always have a feeling of sympathy and brotherhood with the Jewish

---

[1] *Zionism: a Jewish Statement to the Christian World*, p. 4; published by the Federation of American Zionists, New York, 1907.
[2] *Ibid.*, p. 7. [3] *Loc. cit.*, p. 10.

people in all other parts of the world, and must always, in some degree, remain socially separate if they are to continue loyal to their religion. There is no use disguising this fact. To me it seems impossible to separate religion from nationality in Judaism without destroying both. The Jewish religion is and must for ever remain national, and Jewish nationalism is and must ever be religious. . . . The fundamental cleavage between Judaism and Christianity was that the Christian community rejected the national law, while the Jews felt it to be essential."[1] Amplifying this statement, after being taken to task by eminent British Jews, the same writer says: "'Englishman' is a word used in two senses: it means either a person who is a citizen of the British nation—and in this sense a Jew may, of course, be fully an Englishman and born of English parents—or a person who is a member of the Anglo-Saxon people as distinguished from a Welshman, a Scotchman, or an Irishman. Try as he may, a Jew cannot become fully English in this sense unless by intermarriage he 'mingles his blood'; and then he ceases to belong to Jewry. Not only is the Jew different from other members of the nation in blood, but he has a history, a literature, a culture, and traditions of his own—these are among the chief elements of nationality which he does not share with other Englishmen; and he can only disown this splendid heritage at the price of disloyalty to his people and the certain disintegration of his religion."[2]

This fear of the disintegration of Judaism which is at the bottom of Zionism had already been indicated by Spinoza, who stated that the emancipation of the Jews must inevitably lead to the extinction of Judaism wherever the process is extended beyond the political to the social sphere, and throughout it has been evident that such is the case with the modern Jews. Moreover, the Zionists see no relief in emancipation. "The attempt to make the Jews of France and Germany entirely French and German in thought, and to identify them entirely with the French and German nations, has been tried in the last one hundred

[1] Norman Bentwich, in *Jewish Chronicle*, p. 22; London, March 26, 1909.
[2] N. Bentwich, "Zionism at the Universities," *Jewish Chronicle*, p. 13; April 16, 1909.

years. It has succeeded in detaching many of them from Judaism, but it has failed to avert Anti-Semitism. The attempt to make young English Jews entirely English in thought and to identify them entirely with the English people has already succeeded in weakening English Judaism; by cutting at the root of Jewish idealism and impairing the hold of the religion with all that it means for the strengthening of moral character and the suppression of material aims, it may even foster Anti-Semitism in this country."[1]

It is thus evident that the Zionists' *raison d'être* is not only their sympathy with their suffering co-religionists in Eastern Europe, where they are being discriminated against politically, but is a sense of fear, of apprehension for the future of Judaism. In other words, although they maintain that the modern Jews are a race quite distinct from the other racial elements in Europe and America; although they claim that they are a separate nation, with tendencies, hopes, and aspirations differing greatly from the tendencies and aspirations of the non-Jews around them; and although they state a Jew can never become entirely a German, Frenchman, Englishman, or Italian in feeling and thought, they also confess that the most important fear they entertain is that the Jews are becoming estranged from the religion of their forefathers, discard their traditions, ideals, and aspirations as soon as they come in intimate social contact with the Christians. It is to preserve Judaism and to prevent the impending assimilation and perhaps fusion with the non-Jews that the Zionists are aiming most of their energies, indicating thereby their recognition that the assimilation of the Jews is not only possible, but has been going on since they have been emancipated in Western Europe. Knowing well

[1] *Ibid.*, p. 14. The Jewish nationalists cannot conceive a country in Europe without anti-Semitism. Wherever it is not yet evident they foresee its imminence as soon as Jews shall settle there in substantial numbers. (*Cf.* T. Herzl, *Der Judenstaat*, p. 47.) Zangwill (*Jewish Chronicle*, August 7th, 1908) maintains that although the ratio of Jews in Great Britain and Ireland is only one to every two hundred non-Jews, he already sees that England feels unable to digest this alien mass and is beginning to complain of her suffering from indigestion. "We may be sure," he concludes, "that if the number in this country reached only five per cent. of the Jews in the world—*i.e.*, under half a million, we should have violent anti-Semitism."

that it is the separative tenets of their religion which, above all, have kept the Jews from amalgamating with their non-Jewish neighbours for centuries, and realizing that, with the entry of the Jew into modern life, he must also give up most of his exclusiveness, they find that the only way to keep him true to the faith, traditions, and ideals of his forefathers is to separate him from foreign influences. Inasmuch as the Ghetto is not to be thought of again, and the Russian Pale of Settlement has its peculiar perils, the Zionists find that only repatriation and renationalization will preserve Judaism, and they are exerting their efforts in these directions. Their success we will discuss further on. Meanwhile, it is important to inquire in detail into the fundamental problems of Zionism. The question of race has already been discussed, and we arrived at the conclusion that the alleged purity of the Jewish race is visionary and not substantiated by scientific observation.[1] There remains yet to inquire into the problem, "Are the Jews a nation?" Are they a separate nation living among other nations, and have they their own tendencies in life, ideals, aspirations, hopes, often organically opposed to the tendencies, aspirations, and ideals of their non-Jewish neighbours; in short, are they a state within a state in the various European countries? The Anti-Semites have maintained that this is the case. Hamman, the first Anti-Jewish agitator, charged them with being a "people scattered abroad and dispersed among the people in all provinces of Thy kingdom; and

---

[1] Max Nordau, an avowed disciple of Lombroso, knows that anthropological research has dissipated the notion of Jewish racial purity, but he places more confidence in the acute powers of observation of the street loafer who recognizes a Jew by his nose. "To be sure, the street loafer's diagnosis is not infallible, still it fails him only rarely. But then the scientific diagnosis is not always reliable. The acute eye of the street loafer," concludes Nordau, "is sufficient proof that the Jews are a race, or at least a variety, or, if you please, a sub-variety of mankind." (*Le Siècle*, 1899; *Zionistische Schriften*, p. 305). Zangwill asks, "Whoever heard of a religion that was limited to people of particular breed? Of divine truth that was only true for men of dark complexion?" (*Jewish Chronicle*, June 18th, 1909). But in Zangwill's novels there are many blonde Jews. Thus in the *Children of the Ghetto* Daniel is described as "flaxen-haired, blonde-faced" (p. 122-123); at the Purim Ball in the Jewish Club there were many blondes (p. 128); "the fish trade was almost monopolized by English Jews—blonde, healthy-looking fellows" (p. 272).

ASSIMILATION *versus* ZIONISM.

their laws are diverse from all people; neither keep they the king's laws; therefore it is not for the king's profit to suffer them."[1] Similar charges were made against them in ancient Greece and Rome,[2] during the Middle Ages, and by the modern Anti-Semites. It must be acknowledged that in former times these notions about the Jewish nation were not without foundation. It is problematical whether this holds good with the modern European Jews, especially those who have been emancipated and naturalized in the countries in which they live. This will be the subject of our inquiry in the following pages.

A study of the history of the Jews in dispersion up to the end of the eighteenth century shows that as long as religion was part and parcel of the European states the Jews were undoubtedly a nation. In ancient Greece and Rome they demanded and received perfect political and civil autonomy. They had their own quarters, not as distinct as the mediæval Ghetto, but where they preferred to live apart from the pagans. "Every Jewish community was authorized, at least tacitly, to form for itself an autonomous organization: administrative, financial, and judicial."[3] They possessed the right to levy taxes upon their members to defray common expenses, especially in connection with the maintenance of the synagogue.

---

[1] Esther, iii. 8.

[2] Most of the Greek and Roman classical writers who spoke of the Jews mention that the Jewish religion is anti-social. Hecatæus says Judaism prohibits humanity and hospitality; Apollonius Molo considers the Jews "godless and hostile to other men"; Apion, speaking of their abstinence from pork, circumcision, the Sabbath, etc., adds that Judaism is antagonistic to the laws of the people of other faiths; Philostratus is more outspoken when he says: "From olden times they have been opposed, not only to Rome, but to the rest of humanity. People who do not share with others their table, their libations, their prayers, their sacrifices, are further removed from us than Susa, or Bactria, or even farthest India." Juvenal and Tacitus speak in the same vein. *Cf.* Reinach, *Textes d'Auteurs Grecs et Romains relatifs au Judaisme,*; Paris, 1895. The charges of unfair business dealings, usury, etc., are not met with in the literature on the Jews written during the first millennium of the common era. It was only after they were prohibited from working at any occupation they may choose and forced to depend mainly on money exchange, banking, business, etc., during the Middle Ages that we meet with the latter charges. See B. Lazare, *L'antisémitisme;* F. Hertz, *Antisemitismus und Wissenschaft;* Vienna, 1904.

[3] Reinach, article "Diaspora," *Jewish Encyclopædia*, vol. iv. p. 565.

They also possessed the privilege of settling their own legal affairs; they had their own judges and their own code. This code—which was simply the Mosaic law, sedulously commented on by the Rabbis—was the sole study of the Jews and Judaizers to the exclusion of the Roman law, a fact mentioned by Juvenal.[1] In civil suits the autonomy of the Jewish courts applied only in cases when both parties were Jews; in penal cases, at the commencement of the common era, the Jewish magistrates exercised a wide disciplinary jurisdiction, including the right of incarceration and flogging. This judicial autonomy of the Rabbis was kept up even after the admission of the Jews as Roman citizens. Because of the requirements of the dietary laws and the Sabbath rest, they could not perform military service, and they obtained decrees of exemption. These and many other peculiarities show plainly that they could not be considered an integral part of the nation, but that they formed a nation by themselves.

Conditions at later periods and in other countries were not much different. Milman says of the Jews in Spain: "Whatever they were in other lands, in Spain they were more than a people within a people—they were a state within a state. The heads of the community, whether as princes or rabbins, exercised not only religious, but civil authority also; they formed a full judicial tribunal in criminal as well as ecclesiastical affairs; adjudged not only in cases of property but of life; passed sentences beyond that of excommunication, sentences of capital punishment. Many of the hostile statutes of the kings and of the Cortes aim at depriving them of this judicial power; they are to cease to have judges. Even as late as 1391 they put to death, as unsound, Don Joseph Pichon. It was only at that time, under John I., that they were deprived of this right."[2]

In Poland conditions were not different. In addition to the usual communal organization of every town, they also had a central organization, the Council of the Four Lands, which was in control of the administrative, judicial, religious, and charitable institutions of the Jews. They

---

[1] *Sat.* xiv., 100 *et seq.*
[2] H. H. Milman, *History of the Jews*, new edition, vol. ii. p. 370.

collected taxes for the Crown as well as for communal purposes; they tried civil cases "in accordance with their own law." The king even approved in 1533 their decision in a private case as a decision of a private court; they had jurisdiction over all the Jews in the kingdom of Poland, with powers to issue injunctions and binding decisions, and to enforce penalties at their discretion. Their province included many fields of activity: they had a censorship over Jewish books; prescribed the conduct of Jews in relation to Christians, and ordered that the dress of the Chosen People must differ from that worn by the Christians.[1]

This was the case, to a greater or lesser degree, with the mediæval Jews in other countries, in Germany, England, France, Italy, etc. They practically had their own government. And if in addition it is borne in mind that they often spoke languages different from those of the surrounding people, dressed in costumes which distinguished them from their neighbours; married and divorced in accordance with the Rabbinical laws; wrote their letters, legal contracts, wills, and kept their ledgers in the Hebrew language; had their own calendar; refrained from eating at one table with the Christians among whom they lived, etc., it is evident they were an alien element, living among people whose sympathies they could not gain. They were everywhere a nation within a nation, a state within a state.

As has been already shown, they were not wholly responsible for this condition of affairs. To be sure their separative religion demanded such autonomy, and to this exclusiveness can practically be ascribed the survival of the Jews as a social unit after two thousand years of dispersion. But Christendom materially helped in this direction by urging on the separativeness of the Jews, by inaugurating laws aiming at keeping them apart by segregating them in ghettoes, ordaining them to wear costumes differing from those worn by Christians, and even labelling them with badges; excluding them from nearly all the honourable occupations and keeping them out of schools, etc.

[1] See article "Council of the Four Lands," *Jewish Encyclopædia*, vol. iv. pp. 304-308, by S. M. Dubnow, from which the main facts are drawn.

Indeed, the Jews, in spite of all obstructions from within and without, often did break away from tradition and law and attempted to assimilate, by discarding their national characteristics, but in such cases they were baulked sooner or later. This is evident from a study of the languages spoken by the modern Jews, their names, dress, cookbook, etc. It appears that they were most of the time in a state of "arrested assimilation," as Lucien Wolf calls it.[1] Moreover, the Jews were not the only religious group which was forced to live apart in mediæval times. In those days all those who disagreed with the dominant Church were forced to live apart. Other religious minorities, especially those who suffered from cruel persecutions, have had to content themselves with some degree of isolation. The Protestants in France, and the Catholics in England, and in the Orient the Copts, the Armenians, the Druses, and the Parsees were in those days nationally distinct from those who followed the predominant creeds. In Morocco, Persia, etc., the Mohammedans of to-day cannot conceive a Christian or Jewish infidel to be of the same nation as themselves. In Russia, where the Greek Church is a state institution, the Jews of to-day show some national characteristics. They speak their own language, *Yiddish*, and many conduct their affairs, keep their ledgers, write contracts, wills, and many other documents in this dialect; the registration of births, marriages, and deaths is done by their Rabbis, and the divorces granted by them are recognized by the state as valid; in the smaller towns they prefer to settle their differences before their own judiciary (*Beth din*), and not in the state courts; they collect the greater part of their own taxes for the Government in the name of the Jewish community; not only is each individual Jew required to do military duty, but the Jewish community as a whole is held responsible for delivering annually a certain number of recruits. This separativeness goes as far as the calendar with many Jews, who date their letters and documents according to the Hebrew and not the Russian calendar. Up to about fifty years ago it was a disgrace for a Jew to be able to

---

[1] Lucien Wolf, "The Zionist Peril," *Jewish Quarterly Review*, vol. xvii. pp. 1-25.

read Russian or German, or even to have in his possession a book in one of these vulgar languages; it was a sin next to apostasy. But during the last two generations a profound change has been taking place. In the large cities of Russia it is difficult to find a Jew unable to speak Russian, and the younger generation give it preference in their intercourse among themselves, and with others; the majority of the business men conduct their affairs, keep their books, write their documents in that language, and date their letters in accordance with the Russian calendar. If Government restrictions should not hinder these Jews with exceptional laws, they would in the course of one or, at most, two generations assimilate to the same extent as those Jews in western countries. As it is, the Government hinders in all possible ways the de-nationalization of the Jews, prevents them from learning the Russian language in the public schools, keeps them segregated, and thus interferes with their adoption of the culture, habits, and customs of the people of other faiths.

It is different with the Western Jews who have been emancipated during the nineteenth century. They prove that there is nothing within the Jew that keeps him back from assimilating with his neighbours of other creeds; that as soon as the political and civil laws which previously kept him apart from the general population are abrogated, he begins to adapt himself to the new surroundings in a wonderful manner. Moreover, most of the separative laws of his religion, which previously were just as effective as the civil and political disabilities imposed on him by the Christian states, are sooner or later discarded by him after a few years of freedom and equality. The Western Jews cannot any more be distinguished from their non-Jewish neighbours by their dress, language, and even most of the national characteristics, such as manners and customs. Very few native Western Jews know anything of the Hebrew language, and fewer yet know the exact day of the Hebrew calendar on a given day; they marry in conformity with the general civil laws, and apply for divorces to the proper civil authorities, and not to their Rabbis; and in their synagogues and temples the language of the country is exclusively used in the prayers. If to this be added the laxity they display in regard to the separative tenets of their religion, such as the dietary laws, the Sabbath, the holidays, etc., it is evident that they have practically discarded all their former particularisms in exchange for the culture, civilization, habits, customs, and manners of the people among which they live. They no more claim to be German, French, English, or American Jews, but insist that they are Germans, Frenchmen, Englishmen, Americans of Jewish faith. Even their former solidarity is more or less on the wane. Claude Montefiore recently stated that he has much more in common with the British noble or the British workman than with the newly-arrived Polish Jew, except in matters of religion.[1] Even in Poland the *élite* of Jewish society resent the idea of being considered Jews from the national standpoint; they insist that they are " Poles of Mosaic faith."

It is evident from what has just been stated that the Jews of to-day cannot be considered a nation. The national traits of the Jews were distinct during the Middle Ages, when they lived in Christian theocratic countries; some of these traits have been lingering in Russia, because the government is there to a high degree a Greek Orthodox theocracy, but during the last thirty years the national characteristics of the Jews have even there been on the wane. And when we consider the Jews of the world, scattered as they have been all over the face of the globe, we find that they are not at all a nation. The only thing they have in common is their religion. It is the consensus of opinion of all modern statesmen as well as ethnographers that religion alone cannot be considered a basis of a modern nationality. It is true that "in the beginning religion was essential to the very existence of the social group. The social group was an extension of the family. Religious rites were family rites. The Athenian religion was the cult of Athens itself, of its mythical founders, of its laws and customs. It implies no dogmatic theology. This religion was in every sense of the term a state religion. If any one refused to practise it, he was no longer an Athenian, . . . to refuse to participate in such a worship was like a refusal of military service in our modern societies. It was a declaration that one was not an

[1] *Jewish Chronicle*, p. 22; March 26, 1909.

Athenian.[1] But in modern nations we find that "no longer are there masses of people professing a uniform belief. Every one believes and practises after his own fashion, what he can, as he pleases. The state religion is a thing of the past. One can be a Frenchman, an Englishman, or a German, and at the same time be a Catholic, a Protestant, or a Jew, or else be of no creed at all." Moreover, in the case of the Jews there is another point which militates strongly against religion as a test of nationality. While an Englishman adopting the Catholic or Buddhist religion still remains nationally an Englishman, and a German converted to Mohammedanism does not forfeit his national allegiance, the Jewish nationalists look at their nation differently. They agree that a Jew who abandons his faith in favour of Christianity or Mohammedanism loses his claim to allegiance to the Jewish nation. This conception of nationality is not in agreement with the modern view as to what constitutes a nation.

For the modern Jew to insist that religion is the most important basis of nationality is absurd. It is against his own interests. If this be true, Jews have no place in Europe and America, where the majority profess Christianity. It, indeed, justifies the claims of the Anti-Semites, who assert that the Jews are aliens in the Occident, and should be treated as such. In fact many of the Russian and Roumanian statesmen have expressed themselves in favour of Zionism for just this reason. The cultured Jews, those who have assimilated with the general population of the countries in which they have lived for centuries, on the other hand, state that they do not acknowledge that religion is the basis of nationality. They realize that their relief came solely from the separation of the Church from the State. Says Lucien Wolf:—"Broadly speaking, our victories were due not to any special tolerance or sympathy for the Jewish people, but to a revolution in the conception of nationality, which is fundamental to the modern constitution of society. Religious toleration and the acceptance of naturalization in lieu of the old doctrine of the indelibility of allegiance were the principles which governed Jewish emancipation. They established a sort of economic

[1] E. Renan, *What is a Nation?* English translation, pp. 77-78.

Brotherhood of Man in place of the old theologico-racial classification of nations. Consequently it is impossible to repeal the emancipations of dissenting religious communities, or even to hinder their full development, without seriously imperilling the new and already deeply rooted national principles."[1] When an English Jewish nationalist recently declared that Jews can never feel entirely English, nor completely identify themselves with the English nation, the most eminent Jews in London resented the imputation. In a letter signed by twenty-five Jews, including I. Gollancz, A. Eicholz, O. E. D'Avigdor-Goldsmid, Laurie Magnus, Claude G. Montefiore, Leopold de Rothschild, etc., they stated that they object to the distinction made between Jews and persons born of English parents, "for we contend that Jews can be, and are, born of English parents, even though their parents are Jews." They also hold that the suggestion that the Jews cannot become entirely English in thought is not well founded, and express their conviction that even Jewish immigrants who naturalize in England can become as good Englishmen in thought, aspirations, interest, and zeal as those who are descended from ancestors who have mingled their blood with other Englishmen.[2]

The fact of the matter is that the Jews cannot claim national unity to-day when they are scattered all over the world; and their ancient home, Palestine and Syria, has only about 100,000 Jewish inhabitants, or one of 150 in the world. Nor can they claim unity because of unusual community of descent, because, as we have seen, they are not as pure a race as has been generally supposed. They are polyglot, speaking the languages of the peoples around them. To be sure, language is not always a safe criterion of nationality. The Swiss are a nation, in spite of the

---

[1] L. Wolf, "The Zionist Peril," *Jewish Quarterly Review*, vol. xvii., p. 7.
[2] *Jewish Chronicle*, April 9, 1909. In an interview published in the *Manchester Daily Dispatch*, the Chief Rabbi of England said: "I am at one with the signatories in regard to the main point. Since the destruction of the Temple and our dispersion we no longer constitute a nation; we are a religious communion. We are banded together with our brethren throughout the world, primarily by the ties of a common faith. But in regard to all other matters we consider ourselves Englishmen."—*Ibid.*, p. 11, April 23, 1909.

fact that they speak three languages, German, French, and Italian; English is the mother tongue of the British as well as the Americans; Spanish that of the Spanish as well as of the citizens of the South American republics; still this does not unite them into nations. On the other hand, in the struggle of the different nationalities in Austria the only test of allegiance is considered the linguistic. One who speaks Polish is considered a member of the Polish nation; one speaking Bohemian is considered a Czech; and so it is with the Ruthenians, Roumanians, Servians, Bulgarians, etc. Indeed the Jews who speak in that country German, or Yiddish, which is a German dialect, are looked at by the Poles, Ruthenians, Czechs, etc., as representatives of German culture and a source of disunion. Some of the more enthusiastic Jewish nationalists, almost exclusively such as have not succeeded in assimilating to any marked degree, noting that the test of nationality is language, have put up a claim that Yiddish is as good a language as any, and they demand "cultural autonomy" for the Yiddish-speaking inhabitants of Austria and Russia. But after all Yiddish is not the national language of all the Jews; there are several other dialects spoken by the modern followers of Judaism—Spagnuoli, Judæo-Arabic, Judæo-Persian, etc. These are dialects which are the result of extreme isolation for long periods of years. They, however, prove that at some former time they have assimilated linguistically; but later, owing to persecution, expulsion, separation, and segregation, they have remained in a state of "arrested assimilation." Moreover, while during previous ages they often tenaciously held on to their dialect, among the Spanish Jews Spagnuoli, and among the Eastern Jews Yiddish, were considered with a certain degree of sacredness, conditions have changed at the present. They discard these dialects wherever they are released from the strict isolation of the Ghetto. The Jews in Germany who spoke a Yiddish dialect up to one hundred years ago speak at present a pure German; the Jews in Italy, Holland, France, and England, among whom a large proportion spoke Spagnuoli, speak to-day the languages of their Christian compatriots. In Turkey, Morocco, Syria, and some of the Balkan States these Sephardim speak that Spanish dialect to-day. The fact that they still hold on to most of the separative tenets of their religion, as well as that in some of these countries they are legally isolated from their Mohammedan neighbours, accounts for it. The Eastern European Jews who migrated westward during the last forty years, where they are admitted freely into the public schools, soon drop their Yiddish. This is the case with the children of the Jewish immigrants in England, Germany, France, and the United States. It is thus evident that Jewish dialects are in a state of transition, and forgotten as soon as the Jews are given a chance to learn the languages of their non-Jewish neighbours.

Renan's conception of the cohesive principle of modern nationalities consists in the "actual consent, the desire to live together, the will to preserve worthily the undivided inheritance which has been handed down." To have a great inheritance of glory and regrets, to have suffered and rejoiced and hoped together, is not enough to cement people into a nation. There is necessary a common will to do things again, aspirations for future aims and ideals to be realized, for which a common effort is made—these are things which constitute a nation. "A nation is then a great solidarity, constituted by the sentiment of the sacrifices that its citizens have made, and of those that they feel prepared to make once more. It implies a past; but it is summed up in the present by a tangible fact—consent, the clearly-expressed desire to live a common life."[1] It is important to inquire whether the Jews, especially those who live in Western countries, can be considered a nation from this standpoint.

The culture, the literature, arts, as well as the ideals, aspirations, and hopes of a nation are originated and developed by the upper classes of the population and diffused by them among the lower strata of society. The masses, the peasants, the artisans, and labourers are always teachers, scientists, litterateurs, artists, and even the great following their leaders, the ruling classes, including the commercial and industrial leaders, in matters of culture. The knights of the Middle Ages and the learned and cultured classes of the present have been the champions of civilization and culture, and imbued the general popula-

[1] Renan, *loc. cit.*, pp. 80-81.

tion with the ideals and aspirations which are considered national. With the Jews these classes are just those who have a clearly expressed desire to merge, often even to fuse, with the people around them; who are convinced that they are citizens of the countries in which they live, and are ready to make any sacrifice for the future of their country. They call themselves Russians, Germans, Austrians, Englishmen, Americans of Jewish faith. They do not await a Messiah to lead them back to the land of Israel, and even if the Zionists succeeded in renationalizing the Jews in Palestine and organizing a Jewish government, they would not go there. "If the Zionists should succeed in their efforts to obtain and establish an autonomous government in Palestine," said a Jew, "I should like to be their ambassador in Paris."

The denationalization of the Jews goes much further. Their past glories, their historical heroes, victories and greatness are not worshipped and commemorated in the manner done by all other nationalities. Names reminding of their great patriarchs and kings, such as Abraham, Jacob, Joseph, David, Solomon, Esther, Rachel, Sarah, etc., are practically tabooed by the modern cultured Jews. They choose for their children names common among the general population. They do not learn Hebrew, the language which can remind them of their past achievements and glory. Even in Eastern Europe, where up to fifteen years ago Hebrew was not only the sacred but also the secular tongue of the Jews, no periodical in that language can now exist; all attempts to publish a Hebrew periodical meet with failure for lack of subscribers. In Western Europe it has long ago been practically forgotten, excepting as a matter of philological and theological study. In the United States, where nearly two millions of Jews live at present, most of whom are of the orthodox type, a Hebrew periodical could never exist for more than a few months. Citizens of a nation to whom their past is dear, who look back at their departed historical heroes, take great pride in the names of those who made them what they are; they glorify their language and literature. But it appears that the language and literature of the modern cultured Jews is not Hebrew, but that of the people among which they live. They discard the holidays which commemorate their greatest past achievements, such as the feast of the Maccabeans (*Chanuka*); the feast of Esther and Mordecai (*Purim*), who scored a great victory over the first Anti-Semite, Hamman. Few cultured Jews in Western Europe and America know even the date of these holidays, nor do they care to know them. Instead, they send gifts to their friends at Christmas, and their New Year's greetings on the first of January. In the Jewish press in the United States there are annually advertisements during December announcing articles suitable for Christmas presents. No such advertisements are to be seen during the *Purim* and *Chanuka* seasons.

Intellectually also there are no indications of any cultural aspirations of the modern Jews, excepting as citizens of the countries in which they live. The Zionists acknowledge this fact, and are "everywhere engaged in providing facilities for their members, and the mass of the Jews, to become especially acquainted with the history of their people and intimate with the sacred and profane literature in the Hebrew language," says Max Nordau. "They teach the Jews to carry the head high, to be proud of their descent, and to scorn the lies, calumnies, and insults of the Anti-Semites. . . . They preach the abandonment of gross materialism, into which assimilated Jews sink only too easily for want of a worthy ideal in life. . . . They give a new impulse to the celebration of Jewish historical festivals and days of memorial. They even make themselves outwardly distinguishable in many cases by badges. The Zionist holds it to be contemptible to conceal his nationality. He insists on being known as a Jew."[1] Their success in these directions has, however, not been encouraging, as is evident from the fact that the number of assimilated Jews is growing as never before; the number who celebrate their historical festivals is diminishing at a rate appalling to the unassimilated, going hand in hand with the increase in the number of Jews who have Christmas trees in their homes for the amusement of their children. These are social phenomena which have in some measure called forth the energies of those Jews, who consider their past as a great heritage, to combat. The Zionists logically claim that, on the

---

[1] Max Nordau, *Zionism: its History and its Aims*, p. 13.

whole, Judaism cannot thrive under modern conditions in Western countries among surrounding peoples of different faiths, and work for the renationalization and repatriation of their people. But so far as social conditions of the Jews can be taken as an index, their success in these directions has been far from encouraging.

The denationalization of the Jews has gone too far during the last two thousand years to admit of speedy renationalization. An attempt was made recently in New York City to organize a society of Jewish art, to bring together all those who are interested in Jewish art, literature, and science. The first few meetings of those who expressed willingness to promote and foster the aims of the society brought out the fact that there is no such thing as "Jewish" art. The problem, What is Jewish art? was answered in various and contradictory ways. Some maintained that any art object produced by a Jew is a work of Jewish art. But it was shown that many productions of Jews have nothing to do with Judaism, as the statue of Ivan the Terrible by Antokolsky, or Joseph Israel's paintings of Dutch peasants' and fishermen's life, Meyerbeer's *Les Huguenots* or *Robert le Diable*, Heine's *Romancero*, and the like. Some have suggested that Jewish art comprises works and productions inspired by Jews, or by Jewish historical events; but then are the paintings of Biblical scenes in the Vatican and Italian cathedrals, and Doré's works, as well as music by Christian composers on Jewish topics, as Strauss' *Salome*, and literature on the Jews as George Eliot's *Daniel Deronda*, or Scott's *Ivanhoe*, or Byron's Hebrew Melodies, to be included among the Jewish works of art and literature? Moreover, the problem, Is there a Jewish literature? has not been satisfactorily answered. Karpeles believes that it "embraces the collective writings of Jews from the dawn of history until the present age, without any reference to the form, language, or contents of those writings,"[1] and thus lays a racial foundation for his definition. There is no analogy in any other of the modern national literatures, which are usually defined on linguistic grounds. Thus Zangwill's *Children of the Ghetto* is considered a contribution to English literature, just as is

[1] G. Karpeles, *Geschichte der jüdischen Literatur*, p. 1; Berlin, 1886.

Daniel Deronda; Ludovic Halévy's *L'Abbé Constantin*, or *La Famille Cardinal*, cannot be considered Jewish literature, inspired by Judaism or Jewish history; it is French literature in spite of the fact that it was written by one whom the Jews claim. Otherwise the Jews may claim as their literature such works as Renan's *Vie de Jesus*, and even Drumont's *La France Juive*, because they treat of Jewish topics. The Hebrew, Yiddish, Spagnuoli, Judæo-Arabic and Judæo-Persian works, written for and by Jews, can only be considered polyglot Jewish productions, but which is Jewish literature is difficult to define. There is a Hebrew literature,[1] to be sure. But it is understood by only a small fraction of Jews who can read. There is a Yiddish literature understood by many, but not by all the Jews. Moreover, this language is not even uniformly spelled by any two Yiddish writers of note, and it has no grammar. Nor has it a future as a language, because as soon as the Jews have opportunities to enter the common schools they do not learn it. There are practically no native Jews, even descendants of eastern immigrants, in Western Europe and America who can write in the language. It persists in Eastern Europe because the Jews are shut out of the schools and not given an opportunity to learn the language of their neighbours.

Painting and the plastic arts have only recently been cultivated by the Jews. Before their emancipation, when they adhered strictly to the letter and spirit of their law, it was rare indeed to find a Jewish painter or sculptor, because these arts were tabooed by the Biblical and Rabbinical law. The Rabbis extended the prohibition of idols in the Decalogue[2] to include all images, whether intended as objects of worship or not. It is even stated in the Talmud that the pious avoided gazing at pictures engraved on Roman coins. The absence of painters and sculptors of Jewish origin, as a result of this prohibition, was interpreted by many as an indication that Jewish ability is one-sided, only some of the arts being accessible to them to the exclusion of others, especially the plastic arts. Others, like Jacobs, were inclined to attribute the

---

[1] S. Levy, "Is there a Jewish Literature?" *Jewish Quarterly Review*, vol. xv., pp. 583-603.

[2] Exodus, xx. 4.

rarity of Jewish painters to the high proportion of colour-blindness among them. But all these theories have been shattered within the last century since an enormous number of excellent sculptors, and especially painters, some of whom have attained international eminence, have sprung up among the Jews, showing that the absence of painters among them was not a racial trait of the "Semite," but was solely the result of the Biblical prohibition to paint or carve images. Needless to say that the productions of Jewish artists have nothing nationally Jewish to show, but simply reflect the æsthetic tendencies of the times and localities in which they were produced.

Even in music, which was cultivated by the Jews for centuries in their synagogues to the exclusion of all other forms of art, we can find little which can be considered peculiarly "Jewish." During their wanderings over the face of the globe Jews have picked up much of the style and structure of musical composition common among the various peoples who were at different times their neighbours. Most of the sacred melody of the synagogues differs but slightly from the sacred musical compositions of the Mohammedan and Christian Churches at various periods of their history. It is more curious, however, that the Jews have "preserved" in the music of the synagogue a considerable mass of melody directly adapted from the folk-song of Gentile neighbours or constructed on the general lines of musical development in the outer world. In the latter class falls almost the whole of the choral music of the synagogue, the work of composers who either avowedly shaped their work upon the wider, as contrasted with the purely ecclesiastical, lines of art, or were unconscious of the historic and æsthetic value of the traditional material. The borrowed or adopted melodies, on the other hand, were already associated in the outer world with the secular song or dance, and were taken into the synagogue simply from the lack of available melody as the number of Neo-Hebraic hymns rapidly increased. . . . Not all the airs which reproduce external folk-song, however, were thus actually and directly borrowed, for a goodly number must have been the composition of *Hazzanim*. But even so, they were close imitations of the popular melody of the day, and they lack any Jewish characteristics to bring them into line with the older traditional elements.[1]

After all this, the Jews as well as the Anti-Semites say that there is a distinctive national Jewish music. On the one hand, the Jews take great pride in the large number of Jewish composers, such as Meyerbeer, Mendelssohn-Bartholdy, Rubinstein, and many others displaying the great creative powers of their co-religionists in this particular branch of art. But the Anti-Semites, on the other hand, call attention to the inferiority of "Jewish" musical composition. Wagner was one of the first to speak of it in his pamphlet, *Das Judenthum in der Musik*, and later in his *Oper und Drama,* in which he condemns the "Jewish" music of Mendelssohn and his former friend, Meyerbeer, as sweet and tinkling but lacking in depth. Many others followed suit, showing that the French operetta, the Opera Bouffe of the Second Empire, as well as the later comic opera, is distinctly Jewish, and with its lightness of style and touch has degenerated the taste of the public. As a matter of fact, there is nothing distinctly Jewish about these productions of Hector Crémieux, Offenbach, and their more recent imitators, the majority of whom are not Jews.

It is noteworthy in this connection that there is no Jewish folk-music in any country. The popular songs of the Jews in the Orient are sung with melodies common among the Orientals among whom they live; in Eastern Europe Slavonic, Vallachian, Magyar and Gypsy airs are at the foundation of nearly all the Jewish folk-songs, and even ceremonial and ritual airs at weddings, betrothals, festivals, etc., are from this source.[2] In the United States the negro melodies, known as "Coon songs," which have

---

[1] See F. L. Cohen, article "Music," *Jewish Encyclopædia*, vol. ix., pp. 119-135. He shows that most of the synagogal music has been borrowed from popular airs, and as a method of recognizing the melody with which certain prayers are to be sung Jews even prepared special prayers. Thus to the tune of "En Toda la Tramontana" was written a Hebrew prayer, "Shir Todah le-Helohim Tanah"; to a hymn, "Shem nora," was adapted the music of a popular song, "Senora," etc.

[2] It is noteworthy that the Jewish national hymn, *Hatikvah,* officially adopted by the Zionists, is of Bohemian origin, for this march occurs in Smetana's Bohemian Symphony.

been much in vogue in recent years, have also been adopted by the immigrant Jews for their Yiddish songs.

The absence of peculiarly national Jewish productions in the arts manifests itself even in the architecture of their synagogues, which are built in all conceivable styles but Jewish. In Russia, many follow the architectural designs of Slavonic churches; in Italy, some follow the style of the Italian Renaissance; in England, "the interiors of Great St. Helens and Duke's Place in London are well designed and strongly suggest some of the work of Sir Christopher Wren and Inigo Jones. Similarly, in Paris pure styles of French architecture are found; and throughout Europe there are synagogues in Romanesque, Gothic, and many variations of the style of the Renaissance."[1]

This lack of national characteristics in the modern Jews manifests itself in many other ways. The folk-lore, folk-tales, folk-medicine, and most of the popular superstitions among the Jews in various countries are similar to those met with among their non-Jewish neighbours, or among the peoples who were their neighbours formerly. "Altogether some sixty or seventy tales have been found among the Jews of the present day; but in scarcely a single case is there anything specifically Jewish about these stories, while in most cases they can be traced back to folk-tales current among the surrounding peoples."[2] "Even in the tales having a comic termination, and known to the folklorists as drolls, there are no signs of Jewish originality. . As in other branches of folk-lore, modern Jews give strong evidence of having borrowed from their neighbours and show little originality of invention."

The cultured Western as well as Eastern Jews of to-day agree that there is no Jewish nation. "To which nation do we belong?" asks Professor Lazarus. "We are Germans, nothing but Germans; when the conception of nationality is considered, we belong only to one nation, the German . . . It is not only our mother-tongue that makes us Germans. The land we inhabit, the State we serve, the law we obey, the science which enlightens us, are all German. Mother-tongue and fatherland are

---

[1] See article "Synagogue," by A. W. Brunner, *Jewish Encyclopadia*, vol. xi., p. 632.
[2] J. Jacobs, *Jewish Encyclopadia*, vol. v., p. 428.

German, both intrinsically our own; here stood our cradles, here are the tombs of those from whom we descend for several generations. Our beginning as well as the end of our life is here."[1] Lazarus argues that there is no German religion. "Christianity, Catholicism, and Protestantism are just as much French, English, Italian, etc., as they are German. The same holds good for Judaism. It is French, English, Italian, because Frenchmen, Englishmen, and Italians are Jews. Judaism, on the whole, in the same sense as Christianity, is German. Every nationality embraces to-day several religions, just as every religion embraces several nationalities."[2] About the Jewish spirit the same authority has this to say: "There is no more a Jewish nationality; there is absolutely not a Jew who has a Jewish spirit or mind. They necessarily draw for this reason from the national minds of peoples among which they live, of which they became an integral part, and on whom they react. Even in their religion, which is their only distinctive characteristic, they differ according to the country in which they live. This is evident from the way in which they designate their co-religionists, saying: "This one is a Pole," "that one is a Russian," "that one is a German." By this they do not mean to imply the geographical home of the particular Jew, but refer to his character, the disposition and sentiment, even to his mode of study of the Talmud. Even the difference in the ritual and liturgy of the synagogue is designated, as can be seen on the title-pages of the prayer-books, as nationally French, Spanish, German, Polish, Moravian, Bohemian, etc. Owing to this differentiation of the national traits of the Jews in various countries, they can energetically participate in the culture of their non-Jewish neighbours, and contribute their own share to the civilization of the nation. Philo wrote in Greek, Maimonides in Arabic, Spinoza in Latin, Munk and Derenbourg in French, Mendelssohn in German."[3]

It is thus evident that Zionism, based as it is on the erroneous notion that the Jews are a nation, fails at the outset, because it is founded on false premises. There are, however, other reasons, not of an academic kind, why

---

[1] M. Lazarus, *Was heisst National?* pp. 18-19; Berlin, 1880.
[2] *Ibid.*, pp. 24-25.   [3] *Ibid.*, pp. 43-44.

this movement does not and cannot make substantial progress among the Jews. The most important fact is that Palestine, the land which they consider their legitimate home, is rather small, and could not accommodate twelve millions of Jews, even if all wanted to go there. "The whole of Syria could shelter only a small minority of the Jews now in the world," says Leroy Beaulieu. "Must we, to make room for them, expel the Christians and the Moslems? Shall we confide the care of the Holy Sepulchre to the Synagogue? What Christians would propose or tolerate such a thing?"[1] This, coming from the most philo-Semitic of Catholics, is to be considered. It must be remembered that even if Turkey ever cedes Palestine to the Jews, which is far from likely, there are grave doubts whether Christendom, particularly the Roman and Greek Churches, would allow the Holy Land to be in the hands of the Jews.[2] The suggestions made by the Zionists that the places sacred to the Christians and Mohammedans be treated as extra-territorial zones will hardly induce Christendom to part with them.

But "supposing we were to relinquish to Israel all the unoccupied tracts of Syria," says Leroy Beaulieu, "including the desert as far as the Euphrates, not a third, nor even a quarter of the European Jews could find subsistence there. The ancient country of Canaan and the neighbouring regions are certainly not able to accommodate more than a few hundred thousand."[3] Palestine is not a large country. According to the English Palestine Exploration Fund Survey, the region west of the Jordan is about 6,040 square miles; the district east of the Jordan is much smaller, hardly exceeding 4,000 square miles. Altogether it is somewhat smaller than Belgium. The fertility of the land varies greatly in quality. On the whole it is not of a superior quality. The fact is it has never been a very fertile place. The reference to "a land flowing with milk

---

[1] Leroy Beaulieu, *Israel Among the Nations*, p. 354.
[2] Even Zangwill, who has been working earnestly for the renationalization of the Jews, acknowledges that, "not only is Mount Zion private property politically, it is a holy mountain for Mohammedanism and Christianity as well as for Judaism, and this makes it rather like a volcano, very dangerous to those who dwell on its slopes." (*Jewish Chronicle*, August 7th, 1908).
[3] *Loc. cit.*

and honey" does not allude to the fertility of the soil, but to a country with great pasturage for cattle, the land probably not being cultivated in antiquity at all. It is deficient in water in that the arable land has not a quantity sufficient for its productive capacity. If sufficient rain does not fall in time many of the springs dry up, and the land cannot be properly cultivated; the crops wither, there is no harvest, and a general scarcity of grain results, so that the price of bread is closely connected with the rainfall.[1] Irrigation, to be sure, might be effective in improving the soil, but it is problematical whether it would pay to bring thousands of people, as well as a great capital, for the purpose.

It is to this inhospitable soil that the Zionists intend to take the Jews and make farmers of them. After two thousand years of city life, the small traders, the merchants, and the artisans of Eastern Europe are expected to be at once transformed into pioneer farmers and become efficient workers of the soil. It is well known that the tendencies observed among modern peoples are quite the reverse of this process. The stream of migration is to-day from the country to the city. All successful colonization has been accomplished by the transportation of people who have been farm hands for generations. There is no instance in history in which a large number of city-dwellers have gone to a virgin soil or a desert and soon developed its natural resources. The fact of the matter is, that while some Jews have become excellent agriculturists in Russia, the United States, Canada, and Argentine, it seems that in Palestine the results thus far obtained have not been very encouraging. There are in that region about seven or eight hundred Jewish families engaged in agriculture. Nearly all have been subsidized by the Jewish Colonization Association, by the Zionist societies, and through the munificence of the Paris Rothschild. As to their success, I will quote an article published in a Yiddish Zionist weekly, *Das Yiddishe Folk*, in Wilna, and written by an ardent Zionist. He says: "Land is bought for the purpose of cultivation—to plough, to till, to sow, to plant. Are there many Jews who till the land of Israel with their own hands? I know nearly all the colonies and colonists,

---

[1] See I. Benzinger, *Jewish Encyclopædia*, vol. ix., pp. 495-496.

but colonists who hire Arabs and are paid by Rothschild for their task, Jews who only take pensions from Zionist societies, are not agriculturists. Rothschild's riches, combined with the funds of the various groups of Zionists, will be inadequate to settle all the land of Israel with this type of colonists, who receive regular salaries for hiring Arabs to cultivate their land. It is all useless. The idea of the repatriation of Zion is that the Jewish land should be settled with real Jewish farmers, and thus develop a great Jewish population. But now quite the contrary is being done. All the money collected for our purposes ultimately finds its way into the hands of the Arabs. It is no secret that only a small percentage of the colonists are working with their own hands. The majority are small landlords whom Rothschild or the Jewish Colonization Association or the Zionists pay salaries to, because they live in the land of Israel. I do not know what might happen should the relief be withdrawn. Nor do I see how they contribute to the promotion of the national Jewish ideals, and I doubt whether they are desirable elements to assist in the regeneration of the Jews in Palestine."[1]

Realizing the defects in the soil of their sacred land, as well as in the shortcomings of their people as regards their deficient proclivities to agriculture, the Zionists have recently changed their programme. They declare that the most important task is to develop the country industrially and commercially. There are plenty of merchants and artisans among the Jews, and they could find subsistence in Palestine just as well as in other countries, and, considering that they would have their own government and not be exposed to political restrictions and social ostracism, they could live much more happily than in other lands. This is worth looking into closely. Palestine is about the size of Belgium, or a little smaller than the Netherlands. These last two countries support a population of nearly six millions each. But they have excellent means of transportation, a close network of railroads and good highroads, harbours supplemented by canals, combined with an industrial and commercial development of centuries. This has made these countries capable of

[1] M. Chashmonoi, "Praktische Arbeit in Eretz Ysroel," *Das Yiddische Folk*, No. 19, pp. 5-7; Wilna, 1906.

supporting large populations. In Palestine things are different. It was never a fertile land, and centuries of neglect have made the greater part of that region practically a desert. The means of transportation are primitive, the mileage of railroads insignificant, the highroads are bad, and there are no navigable rivers or canals, no first-class harbour. Speedy industrial and commercial development cannot be expected in this kind of land. It will take many years, with even the indefatigable energies of pioneers, which are lacking among the Jews, to bring Palestine to a degree of development adequate to support a population of the size of that of Belgium. Even then it will hardly provide accommodation for half the number of Jews in the world. Meanwhile, not many over one million people can find profitable employment and subsistence there. Considering that there are about 600,000 Moslems and Christians there, it is evident that, even if the Zionists brought over the same number of Jews, the country would be overcrowded for the time being. This would by no means contribute anything to the solution of that vexing Jewish problem. No perfect autonomy or Jewish theocracy could be expected in a country in which half the population is non-Jewish. Indeed there are many Jewish cities in Russia and Galicia in which the population is more than fifty per cent. Jewish. But what is of more importance, it would not at all help the Jews in Russia and Roumania. In these countries there are about 6,000,000 Jews, and the removal of 600,000, leaving 5,400,000, would not by any means convince the Anti-Semites that they have been relieved of the Jews. More than double that number have emigrated from those countries within the last twenty-five years, and conditions have aggravated, if changed at all.

The Zionists have realized all this, and they speak of establishing their Jewish government not alone in Palestine, but also in the neighbouring countries, such as Syria, Mesopotamia, and other parts of Asia Minor. But disregarding the fact that they have less claims on the greater parts of these countries than on the lands in which they live at present, and also the fact that Turkey will never cede that region to anybody for the establishment of an autonomous government, it must be recalled that there are living there about 15,000,000 Moslems and Christians. They cannot be driven out to make place for the Jews. Now, the establishment of a Jewish government in which the majority of the population is non-Jewish—granting that all the 12,000,000 Jews in the world go thither—will not be satisfactory to those enthusiasts who see salvation for the Jew only in isolation from foreign influences.

On the whole this movement has not made great progress among the Jews. Soon after the publication of *Der Judenstaat* by Herzl in 1896, many Jews, especially from Russia, have rallied around him, and the first six International Zionist Congresses showed a steady increase in the number of delegates.[1] At the first Congress the number of Zionists in Russia who were represented by delegates was 47,131; during succeeding congresses the increase was steady and marked, reaching 125,220 at the sixth congress. At the next two conferences their number fell to 66,529 and 69,624 respectively.[2] In other countries the movement has been much weaker. The membership of the Zionists' societies is very small, especially in Western Europe and America; considering that the dues are small, only one *shekel* annually, equivalent to one shilling, so that the poorest may be able to enrol, it is noteworthy that comparatively few Jews find it advisable to join Zionist societies.[3] The official organ of the party, *Die Welt*, has of late been lamenting the enormous decrease in the number of *shekel*-payers in every country.

The failure of this movement is thus summarized by

[1] For the history of Zionism see article "Zionism," *Encyclopædia Britannica*, tenth edition, by Lucien Wolf.

[2] Detailed statistics are given by S. Weissenberg, "Die zionistische Bewegung in Russland," *Zeitsch. Demogr. Stat. Juden*, p. 136; 1906.

[3] In the United States the Zionists' Federation has an annual income of about $3,000.00 from *Shekel*-payers. Considering that ardent Zionists enroll their children, relatives, and friends, it has been estimated that hardly more than 6000 adult Jews consider it worth while to spend 25 cents a year for the movement. Compared with several Jewish fraternal societies with memberships of over 100,000, and with literary societies having thousands of members, the Zionists play no rôle in the life of the Jews in this country. In England the reports of the Zionist Federation show a similar state of affairs. The membership has always been comparatively small and of late decreasing.

Zangwill:—"After twelve years of Zionism the Jew is still forbidden to enter Palestine (his stay is limited to three months). Even under the Turkish Constitution, of the four members returned to Parliament not one is a Jew. Nor have the Jews numerically a right to a Jewish representative, since out of every seven inhabitants of Palestine only one is a Jew. Of a population of 600,000 only 86,000 are Jews. Nor are these the sort of people who can assert themselves even as a minority and form the nucleus of a larger growth. . . . They do indeed constitute a two-thirds majority in Jerusalem; but as few possess Turkish citizenship, even the member for Jerusalem is not a Jew. . . . If the Jews are such a small fraction of the population in Palestine, still smaller is their holding of land. Despite all the Jewish colonies established by Baron E. Rothschild, and by so many societies in Europe, the Jews hold only 2 per cent. of the land in Palestine."[1] The constitution of Turkey appears to have altogether dissipated the idea that Palestine will grant autonomy to the Jews. Herman Bernstein, interviewing the leaders of the Young Turks for the *New York Times*, elicited the information that they have nothing against Jewish immigration, provided it is directed to parts outside of Palestine; that it is not concentrated in any one district, but more or less distributed all over the country; and above all provided the new immigrants are willing to become Turkish subjects. This has since repeatedly been stated by the statesmen at the head of the new Turkish Government.

The causes of this failure of the movement are manifold. In general it is due to the fact that the bulk of the modern Jews are entirely opposed to repatriation. The strictly orthodox class in Eastern Europe is against it because they do not believe in "forcing the hand of Providence"; they believe that Messiah will come sooner or later to redeem the scattered children of Israel without any assistance of mortal man. The reformed Jews in Western countries insist that the Jews are not, like the Turk, only encamped in Europe, ready to retreat to Asia at the first favourable or unfavourable opportunity. Their Rabbis teach that the Jews are only a religious community, and condemn all attempts at repatriation. In England the

[1] *Jewish Chronicle*, May 14, 1909, p. 14.

Chief Rabbi warned several Rabbis against preaching Zionism in their synagogues, and the Haham of the Spanish and Portuguese synagogue in London was admonished from touching upon this subject from his pulpit.[1] In the United States the Conference of American Rabbis declared itself officially against the Zionist movement because "America is the Jews' Jerusalem and Washington their Zion"; during its session of 1908 they again declared that the Jews are only tied together by religion, and not by nationality. The Hebrew Union College in Cincinnati found it advisable to remove several professors who were Zionists and were trying to imbue the embryo Rabbis with the ideal.

The assimilated Jews in Western Europe, and many also in the East, oppose this movement vigorously. "How can the European countries which the Jews propose to 'abandon' justify their retention of the Jews?" asks Magnus. "And why should civil equality have been won by the strenuous exertions of the Jews, if the Jews themselves be the first to 'evacuate' their position, and to claim bare courtesy of 'foreign visitors'?"[2] Lucien Wolf looks at Zionism as a great peril to the Jews, "the natural and abiding ally of Anti-Semitism and its most powerful justification. It is an attempt to turn back the course of modern history, which hitherto, on its political side, has had for its main object to secure for the Jewish people an equal place with their fellow-citizens of other creeds in the countries in which they dwell, and a common lot with them in the main stream of human progress. It is essentially an ignorant and narrow-minded view of a great problem—ignorant because it takes no account of the decisive element of progress in history; and narrow-minded because it confounds a political memory with a religious ideal."[3] "The German Jew who has a voice in German literature must, as he has been accustomed to for the last century and a half, look upon Germany alone as his fatherland, upon the German language as his mother tongue, and the future of the nation must remain the only

---

[1] *Jewish Encyclopædia*, vol. xii., p. 673.
[2] L. Magnus, *Aspects of the Jewish Question*, p. 18; London, 1902.
[3] L. Wolf, "The Zionist Peril," *Jewish Quarterly Review*, vol. xvii., pp. 22-23.

one upon which he bases his hopes," says Ludwig Geiger. "Any desire to form together with his co-religionists a people outside of Germany is, not to speak of its impracticability, downright thanklessness toward the nation in whose midst he lives—a chimera; for the German Jew is a German in his national peculiarities, and Zion is for him the land only of the past, not of the future. The withdrawal of citizens' rights appears to be the necessary consequence of German legislation against Zionism, the only answer that German national conscience can give."[1]

These are the views held by the majority of the cultured Western Jews. They recognize that the oppression of their co-religionists in Russia and Roumania is an important problem, but it cannot and must not be met with repatriation. Persecution drives the Eastern Jews to western countries where they find an asylum, especially in Anglo-Saxon countries. In their new homes they are again creating a problem. It is true that they soon adapt themselves to their new environment, as is shown elsewhere in this work; in fact they assimilate within one or at most two generations in a wonderful manner. Still they are looked at with suspicion by both the Christians and the native Jews. The latter, following their traditional charity toward their unfortunate co-religionists, assume a great burden in trying to assist these newly arrived brethren. The Christians, on the other hand, have many Chauvinists in their midst who look with disfavour upon the "invasion" of an "alien race, with alien speech, religion, traditions, etc." This was the main cause of the investigation of the Royal Commission on Alien Immigration and the resulting "Aliens Bill" which passed the English Parliament; and in the United States the Jewish immigrants have been, together with the Italians, Hungarians, and Slavs, looked at with disfavour by some "nativists." In addition, the Jewish immigrants, having been town-dwellers for centuries, again segregate in western cities, with the result that there is at present about 60,000 Jews in Paris, 150,000 in London, and even a million in New York. Attempts to scatter them all over the country have been made by the native Jews, especially in the United States; the results have been quite encouraging.

[1] L. Geiger, *Stimmen der Wahrheit*, p. 165; Berlin, 1905.

Moreover, segregation is a great obstacle to assimilation, and the native Western Jews do not want to see their co-religionists remain backward in their new homes. The English Jews do their best to induce their co-religionists in the East End of London to emigrate to other cities in Britain or its colonies, especially Canada. The Jewish Colonization Association no more assists Jewish immigrants on the way to England and the United States, but helps them to go to Canada, Argentine, Brazil, etc. The main aim is the exact opposite of that to which the Zionists strive. It is done with the object of dispersing the Jews and thus facilitating assimilation. Even Zangwill's Jewish Territorial Organization, which aims at "acquiring a territory in any place in the world upon an autonomous basis for those Jews who are unable or unwilling to remain in the lands in which they are at present," has received moral and material support from some, though few, Western Jews of prominence and power. This support has been granted not so much to assist in the ultimate aims of Zangwill's scheme, the autonomous territory, but more for the purpose of assisting that organization in its attempt to regulate Jewish migrations, to diffuse information among the Eastern Jews as to the opportunities in countries other than the United States and England. The attempts to divert the stream of Jewish immigration from the port of New York to Galveston, Texas, which has been endowed by a Jewish philanthropist, is fostered by the Territorialists. However, the scheme of obtaining a territory upon an autonomous basis has not been endorsed by many influential Jews in Western Europe and America. They see no reason for autonomy. "As to the pretension that autonomy is required in the interests of the national customs of the Jews," says Lucien Wolf, "that is a gratuitous reflection on the orthodoxy of the non-Zionist. When I challenged Mr. Zangwill in the *Times* to produce a list of those national customs which cannot be observed in a British colony without political autonomy, I was referred (not by him but by somebody else) to one only—the Sabbath. But there is no essential restriction on the observance of the Jewish Sabbath or in the substitution of Sunday work for it in England; and where Jews mostly congregate, as in the East End of

London, the observance is fraught with little or no inconvenience. The only restrictions the emancipated Jews have to observe are that they cannot make the stranger within their gates observe the Sabbath or stone to death the Jew who desecrates it. I do not imagine that the *Nacht Asyl* is designed to correct these anomalies. Latterly, Mr. Greenberg has given us another national custom for the observance of which we are said to require a political free hand—the Jewish law of Marriage and Divorce. May I ask him what law? Is it the Deuteronomic or the Rabbinic law of divorce? Is it the ancient polygamy which lingered among the Italian Jews as late as the seventeenth century, or Rabbi Gershom's monogamous 'custom of the Gentile' of the tenth century, or Mr. Zangwill's recent repudiation of the marriage regulations of Ezra and Nehemiah which even the Paris Sanhedrin upheld?"[1]

There are thus seen two tendencies among the modern Jews. One class, represented by the various factions of nationalists, is aiming at the segregation of their co-religionists in Palestine, or in some other territory, where they may live under an autonomous government. Meanwhile they strive to re-awaken the national consciousness of the Jews, keep them together in the cities in which they live and thus prevent assimilation with its concomitant dangers of disintegration of Judaism, fusion with their non-Jewish neighbours, and ultimate absorption by the other elements in the "melting pot" of modern society. Against this tendency are to be seen arrayed all the assimilated Jews, those who have adopted the culture, habits, and customs of the non-Jewish neighbours, and who consider themselves citizens of the countries in which they live. They have given up most of their separative rites and practices in order to facilitate adaptation to their environment and to be fit for the intimate social contact with their neighbours. They do their best to disperse their co-religionists who cannot or will not remain in their native lands in Eastern Europe and are compelled to migrate westward. Considering that this class is represented by the vast majority of the Jewish *élite* society,

---

[1] L. Wolf, "The Zionist Peril," *Jewish Quarterly Review*, pp. 21-22; 1904.

the money powers, the students, littərateurs, professional men and merchants, and that they in addition control the millions left by the Baron de Hirsch for the purpose of alleviating the lot of his co-religionists, it is evident that they are more effective in their work. If in addition it is considered that history shows conclusively that as soon as the Jew is emancipated and given human rights he always discards his separative practices and does his best to assimilate, and that reactions, such as were witnessed in Spain and in other countries during mediæval ages, are at present unlikely, it is not difficult to foresee which tendency will prevail among the Jews in the near future.

CHAPTER XXIII.

RECAPITULATION AND CONCLUSIONS.

Race pride of the Jews—The Semite and the Aryan—Influence of the environment on racial characters—The difference between the social and anthropological type of the Jew—Anthropologically the Jews are not a pure race—Mixed marriages and their significance—Failure of hostile legislation against the Jews—Decline of fertility of Western Jews—Demography an index of the social and religious status of the Jews—Decadence of Western Jews—Alleged racial immunities—Isolation often spared the Jews during epidemics—Natality—Mortality of the Jews depends more on economic conditions than on "inherent tenacity of life"—Psychic trauma as causes of the nervousness of the Jews—Isolation—Mediæval legislation always aimed at the isolation of the Jew—Judaism the most separative of religions—Effects of the dietary laws and the Sabbath—Judaism the best ally of the Church in keeping the Jew isolated from the Christian—Economic and social effects of isolation—Alleged superiority of the Jew as a trader Characteristics of the Jewish artisan—The "inherent thirst for knowledge" of the Jews—Causes of peculiar criminology of the Jews—Assimilation of the Jews—Large number of baptisms prove capacity for assimiliation—Disabilities in Eastern Europe the greatest barrier in the way of assimilation of the Jews.

HAMPERED on the one hand by their strict and separatist religion, and on the other by the disabilities imposed on them by the laws of Christian states in Europe, the Jews have for centuries lived apart from the people around them. Up to the end of the eighteenth century the social and political environment in which they found themselves was almost alike in every country in Europe. Though scattered in various countries, among diverse races and peoples of different culture, language, traditions, and religion, the Jews, owing to the homogeneity of their own Ghetto environment, presented a uniform social type. Basing their assertions on superficial observation, writers have confounded this uniformity of the social type of the Jew with homogeneity of the physical or anthropological type. The "Semite" was supposed to differ radically from the

"Aryan," not only in religious belief and traditions, but also in descent. The Jew boasted of his own superior lineage, which he believed he could trace back to the time of the great patriarch Abraham. He was proud of the fact that he alone among the nations was able to trace back his ancestry for over four thousand years, having maintained the purity of his breed, unpolluted by the infusion of foreign blood, in spite of all the historical vicissitudes under which he has laboured for centuries, living under the most varied influences of the physical and social environment. It was not the Jew alone who was of this exalted opinion about the seed of Israel. Many non-Jewish writers speak of this "great," "superior," and "remarkable" race, displaying such a striking prepotency of blood which survives victoriously, in spite of all attempts made by other races to vanquish and absorb it. But of late, since the race theories have been taken up by several pseudo-scientists, some authors have turned round and discovered that the Semite is altogether an inferior race when compared with the "Aryan." He is a stranger in Europe, an alien in race, speech, tradition, religion, aspirations, ideals, and the like. Judging from the abundant literature about the Jews which has appeared within the last fifty years, it seems that they have been an interesting topic not only to the philosopher, scientist, and theologian, but more so to the pamphleteer, publicist, statesman, and demagogue. Our study of the racial characteristics of the modern Jews is thus seen to be of more than academic interest. It is of vital importance to the Jews, as well as the people among whom they live, whether they really differ radically, whether they are of different race stock when compared with the *Homo Europœus*, and whether their prepotency is so strong that they can never be assimilated by people of different origin.[1]

---

[1] It was Christian Lassen, in his *Indische Alterthumskunde* (vol i., p. 414; Bonn, 1844-61) who first made the distinction between the Semite and the Aryan. He claimed that the Semite is selfish and exclusive, and not endowed with the harmony of psychic forces which is characteristic of the Aryan. E. Renan, in his *Histoire générale et système comparé des langues sémitiques* (Paris, 1878), and also *Étude d histoire religieuse* (Paris, 1862), speaks of the Semites, and especially the Jews, as differing radically from the Aryan. Renan's opinion was often quoted in favour of the view of the purity of the Jewish race. But later Renan himself has emphatically

This problem can only be studied by the anthropologist. Only somatic traits, only anatomical peculiarities, are stable and persistent, and comparatively unaffected by external conditions. Morphological traits alone depend mainly on heredity for their transmission. Individuals, or groups of individuals, may change their language, their religion; may forget their most sacred traditions within one or two generations. But there is no known way of changing the complexion, the head-form, the height, and the like, and to assure their transmission to the progeny in the new shape. If the Jews have really preserved their original "Semitic" traits, it is in their morphology that we should look for proof. In our study of the Jews we found that language, dress, deportment, manners, and customs, and even religion, are by no means sufficient to prove identity of origin.

It was evident when we detailed the physical characteristics of the modern Jews that they do not by far present a homogeneity of physical type. Renan's apt statement, "Il n'y pas un type juif, il y a des types juifs," is confirmed by a careful study of the somatic traits of the Jews in various countries, and often by the study of the Jews in a single country. These differences are mainly evident in the most persistent traits, which depend solely on heredity for their transmission and constant re-appearance from generation to generation. Some of the differences displayed by Jews in different countries can indeed be attributed to the action of the physical and social environment. The height of an individual may be modified to a certain extent by the mode of life; a plentiful supply

---

denied the existence of a Jewish race in the following words:—"J'ai la conviction qu'il y a dans l'ensemble de la population juive, telle qu'elle existe de nos jours, un apport considérable de sang non sémitique; si bien que cette race, que l'on considére comme l'idéal de *l'ethnos* pur, se conservant á travers les siécles par l'interdiction des marriages mixtes, a été fortement pénétrée d'infusions étrangéres, un peu comme cela a eu lieu pour toutes les autres races. En d'autres termes, le judaïsme à l'origine fut une religion nationale; il est redevenu de nos jours une religion fermée [At the time Renan wrote this mixed marriages were yet infrequent, and the few that did take place were not studied. It cannot be said to-day that Judaism is closed to all admixture of foreign blood]; mais, dans l'intervalle, pendant de long siécles le Judaïsme a été ouvert; des masses très considérables de populations non israélites de sang ont embrasé le judaïsme."
—*Le judaïsme comme race et comme religion*, p. 24; Paris, 1883.

of nourishment, combined with proper physical exercise, may develop the muscular system; example, training, and education may influence for good or evil the psychic, moral, and intellectual capacities. All these human qualities may be influenced by the environment. But these factors are impotent to transform a dark-haired individual into a blonde, or a round-headed person into a long-headed one. The descendants of the German immigrants who settled in the Caucasus about one hundred years ago are to-day just as blonde-complexioned as their compatriots in Central and Northern Europe. The physical environment has not transformed them into dark-complexioned people, the prevalent type in that region. The descendants of the English immigrants in Australia are to-day, after long residence in the Antipodes, and under a different physical environment, of the same physical types as those prevalent in England.

When we find that the European Jews have between fifteen and thirty per cent. of blonde-haired, and even up to fifty per cent. of fair-eyed, persons in their midst, we can by no means take it as evidence of pure breed. When we find in addition that, with a few insignificant exceptions, these blonde Jews are met with in different proportion in various parts of the world; that in Arabia, Africa, and the Caucasus, where the non-Jewish population is distinctly brunette, only from one to five per cent. of Jews are blonde, while in Germany the proportion of blonde Jews reaches thirty per cent., we are forced to the conclusion that the fair-complexioned Jews are a European acquirement of Judaism. This is important, because it throws light on the most crucial point of the anthropology of the Jews. Some have, namely, suggested that the blonde Jews are the descendants of the blonde elements mentioned in the Bible, such as the Amorites, and that since their dispersion in Europe they have kept themselves free from intermixture. If this were the case, the proportion of blonde Jews in every part of the world should be about the same. The different proportions of blonde Jews in various countries shows that other factors were responsible. Was it climate? As far as our present knowledge goes, this cannot be confirmed. There are blondes living in countries where the bulk of the population is brunette. This is, for instance, the case with the blondes in North Africa, which have been discussed so much in anthropological literature,[1] or the large proportion of brunettes in Northern Germany. Such cases are known to be the result of differences in racial derivation. Why should the Jews be considered an exception in this respect? No good reason has been advanced against the opinion that we deal here also with different race types of Jews. In Northern Europe, where the population is predominantly blonde, the Jews could by fusion acquire mostly blonde elements; while in Italy, where the bulk of population is distinctly brunette, or in the Caucasus, Persia, Arabia, and Africa, where the proportion of blonde Jews is practically insignificant, the Jews could not, even if they did intermarry openly or clandestinely, or admit proselytes, acquire anything else but brunette traits. It is conceded by all, except themselves, that the black Jews in India and the Malabar Coast are of undoubted Hindu derivation. It is their misfortune that they are of an extremely different type when compared with white humanity, and could not be incorporated into the body of Judaism as easily as blondes were, owing to the usual prejudices against coloured people. They are, in fact, treated by their white co-religionists with about the same amount of contempt as the coloured population is treated by the whites in the southern states of America. And when the Falasha Jews in Abyssinia are considered, there is hardly any one who would not agree that they are of a distinctly different racial type from the Jews of Europe.

These dark Jews in India and Abyssinia offer excellent proof that the Jews have made proselytes after their dispersion among the nations, in spite of the fact that Judaism is such an exclusive religion, barring the stranger at the gate, and practically never sending forth missionaries to make converts. Jews have, however, incorporated into their communities, at various times, foreign racial elements. It appears that the suggestion that the origin of the black Jews in India dates back to the days when white Jews had native Hindu slaves and forcibly converted them to Judaism is correct. Similar cases are

---

[1] See especially G. Sergi, *The Mediterranean Race*, pp. 59-75, for discussion of the African blondes.

recorded in the history of the Jews in various parts of Europe, particularly Gaul, Spain, Italy, and Hungary. There are records showing that the Church has at various times taken measures to prevent them from converting their Christian slaves to their own faith.[1] That all these measures were of no avail, is seen from the fact that finally the Church was compelled to forbid them to own slaves altogether.[2] The descendants of white slaves have been fused with the rest of the Jews, and cannot to-day, after several generations of liberty, any more be recognized. It is, however, different with the descendants of the Hindu slaves converted to Judaism. They are to-day recognized as of different stock, and treated according to the notions held by the white Jews about the superiority of the white man. But they serve as an excellent example of the proselytism practised by the Jews, and we are justified in assuming that if the differences between Jews and other white folk were extreme, we should undoubtedly recognize at present the descendants of these slaves just as they are recognizable in India.

Turning now to a more stable trait, the head-form, we find the lack of homogeneity is extreme. It is doubtful whether the most mixed of European nations, like the Italians or French, display any greater heterogeneity of cranial type than the Jews. In the Caucasus there are extremely brachycephalic Jews with heads almost round;

---

[1] *Vide* Chapter VIII. *supra*. Even Jacobs, who denies altogether any intermarriage and proselytism among the Jews since their dispersion in Europe, concedes slavery to have been the cause of the infusion of "Aryan" blood into Judaism.—*Journal Anthrop. Institute*, vol. xv., p. 21 of reprint.

[2] For details see I. Abrahams, *Jewish Life in the Middle Ages*, pp. 95 *et seq*. The Talmud and all later Jewish codes forbade a Jew from retaining a slave who was uncircumcised, because a Jew must not profit from a slave's disobedience of the Law of Moses, and no Jew might drink wine touched by a non-Jew. With the female slaves conversion to Judaism was easier and more frequent. The Rabbis even relaxed somewhat in their decisions on female slavery "in order to preserve the morality of Jewish women." The solicitude of the Church in its desire to prevent Jews from owning Christian slaves had a good reason. On the other hand, offences between Jewish masters and their female slaves were punished by the Rabbis, and in order to escape the penalty the owner often voluntarily gave his slave her liberty and recognized her sons as his legitimate offspring. It cannot be said that such practices left the seed of Abraham free from foreign blood.

in Africa and Arabia there are dolichocephalic Jews, with long heads like those of the nomadic tribes of these regions; and there are mesocephalic Jews in Europe, standing mid-

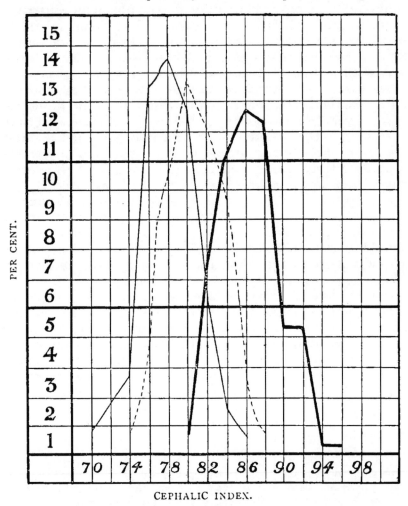

Fig. 142.—The Three Types of Head-form among Jews.
————————— Jews in Tunis.
━━━━━━━━━ Jews in the Caucasus.
. . . . Jews in Lithuania.

way between the above two extreme types. The accompanying diagram (Fig. 142) shows three curves, each representing measurements of heads of Jews. The one to the right represents measurements of Jews in Caucasia; the one to the left, Jews in North Africa; and the middle curve, Jews from Lithuania. This diagram shows in a striking manner that all the three main types of head-form are to be found among the Jews. In other words, as far as the head-form can show, these three different groups of Jews represent three different races, just as if they were of white, yellow, and black complexion. When further inquiry reveals that in Caucasia their non-Jewish neighbours are also brachycephalic, that in Tunis the predominant type is dolichocephalic, the inference forces itself on us that the differences in head-form between these three groups of Jews have been acquired in the countries in which they live. When we further learn that in Europe also the slight differences between the head-form of the Jews in various countries coincides, in a measure, with the differences displayed by the Christians around them, there is no way out but to conclude that the heterogeneity of the cranial type among both Jews and Christians is due to the same causes. As far as our present knowledge of the origin of cranial types goes, only racial intermixture can alter the shape of the head. And when we find that the cranial type of the Jews in countries where they have lived for centuries coincides with the cranial types of the people around them, we may safely conclude that only inter-marriage,—it is immaterial whether open or clandestine,—or conversions, could be the cause. Indeed, if the ancient Hebrews were long-headed, as some are inclined to believe, then only those in countries where the non-Jewish population is of the same cranial type have remained unchanged in this regard; the bulk of the Jews in Europe have diverted from the original type, and are not at all of the race-type of the ancient Hebrews. The same is true if we consider that the ancient Hebrews were brachycephalic. Then only the Jews in the Caucasus have remained true to the type, and the rest have more or less diverged from it. Nor can we imagine for a moment that an assumption that the ancient Hebrews had been a mixed race, and all the cranial types were found among them, will help us to solve the problem. We cannot conceive that all the brachycephalic Jews at the time of their dispersion went to Caucasia, the dolichocephalic to Africa, etc. The only plausible explanation is that by intermixture with their non-Jewish neighbours they have slowly acquired the cranial types prevalent in the countries in which they have lived for a long time.

Stature, though a fluctuating character depending to a certain extent on nourishment, also confirms the racial heterogeneity of the modern Jews. It must be emphasized that social misery with its concomitant defective nutrition may cause a retardation or even an arrest of growth, and thus lower the average stature of a people. But this defect, as an acquired character, does not become a permanent trait by hereditary transmission. Thus, the poorest of the population of England, Scotland, or Norway may be of lower stature than the average of their compatriots, but they are taller than the best nourished of the Hungarians, Poles, Sardinians, or Japanese [1] We have seen that the Jews in Eastern Europe are almost everywhere shorter by about one inch on the average than their Christian neighbours. This may be due to the miserable social and economic conditions under which they labour. But we have found that they also differ among themselves. Thus, the Jews in South Russia are taller than their co-religionists in Poland. Moreover, the Jews give ample evidence that stature is not altogether dependent on social and economic conditions. Those in Bavaria and Turin, for instance, are on a superior plane economically, still they are much shorter than those in the Bukowina, in Roumania, or in Tunis, the majority of whom are living from hand to mouth in abject poverty. This goes far to show that the *milieu* alone is not sufficient to explain the differences in stature of Jews in various countries. But when we bear in mind that the non-Jewish population in Bukowina, Roumania, and Tunis is also taller than the non-Jews in Bavaria and Turin, we may safely conclude that the origin of the differences in stature of the Jews in these countries is due to the same causes as the differences in their complexion and head-form.

Additional confirmation of the heterogeneity of the racial affinities of Jews is found in the different types of

---

[1] See J. Deniker, *The Races of Man*, p. 32.

the modern followers of Judaism met with in different countries. It is an undeniable fact that the cast of countenance depends as much, probably more, on the social *milieu* than on the anthropological traits. Moreover, the cast of countenance changes very easily under a change of the social environment. I have noted such a rapid change among immigrants to the United States. While here they are often easily taken for "foreigners"; still when they have remained in America for a long number of years and have adopted some or most of the habits and mannerisms of Americans, they assume quite a new general appearance. This new physiognomy is best noted when some of these immigrants return to their native homes; it is then evident even to the casual observer that they radically differ in appearance from their compatriots who have not been in the United States. This fact offers excellent proof that the social elements in which a man moves exercise a profound influence on his physical features. In our study of the types of Jews it was evident that the social type is the one which is commonly recognized among the inhabitants of the Ghetto and their descendants. "We distinguish different nationalities not so much by physiognomy, figure, complexion, or proportions, for our eye is not sensitive enough to perceive all this without practice and without the aid of scientific apparatus. But what strikes us is the type—something inexpressible and indefinable—which is the effect of social influence—*i.e.*, of the influence of the social factor. . . . The type or physiognomical character of a folk or social group is not anthropological but social."[1] It is this social type of the Jew which popular opinion considers peculiarly Jewish, and which is an expression of the prolonged action of a uniform environment. That the anthropological type of the Jews escapes our attention is due to the fact that "we are in general more impressed by what is human in man—*i.e.*, by his intellectual and moral faculties—than by what is animal. . . . Thus when an individual has certain outward marks denoting membership in a group, such as costume, head-dress, and the like, the moral type of the group is still more striking in

[1] L. Gumplowitcz, *The Outlines of Sociology*, pp. 161-162; Philadelphia, 1899

him, and we do not notice his anthropological type or deceive ourselves about it, unless it is very conspicuously unusual "[1] Mainly for this reason most of the Jews in Eastern Europe, who are anthropologically of various types, deceive the casual observer into believing that they all present physiognomical homogeneity. If in addition his dress is peculiar, as is the case in Poland and Galicia, the Jew can be diagnosticated without looking at his anthropological traits at all. Many of the Western Jews who recently emerged from the Ghetto have not succeeded in ridding themselves of the expression peculiar to that social type. But closer examination has shown that this is but the expression of the mental man, the mirror of his soul, which is reflected in his cast of countenance. Anthropologically we have seen that there are many types of Jews. In addition to the extreme types, such as the Black Jews in Malabar Coast, the Falashas in Abyssinia, or the Chinese Jews, there are in Slavonic countries Jews who do not differ physically from the Slavs; there are Teutonic, Mongoloid, Negroid types to be met with in all parts of the world. But it must be emphasized in this connection that while the social *milieu* may alter the expression of an individual, may influence his bearing and deportment—as the transformation which many of the immigrants to the United States undergo proves—it cannot alter the anthropological type. A dark-complexioned individual cannot become blonde by a change of *milieu;* a long head cannot be transformed into a round one, a hook into a snub nose, or straight into oblique eyes. And when we find that many Jews with thick upturned lips are also prognathous, have long heads, frizzly hair, and other negroid traits; when we find other Jews with oblique eyes who have also prominent cheekbones, flat noses, thin, straight, long hair, and often Mongolian beards; when we find that many Jews present all the physical traits of Slavonians, Teutons, etc., we cannot attribute these different morphological characters to the action of the *milieu*. Such transformations of the physical type are not known to have taken place among any other people. They are always due to racial intermixture. It appears thus that the Jews during their

[1] L. Gumplowitcz, *ibid.*, p. 166.

migrations in various parts of the world have taken up almost everywhere new racial elements and incorporated them by fusion into the body of Judaism. There is no more justification for speaking of ethnic unity among the modern Jews, or of a "Jewish race," than there is justification to speak of ethnic unity of the Christians, or Mohammedans, or of a Unitarian, Presbyterian, or Methodist race. There are more differences to be seen in the anthropological type of the Jews in the Caucasus when compared with their co-religionists in Tunis than between each of these groups of Jews and the peoples around them. A considerable proportion of Jews in Eastern Europe have more Slavonic blood flowing in their veins than so-called "Semitic" blood, whatever this may imply.

Viewed from this standpoint, the question of the origin of the Jewish "race" loses its significance. It is immaterial whether they were a homogeneous ethnic type in their home in Palestine, or whether at the time of their consolidation into a national unit they were already a conglomeration of the diverse racial elements common at that time in Egypt, Palestine, Asia Minor, and Mesopotamia. Nor is it important in this connection to make a pedantic attempt to trace the "cradle of the Semites," as has been done by many authors, with a view to determining whether the ancient Hebrews were of Asiatic or African physical type.[1] Considering their present ethnic heterogeneity, it is immaterial which type of mankind was predominant among their precursors as carriers of monotheism. We have seen that to-day the bulk of the Jews who have lived for centuries in Africa present predominantly an African physical type; those in Asia are mostly of Asiatic type, and the European Jews are mostly of the anthropological types met with among the European races. The Jew in Russia has less kinship in blood with his co-religionist in the interior of Morocco than with the Slavs among whom he lives; the thirty per cent. of Jewish blondes are nearer in blood relationship to the North European Teutons, or the East European blondes, than to their co-religionists in Yemen, Arabia; the

---

[1] See D. G. Brinton and M. Jastrow, *The Cradle of the Semites*, Philadelphia, 1890; W. Z. Ripley, *The Races of Europe*, pp. 368 *et seq.*

brachycephalic Jews in the Caucasus are further removed racially from the dolichocephalic Jews on the oasis M'zab than are the Christian Lithuanians from the Germans in Europe.

This point cannot be too strongly emphasized. It not only dissipates the exalted notion of the "Chosen People," who believe that they can trace back their ancestry for over four thousand years, as far back as their patriarch and progenitor, Abraham, but it also shows the baselessness of the position of their enemies, the Anti-Semites. In accordance with the spirit of the times, the Anti-Semites have also attempted to put a pseudo-scientific veneer on their agitation, and propounded a theory that the "Jewish race" constitutes a branch of the Semitic race, and is entirely alien in Europe, incapable of assimilating European standards of morals and fair-play; that the antipathy between the Aryan and Semite is quite natural, considering the differences in racial affiliation; that fusion between the Aryan and Semite is almost impossible, and that the gulf between them will always remain wide enough to keep them apart. The differences between these two races, the "Aryan" and the "Semitic," being natural and depending on hereditary transmission, cannot be wiped out by a change of the environment. This alleged gulf between the Jew and his non-Jewish neighbours, being purely social and having no ethnic basis, has, however, been narrowed of late. The large and increasing number of mixed marriages which have been taking place in recent years bear testimony that there is no ethnic reason for the separation of the Jew and Christian. Indeed, as we already know, it was the Church as well as the Synagogue which prevented the amalgamation of the Jews and kept them apart as a religious minority for centuries. As long as the Church held all matrimonial affairs with an iron hand, no intermarriage was allowed. Mixed marriages were only permitted by law since civil marriage was established in some countries. In Russia, Austria, etc., they are not yet allowed. When the question of legalizing marriages between Jews and Christians was discussed in the German and Hungarian Parliaments, the clergy, as well as many pious Christians, petitioned the representatives against the passage of the law. It was stated that this will prove to be a relapse into paganism, that Christianity will lose many adherents, and that the general population may become Judaized. But from all the historical evidence available it appears that the Synagogue and the Church are both powerless to prevent intermarriage between Jews and Christians unless the State comes to their rescue. In Germany such unions were only legalized in 1875, and during 1900-08 one-fifth of all the Jewish marriages were contracted with Christians; in Hungary they were only legalized in 1895, and one-sixth of the Jewish marriages in Budapest are with Christians; in Scandinavia mixed marriages are as frequent as "pure" marriages. Two forces only are capable of preventing mixed marriages—the State, and isolation of the Jew. In Russia and Austria, where the law prohibits such unions, there are officially no mixed marriages,[1] nor can we expect mixed marriages in Moslem countries for the same reasons. Isolation of the Jews from the general population, which is to be observed in the East, where they differ from the Christians not only in religion but also in language, dress, etc., is even a better preventive of intermarriage. This is best illustrated by conditions in New York City. The Jews who have been here for two or more generations are marrying with Christians as frequently as the Jews in Berlin, Paris, Rome, and Copenhagen. The Spanish and Portuguese Jews in the United States have in this manner practically disappeared. Having adopted the habits and customs of the general population, they come into social contact with Christians, and alliances follow as a result. In contrast with these native Jews are to be seen the immigrants, who less often, though not as rarely as is generally supposed, marry out of their faith. The reason is that they are practically isolated from the Christians. Like all other immigrants, they are clannish, perhaps more clannish than others, and live only among their own countrymen. It is

[1] The spirit of the times is to-day, however, much stronger than legislation. In Austria mixed marriages are as yet not permitted legally; still, in Vienna a large proportion of Jews marry with Freethinkers, thus evading the prohibition to marry with Christians. In Galicia and Bukowina practically no intermarriages are taking place, not because the law is in the way, but because the Jews, adhering strictly to their faith, do not want to marry out of their pale.

noteworthy that the largest number of Jewish marriages among the immigrants are contracted between natives of the same city in Europe, while international marriages, considering as such those which are contracted between Russian and German, Austrian, Roumanian Jews, are in the minority. Indeed one often hears among the New York Jews that a marriage between a Russian and German Jew is bound to prove a failure; even the Lithuanian and South Russian Jews are said to find it hard to get along in matrimonial affairs. Yet such marriages are taking place because these different classes of Jews come socially in contact. There is one class of immigrant Jews which often intermarries with Christians. We refer here to public school teachers, especially male teachers of Jewish origin, who very often marry out of their faith. The main reason is that they come in social contact with their non-Jewish colleagues at school. Here also the rule observed in Europe is confirmed. More Jewish men marry Christian wives than Jewesses marry Christian husbands.

In the present age when marriage is a civil and not a religious affair, when the Church and the Synagogue have no support from the State in their prohibition of intermarriage between persons of different creeds, religion is powerless to prevent mixed marriages. The effect on the Jews and Judaism is immense. The gulf which separated them from their Christian neighbours in the past is narrowing with the increase of these unions, and the way is paved for the solution of that problem of the Jew and the Christian which only thirty years ago was considered hopeless. This is an indication that the social isolation of the Jew is coming to an end, and that in the near future all the real and alleged differences between Jews and Christians will completely disappear in progressive communities.

The demographic phenomena presented by the Jews in various countries are very instructive. In addition to the fact that no uniformity can be observed, which practically excludes ethnic causes, they are also valuable in giving us a striking picture of the social conditions of the Jews in various parts of the world. The demographic phenomena of the Jews may be taken as an index of their social, economic, and intellectual conditions, which again are mostly dependent on their political position in the countries in which they live. Wherever they are isolated by hostile legislation, compelled to live apart from their non-Jewish neighbours, confined within the walls of the Ghettoes, and thus deprived of every opportunity to enter into intimate social intercourse with Christians; wherever, largely as a result of this isolation, they are on a low economic and intellectual standard, their birth-rates and marriage-rates are high, and practically no inter-marriage with Christians takes place. Hostile legislation against the Jews is thus shown to fail utterly in its aims, as can be seen from the detailed evidence presented in the course of this work. Legal repression of the Jews, as practised during the centuries preceding the beginning of the nineteenth, and even to-day in Russia and Roumania, has had mainly one aim in view: to render their life so miserable and unbearable as to make it more advantageous for them to adopt Christianity, and thus rid themselves of all disabilities.[1] How far this policy fails in its aims and purposes can be seen from the fact that conversions to Christianity are comparatively rare in Russia and Roumania. On the other hand, in common with all other classes of people who are on a low social and economic level, their natural increase—*i.e.*, the excess of births over deaths—is enormous among them. They increase in number in spite of all the cruel attempts to check them. This is substantiated by the statistical evidence given in the first chapter of this book dealing with the number and distribution of the Jews. In Russia, Poland, and Roumania they have kept on increasing in number.

Conditions are different in Western and Southern Europe. In Germany, France, Italy, England, and also in America and Australia, where the Jews enjoy civil liberty on an equal basis with the general population, and where they are, as a result, on a superior plane socially, intellectually, and economically, their marriage-rates and birth-rates are so low, that even with a phenomenally low mortality, there is left a very small excess of births over

---

[1] A Russian statesman recently said that repression of the Jews will, he hopes, result in converting to Christianity one-third of their number; another third will emigrate, and the last third will die. Thus he expected to solve the "Jewish problem" in Russia.

deaths, which excess keeps on dwindling. Indeed the Western Jews display a striking retrogression and decadence, which is by no means accidental. It can be traced mainly to the remarkable development they have been undergoing during the last seventy-five years, and especially to the social intercourse with the Christians around them, which is responsible for the large and growing tendency to inter-marriage. The children born to these mixed couples, as was shown above, are practically lost to Judaism; hardly ten per cent. are raised as Jews, and the rest is a gain to Christianity. On the whole, the native Jews in western countries are being diminished by low birth-rates and absorbed by the Christian population through inter-marriage, and in Germany and Austria partly also through baptism.

These phenomena have been kept in abeyance by two redeeming factors: the favourable mortality rates of the Western Jews and the high birth-rates of the Eastern Jews have both been effective in keeping the total number of Jews in the world on the increase. It must, however, be borne in mind that while the birth-rate can keep on sinking, in fact natality may go down till the annual number of births is insufficient to replace all those lost by death, the low mortality must reach its limit. It seems that mortality rates of ten to fourteen per 1000 population are quite low, and it is doubtful whether they can ever be much lower. To date the Western Jews hold their own by immigration from Eastern Europe. But the reservoir of Jews in Russia, Poland, and Roumania is by no means inexhaustible. The seven or eight millions of poverty-stricken humanity of Jewish faith also show signs of lesser vigour as regards multiplication in number. Their fertility begins to abate as we have seen from statistical evidence gathered in Warsaw, Bucharest, and especially Budapest. Even in Austria the natural increase of the Jews has been declining. During the period 1869-1880 they increased 22.88 per cent.; in 1880-90, 13.42 per cent.; while the general population increased during these periods only 8.58 and 7.91 per cent. respectively. During the decade 1890-1900 the Jews only increased 7.14 per cent., as against 9.12 per cent. of the Roman Catholics, 15.71 per cent. of the Protestants, and 11.38 per cent. of the

Greek Catholics.[1] During the last ten years the excess of births over deaths among the Eastern Jews has been more or less drained off by emigration to western countries, where they replaced the large number lost by a vanishing birth-rate, mixed marriages, and baptism. But with the improvement of the political status of the Jews in Russia and Roumania, which is bound to come sooner or later, their demography will approach that of the Jews in Western Europe. That such is the tendency is proven by conditions in Austria and Hungary, where the birth-rate has fallen perceptibly, and the number of mixed marriages has increased within the last ten years to an alarming degree; in the large cities of Russia, according to reports, "prudential limitation of the size of the family" is no more unknown among them;[2] while among the immigrants from that region who have lived for some time in western countries, it appears that "race suicide," intermarriage, etc., are just as frequent as among the native Western Jews.

We do not want to be misunderstood on this point. In showing the tendency to retrogression of the Jews we do not at all mean to imply that this is a sign of physical degeneration of a physiological or pathological nature. The decline of the birth-rates of the Jews is no indication that they have recently suffered from a diminution of their procreating capacity. Nor are they in any way unique in this respect. The same phenomena are to be observed among all civilized peoples in varying degrees of intensity. "Prudential foresight" goes hand-in-hand with an improved standard of life, with greater ambition to raise children who are fortified with a proper education, the best weapon in the fierce struggle for existence which has been going on in modern commercial and industrial life.

[1] J. Thon, *Die Juden in Oesterreich*, pp. 40-42; Berlin, 1907.
[2] A considerable number of pamphlets on methods of prevention of conception have recently appeared in Yiddish, and they have had a wide circulation in Russia. The effect of this kind of literature on the birth-rate is well known. Then it must be mentioned that recently the marriage rates have declined among the Jews in Russia; late marriages and celibacy have made their appearance. (See p. 247 *supra*.) This must, in the near future, have an immense effect in diminishing the birth-rates. To expect that they will increase in number at the same rate as they did during the preceding century is absurd.

The birth-rate of the city population has been declining for this reason in every country; celibacy and late marriages are the order of the day. In a great measure this is due to the changes brought about in modern times by the intense development of industrial activity, and the increased demands for skilled artisans who are educated. The agricultural labourer is thus attracted to the city where he can find greater opportunities for his advancement, as well as for the education of his children. The fecundity of modern peoples thus depends, in an inverse ratio, on the number of town-dwellers, and people who are engaged in mercantile and industrial pursuits and in the liberal professions. The main difference between Jews and Christians in Europe is therefore evident: while among the Christians the accretion of the city population is a recent phenomenon, and the rural districts are still recruiting heavily from their loins population for the "man-killing" urban centres, the Jews have been town dwellers for centuries, and thus have all the attributes of the town-dwellers in a more accentuated degree. In other words, the difference between the Western Jews and their Christian neighbours is only one of degree. They are going more rapidly on the frenzied path of modern life. With birth-rates of 12 to 18 per 1000, the Western Jews have outstripped France with its birth-rate of 20, which has been considered alarming. In this respect as well as in many other respects, the Jews are merely the *avant-coureurs*, showing whither modern society is travelling. Christianity, however, has yet large reserves to draw upon to replace the losses incurred by the conditions just described, while Judaism cannot count very much on its reserves in Eastern Europe, for reasons indicated in the preceding pages.

The demographic phenomena presented by the Jews can also be taken as an index of their religious status. In the Orient and Eastern Europe, where their devotion to faith and traditions is intense, they have high birth rates; they marry early, have a substantial excess of births over deaths, and hardly ever intermarry with Christians. In western countries conditions are the exact opposite, indicating a lessened intensity of faith in their religion and traditions, often amounting to religious indifference. The result is that "race suicide," late marriages, celibacy and the like are frequent, and Jews do not increase, and in some places even retrogress, in number. Indeed, the cruel persecutions and massacres to which they have been exposed during the last two thousand years have not robbed Judaism of as large a number of adherents as modern emancipation, with its concomitant adoption of the habits and customs of modern life in Western Europe. The orthodox Jewish rabbis of yore, who were against all intercourse between Jews and Christians and placed almost unsurmountable barriers in the way of those of their followers who might have come in intimate contact with non-Jews (such as, for instance, the dietary laws), were right from their standpoint. Judaism prospers best under the iron rule of isolation. Russia offers perhaps the best illustration of the point. The oppression of the Jews in that country has but one aim in view—to gain them for the Greek Catholic Church. The Russian bureaucracy believes that religious unity will greatly strengthen their hold of the people. As soon as he is baptized, the Jew, besides receiving a bonus of thirty silver roubles, is also granted all the rights and privileges enjoyed by the Christian population. The world which was denied to him in a great measure, is at once opened to him as soon as he is immersed in the baptismal waters. But notwithstanding all the tempting advantages offered, less than 90,000 Jews were baptized in Russia during the nineteenth century.[1] In contrast with Russia may be taken conditions in Prussia, where the number of Jews is only about 400,000, less than one-tenth the number in Russia. Here, according to De le Roi, as many as 13,128 Jews have been baptized during the nineteenth century, and since mixed marriages have been legalized in 1875, about eleven thousand Jews have married Christians. In Russia no such marriages have taken place, excepting among those who adopted Christianity, and are thus included among the converts. In Russia the birth-rate of the Jews was 37.43 in 1897, not much lower than it was in the beginning of the nineteenth century. As a result, the number of Jews in Russia has

---

[1] See J. de le Roi, *Judentaufen im 19 Jahrhundert*, pp. 31-32, 40-45; Berlin, 1903.

at least tripled within one hundred years, in spite of the vast exodus to Western Europe, America, and other continents. On the other hand, in Prussia the birth-rate of the Jews, which was high in 1822-40—35.46, the same as that of the Jews in Russia—began to sink since their emancipation, reaching only 18.72 in 1906. In other words, if the Prussian Jews had remained in their original political and social condition, unaffected by modern life and by contact with the Christians, they undoubtedly would have maintained their birth-rate, just as their co-religionists in Russia, and the number of Jews born in 1906 would have been about 15,000 instead of 7,541, as was the case. Moreover, the number of Jews born in Prussia during 1875-1906 was altogether 281,500; if they had maintained their birth-rate at 35 per 1,000 the number born would have been about 400,000 during that period. The decline in fertility has consequently caused a loss to Judaism of about 118,000 souls. If to this are yet added the large number of conversions to Christianity and of mixed marriages which have taken place during these thirty-two years, it is evident that the total loss sustained by Judaism was larger in Prussia during 32 years where there are only 400,000 Jews, than among the 5,500,000 Jews in Russia during the entire nineteenth century.

What are the effects of this decadence on the number of Jews residing in western countries? They are decreasing in number in an unprecedented manner, and will hardly be able to maintain themselves from their own loins as a religious minority among so many Christians. Although an enormous number of Germans have left their native country for America and the German colonies, still the population keeps on increasing. In contrast with the Christians, the Jews in that country have not kept pace with the general increase of population, and in fact show a relative decrease in number, and this in spite of the fact that comparatively few have emigrated and many Eastern European Jews have immigrated to Germany. If the constantly increasing number of mixed marriages, baptisms, as well as the declining marriage-rate and vanishing birth-rate be taken as a criterion, the future of Judaism in Germany is, to put it mildly, not very bright. The same process of decadence is to be seen among the native Jews in Italy, France, England, America, Australia, etc., in varying degrees of intensity. About conditions of the Jews in France Max Nordau says that, since the law for the separation of Church and State has been enforced, there has been "disclosed a situation which hitherto had been hidden from most people by a deceptive cloak. The official organization of French Judaism formed a façade which was very imposing, but which had nothing behind it. Now that the State has separated itself from the Synagogue, as it has done from the Church, the official façade of French Judaism has collapsed and it is disclosed in all its pitiful weakness and decrepitude." As is the case with other Jewish communities in western countries, the defections have been replaced by immigration from the East of Jews who preserved Judaism with zeal. But this is only observed during the first and often also in the second generation. " In the third generation they were mostly swallowed up. The grandchildren of the immigrant German Jews are no longer to be distinguished from the old French Jews; they are alienated from Judaism and everything that is Jewish to as great an extent as the others." It is doubtful whether the recent immigration of Russian Jews will save the situation. "Sooner or later the descendants of the Russians and Poles will freely adopt the French local colour," says Nordau, and concludes that "The decay of French Judaism is not in doubt. French Judaism has no future, for it has no present. . . . *If Judaism is only a religion, then religious indifference will soon put an end to Judaism.*"[1] This situation is not confined to France. Exactly the same conditions have been observed in England, Italy, Scandinavia, Australia, and the United States. In exactly the same manner the original Jewish settlers, the Spanish and Portuguese Jews of the seventeenth and eighteenth centuries who refrained from intermarriage with their German and Polish co-religionists, have practically disappeared; very few of them have been left. If immigration from Eastern Europe should for some reason cease, the number of native Jews in the United States would dwindle away at a rate appalling to those

---

[1] Max Nordau, "The Decadence of Judaism in France," *Jewish Chronicle*, p. 10; London, Jan. 18, 1907.

who have the interests of their faith at heart. It appears that the Jews pay an exorbitant price for their liberty and equality,—self-effacement.

A Jewish physician who devoted long years to the practice of his profession among his co-religionists in the Russian Pale of Settlement, describing the miserable social, sanitary, and hygienic conditions of the Jews, said that they are a most remarkable people from the medical standpoint. They lend themselves best to experimentation on the beneficial effects of adverse sanitary and hygienic surroundings on the health and well-being of the human species. From the evidence presented in the chapters dealing with the pathological characteristics of the Jews, it appears that there is a considerable amount of truth in this statement. It is evident that, notwithstanding the fact that from the standpoint of sanitation the bulk of the Jews in Eastern Europe, and to some extent those in the Jewish quarters of London, New York, Philadelphia, Chicago, etc., live under conditions comparable only with those encountered in the "slum" districts of the modern large urban centres, they still do not pay so heavy a penalty for their disregard of the first principles of hygiene as does the slum population of non-Jewish origin. This singular peculiarity of the Jews has been spoken of by many writers as showing that they possess a "remarkable tenacity of life," an "inherent power of resistance to the noxious effects of contagious disease," and as demonstrating the race element in the etiology of disease. But as has already been intimated, a careful study of the morbidity and mortality of the Jews in various countries does not reveal any ethnic basis for the peculiarites shown by the Jews in this regard. The differences displayed by Jews at different times and in different places show conclusively that other factors are responsible. Thus, they were not altogether spared by the epidemic of Black Death during the Middle Ages, as was alleged by many writers. Haeser says that in some places they were attacked by the scourge to a lesser degree than the Christians.[1] "In Avignon those mostly affected by the plague were the poor, especially the Jews and the very

[1] Haeser, *Geschichte der epidemischen Krankheiten*, vol. iii., p. 153; Jena, 1865.

intemperate Spanish. Among the Jews, one-tenth of whom succumbed, the scourge manifested itself as fully developed bubonic plague.[1] There are similar reports about the epidemics of plague in Prague during 1713 and in Poland in 1770. Haeser also reports that during the cholera epidemic in 1831 the Jews were especially often and severely attacked, and adds that, while during the Middle Ages they were burned at the stake because of their alleged immunity, they were persecuted and driven from many cities in 1831 as carriers of the nidus of cholera,[2] and in Warsaw they were very severely attacked.[3] The mediæval immunities of the Jews thus appear to be one of the many myths in circulation about them.[4] We have also seen that there are practically no differences between the Jews and Christians as regards the incidence of typhoid fever, scarlet fever, measles, diphtheria, etc. While in some cases there are reports of a lesser morbidity of mortality, there are also reports of other places and periods when the Jews suffered just as much and even more than the Christians around them. The fact that they generally lived in former times isolated from the non-Jewish population will often explain a difference in regard to epidemic diseases. It is well known that contagious diseases often attack one part of a city while the rest is spared, irrespective of the racial, social, or economic condition of the population. Moreover, inasmuch as infectious and contagious diseases are not filth diseases *per se*, but depend on specific germs for their transmission and propagation, it is evident that it is not necessarily the richer part of a city that will invariably be spared in every epidemic. Indeed, there often occur epidemics in parts of the city inhabited by the richest class of people, while a neighbouring quarter, inhabited by poor, is either partially or completely spared. It must be borne in mind that the enemies of the Jews always had their eyes open to every peculiarity they may present. In case the Ghetto was spared by an epidemic the Jews were accused of poisoning the wells of the city, while in cases when they were attacked by the scourge they were accused of being the source of infection. This is mainly the reason why we

[1] Haeser, *ibid*, p. 183.
[2] *Ibid*, vol. iii., p. 807.
[3] *Ibid.*, p. 810.
[4] See Chapter XIII., *supra*.

have so many reports about the pathological peculiarities of the Jews during the Middle Ages.

Their favourable death-rates are also not by any means shown to be the result of an ethnic "tenacity of life," but are mainly explained by social differences when Jews are compared with Christians. In general it appears that their mortality rates are greatly influenced by their economic conditions. In Germany, Holland, Italy, France, etc., where they are on a superior economic plane, their death-rates are low, ranging from 11 to 14 per 1,000; in Russia, Austria, Hungary, Roumania, Algeria, etc., where the majority live in poverty and want, their mortality rates range between 16 and 22 per 1,000. Austria shows the influence of economic conditions on the mortality rates of the Jews in a striking manner. During 1895-1900 the rates in the various countries of the Austrian Empire were as follows:—Silesia, 13.2; Lower Austria, 14.1; Moravia, 14.8; Bohemia, 15.7; Bukowina, 17.9; and Galicia, 21.0.[1] It thus appears that in the parts of the country where they are on a high economic level, as in Silesia, Lower Austria (Vienna), Moravia, and Bohemia, their mortality is quite low; while in Bukowina and Galicia, where the poverty of the Jews rivals that observed in Roumania and the Orient, their mortality rates are very high. Their favourable mortality in Western countries is also a result of their lower birth-rates, which influences greatly the infant mortality. A lesser number of children born means a lesser number of deaths in the early years of life. In Austria, the provinces where the Jews have high birth-rates, like Galicia and Bukowina, their mortality is also high; while in Silesia, Lower Austria, Moravia, etc., where the birth-rates are low, their mortality is also low. If, in addition, it is borne in mind that Jewish mothers take greater care of their children, that their devotion as parents is unprecedented among the poor of other creeds, that they nearly always nurse their children at the breast, that Jewesses only rarely go to work in factories after marriage, and other social peculiarities, it is evident that the so-called "tenacity of life" of the Jew can equally be achieved by people of any race by adopting their mode of life.

[1] See J. Thon, *Die Juden in Oesterreich*, pp. 28-34; Berlin, 1907.

RECAPITULATION AND CONCLUSIONS.

Their lesser liability to consumption is remarkable, considering the adverse conditions under which they find themselves, all of which are favourable to the development and spread of tuberculosis. That it is not a racial trait is seen from the fact that in the United States the number of Jewish consumptives is growing to an alarming extent. Racial immunities are not lost by a residence for a few years in a new country, or by a change of *milieu* for one generation. The negro has not lost his immunity to yellow fever after residing in the United States for two or three centuries. Nor can we attribute it to the ritual inspection of meat practised by the Jews, because in western countries, where they are not loth to consume meat not prepared according to the dietary laws, their tuberculosis mortality is lower than in the East, where they are very strict in this regard. They are better adapted to city life and overcrowding by a long sojourn in the Ghetto, and by a process of natural selection there were eliminated most of those who were predisposed to tuberculosis, thus giving them an advantage. The lesser number of Jews who succumb to pulmonary and bronchial diseases may also have been acquired in a similar manner. In addition, it must be recalled that their indoor occupations, which do not necessitate frequent exposure to the inclemencies of the weather, and also their abstemiousness, which gives them a better chance to survive an attack of pneumonia and the like, may greatly influence their mortality from these diseases. This indoor life is, however, responsible for the large number of Jews who suffer from chronic pulmonary and bronchial diseases, such as bronchitis, emphysema, asthma, etc.

From the facts presented in Chapter XIV. it is evident that there are hardly any differences between Jews and others in regard to their liability to diseases of the circulatory and digestive organs, as well as to cancer, or to diseases of the skin and eyes. The lesser number of Jewish infants dying of acute digestive disturbances during the summer months is not due to any peculiar congenital vitality with which they have been alleged to be endowed. This is evidently the result of the care bestowed upon them by their mothers, the feeding at the breast, and the domestic habits of the Jewish mother, who rarely goes to work after marriage. Indeed, since a change has taken place in this regard among Jewesses in New York City, since many go to work and are compelled to feed their infants artificially, the number of children who suffer and die as a result of these diseases during the summer months has been increasing, and similar conditions have been observed in London and Manchester.

The traditional purity of the Jewish home and family life, which was one of the characteristics of the Ghetto Jew of the past, was responsible for the smaller number affected with venereal diseases among them. Some authors have attempted to attribute this to a remarkable immunity to these diseases, while others saw one of the most beneficial effects of ritual circumcision in the fact that only rarely was a Jew affected with any of the social diseases. Some writers went even so far as to recommend the general adoption of circumcision by Christians as an excellent preventive of many ills of modern man. But what a change the Jews have recently undergone in this respect can only be attested by physicians who practise among them. Indeed, there are now hardly any differences between Jews and others as regards the liability to suffer from these diseases. The number of Jews affected with venereal maladies is commensurate with the number who expose themselves to infection. And inasmuch as the traditional purity of their family life has more or less changed since they have emerged from the Ghetto, these diseases have been on the increase among them.

The only pathological processes which are more frequently met with among Jews are the derangements of the nervous system. The nervous and mental diseases, and also diabetes, are apparently the privilege of the Jews. But that even this is not a result of any anatomical or physiological peculiarity is evidenced by the fact that only the functional nervous derangements are thus frequently encountered. Hysteria, even in the male, which is very common, may be considered almost natural among people with such an enormous amount of suffering and martyrdom as the Jews. "They cry before they are hit," not only individually, but also as a class. One has to read the Jewish press, especially the Yiddish press, to appreciate the hysterical grief and terror displayed on every occasion when some misfortune is threatening their co-religionists in Russia, Roumania, or Morocco. The hysterical mood of the Jew is also evident when one sees the plays which are most successful on the Yiddish stage. The morbid, melancholy phases of life, full of grief, sorrow, and sadness, are those which succeed best. Even the humour of the Yiddish poet and playwright almost invariably has a sombre tinge. Considering their history, and how often they have been abused during the last eighteen hundred years, this is not at all surprising. Similarly, with the average Jew who suffers from some malady the hysterical element often predominates. Not only is the patient liable to exaggerate his sufferings, but also all those who take an interest in his health and well-being are thrown into a state of terror and grief at each change for the worse. It is noteworthy, however, that these hysterical manifestations are on the decline. The Western Jews are ridding themselves of them in a most remarkable manner. The Jews in Russia also have shown recently that they can meet misfortune with fortitude and with manly resistance, instead of hysterical appeals for mercy. During the recent pogroms in Russia they have defended themselves in a manner with which they would have never before been credited. All this goes to show that it is all a question of education and example. Nowadays that they have been acquiring many of the habits and manners of life of their Christian neighbours, they are also learning that self-possession and calmness are usually of more benefit than alarm and excitement.

There is no wonder that they have been controlled more by their emotions than by their will power. These emotional temperaments are known to be the result of traumatism—*i.e.*, of either physical or psychic injuries. No people has been more harassed for centuries than the Jews. It is because of the cumulative effects of repeated psychic injuries that we find him to-day as a *temperament Mensch*. If to this is added the fact that Jews are pre-eminently town-dwellers, and to a large extent engaged in mercantile and speculative pursuits, it is quite in accordance with our present knowledge of the etiology of neurasthenia that the stress of mind incident to the intense application to business should claim a great number of victims among them. Commerce, banking, speculating, small trading, and the professions known as *precarious occupations* entail a large amount of care, worry, and anxiety. It is well known that the speculator and the merchant, on meeting with reverses, often lose their mental balance. In the case of the Jews, the majority of whom are what are known in the vernacular as "bundles of nerves," this over-exertion of the nervous system is liable to do more harm than in others. The disproportion between the inadequately developed physique and the constantly active mind, with its restlessness and ceaseless mental activity, have had a particularly degenerative influence. His fatigued, weary, and exhausted brain is easily deranged under the least exciting cause; it gets "out of gear," and even collapses under circumstances which might produce little harm in others.

The *psychic trauma*, or injuries to the soul, already spoken of, to which he has been subjected repeatedly during the eighteen centuries of his dispersion among the nations, have greatly contributed to his nervous disposition. He is ambitious and persevering, possessing an enormous amount of "push," which he cannot always bring into play while struggling against adverse circumstances. If to struggle against adversities taxes the nervous system, then what class of people has more enormous odds to overcome? To this must be added the massacres, which have not ceased during the twentieth century, and which in mediæval times were of more frequent occurrence, the *autos da fe,* the expulsions from the native country, etc. Could the survivors after a massacre remain with stable nerves? Could children who witnessed their parents' violent death, their mothers, sisters, and relatives maltreated, remain with well-balanced brains? Physicians report that after the recent pogroms in Russia the number of insane Jews was appalling. Considering that in mediæval times massacres of Jews were quite frequent, and the number of Jews was much smaller than at present, it may be said that many of the survivors have remained with unstable nerves, and that a fair proportion of the neurotics and psychopathics have inherited their nervous dispositions from their maltreated grandparents. Any people, no matter of what race, could not remain with healthy nerves under the ban of abuse and persecutions to which the Jews were subjected.

How far the nervousness of the Jews depends more on their environment than on ethnic peculiarities is shown by the large number of suicides among them. In former years, when they adhered strictly to their faith and traditions, a Jewish suicide was very rare. But within the last twenty-five years they have outstripped the Christians in Germany and Austria (excepting Galicia) in their tendency to self-destruction. Of course this goes hand-in-hand with their nervousness, their precarious occupations, and their life in cities. Formerly they were isolated from their Christian neighbours, but since they have adopted most of the habits and customs of the people around them they have also learned from them voluntary destruction of life under severe stress of mind.

The effect of isolation is best seen in a study of the social characteristics of the Jews. If their sojourn in the Ghetto for many generations was potent in producing the ethnic type of the Jew, it has been more effective in producing and maintaining the social conditions which may be called characteristic of the Children of Israel. Isolation, which has been called by Darwin the corner-stone of breeders, is more effective in engendering social types than ethnic types. In man isolation is seen to be mostly of two kinds, geographical and social, and it was mostly social isolation which was operative in moulding the Jew as we meet him to-day. In fact, geography played only a minor rôle in his case. Notwithstanding that the seed of Israel were scattered in various parts of the habitable globe, in spite of the fact that the different Jewish communities have been separated geographically from each other in a manner unknown among any other social group, they still lived everywhere in the same *milieu*. It was only after their emancipation in Western Europe during the first half of the nineteenth century that there were to be noted differences in the environments of the Jews in different countries. It has been often emphasized that mediæval legislation against them was responsible for most of the social characteristics to be observed among the modern Jews. The uniformity of these phenomena is easily explained by the fact that, inspired from the same source, the Church which ruled Mediæval Europe, the anti-Jewish legislation was almost everywhere of the same character. They were everywhere limited as to the choice of residence, sequestrated in the *Ghetto, Judengasse,* or *Jewry,* and not allowed to leave their quarters without special permission; they were prohibited in every country from owning or even leasing land; the guilds nowhere permitted them to choose their occupation, and in most countries they were compelled to wear the infamous "badge," so that they might be ostracized as if they were of different colour from their neighbours of other creeds. To all this must yet be added that in no country were they allowed to participate in the political, civic, and social functions of the citizen, being thus branded as an alien element. The fact that almost everywhere the same methods were used to isolate them was taken by some writers as a satisfactory explanation of the uniformity of the social phenomena among them. "Who can say what would have been the effect on any other religion of such a treatment prolonged throughout several hundreds of years?" asks Leroy Beaulieu. "If the Mohammedans could have tried the experiment on the Christians, they would probably have obtained as clearly marked a type in ten generations."[1]

But it must be conceded that such an experiment could hardly be tried successfully on followers of Christianity. They would be absorbed by the surrounding majority within several generations. In his zeal to prevent such absorption the Jew himself welcomed at all times the isolation in which Christendom has placed him. By the nature of his religion he could not exist as a Jew if he attempted to commingle with his neighbours of different faith. Judaism is the most separative of religions. It is not universal, like Christianity, but tribal. It has a great distaste for the stranger at the gate, and does not send forth any missionaries among people of different creeds, or among the pagans. It is not eager for proselytes like Christianity or Mohammedanism. In fact it rather repels most of those who might be attracted by its ethical teachings. Ritual circumcision is not calculated to make

[1] A. Leroy Beaulieu, *Israel among the Nations*, p. 122.

Judaism attractive to Christian or pagan. Then the dietary laws are by no means conducive to promote intimate social intercourse between Jews and their neighbours of different faith. Writers on the sociology of the Jews often neglect to appreciate the effects of these dietary laws as they have been obeyed by all the Jews before their emancipation in some European countries, and as they are being obeyed to-day by the Jews in the Orient and Eastern Europe, and some of their co-religionists in America. These laws are not limited to the avoidance of pork and to a special method of slaughter and meat inspection with a view of preventing diseases among the Chosen People. Only apologetic theologians speak of Moses as the greatest sanitarian, the ancient precursor of modern hygiene. It has been well established that these rules had their origin much before the time of Moses, and are in fact survivals of a system of Totemism which must have existed among the primitive Hebrews. As members of Totem clans they tabooed animals which they worshipped—the totems. The list of forbidden animals given in Leviticus xi. and Deuteronomy xv. was only later codified with the object of keeping the Jews isolated from the heathen.[1] "I am the Lord your God, which have separated you from other people. Ye shall therefore put difference between clean beasts and unclean, and between unclean fowls and clean. ... And

---

[1] See Robertson Smith, *Animal Worship and Animal Tribes among the Arabs and in the Old Testament*, and his *Kinship and Marriage in Early Arabia*, chap. vii. ; also *Religion of the Semites*, p. 270 f. Joseph Jacobs, in his *Studies in Biblical Archæology*, pp. 64-103 (London, 1894) gives an excellent summary. Salomon Reinach has recently pleaded with his co-religionists in favour of discarding these dietary laws as relics of barbarism, and only interfering with friendly intercourse with their neighbours. See *Cultes, Mythes, et Religions*, vol. ii., pp. 12-36, 418-436, 443-446 (Paris, 1906). He says that "les idées de *pureté* et d'*impureté* n'ont rien de commun avec celles de bonté, de chasteté, d'utilité, d'une part, ni, de l'autre, avec celles de méchanceté, de lubricité, d'insalubrité. Ce que l'on ne tue pas et ce que l'on ne mange pas est précisément ce qui provoque le respect, l'abstention, le *Hands off*; c'est donc, à proprement parler ce qui est sacré" (p. 12). He argues that the political emancipation of the Jews is not sufficient. They must inaugurate an *émancipation intérieure* in order to succeed in life. The reform Rabbis in the United States take about the same position. "In this country, with our free environment, traditional *Shulchan Aruk* Judaism has no place," says Rabbi D. Philipson (*American Hebrew*, p. 91; Nov. 27, 1908).

ye shall be holy unto me : for I the Lord am holy, and have severed you from other people, that ye should be mine."[1] In the opinion of the Rabbis the Biblical prohibitions were insufficient to keep the Jew away from friendly intercourse with his non-Jewish neighbours, and they added many new prohibitions and interdictions with the object of precluding any intimacy between Jew and Gentile. A Jew must not eat at the same table with a Gentile, nor any food prepared by the latter ; must not eat or drink from dishes, with spoons, forks, knives, etc., which have been used by a Gentile ; must not drink wine the container of which has been touched by a Christian, Mohammedan, or heathen. This has actually engendered an instinct in the Jew against *Terefa*, unclean food—*i.e.*, unfit for consumption by the Chosen People, or prepared by non-Jews. I have known Jews to feel nauseated and even vomit when told that the food they have consumed was not *Kosher*.

This separatism of the Jew was yet intensified by the Jewish Sabbath. He rested when others were working, and worked when the majority were resting. His joys and sorrows which are reflected in his holidays were different from those of the people around them. He often spoke a different tongue, wore different dress, both of which, though not nationally Jewish, yet differ from those of the majority. Thus he was isolated from the people among whom his lot had thrown him. The Church in its attempts to isolate the Jew found in his religion a most powerful ally. Indeed, it can be stated that if not a severely separative religion, the Church, even with the assistance of the State, could by no means keep the Jews from merging with the general population. Social sympathy, if not interfered with by differences in colour, is much stronger than the law. It was the intense tribal spirit engendered by his religion which kept the Jew from intimate contact with the Gentiles more than the laws promulgated by Christian States for the purpose.

The effects of these disabilities inflicted on the Jew from without by the Church and from within by his rabbis are seen to-day when a study is made of their social and economic conditions in various countries. During

[1] Leviticus xx., 24-26.

mediæval ages they were practically all, with very few exceptions, living in poverty and misery. The exception was chiefly to be seen in Spain, for a hundred years before their final expulsion. But it must be borne in mind that the vast majority of the rich Jews were either *Marranos* (Jews who adopted Christianity officially and observed some of the Jewish rites secretly) or assimilated Jews— *i.e.*, such as had adopted the language, manners, and customs of the Christians among whom they lived. The isolated Jew—the Ghetto Jew—was always poor as a rule. Ruppin's statement that *orthodoxy and poverty, assimilation and prosperity, are almost synonymous terms with the Jews*[1] is borne out by most of the facts of their history in Europe. Even to-day most of the Jews in the East European Ghettoes are poor, while their co-religionists in western countries, who have given up most of the separative practices of Judaism, are well-to-do.

Jewish ritualism is rather costly to its followers. The Sabbath can only be kept in isolation; but when living in the midst of a Christian majority in large industrial centres it is difficult, often impossible, to rest on a day when all others are working. The economic reason is mostly responsible for the recent disregard of the Sabbath by western Jews, especially in America. The ritualism of the dietary laws is yet harder to bear. *Kosher* meat costs about twenty-five per cent. more than ordinary meat all over the world, and the poor must bear the burden because the rich Jews, as a rule, disregard them more or less. In the United States there are frequent "meat riots," the Jewish workmen resenting the extortionate prices exacted by the Kosher butchers endorsed by the rabbis. In England the Chief Rabbi recently relaxed in this direction, permitting the consumption by Jews of packed Argentine meat; but the more orthodox rabbis repudiated him, and urged their flocks to consume only meat slaughtered in London, irrespective of cost.

These dietary laws keep the Jews segregated. They cannot become pioneers or colonists,—they must not eat game, nor can they eat many species of fish. The result is that they must live in Ghettoes. The attempts made by Jewish philanthropists to scatter them all over the United

[1] Arthur Ruppin, *Die Juden der Gegenwart*, p. 189; Berlin, 1905.

States or Britain, thus relieving the congestion of the Jewish quarters in New York and London, is to a certain extent thwarted for this reason. They will not move unless they know they can get Kosher food in their new places.

It is for these reasons mainly that these laws are of late disregarded by many Jews in Eastern Europe to a certain extent. In Western Europe and America the number of native Jews who disobey the Sabbath and the dietary laws has been growing as never before. Even the large Jewish hospitals, orphan asylums, and other institutions in America make no pretence of having Kosher food, for reasons of cost and inconvenience. These relaxations of Jewish ritualism are more effective in the direction of disintegration of Israel and assimilation than is generally appreciated. The greatest factor in the isolation of the Jew is thus removed. When he can eat at the table of his Christian neighbour he comes in closer social contact with him, and they both learn each other intimately. The greater part of the perennial prejudice is removed, and even mixed marriages are the result, as has already been shown.

All the facts presented in the chapter dealing with the occupations of the Jews showed conclusively that the preference for sedentary occupations which was characteristic of the mediæval Jews, and their abstinence from certain trades, especially such as require excessive muscular exertion, are by no means racial. They are mainly the result of the peculiar *milieu* into which mediæval legislation, as well as the requirements of their religion, have plunged them. There were always good Jewish butchers, bakers, printers, and bookbinders, because they could not leave their food and sacred books to be prepared by Christians. They could not work with Christians because their days of rest do not coincide. Even to-day many Jews who follow their religion implicitly cannot work in factories and mills where it is insisted that workmen must work on the Sabbath. W. Evans-Gordon shows that few Jews are employed in the mills owned by Jews in Poland, because, "unless the machinery is to lie idle two days in the week, the workpeople must be either all Jews or all Christians."[1] Similar testimony is given by many other

[1] W. Evans-Gordon, *The Alien Immigrant*, pp. 143-144; London, 1903.

RECAPITULATION AND CONCLUSIONS.   539

writers on the economic conditions of the Jews in Eastern Europe.[1] Of late conditions have been changing rapidly, even in Eastern Europe. I have seen many Jewish workmen at work during the Sabbath in Russia, Poland, and Roumania when I visited these countries during 1905 and 1907. Twenty years ago such open violation of the Sabbath in a Jewish community would not have been tolerated by the Jews, and the offenders would surely have been persecuted to any possible extent. In the United States there are many Jews who keep the Sabbath, and who will not even light a match during the tabooed day. But the majority work Saturdays and rest on Sundays. Even recent immigrants know that the way to assure success in a trade is to discard the Sabbath. The majority of the shops and stores in the east side of New York City are open for business on Saturday; and on *Rosh Hashana*, the Jewish New Year, one of the most sacred of holidays, many Jewish business establishments in the east side are open.[2] Conditions in Eastern Europe are approaching those observed among the Jews in western countries, as far as I can judge from my recent visit to the Jewish settlements in that region. Thus one of the important factors in the separativeness of the Jew is being obliterated.

Since the guilds which have kept the Jew from engaging in certain trades have lost their power over him, we meet him in almost every conceivable occupation. The suggestion made by some authors that one of their racial traits is a characteristic abhorrence of manual labour and excessive muscular exertion proves to be pure fiction. Only about one hundred years ago, and even later, it was said by many writers that the Jews were not fit for military service, because of their deficient physical capacity, as well

---

[1] See B. C. Baskerville, *The Polish Jew*, pp. 41-80; London, 1906. This author mentions some factories which are open both Saturdays and Sundays for this reason, while others must be kept closed two days a week in order to keep the Jewish hands.

[2] The Yiddish theatres in New York are open on the Sabbath and all the Jewish holidays, even the most sacred, such as *Rosh Hashana*, when they play twice, matinee and evening, to large audiences of Jews, who thus openly desecrate their most inviolable holidays. It appears that in London the Jewish community resented an attempt on the part of Jewish actors to play on the Sabbath. In New York no such resentment has ever been displayed by responsible Jews.

as for their proverbial cowardice. The fact that up to about seventy-five years ago they were never admitted into European armies was not considered in this connection. But since they have been drafted into the European armies it was discovered that they make fair soldiers. Some have even testified that they make excellent warriors. Their alleged cowardice was also true in mediaeval times, when they were degraded as pariahs, and they practically never raised a hand in their own defence. Recently they have changed even in this direction, and Russia has discovered that they have been misjudged in the past. In their activity in the revolutionary movement, as well as in many terrorist plots, the Jews have displayed bravery and courage equalled only by their martyrdom during the Middle Ages. In addition, it is also a fact that they fight duels in Germany and Austria more often, proportionately, than the Christians, as has already been shown.[1]

Friendly critics have not neglected to point out the Jew's incapacity for hard manual labour. He lives more on brain than on brawn, it has been said by one writer; while some enemies have said that he can only thrive as a merchant, a middle-man, a usurer, and the like. Others, like Andree, have been more cautious, and said that the range of occupations for which the Jews are fit are one-sided. Only certain arts, industries, sciences, and handicrafts are pursued by the Jew, to the exclusion of all other productive occupations, and that this is a "natural and hereditary racial characteristic."[2] This author based his assertions on conditions of the Jews before the middle of the last century, when they were not yet allowed to pursue every occupation for which they might have been fit. The mistake here made is the same as the mistake made by this author about the excessive prolificacy of the Jews, which has disappeared recently with a change of the environment. In their occupations they also show plainly that they are a product of the *milieu* in which they found themselves during eighteen hundred years. With a change of the *milieu*, there is at once manifested a change of their sociological condition in this regard. Their

[1] See p. 413, *supra*.
[2] R. Andree, *Zur Volkskunde der Juden*, pp. 186-187.

RECAPITULATION AND CONCLUSIONS.

historical vicissitudes explain clearly why they have not tilled the soil, or worked at manual labour. The legislation about the Jews during the Middle Ages had one basic principle which paralyzed them in their choice of occupation: they were legally considered aliens, and treated as such—*i.e.*, they could at any time be expelled and their property confiscated; they were not admitted into the trade guilds, thus depriving them from pursuing most of the skilled trades, while money-lending, which was prohibited to the Christians, was rather encouraged among the Jews.[1] From within they also had many obstacles, as has been shown. Their religion demanded that they should rest on the Sabbath, when the majority is working; their dietary laws have isolated them from every friendly intercourse with their neighbours, thus confirming that they are aliens. Keeping apart from the majority had as a concomitant the effect of creating special social conditions.

Certain peculiarities have been noted by many authors while speaking of the Jewish merchant and artisan. There appears to prevail a superstition that the Jew is superior to any merchant of other faith, as a trader. Some think he is more "smart," "clever," "calculating," etc. Ruppin thinks that all these and other terms are inadequate, and do not completely describe the Jewish superiority in this regard. He coins the word "*intellectualismus*," and says that the superior intellectuality of the Jew explains his success in business. He agrees, however, that the English are just as good as the Jews, while they are no match at all for the Americans, who are much better business men.[2] Both friends and enemies of the Jews thus often exaggerate the so-called Jewish commercial spirit, which on investigation proves to be a pure legend. There is no question that during the Middle Ages, when the higher classes of the European population looked down

---

[1] Roscher points out that when during the fourteenth and fifteenth centuries the Christians had themselves begun to take a hand in commerce, which then became considered a respectable occupation, they have framed laws excluding Jews from every kind of commerce, thus eliminating them as rivals. Only peddling, petty trading, and money-lending were left for them.—See "Die Juden im Mittelalter," *Ansichten der Volkswirtschaft*, vol. ii., p 221.

[2] A. Ruppin, *Die Juden der Gegenwart*, pp. 176-178.

at commerce, the Jews, meeting with little or no competition, excelled as merchants. At the present, also, in Eastern Europe they excel because the bulk of the population is agricultural, while the cultured classes devote themselves mostly to military or professional pursuits. This is especially the case in Roumania, where the Christian natives sadly neglect mercantile pursuits; the richer class live on the incomes from their estates, or pursue military or professional pursuits, while the common people are mostly peasants, and to a smaller degree artisans who are kept in ignorance, so that over ninety per cent. of the population is illiterate. Of course here the Jew excels in business, though the Greeks in that country are at least as good, if not better, at commerce. For similar reasons the Jews succeed in other parts of Eastern Europe. But many of the Russian and Polish merchants are unquestionably shrewder and more successful in business than the Jews. A good public school system for the Christian population of Eastern Europe could within a few decades educate the common people so that they would rival the Jews in commerce. In addition it must be mentioned that most other religious minorities seem to develop good business capacity while living among a hostile majority. The Greeks and Armenians in Turkey are good examples. "The Armenian in a foreign land is an artisan, labourer, trader, merchant, banker, speculator, etc., but never an agriculturist, as at home," says Rohrbach. It is particularly interesting to note that the Armenian merchants enjoy about the same evil reputation as the Jewish merchants in Eastern Europe. When inquiries are made in the Caucasus about the Armenians, a German, Georgian, Russian, or anybody else volunteers the information that they are despicable swindlers. It is well known that in the Orient three ascending degrees of fraudulent business men are proverbially known: one Greek is as bad as two Jews; one Armenian is as bad as two Greeks; and two Armenians are as bad as the devil. The opinion about the Armenian is not unanimously accepted. Sometimes it is said that two Greeks are as bad as the devil.[1] It is

---

[1] P. Rohrbach, *In Turan und Armenien*, pp. 214, 203. Quoted from Ruppin, *Zeitsch. Demographie und Statistik der Juden*, pp. 177-181; 1907.

RECAPITULATION AND CONCLUSIONS. 543

curious to note that Rohrbach's description of the condition of the Armenians in the Caucasus is exactly the same as that commonly given of the Jews in Eastern Europe. It appears that they are mainly the merchants and middlemen of that region. Any one who wants to do any kind of business must come in contact with them. The result is that there is hardly an inhabitant of the Caucasus who has had no business transaction of any kind with an Armenian, and perhaps has even been cheated by him, which is almost inevitable, considering the bargaining and business methods of the East. The result is that nearly everybody bears testimony as to the unscrupulousness of the Armenian. The same is true about the Jews in Eastern Europe. The Russians, Poles, and others cannot successfully compete with the Jews, simply because the latter never drink to excess, and assiduously attend to their affairs. When they meet, however, with Greeks, Armenians, and others, who are equally sober and persevering, they do not excel at all; while with the Chinese they cannot even compare as traders, as has been repeatedly shown by many observers. Their poverty in Eastern Europe bears good testimony that they are not such good business men as they are reputed to be. To ascribe to them superior qualifications in this regard is absurd. Any other civilized people placed in the same position would be as successful in business as the Jews.

In a study of the Jewish spirit in modern commercial life Sombart brings forward considerable evidence to the effect that the Jews in Europe were the first to discard the ancient trade traditions which considered it unethical for a merchant to undersell another; to be satisfied with small profits on large and brisk sales; to occasionally sell at a loss when advisable to get rid of a certain line of goods or to push out a competitor; to sell on the instalment plan; and above all, to advertise in newspapers and otherwise, and thus create a demand for their goods.[1] It is problematical whether they were alone in the field with these business methods during the seventeenth and eighteenth centuries. It seems to me that because they constituted

[1] Werner Sombart, "Judischer Geist in modernen Wirtschaftsleben," *Die Neue Rundschau*, pp. 585-615, May, 1910.

the majority of the people engaged in commerce in those days, they were the most conspicuous, and for that reason Christian merchants of Germany, France, England, etc., have complained that they are crowding them out, as Sombart shows. At any rate, at present they are not alone in this field. All successful business of to-day is conducted on these principles. To call this the "Jewish capitalistic method," as Sombart does, and ascribe it to race characteristics of the Jews is not justified. The most that can be said is that being the first merchants in Europe with international connections, brought about through historical vicissitudes, they were ahead of their time. Even at this game the English, and especially the Americans, have outdone them during the last fifty years.

Sociological works, particularly in England and America, abound in descriptions of the characteristics of the Jewish workman. It is claimed that the Jew is a labourer and artisan only temporarily, and at the first opportunity leaves his work and becomes a trader, a merchant; in short, that he considers himself in a stage of transition. While at work, he is an individualist and will not submit to the routine rules of a factory, and for that reason prefers to work in "sweat-shops," where there are no rules and regulations to be obeyed; where he can smoke, talk, and have his own hours for labour and rest. Considering himself in a stage of transition, he does not look for any improvement in his trade, as the English or American workman, but is ambitious to climb higher.[1] These and many other characteristics are ascribed to the "Jewish race." The fact of the matter is that in England and the United States there are two classes of Jewish workmen. One class consists of artisans who have worked at their trade since childhood, and perhaps learned it from their parents. These artisans are just as zealous to improve conditions in their occupation as any American or English mechanic; they are also proud of the kind of work they turn out, and submit to any reasonable discipline of the factory in which they are employed. The second class of Jewish workmen in England and America consists of

---

[1] See C. Russell and H. S. Lewis, *The Jew in London*, 1901; John A. Dyche, "The Jewish Workman," *Contemporary Review*, January, 1898; idem, "The Jewish Immigrant," *ibid.*, March, 1899.

immigrants who, in their native land, were not workmen at all. There they were merchants, students, or simply people without any occupation. In their new home they had to adopt some occupation to sustain themselves, and found that tailoring is quite easy to learn, especially work at ready-made clothing in which the division of labour has been brought almost to perfection. It is this class of Jewish workmen who do not want to submit to the strict discipline of the modern factory, and who are constantly on the look-out for an opportunity to raise themselves out of the submerged condition in which, according to their notion, they find themselves. People of this class often succeed in changing their vocation and become merchants, real estate brokers, and even professional men. Moreover, this is to be seen also among immigrants of other than Jewish faith. There are many in England, and especially in the United States, who began in a quite lowly position on their arrival, but later branch out in other directions and succeed in becoming even captains of industry. The Germans, Scotch, and Irish in America and Australia show similar proclivities. The Jew is by no means unique in this regard.

The high proportion of Jewish students in universities and high schools is not at all an indication of a "greater thirst for knowledge" of the Jewish youth. It must be borne in mind when considering social conditions in Eastern Europe, that the bulk of the non-Jewish population belongs to an agricultural class which rarely send its children to high schools and universities. Even elementary education is obtained with difficulty in those regions. The Russian, Austrian and Hungarian peasantry cannot be compared with Jews, who are mainly town-dwellers and have a very large proportion of merchants and traders in their midst. This latter class is just the class from which the greater number of modern university and high school students are recruited. Among the Christians in those countries an enormous number of the educated youth finds an outlet in either the civil service or the military service, both of which are closed to the Jews. There is no doubt that if the children of Jewish merchants and professional men were compared with the children of Christians of the same class, excluding of course civil and military service, there would hardly be found any differences in favour of the Jews.

In the United States a noteworthy peculiarity is to be observed among the Jewish immigrants from Eastern Europe. The poorer mechanics and small traders are more apt to send their children to high schools and universities than the Christians of the same social and economic status. In New York City the number of students in the City and Normal Colleges is very large; a conservative estimate is that seventy per cent. of the students in these institutions are Jewish. That this also is not an indication of any special, inherent proclivities of the Jews to overcome all obstacles in their search for education and knowledge is evident when their condition in Eastern Europe is considered. There industrial development is not on as high a scale as in the United States. Only very rarely is a mechanic seen raising himself above the class of wage-earners, no matter how able he may be. The children of merchants and the higher class of artisans are therefore apt to flock to the professions, the civil and military careers, as the only means of crossing the great chasm which lies between them and the so-called higher classes. In Russia and Roumania the *élite* of society is made up, next to the noble and military classes, of persons of the learned professions. In attempting to uplift himself in the United States, the Jew simply follows Eastern European notions and experience. But after one or two generations even this is changed for the American standard of proficiency, and we find many native Jews in nearly all mechanical pursuits. There are numerous Jews working as electricians, telegraph operators, engineers, etc., with as much success as any other class of people have achieved in these occupations. In addition, it must be recalled that the Jewish immigrant is not drawn from the class of European agriculturists, as is the case with the Irish, Italian, and Hungarian immigrants. Many of the Jewish immigrants in New York City were well to do in their native home in Russia, and were compelled to emigrate by the cruel persecutions to which they were subjected. While here they live in poverty, their standard is different, I may say superior, to that of persons who were peasants at home. It is quite natural that they should make all kinds of sacrifices to give their children a higher education.

Nor are there to be seen any racial peculiarities when the criminality of the Jews is considered. It must be borne in mind that with the advance of civilization crimes of violence are declining in every country, while transgressions of fraud are increasing in frequency. Highway robbery, murder, and other extreme types of violent crime have decreased in every civilized country in Europe and America within the last thirty years. But the relative number of criminals arrested and convicted for anti-social acts has remained about the same, or has even increased. It thus appears that of late years, going hand-in-hand with the advance of civilization, the character of the crimes committed by individuals who have anti-social proclivities has changed. It pays more and is safer to organize some fraudulent stock company, to forge cheques and notes, to manipulate with securities and the like, than to steal or rob in primitive fashion. The result is that criminal proclivities of individuals of any race, nation, or religious community manifest themselves in crimes of certain types, in accordance with the number of town-dwellers, the degree of education of the average citizen, the proportion of persons engaged in mercantile, industrial, and agricultural pursuits. The larger the proportion of illiterates, of alcoholics, or of agricultural population—in a word, of persons who have not been affected by that complex condition of life which we style "civilization"—the larger the number of crimes of a violent and brutal character are committed. Brute force plays a very important rôle in the struggle for existence of such people. On the other hand, with the advance of culture, education, civilization, success in the struggle for life depends more on the mental capacity of the people than on their physical prowess. The number of criminals does not decrease, however, in civilized communities. There has only been observed a distinct transformation in the types of crimes committed. Fraud, cunning, and lust replace robbery and murder under the stress of modern industrial, commercial, and financial activities. This is the main reason why crimes of violence are proportionately more often committed in countries which have lagged behind in the march of modern civilization; also in rural communities, than in urban centres. Many private wrongs in backward communities are often privately avenged by the wronged party or his friends, while in communities in which an industrial and commercial spirit prevails many of these individual wrongs are settled by claims for damages. A comparison between conditions in countries like the United States and England, representing modern conditions, and Turkey or Sicily, as lagging behind in civilization, will make this point clear. In the former countries there are thousands of suits for damages tried in the courts, and wrongs are compensated by money; in the latter, assault and murder is the method of choice when a wrong has to be avenged.

The application of these observations to the criminology of the Jews is evident. For centuries they have lived in cities, have engaged largely in mercantile and financial pursuits. Up to one hundred years ago there were practically no Jews engaged in agricultural pursuits, and few were artisans. Even to-day a very small, almost insignificant, number are agriculturists. Their occupations are just those in which crimes against property are usually committed by various fraudulent methods, instead of crimes of violence and against the person, which are characteristic of rural populations and of the lower strata of city population. As a religious minority living amid hostile neighbours, they developed a distaste for alcohol, excessive drinking being very injurious in the struggle for existence. This again reduces the number of Jews liable to commit violent acts. As a matter of fact, in countries where their disabilities have been diminished, and they have, as a result, adopted most of the habits and customs of the Christians of the same social status around them, the number of Jews who commit crimes of violence has increased. This is the case in Amsterdam and New York, as has already been shown. In Russia, also, it was thought only two decades ago that the Jew could never commit murder, either because of his alleged cowardice or his innate abhorrence of violence. But of late they have proven the contrary. The number of Jewish terrorists in the Russian revolutionary movement is enormous, far in excess of their proportion in the total population.

RECAPITULATION AND CONCLUSIONS. 549

With the advance of civilization, with the change which is going on in the social, economic, and industrial life in modern European and American populations, the difference in the criminology of the Jews and others is being rapidly obliterated. This is largely a result of the enormous increase in the city population and in the number of persons engaged in industrial and commercial pursuits. The Jews, on the other hand, giving up most of their social and economic peculiarities, engage in industrial occupations more often than formerly, so that there is at present a large labouring class among them. The crimes committed by the Jews of this class do not differ materially from those observed among labourers and artisans of other religious denominations. Fifty years ago the criminology of the Jews was a good indication of what modern society is coming to under the stress of intense commercial and financial activity. In this respect, as was the case with many other peculiarities, such as the excessive number of psychopathics and neuropathics, the Jews have only been the advance agents. Many publicists of Europe have, in fact, often designated conditions in the United States as "Jewish." But to-day Western Europe is marching, though somewhat slowly, on the same path, in order to obviate the intense competition of the Americans. It is noteworthy that the Jews of Europe are the best competitors of the Yankees in the battle for commercial supremacy.

Taking to-day one hundred thousand Jewish manufacturers, merchants, and bankers in Germany, France, and England, and comparing them with a similar number of Americans of the same social and industrial class, no differences in their methods of dealing with their fellow-man will be found. Nor will there be found any difference between the criminal proclivities of the average Jewish artisan in Russia or America and his Christian neighbour, if we except alcoholism and its consequences, which are more prevalent among the latter. The criminology of the Jews is purely a result of their social and economic conditions.

We have found no differences between Jews and Christians which can justly be attributed to racial causes, and which depend solely on hereditary transmission, unaffected by the environment. A study of the characteristics presented by the Jews shows better than anything else the truth of Herbert Spencer's repeated assertion to the effect that the vulgar errors committed by sociological writers are in a great measure due to a failure to recognize the extraordinary complexity of the problems involved in the phenomena and the subtle relations of cause and effect. Religion, the Jewish, as well as the Christian and Mohammedan, with the assistance of the State, artificially created the type of the Jew of the beginning of the nineteenth century. There is nothing unusual in the fact that an isolated community should evolve peculiar characteristics. As a matter of fact, in those countries in which the Church has been separated from the State the type of the Jew has undergone a transformation and approached more or less the type of the people among which he lives. There was nothing in the way of such a transformation as soon as the barriers placed by religion and the State were removed, because ethnically there are practically no differences between Jews and other Europeans. Both consist of conglomerations of various racial elements blended together in a manner that makes it impossible to disentangle the components, or even the predominant race, out of the ethnic chaos of most nations.

Those Jews who have been treated for some time on an equal plane with their Christian fellow-citizens have shaken off their ancient peculiarities to such an extent, that there are to-day more differences between the native French Jews and their Russian co-religionists than between Jews and Catholics in Florence, Rome, and Naples. As a town-dweller for centuries he has become very plastic, often quick of intelligence, and eager to acquire all the attributes that make a good citizen of a country where he is given a square deal. He is even ready to shake off the traditional separative ritualism of Judaism when the law does not degrade him by segregation in the Ghetto, and is willing to contribute more than his share to the narrowing of the gulf which lies between him and others.

The doubt expressed by some writers as to the possibility of assimilating the Jews is not based on facts. The fact is that the specific difference between Jews and other white people consists mainly in the difference in religious belief. Christendom has assimilated more Jews during the past eighteen centuries than is generally appreciated. If the differences between the "Semite" and the "Aryan" were really differences in kinship, the baptismal waters could not transform a Jew into an "Aryan" within two or three generations beyond recognition. The non-Jewish population of Europe and America contains an enormous number of families who are derived from baptized Jews or from mixed marriages. The Spanish nation of to-day is supersaturated with "Jewish blood," derived from the Marranos who remained in that country after the final expulsion of the Jews during the last decade of the fifteenth century. "The blood, both in Spain and Portugal," says Milman, "was ineffaceable as the negro blood in the United States of America—the pure red of princes even kings was tainted. The shrewd Venetian ambassador in the reign of Philip the Second and his successor, observing how deeply the priesthood as well as the laity were polluted with Jewish blood, doubted whether their Christianity was more pure than their descent; and as late as towards the close of the last [eighteenth] century it is told of Pombal, that the King of Portugal, Joseph I., proposed to issue an edict that all who descended from Jews should wear a yellow cap. Pombal appeared in the Council with three yellow caps. The king demanded the meaning of this strange accoutrement. 'One is for your Majesty, one for the Grand Inquisitor, one for myself.'"[1] In a book written by Cardinal Mendoza, published in 1560 under the title *El tizan de la nobleza española*, the author enumerates an enormous number of Spanish noble families derived from Jews. Llorente, author of a well-known history of the Inquisition in Spain, maintains that on the female line of descent all the Spanish grandees are derived from Jews. It is indeed noteworthy that in spite of the alleged prepotency of Jewish blood spoken of by some Jews as well as by many of their enemies, the Jewish blood which presumably circulated in the veins of many of these Spanish nobility by no means prevented them from treating the Jews with the utmost cruelty. Many of the in-

[1] M. H. Milman, *History of the Jews*, vol. iii., p. 329; London, 1864.

quisitors were of Jewish origin, and even Ferdinand the Catholic, who expelled the Jews from Spain in 1492, had Jewish blood in his veins, and Kayserling shows that his mother was a grand-daughter of the beautiful Jewess Palama from Toledo. Nobody will claim that the Spanish inquisitors and Ferdinand the Catholic were not assimilated and acted in accordance with the tendency of the times. That it was not only among the noble classes which assimilation took place is evident from the fact that in the Castilian kingdom there was a diminution in the number of Jews from 1290 to 1474 from 850,000 to 150,000, judging by the head tax they paid.

Spain is not unique in this regard. In a recent book on the history of nobility,[1] it is shown that there have been over 1,000 noble Jewish families,[2] and the author enumerates by name 480 Jewish noble families.[3] Most of them are found in Germany, England, Italy, France, and even in Russia.[4] The descent of "noble" families is more or less easily traced, and they give us an idea of the extent to which Jewish people may be assimilated, often beyond recognition. But it is not only in the nobility where Jews may adapt themselves, that even their alleged "prepotency" does not help them to maintain their characteristics. The fact that they become champions of Christian ideals, of "Aryan" culture and civilization to the extent of persecuting the co-religionists of their forefathers belies a prepotent Jewish spirit. The millions of Jews who have been baptized within the last eighteen hundred years, without attaining nobility in caste, have become "Aryans" without either themselves, or anybody else being able to trace their descent. Lombroso was right in his statement that if all the Jews were baptized, their descendants, after two or three generations, would probably not exhibit any peculiarities.[5] It must be recalled that very few of the distinguished Jews of the nineteenth century have left descendants within the fold of Judaism. Max Nordau says that of all the Jews who

---

[1] Von Bülow, *Geschichte des Adels;* Berlin, 1903.
[2] *Ibid.*, p. 37.   *Ibid.*, pp. 99-104.
[4] See N. Samter, *Judentaufen im 19 Jahrhundert* pp. 86-93; Berlin, 1906.
[5] *L'antisemitismo e le scienze moderno,* Torino, 1894.

gained fame and distinction or only recognition in any field within the last thirty or forty years, hardly one-fifth have remained true to Judaism;[1] and Arthur Ruppin says that there was not a distinguished Jew during the first half of the nineteenth century who was not sprinkled with baptismal waters, and he enumerates some, as Heine, Börne, Benfey, Mendelssohn-Bartholdy, Marx, Stahl, Ricardo, Disraeli, and many others.[2] The vast majority of Jewish professors in Germany and Austria have been baptized. Of the few who have not undergone it themselves, a large proportion have at least baptized their children at birth, in order to remove the disabilities which threatens those of Jewish faith. It is thus substantiated that distinction gained by a Jew is one of the first indications that he will soon be lost to Judaism. It is related that Maria Theresa once asked her State Chancellor how she could easily gain the Jews for the Christian Church. "Majesty," the latter answered, "when you raise them to the rank of nobility."

These facts are of more than passing importance in connection with the question as to the source of the differences between Jews and others. If these were due to ethnic differences between the "Semite" and the "Aryan," as has been alleged by many writers, the baptismal waters could by no means wash away all their characteristics within two or three generations. It is evident that the differences between the Jew and the Christian in Europe are due to differences in religious belief. It was solely the separative tenets of Judaism, coupled with the isolating laws of Christian nations which have created that type generally known as the Jewish. Within the last century, however, both Judaism and Christianity have begun to break down the barriers which have always separated classes that differ in religious belief. The Jews have fairly advanced on the path of discarding most of their separative dogmas and practices. The most potent factor in keeping them from social intercourse with their non-Jewish neighbours, the dietary laws, have recently been either completely discarded, or

---

[1] *Allgemeine Israelitische Wochenschrift*, p. 663; 1896.
[2] *Jahrbücher für Nationalokonomie und Statistik*, vol. xxiii., pp. 766-767; 1902.

more liberally interpreted. There are to-day very few Jews, natives of western countries, who refuse to partake at a Christian table, or who will not eat from dishes previously used by non-Jews. A large proportion of Western Jews also intermarry with people of other faiths, which is more potent in merging the Jews with their Christian neighbours than any other factor. Considering that the rates of intermarriage in some countries where the law permits such unions are about the same as the rates of intermarriage between Catholics and Protestants, and in some countries, like Scandinavia and Italy, even higher, it is evident that the isolation of the Jew has not a very long lease. In addition it must be borne in mind that most of the other separative characters of the Jews are loosing their significance. The Sabbath is a dead letter to the majority of Western Jews, they rest when the general population rests, and work when everybody is working. They have adopted many of the manners and customs of the people around them; I believe that just as many, probably more, native Jews in the United States send New Year greetings to their friends on January the first than on *Rosh Hashana*, the Jewish New Year; and on Purim very few Jews indeed send gifts to their friends, while Christmas gifts are very much in vogue among them. Seventy-five years ago a Jew, no matter whether he lived in a eastern or western country, would have been put under ban and persecuted by his co-religionists much more severely than an apostate, for acting in this way. To-day public opinion among them has so changed that they look with equanimity at those who discard their sacred religious laws and traditions. To this must be added that they no more employ peculiar jargons, such as Spagnuoli or Yiddish, but that the vernacular of their non-Jewish neighbours becomes their own in western countries, and that even their names, dress, and the like are being changed for those common among the Christians among whom they live. When all this in borne in mind, it must be conceded that they assimilate much better than some writers on the "race question," as well as many Jews, are willing to admit. In fact they assimilate in countries where the laws of the state do not interfere with them in this direction much better than some minorities of so-called "Aryan" origin in Germany and Austria. The latter, though not radically differing in religious confession from the ruling majority, still each having most of the attributes of a nation, such as language, soil, dress, and the like, which they consider their own, are not inclined to part with them for the national attributes of their rulers. Perhaps because the Jews have none of these national characteristics, as was obvious from the evidence presented in the preceding chapter, they are more plastic and have a greater aptitude for adaptation to a new environment as soon as they are liberated from the disabilities imposed upon them by the Synagogue, Church, and State.

Judaism has been preserved throughout the long years of Israel's dispersion by two factors: its separative ritualism, which prevented close and intimate contact with non-Jews, and the iron laws of the Christian theocracies of Europe, which encouraged and enforced isolation. The Jewish nationalists rightly realize that only isolation can prevent defilement and absorption through contact with Christendom, and finding that theocracies are no more to be thought of in Europe, they urge repatriation in a Jewish territory in Asia, or anywhere else, as the only means of saving the scattered remnants of Israel.

But we found that denationalization has gone too far to admit repatriation of the Jews, and the solution of the perennial Jewish problem can be, and is being, accomplished in the countries in which they live at present. The emancipated Jew cannot and will not return to a Ghetto environment. The hardest struggle they have at present is to free their Russian co-religionists from enforced segregation and isolation. We have also seen that when liberated from the Ghetto they soon begin to free themselves from their ritualism, which has as a concomitant a strong and growing tendency to intermarriage. This, coupled with voluntary baptisms, low marriage and birth rates, characteristic of emancipated Jews everywhere, points to the road modern Israel is pursuing. We have also found indications that the Eastern Jews manifest a tendency to proceed in the same direction, but that the Russian autocracy has placed unsurmountable barriers in their way. Indeed, it is clear that the removal of the disabilities under which they labour, as well as the legalization of intermarrige in Russia, would emancipate the Jews in a couple of generations, not only politically, but also as regards their ritualism, bringing them there where their Western co-religionists are at present after two generations of freedom. The number of Jews ready to replace those lost through assimiliation might thus be diminished.

Meanwhile the political disabilities in Eastern Europe, and to a certain degree also social ostracism in western countries, are the most potent factors working in favour of Judaism. The laws enacted and enforced by the Christian governments in Russia and Roumania are more instrumental in maintaining Judaism than all the Rabbis in the world. Moreover, these laws are keeping up Judaism numerically not only in their own countries, but by producing a surplus of Jews who, by emigration to western countries, replace those who have been lost through assimilation.

BIBLIOGRAPHY

ABBOT, G. F., *Israel in Europe.* London, 1907.
Abrahams, I., *Jewish Life in the Middle Ages.* London, 1896.
Abramowitsch, M., Die Bewegung der judischen Bevölkerung in Wilna. *Zeitschr. f. Demogr. u. Statist. d. Juden*, pp. 23-29; 1906.
Adler, E. N., *Jews in Many Lands.* London, 1905.
Alsberg, M., Rassenmischung im Judenthum. *Samml. gemeinverständl. wissen. Vortrage*, N.S., V., Part 116. Hamburg, 1891.
Ambrunn, L., Die Kriminalität d. Juden in Russland. *Zeitschr. f. Demogr. u. Stat. d. Juden*, pp. 6-9; 1909.
Ammon, Otto, *Zur Anthropologie der Badener.* Jena, 1899.
Andree, R., *Zur Volkskunde der Juden.* Leipzig, 1881.
Aspects of the Jewish Question, by a Quarterly Reviewer. London, 1902.
Auerbach, E., Die jüdische Rassenfrage. *Archiv fur Rassen- und Gesellschaftsbiologie*, pp. 332-361; 1907.
—— Die Sterblichkeit der Juden in Budapest. *Zeitschr. f. Demogr. u. Statist. d. Juden*, pp. 145-158, 161-168; 1908.

BARTON, G. A., *A Sketch of Semitic Origins.* New York, 1902.
Baskerville, B. C., *The Polish Jew.* London, 1906.
Beadles, M., The Insane Jew. *Journ. of Mental Science*, XXVI., pp. 731-737.
Beddoe, John, On the Physical Characters of the Jews. *Trans. of the Ethnological Soc.*, Vol. I., pp. 222-237. London, 1861.
Benedict, M., The Insane Jew. *Journ. of Mental Science*, Vol. XXII., pp. 503-509.
Billings, J. S., Vital Statistics of the Jews in the United States. *Census Bulletin No. 19.* Washington, 1890.
Blau, Bruno, Austritte aus dem Judenthum in Berlin. *Zeitschr. fur Demographie u. Statist. d. Juden*, pp. 145-153, 1907; pp. 87-90, 1909.
Blechmann, B., *Ein Beitrag zur Anthropologie der Juden*, Inaugural Dissertation. Dorpat, 1882.
Boas, Franz, Heredity in Head-form. *American Anthropologist*, N.S., Vol. V., pp. 530-538.

Boas, Franz, Heredity in Anthropometric Traits. *American Anthropologist*, Vol. IX., pp. 453-469.
—— Changes in Bodily Form of Descendants of Immigrants; Washington, 1910.
Brinton, D. G., and M. Jastrow, *The Cradle of the Semites*. Philadelphia, 1890.
Brosius, Die Psychose der Juden. *Allgem. Zeitschr. f. Psychiatrie*, Vol. LX., p. 269.
Buschan, G., Einfluss der Rasse auf die Form und Haufigkeit pathologischer Veränderungen. *Globus*, Vol. LXVII., pp. 21-24, 43-47, etc.; 1895.
—— Einfluss der Rasse auf die Häufigkeit und die Formen der Ceistes- und Nervenkrankheiten. *Allg. med. Central-Zeitung*, No. 9; 1897.

CHEINISSE, L., La Race juive, jouit-elle d'une immunité á l'égard de l'alcoholisme? *Semaine Médicale*; Dec. 23, 1908.
—— La tuberculose chez les Juifs, *Semaine Médicale;* April 27, 1910.
Cohn, W., Sterblichkeitsverhältmisse der Stadt Posen. *Vierteljahresschrift f. gerichtl. Medicin*, pp. 268-285; 1869.

DE LE ROI, JOH., *Judentaujen im 19 Jahrhundert*. Leipzig, 1899.

ELKIND, A. D., Evrei. *Trudi anthropol. otdiela*, XIX., 1899. Moscow, 1903.
—— Evrei, *Russian Anthrop. Journ.*, No. 3, pp. 1-45; 1902.
—— Versuch einer anthropologischen Parallele zwischen den Juden und Nichtjuden. *Zeitschr. f. Demogr. u. Statist. d. Juden*, Nos 1 and 2; 1908.
Engländer, M., *Die auffallend häufigen Krankheitserscheinungen der jüdischen Rasse*. Vienna, 1902.
Erckert, R. von, *Der Kaukasus und seine Völker*. Leipzig, 1887.
—— Kopfmessungen kaukasischer Völker, *Archiv fur Anthropologie*, Vol. XVIII, pp. 263-281, 297-335; Vol. XIX., pp. 55-87, 211-249, 231-256.
Errera, L., *Les Juifs Russes, Extermination ou Emancipation?* Bruxelles, 1903. English translation, *The Russian Jews;* London, 1894.
Evans-Gordon, W., *The Alien Immigrant*. London, 1903.

FISHBERG, M., The Comparative Pathology of the Jews. *New York Medical Journal*, Vol. LXXIII., pp. 537-543, 576-582; 1901.
—— The Relative Infrequency of Tuberculosis among Jews. *American Medicine*; Nov. 2, 1901.

Fishberg, M., Physical Anthropology of the Jews: I, The Cephalic Index, *American Anthropologist*, N.S., Vol. IV., pp. 684-706, 1902; II., Pigmentation, *Ibid.*, Vol. V., pp. 89-106.
—— Articles in *Jewish Encyclopædia*: "Apoplexy," "Craniometry," "Diabetes," "Eyes," "Hair," "Girth of Chest," "Growth of the Body," "Idiocy," "Insanity," "Morbidity," "Mortality," "Nervous Diseases," "Nose," "Stature," "Types."
—— The Jews: a Study of Race and Environment. *Popular Science Monthly;* Sept., Nov., Dec., 1906; Jan. 1907.
—— Beiträge zur physischen Anthropologie der nordafrikanischen Juden. *Zeitschr. f. Demographie u. Statist. d. Juden*, No. 11; 1905.
—— Zur Frage der Herkunft des blonden Elements im Judentum. *Ibid.*, pp. 7-12, 25-30; 1907.
—— Die Korpergrosse. *Ibid.*, pp. 101-104, 120-129.
—— Die Armut unter den Juden in New York. *Ibid.*, pp. 113-114; 1908.
—— Die angebliche Rassenimmunität der Juden. *Ibid.*, pp. 177-188.
—— Materials for the Physical Anthropology of the Eastern European Jews. *Annals of the New York Academy of Sciences*, Vol. XVI., pp. 155-296; 1905. *Memoirs of the American Anthropological and Ethnological Societies*, Vol. I, pp. 1-146; 1905.
—— North African Jews. *Boas Anniversary Volume*, pp. 55-63; 1906.
—— Tuberculosis among the Jews. *Transactions of the Sixth International Congress on Tuberculosis*, Vol. III., pp. 415-428; *Medical Record*, Dec. 26, 1908.
Fligier, C., Zur Anthropologie der Semiten. *Mitteilungen der Anthropologischen Geselschaft in Wien*, Vol. IX., pp. 247-253; 1881.
Frederic, Harold, *The New Exodus: a Study of Israel in Russia.* London, 1892.
Freeman, E. A., The Jews in Europe. *Historical Essays*, Series 3, pp. 225-231.

GILTCHENKO, N. W., Vies golovnavo mosga . . . u raslichnikh plemen naseliaiushchikh Rossiu. *Trudi antropolog. otdiela*, Vol. XIX., pp. 151-153.
Glatter, Das Rassenmomment in seinem Einfluss auf Erkrankungen. *Vierteljahresschrift fur gerichtliche Medicin*, Vol. XXV.
Gluck, L., Beiträge zur physischen Anthropologie der Spanionlen. *Wissenschaftliche Mitteilungen aus Bosnien und der Hercegovina*, Vol. IV., pp. 589-592; 1896.

Goldberg, B., Ueber die sprachliche Verhältnisse der Juden Russlands. *Zeitschr. Demogr. Stat. d. Juden*, Nos. 6 and 7; 1905.
—— Die Juden unter der städtischen Bevölkerung Russlands. *Ibid.*, No. 10.
—— Die Gebrechlichen unter den Juden Russlands. *Ibid.*, pp. 72-74; 1908.
Goldstein, E., Des circonférences du thorax et de leur rapport à la taille. *Revue d'anthropologie*, Serie 2, Vol. VII., pp. 460-485; 1884.
—— Introduction ? l'étude anthropologique des Juifs. *Ibid.*, Vol. VIII., pp. 639-675.
Goldstein, F., Die Herkunft der Juden. *Globus*, Vol. XCI., pp. 124-128; 1907.
Graetz, H., *Geschichte der Juden*, 11 vols.; Leipzig, 1882. English translation, *History of the Jews*, 6 vols.; London, 1892.

Herzl, Theodor, *Zionistische Schriften*. Cologne, 1905.
Hertz, F., *Antisemitismus und Wissenschaft*. Vienna, 1904.
Halpern, G., *Die jüdischen Arbeiter in London*. Stuttgart, 1903.
Hartmann, Eduard von, *Das Judenthum*. Leipzig, 1885.
Hoppe, H., *Krankheiten und Sterblichkeit bei Juden und Nicht-Juden*. Berlin, 1903.
—— Zur Statistik der Juden in Ungarn. *Zeitschr. f. Demogr. u. Statist. d. Juden*, No. 12; 1905.
—— Die Kriminalität der Juden u. der Alkohol. *Ibid.*, Nos. 3 and 4; 1907.
Hough, J. S., Longevity and other Biostatic Peculiarities of the Jewish Race. *Medical Record*, pp. 241-244; 1873.
Hovorka, O., *Die aeussere Nase*. Vienna, 1893.
Huguet, M., Les Juifs du Mzab. *Bull. Soc. d'anthropol.*, p. 559; 1902.
—— Recherches sur les habitants du Mzab. *Revue de l'école d'anthropologie*, Vol. XVI.; Jan. 1906.
Huxley, H. M., article: Anthropology of the Samaritans. *Jewish Encyclopædia*, Vol. X. pp. 674-676.
Hyde, Frank G., Notes on the Hebrew Insane. *American Journal of Insanity*, Vol. LVIII., pp 469-471.

Ikoff, K. N., Neue Beiträge zur Anthropologie der Juden. *Archiv für Anthropologie*, Vol. XV., pp. 369-389; 1884.
Ivanowski, A. A., Ob antropologitcheskom sostave nasielienii Rossii. *Trudi antropol. Otdiela*, Vol. XXII. Moscow, 1904.

Jaques, V., Types Juifs, conference. *Revue des études juives*, Vol. XXVI., pp. 49-80; 1893.
—— Les origines ethniques des juifs. *Bull. de la soc. d'anthrop. de Bruxelles*, Vol. XXI.; 1894.

BIBLIOGRAPHY.

Jacobs, Joseph, On the Racial Characteristics of Modern Jews. *Journ. Anthrop. Institute*, Vol. XV., pp. 23-62; 1886.
—— with I. Spielman, On the Comparative Anthropometry of English Jews. *Ibid.*, XIX., pp. 76-88; 1890.
—— Are Jews Jews? *Popular Science Monthly*, Vol. LV., pp. 502-510.
—— *Studies in Jewish Statistics.* London, 1891.
—— The Comparative Distribution of Jewish Ability. *Journ. Anthrop. Institute*, Vol. XV.; August 1886.
Judt, J. M., *Zydzi jako rasa fizyczna;* Warsaw, 1902. German translation, *Die Juden als Rasse;* Berlin, 1903.
Jewish Colonization Association, *Materials on the Economic Condition of the Jews in Russia*, 2 volumes; St. Petersburg, 1904 (in Russian). French translation, *Récueil de Matériaux sur la Situation économique des Israélites de Russie*, Vol. I.; Paris, 1906.
Jewish Encyclopædia. 12 vols. New York, 1901-06.

KATZ, A., *Die Juden in China.* Berlin, 1900.
Knopfel, L., Die jüdische Mischehen im Deutschen Reich u. d. konfessionelle Erziehung der Kinder. *Zeitschr. Demogr. Statist. d. Juden*, pp. 107-108; 1906.
Kollmann, J., Schädel und Skeletreste aus einem Judenfriedhof des 13 und 14 Jahrhundert zu Basel. *Verhandl. d. Naturforsch. Gesellsch.*, Vol. VII., pp. 648-656. Basel, 1885.
Körösi, J. von, *Einfluss der Confession, des Wohlstandes und der Beschäftigung auf die Todesursachen.* Berlin, 1898.
—— Couleur de la peau, des cheveux et des yeux à Budapest. *Annales de Démographie*, Vol. I., pp. 136-137.
Kretzmer, M, Ueber anthropologische, physiologische, und pathologische Eigenthümlichkeiten der Juden. *St. Petersburger medicinische Wochenschrift*, Vol. XXVI., pp. 231-234.
Kurdoff, K. M., Gorskie Evrei Dagestana. *Russian Anthrop. Journal*, Nos. 3 and 4, pp. 57-87; 1907.

LAGNEAU, Sur la Race Juive. *Bull. de l'Académie de Médicine de Paris;* Sept. 8, 1891.
Laufer, B., Zur Geschichte der chinesischen Juden. *Globus*, Vol. LXXXVII., pp. 245-247; 1905.
Lazare, Bernard, *L'Antisémitisme, son Histoire et ses Causes;* Paris, 1892. English translation, *Anti-Semitism;* New York, 1903.
Leroy Beaulieu, A., *Israel chez les Nations;* Paris, 1893. English translation, *Israel among the Nations;* London, 1894.
Livi, R., *Antropometria Militare.* Roma, 1896.
Lombroso, C., *L'antisemitismo e le scienze moderne.* Torino, 1894.
Luschan, F. Ritter von, Die anthropologische Stellung der Juden, *Correspondenzblatt d. Deutschen Gesel. f. Anthropol.*, etc., Vol. XXIII., pp. 94-102; 1892.

Luschan, F. Ritter von, Zur physischen Anthropologie der Juden. *Zeitschr. Demogr. Stat. d. Juden*, No. 1; 1905.
Lux, H., *Die Juden als Verbrecher*. Munich, 1893.

MAJER, J., and J. Kopernicki, Charakterystyka fizyczna ludnosci Galicyjskiej., *Zbior Wiadmosci do antropologii krajowej*, Vol. I., pp. 1-181, 1877; Vol. IX., pp. 1-92, 1885.
Majer, J., Roczny przyrost ciala u Zydow Galcyjskich. *Ibid.*, Vol. IV., pp. 3-32; 1882.
Minor, L. S., Contribution á l'étude de l'étiologie du tabes. *Archives de Neurologie*, Vol. XVII., pp. 183-382.
Minutes of Evidence taken before the Royal Commission on Alien Immigration. London, 1902-03.
Mitteilungen der Gesellschaft fur jüdische Volkskunde (M. Grunwald, editor). Hamburg, 1897, etc. Current.
Milman, M. H., *History of the Jews*. 3 vols. London, 1866.

NEUBAUER, A., Notes on the Race-Types of the Jews. *Journ. Anthropol. Institute*, Vol. XV., pp. 17-23; 1886.
Nordau, Max, *Zionistische Schriften*. Cologne, 1909.
Nossig, A., *Jüdische Statistik*. Berlin, 1903.
Nott, J. C., and A. R. Gliddon, *Types of Mankind*. Philadelphia, 1860.

OPPENHEIM, H., Zur Psychopathologie und Nosologie der russisch-jüdischen Bevölkerung. *Journal für Psychologie und Neurologie*, Vol. XIII.; 1908.

PANTIUKHOF, I. I, Observations anthropologiques au Caucase. *Memoires Section Caucasienne de la Société Imperiale Russe de Géographie*, Vol. XV. Tiflis, 1893 (in Russian).
—— *Les Races du Caucase.* Tiflis, 1893 (in Russian).
Pilcz, A., Geistesstörungen bei den Juden. *Wiener klinische Wochenschrift*, Vol. XV., pp. 888-890, 908-910; 1901.
—— *Beitrag zur vergleichenden Rassen-Psychologie.* Leipzig, 1906.

RABINOWITSCH-MARGOLIN, Sara, Die Heiraten von Juden im europäischen Russland. *Zeitschr. f. Demogr. u. Statist. d. Juden*, Nos. 10-12; 1909.
Ranke, J., Zur Statistik und Physiologie der Korpergrösse der bayerischen Militärpflichtigen. *Beiträge zur Anthropologie Bayerns*, Vol. IV., pp. 1-35; 1881.
Raseri, E., La Populazione Israelitica in Italia. *Atti della Società Romana di Antropologia*, Vol. X., pp. 82-93; 1904.
Reibmayr, A., *Inzucht und Vermischung beim Menschen*. Leipzig, 1897.
Reinach, S., La prétendue race juive, *Rev. des Études juives*, 1903; *Cultes, Mythes et Religions*, Vol. III., pp. 457-471, Paris, 1908.

Renan, E., *Le Judaïsme comme race et comme religion.* Paris, 1883.
Rosenfeld, S., Die Sterblichkeit der Juden in Wien. *Archiv für Rassen- und Gesellschaftsbiologie,* Nos 1 and 2; 1907.
—— Todesursachen bei Juden in oesterreichischen Städten. *Zeitscr. f. Demogr. u. Statist. d. Juden,* pp. 161-167; 1907.
Rosenthal, H., The Chazars. *Jewish Encyclopædia,* Vol. IV, pp. 1-7.
Ripley, Wm. Z., *The Races of Europe.* New York, 1899.
—— The European Population of the United States. *Journal of the Royal Anthropological Institute,* Vol. XXXVIII., pp. 221-240; 1908.
Rosenbaum, S., A Contribution to the Study of the Vital and other Statistics of the Jews in the United Kingdom. *Journ. Royal Statistical Society,* Vol. LXVIII., pp. 526-562; 1905.
Rubinow, I. M., Economic Condition of the Jews in Russia. *Bull. of the Bureau of Labour,* No. 72, pp. 487-583. Washington, 1907.
Ruppin, Arthur, Die sozialen Verhältnisse der Juden in Preussen und Deutschland. *Jahrbücher f. Nationalökonomie u. Statistik,* 3rd series, Vol. XXIII., pp. 374-386, 760-785; 1902.
—— *Die Juden der Gegenwart.* Berlin, 1904.
—— Die Kriminalität der Juden in Deutschland. *Zeitschr. f. Demogr. u. Statist. d. Juden,* No. 1; 1905.
—— Die jüdischen Handwerker in Rumänien. *Ibid.,* No. 7.
—— Juden und Armenier. *Ibid.,* pp. 177-181; 1906.
—— Die bestehende Mischehen in Preussen. *Ibid.,* pp. 74-76; 1908.
—— Die Juden in Bulgarien. *Ibid.,* pp. 88-89.
—— Die Mischehe. *Ibid.,* pp. 17-23
—— *Die sozialen Verhältnisse der Juden in Russland.* Berlin, 1906.
—— *Die Juden im Rumänien.* Berlin, 1908.
Russel, C., and H. S. Lewis, *The Jew in London.* London, 1901.

SALOMAN, J., Eheschliessungen zwischen Juden und Christen in Kopenhagen. *Zeitschr. f. Demogr. Stat. d. Juden,* No. 1; 1905.
Samter, N., *Judentaufen im 19 Jahrhundert.* Berlin, 1906.
Sayce, A. H., *The Races of the Old Testament.* London, 1891.
Scheiber, S. H., Untersuchungen über den mittleren Wuchs der Menschen in Ungarn. *Archiv für Anthropologie,* Vol. XIII., pp. 133-267; 1881.
Schimmer, G. H., Erhebungen über die Farbe der Augen, der Haare und der Haut bei den Schulkindern Oesterreichs. *Mitt. d. Anthrop. Ges. Wien;* 1884.
—— *Statistik des Judenthums.* Vienna, 1873.
Schweig, M., Die jüdischen Handwerker in Rumänien. *Zeitschr. Demogr. u. Stat. d. Juden,* pp. 60-63; 1909.

Sichel, M., Ueber die Geistesstörungen bei den Juden. *Neurologisches Centralblatt*, Vol. XXVII., pp. 351-367, 1908; *Umschau*, Vol. XII., pp. 507-509.
—— Psychiatrisches aus der Literatur und Geschichte des jüdischen Volkes. *Neurolog. Centralbl.*, Nos. 5 and 6; 1909.
Silvagni, Luigi, La Patologia comparata negli Ebrei. *Rivista Critica di Clinica Medico*, Nos. 35 and 36; 1901.
Singer, H., *Allgemeine und Spezielle Krankheitslehre der Juden*. Leipzig, 1904.
Slouschz, N., Hebræo-Phéniciens et Judéo-Berbers. *Archives Maroccaines*, Vol. XIV.; 1908.
Sofer, Leo, Chuetas, Maminen und Falascha. *Politisch-Anthropologische Revue*, Vol. V., p. 100-105; 1906.
Snigireff, Materiali dlia medizinskoi statistike i geografii Rossii. *Voenno Medizinski Zhurnal*, 1878-79.
Sombart, W., Jüdischer Geist im modernen Wirtschaftsleben, *Die Neue Rundschau;* 1910.
Stieda, L., and W. Dybowski, Ein Beitrag zur Anthropologie der Juden. *Archiv für Anthropologie*, Vol. XII., pp. 61-71; 1883.
Stratz, C. H., *Was sind Juden?* Vienna, 1903.
Struck, A., Die Verborgenjüdische Sekte der Dönmeh in Salonika. *Globus*, Vol. LXXXI., pp. 219-224; 1902.

TALKO-HRYNCEWICZ, J., Charakterystyka fizyczna ludnosci Zydowskiej Litwy i Rusi. *Zbior Wiad. do antropol. kraj.*, Vol. XVI., pp. 1-62. Cracow, 1892. (Summarized in *Archiv f. Anthropologie*, Vol. XXIV., p. 380.)
—— *Karaimi v. Karaici Liteswscy*. Zarys anthropologo-etnologiczny. Cracow, 1903.
Teumin, S., *Topographisch-anthropometrische Untersuchungen über die Proportionsverhältnisse des weiblichen Körpers*. Brunswick, 1901.
Thon, J., Die Bewegung der jüdischen Bevölkerung in Bayern. *Zeitschr. f. Demogr. u. Statistik d. Juden*, No. 8; 1905.
—— Die Kriminalität der Christen und Juden in Ungarn. *Ibid.*, pp. 104-107; 1907.
—— Taufbewegung der Juden in Oesterreich. *Ibid.*, pp. 6-12; 1908.
—— *Die Juden in Oesterreich*. Berlin, 1907.
Tostivint, with Remlinger, Note sur la rareté de la tuberculose chez les Israélites Tunisiens. *Révue d'hygiéne et de Police Sanitaire*, Vol. XXII., p. 984; 1900.
Trap, Cordt, Die Juden in Kopenhagen. *Zeitschr. Demogr. Stat. d. Juden*, pp. 97-101; 1907.

VIRCHOW, R., Gesamtbericht . . . über die Farbe der Haut, der Haare und der Augen der Schulkinder in Deutschland. *Archiv für Anthropologie*, Vol. XVI., pp. 275-475; 1886.

WADLER, A, Die Juden in Serbien. *Zeitschr. Demogr. Stat. d. Juden*, pp. 145-148, 168-173; 1906.

Waldenburg, A., *Das isocephale Element unter Halligfriessen und jüdischen Taubstummen*. Berlin, 1902.

Waldstein, Chas., *The Jewish Question and the Mission of the Jews*. London, 1902.

Wateff, S., Anthropologische Beobachtungen der Farbe der Augen, der Haare und der Haut bei den Schulkindern von den Turken, Pomaken, Tataren, Armenier, Griechen, und Juden in Bulgarien. *Correspondez-Blatt der Deutschen Gesel. f. Anthrop*, etc., Vol. XXXIV., Nos. 7, 8; 1903.

Wassermann, Rudolf, *Beruf, Konfession und Verbrechen*. Munich, 1907.

—— Kritische und ergänzende Bemerkungen zur neuen Literatur über die Kriminalität der Juden. *Zeitschr. Demogr. Statist. d. Juden*, pp. 172-174; 1908.

—— Die Kriminalität der Juden in Deutschland in den letzten 25 Jahren. *Monatschrift für Kriminalpsychologie und Strafrechtsreform;* 1909.

Weinberg, R., K-ucheniu o forme mosga cheloweka. *Russian Anthropl. Journal*, Part IV., pp. 1-34; 1902.

—— Ueber einige ungewöhnliche Befunde an Judenhirnen. *Biologisches Centralblatt*, Vol. XXIII., pp. 154-162; 1904.

—— Das Hirngewicht der Juden. *Zeitschr. f. Demogr. u. Statist. d. Juden*, No. 3; 1905.

—— Die Transkaukasische Juden. *Ibid.*, No. 5.

—— Zur Pathologie der Juden. *Ibid.*, No. 8.

—— Soziales und Biostatisches Verhalten der livländischen Juden. *Ibid.*, pp. 69-73; 1906.

Weisbach, A., Körpermessungen verschiedener Menschenrassen. *Zeitschrift für Ethnologie;* 1877, Ergänzungsband.

Weissenberg, S., Die südrussischen Juden. *Archiv für Anthropologie*, Vol. XXIII., pp. 347-423, 531-579.

—— Die Karäer der Krim. *Globus*, Vol. LXXXIV., pp. 139-143; 1903.

—— Das jüdische Rassenproblem. *Zeitschr. Demogr. Statist. d. Juden*, No. 5; 1905.

—— Der Gesundheitszustand der Juden in Odessa. *Ibid*, pp. 90-93; 1909.

—— Die zentralasiatischen Juden in anthropologischer Beziehung. *Ibid.*, pp. 103-110.

—— Die autochthone Bevölkerung Palästinas in anthropologischen Beziehung. *Ibid.* pp. 129-139.

—— Pekin und seine Juden. *Globus*, Vol. XCVI., No. 3; 1909.

—— Die Spaniolen. *Mitteil. Anthropol. Ges. Wein*, Vol. IX., pp. 225-239; 1909.

—— Beitrag zur Anthropologie der Juden. *Zeitschr. f. Ethnologie*, Heft VI., pp. 961-964; 1907.

Weissenberg, S., Die jemenitischen Juden. *Ibid.*, Heft III. and IV., pp. 309-327; 1909.
―― Die kaukasische Juden in anthropologischer Beziehung. *Archiv fur Anthropologie*, N.S., Vol. VIII., pp. 237-245; 1909.
Weldler, N., Die Bevölkerungsbewegung des Jahres 1906 bei den Juden in Ungarn. *Zeitschr. Demogr. u. Stat. d. Juden*, pp. 118-122; 1908.
White, Arnold, *The Modern Jew.* London, 1899.
Wiener, L., *The History of Yiddish Literature.* New York, 1899.
Wolf, Lucien, The Zionist Peril. *Jewish Quarterly Review*, Vol. XVII., pp. 1-25; 1904.
―― Article, "Zionism," in *Encyclopædia Britannica.* 10 ed.

YAKOWENKO, M. G., *Materiali k antropologii evreiskoi naselenii.* St. Petersburg, 1898.

ZACK, N. W., *Fizicheskoye rasvitie dietei.* Moscow, 1892.
Zakrzewski, A., Wzrost w Krolestwie Polskiem. *Zbior Wiad. do antrop. kraj.*, Vol. XV., pp. 1-39; 1891.
―― Ludnosc miasta Warszawy. *Mater. antrop.-archeolog. Akadem. umiej*, Vol. I. pp. 1-38. Cracow, 1895.
Zollschan, I., *Das Rassenproblem.* Vienna, 1909.

INDEX OF AUTHORS.

ABRAHAMS, I., 378, 381, 393, 396, 421, 509
Abramowitsch, M., 261
Adachi, B., 316
Adler, E. N., 126, 161
Allbutt, 348
Allen, Grant, 60, 214
Alsberg, M., 118
Ammon, Otto, 64, 74, 88
Andree, R., 17, 94, 99, 124, 136, 188, 205, 226, 315, 399, 540
Anutchin, 33
Apion, 475
Auerbach, E, 77, 231, 260, 263, 278, 284, 287, 298, 301, 328, 352
Aurelius, Marcus, 314

BARAZHNIKOFF, 281
Baskerville, B. C., 539
Bastian, A., 149
Beadles, C. F., 341, 344
Beddoe, J., 33, 65, 84, 99, 169
Behrend, 290
Beloch, 2
Bendt, J. T, 161
Bentwich, N., 472
Benzinger, I., 60, 491
Berliner, 396
Bershadsky, 4
Bertillon, 19, 300
Bewer, Max, 446
Billings, J. S., 233
Binzerbach, 446
Bismarck, 210
Blau, B., 408, 459
Blechmann, 13, 86, 106
Boas, Franz, 25, 27, 36, 219, 220
Boldt, J., 320

Bordier, A. 311, 337
Borrow, 160
Botwinick, 323
Boudin, 17, 280
Bovis, R. de, 313
Braithwaithe, J., 311
Brandes, Georg, 3 2, 167
Brinton, D. G., 515
Broca, 17, 69, 106
Brodowski, J., 363
Brosius, 348
Brunner, A. W., 491
Bülow, von, 552
Burchard, H., 126
Busch, M., 210
Buschan, G., 272, 280, 311, 337, 348
Bushee, F. A., 409

CAMMEO, G., 215
Castro, M. de, 147
Chamberlain, H. S., 445
Charcot, 296, 324, 329
Chashmonoi, M., 495
Cheinisse, 275, 313
Cohen, F. L., 490
Cohn, 278, 322
Costello, Percy M., 360
Curzon, 128
Czacki, T., 4
Czerning, 189

DARWIN, 533
Davis, 49
Degner, 278
De le Roi, J., 454, 523
Delitzsch, 92

INDEX OF AUTHORS.

Deniker, J., 28, 32, 41, 68, 76, 106, 108, 114, 512
Deutsch, G., 277, 386
Dilthey, W., 445
Dohm, C. W. von, 434
Dolgopol, 259
Drumont, 154
Dubnow, S. M., 477
Dyche, John A., 544

EBSTEIN, W., 337, 338
Eichholtz, 309
Einhorn, 224
Einsler, 318
Eisenmann, 278
Elkind, 40, 74, 80, 99, 104
Ellis, Havelock, 32, 315, 344
Erb, W., 327, 348
Evans-Gordon, W., 455, 538

FAITLOVITCH, 146
Feldman, B, 183, 221
Felkin, 18
Féré, 296
Fishberg, 32, 41, 49, 74, 278, 283, 287
Fishkin, 317
Flad, 146
Fracastor, 277
Frankel, L. K., 367
Frederic, Harold, 429
Frerich, F. T., 298
Fortunatus, 314

GAJKIEWICZ, 326
Galton, F., 100, 176
Geiger, L., 500
Gerster, A. G., 305
Gilfoy, 283
Giltschenko, N. W., 57
Glatter, 283, 309
Gliddon, 90, 92
Glück, 65
Goldberg, B., 12, 321
Goldscheider, A., 236, 257, 268
Goldstein, E., 85
Gollanz, I., 483
Gould, G., 317
Graetz, H., 183, 184, 189, 190, 277

Grandidier, 306
Gumplowicz, L., 513, 514
Gutzkow, K., 454

HAESER, 526, 527
Hahn, C, 131
Hale, II., 388
Hall, 308
Hamy, 49
Hannauer, W., 293
Hardy, 316
Harnack, A., 445
Hartmann, Ed. v., 205, 445
Haushoffer, 1
Hebräus, A., 383
Hecatæus, 475
Hellwald, 102
Herzl, Th., 473, 497
Higier, 327
Himmel, 28, 40
Hirsch, A., 280
Hirsch, E. G., 182, 224, 464
Hoffmann, F. G., 262
Hope, E. W., 261
Hoppe, Hugo, 269, 385
Hough, J. S, 277
Hovorka, O, 80
Huguet, J., 145
Hutchinson, II. N., 175
Huxley, H. M., 50, 124
Huxley, Thomas, 389, 391
Hyde, F. C., 340

IKOFF, 48, 106, 151, 194
Ivanowski, A. A, 40, 52

JACOBS, Joseph, 3, 54, 56, 64, 84, 239, 395, 509
Jaeger, G., 315
Jastrow, M., 515
Josephus, 2, 60
Judt, J. M., 89, 99
Juvenal, 475

KAJEWNIKOFF, 342
Kalgut, 313
Kayserling, 160
Keane, A. II., 389

Kempster, 429
Kleen, 301
Kleinpaul, R., 315
Knopfel, 200
Kohler, K., 221, 404
Kohler, M. J., 150
Kollmann, 24, 48
Körösi, 64, 258, 283, 302, 306, 309
Kopernicki, 29, 40, 68, 74, 82, 86
Kovalevsky, P., 415
Kowarsky, S., 308
Krafft-Ebbing, 327
Krose, H. A., 207
Külz, 298
Kurdoff, K., 41, 49, 65, 131

LAFONTAINE, 317
Lagneau, G., 69, 311
Lancereaux, 296
Lasson, Christian, 505
Laufer, Berthold, 135
Layard, 92
Lazare, B., 420, 425, 475
Lazarus, M., 492
Lea, Ch. H., 155, 157, 158
Leake, W. M., 161
Lecky, 393, 460
Leroy-Beaulieu, A., 108, 124, 267, 449, 493
Levy, S., 488
Lewis, H. S., 444
Libreich, R., 321
Linetzky, 386
Livy, Michael, 278
Loane, J., 233, 256
Loeb, J., 145
Loeb, Morris, 376, 378
Lombroso, C., 41, 47, 65, 239, 302, 309, 328, 552
Lotze, 149
Luschan, 53, 69, 83

MAGNUS, Laurie, 482, 499
Majer, J., 29, 40, 74, 82, 86
Maltzan, 126
Mapother, 280
Marcellinus, Ammianus, 314
Martin, 136
Maspero, 92
Maurer, 106

Maximoff, 340
Mayo-Smith, 207
McLeod, N., 173
Meakin, 159
Meyenberg, 277
Michel, F., 316
Milman, 452, 476, 551
Minor, L. S., 325, 342
Molo, Apollonius, 475
Montefiore, C. G., 223, 482
Moretzki, 213
Morselli, 351
Moses, J., 306
Murphy, S. F., 232, 261

NAGEL, F., 239
Nahoum, H., 148
Newsholme, 234, 237
Nichols, J. B., 238
Niven, 285
Noah, M. M., 8
Noorden, Carl von, 298, 300
Nordau, Max., 154, 449, 463, 470, 474, 486, 525, 552
Nossig, A., 1, 363
Nott, 90, 92

OPPENHEIM, H., 309, 327
Orelli, 123
Ottolenghi, 322

PANTIUKHOF, 28, 40, 49, 64, 74, 88
Papratz, 336
Paulsen, F, 445
Pennel, T. L., 174
Peretz, 386
Petrie, Flinders, 1
Philipson, D., 535
Philo, 2, 184
Philostratus, 475
Pilcz, A., 329, 339, 341, 348
Pittard, E., 40, 52
Pollatscheck, A., 298
Pouchet, 251
Prinzig, 414
Pruner-Bey, F., 49, 69
Pyle, 317

QUATREFAGES, 49

INDEX OF AUTHORS.

RAMAZZINI, 278, 396
Ranke, J., 28, 33, 83
Ratzel, F., 174
Rau, 278
Rawlinson, 92
Raymond, 324
Reich, M., 315
Reid, G. A., 274
Reinach, Salomon, 156, 535
Reinach, Theodore, 2, 186, 188, 475
Remilinger, 288
Renan, E., 188, 481, 484, 505
Ripley, 25, 33, 51, 77, 85, 171, 176, 202, 515
Robert, Ulysse, 92
Rohrbach, P., 542
Rosenbaum, S., 6, 13
Rosenfeld, S., 278, 287, 302, 307, 328, 352
Rosenthal, H., 191
Rothschild, N., 306
Rubinow, I. M., 362, 399, 405
Ruppin, A., 2, 16, 229, 244, 246, 252, 264, 268, 321, 336, 379, 397, 416, 454, 537
Russel, C., 544
Ryazansky, 340

SACK, 29
Salomon, J., 196
Samter, N., 198, 213, 444, 454, 459, 552
Sarur, R. M. abi, 145
Savage, G. H., 343, 348
Sayce, 91, 118, 181
Scalzi, 279
Scheiber, 28
Schellong, 19
Scherer, 422
Schick, L., 201
Schimmer, 63, 226
Schleich, 171
Schleiermacher, 445
Schmidt, Emil, 137
Schwartz, I., 277, 293
See, 300
Segal, J., 241
Senn. N., 318
Sergi, 118, 508
Shaler, N. S., 448

Sibree, 149
Sichel, 329, 338, 345, 347
Sidgwick, A, 442
Sikorski, 340
Singer, H., 298, 319
Slouschz, N., 145
Smith, Eustace, 309
Smith, Goldwin, 154
Smith, Robertson, 535
Snigireff, 28, 36, 39, 86
Sofer, Leo, 157, 160
Soler, T. B., 160
Sombart, Werner, 543
Spencer, Herbert, 550
Spielman, 41
Stead, W. T., 210
Steinen, von den 174
Stembo, L., 326
Stern, H., 299
Stevenson, 234, 237,
Stieda, 106
Stokvis, 282
Stratz, 175, 176
Struck, 153
Sundbärg, 230
Swiderski, 41

TACITUS, 2, 475
Talko-Hryncewicz, 36, 151
Taronji, 160
Taylor, I., 389
Ten Kate, 173, 176
Thackeray, 98
Theilhaber, F., 193
Thon, J., 13, 200, 211, 241, 269, 301, 328, 334, 379, 415, 528
Tobler, 324
Tolwinsky, 28, 40
Topinard, 68, 79, 106
Tormay, 279
Tostivint, 288
Trap, Cordt, 198, 215, 268
Treitschke, 445
Tschudi, 277

VIRCHOW, 17, 18, 62, 64
Vogt, Karl, 106

WACKERNAGEL, 122
Wadler, 372, 385

Wagner, 490
Wallace, A. R., 17, 19
Wallach, 298
Ward, 285
Wartegg, 145
Wassermann, L., 354, 375
Wassermann, R., 418
Wateff, 64
Weber, 429
Weinberg, R., 57, 317, 408
Weisbach, 57
Weissenberg, S., 29, 35, 40, 49, 55, 99, 106, 118, 151, 497
Weldler, N., 339, 346
Westermarck, 251
Weyl, 19
White, A., 154
Wiener, L., 386, 391

Wolf, Lucien, 478, 481, 497, 499, 502
Wolff, 280
Woodruff, Ch , 17
Worms, 329
Wright, 118

YAKOWENKO, 36
Yashchinsky, 29

ZAKRZEWSKI, 28, 33, 35, 39
Zangwill, 99, 178, 223, 470, 473, 474, 493, 498
Zevin, I., 386
Zombacco, 319
Zunz, L., 453

INDEX OF SUBJECTS.

ABYSSINIA, number of Jews in, 10. *See also* Falashas.
Acclimatization, 16 *et seq.*
A'ghans with Jewish physiognomy, 174
Africa, number of Jews in, 10; North, anthropological types of Jews, 136 *et seq.*
Agriculture, Jews engaged in, 403; in Russia, 404, 494; in Palestine, 405, 494; in the United States, 405; in Argentine, 406
Alcoholism, 273 *et seq.;* Jews rarely total abstainers, 275; in England and United States, 275; and tuberculosis, 292; and insanity, 342; and poverty, 367
Algeria, Jewish types in, 140
Aneurism, 305
Anti-Semitism, causes of, 447 *et seq.;* Zionist view of, 473; retards assimilation, 470; Zionism no remedy against anti-Semitism, 496
Apoplexy, 329
Architecture, there is no Jewish, 491
Armenians and Jews, 542
Armies, Jews in, 540
Art, there are no Jewish forms of, 487
Arthritism, 297
Aryan type among Jews, 72, 76
Aryans and Semites, 505
Ashkenazim, 106; physical types of, 111 *et seq.*
Asia, number of Jews in, 9
Assimilation, 446 *et seq.;* Zionist view of, 154, 470 *et seq.;* "arrested," 478; and emancipation, 479; and language, 381, 387, 391, 483; desire for, 485; capacity for, 154, 516, 550; in Spain, 158 *et seq.*, 551; in Roumania, 425; in France, 525; and economic conditions, 537
Australia, number of Jews in, 10; in cities, 14; mixed marriages, 203, 215
Austria, number of Jews in, 5; complexion, 63; mixed marriages in, 195, 200; birth-rates, 228, 520; fecundity, 235; marriage rates, 249; illiteracy, 373; languages spoken by Jews, 384; occupations, 398, 400; emancipation, 432; Jews in army, 439; baptism in, 455 *et seq.*

BADGE, 92
Baptism, voluntary, 451; and emancipation, 451, 455; in Greece, 452; in Spain, 452; during nineteenth century, 454; incentives for, in Russia, 430; causes of, 460; effects of, 461; social conditions of Jews submitting to, 456, 459; of Jewish professors in Germany, 453; of Jewish children, 454; of English Jews, 454; and assimilation, 552
Bend, the Ghetto, 164
Beni Israel in India, 134
Berber Jews, 144, 146
Births, 225 *et seq.; see also* Fertility, race influence, 227; geographical influences, 230; in Eastern Europe, 228; in Western countries, 229; excess of, over deaths, 265 *et seq.*

INDEX OF SUBJECTS.

Birth-rates, decline of among Jews, 231, 234, 268, 520; economic influences on, 237, 266, 519; and isolation, 519; in London, 232; in the United States, 233
Black death, 276
Black Jews in India, 131 *et seq.*, 508
Blindness, 321
Blondeness, *see also* Hair; among the ancient Hebrews, 60, 507; origin of, among the Jews, 69, 190, 507; proportion among modern Jews, 64, 65, 507; and stature, 74; and head-form, 74; distribution of, in Germany, 70; climatic influences, 70, 507; and artificial selection, 77
Blonde type, 66
Bokhara, Jews in, 126
Brain, weight of, 57; characteristics of, 58
Bright's disease, 310
Brunette type, 66
Bulgaria, number of Jews in, 6; birth rates, 228; illiteracy in, 372; naturalization of the Jews, 433

CANAANITES, 121
Canada, number of Jews in, 6
Cancer, 311 *et seq.*; rarity of, among Jewesses, 312
Caucasus, Jews in the, 130
Cave-dwellers, Jewish, 145
Celibacy, 246
Cephalic index of African Jews, 49; in the Caucasus, 49; Samaritans, 50; European Jews, 50, 52 *et seq.*; autochthonous Jews in Palestine, 55. *See also* Head-form.
Chest, girth of, 85; as a racial trait, 88
Chinese Jews, 134
Cholera, 279, 527
Chozars, 114, 191; intermixture with Jews, 194
Christãos Novos, 155
Christian Scientists, Jewish, 467
Chuetas, 157
Church, and legislation concerning the Jews, 420; and Zionism, 493

Circumcision, ritual, and proselytism, 184, 186, 534; of slaves, 189, 509; and fatal bleeding, 306; and syphilis, 318, 530
City dwellers, Jews as, 11 *et seq.*; effects of, on birth-rate, 237; and insanity, 339, 350, 531; and occupation, 394; and illiteracy, 372; and criminality, 412, 548
Cochin, Jews in, 131
Colour-blindness, 322
Colour, correspondence between hair and eyes, 66 *et seq.*
Commercial pursuits, 399
Commercial spirit of Jews, 541, 543
Complexion of ancient Hebrews, 60
Consanguinity, 250; its effects on pathology, 251; and nervous diseases, 331; and deaf-mutism, 337; and insanity, 349
Contagious diseases, 537 *et seq.*
Conversions in Spain, 155. *See also* Baptism
Conversos, 155; persecution of, 156; isolation of, 158
Converts to Judaism, classes of, 184; treatment of, by Jews, 185
Crimes, forms committed by Jews, 412 *et seq.*, 548; of violence, 413, 549
Criminality, 407 *et seq.*; and occupation, 411, 418, 548; and race, 410; characteristics of Jewish, 416; effects of political disabilities, 411; Jewish, in England, 409, 417; in the United States, 409, 416
Croup, 282
Crypto-Jews, 152
Cushites, 120

DAGGATOUNS, 144
Daghestan Mountain Jews, 131
Deaf-mutism, 336
Death-rates, 255 *et seq. See* Mortality
Decadence of Western Jews, 520; effects of, 524
Defectives, 332; and marriage of the unfit, 245
Dementia præcox, 343
Demography, 225 *et seq.*

INDEX OF SUBJECTS.

Denationalization, 485
Diabetes, 297 et seq.
Diathesis, 296
Dietary laws, origin of, 535; economic and social effects of, 420, 536 et seq.; and tuberculosis, 290; disregarded by modern Jews, 538
Diphtheria, 282
Disabilities, political, 419 et seq.; in Roumania, 422; in Russia, 426; and poverty, 361; effects of, 434; social, 438
Discriminations, political, 420 et seq.; social, 440
Diseases, endemic, 282 et seq.; contagious, 276; of digestive organs, 306, 529; or circulatory organs, 393; of respiratory organs, 302; of nervous system, 324, 530; external causes of, 273; alleged immunities against, 276; during Middle Ages, 277, 526; and indoor occupations, 303
Divorce, 251 et seq.; and mixed marriages, 217
Dönmeh, 152, 160; physical type of, 153
Drug-addiction, 347

Economic conditions, 356 et seq.; and assimilation, 537
Eczema, 316
Education, 370 et seq., 545; Restrictions in Roumania, 423; in Russia, 428
Emancipated Jews, number of, 419, 433
Emancipation of Jews, 431 et seq.; and baptism, 453, 455, 460
England, number of Jews, 6; stature, 31, 41; complexion, 64; mixed marriages in, 202, 223; birth-rate in, 232; decline in marriage-rates, 249; mortality, 256; infant mortality, 261; languages spoken by Jews, 386; criminality, 409, 416; immigration, 436; emancipation, 431; Jews in army and navy, 440; baptisms in, 454, 461, 464; nationality of Jews in, 472, 482
English-speaking Jews, number of, 10

Epilepsy, 328
Erythrism, 68
Expectation of life, 261, 263
Eye, the Jewish, 169; diseases of, 319 et seq.
Eyes, colour of, in Biblical times, 61; fair, percentage of, 64, 65, 507

Face (see also Physiognomy), the Ghetto, 166, 171; in composite photographs, 102
Facial expression and occupation, 166; as a product of social selection, 176
Falashas, 146, 508; physical type, 147; origin of, 148
Favus, 317
Fecundity, 235; decline of, 236
Feeble-mindedness, 332
Fertility, of ancient Hebrews, 226; decline among modern Jews, 235, 520
Fœtor Judaicus, 314
Folk-lore, 491
France, number of Jews, 7; mixed marriages, 201, 215; emancipation, 431; decadence of modern Jews in, 463, 525;
Freethinkers, Jewish, 195

G'did al Islam, 152
General paralysis, 341
Gerim, 193
Germany, number of Jews, 6; in cities, 16; complexion of Jews, 62; mixed marriages, 197, 198 et seq., 215, 222; birth-rates, 229; fecundity, 235; celibacy, 246; mortality, 257; criminality, 408, 411 et seq.; ostracism in army and navy, 439; social ostracism, 442; baptisms, 444. 523, 459 et seq.
Ghetto, 534; origin of, 421
Glaucoma, 320
Goitre, 311
Greece, number of Jews, 6
Growth of the body, 29
Gypsies and Jews, 447

Habitus phthisicus, 286
Hæmophilia, 305

Hair, colour of, 60 *et seq.;* red, 68. See also Blondeness
Head, size of, 56
Head-form, 47 *et seq.;* of ancient Hebrews, 47, 511; of modern Jews, 48; variability, 49; types of among Jews, 50, 509; and intellectuality, 54; and race purity of the Jews, 55, 511; and blondeness, 76. *See also* Cephalic index
Heart, diseases of the, 303
Hebrews, ancient, stature of, 27, 53; cephalic index, 47, 55, 511; complexion of, 60
Hemorrhoids, 305
Herpetisms, 297
Hindus, with Jewish physiognomy, 175
Hittites, 118
Holland, mixed marriages in, 200; criminality, 408, 417; emancipation of Jews, 432
Hungary, number of Jews in, 6; stature, 28; cephalic index, 64; mixed marriages, 197, 201, 214; birth-rates, 229; fecundity, 235; mortality, 257; languages spoken by Jews in, 385; criminality, 415; baptisms in, 458
Hysteria, 324, 330, 530

Idiocy, 332; amaurotic family, 335; Mongolian type of, 335
Illegitimacy, 242 *et seq.;* as an index of morality, 242
Illiteracy, 371; in Russia, 371; in London, 372; in Australia, 374
Imbecility, 332
Immigration to the United States, 436
Incas, with Jewish physiognomy, 175
India, number of Jews in, 10; types of Jews in, 131 *et seq.;* origin of black Jews in, 508
"Indo-Germanic Jews," 64
Infantile diarrhœa, 306
Infectious diseases, 263
Inquisition in Spain, causes of, 156
Insane, high proportion of Jewesses, 344
Insanity, 237 *et seq.;* among ancient Hebrews, 337; in Prussia, 338; in Austria, 339; in Hungary, 340;

in the United States, 341; clinical forms among Jews, 341; puerperal, 344, 346; moral, 343; prognosis of, among Jews, 347; and religion, 348; and consanguinity, 348; causes of excessive rate among Jews, 530 *et seq.*
Insurance, 261
Intermarriage (*see also* Mixed marriages), common among kings and patriarchs of Israel, 181; with Canaanities, 182; Biblical prohibition, 181, 221, 467; Ezra's prohibition, 182; in Greece and Rome, 183; in Spain and Portugal, 158, 189; prohibited by Church Councils, 188, 221; prohibited in Russia and Austria, 195, 224, 517; between Protestants and Catholics, 206; effect of legalization on frequency, 207, 222; opposition to, by Church and Synagogue, 205, 221, 516; Jewish theological attitude toward, 221 *et seq.*, 467; religion no strong barrier to, 223; more Jews than Jewesses apt to enter, 205; loss sustained by Judaism through, 216, 218, 524; desirability of, 209, 518; racial antipathy no barrier, 209; ethnic effects, 219; fertility of, 210; physical condition of children born to, 213; intellectuality of descendants from, 214; Ghetto isolation the best preventive of, 209, 224, 517; effects of, on social conditions of the Jews, 462 *et seq.*, 518
Intermittent claudication, 327
Isolation, welcomed by Jews, 421; as a preserver of Judaism, 437 *et seq ;* and fertility of Jews, 519; dietary laws and, 535; in Rome, 475; effects of, 535; enforced by Church and State, 431; Jewish physiognomy and, 177; of Jews by Christian society, 477; and language, 387
Italy, number of Jews in, 7; complexion of Jews, 65; mixed marriages, 202, 215; emancipation, 433

INDEX OF SUBJECTS.

JAMAICA, Jews in, 149
Japanese, with Jewish physiognomy, 173
Jesus, race of, 445
Judæus primigenius, 121
Judaism and nationality, 491; as a separative religion, 534 *et seq.*

KARAITES, 150, 319

LADINO, see *Spagnuoli*
Language, as a test of race, 389; and nationality, 483; and assimilation, 381
Languages spoken by Jews, 379 *et seq.*
Law, study of, by Jews, 378
Legislation, mediæval, concerning the Jews, 422, 434
Leprosy, 318
Limpieza, 158
Literature, is there a Jewish? 487
Loango Coast, Jews on, 149
Locomotor ataxia, 326

MADAGASCAR, Jews in, 149
Malabar, Jews in, 131
Male births, excess of, 238 *et seq.*
Marranos, 157; persecution of, 156; removal of disabilities from, 159
Marriage, 245 *et seq.*; Rabbinical ordinance concerning, 245; age at, 246; social factors in, 248; decline in rates in England, 249; consanguineous, 250; dissolution of, see Divorce, 251
Marriages, mixed, 195 *et seq.* (*see also* Intermarriage); legal status of, 195, 224; definition of, 196; statistics of, 197; in Scandinavia, 196, 517; in Germany, 198, 222, 524; in Amsterdam, 200; in Austria, 200, 517; in Hungary, 201, 517; in England, 202, 223, 249; in the United States, 203, 222, 518; in Australia, 203, 215; religion of children born to, 214; frequency of divorce, 217
Mavambus, 149
"May Laws" in Russia, 426 *et seq.*
Medicine, study of by Jews, 377

Merchant, characteristics of Jewish, 541
Migrations of Jews, 434, 471; from Russia and Roumania, 435
Military service, fitness for, 86
Mission to the Jews, failure of, 218, 461
Mixed type, 66
Mongoloid type of Jews, 118
Mortality, 255 *et seq.*, 528; influence of economic conditions, 258, 528; influence of occupation, 265
—— infantile, 259 *et seq.*; and birth-rates, 260, 264
Music, Jewish, 489
Myopia, 323
M'zabite Jews, 145

NAMES of Jews, 485
Natality, 225 *et seq.*
Nation, Jewish, 471; is there a Jewish? 474; what is a? 484
Nationality and religion, 478, 480; and language, 483; of German Jews, 491
Natural increase, 267 *et seq.*
Negroid type of Jews, 120
Negro Jews, 146, 149
Nervous diseases, 324 *et seq.*
Neurasthenia, 324, 330, 531
"Noble" Jews, 531 *et seq.*
Nomadic tribes of Jews, 144
North-European types of Jews, 114
Nose, Jewish, 79, 82, 84; forms of, 79
Number, total, of Jews, 3; in ancient times, 1; in mediæval times, 3

OCCUPATIONS, 393 *et seq.*, 538 *et seq.*; in Russia, 397; in Austria, 398; in the United States, 399, 401; during the Middle Ages, 393; and religion, 394; and race, 538; and criminality, 411 *et seq.*; and political disabilities, 393
Odours, racial, 315

PAINTERS, Jewish, 488
Pale of Settlement, Russian, 4, 11, 427

INDEX OF SUBJECTS.

Palestine, types of Jews in, 121; number of Jews in, 10, 482; size of, 493; resources of, 494
Paralysis agitans, 326
Paranoia, 343, 346
Parvenus, Jewish, 451, 461 *et seq.*; characteristics of, 462
Pathological characteristics, 270 *et seq.*, 526 *et seq.*
Persia, Jews in, 127
Physiognomy, Jewish, 94, 513; in Rembrandt's paintings, 62, 93; painter's conception of, 97; novelist's conception of, 98; among non-Jews, 171 *et seq.*; a product of isolation, 176; among old noble families, 175 *et seq.*
Plica Judaica, 317
Pneumonia, 302
Political conditions, 419 *et seq.*
Poor, characteristics of Jewish, 360; regeneration of, in England and America, 367
Poverty, among the Jews, 361 *et seq.*; and Jewish ritualism, 537
Prepotency, 99, 102, 220
Professors, Jewish, 442
Proselytes, Russian, 193
Proselytism, 179, 508; in Greece and Rome, 183; in Palestine, 184
Psychosis Judaica, 348

RACE-PRIDE of the Jews, 505, 516
Race, purity of Jewish, 21, 506; traits, persistent, 24; traits, fluctuating, 26; and environment, 25, 506; effects of intermixture of, 25; and birth-rates, 227; and head-form, 49 *et seq.*, 509; and suicide, 351; and disease, 270 *et seq.*; and language, 389; and nationality, 474; and criminality, 547 *et seq.*, 410; and occupation, 538 *et seq.*; there is no Jewish, 515
Race theory of anti-Semitism, 448
Religion and intolerance, 449; and nationality, 480; and the social type of the Jew, 550; and occupation, 394
Retinitis pigmentosa, 320

Rickets, 308
Ritualism, economic effects of Jewish, 537
Roumania, number of Jews in, 6; cephalic index, 50; complexion of Jews in, 64; mixed marriages, 197; birth-rates, 229; fecundity, 235; poverty of Jews, 365; disabilities in, 423 *et seq.*; emigration from, 435
Russia, number of Jews in, 3; distribution, 11; stature, 28; cephalic index, 50; complexion, 64; birth-rates, 229; fecundity, 235; marriage-rates, 247; poverty, 361; illiteracy, 372; languages spoken by Jews in, 384; occupations, 396 *et seq.*; Jewish agriculturists in, 404; criminality in, 408, 418; disabilities in, 426 *et seq.*; emigration from, 435; baptisms in, 454, 523; assimilation in, 479; failure of repression of the Jews in, 519; origin of Jews in, 192
Russian sectarians, 193

SABBATH, the Jewish, 536; and economic conditions, 538 *et seq.*; disregard of, 538
Sahara, Jews in, 143
Samaritans, 121
Scandinavia, number of Jews in, 7; mixed marriages in, 196, 215
Scarlet fever, 284
Sculptors, Jewish, 488
Selection, artificial, of Jewish physiognomy, 176
——— social, and complexion, 77
Semite, in Europe, 445, 448
Semites, ancient, distribution of, 54; characteristics of, 505; cradle of, 515; capacity for assimilation in Europe, 516; effects of baptism on their racial traits, 533
Sephardim, 106; characteristics of, 108; compared with Ashkenazim, 110; distribution of, 106; race mixture of, 111; intermarriages of, with Christians, 111
Servia, number of Jews in, 6
Sex at birth, 238

INDEX OF SUBJECTS.

Skin diseases, 313 *et seq.*
Skulls of Sephardim, 49. *See also* Cephalic index
Slaves, conversion to Judaism, 189, 509
Slavonic type of Jews, 114
Small-pox, 284
Solidarity, Jewish, 361
Spagnuoli, 380, 382
Spain, number of Jews in, 7; political status of Jews in, 476; expulsion of Jews from, 155; baptisms in, 452
Stature, 27 *et seq.*; of ancient Hebrews, 28; of Jewish recruits, 28; of Jewesses, 31; and environment, 32, 512; and occupation, 34; social selection and, 45; race effects on, 38, 512; variability of, 44
Stillbirths, 241 *et seq.*
Stock Exchange, Jews in, 360
Subbotniki, 192
Suicide, 350 *et seq.*, 533; and religion, 351; effects of social conditions on frequency of, 352; and occupation, 354
Surinam, Jews in, 149
Switzerland, number of Jews, 7; emancipation, 433
Syphilis, 318, 326, 342, 530

TAILORING, preference for, by Jews, 396
Ten Lost Tribes of Israel, 172
Territorialism, 470, 501
Teutonic type among Jews, 114
Totemism, 525
Trachoma, 320
Tripolis, Jews in, 145
Troglodyte Jews, 145
Tuberculosis, 286 *et seq.*, 529; clinical forms among Jews, 294; during the Middle Ages, 293; and dietary laws, 291; adaptation to, 293; urbanization and, 294
Tunis, Jews in, 140
Turanian type of Jews, 114

Type, of ancient Hebrews, 90; Jewish, persistence of, 92, 94; prepotency of, 99; composite, 100; and social selection, 178; origin of, 102 *et seq.*; dress and deportment influencing the, 163, 513; psychic or social, 165, 513; Slavonic, 114; Turanian, 114; Teutonic, 114; Mongoloid, 118; Negroid, 120
Types of Jews, 90 *et seq.*
Typhoid fever, 278

UNITED STATES, number of Jews, 7; distribution of Jews, 13; stature, 31, 36; complexion, 64; mixed marriages, 203, 222; birth-rates, 233; divorces, 253; mortality, 256; languages of Jews, 386; occupations, 399, 401 *et seq.*; Jewish agriculturists in, 405; criminality, 409, 416; immigration, 434 *et seq.*; social ostracism of Jews, 440 *et seq.*; baptisms, 460, 464
Universities, Jews in, 375 *et seq.*, 545

VACCINATION, 285
Venereal diseases, 530

WHOOPING cough, 284
Workman, characteristics of Jewish, 544

YEMEN, Jews in, 124
Yiddish, 380, 383; non-Jews speaking, 384; in England and America, 386; relation to German, 391; discarded in western countries, 483; as a national language, 483

ZIONISM, 466 *et seq.*; programme of, 469, 495; doctrines of, 486; impotent against anti-Semitism, 496; failure of, 497; Jewish opposition to, 499
Zionists, number of, 497
Zafy Ibraim, 149

NEW BOOKS

IMPORTED BY

CHARLES SCRIBNER'S SONS,

NEW YORK CITY.

GREAT WRITERS.

A NEW SERIES OF CRITICAL BIOGRAPHIES OF FAMOUS WRITERS OF EUROPE AND AMERICA.

LIBRARY EDITION.

Printed on large paper of extra quality, in handsome binding, Demy 8vo, price $1.00 each.

ALPHABETICAL LIST.

PRESS NOTICES.

Life of Jane Austen. By Goldwin Smith.

"Mr. Goldwin Smith has added another to the not inconsiderable roll of eminent men who have found their delight in Jane Austen. Certainly a fascinating book."—*Spectator.*

Life of Balzac. By Frederick Wedmore.

"A finished study, a concentrated summary, a succinct analysis of Balzac's successes and failures, and the causes of these successes and failures, and of the scope of his genius."—*Scottish Leader.*

Life of Charlotte Brontë. By A. Birrell.

"Those who know much of Charlotte Brontë will learn more, and those who know nothing about her will find all that is best worth learning in Mr. Birrell's pleasant book."—*St. James's Gazette.*

Life of Browning. By William Sharp.

"This little volume is a model of excellent English, and in every respec it seems to us what a biography should be."—*Public Opinion.*

New York: CHARLES SCRIBNER'S SONS.

Life of Bunyan. By Canon Venables.
 "A most intelligent, appreciative, and valuable memoir."—*Scotsman*.

Life of Burns. By Professor Blackie.
 "The editor certainly made a hit when he persuaded Blackie to write about Burns."—*Pall Mall Gazette*.

Life of Byron. By Hon. Roden Noel.
 "He [Mr. Noel] has at any rate given to the world the most credible and comprehensible portrait of the poet ever drawn with pen and ink." *Manchester Examiner*.

Life of Thomas Carlyle. By R. Garnett, LL.D.
 "This is an admirable book. Nothing could be more felicitous and fairer than the way in which he takes us through Carlyle's life and works." —*Pall Mall Gazette*.

Life of Cervantes. By H. E. Watts.
 "Let us rather say that no volume of this series, nor, so far as we can recollect, of any of the other numerous similar series, presents the facts of the subject in a more workmanlike style, or with more exhaustive knowledge."—*Manchester Guardian*.

Life of Coleridge. By Hall Caine.
 "Brief and vigorous, written throughout with spirit and great literary skill."—*Scotsman*.

Life of Congreve. By Edmund Gosse.
 "Mr. Gosse has written an admirable and most interesting biography of a man of letters who is of particular interest to other men of letters." —*The Academy*.

Life of Crabbe. By T. E. Kebbel.
 "No English poet since Shakespeare has observed certain aspects of nature and of human life more closely; and in the qualities of manliness and of sincerity he is surpassed by none. Mr. Kebbel's monograph is worthy of the subject."—*Athenæum*.

Life of Darwin. By G. T. Bettany.
 "Mr. G. T. Bettany's *Life of Darwin* is a sound and conscientious work."—*Saturday Review*.

Life of Dickens. By Frank T. Marzials.
 "Notwithstanding the mass of matter that has been printed relating to Dickens and his works, ... we should, until we came across this volume, have been at a loss to recommend any popular life of England's most popular novelist as being really satisfactory. The difficulty is removed by Mr. Marzials' little book."—*Athenæum*.

Life of George Eliot. By Oscar Browning.
 "We are thankful for this interesting addition to our knowledge of the great novelist."—*Literary World*.

New York: CHARLES SCRIBNER'S SONS.

Life of Emerson. By Richard Garnett, LL.D.

"As to the larger section of the public, to whom the series of Great Writers is addressed, no record of Emerson's life and work could be more desirable, both in breadth of treatment and lucidity of style, than Dr. Garnett's."—*Saturday Review.*

Life of Goethe. By James Sime.

"Mr. James Sime's competence as a biographer of Goethe, both in respect of knowledge of his special subject, and of German literature generally, is beyond question."—*Manchester Guardian.*

Life of Goldsmith. By Austin Dobson.

"The story of his literary and social life in London, with all its humorous and pathetic vicissitudes, is here retold as none could tell it better."—*Daily News.*

Life of Nathaniel Hawthorne. By Moncure Conway.

"Easy and conversational as the tone is throughout, no important fact is omitted, no useless fact is recalled."—*Speaker.*

Life of Heine. By William Sharp.

"This is an admirable monograph, . . . more fully written up to the level of recent knowledge and criticism of its theme than any other English work."—*Scotsman.*

Life of Victor Hugo. By Frank T. Marzials.

"Mr. Marzials' volume presents to us, in a more handy form than any English, or even French, handbook gives, the summary of what, up to the moment in which we write, is known or conjectured about the life of the great poet."—*Saturday Review.*

Life of Hunt. By Cosmo Monkhouse.

"Mr. Monkhouse has brought together and skilfully set in order much widely scattered material."—*Athenæum.*

Life of Samuel Johnson. By Colonel F. Grant.

"Colonel Grant has performed his task with diligence, sound judgment, good taste, and accuracy."—*Illustrated London News.*

Life of Keats. By W. M. Rossetti.

"Valuable for the ample information which it contains."—*Cambridge Independent.*

Life of Lessing. By T. W. Rolleston.

"A picture of Lessing which is vivid and truthful, and has enough of detail for all ordinary purposes."—*Nation* (New York).

New York: CHARLES SCRIBNER'S SONS.

Life of Longfellow. By Prof. Eric S. Robertson.
"A most readable little book."—*Liverpool Mercury*.

Life of Marryat. By David Hannay.
"What Mr. Hannay had to do—give a craftsman-like account of a great craftsman who has been almost incomprehensibly undervalued—could hardly have been done better than in this little volume."—*Manchester Guardian*.

Life of Mill. By W. L. Courtney.
"A most sympathetic and discriminating memoir."—*Glasgow Herald*.

Life of Milton. By Richard Garnett, LL.D.
"Within equal compass the life-story of the great poet of Puritanism has never been more charmingly or adequately told."—*Scottish Leader*.

Life of Renan. By Francis Espinasse.
"Sufficiently full in details to give us a living picture of the great scholar, . . . and never tiresome or dull."—*Westminster Review*.

Life of Dante Gabriel Rossetti. By J. Knight.
"Mr. Knight's picture of the great poet and painter is the fullest and best yet presented to the public."—*The Graphic*.

Life of Schiller. By Henry W. Nevinson.
"This is a well-written little volume, which presents the leading facts of the poet's life in a neatly rounded picture."—*Scotsman*.

"Mr. Nevinson has added much to the charm of his book by his spirited translations, which give excellently both the ring and sense of the original."—*Manchester Guardian*.

Life of Arthur Schopenhauer. By William Wallace.
"The series of Great Writers has hardly had a contribution of more marked and peculiar excellence than the book which the Whyte Professor of Moral Philosophy at Oxford has written for it on the attractive and still (in England) little-known subject of Schopenhauer."—*Manchester Guardian*.

Life of Scott. By Professor Yonge.
"For readers and lovers of the poems and novels of Sir Walter Scott this is a most enjoyable book."—*Aberdeen Free Press*.

Life of Shelley. By William Sharp.
"The criticisms . . . entitle this capital monograph to be ranked with the best biographies of Shelley."—*Westminster Review*.

New York: CHARLES SCRIBNER'S SONS.

ife of Sheridan. By Lloyd Sanders.

"To say that Mr. Lloyd Sanders, in this volume, has produced the best existing memoir of Sheridan is really to award much fainter praise than the book deserves."—*Manchester Guardian.*

"Rapid and workmanlike in style, the author has evidently a good practical knowledge of the stage of Sheridan's day."—*Saturday Review.*

ife of Adam Smith. By R. B. Haldane, M.P.

"Written with a perspicuity seldom exemplified when dealing with economic science."—*Scotsman.*

"Mr. Haldane's handling of his subject impresses us as that of a man who well understands his theme, and who knows how to elucidate it."—*Scottish Leader.*

"A beginner in political economy might easily do worse than take Mr. Haldane's book as his first text-book."—*Graphic.*

ife of Smollett. By David Hannay.

"A capital record of a writer who still remains one of the great masters of the English novel."—*Saturday Review.*

"Mr. Hannay is excellently equipped for writing the life of Smollett. As a specialist on the history of the eighteenth century navy, he is at a great advantage in handling works so full of the sea and sailors as Smollett's three principal novels. Moreover, he has a complete acquaintance with the Spanish romancers, from whom Smollett drew so much of his inspiration. His criticism is generally acute and discriminating; and his narrative is well arranged, compact, and accurate."—*St. James's Gazette.*

Life of Thackeray. By Herman Merivale and Frank T. Marzials.

"The book, with its excellent bibliography, is one which neither the student nor the general reader can well afford to miss."—*Pall Mall Gazette.*

"The last book published by Messrs. Merivale and Marzials is full of very real and true things."—Mrs. ANNE THACKERAY RITCHIE on "Thackeray and his Biographers," in *Illustrated London News*

Life of Thoreau. By H. S. Salt.

"Mr. Salt's volume ought to do much towards widening the knowledge and appreciation in England of one of the most original men ever produced by the United States."—*Illustrated London News.*

Life of Voltaire. By Francis Espinasse.

"Up to date, accurate, impartial, and bright without any trace of affectation."—*Academy.*

Life of Whittier. By W. J. Linton.

"Mr. Linton is a sympathetic and yet judicious critic of Whittier."—*World.*

Complete Bibliography to each volume, by J. P. ANDERSON, British Museum, London.

New York: CHARLES SCRIBNER'S SONS.

"*An excellent series.*"—TELEGRAPH.

"*Excellently translated, beautifully bound, and elegantly printed.*" LIVERPOOL MERCURY.

"*Notable for the high standard of taste and excellent judgment that characterise their editing, as well as for the brilliancy of the literature that they contain.*"—BOSTON GAZETTE, U.S.A.

Library of Humour.

Cloth Elegant, Large 12mo, Price $1.25 per vol.

VOLUMES ALREADY ISSUED.

The Humour of France. Translated, with an Introduction and Notes, by ELIZABETH LEE. With numerous Illustrations by PAUL FRÉNZENY.

The Humour of Germany. Translated, with an Introduction and Notes, by HANS MÜLLER-CASENOV. With numerous Illustrations by C. E. BROCK.

The Humour of Italy. Translated, with an Introduction and Notes, by A. WERNER. With 50 Illustrations and a Frontispiece by ARTURO FIELDI.

The Humour of America. Selected, with a copious Biographical Index of American Humorists, by JAMES BARR.

The Humour of Holland. Translated, with an Introduction and Notes, by A. WERNER. With numerous Illustrations by DUDLEY HARDY.

The Humour of Ireland. Selected by D. J. O'DONOGHUE. With numerous Illustrations by OLIVER PAQUE.

The Humour of Spain. Translated, with an Introduction and Notes, by SUSETTE M. TAYLOR. With numerous Illustrations by H. R. MILLAR.

The Humour of Russia. Translated, with Notes, by E. L. BOOLE, and an Introduction by STEPNIAK. With 50 Illustrations by PAUL FRÉNZENY.

New York: CHARLES SCRIBNER'S SONS.

In One Volume. Crown 8vo, Cloth, Richly Gilt. Price $1.25.

Musicians' Wit, Humour, and Anecdote:

BEING

ON DITS OF COMPOSERS, SINGERS, AND INSTRUMENTALISTS OF ALL TIMES.

By FREDERICK J. CROWEST,

Author of "The Great Tone Poets," "The Story of British Music"; Editor of "The Master Musicians" Series, etc., etc.

Profusely Illustrated with Quaint Drawings by J. P. DONNE.

WHAT ENGLISH REVIEWERS SAY:—

"It is one of those delightful medleys of anecdote of all times, seasons, and persons, in every page of which there is a new specimen of humour, strange adventure, and quaint saying."—T. P. O'CONNOR in *T. P.'s Weekly.*

"A remarkable collection of good stories which must have taken years of perseverance to get together."—*Morning Leader.*

"A book which should prove acceptable to two large sections of the public those who are interested in musicians and those who have an adequate sense of the comic."—*Globe.*

THE USEFUL RED SERIES.

Red Cloth, Pocket Size, Price 50 Cents.

NEW IDEAS ON BRIDGE. By ARCHIBALD DUNN, JUN.

INDIGESTION: Its Prevention and Cure. By F. HERBERT ALDERSON, M.B.

ON CHOOSING A PIANO. By ALGERNON ROSE.

CONSUMPTION: Its Nature, Causes, Prevention, and Cure. By Dr. SICARD DE PLAUZOLES.

BUSINESS SUCCESS. By G. G. MILLAR.

PETROLEUM. By SYDNEY H. NORTH.

✱ INFANT FEEDING. By a PHYSICIAN.

THE LUNGS IN HEALTH AND DISEASE. By DR. PAUL NIEMEYER.

HOW TO PRESERVE THE TEETH. By a DENTAL SURGEON.

MOTHER AND CHILD. By L. M. MARRIOTT.

New York: CHARLES SCRIBNER'S SONS.

The Music Story Series.

A SERIES OF LITERARY-MUSICAL MONOGRAPHS.

Edited by FREDERICK J. CROWEST,

Author of "The Great Tone Poets," "Musicians' Wit and Humour," etc.

Illustrated with Photogravure and Collotype Portraits, Half-tone and Line Pictures, Facsimiles, etc.

Square Crown 8vo, Cloth, $1.25 net.

VOLUMES NOW READY.

THE STORY OF ORATORIO. By ANNIE W. PATTERSON, B.A., Mus. Doc.

THE STORY OF NOTATION. By C. F. ABDY WILLIAMS, M.A., Mus. Bac.

THE STORY OF THE ORGAN. By C. F. ABDY WILLIAMS, M.A.

THE STORY OF CHAMBER MUSIC. By N. KILBURN, Mus. Bac. (Cantab.).

THE STORY OF THE VIOLIN. By PAUL STOEVING, Professor of the Violin, Guildhall School of Music, London.

THE STORY OF THE HARP. By WILLIAM H. GRATTAN FLOOD, Mus. Doc.

THE STORY OF ORGAN MUSIC. By C. F. ABDY WILLIAMS, M.A., Mus. Bac.

THE STORY OF ENGLISH MUSIC (1604-1904): being the Worshipful Company of Musicians' Lectures.

THE STORY OF MINSTRELSY. By EDMONDSTOUNE DUNCAN.

THE STORY OF MUSICAL FORM. By CLARENCE LUCAS.

THE STORY OF OPERA. By E. MARKHAM LEE, Mus. Doc.

LATEST ADDITIONS.

THE STORY OF THE CAROL. By EDMONDSTOUNE DUNCAN.

THE STORY OF THE BAGPIPE. By WILLIAM H. GRATTAN FLOOD, Mus. Doc.

New York: CHARLES SCRIBNER'S SONS.

The Makers of British Art.
A Series of Illustrated Monographs
Edited by
James A. Manson.
Illustrated with Photogravure Portraits; Half-tone and Line Reproductions of the Best Pictures.

Square Crown 8vo, Cloth, $1.25 net.

LANDSEER, SIR EDWIN. By the EDITOR.
"This little volume may rank as the most complete account of Landsee that the world is likely to possess."—*Times.*

REYNOLDS, SIR JOSHUA. By ELSA D'ESTERRE KEELING.
"An admirable little volume . . . Miss Keeling writes very justly anc sympathetically."—*Daily Telegraph.*
"Useful as a handy work of reference."—*Athenæum.*

TURNER, J. W. M. By ROBERT CHIGNELL, Author o "The Life and Paintings of Vicat Cole, R.A."
"This book is thoroughly competent, and at the same time it is in the bes sense popular in style and treatment."—*Literary World.*

ROMNEY, GEORGE. By Sir HERBERT MAXWELL BART., F.R.S.
"Sir Herbert Maxwell's brightly written and accurate monograph will no disappoint even exacting students, while its charming reproductions ar certain to render it an attractive gift-book."—*Standard.*
"It is a pleasure to read such a biography as this, so well considered, anc written with such insight and literary skill."—*Daily News.*

WILKIE, SIR DAVID. By Professor BAYNE.
CONSTABLE, JOHN. By the EARL OF PLYMOUTH.
RAEBURN, SIR HENRY. By EDWARD PINNINGTON
GAINSBOROUGH, THOMAS. By A. E. FLETCHER.
HOGARTH, WILLIAM. By Prof. G. BALDWIN BROWN
MOORE, HENRY. By FRANK J. MACLEAN.
LEIGHTON, LORD. By EDGCUMBE STALEY.
MORLAND, GEORGE. By D. H. WILSON, M.A., LL.M
WILSON, RICHARD. By BEAUMONT FLETCHER.
✱ **MILLAIS, SIR JOHN EVERETT.** By J. EADIE REID

The Contemporary Science Series.

Edited by Havelock Ellis.

12mo. Cloth. Price $1.50 per Volume.

I. **THE EVOLUTION OF SEX.** By Prof. PATRICK GEDDES and J. A. THOMSON. With 90 Illustrations. Second Edition.

"The authors have brought to the task—as indeed their names guarantee—a wealth of knowledge, a lucid and attractive method of treatment, and a rich vein of picturesque language."—*Nature.*

II. **ELECTRICITY IN MODERN LIFE.** By G. W. DE TUNZELMANN. With 88 Illustrations.

"A clearly written and connected sketch of what is known about electricity and magnetism, the more prominent modern applications, and the principles on which they are based."—*Saturday Review.*

III. **THE ORIGIN OF THE ARYANS.** By Dr. ISAAC TAYLOR. Illustrated. Second Edition.

"Canon Taylor is probably the most encyclopædic all-round scholar now living. His new volume on the *Origin of the Aryans* is a first-rate example of the excellent account to which he can turn his exceptionally wide and varied information. . . . Masterly and exhaustive."—*Pall Mall Gazette.*

IV. **PHYSIOGNOMY AND EXPRESSION.** By P. MANTEGAZZA. Illustrated.

"Brings this highly interesting subject even with the latest researches. . . . Professor Mantegazza is a writer full of life and spirit, and the natural attractiveness of his subject is not destroyed by his scientific handling of it."—*Literary World* (Boston).

V. **EVOLUTION AND DISEASE.** By J. B. SUTTON, F.R.C.S. With 135 Illustrations.

"The book is as interesting as a novel, without sacrifice of accuracy or system, and is calculated to give an appreciation of the fundamentals of pathology to the lay reader, while forming a useful collection of illustrations of disease for medical reference."—*Journal of Mental Science.*

VI. **THE VILLAGE COMMUNITY.** By G. L. GOMME. Illustrated.

"His book will probably remain for some time the best work of reference for facts bearing on those traces of the village community which have not been effaced by conquest, encroachment, and the heavy hand of Roman law."—*Scottish Leader.*

VII. **THE CRIMINAL.** By HAVELOCK ELLIS. Illustrated Fourth Edition, Revised and Enlarged.

"The sociologist, the philosopher, the philanthropist, the novelist—all, indeed, for whom the study of human nature has any attraction—will find Mr. Ellis full of interest and suggestiveness."—*Academy.*

New York: CHARLES SCRIBNER'S SONS.

VIII. SANITY AND INSANITY. By Dr. CHARLES MERCIER. Illustrated.

"Taken as a whole, it is the brightest book on the physical side of mental science published in our time."—*Pall Mall Gazette.*

IX. HYPNOTISM. By Dr. ALBERT MOLL. New and Enlarged Edition.

"Marks a step of some importance in the study of some difficult physiological and psychological problems which have not yet received much attention in the scientific world of England."—*Nature.*

X. MANUAL TRAINING. By Dr. C. M. WOODWARD, Director of the Manual Training School, St. Louis. Illustrated.

"There is no greater authority on the subject than Professor Woodward." *Manchester Guardian.*

XI. THE SCIENCE OF FAIRY TALES. By E. SIDNEY HARTLAND.

"Mr. Hartland's book will win the sympathy of all earnest students, both by the knowledge it displays, and by a thorough love and appreciation of his subject, which is evident throughout."—*Spectator.*

XII. PRIMITIVE FOLK. By ELIE RECLUS.

"An attractive and useful introduction to the study of some aspects of ethnography."—*Nature.*

XIII. THE EVOLUTION OF MARRIAGE. By Professor LETOURNEAU.

"Among the distinguished French students of sociology, Professor Letourneau has long stood in the first rank. He approaches the great study of man free from bias and shy of generalisations. To collect, scrutinise, and appraise facts is his chief business. In the volume before us he shows these qualities in an admirable degree."—*Science.*

XIV. BACTERIA AND THEIR PRODUCTS. By Dr. G. SIMS WOODHEAD. Illustrated. Second Edition.

"An excellent summary of the present state of knowledge of the subject." —*Lancet.*

XV. EDUCATION AND HEREDITY. By J. M. GUYAU.

"It is at once a treatise on sociology, ethics, and pedagogics. It is doubtful whether, among all the ardent evolutionists who have had their say on the moral and the educational question, any one has carried forward the new doctrine so boldly to its extreme logical consequence."—Professor SULLY in *Mind.*

XVI. THE MAN OF GENIUS. By Prof. LOMBROSO. Illustrated.

"By far the most comprehensive and fascinating collection of facts and generalisations concerning genius which has yet been brought together."— *Journal of Mental Science.*

New York: CHARLES SCRIBNER'S SONS.

VII. THE HISTORY OF THE EUROPEAN FAUNA.
By R. F. Scharff, B.Sc., Ph.D., F.Z.S. Illustrated.

VIII. PROPERTY: ITS ORIGIN AND DEVELOPMENT.
By Ch. Letourneau, General Secretary to the Anthropological Society, Paris, and Professor in the School of Anthropology, Paris.

"M. Letourneau has read a great deal, and he seems to us to have selected and interpreted his facts with considerable judgment and learning."—*Westminster Review.*

XIX. VOLCANOES, PAST AND PRESENT. By Prof. Edward Hull, LL.D., F.R.S.

"A very readable account of the phenomena of volcanoes and earthquakes."—*Nature.*

X. PUBLIC HEALTH. By Dr. J. F. J. Sykes. With numerous Illustrations.

"Not by any means a mere compilation or a dry record of details and statistics, but it takes up essential points in evolution, environment, prophylaxis, and sanitation bearing upon the preservation of public health."—*Lancet.*

XXI. MODERN METEOROLOGY. An Account of the Growth and Present Condition of some Branches of Meteorological Science. By Frank Waldo, Ph.D., Member of the German and Austrian Meteorological Societies, etc.; late Junior Professor, Signal Service, U.S.A. With 112 Illustrations.

"The present volume is the best on the subject for general use that we have seen."—*Daily Telegraph* (London).

I. THE GERM-PLASM: A THEORY OF HEREDITY.
By August Weismann, Professor in the University of Freiburg-in-Breisgau. With 24 Illustrations. $2.50.

"There has been no work published since Darwin's own books which has so thoroughly handled the matter treated by him, or has done so much to place in order and clearness the immense complexity of the factors of heredity, or, lastly, has brought to light so many new facts and considerations bearing on the subject."—*British Medical Journal.*

XXIII. INDUSTRIES OF ANIMALS. By E. F. Houssay. With numerous Illustrations.

"His accuracy is undoubted, yet his facts out-marvel all romance. These facts are here made use of as materials wherewith to form the mighty fabric of evolution."—*Manchester Guardian.*

New York: Charles Scribner's Sons.

XIV. MAN AND WOMAN. By Havelock Ellis. Illustrated. Fourth and Revised Edition.

"Mr. Havelock Ellis belongs, in some measure, to the continental school of anthropologists; but while equally methodical in the collection of facts, he is far more cautious in the invention of theories, and he has the further distinction of being not only able to think, but able to write. His book is a sane and impartial consideration, from a psychological and anthropological point of view, of a subject which is certainly of primary interest."—*Athenæum*.

XXV. THE EVOLUTION OF MODERN CAPITALISM. By John A. Hobson, M.A. (New and Revised Edition.)

"Every page affords evidence of wide and minute study, a weighing of facts as conscientious as it is acute, a keen sense of the importance of certain points as to which economists of all schools have hitherto been confused and careless, and an impartiality generally so great as to give no indication of his [Mr. Hobson's] personal sympathies."—*Pall Mall Gazette*.

XXVI. APPARITIONS AND THOUGHT-TRANSFERENCE. By Frank Podmore, M.A.

"A very sober and interesting little book. . . . That thought-transference is a real thing, though not perhaps a very common thing, he certainly shows."—*Spectator*.

. AN INTRODUCTION TO COMPARATIVE PSYCHOLOGY. By Professor C. Lloyd Morgan. With Diagrams.

"A strong and complete exposition of Psychology, as it takes shape in a mind previously informed with biological science. . . . Well written, extremely entertaining, and intrinsically valuable."—*Saturday Review*.

XXVIII. THE ORIGINS OF INVENTION: A Study of Industry among Primitive Peoples. By Otis T. Mason, Curator of the Department of Ethnology in the United States National Museum.

"A valuable history of the development of the inventive faculty."—*Nature*.

XXIX. THE GROWTH OF THE BRAIN: A Study of the Nervous System in relation to Education. By Henry Herbert Donaldson, Professor of Neurology in the University of Chicago.

"We can say with confidence that Professor Donaldson has executed his work with much care, judgment, and discrimination."—*The Lancet*.

XXX. EVOLUTION IN ART: As Illustrated by the Life-Histories of Designs. By Professor Alfred C. Haddon. With 130 Illustrations.

"It is impossible to speak too highly of this most unassuming and invaluable book."—*Journal of Anthropological Institute*.

New York: Charles Scribner's Sons.

XXXI. THE PSYCHOLOGY OF THE EMOTIONS. By TH. RIBOT, Professor at the College of France, Editor of the *Revue Philosophique*.
"Professor Ribot's treatment is careful, modern, and adequate."—*Academy*.

XXXII. HALLUCINATIONS AND ILLUSIONS: A STUDY OF THE FALLACIES OF PERCEPTION. By EDMUND PARISH.
"This remarkable little volume."—*Daily News*.

XXXIII. THE NEW PSYCHOLOGY. By E. W. SCRIPTURE, Ph.D. (Leipzig). With 124 Illustrations.

XXIV. SLEEP: ITS PHYSIOLOGY, PATHOLOGY, HYGIENE, AND PSYCHOLOGY. BY MARIE DE MANACEÏNE (St. Petersburg). Illustrated.

XXV. THE NATURAL HISTORY OF DIGESTION. By A. LOCKHART GILLESPIE, M.D., F.R.C.P. ED., F.R.S. ED. With a large number of Illustrations and Diagrams.
"Dr. Gillespie's work is one that has been greatly needed. No comprehensive collation of this kind exists in recent English Literature." *American Journal of the Medical Sciences*.

XXXVI. DEGENERACY: ITS CAUSES, SIGNS, AND RESULTS. By Professor EUGENE S. TALBOT, M.D., Chicago. With Illustrations.
"The author is bold, original, and suggestive, and his work is a contribution of real and indeed great value, more so on the whole than anything that has yet appeared in this country."—*American Journal of Psychology*.

XXVII. THE RACES OF MAN: A SKETCH OF ETHNOGRAPHY AND ANTHROPOLOGY. By J. DENIKER. With 178 Illustrations.
"Dr. Deniker has achieved a success which is well-nigh phenomenal." *British Medical Journal*.

XXXVIII. THE PSYCHOLOGY OF RELIGION. AN EMPIRICAL STUDY OF THE GROWTH OF RELIGIOUS CONSCIOUSNESS. By EDWIN DILLER STARBUCK Ph.D., Assistant Professor of Education, Leland Stanford Junior University.
"No one interested in the study of religious life and experience can afford to neglect this volume."—*Morning Herald*.

XXXIX. THE CHILD: A STUDY IN THE EVOLUTION OF MAN. By Dr. ALEXANDER FRANCIS CHAMBERLAIN, M.A., Ph.D., Lecturer on Anthropology in Clark University, Worcester (Mass.). With Illustrations.
"The work contains much curious information, and should be studied by those who have to do with children."—*Sheffield Daily Telegraph*.

New York: CHARLES SCRIBNER'S SONS.

XL. THE MEDITERRANEAN RACE. By Professor SERGI. With over 100 Illustrations.

"M. Sergi has given us a lucid and complete exposition of his views on a subject of supreme interest."—*Irish Times.*

XLI. THE STUDY OF RELIGION. By MORRIS JASTROW, Jun., Ph.D., Professor in the University of Pennsylvania.

"This work presents a careful survey of the subject, and forms an admirable introduction to any particular branch of it."—*Methodist Times.*

XLII. HISTORY OF GEOLOGY AND PALÆONTOLOGY TO THE END OF THE NINETEENTH CENTURY. By KARL VON ZITTEL.

"It is a very masterly treatise, written with a wide grasp of recent discoveries."—*Publishers' Circular.*

XLIII. THE MAKING OF CITIZENS: A STUDY IN COMPARATIVE EDUCATION. By R. E. HUGHES, M.A. (Oxon.), B.Sc. (Lond.).

"Mr. Hughes gives a lucid account of the exact position of Education in England, Germany, France, and the United States. The statistics present a clear and attractive picture of the manner in which one of the greatest questions now at issue is being solved both at home and abroad."—*Standard.*

XLIV. MORALS: A TREATISE ON THE PSYCHO-SOCIOLOGICAL BASES OF ETHICS. By PROFESSOR G. L. DUPRAT. Translated by W. J. GREENSTREET, M.A., F.R.A.S.

"The present work is representative of the modern departure in the treatment of the theory of morals. The author brings a wide knowledge to bear on his subject."—*Education.*

XLV. A STUDY OF RECENT EARTHQUAKES. By CHARLES DAVISON, D.Sc., F.G.S. With Illustrations.

"Dr. Davison has done his work well."—*Westminster Gazette.*

XLVI. MODERN ORGANIC CHEMISTRY. By DR. C. A. KEANE, D.Sc., PH.D., F.I.C. With Diagrams.

"This volume provides an instructive and suggestive survey of the great range of knowledge covered by modern organic chemistry."—*Scotsman.*

TO-DAY'S ADDITIONS:—

THE CRIMINAL. By HAVELOCK ELLIS. Fourth Edition, Revised and Enlarged.

XLVII. THE JEWS: A STUDY OF RACE AND ENVIRONMENT. By Dr. MAURICE FISHBERG.

"It shows abounding evidence in its pages that it is intended to show, immense industry, consummate pains, vast literary and statistical resources. It contains, to be sure, much information of great value, and it sets forth many facts absorbing in their interest for any who desire to study the Jewish people."—*Jewish Chronicle.*

New York: CHARLES SCRIBNER'S SONS.

IBSEN'S DRAMAS.

Edited by WILLIAM ARCHER.

THREE PLAYS TO THE VOLUME.

12mo, CLOTH, PRICE $1.25 PER VOLUME.

"*We seem at last to be shown men and women as they are; and at first it is more than we can endure. All Ibsen's characters speak and act as if they were hypnotised, and under their creator's imperious demand to reveal themselves. There never was such a mirror held up to nature before: it is too terrible. . . . Yet we must return to Ibsen, with his remorseless surgery, his remorseless electric-light, until we, too, have grown strong and learned to face the naked—if necessary, the flayed and bleeding—reality.*"—SPEAKER (London).

VOL. I. "A DOLL'S HOUSE," "THE LEAGUE OF YOUTH," and "THE PILLARS OF SOCIETY." With Portrait of the Author, and Biographical Introduction by WILLIAM ARCHER.

VOL. II. "GHOSTS," "AN ENEMY OF THE PEOPLE," and "THE WILD DUCK." With an Introductory Note.

VOL. III. "LADY INGER OF ÖSTRÅT," "THE VIKINGS AT HELGELAND," "THE PRETENDERS." With an Introductory Note.

VOL. IV. "EMPEROR AND GALILEAN" With an Introductory Note by WILLIAM ARCHER.

VOL. V. "ROSMERSHOLM," "THE LADY FROM THE SEA," "HEDDA GABLER." Translated by WILLIAM ARCHER. With an Introductory Note.

VOL. VI. "PEER GYNT: A DRAMATIC POEM." Authorised Translation by WILLIAM and CHARLES ARCHER.

The sequence of the plays *in each volume* is chronological; the complete set of Volumes comprising the dramas thus presents them in chronological order.

"The art of prose translation does not perhaps enjoy a very high literary status in England, but we have no hesitation in numbering the present version of Ibsen, so far as it has gone (Vols. I. and II.), among the very best achievements, in that kind, of our generation."—*Academy*.

"We have seldom, if ever, met with a translation so absolutely idiomatic."—*Glasgow Herald*.

New York: CHARLES SCRIBNER'S SONS.

Made in the USA
Coppell, TX
12 March 2021